BEATING TIME
THE STORY OF THE IRISH BODHRÁN

BY THE SAME AUTHOR

The Companion to Irish Traditional Music (3rd edition). Cork University Press, 2024

Ón gCos go Cluas – From Dancing to Listening (edited, with Liz Doherty). Aberdeen University Press, 2020

Catalogue of the Grace Kelly Irish-American song-score collection. Princess Grace Irish Library, Monaco, 2019

Complete Guide to Learning The Irish Flute. Waltons, Dublin, 2013

Crosbhealach an Cheoil, 2003 (ed., with Liz Doherty, Therese Smith, Desi Wilkinson, Paul McGettrick, Colette Moloney and Eithne Vallely). Whinstone, Dublin, 2013

The Companion to Irish Traditional Music (2nd edition). Cork University Press, 2011

The Tailor's Twist – The Life in Music of Ben Lennon of Kiltyclogher (with Jacques Piraprez Nutan). FOBL, Dublin, 2011

A Work of Art – the life and work of painter JB Vallely. Emer Gallery, Belfast, 2008

Sing up! Comic Songs and Satires of Modern Ireland. Dedalus Press, Dublin, 2008

Tuned Out – Traditional Music and Identity in Northern Ireland. Cork University Press, 2008)

Together in Time, the life, times and music of John Kennedy of Cullybackey. Lough Shore Traditions Group, Antrim, 2001

Retrospective: A visual celebration of the life and works of Armagh painter JB Vallely. Emer Gallery, Belfast, 2000

Companion to Irish Traditional Music (1st edition). Cork University Press, 1999

Crosbhealach an Cheoil – The Crossroads Conference Papers 1996 (ed., with Hammy Hamilton, Liz Doherty, and Eithne Vallely. Whinstone, Dublin, 1999

The Blooming Meadows – the Soul of Traditional Music (with Charlie Piggott & Nutan). Town House, Dublin, 1998

Timber – The Flute Tutor. Long Note, Miltown Malbay, 1986; Waltons, Dublin, 1999

BEATING TIME
THE STORY OF THE IRISH BODHRÁN

Fintan Vallely

First published in 2025 by
Cork University Press
Boole Library
University College Cork
Cork, T12 ND89. Ireland

Authorised representative:
Sinead Neville.
Email: corkuniversitypress@ucc.ie

Text © Fintan Vallely
Images © the named sources where credited.
Photographs credited 'EDI' © Fintan Vallely

Library of Congress Control Number: 2025932738
Distribution in the USA: Longleaf Services, Chapel Hill, NC, USA
All rights reserved. No part of this book may be reprinted or reproduced or utilised in any electronic, mechanical, or other means, now known as hereafter invented, including photocopying and recording or otherwise, without either the prior written permission of the publishers or a licence permitting restricted copying in Ireland issued by the Irish Copyright Licensing Agency Ltd., 25 Denzille Lane, Dublin 2.

ISBN 978-178205-046-9

Book design and typesetting,
Martin Gaffney FIDI

Printed in Malta by Gutenberg Press Ltd.

www.corkuniversitypress.com

Contents – The bodhrán story at a glance

Preface ... I
Summary of discussion ... III
Glossary ... V

Chapter 1 The Bodhrán in Traditional Music ... 1
The rise of the bodhrán as we know it ... 1
What it is ... 3
Scarcity of resources ... 6
Assumptions ... 7
The experience of drums ... 8
Suspicion of the drum-kit ... 9
Insecurity and challenge ... 11

Chapter 2 The Urge to Drum ... 15
Material evidence ... 15
No drum visible in ancient Ireland ... 16
Female-centred religion, deities and priests ... 18
Drums and war ... 19
The military tambourine ... 20
Military tambourines in Ireland ... 23
Tambourines and the gentry ... 25

Chapter 3 The Irish *Timpan*: Strings or drum? ... 29
Enter Cambrensis, AD 1188 ... 30
The Fair of Carman, ended *c.* AD 718 ... 31
The *Irish* tympanists, AD 721 ... 32
'The Four Masters', period AD 1328–1616 ... 33
The *Zoilomastix*, AD 1625 ... 35
Charles O'Conor AD 1710–91 ... 35
Joseph Cooper Walker, 1786 ... 36
Bunting 1809: Skin versus strings ... 37
Eugene O'Curry (1794–1862): the 'timpan' was not a drum ... 38
W.K. Sullivan ... 41
English-language translations ... 41
Enter the real drum ... 44
'Cambrensis-ism' in dictionaries? ... 47

Chapter 4 The Word 'Bodhrán' in Documents ... 51
'The Paris manuscript', c. AD 900 ... 51
Rosa Anglica, c. 1550 ... 53
Sifting out the words ... 56
The historic dictionaries ... 57
The Poole Glossary ... 58
Irisleabhar na Gaedhilge ... 59
Dinneen's dictionary ... 60
The Scottish dictionaries ... 63
The modern dictionaries ... 63
The Royal Irish Academy dictionary ... 64
The bodhrán '*in a bodhrán*' ... 64
A distinct, purpose-defining original meaning for 'bodhrán'? ... 65
Spelling, pronunciation and meaning ... 66
Audio evidence ... 67
Wild card meanings ... 67
Linguistic speculation ... 68

Chapter 5 'Bodhrán': sound or function? ... 71
Deafness, noise and dull sound ... 71
The actual, original bodhráns ... 73
Winnowing ... 74
Multi-task bodhráns ... 77
Sieves ... 78
The container bodhrán ... 79
The Halls' 'borrane', *c.* 1840 ... 81
Bodhrán as a music instrument? ... 81
Museum bodhráns ... 82
The National Museum collection ... 82
The Ulster Folk Museum collection ... 84
Sieve-making ... 84
Bodhráns in photographs ... 85

Chapter 6 The Tambourine on the Irish Stage ... 89
Teaching and learning ... 90
Tutor books ... 91
Availability and role models ... 92
The 'minstrels', 1844 – *c.* 1905 ... 93
Authenticity or exoticism? ... 96
Interest in minstrel music ... 98
Impersonating the impersonators ... 100
Attitudes to slavery ... 100
Familiarity ... 101
Influence on music instruments in Ireland? ... 103
Audiences for popular entertainments ... 104

Chapter 7 Tambourines among the People ... 109
Reports from abroad ... 110
Agitational tambourine ... 111
Religion and solemnity ... 112
Tambourine as collection tray ... 113
Decoration and novelty ... 113
Prejudices ... 114
Countrywide availability? ... 114
Tambourine and the law ... 115
The tambourine in folklore ... 116
Rattle or thump? ... 116
Tambourine sizes ... 117
Copying the tambourine ... 118

Chapter 8 Seeing Is Believing: Presence and Absence ... 121
The first tambourine, 1832? ... 123
Interpretation of *Snap Apple Night* ... 123
A Shebeen in Listowel, *c.* 1842 ... 124
The Vinegar Hill tambourine, 1798 or 1854? ... 126
Tambourines in European art ... 128
Tambourines in Irish photographs ... 130
Absence – or out of sight? ... 131
Music at ancient fairs ... 132
Donnybrook Fair 1200s–1855 ... 132
The Sports of Easter Monday, Belfast, 1818 ... 133
Antaine Raifteараí (1779–1835) ... 133
The Halls, *c.* 1840 ... 135
William Carleton, 1843 ... 135
J.G. Kohl, 1843 ... 136
'Aonach Bhearna na Gaoithe' / The Fair of Windgap, *c.* 1876 ... 136
Francis O'Neill, 1903–22 ... 137

Chapter 9 Improvising Tambourine on a Bodhrán? **141**
The Ballinskelligs battery 143
Tomás a' Bhodhráin 144
Drumming on the wecht 145
Foot percussion 147
From bodhrán to actual tambourine 148
The Wren 149
From noise to music 152
Wren catching 154

Chapter 10 The Literary Drum **157**
Twentieth-century tambourine 159
Rosa Mulholland 159
Enter Bryan MacMahon 159
John B. Keane 161
Sive, the Munster finale … 163
Seán Ó Riada, 1960: From tambourine to bodhrán 164
Michael Hartnett 167
The Bodhrán Makers, 1986 167
Gabriel Fitzmaurice, 2006 169

Chapter 11 From Walking to Sitting: Tambourine to Bowran **173**
Tambourines on the sidelines 174
Transformation of the Wren 175
Beating out fervour 177
Seán Ó Riada and the bodhrán in the press 179
The tambourine competition, 1962 180
The silence of the tambourines 182
The *Sive* tambourine legacy 184
Travellers and the 'bowran' 185
Tambourine outside of Munster 186
The 'bowran' eclipse 188
The parallel bochrán soundscape 189
Role of the press 190
Bodhrán women 192
'The Bodhránry of west Limerick' 194
The persistence of 'bowran' 196

Chapter 12 Below the Melodicist's Horizon? **199**
Fife and drum bands 201
Bodhrán territories 202
Visibility of tambourines 204
Connacht 209
Galway 209
Clare 210
Tambourine among the 1950s London Irish 211
Midlands 212
Dublin county 212
Social class and style 213

Chapter 13 The *Actual* Bodhrán Makers **217**
Poverty and making do 218
Making tambourine copies 219
Home-making of instruments 221
Recycling the riddle 222
Specialisation 224
Desperate measures 225
The jingles 226
The 'stick', cipín or 'tipper' 228
First mention of 'stick' in the press 231

Bodhrán makers and the media 232
Part-time specialists 233
Testing the theories 236
Charlie Byrne 238
Seamus O'Kane 240
Malachy Kearns 242
Páiric McNeela 243

Chapter 14 Twentieth-century Bodhrán **247**
Bodhrán soloists 249
Stylistic change 252
Media and myth 253
State representation of bodhrán popularity and status 255
Competitions 256
The bodhrán in the All-Ireland Fleadh 256
Geographic expansion 258
Ulster 258
Munster 259
Leinster 259
Connacht 260

Chapter 15 Bodhrán Theories and Opinions **265**

Chapter 16 Re-thinking the Bodhrán? **279**
The gap – no outside influence? 280
No 'minstrel boys' on the drum? 280
The 'pagan' bodhrán thesis 282
Romantic rhetoric? 284
Closing the file 285
Waving the flag 286
From marching Wren to sit-down music 287

Chapter 17 A Bodhrán Portrait Gallery **289**

Appendices **318**
Appendix 1. The Eugene O'Curry lectures notes on the timpan. 318
Appendix 2. Music-professionalism references in manuscripts 320
Appendix 3. Verses written by Newcastle West poet Michael Hartnett 321
Appendix 4. Contemporary Developments 321
Appendix 5. Caoimhín Ó Danachair / Kevin Danaher, biography. 323
Appendix 6. Video, film and online links 323
Appendix 7. Folklore: *The Schools' Collection* 324
Appendix 8. Gerald Griffin: extract from *The Collegians*, 1829 324
Appendix 9. *The Kerryman*, 1944 325
Appendix 10. The '78' recording discs 326
Appendix 11. Extract: *Our Musical Heritage*, Radio Éireann, 1962 326
Appendix 12. '…Our native drum, the bodhrán…' 326
Appendix 13. Comparison of various players' striking styles 327
Appendix 14. Singing about and slagging off the bodhrán 328

Bibliography **334**

Acknowledgements **340**

Index **344**

"Here and there throughout Ireland there are places, occasions and even festivals which echo the rhythms of an earlier way of life. They draw the imagination into areas where myth, history and religion meet and overlap, areas where scholars speculate and ordinary people do extraordinary things for reasons they no longer understand"

[*prologue to Telefís Éireann programme on Puck Fair, 1969*]

The author and Jim Higgins near Oranmore, 2022

Preface

This book is an investigation into the background of the bodhrán in Ireland, a turning over of stones, a 'cold-case' file. It looks anew at the instrument's past – a tangle of primitive agricultural and domestic life, colonial legacy, popular entertainments, art, literature and cultural renaissance. The story is considerably less glamorous than those that apply to melody instruments, but is every bit as challenging. It is not on the scale of, for instance, the centuries-old prestige, aesthetics and development of the harp, all of which has been documented, and which shows an ongoing advance from a thousand years ago towards that instrument's present-day scale of technique, technological supremacy and participative uptake. Nor does it match the progress of the fiddle from at least the 1600s, the uilleann pipes from the 1700s, or the big nineteenth-century instruments – flute, accordions and concertina. The records which those can draw upon are neither imagined nor wishful: they include everything from surviving objects, through published documents and folklore records, to teaching methods and recording and broadcasting via all forms of media up to the 1960s, the point at which we only first begin to really hear of the bodhrán. This is not to suggest that the drum's history is unimportant or that it is inferior as an instrument; it is just a fresh dimension in Irish music – and it is later. There may have been an ancient thread in shamanism which would give this Irish frame drum a semblance of continuity – a 'pagan' drum as some commentators see it. But no such trail is documented – there is no sequence of bodhrán evidence back from the present day to the ancient past.

Research for this book began in fact with the assumption of the opposite – a lineage for the bodhrán's antiquity as a drum. But as the work progressed, that mission was repeatedly shunted off its target in a never-ending series of always-surprising tangents which irresistibly herded the story to a somewhat contrary destiny, and expanded what had originally been a mere article to its present scale. The initial idea had been that surviving images and the National Museum's collection would alone support, or demonstrate, a genealogy. But instead, they provoked the casting of a wider net to take in transcribed folklore. This, in turn, prompted further searches in a broader span of print literature, uncovering of new bodhrán morsels, leading to the development of a chronology supported by newspaper reportage – which itself raised other challenges. And, not of least significance, has been ongoing, casual feedback from various bodhrán players themselves – how they have chosen to recall, regard and promote the drum.

The study sets new parameters as well as revisiting the existing knowledge. Many of the facts of the investigation may not seem remarkable, for they have always been there, but here they are brought together systematically, and chronologically where appropriate, in the fresh context of new information. The work is, of course, only as complete as resources, contacts and available time and data permit, and in that way cannot claim to be definitive. But it does modestly offer a fresh perspective and a different standard of 'knowing' about the bodhrán, one which is appropriate for the information-age impulse to understand roots and routes alike. The interpretation in the following pages appreciates the valuable work already done by past scholarship. It has much re-contextualising of data from as far back as the first millennium, information which was collated two or more centuries ago. The leads of earlier commentators are acknowledged where appropriate, by consideration of their views of the possible ways in which the bodhrán might have come to be with us in the twenty-first century. And, of course, the issues that are raised are not complete in themselves, but point to areas that need yet more detailed coverage: about the drum's makers, older local players and their styles, regional specialisation, the spiritual dimension and about the influence of military bands and early popular-music minstrelsy on all of Irish music's instrumentation.

Four major information areas are observed – objects, images, writings and folklore. Museum holdings have been examined, etchings, paintings and photographs have been observed; manuscripts, textual descriptions, newspapers and existing publications have been explored, as well as folklore records. All of these point to a conclusion that the bodhrán as we know it is, yes, uniquely Irish, but whether or not such a drum was also a feature of early Gaelic society can only be speculated. For it is at once ancient and modern, a legacy, a borrowing and an invention, imagined and real. It has the name and well-documented, atavistic legacy of a primitive, rural tool, but has the form of a Middle-Eastern, Greek, Roman, Turkish and popular-music success. In name, it does have a material, historic presence in Ireland, but not as a percussion instrument. The bodhrán's earliest-described music attributes in Ireland have been merely peripheral, an inconspicuous improvisation by barely-documented, passionate, rural percussion pioneers on society's back-roads, out of sight and hearing of most chroniclers, contributing nothing obvious to Irish music in the way that we know it for being decidedly melody-based. But in the decade after 1951 and the formation of Comhaltas Ceoltóirí Éireann and its creation of the fleadh, this drum was highlighted, first by one provincial writer, then picked up and dramatically propelled to front-stage by another, and – suddenly – given an establishment imprimatur via national radio by a classical music composer. The creative impulses of a handful of ingenious innovators have subsequently roller-coasted the bodhrán to its present day standing.

Indeed, the drum's most remarkable attribute is that such newness can actually be celebrated by living people, for at the time of writing the creators of most of the bodhrán's modern forms and styles are actually still alive and playing. So, in order to contemporise the writing, and to highlight the drum's modernity as an instrument, portrait images of a number of innovative and pioneering players and stylists who have actually shaped the instrument as we know it today have been commissioned from the Belgian-Irish photographer and traditional-music devotee Jacques Piraprez Nutan. Sligo-based musician and photographer James Fraher has also been brought in to the project with his remarkable archive and contemporary images. And, to aid comprehension and appreciation of these as well as the huge amount of data in the pages, fellow musician and book designer Martin Gaffney elevates the overall study to a high pedestal of artistic presentation.

Fintan Vallely, March 2025

◀ Bodhrán class at Milwaukee Irish Fest, 2000 [*EDI*]

Summary of discussion

First Beats gives the gist of the content. **Chapter 1** gives the backdrop against which the drum has developed, considers the attitudes that have affected acceptance of drumming and of the bodhrán in Irish traditional music. **Chapter 2** looks at the absence of historical drumming in Ireland, the ancient associations of tambourines with religion, the manufacture and movement of the frame drum internationally, in religious cults, and the effect of its presence with the military and among the gentry. **Chapter 3** deals with underlying historical writings relating to the existence or otherwise of a drum tradition in Ireland, detailing misinterpretation arising from early writing, the entry of the military drum and persistence of misinformation. **Chapter 4** takes this investigation back to manuscript and early writings, and details how dictionaries have dealt with terminologies and translation, and discusses pronunciation. **Chapter 5** explores the three meanings of 'bodhrán', focusing on the device bodhráns – the agricultural and domestic tool – thinking guided by examination of museum artefacts and folklore information. **Chapter 6** explores a previously hidden aspect of the story, the tambourine on Irish stages in early popular music, with 'black & white' minstrels and with the local Irish who mimicked them; the nature and origin of their drum is discussed, as are aspects of their impact in Ireland. **Chapter 7** observes the tambourine on the streets in Irish society, from the years prior to the minstrels, its sale by the music trade, with a diversity of applications, and consideration of instrument sizes. **Chapter 8** analyses the historical visual evidence by date, and assesses the absence of written comment on tambourines and/or a percussion tradition. **Chapter 9** details improvisation on the device bodhrán leading to inevitable local making of the tambourine, and its visibility on the Wren. **Chapter 10** looks at the remarkable resurgence sparked by Bryan MacMahon, John B. Keane and Seán Ó Riada, and the subsequent construction of the bodhrán

▸ Johnny 'Ringo' McDonagh [*Nutan*]

pedigree as we have been given it. **Chapter 11** explores through press reports the move of the Wren tambourine from the rural outdoors to urban, sit-down competition and performance, and the start of the name-change from tambourine to 'bowrawn' – the phonetic term for bodhrán. **Chapter 12** notes the takeover of the word 'bodhrán' and its roots as 'tambourine' in west Limerick and Connacht. **Chapter 13** looks at cultural and technical aspects of making the drum, attitudes to it, a sample of well-known makers, and the growth and professionalisation of that business. **Chapter 14** moves from historic tambourine recordings, through to the advent of competitions, analysing All-Ireland Fleadh statistics for terminology, and region and gender of players. **Chapter 15** summarises what has been said of the drum's history by those who have chosen to write and speak about it over the sixty-five years since it was first talked about. **Chapter 16** comments on established opinions in light of the new information, pointing to the need to straighten out terminology and historical commentary. **Chapter 17** has contemporary bodhrán player portraits. **Appendix 1** itemises Eugene O'Curry's manuscript evidence on the *tiompán*, as well as ancient Irish music terminology, making this information easily consultable for the first time in a century and a half. **Appendix 2** lists professional musician manuscript references in ancient Ireland. **Appendix 3** is a poem by Michael Hartnett. **Appendix 4** gives Mícheál Ó Súilleabháin's summary of changes in his time. **Appendix 5** is a biography of Caoimhín Ó Danachair. **Appendix 6** has video, film and online links. **Appendix 7** is Folklore: *The Schools' Collection*. **Appendix 8** has words by Gerald Griffin on mummers in 1829. **Appendix 9** is a *Kerryman* newspaper account of the Wren. **Appendix 10** lists '78' tambourine recordings. **Appendix 11** is Seán Ó Riada's estimation of the bodhrán. **Appendix 12** is an amendment to Ó Riada's words. **Appendix 13** is a comparison of striking styles. **Appendix 14** has the words of four satirical bodhrán songs.

Glossary

Drum terms

'Frame drum' is the generic description for any kind of drum that is formed from a single membrane tensioned over one side of a shallow wooden frame. The bodhrán and the tambourine are such drums. Because the terms 'tambourine' and 'bodhrán' have both been used for the frame drum in Ireland at different times, for music they are generally used throughout this book with regard to the specific period being discussed, i.e. 'tambourine' prior to 1959 and bodhrán' thereafter.

Meanings of the word 'bodhrán'

There has been much confusion over this in the past, and some commentators have variously chosen to dismiss the whole bodhrán-origin affair as 'recondite', involving 'a madhouse of theorising', or just 'lost in the mists of time'.[1] But the term 'bodhrán' has three distinct meanings:

1. Its original form was a device made with skin stretched on a hoop of wood, the primary function of one form of which was as an agricultural tool used in grain processing. A similar, typically smaller, form was used as a container, and a household version saw service as a tray or dish. These have had various alternative names (in many spellings) according to use, place and era – such as *bodhrán*, *dallan*, *dildurn*, *wecht*, *wight*, *wite*, 'winnowing fan' or 'winnower.'

2. The second major meaning of the term bodhrán is related to deafness – *'a deaf person'.*

3. Since c. 1960 'bodhrán' has come to be used to indicate just today's bodhrán drum. But both the 'device' and 'drum' meanings of the word bodhrán apply in the pages which follow.

The tambourine

All forms of the tambourine have 'jingles', which typically are four or five pairs of small metal discs inserted in the rim of the drum, the tinkle of which complements the sound. For modern time there is a need to distinguish between particular forms of what has historically been called 'tambourine'. The first is the one similar to the modern bodhrán, a substantial, c. 35 cm – or more – diameter, c. 10 cm deep, one-sided frame drum with or without jingles. It can be as much as 60 cm diameter and of greater rim depth but both these measurements affect the tone, as does the nature and thickness of the skin.[2] This is a percussion instrument, and is gripped by one elbow or hand and played with the other, or with a stick.

The second is the small, one-hand-operated *con*-cussion instrument, a c. 20cm or so diameter, skin-covered 'rattle', played by shaking, or striking it on the thigh, used widely in popular and in Latin musics; modern forms of it have dispensed altogether with the membrane. Such a rattle-type tambourine is seen often with band singers, and forms of it can be heard on a third of The Beatles' twenty-seven No. 1 singles, although it and the tambourine in general had such an inferior status that it has not ever been listed among their instruments.[3] This form of tambourine is not used in Irish traditional music, but there has been experience of it in Ireland via advertising in Irish newspapers, and through popular musics in the twentieth century.

Percussion tambourines have different names in their various cultures, and those used by the military in the 1700s and the minstrels in the 1800s were in a variety of sizes, often like today's bodhrán. So, for the centuries prior to c. 1960 the term 'tambourine' is used in a generic sense throughout this book to cover all sizes of skinned frame drums with or without jingles.[4]

The term 'music' is used throughout as a noun to denote actual and notated music, and as a descriptor – such as music instrument, performance, show, teaching, event, evening, analysis, history, etc. 'Musical' is only used when describing a person or people with music-making ability, potential or disposition – such as a musical person, family, community, species, race, etc.

Spellings

Spellings of the words 'bodhrán' and 'tambourine' are a major obstacle in web-search negotiation. For in newspaper and written folklore accounts and in dictionaries the drum is found under at least twenty-three different names – bodhrán, bodhrán, badhran, bárán, bodran, bodaran, bodhrahn, bobharan, bodharan, boran, bouran, búdhrán, búran, boarn, boorane, boorawn, bouraun, borne, borran, borrane, bourawn, bowran, bowrawn – and so on. In this book the spelling 'bodhrán' is taken as equivalent to all. So too for 'tambourine', which can also be tambareen, tambarine, tamborine, tamboreen or tambóirín. In quotations from printed sources all of these variants are shown as they were originally spelt, and other mis-spelt words, where they occur, are similarly cited.

The term 'traditional' means the broad field of orally-transmitted, vernacular Irish song, music and dance practices and repertoires in all of the island of Ireland' and its diaspora communities in England, Scotland and north America that were popularly practised in the pre-recording and -broadcasting age, prior to c. 1900. Because the field includes much that was in older court and harp music, some of which is also shared with Classical music, the term 'folk' music is not used in Ireland, except when denoting the more international American and British mid-1900s genre, the style of which spilled over to Ireland in the form of ballad- and folk-groups. The word 'traditional' also implies style, which is passed on only by listening and experiencing, and applies too the wealth of new composition and avant-garde artistry among Irish players.

'Wren' is capitalised in occurrences of aspects of the post-Christmas Wren tradition.

Irish language words

Certain words in Irish recur frequently. These include:

Fleadh / fleadh cheoil – annual traditional-music festivals organised by Comhaltas Ceoltóirí Éireann, one for each of the thirty-two counties on the island, one for each of the four provinces (Ulster, Munster, Leinster and Connacht), each Diaspora region, and one nationally, the All-Ireland.

Feis – a cultural festival which can cover multiple artforms, including Irish dance, as well as traditional, Classical and Choral musics.

Féile – festival or fair.

Precedents

What is given in these pages starts from what has already been on the written and historical record. Established matters – such as the world history of frame drums and tambourines, and the aesthetic and spiritual dimensions of drumming – are regarded as work already done, amply covered in many extant international publications.[5] But most of the numerous studies that have been done on Ireland and the bodhrán are drawn upon or mentioned where it is appropriate, and are evaluated in Chapter 15. Research for this book has been intensive, yet acknowledges that such historically investigative work can never be regarded as complete, and so it is likely – and anticipated – that aspects of the data given here may well come to be clarified, challenged or superceded as fresh digitisation of newspapers, personal correspondence archives and manuscripts brings to light previously-obscured information. Indeed it is hoped that the structure and data here will stimulate fresh and further thinking on aspects of both the present and past.

Accuracy

In folklore accounts and in television and radio interviews the subjects are under a certain amount of pressure, or may be excited, and can inadvertently exaggerate. This is obvious in some cases, but care has been taken to cross-check quotes information where that could be misleading. The same attention has been given to printed data, which may only be as accurate as the reporter's wisdom and skills, or as context and resources at the time permitted. The terms 'bodhrán' and 'tambourine' are endeavoured to be used here as applicable to the periods being discussed at any point.

Abbreviations

RÉ (Radio Éireann) refers to the Irish national radio broadcaster up until 1961; thereafter it was linked to television broadcasting as RTÉ (Radio Telefís Éireann). Its traditional music radio programming is regarded as hugely important in the revival of the music, as associated with it is the name of Seán Ó Riada, whose broadcasts of his newly-arranged traditional music introduced and popularised the bodhrán as a standard instrument. Additionally, television programming introduced the bodhrán visually to audiences all over the island, particularly through annual coverage of fleadh ceoils. TG4 (Teilifís na Gaeilge) is the national Irish language television station which has come to feature traditional music most prominently; RnaG (Raidió na Gaeltachta) is the Irish-language radio station which carries all levels of performance of the music set in a matrix of day-to-day current cultural and political affairs. NFC is the National Folklore Collection; NMI is the National Museum of Ireland; RIA is the Royal Irish Academy, an institute of higher learning in Dublin; UCD is University College Dublin; SC is the *Schools' Collection* of folklore.

Terms: Some terms found in chapters prior to their full explanation include:

Winnowing – the act of separating grain from chaff.

Wren – a seasonal winter tradition which typically involves tambourines or bodhráns.

Wecht and **dallan** – forms of winnowing devices similar to the original non-music bodhrán.

Revival: Two meanings are relevant. The 'Celtic revival' refers to the broad, politics-driven cultural revival in Irish language, literature and theatre in the latter decades of the nineteenth century, which loosely covered music and dance also. 'Revival', however, in these pages generally means the period from the 1950s to the 1990s during which the major transformative initiatives in Irish traditional music were happening in tandem with new economic prosperity and political assertiveness, when the influential music organisations and structures were formed, in particular Comhaltas Ceoltóirí Éireann (CCÉ, in 1951), An Comhairle Ealaíon (ACI, The Arts Council of Ireland, in 1951), Na Píobairí Uilleann (NPU, in 1968), Scoil Samhraidh Willie Clancy (SSWC, in 1972), and the Irish Traditional Music Archive (ITMA, in 1987). CBÉ is Comhairle Béaloideasa Éireann, formerly the Department of Irish Folklore at University College Dublin, and Dúchas is the national folklore digitisation project.

Referencing

Because much of the material and argument is new, references are necessary, but the systems used are varied in order to economise on space and avoid distraction. All references connect to the full title and publisher or interviewee data in the bibliography. There are four referencing formats, depending on what is being quoted:

1/ Where a particular book or source is referenced, there is a note giving the writer's name, the year of publication and the page number, e.g. Murphy 2001, 63. This is typically done as an end-note, but in some passages, where feasible, it is placed at the end of the quotation line where a name or date is important, e.g. [Murphy 2001, 63].

2/ Newspapers are cited with the paper name, followed by year, month and date, and then page number. For example: [*Irish Press* 1938 1230 6] means *Irish Press*, 1938, December 30, page 6. Where the citation is short, the information is given as an end note; but where it is long, it is attached to the quote deliberately in order to make visible the relevant area and period.

3/ References from the NFC's **Schools' Collection** are given in-text in the format (223, 34) where 223 is the collection's book number, and 34 is the page number within it.

4/ References from 'The Four Masters' use the volume number and pages folio. For instance, [4 1016-17] means Vol. IV, pages 1016 and 1017].

5/ 'PC' indicates a personal communication or interview source.

Listen to bodhrán styles on the web

Those not familiar with the bodhrán can listen to a variety of old and modern-day techniques in the playing of nineteen stylists on Robbie Harris' compilation album Pure Bodhrán (log on to bandcamp.com). Among these are performers who are imaged, discussed or quoted in this book: Tommy Hayes, Robbie Harris, Ronan Ó Snodaigh, Jimmy Higgins, Donnchadh Gough, Cathy Jordan, Brian Fleming, John Joe Kelly, Christy Moore, Kevin Conneff, John Reynolds, Colm Murphy, Johnny 'Ringo' McDonagh, Dónal Lunny, Gino Lupari and Glen Velez.

CHAPTER 1
THE BODHRÁN IN TRADITIONAL MUSIC

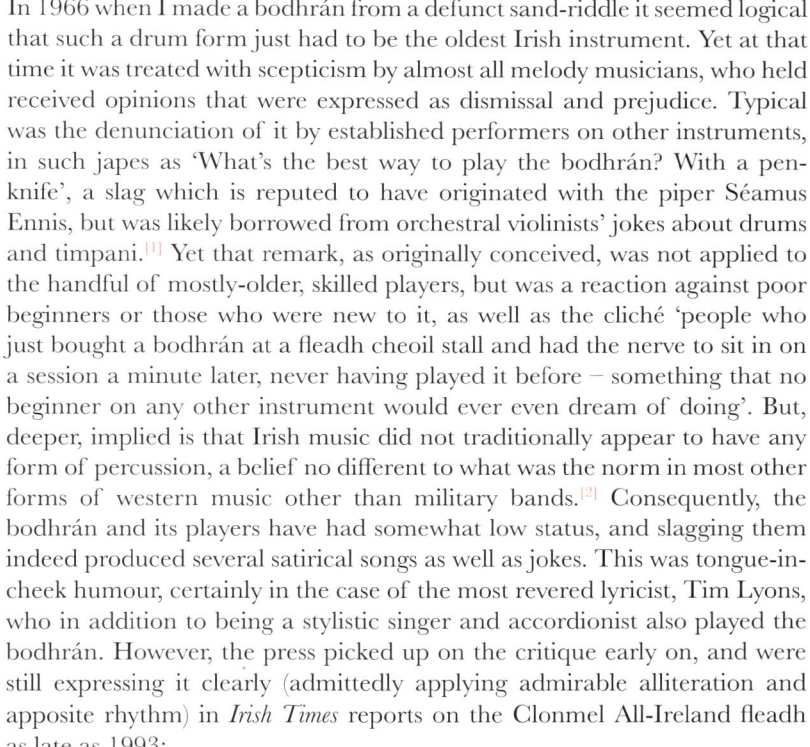

◀ Armagh Pipers' Club performance at the Bogside Fleadh, Derry City, 1969, with Niall Vallely on the bodhrán made by Belfast player Tom Hartley [*Illustration by Lorcan Vallely based on a photo from* The Derry Journal]

▲ The author in Bremen, 1980
[*Photo: Francie Rock*]

In 1966 when I made a bodhrán from a defunct sand-riddle it seemed logical that such a drum form just had to be the oldest Irish instrument. Yet at that time it was treated with scepticism by almost all melody musicians, who held received opinions that were expressed as dismissal and prejudice. Typical was the denunciation of it by established performers on other instruments, in such japes as 'What's the best way to play the bodhrán? With a pen-knife', a slag which is reputed to have originated with the piper Séamus Ennis, but was likely borrowed from orchestral violinists' jokes about drums and timpani.[1] Yet that remark, as originally conceived, was not applied to the handful of mostly-older, skilled players, but was a reaction against poor beginners or those who were new to it, as well as the cliché 'people who just bought a bodhrán at a fleadh cheoil stall and had the nerve to sit in on a session a minute later, never having played it before – something that no beginner on any other instrument would ever even dream of doing'. But, deeper, implied is that Irish music did not traditionally appear to have any form of percussion, a belief no different to what was the norm in most other forms of western music other than military bands.[2] Consequently, the bodhrán and its players have had somewhat low status, and slagging them indeed produced several satirical songs as well as jokes. This was tongue-in-cheek humour, certainly in the case of the most revered lyricist, Tim Lyons, who in addition to being a stylistic singer and accordionist also played the bodhrán. However, the press picked up on the critique early on, and were still expressing it clearly (admittedly applying admirable alliteration and apposite rhythm) in *Irish Times* reports on the Clonmel All-Ireland fleadh as late as 1993:

> Bodhráns packed for the trip to Tipp … Bearing bones, bodhráns, boxes and backpacks, busloads of them were still arriving … [*Irish Times* 1993 0828]

> No escaping bodhrán blight at fleadh cheoil … bodhráns, which constitute something of an affliction. A friend who knows about these things says that true musicians are constantly trying to avoid them. In Clonmel, there was to be no escape: it was a bodhrán blight [*Irish Times* 1993 0830]

The rise of the bodhrán as we know it

The bodhrán first became widely known during the 1960s, helped considerably by radio programming and LP recordings. Remarkably, it went from obscurity to notability all over the island inside a decade, with a captivating, soft timbre and laid-back playing style that was rapidly, progressively developed by a handful of keen, mostly young, innovative, new-professional performers[3] who consulted with various iconic, veteran tambourine players and makers. Their skills and virtuosity gave the drum status, leading to it being seen as synonymous with Irish music both in Ireland itself and internationally. The bodhrán has been adopted by other music genres too, in particular by folk music in England and traditional music in Scotland and by other western cultures. It has been symbolically used as well by major folk/rock bands The Incredible String Band (1966 – '74), Pentangle (1967 – 73) and Steeleye Span (1969 – 78), and latterly by The Corrs and Imelda May in Ireland. The bodhrán's structural simplicity and seductive beat have also projected it into a somewhat ambassadorial role, representative of Ireland itself. So much so that presidents, prime ministers, politicians, sports stars, medical and industrial field leaders have seen fit to be photographed holding it. This endorsement adds to its key sonic and visual roles in Irish music, making it a sought-after memento for tourists of all kinds, for decorative use as well as for casual and professional music-making. A spiritual dimension of the drum has also been kindled (or re-kindled?) and it has developed an additional, more prosaic, use as part of the motivational and provocative paraphernalia of Irish popular sports followers.

It is nothing short of amazing that such a basic instrument could so take over in iconicity from the oldest Irish-identified instrument, the harp, which has been with us for almost a thousand years, or from the authority of the assiduously-revived uilleann pipes, which we have had for close on three centuries. Each of those is at the pinnacle of melodic and rhythmic complexity, and literally hundreds of thousands, if not millions, of pounds and euros, and as many research hours, have been invested in

▲ Ireland soccer personality Jack Charlton poses with Opel-promotion bodhrán [*Courtesy CCÉ and Treoir magazine*]

▼ Instruments aloft, All-Ireland Fleadh Tullamore, 2009 [*Nutan*]

▸ Dublin singer Imelda May [*Donar Ahora, Creative Commons*]

▲ Celebrity poses with bodhrán: Presidents Higgins and McAleese, Taoiseach Bertie Ahern [*Courtesy CCÉ and Treoir magazine*]

their development, revivals and substantial organisational and promotional structures. For it is harp and pipes, joined in the 1800s by a handful of other melody instruments, that have been the vehicles on which Irish recreational and artistic 'traditional' dance music was indeed constructed. Percussion as such has played no apparent pre-twentieth-century role in the music: there is scant evidence of it in Irish music's documented record. So little indeed that one can reasonably ask the question: if Ireland did have a melody-articulating, percussion dimension to its music, where could it have hidden for so many centuries? Why was it not a feature of written and visual antiquarian records of the 1800s and 1900s? And how could it have been so relatively invisible until *c.* 1960? Where indeed did the bodhrán spring from?

What it is

The bodhrán is a single-skin frame drum which is played in a vertical position with a stick, and occasionally with the hand or a knuckle of the first finger; it is gripped with the other hand by means of a cross-bar or wires, or, as generally today, held between the elbow and forearm and the side. With the playing hand the player articulates the beat and rhythm of dance music, most of which is in 4/4, 2/4, 6/8, 9/8 and 12/8 time. This is done while following the melodic contour of the tune, interpreting and accenting its pulse and decorative detail. Pitch can be matched or varied by the action of the holding hand pressing on the inside of the skin for additional colour, volume and resonance: playing the drum is as specialised and demanding as melody-playing and solo step-dance. As with all instruments, there are all calibres of player, from the weak to the mediocre, to the virtuosic. Playing the bodhrán is a skill that involves rhythmic and melodic savvy, close listening, aesthetic judgement and collaborative expertise. It is sophisticated, and – despite the illusion of simplicity – to be done credibly it has to be studied and learnt.

Learn the Bodhrán in 30mins for FREE with me, Paraic McNeela.

Includes a complete beginner's introduction to the bodhrán and a fantastic guide to the various bodhrán beaters and tippers.

First Name

Enter email

Become A Bodhrán Player in 30MIns!

No, I Don't Need Bodhrán Lessons

This drum is a product of the so-called 'revival' period of traditional music in Ireland, which is generally taken as beginning in the 1950s,[4] a process that had eventually emerged out of the strong movements in antiquarianism, history, literature, theatre, sport and the Irish language that fed into the new, partitioned Free State of Ireland in 1921. It has been said, and assumed, that nothing was done for music in that period, but that is not quite accurate when one considers that 'traditional' music, being simply *there*, was in use as the basic social-entertainment medium all through the revolutionary period.[5] Indeed it had already been collected since the mid-1700s, most strongly in the later 1800s. Because it was just 'music', however, indulged in by the less-well-off Irish and some eccentric members of the upper classes, as well as being occasionally played by military bands, it had not been held in any particular regard, or else went unnoticed, by the Anglo-Irish establishment.

▲ The remarkable thing is that a basic technique can actually be quickly learnt, but dedicated playing demands much time and practice [*McNeela Music*]

▼ Tom Murray, James Coleman and Fionn O'Donnell [*James Fraher*]

Yet it can be seen from literature that this Irish music was an essential, functional utility nevertheless, especially among rural, new-urban and emigrant communities, and was always moving seamlessly from old instruments on to modern ones. It was in competition with the easy sounds of the banal and 'popular', and the inferiority-inducing, officially-favoured 'proper' musics, and it was bruised by colonial trivialisation. The harp had been the subject of continued promotion efforts since the 1700s, however, the uilleann pipes had societies in Dublin, Cork and Westmeath, the fiddle retained a universal popularity, the flute passed from military service into recreational music, and the new, factory-produced free-reed instruments – accordions and concertinas – had huge uptake all over the island.

What happened in the 1960s was therefore not so much a revival, as a reconfiguration of the music from once having had a primary purpose for dancing, to now being 'classicised' as a sit-down concert recital or 'listening music'. This, additionally, developed an infectious, sport-like attraction for being participative – played casually by gatherings of otherwise-unaffiliated individuals. For many, it can be consciously nationally-expressive, something which it had not always previously been. The ancestor of today's bodhrán – the tambourine – was originally used mainly in walk-around, minor-theatrical, seasonal ritual on the Wren, and played no significant role in traditional music up until the 1960s. But after that time it got into step with the surge in confidence of Irish identity that marked the economic-change and northern civil rights years. The bodhrán became part of a

▼ Tutors on stage at Craiceann, 2023 [*EDI*]

new popularity, introducing the directive, physical-pulse aesthetics of the military band and popular music, and it was able to achieve a high-point of visibility and consequent approval that led to the emergence of a totally new percussion skills-base and audience.

Scarcity of resources

Establishing an early history for the bodhrán is hampered somewhat by the fact that the island of Ireland has been neither a colonial nor an industrial power that would have supported major material artistic and written historical initiatives and records.[6] On the contrary, Ireland's collective indigenous language and associated arts had once upon a time been politically outlawed,[7] their practice subverted by deliberately-destructive, hostile, formal-education policies and confidence-eroding imperial social mores. Irish cultural and aesthetic artefacts had all therefore to be patiently researched from manuscripts, retrieved and reassembled before, during and following the intensive ideological and, ultimately, military struggle which resulted in the present two Irish states. That we have considerable information on the harp has been due to preservation and revival efforts which have been in train for almost three centuries, as well as the fact that that instrument has, and has had, considerable internationally-applicable and influential variety and performance potential.

The other indigenous instrument, the uilleann pipes, had declined in popularity, but was sheltered by nineteenth-century revivalism, and survived with a degree of respect during the first few decades of the twenty-six county

▲ A 2008 cover of the German Irish cultural magazine *Irland Journal*

▼ Brian Bourke, bodhrán, with Dermot Byrne, Frankie Gavin and Steve Cooney [*Nutan*]

1 THE BODHRÁN IN TRADITIONAL MUSIC

▲ Colm Murphy [*Nutan*]

"I remember Arty McGlynn describing a particular accompaniment of Irish dance music as being 'Loud, confident, and wrong'. To my mind the strength of traditional music lies in its melodic subtlety and verve; augmenting that dynamic is a bodhrán player's primary function, where less is always more"
Colm Murphy

▲ Four Men and a Dog poster illustration

"A history of modern Ireland in a musical instrument: from rural agricultural tool pressed into occasional vernacular percussion use to universally played traditional musical instrument with multiple forms and stunningly developed technique. An example of how Irish musical traditions of the past have been the outcome perhaps of relatively sudden adaptations rather than of slow processes of evolution"
Nicholas Carolan, founding director
Irish Traditional Music Archive

and six-county states, blooming after 1951; its development and status accelerated dramatically following the formation of Comhaltas Ceoltóirí Éireann in 1951, and Na Píobairí Uilleann in 1968. The core melodic repertoires of Irish music are derived largely from Gaelic song and its associated, sophisticated, 'court' harp music, and from borrowing and exchange with the neighbouring island. This, in turn, also had a parallel 'popular' dimension, expressed among the poorer classes in the use of indigenous fiddles, whistles and pipes, and, later, the adopted, sixteenth-century Italian violin, as well as the flute, concertina and accordions in the nineteenth century, all of them used to create and perform – variously – aesthetically-pleasing, artistically-satisfying, social and community-cohesive dance music.

It need not be surprising that, in the midst of such historical melody-centrism, a sighting or record of any form of indigenous percussion would be absent, or, more likely, scattered, and so appear insignificant, if it was observed at all. But there are occasional reports of it – tantalising word of drum-improvisation on the original bodhrán, which, as will be shown, was a ubiquitous household utensil.[8] By contrast, there is considerable 1800s newspaper evidence of the actual tambourine – but rarely in Irish dance music – though such a use was documented occasionally in the 1800s.[9] Then there is some modern-day comment on the tambourine between the 1920s and 1960s. But the earliest stylistic evidence of the sound of a frame drum in Irish dance music is limited to only a handful of early-twentieth-century commercial gramophone recordings that have tambourine accompaniment.

Assumptions

There are many differing beliefs about the origins of the bodhrán, not all of them true. The wrong, the daft, the hazy, the romantic and the good are all promulgated on the live personal-contact grapevine and the internet alike. Among them are numerous factually accurate accounts which, though they may not be complete, are nevertheless key, even where they do not give any obvious or identified sources. The most comprehensive are by Caoimhín Ó Danachair (1947, 1955), Mícheál Ó Súilleabháin (1974, '83, '84, '96), David Such (1985), Janet McCrickard (1987), Svend Kjeldsen (2000, '12, '13) and Rina Schiller (2001); these and others are covered in Chapter 15. International authorities like Glen Velez, Layne Redmond and Richard Graham have explored other related frame drums, their research and knowledge covering the whole planet; the variety of frame drum histories, applications, styles and social functions they deal with are, so to speak, the full jigsaw puzzle to which this book merely adds pieces.

It is taken for granted in the writing that follows that the bodhrán is a form of tambourine, and that the term 'bodhrán', though Irish, is originally known to have indicated an agricultural and domestic tool or utensil.

But since opinions are open, or divide, on the issue of whether or not it was merely *also* a drum, or had once been *primarily* a drum, much old historical detail has been gone into. Each of the major bodhrán commentators acknowledges as relevant, or explores, three or four dimensions of international prevalence and spread of forms of the tambourine: Roman (*c.* AD 100) via their occupation of England; Shamanistic practices associated with the Vikings (AD 800s – 1000s); and

Islamic influence (AD 800 on). On balance, it is concluded that, since the Romans did not occupy Ireland, their direct influence is unlikely, and, also, that there is no obvious evidence of shamanistic use. It seems generally accepted, however, that there is a strong likelihood of an Islamic and southern Italian influence, facilitated by ongoing trade and sea-travel as well

▲ The early Tulla Céilí Band c. 1954 [CCÉ]

as music migrations both before and following the 'Crusades'.[10] Military bands are another important source of influence. These various, and varying, opinions raise questions, among which are:

- What is the relationship of the imported tambourine to today's bodhrán?
- Did the original bodhrán have two distinctly different functions – as both utensil and instrument? And if so …
- Which is the older and which one of them gave the device its name? i.e.
- What does *bodhrán* – literally – mean?

The experience of drums

As an instrument, the 'bodhrán' was little known outside of pockets in Connacht and Munster before the 1960s. And most musicians had never heard of or noticed (or heeded?) its pre-1960s progenitor, the tambourine, even though it had been played on a few early American Irish-music recordings. But they did have experience of some céilí bands using the standard jazz-style drum-kit, a practice which had begun in America and had become popular in Ireland by c. 1938.[11] The justification for those bands' use of the snare-and-bass combination was that in the céilí-dance halls where it was occasionally used, it was said to add solidity as well as some cover for musicians on account of the fact that it emphasised beat, and could articulate rhythm desired by dancers. Most dancers liked the sound of Irish music, but did not necessarily 'know' or follow too many tunes. But

> "When, in 1971, I asked Sonny Davey in Killavil not to include rattles on the bodhrán that he was making for me, I believed that I was buying into an already ancient tradition. But I was in fact a participant in the delivery of a new tradition–the full development within Irish music of a percussive note that had previously had only an insignificant presence"
> *Terry Moylan, piper and music historian*

1 THE BODHRÁN IN TRADITIONAL MUSIC

▶ Drum kit played along with a large bodhrán in a Kerry band at Rathmore fleadh, May 1969 [Kennelly Archive]

> "As a young musician I teamed-up with my Coláiste Eoin classmate Dónall Ó Laighin, a fine bodhrán player; as a duet we entered competitions using that format to show-off our arrangements thus allowing our roles as 'musician' and 'accompanist' to become blurred. We were so fortunate to have been surrounded by great music in that school, including elder bodhrán players Feargal Ó Brolcháin and Stiofán Ó Riain"
> **Cormac Breatnach,** *Musician*

> "While at school in the 1970s I cannot recall the presence of the bodhrán at any of the sessions in the Gorey, Ferns or Enniscorthy areas, but it became part of the early scoraíocht groups, particular players emancipating it by following its tonal nuances rather than just providing a uniform rhythmic beat, more in keeping with the intricacies of the music. A new generation of solo percussionists now take a seat alongside the melodic instruments"
> **Nora Byrne Kavanagh,** *Flute player, music teacher*

they were adept at responding to rhythm and beat, something they had been doing instinctively, often in small spaces, when dancing to percussion-less music for at least the previous two and a half centuries.

A more simple solution can be found for understanding the introduction of drum-kits, however. This was the glamour and power of bass and side drums that had already been established by military and marching bands and, indeed, by the American and British popular music which had entered Irish towns and was coming through on radios and records increasingly after the 1920s. There was also the fact that dancing to céilí bands was being done in halls – bigger spaces with more people – where volume, rhythm and some authority were critical. Beat- and rhythm-marking had previously been unnecessary in the smaller intimate gatherings where no more than two or four couples might be on the floor. Yet, since public response to the céilí band that had a drum was positive, it must be the case that, previous to that, people had an innate and personally-interpreted understanding of the rhythm in the music, and in the new dance-hall environment they permitted expression of that to be mediated for them by the drummer. Either way, by the 1960s drums had become an almost essential ingredient in music for social dancing,[12] and in the hands of a savvy performer they have always contributed to the danceability of dance music and so could enhance the reputations of particular bands. The drum-kit has indeed for long been ratified by Comhaltas Ceoltóirí Éireann by its inclusion in All-Ireland fleadh competitions since 1964.

Suspicion of the drum-kit

This use of the multiple-drum 'kit' in céilí bands is a factor which underlies the tendency towards an unease with céilí bands among many musicians, especially during the revival, in particular the 1960s. From then on, 'real' traditional music was being seen as what was performed by solo, duet, trio and ensemble players, not by céilí bands, as highlighted by Seán Ó Riada (Chapter 10), who held that 'The modern notion of using a jazz drum-kit

▲ Céilí band wood-block player Frank Leahy in The Haymakers band with Andrew McNamara, accordion, and Mike Fitzpatrick, harmonica, at Ennis Trad Fest, 2008 [*Nutan*]

is entirely out of tune with Irish music. Their sound is coarse and without subtlety'.[13] He himself preferred, and introduced, the one-voice tambourine (he used the term 'bodhrán' rather than the then-common term 'tambourine', possibly to suit his aesthetic sense) as a form of bass, and with the valuable potential to play with varying pitch, loudness and texture[14]. Yet, apart from stage concerts, the 'solo tradition' that he spoke of in Irish music[15] (which remains satisfying to most individual players today) is not at all the norm, and in fact all session playing, being unison, could be said to be close to a multiple-instrument céilí band sound at times. 'Solo tradition' is a convention which prioritises the skill and artistic satisfaction of the player. It became psychologically established as a consequence of limits on space, and the need for, or the availability of, only one musician to play at a time in small, cramped household rooms prior to social dances being held in halls; dancers did not need high volume or a sophisticated melody-line. Yet, even though unison playing by multiple musicians in sessions may seem to mimic the céilí band, in that both are built around a melody-centred rhythm or pulse, it does have a significant difference. For while the band members strive to play the same versions of tunes with the same rhythm, session players will not necessarily be doing so. That sense of aesthetic space or non-confinement contributes to the view that céilí bands are not 'traditional music' per se, but are rather an application of it.

Social playing practices have changed, and accompanying rhythm has by now become totally accepted, if not de rigueur, since the 1970s, in the form of the guitar and bouzouki as well as the bodhrán and keyboards, and is generally regarded as being part of the sophistication of traditional music. This is the realm that the bodhrán occupies today, and which has

"The bodhrán brings a magical quality to traditional music, awakening a depth of sonority from its first sounding. It can lighten and enrich music texture through filigree micro-rhythmic interaction with the melodic line, and its versatility can simultaneously carry a pulsating bass and complex rhythmic patterning. Today's performers, supported by responsive advances in bodhrán construction, now bring virtuosity and imagination to music expression"
Helen Lawlor, harp player and lecturer, TU Dublin Conservatoire

▲ Rathaspick Céilí Group, Ferns, County Wexford [CCÉ]

attracted the participation of percussion-oriented performers in what is otherwise a melodic tradition. It is not surprising therefore that varying, and new, opinions will be found in writings on the bodhrán, the first of which appeared in 1947. Many of those are minor parts of tutor publications, but some are dedicated, conscientious and detailed research. Overall, their variety illustrates both the value of original research and the pitfalls of blind acceptance of received wisdom and unchecked information. Forty-one of them are critically assessed or noted in Chapter 15.

Insecurity and challenge

One way or another, percussion has persisted, even though prejudice, practicality and a common sense of music appreciation have kept a lid on over-indulgence in it in the traditional-music session scene. Scoil Samhraidh Willie Clancy in Clare, for instance, has resisted the inclusion of bodhrán teaching, in order to enhance appreciation of melody and style, and to avoid the music venues being overwhelmed by the drum. The end result is a consensus that generally there will only be one bodhrán as percussion, and, indeed, in accompaniment, guitar numbers will be limited too. This is only since the 1960s, as before then there was rarely a bodhrán to be found, and, where it was, it was always called 'tambourine'. The tambourine had indeed been used here and there all through the earlier twentieth century, occasionally part of casual and formal music-making in the hands of such as Thady Casey in County Clare; he was one of a number of resolute, expert players who clearly must have been playing all the year round.

> "Bringing out a tune's rhythm rather than imposing it, a good bodhrán player is a complex animal who combines oxymoronic qualities of drive and subtlety, inspiration and repetition"
> **Verena Commins,** U.G., All-Ireland Minor bodhrán winner 1985, and U-18, 1986

References to tambourines in conjunction with Irish dance-tunes, however, are scarce in any literature prior to the 1950s, whereas, for instance, flutes, fiddles, accordions and uilleann pipes are frequently cited. This would suggest that percussion was not seen as part of, or necessary for, the music – as indicated by statistics published in *A Directory of Traditional Musicians in the Mid-west of Ireland* by Niall Ó Beacháin in 1986. Although only dealing with one region, its figures show that, out of 666 named musicians, only six played bodhrán (five of these from Clare, one from Limerick), seven played the drum-kit, and one the spoons; two of the bodhrán players were women. There can be no doubt that there were many more players on the bodhrán in all of those counties at that time, particularly in County Limerick, but the figures suggest that it was either not played outside of the Wren season and events, and/or was not thought of or regarded with confidence as a bona fide instrument. Such press references as do exist prior to the 1960s show that non-melody contribution to traditional music was more the territory of eccentricity, or a novelty. Yet the fact that there were a number of early-1900s recordings of tambourine players[16] shows that 1/ the tambourine was around in both the USA and Ireland, 2/ there was an accepted, developed, skilled playing technique, and, consequently 3/ it can be deduced that such drumming likely had a historical, if sporadic, basis.

Despite cold-shouldering, resistance, cautious reception, reservations and patronisation, bodhrán playing has prevailed, and developed. Major players have kept their heads both down and up and have pushed out the drum's boundaries from once just being supplementary, to now having equal and even solo status. This will be explored in detail in the chapters that follow.

> "I have been blessed to play with some of the greatest musicians to ever beat the goat skin. The main thing I have learnt is that there is nothing better than a great bodhrán player – one who plays 'in the pocket' – who syncs up everyone while driving them on, raising the bar and making you want to play. I am also aware that there is nothing like a bad bodhrán player to destroy a session!"
> **Joanie Madden,** *Cherish the Ladies*

> "Sé'n bodhrán a chur ar mo thuras mé chun Ceol Gaelach a chasadh ar na píopaí mé! / T'was the bodhrán that set me on the path to playing Irish music on the uilleann pipes!"
> **Pat Mitchell,** *piper and researcher*

◀ Tom Hartley in a renowned northern session at *Pat's Bar*, Belfast with Ballycastle fiddle-player John Mag, c. 1969 [*Courtesy Tom Hartley*]

NOTES TO CHAPTER 1

Notes to Terminology

[1] Respectively, Such 1985, McCrickard 1987 and Houlihan 2007.

[2] The fundamental tone of a drum skin depends on which animal it originates from. Skins have three layers, which can be processed, split, used separately and treated to generate specific pitches. (Kjeldsen 2022, ref. Fletcher and Rossing 1998; Rossing 2000).

[3] Hamelman 2011, 95.

[4] This convention of using a term appropriate to era, even if a new term is later applied, has been used also by Reg Hall in his 2016 thesis on Irish music in London (Hall 2016).

[5] Such as Redmond, Scholes, Montagu, Hart, etc. (see bibliography and references).

Notes to Chapter 1

[1] Groce 1996, 105–12. This writer has a dozen jokes at drummers' expense, several of which have been recycled as bodhrán jokes, but there are as many more bodhrán-specific ones.

[2] Schiller 2001, 103.

[3] Ó Súilleabháin 1974, 5; 1996. The bodhrán's visibility has been heightened nationally by Ó Riada's band Ceoltóirí Chualann (with Peadar Mercier), by Ó Súilleabháin's own work with Mel Mercier, and internationally by touring bands such as The Chieftains (with Kevin Conneff), The Bothy Band (Dónal Lunny), De Dannan (with Johnny Ringo McDonagh and, subsequently, Colm Murphy), Planxty (with Lunny and Christy Moore), Flook with John Joe Kelly and Dervish (with Cathy Jordan).

[4] See Vallely 2020; also 2011, 576 (revival), and 686–90 (tradition).

[5] RTÉ's dance documentary *Steps to Freedom*, broadcast first in January 2022.

[6] Cleary 2006, 78.

[7] For instance, the Statutes of Kilkenny in the 1360s which proposed the outlawing of major Irish cultural pursuits, language, music and sports.

[8] Fenton 1914, 106–7.

[9] O'Daly 1876, 53.

[10] Such 1985, 9.

[11] Ní Fhuarthán 2022, PC. John Lynch writes of the Kilfenora Céilí Band having a bass drum and snare strapped to the roof of the car on the way to a venue in that year.

[12] There were exceptions of course, these included the Laichtín Naofa Céilí Band in Miltown Malbay County Clare, with which Pat Kelly once played bodhrán.

[13] Ó Riada 1972, 76.

[14] Kinsella 1982, 76.

[15] Ó Riada 1972, 73

[16] See Chapter 14 for these.

▼ Peadar Mercier playing with Dan Dowd, Séamus Ennis and an unidentified flute player [*Photographer anon, courtesy of the Irish Traditional Music Archive*]

CHAPTER 2
THE URGE TO DRUM

School musicians at Listowel Feis, County Kerry, May 1955 [*Kennelly Archive*]

Lyre and tambourine players, Babylon, Iraq, 1900–1700 BC. [*Pergamon Museum, Berlin, Germany. Image copy by Patricia Vallely*]

Hundreds of bodhráns are made and sold in Ireland each year, most of them bought by tourists. Many are also acquired by both established and aspiring players, so there is no doubt that there is a 'drum constituency' in the traditional music psyche. As in other societies, percussion music is the easiest to improvise and, because it has most often been the territory of the poorer classes, it can go undocumented. Assumptions and guesswork are therefore understandable, and necessary, as long as they are guided and scaffolded by evidence. Starting with basics, noise-making which can sometimes appear rhythmic is a feature even of animal life.[1] So it is hard to imagine any human society that would not want, or feel compelled, to make noise as a physical, rhythmic response to music.[2] Rhythmic movement and noise-making – dictated by heartbeat and breathing – came before vocal music, and all predate instrumental music.[3] Melody as we know it is unique to the human species, and instruments for producing it have been made for millennia; bone flutes are the oldest, one early specimen of which, found in Slovenia, is said to date back 50,000 years. But such instruments, adapted from nature-formed bone tubes, are a long way from the technique of tensioning and fixing a skin on a hollow frame to make a drum in order to create a desired sound and effect.[4] That was not being done until much later, *c*. 5600 BC, as can be seen in shrine painting of instruments at Çatal Hüyük, Anatolia, Turkey, and in the Louvre museum, Paris sculptures of female tambourine players from Mesopotamia (modern-day Iraq), *c*. 2340–1500 BC. Drawings from *c*. 2700 BC Babylonia give the earliest surviving depiction of round frame drums.[5] That those are shown being played alongside female dancers as an established practice at that time means that the drums were already being made and used earlier than that.

Material evidence

It may not be possible to know when drums were first created, but it is established that they were initially made from pre-existing containers like shells, gourds, hollow tree-trunks and, latterly, discarded everyday utensils.[6] Yet while bone flutes can survive the ravages of time in damp climates, skin, wood and fibre generally do not, so, if there was a drum in ancient Ireland, appropriate archaeological instrumental information would simply be absent. But there is much evidence worldwide – written in iconology and in imagery. For the Middle East it can be found first in the Old Testament, which often mentions the timbrel. This is corroborated by archeological finds in Palestine – clay, female figurines playing the '*tof*', a tambourine.[7] Surviving occurrences of this kind of artefact, as well as carved relief panels, show that there has been a presence of frame drums across the Asian continent from Mesopotamia to Japan, as far back as the third millennium BC.[8] Material evidence elsewhere shows that they have been in many cultures in all eras, in different sizes, and under different names, 'the most geographically spread drum in history',[9] and 'that with the longest continuous history'.[10] They are seen in sculpture and visual art, most of the time with spiritual significance, and, as stated already, played by women.[11] A later Christian example of such is a multi-jingled tambourine played by a woman which is part of a remarkable fourteenth-century stone frieze known as 'The Minstrels' Gallery' in Exeter Cathedral, England; jingles were an early Christian era Roman addition to the tambourine, and were eventually adopted by the Turkish.[12] Frame drums have also had a major association with shamanism, 'a traditional belief system that survives among' Arctic, native American, native Australian and some African peoples that links the temporal with the otherworld, dealing with healing and counselling. Such practice was most likely the case in Ireland, too and for this reason, the Irish frame drum, the bodhrán, is utilised today by Newgrange, County Meath winter-solstice celebrants who intuit that it is historically relevant for Ireland.[13]

If this is the case, however, it is about a more ancient humanity – for no such instances have been documented over the first two millennia. But it is known for sure that frame drums not unlike the bodhrán – the timbrel, tympanon or tympanum – did play ceremonial, sacred roles in ancient Egyptian, Greek and Roman societies.[14] This is mentioned in Latin-language manuscripts, and there are many surviving objects to prove it; the tympanum indeed is reported as 'an impressive percussion instrument'.[15] However, the fact that the terminology used in the past varies, as do translations, can lead to errors in modern-day understanding.

▲ Figurine of the Goddess Cybele with tambourine, c. 200 BC [*Courtesy of the Master and Fellows of Christi College, The Fitzwilliam Museum, Cambridge*]

No drum visible in ancient Ireland

Settlement in Ireland, which dates to at least 10,500 BC, has preserved no material evidence of music, but early immigrants to the country c. the fifth century BC are associated with found wind instruments, not with drums.[16] Writing, in the form of ogham, is limited to memorial and boundary stones, so there is no written information about music from earlier times. More complex melody instruments do survive, however – harps from substantially

▲ Bodhráns used for spiritual ambience to mark the winter solstice at Newgrange, County Meath, 2022 [*Dúchas*]

> "In 1979 I became enchanted by the magical music of The Chieftains. That's where I first saw the bodhrán, and was swept away by its dignity and the intricate way it is played … that heart-stirring, throbbing beat … The ancient lingering connection between the frame drum and the Great Mother Goddess can be traced in the bodhrán too"
> **Janet E. McCrickard**

later, from the fifteenth to the nineteenth centuries. And since the Irish climate does not preserve organic materials, the only information on earlier instruments that we have comes from texts dating to around a thousand years ago. Also, because nothing can be taken at face value in medieval writings, to know what kind of music was being played at that time we have to depend on comparative information from British and continental sources for suggestions and implications. As for the types of instruments played, music archaeologist Ann Buckley says that 'it is impossible to establish conclusively whether there were characteristically Irish instruments in existence during the early middle ages.' And whether or not there were drums – they are not present in records – is debatable, on account of the fact that 'Scant references to other instruments in the early sources should most probably be understood that they did not feature prominently in court life'. The main reported instruments were *cruit/crot* (harp) and the *tiompán/timpan*, 'both stringed instruments'; the *timpan* was initially plucked, but would have come to be bowed around the eleventh or twelfth century, when the bow was adopted in western Europe.[17] Still, it is likely that shamanism was a feature of ancient Irish culture, this involving using a drum to reach self-induced trance and ecstatic experience. And we could have had such an influence from Scandinavia in an earlier period, for Ireland was not isolated in the world, and 'entertainers from Iceland were said to have visited the courts of Hiberno-Norse kings in Dublin in the 10th century'.[18] How much influence that might have exercised on the greater native population outside of the courts, however, is a matter for debate. There are a few images relating to music from the Irish Middle Ages, one being the drawing of a harper in one version of Giraldus Cambrensis' account from *c*. 1188. (see p. 28). There is but one depiction of a frame drum player, which appears on a small, sixteenth-century engraved ivory book cover panel that was found in a house in Donabate, County Dublin in 1850 and is now in the National Museum. This shows four men in a sword dance, with a fifth figure holding a small frame drum. But considering the material that the book cover is made from, it is certainly not an artefact representing vernacular music-making; Ann Buckley suggests it may depict a pageant, or seasonal play. The object most likely did not originate in Ireland, but it is the only evidence that there could have been knowledge or awareness of a frame drum in Ireland at that point in time.[19] We have indeed copious records of tambourines in Ireland in the eighteenth and nineteenth centuries, so the history of that drum is important to explore.

Female-centred religion, deities and priests

Much fascinating research has been done on the tambourine internationally, an instrument at the core of pre-Christian religions which worshipped female deities, female-centred belief linking the moon, fertility and sexuality, something addressed in an Irish context regarding an Irish frame drum by Janet McCrickard in 1987. Among celebrated goddesses from some 1400 years before Christianity were Hathor (at Dendera) and Isis in Egypt, Cybele in Anatolia, Aphrodite, at Kition in Cyprus, Ariadne on Crete. Associated with them was an ecstatic, prophetic religion.[20] Birth and death were occasions marked with tambourine-playing and music. Many of the symbols from these religious practices were to be later adopted – but masculinised – by Christianity. Hundreds of tambourine-bearing images, carvings and statuette castings celebrate these deities and female priests, prime among them being Cybele; two painted frame drum skin heads celebrating Isis from *c*. 1600 to 1100 BC Egypt still survive. Layne Redmond's extraordinary study *When the Drummers Were Women* details the millennium and more of their being worshipped, as well as their usurpation and condemnation as demonic following the transition to male-deity, one-God worship. With the ancient Greeks' elevation of strings music to superior status, tambourine played by women was demoted;[21] the drum was converted from female, sacred instrument to male device of war. Roman sculpture and friezes in the early Christian era show women with tambourines in ecstatic Dionysian celebration. But over the course of the fourth century AD, Christianity eliminated the tambourines, the women and explicit genitalia. Women in music and dance were banned in 300 AD,

▲ The earliest depiction of jingles on a tambourine, on a Roman sarcophagus, second century AD [*Walters Art Museum, Baltimore, USA*]

▼ Military band, late 1700s, with tambourine [*Farmer*]

2 THE URGE TO DRUM

again in 850 AD: 'Actors, athletes and professional musicians could not be baptised. In the sixth century, Pope John III outlawed the tambourine'. The older religious practice went somewhat underground, surviving marginally for instance in Gypsy/Roma performance-traditions in modern time, and in the association of the drum with women and sexuality that lingered as part of wedding customs in present-day Afghanistan.[22] A continuity with the older, female practice is seen in the 1930s women's bands (featuring *daireh* frame drum players) in Herat, which are described as linking 'sieves, frame drums, dancing, prostitution', the menfolk playing on *sarinda* strings, the women performing seductive dance.[23] Among the ancient Jews women danced, sang and played the *tof* frame drum too, as seen in figurines from 1000 BC, and indeed this instrument appears in Christian celebratory images as well under its biblical name 'timbrel',[24] a practice continued in a rudimentary way by Salvation Army bands. In the Marche region of Italy a highly-developed tradition of singing narrative, social-commentary lyrics by older women and men in an open-metre, nasal, *sean-nós* style with fabulous hand-struck *tamburello* tambourine persists today,[25] and there are similar music-accompaniment practices in Albania, Ukraine and Estonia. The cults of Isis and Cybele ultimately spread in Europe, including to Paris, their association of the tambourine with women being one route by which the frame drum travelled into Europe from the Middle East; a second-century AD Roman-sculpted sarcophagus shows a woman playing a tambourine with mounted jingles.[26] In the Romantic period, late 1700s to mid-1800s, the tambourine was visually highlighted in art, and it became a fashionable instrument for song, piano and harp accompaniment by women, some of their abilities and styles reported as virtuosic.[27]

But aside from the ancient links between women, dance and tambourine in spiritual practices, in Europe there does not generally appear to be an elemental link between drumming and secular social dancing. Indeed, drums can be seen to have not been universally needed for such dance in modern time, notably in Ireland, where, from the seventeenth to the early twentieth centuries, reporting and images show that dancers used only melody, with no formal instrumental percussive rhythm.[28] There are, however, occasions of informal dance in art images showing children dancing to a mother playing a tambourine (see p. 25). But a major European exception is the use of the tamburello with tarantella dance which emanates from Sicily, a practice which with migration spread the tambourine from there to England and America, and filtered out to influence the forerunners of popular music, the nineteenth-century 'minstrel' troupes.[29]

Drums and war

Drums, like people, moved with migrations, as agents in politics, religion and ceremony alike, and by the Middle Ages they were a major instrument in Islamic societies and on the African continent in many variations, trickling into southern Europe. War was a major force in driving this, utilising the excitement and intimidatory aspects of drumming:

> Music is an essential to war, and an army would as soon think of leaving its gunpowder as its harmony at home. In all nations from the earliest times music has been the accompaniment of feats of arms, and served the two-fold

▲ Colm Murphy with Sami Lapp drum [*Nutan*]

▲ Carved 'monster' tambourinist, India

purpose of inspiring the troops to fight, and as a means of conveying orders or commands. The noisiest instruments were naturally the best adapted for this purpose: 'The shrill trump, the spirit-stirring drum'.[30]

One major era of this military drum usage is found in 400–200 BC India, documented in the 'Bhagavad Gita' [Song of God] in the Hindu Sanskrit epic poem the Mahabharata:[31]

> On hearing Bheeshma's call for battle, everyone in the Kaurava army also started playing various instruments eagerly, creating tumultuous sound. *Shankhāh* means conches, *panav* are drums, *ānak* kettledrums, *bhreyah* bugles, and *go-mukh* are blowing horns. All these instruments playing together created a loud pandemonium.[32]

Of more relevance to Europe was the use of drums by Saracens to inspire their armies in Palestine in the course of their expansionism and during the Crusades from 1095 to 1291 AD, and thereafter up until the 1500s. Drums were a key part of their military efficaciousness, as a result of which *nakeres* (kettledrums) and other drum forms, including the frame drum, came to be adopted by Europeans;[33] the Ottoman Empire had additional influence in southern Spain and in the Balkans. Drums were such a vivid part of warfare and soldiers' experience in all centuries up to the twentieth that it is not surprising that percussion had slipped into recreational favour and vernacular music as early as the fifteenth. Exceptionally popular then was the 'tabor',[34] a small one-hand-operated drum played along with a one-handed flute. Textual evidence of this in England is supported in stone carvings as far apart as Exeter (1240 AD) and Beverly (early 1500s).[35] This instrumental combination also still thrives today in the Basque Country of Spain as *dambolina* (drum) and *txistu* (three-hole flute), a practice which was in turn brought by the Spanish and Portuguese to Ecuador and the Americas.[36] The 'kettledrum', of specific military origin, came to orchestras following the Crusades as 'timpan/timpani', a term which, sounding similar to the Roman *tympanum* frame drum, has caused such confusion in the Irish context. Early Irish military activity had music, in the form of the bagpipes, and it also used 'vocal sounds, battle-cries and drones … wind instruments producing terrifying sounds to put the enemy at a psychological disadvantage'.[37] But drums were not part of it until 1601.

▲ Pipe and tabor player, detail from 'Introduction of the Cult of Cybele to Rome' (c. 1505) by Andrea Mantegna. [*Image copy courtesy Patricia Vallely*]

▼ 1750 military tambourine [*St Cecelia's Hall, Edinburgh*]

The military tambourine

Internationally, the military came to have the most dramatic application of percussion, in marching bands as snare and bass drums, a compellingly attractive and authoritative use of sound which by the second half of the

2 THE URGE TO DRUM

twentieth century became incorporated into and taken over by popular and rock musics.[38] Apart from those, and the huge, Irish-invented bass drum the Lambeg, the issue most relevant to the bodhrán story is likely to have been the experience of frame drums that followed European military borrowing of percussion from Islamic forces in the 1200s and 1300s.[39] The purpose of those was to inspire troops and frighten the opposition, a dramatisation of warfare which gradually became a practice of all European armies, being used by the English by 1333:

> Then the Englieshe mynstrelles beten ther tabers, and blewen their Trompes and pipers pipedene loude and made a grete schowte upon the Skottes . . .[40]

Nicholas Carolan's translation of accounts of music instruments used in Ireland prior to the seventeenth century shows that drums proper were at that period very much instruments typical of the English,[41] and that their adoption in Ireland was as spoils of war:

> Captured at the Yellow Ford were thirty-four military banners, all the military drums, the war-cannons, a great number of weapons and all the provisions . . .[42]

Drums were standard English army equipment by the 1500s, as seen in John Derricke's accounts of the military in Ireland, by which time the French term 'bande' had come to be used for military music ensembles.[43] Drums and fifes were the instruments used for regiments of foot-soldiers, but for demonstrative, ceremonial use, more formal music and structures were developed. Such military-music ensembles in Europe and England copied the Ottoman empire's Janissaries' range of percussion and concussion instruments, adding a tambourine, creating their own Janissary-style music. The frame drum model which this music adopted was the large

▲ Tambourine player, British Regiment of Foot, 1830 [www.armoury.co.uk]

▲ Tambourine player in Duke of Gloucester's Band [britishempire.co.uk]

▶ Lambeg drummer, Belfast, 1969 [Nutan]

bejingled Italian tamburello that by the early 1700s was an immigrant Italian buskers' instrument[14] in London, and went on to be part of popular, orchestrated music.

Janissary – 'Turkish' – music was taken up by the Austro-Hungarian military *c.* 1741, then formally by the British *c.* 1785.[46] One British regiment, the 29th, known also as 'The Ancient Britons', had already adopted the Janissary visual and instrumental formula earlier, *c.* 1759, involving black players – Guadeloupe boys who were considered to be 'very ornamental as drummers'. That regiment had been sent to Boston during the American Revolutionary War, 1775–83. During the 1798 rebellion in Ireland, it was routed at Ballyellis, County Wexford where one of the black drummers was killed; a later, 1832, image from the regiment shows a black tambourine player.[46] Military bands also had a popular-music function, the earliest being the band of the Coldstream Guards which began a regular stint at London's Vauxhall Gardens entertainments in 1790, playing there until 1805; thereafter its members played under the name 'The Duke of Gloucester's Band', later 'The Coldstream Band'. The 'pleasure gardens' was the centre of the fashionable cultural life of England at the time, patronised by all social classes from royalty to servants. It thereby linked high and popular culture, and was a site of experience of new styles, instruments and dances for all classes. One of the instruments utilised in the military-band performances there was the tambourine, which in 1821 was depicted by George Cruikshank being played by a black, turbaned performer. In 1798 it had already been reported in *The Morning Post* and *Gazetteer* that the duchess of York was being taught the instrument by one of the band's black musicians. Tambourines were acoustically a minor part of drumming volume in each ensemble, but were visually symbolic: 'Three black men were employed to beat the tambourine',[47] for spectacle. Exemplifying their dramatic role is the report that in one such British band these played while 'marching in front, performing all sorts of contortions and evolutions whilst playing their tambourines'.[48] This description suggests a prototype of the performance style adopted in the following century by civilian 'minstrels', troupes of whom toured in Ireland in the 1800s, and indeed by twentieth-century loyalist flute and drum bands in Ulster, if not indeed by Wrenboys. It also suggests a precedent for the idea of 'blacking up' in connection with physically-demonstrative music.

The tambourines used in the Janissary-inspired bands are reported as being 'very large'.[49] One which is similar in size to tambourines of the time, and indeed to today's bodhrán, is seen in an eighteenth-century painting being played with the hand.[50] A tambourine with a larger diameter and deeper rim would give a more booming sound,[51] its loudness demanding attention and giving it some authority. This quality would have been a reason for use in military or political contexts, such as that reported in Fifeshire, Scotland, where the suburb of Nethertown had preserved an old sort of drum , hidden away in Thresher Charlie's Garrett. This so-called Nethertown Weicht belonged to a secret political society, 'The Friends of the People', founded in 1796 on French revolutionary principles[52]

▲ Tambourine Frazier, Royal Tyrone Regiment [*royal-Irish.com*]

▼ George Cruikshank's depiction of the tambourine with the Duke of Cambridge's military band at Vauxhall gardens in 1821 [*Sir John Soane's Museum, London*]

Bodhrán player Svend Kjeldsen gave this military aspect some attention in 2012, also noting that British military tambourines were large, this to do with volume:

> To fill the needs of London's military percussionists, instrument makers such as Joseph Dale and Cornelius Ward created oversize tambourines that could be heard above the din of a marching band[53]

Military tambourines in Ireland

These drums are likely to have been the role models for the larger Munster bodhráns in the mid-1900s, where knowledge of drumming and making drums could have been brought home by any local man who had been in a regiment that had used them. One such was the Tyrone militia, the band of which had a large bodhrán-sized decorated, hand-struck tambourine played by a black man known as 'Tambourine Frazier'. In 1797 the regiment was at Bantry Bay, Cork in anticipation of a French landing, and in 1798 they were deployed against the United Irishmen in County Kildare, at Tubberneering and at Vinegar Hill, County Wexford.[54] Indeed a later sketch of the Vinegar Hill battle shows what is possibly a captured tambourine being paraded (see p. 127). Music was a feature of their marching, and they are reported as playing *c.* 1809 at a party in Wexford for a politician's birthday, and 'contributed not a little in detaining the joyous party to a late hour next morning'. They also 'accompanied the Lord Lieutenant on a tour on the Grand Canal and played concerts in Dublin that year, including at the Rotunda Gardens'.[55] 'Seven or eight' of the players were black, said to have come from America following the War of Independence, where, as slaves, they got their freedom in return for fighting for the British. Their colour was considered to add 'a degree of exotica' to the band who all were 'extravagantly uniformed'.

The militia was posted variously to Dublin, Wexford and Limerick and other counties.[56] Some of the Irish bandsmen among them may have returned to home communities in Ireland after the fighting and, certainly, many non-musician soldiers would have done so. Also, those in other

▲ Regimental tambourine of the First Food Guards regiment as played by 'tambourine Frazier', made by Goulding, Soho Square, London [*National Army Museum, London*]

▼ *Illustrated London News* supplement banner showing a tambourine among military weapons and music instruments

regiments would have observed instruments and style too. There was indeed a variety of means through which awareness of the military tambourine would have spread.

As for early use of such a military tambourine in Ireland, one tale may be relevant, that of a 'rousing' association implied in schoolteacher William Ó Danachair's passing on of lore about how in the sixteenth century 'the *bodhrán* was used formerly to provide martial music in west Limerick'.[57] This story does seem a fanciful hear-say, for taking it at face value it would have had to be a large bodhrán with a tightly stretched skin, a tambourine copy. Since the first historically mentioned drums in Ireland were British, in the same period, the late 1500s, it seems more likely that it was such an actual captured military drum that the folk memory is referring to in this story. Also, at the time the source of the information was speaking (*c.* 1930), it was within the experience of educated people that in dictionaries the words 'drum' and 'big drum' were among the translations being given for the word 'bodhrán'.[58]

Historical tambourines in various museums support the idea of the role of the British military in that drum-type's introduction to Ireland. One of them which is displayed at St Cecelia's Hall in Edinburgh (see image on p. 20), a fine specimen of a military-style orchestral tambourine dated 1750,[59] is of a similar size to the north Munster tambourines. This gives shape to a story told to journalist Tom Aherne by the Sheehys of west Limerick that tambourine-making and -playing skills were brought to the region originally by an ex-British-

▲ Scotish painter David Allan's 'Sir John Halkett of Pitfirrane, 4th Bart (1720–1793), Mary Hamilton, Lady Halkett and their Family'. The tambourine was a fashionable instrument for young upper-class women in the late 1700s. [*National Galleries Scotland (NG 21)*]

▶ 'Private House Concert with Two Children Dancing', by Pietro Fabris (1756–92) [©*Hampel Fine Art Auctions*]

army drummer.[60] Considering the army's deployment all over Ireland, and the fact of numerous Irish men being part of it, some of them later teaching music and band-marching skills in local communities, it is indeed likely that the large, Italian-influenced military tambourine was one early role model for Irish tambourines.[61]

Tambourines and the gentry

The military-band adoption of the tambourine did contribute in a formal and documented way to familiarising the European music world with that drum. The consequences of the flamboyant disposition of non-white tambourine players in the Janissary practice would have been memorable and influential as well, and very likely to have played a role in subsequent peacetime interest in tambourines, the best-documented of which was the 'blackface' minstrel practice that was hugely popular after the 1830s on music-hall and vaudeville stages. But aside from the military band influence in the late 1700s, the tambourine had already come into western society through commerce, sailors, travel and the music trade. Richard Graham and Sam Girling point to the presence of the tambourine in fashionable music education of wealthy-society young women in the late 1700s

▲ Strolling players at the Fuochi di San Giuseppe festival in Itri, Lazio, central Italy, 2025 *[Helen Walker]*

and early 1800s.[62] This is seen often in art from the period, such as the 1781 Scottish painting on page 24 which has a tambourine with jingles being played 'up' and with the fingers, in the Italian or Arabic fashion, along with a long-neck lute.[63] The fact that this was Scotland, and no symbolic bagpipe or fiddle was present, and that all those taking part seem at ease with the instruments, suggests not just approval for the fashion, but familiarity with it. This of course was a depiction of the upper classes, but the use of drums did gradually filter out into entertainment experience through orchestras.[64]

The *Illustrated London News*, a graphically illustrated magazine which ran weekly from 1842 to 1971, reflected this commonality, having a tambourine at the centre of its supplement's banner logo (see p. 23). The tambourine was also in British folk music by the 1700s, and – in the opinion of Reg Hall, who has documented Irish music in London – through the experience of Irish migrants it would have likely had an influence in Ireland: 'what happened in England, happened in Ireland'.[65] The tambourine made its way into theatre productions, and it was already on stages in Ireland by the 1740s. In this way, both the object 'tambourine', and knowledge of it as a hand-struck frame drum, entered the urban public experience. Irish big-house people had knowledge and experience of its fashionable application in music education, and deployment on the popular stage. And, as in all matters, serving house staffs from the poorer classes were witnesses to this, observers who disseminated such awareness and information back to their communities.

There are in fact numerous occasions of music influence and experience being shared among social classes in Ireland, not least in singing, as seen in 1842 advertising for mass teaching of sight reading to singers in William Forde's *Voice of the People* project, and by the Temperance movement's alliance with the German mass sight-singing instructor Joseph Mainzer[66] in the same period. In instrumental music in Ireland, big-house activity included balls and parties, accounts of which indicate that favoured local people from lower social classes were present from time to time. The servants, coach drivers, ground staff and such who were on the premises certainly could witness what took place, so information was constantly passing in and out, among classes – upstairs to downstairs, so to speak: servants were well placed to be aware of music instruments. Such potential for an interchange interface between music practices can be seen for instance in Hilary Pyle's account of one big-house butler, Gorman, who 'had come to Skreen from the Leitrim Militia when it was disbanded … was also a flute player, and played at all the Skreen dances'.[67] This has also been described for the nature of the gathering depicted in Daniel Maclise's 1832 painting *Snap Apple Night*.[68] But there are additional factors to consider in Ireland, not least the widespread use of frame drum types in many other countries.

This chapter introduced the idea of the spread of drums in Europe over an almost 2,000 year time span, and of how the tambourine would have been known in Ireland. The chapters which follow will show how this drum became embedded in Irish social life; but first, the idea of an Irish percussion needs to be looked at in order to establish whether or not the adopted tambourine was a replacement for an indigenous Irish drum. There has been much confusion about this, and many questionable assumptions have resulted, these emanating from differing interpretations of the name and nature of an old Irish instrument, the *timpan*. This will be considered in the next chapter.

▲ East African percussionist playing a square tambourine, c. 1995 [EDI]

▲ A woman sings to her own vigorus tamburello playing, Marche region, Italy

▲ Gian Franco Santucci from the Campania region of Italy, with the *tammorra*, a form of the Italian tamburello, a performer at the final William Kennedy Piping Festival in Armagh, 2025 [EDI]

▶ *'A Dedication to Bacchus'*, fanciful, ecstatic tambourine–women association in ancient Greece depicted in an 1889 Romance-theme painting by the Dutch artist Lawrence Alma-Tadema

NOTES TO CHAPTER 2

[1] Dean 2011, 4 cites a report that in Taï Forest, Ivory Coast, chimpanzees 'seem to use drumming on buttressed trees to convey information' (Boesch 1991, 81).

[2] Ibid., 4, and Dowling 2009, PC.

[3] Quirey 1976, 10.

[4] Dean op. cit., 6.

[5] Skinner 2012, 3.

[6] Skinner op. cit., 7.

[7] Galpin 1956, 62.

[8] Ibid., 111, 145.

[9] Ibid., 5.

[10] Montagu 2010, 11.

[11] Redmond 2018, 1–11; McCrickard 1987, 19–25. Redmond's book carries scores of remarkable images of pottery figurines, reliefs and paintings showing female tambourine players, many with bodhrán-size instruments, dating from 2300 BC up to the 1500s AD.

[12] Graham op. cit.

[13] Newgrange is a neolithic site dating to 3100 BC (see bodhrán footage on Irish Central, 2022).

[14] Redmond op. cit.; McCrickard 1987, 21–6.

[15] McCrickard op. cit., 23.

[16] Buckley 2005, 745.

[17] Ibid., 749–50.

[18] Ibid., 764.

[19] Ibid., 773.

[20] Doubleday 1999, 104; McCrickard 1987, 21–5.

[21] Kartomi 1990, 110.

[22] Ibid., 4.

[23] Baily 1988, 34.

[24] McCrickard 1987, 17–19.

[25] See 'Italian tamburello' on page 323.

[26] Graham 2022, PC. One such second-century AD, Roman sculpted sarcophagus held at the Walters Art Museum, Baltimore, USA, carries a stone relief carving *The Triumph of Dionysus*. This depicts a woman playing a tambourine with jingles. Because other carved and mosaic depictions of the same story do not have jingles on the instrument, Richard Graham believes this to be the earliest appearance of jingles, meaning that their addition was a Roman innovation.

[27] Skinner 2012, 10; Scholes 1987, 781.

[28] Feldman and O'Doherty 1979, Preface.

[29] Roth 2022, PC.

[30] Farmer 1904, 5. The end quote is from William Shakespeare's *Othello*, act 3, sc. 3, l.

[31] *Encyclopedia Brittanica* online, 1998–2022.

[32] 'Bhagavad Gita', 2022.

[33] Ibid., 12–13. This is widely reported, notably also in Scholes 1987, 777; Dean 2011, 11; McCrickard op. cit., 19.

[34] Scholes 1987, 777; Dean 2011, 162.

[35] Montagu 2010, 209.

[36] Ibid., 211.

[37] Buckley 1990, 40.

[38] Dean op. cit., 199–200.

[39] Galpin op. cit., 62.

[40] From a ballad in the Harleian MS on the victory of Edward III over the Scots at Hallidon Hill, 1333 (Farmer 1904,15).

[41] Carolan 2001, 51.

[42] Ibid., 50, translated from O'Sullivan Beare 1625.

[43] Farmer 1904, 25. By 1661, the previous English word for a combination of musical instruments in performance had been, simply, 'noise' (ibid.). However, in his 1912 study (p. 55) Farmer says that the general use of 'band' was not the case until the nineteenth century.

[44] Graham 2022, PC.

[45] Farmer 1904, 51. Farmer (1912, 73) refers to the Turkish music craze.

[46] Worcestershire Regiment, 2022.

[47] Farmer 1912, 69, 75.

[48] Farmer 1904, 51.

[49] Farmer 1912, 75.

[50] Ibid., frontispiece.

[51] McCrickard 1987, 11.

[52] Ibid., 8.

[53] Kjeldsen 2012, 50.

[54] An image of the Vinegar Hill battle published fifty years later shows a woman with a tambourine. This is speculated in Chapter 8 as the (later) artist's artistic licence, but one could of course have been captured from a British regimental drummer.

[55] Doherty 2022.

[56] Inniskillings, 2018.

[57] Uí Ógáin 2002, 142. Information on Desmond on odonohoearchive.com; The *Schools' Collection*, Cáit Ní Tarrant, as related by Mr Jerh. Sullivan, Glounawaddra, Kingwilliamstown, Gleanntán, Scairteach an Ghleanna (Cordal east), p. 257.

[58] Foley 1855, 47; Fournier 1910, 89; MacCionnaith 1935, 365; Dinneen 1927.

[59] The inscription for this item, no. 3332, says that such tambourines 'joined the orchestra in the 18th century'. While drums in general 'provided rhythm, excitement and a touch of pomp and ceremony, hand-held percussion instruments provided special effects where needed'.

[60] Aherne 2011, 26.

[61] Graham op. cit.

[62] Ibid.; Girling 2018 and 2022.

[63] Harte 2020, 10.

[64] Scholes 1987, 781.

[65] Hall 2023, PC.

[66] McHale 2007, 166.

[67] Pyle 1997, 35.

[68] Murray 2008, 96: '… persons of superior position in society were to be found unaffectedly mingling with the poorest peasantry of the parish' (Anon, 1845).

quodam alio sunt. tam remoti
z a modestis z mongeranis popu-
lis tam segregati. solam uirurū bar-
bariem in qz uiuūt sunt z nutri-
ti sapiunt. z assuescunt. z tanqz
altam naturam amplectunt. Qd
gz in huis nature illud optimum. de
quo fere industrie. illud pessi-
mum. De gentis istius z muitis
instrumentis peritia incomparabili.
In musicis solum instrumentis com-
mendabilem inuenio gentis istius
diligentiam. in quibus pre omni na-
tione quam uidimus incomparabiliter z
structa e. Non in hiis sunt in qz
tranuolu ciubs; assueti sunt, tarda
z morosa. instrumentis modulatio.
uerum uelox z preceps. Suauis tñ z
iocunda sonoritas. Mirum qd
in tanta tam preipiti digitorum ra-
pacitate. musica seruatur propor-
tio. z arte p omnia indempni. int'
tripartos modulos organaqz multi-
pliciter intricata. tam suaui uelo-
citate. tam dispari paritate. tam di-
scordi concordia. consona reddit' z
completur melodia. seu diatessa-
ron. seu diapente corde concrepent.
Semp tñ a B. molli incipiunt. z i
idem redeunt. Vt cuncta sub iocūde
sonoritatis dulcedine compleant'
tam subtiliter modulos intrant
z exeunt. sicqz sub obtuso grossioris
corde sonitu. gracilium tinnitus lice-
ti ludunt. latentius delectant. laci-
uiusqz demulcent. Vt pars artis max-

ima uideat' artem uelare. tamqz
si lateat prosit. serata ars depren-
sa pudoreni. Hinc accidit ut
ea que subtili' intuentibz. z artis
archana acutius discernentibz. int-
nas z ineffabiles comparant ani-
mi delicias: ea si attendentibz. si-
cut uidendo si uidentibz. z auditu
si intelligentibz. aures poth' hone-
rent qm delectent. z tanqm con-
fuso inordinato qz strepitu muitis auditoribz. fastidia pariant
tediosa. Notandum uero qz
Scotia z Gwallia hec ypagarionis
illa coniuratonis. z assimilatis
gz hiberniam immodum emu-
la imitari nititur disciplina.
Hybnia quidem tm duobs. uti-
tur z delectatur instrumentis.
Cythara. s. z tympano. Scotia tri-
bz. Cythara. tympano. z choro.
Gwallia uo. cythara. thubiis z
choro. E'neis magis utuntur
cordis. quia de corio fctis. Multor
autem opinione hodie sco-
tia ñ tm magistram equiparat
hyberniam. Im z in musica pi-
tia longe prualet z precellit.
Vn t ibi qz fontem artis iam re-
quirunt. De comodis z effecti-
Musice sonoritatis h; que sue
dulcedo nõ tm delectat
modicū. qu imo iuuat z cō-
modis. Animos itaqz tristes si
mediocriter exhilarat. Nubilos
uultus serenat. supcilium ponit

F
de instrumētis hybin-
ie. Guallie
z scoci-
e

VII

CHAPTER 3

THE IRISH TIMPAN: STRINGS OR DRUM?

Percussion in the form of the bodhrán is taken for granted in Irish music today, despite the fact that historically the music has been defined by solely instrumental melody and song. No form of drum can be found to have been associated with it in the ancient past. Yet some form of independent existence for a basic drum in Ireland should not be ruled out, not least because to have a drum would seem so logical. There is evidence that Ireland possibly had castanet-style *crotals* as an instrument, but from the BC period it certainly did have melodic instruments in the form of bronze horns and trumpets, 120 of which have been found in various parts of the island, made first between 1500 and 1100 BC.[1] These would have been used for ceremony and war, and possibly had a role in celebration or recreation.[2] Their use had died out by 500 BC after the end of the Bronze Age, and, following that, there is much manuscript information, from as early as AD 592, that the formal, and taught, music-making in Ireland was based on strings, some form of harp being earliest.[3] Associated with that was another widely-mentioned stringed instrument, the *tiompán* or *timpan*. The understanding or acceptance of what that one word meant in ancient Ireland has led to considerable speculation. The Irish timpan was a stringed instrument, even though the

◂ Page 75 of the National Library's edition of *Topographia Hibernica* which gives detail on music [*National Library of Ireland MS 700*]

▸ Harp drawing in *Topographia Hibernica* [*Topography of Ireland*]

◀ Cambrensis' lines 1–3 mentioning 'cythara & tympano'

term sounds the same as 'timpanum', which at that time in England and Europe was a drum, like a tabor drum, or a tambourine, and also the Biblical 'timbrel'. Irish manuscripts are clear about this distinction, but the picture became clouded on account of later misunderstanding of words written by the Anglo-Norman chronicler Giraldus Cambrensis.

Enter Cambrensis, AD 1188

'Cambrensis' was born Giraldus de Barri in Pembrokeshire, Wales *c.* AD 1146, and educated at the Benedictine abbey of Gloucester. He 'was drawn to literature and an ecclesiastical career', and learnt Latin in Paris where he spent thirteen years studying law, philosophy and theology. In 1183 he visited Ireland 'where his family were the chief instruments in the conquest', and returned again in 1185, 1199 and 1204.[4] He 'diligently explored the site and nature of the island and primitive origin of its race',[5] out of which he wrote *Topographia Hibernica* [Topography of Ireland]. From a colonist perspective this was 'all that is known of the state of Ireland during the whole of the middle ages, a few barren Chronicles excepted'.[6] But from an Irish perspective it was considered by Geoffrey Keating 'the false history of Ireland'.[7] Cambrensis' account of the nature of Ireland and its society was based on time spent in counties Cork and Waterford, with visits to Dublin, Wicklow, Kildare, Meath and Westmeath – an investigation of interest to English colonial expansion. He added material from other writers, the substance of which had, according to one editor 'as much to do with Ireland or its people as with the moon and the man in it'.[8] The work was completed and presented with great ceremony in the three years after AD 1185. Cambrensis' opinion of the native Irish was somewhat contemptuous, but, in spite of that, John O'Meara, the 1951 translator of his work, believes that without it 'our knowledge of the Ireland of the twelfth century could be much the poorer'.[9] Cambrensis did say some favourable, and often-cited, glorifying things about music style, but what he said about music instruments was limited. Writing in Latin, he noted that associated with the harp in Ireland was another instrument that he spelt 'tympano',[10] his approximation of the sound of the Gaelic term *tiompán* or *timpan*:

> Hybernia quidem unn duob; utitur et delectatur instrumenti. Cythara et *tympano* / Ireland uses and delights; in two instruments only. The harp and the timpanum[11]

Subsequent assumption that his Latin word 'tympano' translates into English as 'drum' has resulted in much confusion. This happened later, attention drawn to it by Edward Bunting in 1809, who initially was not aware of the nature of the instrument that Cambrensis had actually been referring to, and had assumed that he meant the European timpanum, a drum. So, considering the passing of years, and going by what was a European standard, the mistranslation of 'tympano' as 'tabor', drum, isn't an unreasonable error – but nonetheless it is inaccurate.[12] John O'Meara's more authoritative, modern interpretation explains that for Ireland in the period being described, 'one played on the timpanum with one's fingers, or a plectrum'.[13] A rebuttal of the 'drum' meaning for timpan had already been made before Bunting's time, first by Charles O'Conor (1710–91), Joseph Cooper Walker (in 1786) and Edward Ledwich (in 1804), then emphasised later by the Gaelic scholar Eugene O'Curry[14] (c. 1862) and by Grattan Flood in 1927,[15] to the extent that it could be said categorically that 'the Latin tympanum signifies a drum or tambourine … the Irish timpan was, in fact, a stringed instrument which was sounded with a bow'.[16] The timpan issue has caused such mis-direction in thinking about today's bodhrán that its history will now be looked at.

The Fair of Carman, ended c. AD 718
The earliest mention of the timpan occurs in a description of a variety of instruments in a social context that is found in a poem describing the Fair of Carman in County Kildare that took place prior to AD 718. This is in a lengthy verse which appears in a manuscript, the *Book of Leinster*. The poem mentions 'timpan', along with harp, trumpet, horns and pipes:

> *Is iat a ada olla* / These are its many great privileges
> *Stuic, cruiti, cuirn chraestolla* / Trumpets, cruits, wide-mouthed horns
> *Cuisigh, timpaig cen triamna* / Cuisig, timpanists without weariness
> *Filid ocus saen chliara* / Poets and petty rhymesters[17]

Allowing for the fact that this account was written c. 1160,[18] and may have been listing what were the contemporary norm at fairs at that time, it would still show that the instrument known as timpan was on the island at least in Cambrensis' time, indeed corroborating his reporting of it. As for ascribing a meaning to timpan for that period, there is nothing in the quoted poem to indicate what it actually was, though subsequent writing gives much clarity. The idea of it being a drum in these circumstances would be fascinating, as thrilling as a late-night, town-square All-Ireland fleadh scenario, or a drumming display under a bridge in Portadown on July the twelfth. But if that was the case it is unlikely that it would not have been documented elsewhere.

The *Irish* tympanists, AD 721

The nature of the Gaelic timpan as a stringed instrument is, naturally, accepted by scholars today, but its drum meaning for English and European contexts still stands – and this can cause problems. One such instance is seen in translations of a paragraph from *The Fragmentary Annals of Ireland* concerning the year AD 721, which describes a rowdy party scene with music:

> dream occ cusleannaigh & oc featchuisigh; timpanaigh & cruitiri og seanmain

John O'Donovan translated this in 1860 as 'some piping, some whistling … tympanists and harpers were playing'.[19] But a 1978 translation, presently on the CELT website, erroneously applies the drum meaning to timpan: 'some piping, some whistling … drummers and harpers playing'.[20] This is out of step with established thinking, and is misleading,[21] as will be seen in the chronology of the progress of establishing the nature of the timpan that is given in upcoming pages. Yet, despite this, it is not unreasonable to think that the European drum tympanum, or knowledge of it, was also present in Ireland at that time, through south-east-coast settlement by Normans (these including some of Cambrensis' family), people who would have been influenced by Roman culture in England. And while Roman influence is not considered likely to have been of significance in Ireland, nevertheless its associated terminology could well have found its way here.[22] Anyway, Cambrensis himself had little experience of the real Ireland and its cultural pursuits, since he dealt only with occupied Ireland. Yet, even there, as well as colonial and court instrumental music, there would also have been a vernacular music which could well have included percussion that he did not observe. Yet that would indicate all the more that he was aware of the indigenous nature of the timpan as a stringed instrument in court music, and that he intended just that by using the term 'tympano'. There is also the point that in Cambrensis' 'third book', in which his music comments appear, he acknowledges that he did consult some written sources from which he could not have avoided knowing about the timpan as a stringed instrument.[23] Looking at other documents' mention of timpan and timpanists verifies this, and reinforces the belief that Cambrensis knew well that he was referring to a stringed instrument, not a drum.

▲ Manuscript detailing instruments at a gathering in AD 721 [*Corpas of Electronic Texts, courtesy celt.ucc.ie*]

▶ Comment on the Fair of Carman from O'Curry [*Sullivan 1873, 530–1*]

▶ From Joseph Cooper Walker's 1818 *Historical Memoirs of the Irish Bards*

Thus it is they used to hold this fair, by their tribes and families and households, to the time of Cathair Mor; and Cathair, however, bequeathed not Carman unto any but to his own descendants, and the precedence he bequeathed to the race of Ros Failge, their followers and their exiles, to continue the fair *ut* the seven Laigsechs and the Fotharts; and to them belongs [the right] to celebrate it, and to secure it from every disaster [while] going thither and returning thence. There were seven races there every day, and seven days for celebrating it, and for considering the laws and rights of the province for three years. It was on the last day of it the Ossorians held their fair, and they coursed it every day before closing; and hence it was called the steed contest of the Ossorians. The Forud of their king was on the right hand of the king of Leinster, and the Forud of the king of Ua Failge was on his left hand; and in the same manner their women.

On the Kalends of August they assembled there, and on the sixth of August they left it. Every third year they were wont to hold it; and [it took] two years for the preparations. It was five hundred and eighty years from the holding of the first fair in Carman, to the forty-second year of [the reign of] Octavius Augustus, in which year Christ was born.

Three markets there, viz., a market of food and clothes; a market of live stock, cows and horses, etc.; a market of foreigners and exiles selling gold and silver, etc. The professors of every art, both the noble arts and the base arts, and non-professionals were there selling and exhibiting their compositions and their professional works to kings; and rewards were given for every [work of] art that was just or lawful to be sold, or exhibited, or listened to.

Corn and milk [were promised] to them for holding it, and the sway of any invading province should not be over them, but that they should observe the Fridays, and that they should fast, men, women, boys, maidens, as well as exiles, chiefs, champions, and clerics. [They were also promised] prosperity and comfort in every household, and fruits of every kind in abundance, and abundant supplies from their waters, and fertility to the land of Leinster. And, moreover, that decay and failure and early grayness should come upon their men, kingly heroes, and women; and the forfeiture of his land or its price from him who evades it, men, kingly heroes, and women; and that failure [of] young kings, mean clothes, and baldness would come on them unless they celebrated it, Ut Fulartach cc.

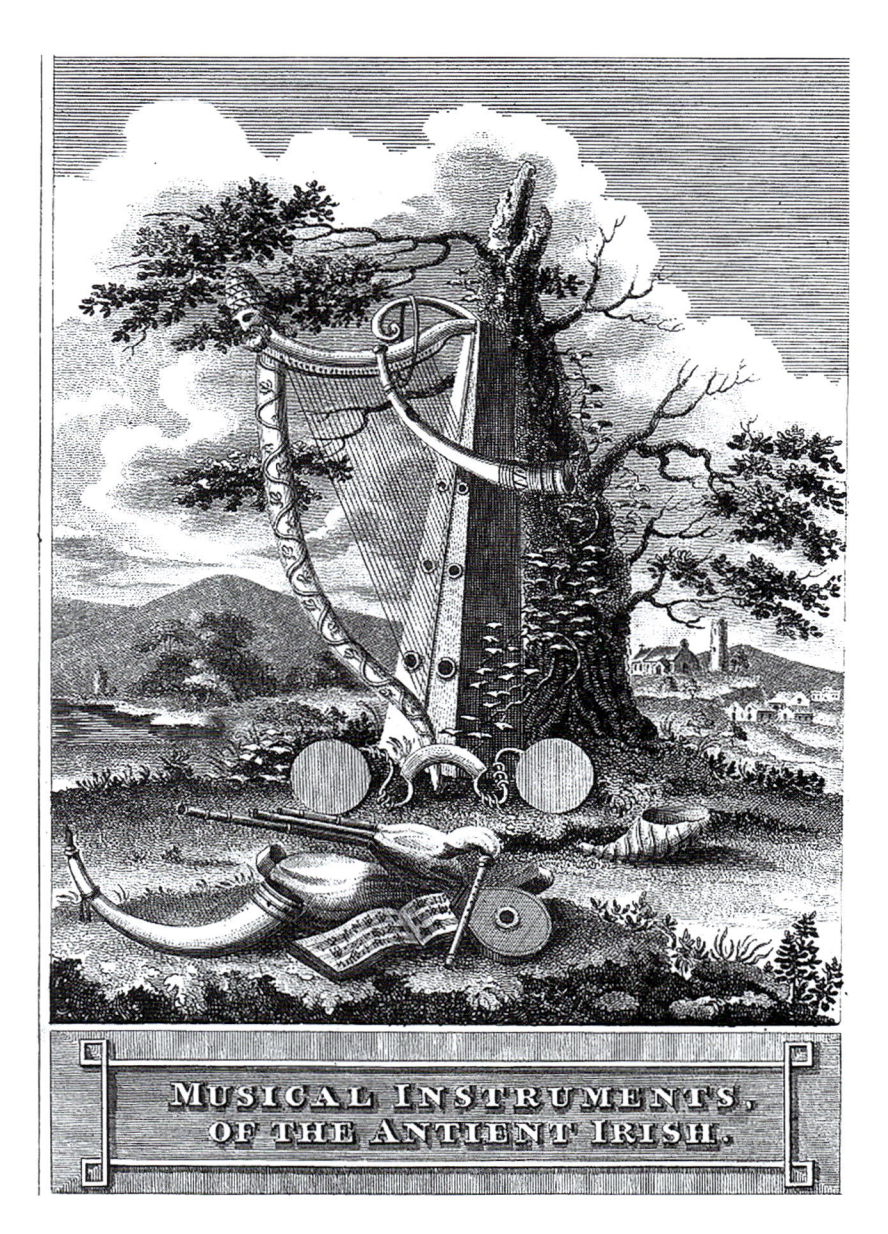

MUSICAL INSTRUMENTS, OF THE ANTIENT IRISH.

'The Four Masters', period AD 1328–1616

Sixteen separate entries give the names of eight timpan players among the dozens of musicians who are named in the various Irish historical annals manuscripts,[24] typically as notices of their deaths as high-status performers or teachers. The seventeenth-century *Annals of the Kingdom of Ireland*, popularly referred to as 'The Four Masters',[25] is one of the documents concerned, a six-volume history of Ireland covering from 2951 BC up to 1616. Its information on the pre-Christianity period is quite arbitrary and uncertain, mythic indeed, bordering on fictional and fantastic.[26] But the AD years chronology is more substantial, being a vivid record of kingship, chieftains, deaths, destruction, hostage-taking, depredation, plundering and warfare in Ireland, that progresses from internecine struggles, through Danish and Norse invasions to, finally, resistance to Normans and the English. It was commissioned by the Sligo chieftain Fearghal Ó Gara, and was compiled near Donegal town over the years 1632–46, hosted by the Franciscan friars there in huts close to the ruins of their monastery which had been occupied as a garrison by the English in 1601. The work was copied on to vellum from earlier manuscripts by Michael Ó Cléirigh and Ferfeasa Ó Maelchonaire, from Roscommon, and Cucogcridhe Ó Cléirigh and Conaire Ó Cléirigh from Donegal. A section covering 1171–1616 was published by John O'Donovan in 1848, followed by the full work in 1856, a translation based on original papers the provenance of which was verified by the pioneering archaeologist and music collector George Petrie in 1831. O'Donovan added extensive footnotes, some on music, and corrected many earlier translation errors. Among the history's myriad references to plagues, famines and weather extremes there are numerous mentions of 'keepers of a house of general hospitality', a term which implies socialising and intellectual life, likely sites of music-making, as well as music patronage.[27] As in other such documents, the music and instruments which are indicated are not necessarily those of the plain people, but are of the courts, so it cannot be assumed that there were not also other instruments.[28] In the earliest among the Annals' listing of deaths, in AD 1328 O'Donovan translates 'tiompánach' as 'minstrel':

> Maolruanaidh, an rogha tiompánach ereann, 's alban esidhe ina aimsir / Mulrony, Chief Minstrel of Ireland and Scotland in his time.

And elsewhere, the word timpan is assumed to mean the stringed instrument:

> Mulronie Mac Kervel, chief Musician of the Kingdome, and his brother Gillekeigh, were killed in that company, of whom it's reported that no man in any age ever heard, or shall hereafter hear, a better Timpanist[29]

In AD 1361 'Magrath O'Finnaghty, Chief Musician and Tympanist to the Sil-Murray, died',[30] and in AD 1490 so too 'Finn O'Haughluinn, Chief Tympanist of Ireland'.[31] There is no indication of the presence of music used by the Irish in battle at any point, but drums are indicated on the English side. This is in the comment by Cucogry O'Clery on the 1598 battle of The Yellow Ford near Armagh, in which he cites Irish chieftains O'Neill's and O'Donnell's words of exhortation to their troops prior to the battle, which suggests that drums – called 'tábúr' – may have been strange to the Ulster fighters:

> 'A dhéaghmhuintir', ar siad, 'na huaimhnighthír sibh, 's na gabhaidh gráin siar na gallaibh ar allmhurdhacht a ninnill, 's ar iongghnaithchiu a n-eittigh 's a narm, 's la toirann beice a trompa, a tábúr 's a caismearta catha'

> 'Brave people', said they, 'be not dismayed or frightened at the English on account of the foreign appearance of their array, and the strangeness of their armour and arms, the sound of their trumpets, and tabors, and warlike instruments'[32]

Detailed description is given at times of the Irish disposition of weaponry, such as O'Donnell's preparation for an attack in 1599 which includes

> shooting parties [muskets, javelins, stone-pelting], with their high-sounding, straight-shooting guns ... strong, smooth-surfaced bows ... bloody, venomous

▲ Irish military piper, by John Derricke, 1581 [*Courtesy Wesley Boyd and The Blackstaff Press*]

javelins and other missile weapons. Over these soldiers he appointed a fight-directing leader, and a battle-sustaining champion.

But there is no mention of drums, indeed not even of a piper, with the Irish, even though the English troops are described as sounding their trumpet and other martial instruments. Regarding the same incident, another chieftain, O'Rourke, who was nearby, is reported as having heard the sound of the English trumpets and drums.[33]

The Annals of Ulster also carries references to timpan and timpanists, first in 1177: 'The Timpanist Ua Coinnecen, arch-ollam of the north of Ireland, was killed by the Cenel-Conaill with his wife and with his people'.[34] It also details a mass killing in 1329, in the course of which the instrument is identified as stringed:

> And on the same day, in this massacre, Ó Cearbhaill, that famous timpanist and harpist, supreme in his art, mighty in precedence and excellence, lay in the grave in the same place with about twenty other timpanists, his students. He was called Cam Ó Cearbhaill because he was one-eyed and could not see straight … and if he was not the the first inventor of the art of string music, nevertheless, of all his predecessors and precursors, he was corrector, scholar and director.[35]

The Zoilomastix, AD 1625[36]

Further writing by Philip O'Sullivan Beare, *c.* 1625, casts some more light. For he strongly refuted elements of the picture of Ireland that had been presented by Giraldus Cambrensis:

> I can give no thanks to this most petulent and abusive man; I have no high opinion of belated and untimely praise. I refuse the rock-hard bread given by this most malevolent little man; I am wary of a sword smeared with honey. For I think he celebrates Irish music with such great praise, not so that he may make us famous by some commendation, but that he may demonstrate the sharpness of his own intelligence[37]

He also challenged the writings of Richard Stanihurst (1547–1618) who he said

> can be seen to have neither ears nor understanding when, in contradiction of experience and the unanimous evidence of writers, he disparaged Irish musicians … Hardly any harper could be found … more impaired in his sight than you are in your mind, you who, if you were to be faithful to the historical truth, would pass on [miss] the fact that the strings of the harp are never of iron, but are of brass or silver, and are used also by musicians on the tiompán. They strike the harp with the tips of their fingers, but the tiompán with plectra.

> The Irish play on the harp, on the tiompán … and on the … bagpipe … and on the later lute, trumpet, military drum, and pipe or flute or reed-pipe.[38]

This reference to the military drum may reflect the idea that the drum came from outside, with the English military, as described in Chapter 2.

Charles O'Conor (AD 1710–91)

The earliest modern-day commentator on the actual nature of the timpan in Ireland was Charles O'Conor, an Irish-language scholar, antiquarian and Catholic activist, of Belanagare, County Roscommon, a direct descendant of the kings of Connacht and the last high-kings of Ireland. As Catholic schools were proscribed by law, he was educated at local hedge schools, in their classical mould that was typical of education of those times. He started Latin at the age of seven, and went on to read Ovid, Suetonius and Erasmus, later studying mathematics, science, and French. In his lifetime he is said to have acquired or seen practically every major Irish manuscript, and read the important writers of his time in English and French, and studied the Irish literary tradition, a broad erudition which places him as an authority on ancient Ireland.[39] Bunting (1840), O'Curry and Sullivan (1873) all cite him as the person who was the first to show clearly that the timpan was a stringed instrument.[40] This O'Conor had done from the study of old manuscripts, a process which O'Curry then retraced in detail in the following century. O'Conor's translations have been corrected by subsequent scholars, notably by John O'Donovan in 1856, but none of the critique of his work concerns the timpan, the source for the data on which was the Stowe MS.

Joseph Cooper Walker, 1786

Subsequent dealings with Cambrensis' *tympano* have, however, generated a muddiness. The earliest in print was by Walker in 1786, who, without giving any source, said:

> the Tabour was always a favourite instrument amongst the Irish, of which the Flute, or an instrument of the same species, has ever been the associate.[41]

Because of his absence of a source, it could be presumed that he was interpreting Cambrensis 'tympano' as a drum. But as he goes on it becomes clear that he merely means that the drum, which had been imported, had become a favoured instrument, for he continues:

> the DRUM, which we had either from the English, or from the Holy Land, by means of some of our Quixote-like adventurers, who turned their arms against the Pagans. The Drum, according to le Clerc, was an Oriental invention; a circumstance which seems to make for the latter conjecture.[42]

And he proceeds to rationalise that Cambrensis' 'tympano' could not be a drum, drawing as evidence on a manuscript from AD 1340 which extolls the merits of O'Carrol, the Harper, and his pupils who were described as 'tympanista' (as discussed also on the previous page). Walker says that if it is clear that in Cambrensis' time harping was a sophisticated art, and – since O'Carrol performed on two instruments, the tympanum and the harp – if the tympanum was a drum, then

> what great execution could be expected on the Tabour, so as to merit so high an eulogium*?[43] Even if he played on Tabours of different sizes, of which we have no intimation, the merit must come short of the praise.

This leads him to think that by 'tympanista', Clynn, the scribe, would understand O'Carrol to have been 'a master of music', and his twenty scholars were

> tympanists, that is, masters of the science ... He does not say those scholars were Harpers, for that they were in perfection; they were more, they were Composers and Masters of music, or Tympanists.[44]

Lending weight to Walker's deduction that the tympanist was not a drummer is an appendix in the same volume, an explicit letter from the antiquarian

▼ Walker's comment on the drum as having come from the English

3 THE IRISH TIMPAN: STRINGS OR DRUM?

Edward Ledwich, a passage which Ledwich himself indeed felt it important to repeat in the first edition of his own book a decade later:

> a mistake of Cambrensis unfolds itself to view. The Irish, he informs us, used but the Tabor and Harp. Here then could not be a varied combination of sounds; a multiplicity of parts, or such an artificial composition as to constitute counterpoint; a single melody, and that confined within a small compass, was all that could be executed … Cambrensis must have been ignorant of the art he was describing, or extremely inadvertent, as no such effects, as he suggests, could be produced by such instruments … An omission of a transcriber very probably gives rise to the error.[45]

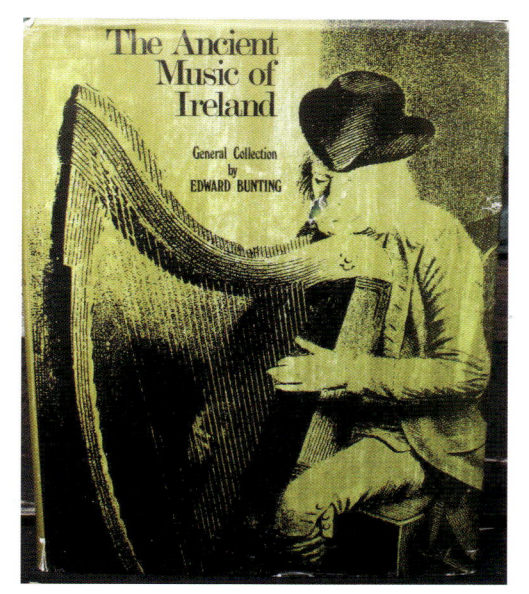

Here, Ledwich was challenging the interpretation of tympano as tabor. The progress of such comments shows that translation and interpretation of Cambrensis are of key importance, something which arose shortly afterwards in the writings of the first major collector of older Irish music, Edward Bunting.

Bunting, 1809: Skin versus strings

None of the nineteenth-century music collectors, commentators or authorities reported or described tambourines or bodhráns being played in indigenous music-making. The most influential of these, Edward Bunting, however, in his 1809, second, *Collection of the Ancient Music of Ireland* is the exception, for he repeated the suggestion of the favouring of a drum in the country. What he published, without a written description, was an image of two drums, one an actual European timpan, or kettledrum, the other a large metal-rimmed frame drum, similar to an Italian tamburello.[46] The fact that he showed two very different drum types, and without comment, suggests that he did not have, or had not himself seen, any evidence of a drum, and was merely showing generic drum images. His comment took its direction from Cambrensis[47] whose 'tympano' he initially interpreted as meaning 'tabor', when he says 'Ireland, indeed, employs and delights in only two instruments, the Harp and the Tabor'.[48] However, contradictorily, in a footnote, Bunting also gives information from the 1300s which challenges that:

> In Trevisa's translation of *Higden's Polychronicon* of the thirteenth century, in describing Irish manners, we find this observation … Irishmen be cunning in two manner instruments of music, in Harp and Tymbre, that is armed with wire and strings of brass, in which instruments, tho they play hastily and swiftly, they make right merry harmony and melody …[49]

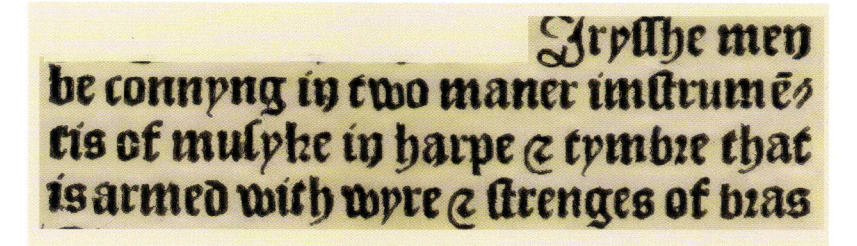

The Ancient Music of Ireland by Edward Bunting, 1969 edition by Waltons, Dublin

▶ Higden's *Polychronicon*, thirteenth century, repeats what Cambrensis wrote

▼ The drums depicted by Bunting, 1809

Not only does this clearly describe strings, but it quotes a source close to Cambrensis' time, which can be taken as meaning that Cambrensis had intended 'tympano' to mean a stringed instrument. But in the same volume Bunting seems to revert, again, when he says that 'the *tympanum* mentioned

37

by Cambrensis as an instrument of Ireland, was a species of drum'.[50] By the time of his much-expanded 1840 third volume this confusion had been somewhat resolved, in that he carried no image, and corrected himself, citing the pre-Norman (1169) and pre-Danish (700s) poem from which Charles O'Conor had deduced that the timpan was stringed. By now he elaborates on how Cambrensis

> states that the Irish used and took delight in two instruments, the harp and tympanum … As to the tympanum, which has generally been supposed to be a drum, Doctor O'Connor [Catalogue of Stowe MSS. vol. i. p. 147] adduces an Irish poem, certainly composed before the destruction of the Irish monarchy by the invasion of the Danes [c. AD 795-980], in which the harper is directed to mind his *cruit*, and the minstrel the strings of his *tiompán*, or his *tiompán* of strings.[51]

Bunting then adds his own deduction as to what the timpan actually was like:

> it seems evident, as the learned writer shows, that this instrument was a species of lute or gittern; for, in a passage of Suetonius [in Aug. c. 68], descriptive of a Gaul playing on it, it is further characterized as being round, and played on with the fingers; and it appears also from Ovid [In Fasti, 1. iv. v. 302], to have been covered with skin, in a word, an instrument in all respects resembling a south Sea islander's guitar. It is very remarkable, that in Shane O'Neachtain's song of Maggy Laider, an Irish composition of the seventeenth century … this primitive instrument is introduced as an accompaniment of the bagpipe: *Seinn duiñ steangcan, piob as tiompán*.[52]

The idea of a circular instrument played with the fingers is tempting to imagine as a drum, but Bunting clearly dismisses this, and reasons tiompán to be a stringed instrument. The example he gives for the latter is not the modern European guitar, but a primitive form of lute which had a skin-covered resonator. Guitar-like instruments were known in Europe from the tenth century, among them the Persian, Chinese, Japanese, west African and Egyptian lutes which were circular, and had a skin-covered wood body.[53] Bunting's statement here suggests that the image of a frame drum that he showed in 1809 was a fanciful one, and an error, not a valid historical record. In a separate glossary of terms in the same 1840 edition he corrects the error, but confuses this by also reprinting from his first edition 'Tiompán' meaning 'A drum, tymbal or tabor'.[54] It may be, however, that his retention of that was less an oversight, and more an effort to include the European meaning of the word. But because he does not mention the Irish timpan in the glossary at all (the very stringed instrument that he has argued for in the same book) suggests a lack of conviction or information. Mícheál Ó Súilleabháin acknowledges this seemingly ambiguous treatment of the word 'tympanum' as 'a mystery',[55] something that is acknowledged too in later scholarship, notably in the *Encyclopaedia of Music in Ireland*:

> Owing to confusion with its Latin translation, *tympanum*, it is sometimes erroneously referred to as a drum … but it is clear both from literary references in Irish and Latin sources that this was a stringed instrument.[56]

Eugene O'Curry (1794–1862): the 'timpan' was *not* a drum

Eugene O'Curry, a close friend of John O'Donovan, was first professor of archaeology and Irish history in the Catholic University of Ireland. He was

▲ Eugene O'Curry

the next major commentator on the fallout from the Cambrensis statement and what he saw as a misinterpretation of 'tympano':

> But, a greater mystery than this attaches to the instrument itself, which the Gaedhil called a Timpan. We know that the English Tymbal and Latin Tympanum mean a drum of some sort; but it is beyond all doubt that the Irish Timpan spoken of in our ancient Irish MSS., was a stringed instrument, one of the kinds of harp.[57]

O'Curry did not live to see his work published, but this was done under the editorship of his colleague William K. Sullivan, a remarkable Cork polymath who was professor of chemistry at the same university. Elected a member of the Royal Irish Academy in 1857, Sullivan went on to be president of Queen's College, Cork (now UCC). Applying his expertise in Celtic studies and Irish history, he voluminously edited O'Curry's lectures for publication a decade after the writer's death. In the course of the introduction to this it was firmly stated that the Irish timpan had been a stringed instrument, and indeed the reader was reminded that O'Curry was not the first to say so.[58] O'Curry himself was a rigorous researcher who was passionate about early Irish cultural practices, an expert on the body of Irish manuscripts which hold orally-passed-on information relating to the earlier centuries of society and life in Ireland. He presented his findings from 1857 to 1862 as a series of thirty-eight lectures on all aspects of early Gaelic culture that he prepared while he was chair of Irish history and archaeology at the then new Catholic University in Dublin (now University College Dublin).

The final eight of these were titled 'Of Music and Musical Instruments in Ancient Erinn', upon the completion of the last of which he died suddenly. All of his lectures, edited by Sullivan, were published in 1873 as three volumes titled *On the Manners and Customs of the Ancient Irish*. Sullivan's wealth of explicatory information in the introduction occupies all 680 pages of Volume 1.[59]

There is no indication of a drum for the Irish context anywhere in the O'Curry lectures. But there are numerous addresses, in lectures 31, 32 and 36 – totalling twenty pages, *c.* 10,000 words – on the timpan. These are concentrated, and are presented with a view to proving O'Curry's belief that the instrument was stringed, if not indeed an indigenous ancestor of the fiddle.

The O'Curry lectures, therefore, are a central issue in investigating the history of a drum in Ireland, and because the timpan – as such – did not survive beyond the seventeenth century, these are the only information sources that are available. They provide some sixteen separate manuscript references to *timpan*, all of which make it obvious both from indication of the performance contexts and description of the instrument that the timpan was stringed. O'Curry's points are summarised in full in Appendix 2, but some are timely to note here. Typically he uses translations from the Irish manuscripts which convey a sense of mystery, wonder and spectacle in the Gaelic past. For instance:

> The word *Timpan* next occurs in the ancient historic tale of the *Battle of Magh Lena* ... where Eoghan Mór, king of Munster in the second century, on his return from Spain to the Island of Cregraidhe In Berehaven, is received by the lady Eadan ... Eadan answers 'Yes ... the pleasant sunny chamber also remains / Where the sweet-stringed *Timpan* was heard'.[60]

Strong among the features of his selection of extracts is the need to demonstrate the nature of the timpan, as in this description of an aisling-style, spiritual meeting:

> He held a silver *Timpan* in his hand
> Of red gold were the strings of that Timpan
> Sweeter than all music under heaven
> Were the strings of that *Timpan*.[61]

The integrity of the music overall is of concern to Eugene O'Curry as a nineteenth-century antiquarian devoted to not only identifying and understanding, but also to formalising, the existence of the intellectual sophistication of classic Gaelic society:

> There are three qualities that give distinction to a *Cruit* (or Harp), namely, the Crying Mode, the Laughing Mode, and the Sleeping Mode. The Timpanist has a wand, and hair, and doubling (or repetition).

Here too he underlines the nature of a timpan by noting the alternative methods by which strings can be sounded – striking, plucking or bowing:

> First it [this] shows distinctly that the Cruit was of a very different and of a higher order than the *Timpan* ... And secondly, it proves beyond all controversy that the *Timpan*, like that described by king *Cormac*, was played with a wand and hair, or, in other words, with a bow.[62]

It is also seen from the passage that both the harp and the timpan were common to the same performer. One citation goes further than merely distinguishing the timpan from a drum, but sets a date by which the instrument was still known, and still being played, as well as raising the possibility of a continuity for fiddle-playing in south County Clare:

> This book, then, having been compiled in the year 1509, the note on the harp and *Timpan* must have been copied from an older book, or written by the scribe himself for the first time, that year. In either case it is plain that at this time, or possibly long before, the playing on the harp and on the *Timpan* had become distinct professions, notwithstanding that, as a matter of course, any person might play both instruments, though [be] the professor of but one. From many sources we have authority to believe that the *Timpan* came down concurrently with the harp to the close of the seventeenth century; but what became of it then, or whether it merged into our present fiddle, I am quite at a loss to know.[63]

Such a dating of the period of the stringed timpan is also given oldest and newest parameters:

> We find the harp, *Timpan*, and fiddle, mentioned in the ancient poem on the fair of Carman [AD 718] ... and we have them again mentioned in Eugene O'Donnelly's poems about the year 1680; but from that time down, I am not certain of having met with any reference whatsoever to the *Timpan*.[64]

From *c.* 1680, in a poem by Eoghan Ó Donnghaile:

> Three strings not of sweet melody / I perceive in the middle of thy Timpan / Small their power; bitter their sound' ...Even so late as the close of the seventeenth century, the *Timpan*, or *Tympanum*, was still known in this country, and not by any means as a drum of any kind.[65]

3 THE IRISH TIMPAN: STRINGS OR DRUM?

Eugene O'Curry's motivation for assembling and presenting this data does not appear to be to dispute with Cambrensis, or to deny the existence of an indigenous Irish form of drum, but to establish what the actual instruments of Irish music were, and thereby the nature of the music. Melody appears as supreme, and no evidence of any kind of drum emerges for Ireland. Informed by the manuscripts, the only evidence available, his firm belief was that he had proved that the Irish timpan was a stringed instrument which was either plucked or bowed, or both.

W.K. Sullivan

Eugene O'Curry's lectures in print were prefaced by W.K. Sullivan who speaks unequivocally on the nature of the timpan. In his introduction he says:

> Timpan, the name of the second, and by far more important, of the bowed instruments mentioned in Irish manuscripts, does not suggest the slightest relationship with any of the continental medieval bowed instruments. It is a puzzle how a stringed instrument could have received a name which ... always meant a drum or tambourine[*]. Nowhere do we find a description of it; our only means for determining what manner of instrument it was, is by induction from the vague and scattered notices which occur in poems, prose tales, and in the laws. O'Curry has brought together all those fragments in the Lectures, and almost everything I could say in addition, I have been obliged to say incidentally in discussing the history of the harp in Ireland, with which that of the Timpan is almost inseparably interwoven. In this place it only remains to draw conclusions as to what the Timpan was. The passage quoted from the Laws in Lecture xxxvi establishes beyond doubt that the name Timpan was certainly given to a bowed instrument. This does not preclude the name being also applied to an instrument played with the fingers ... the instrument must therefore have somewhat resembled the Welsh Crwth ... up to the eleventh century the bowed instruments in Europe did not essentially differ from each other. It is therefore impossible to say whether the Timpan was a Rote or Vielle, but there can be little doubt that the instruments included under this name in Irish documents were practically the same as the instruments of the same class in use in the west of Europe in the eleventh century, and in the absence of positive proof to the contrary, we may safely assume that the Irish Timpan and the Welsh Crwth or Crud of the time of Giraldus Cambrensis were borrowed from the neighbouring continental nations[66]

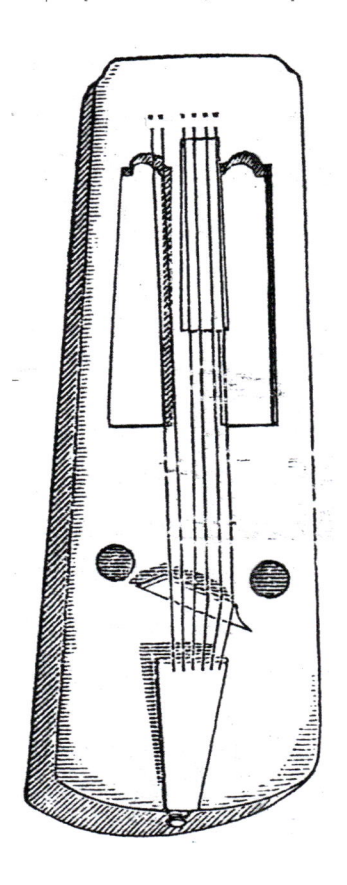

English-language translations

The full *Oxford English Dictionary* actually acknowledges the nature of the timpan for Ireland too, while also giving the English and European meaning:

> Tympan ... 1. A drum or similar instrument, as a timbrel or tambourine ... b. [Ir. *tiompán*.] An ancient Irish stringed instrument played with a bow ... .[67]

The strings reference is taken from the writing of one Ranulphus Higden (1280–1364), a Benedictine monk at St Werburg's monastery in Chester. His printed history was a best-seller for printer William Caxton, covering as it did the known world, including Ireland. His information on music in Ireland is so close to that given by Cambrensis that clearly it was borrowed from him, but with the difference that even at two centuries distance Higden knew to specify the Irish timpan as a stringed instrument:

> Irysshe men be connyng in two maner imstrumentis of musyke ... harpe & tymbre that is armed with wyre & strenges of bras in whiche instrumentes though they playe hastely & swyftly they make right mery armonye & melodye with thyire tewnes werbles & notes.[68]

▲ W.K. Sullivan

▼ Welsh crwth of the type suggested for the timpan [*Sullivan 1873, ccccxcvi*]

> **tym·pan** *also* **tim·pan** \\'timpən\\ *n* -s [in sense 1a, fr. ME *tympan, timpan*, fr. OE *timpana*, fr. L *tympanum*; in sense 1b, fr. IrGael *tiompan*, fr. L *tympanum* drum; in other senses fr. ML *tympanum* eardrum & L *tympanum* drum, architectural panel — more at TYMPANUM] **1 a :** DRUM **b :** a Celtic bowed stringed musical instrument

▲ Tympanum entry in Webster's (USA) dictionary with Irish stringed instrument reference in addition to the European 'drum' [*Merriam Webster Vol. 3 1971: 2475*]

A meaning for 'tympaning' is also given by the Oxford dictionary as 'the playing of a tympan' (the stringed instrument), the definition taken from Eugene O'Curry:

> 1862 O'Curry Anc. Irish xxxvi. (1873) III. 363 The harper has exclusive harping … The Timpanist has exclusive timpaning (or Timpan playing).[69]

But the English and European meaning is also given in the *Oxford*, as 'Timpanist … one who plays the kettle-drums'. Absence of knowledge of the dual meaning continues to direct some modern-day commentators to the drum conclusion. For there is a tendency to translate via the standard Latin dictionary which uses a similar term for the small drum used in Rome 'in worship of Cybele and Bacchus'[70] from *c.* 200 BC into Christian time – known as the *tympanon* (Greek) or *tympanum* (Roman). From the many images of this instrument that survive (see Chapter 2) it can be seen to often have been similar to the bodhrán in size. The religious use of it was already dying out by the end of the western Roman empire (AD 476) but it persisted up to the tenth century,[71] the ancestor of the tamburello/tamburo which is used in Italian folk music.[72] But because 'timpanum' was also a generic European drum term, Latin and other dictionaries continued to carry it, as it is relevant to the study of ancient Rome. However, it is of little consequence in Irish music, since the original instrument is long gone. For instance, a 1773 Latin–English–Latin lexicon translates 'drum' as 'tympanum', and vice versa, and repeats the worship reference with regard to Cybele.[73] Present-day Latin dictionaries tend to still use the tympanum=drum equation, because 'tympanum', from medieval Latin, is applicable to any kind of drum, including the eardrum as well as above-door, architectural panels, and is said to originate in the Greek word for drum, *tympanon*; it first appeared in print in 1619.[74] But the more comprehensive twentieth-century English-language dictionaries do note the Irish strings-related meaning, with Webster's 1977 giving, in addition to 'drum' and 'eardrum', the significant information: 'IrGael *tiompán* … a Celtic bowed stringed musical instrument'.[75] Patrick Weston Joyce, writing in 1908, detailed the tiompán unambiguously:

> The Irish had a small stringed instrument called a Timpan, which had only a few strings. It had a body like a flat drum, to which at one side was attached a short neck: the strings were stretched across the flat face of the drum and along the neck: and were tuned and regulated by pins or keys and a bridge. It was played with a bow or with the finger-nail, or by both together, while the notes were regulated in pitch or 'stopped' as musicians say with the fingers of the left hand, like those of a fiddle or guitar. This little instrument was a great favourite, and is constantly mentioned in Irish literature … The harp and timpan

From many sources we have authority to believe that the *Timpan* came down concurrently with the harp to the close of the seventeenth century; but what became of it then, or whether it merged into our present fiddle, I am quite at a loss to know. We find the harp, *Timpan*, and fiddle, mentioned in the ancient poem on the fair of Carman as already mentioned; and we have them again mentioned in Eugene O'Donnelly's poems, about the year 1680; but from that time down, I am not certain of having met with any reference whatsoever to the *Timpan*.

To the above valuable passage taken from Edmund *O'Deoráin*'s book of 1509, I may be permitted to add one short extract more from an article in the Brehon Laws, which provided as to wounds and injury to the person. The passage is as follows:

" If the top of his finger, from the root of the nail, or above the black, has been cut off a person, he is entitled to compensation for his [injured body], and a fine [for his outraged] honour, in proportion to the severity of the wound. If the blood has been drawn while cutting his nail off, he is entitled to the fine for blood-shedding for it. If it be from the black [circle] out that his nail has been taken off him, he is entitled to the same fine as for a white [or bloodless] blow; and if he be a Timpanist, then there is a quill [or feather] nail for him besides, by way of restitution".(415)

This last reference to the *Timpan* so plainly implies its character, that nothing more need be said upon the subject. A question, however, for the first time arises out of the above extract from the Brehon Laws, and it is this: was the quill really used as a substitute for the bow, or, as we have it in this law, was it used as a substitute for the nail of the finger, or for the thumb, perhaps? It is not easy to determine this question with certainty: but it may easily be conceived as affording an explanation of how the two extra strings of the instrument now called *Cruit* by the Welsh were played. We may imagine the *Timpan* in fact to have been a kind of fiddle, played with a bow, but with two additional deeper strings, struck with the thumb or thumb-nail, so that if that nail were injured, it would be necessary to supply it with an artificial one.

It is remarkable too, as just mentioned above, how constantly we find the *Cruit* and the *Timpan* accompanying each other, and that this is no modern confusion of the one with the other may be seen from a passage of the *Tochmarc Emire*, or courtship of the lady *Emer*, already referred to. The passage has reference to the splendour of the palace of the Royal Branch of the kings of Ulster at *Emania*, in the time of king *Conchobhar Mac Nessa*, and is as follows:

" Great and numerous were the assemblies of that royal house; and of admirable performers, in gymnastics; and in singing; and in playing; for gymnasts contended; and poets sang; and Harpers and Timpanists played there".(416)

▶ Extract on the nature of the timpan from Eugene O'Curry's 'Of music and musical instruments in ancient Erinn' lecture XXXVI, pages 364-5, *Manners and Customs of the Ancient Irish*, Vol. 3, 1873

were the chief instruments of the higher classes, many of whom played them as an accomplishment, as people now play the piano and guitar.[76]

Judging by other publications, among them Karen Ralls' 2000 *Music and the Celtic Underworld*,[77] this appears to be internationally understood today.

Enter the real drum

The timpan disappeared from manuscript reports on music and musicianship in the late 1600s, but comment on the English military's use of drums had by that time been going on for almost a century; in some texts these are translated as 'tabor'. For instance, in 1595:

> The Chief Justiciary of Ireland, Sir William Russell, marched to Baile-na-Cuirre … Upon their arrival in the neighbourhood of the castle, but before they had passed through the gate of the rampart that surrounded it, the sound of a drum was accidentally heard from the soldiers … Fiagh, with his people, took the alarm[78]

> [AD 1599] O'Rourke … had promised O'Donnell that he would be ready to attack the English like the rest, whenever it would be necessary; *and* when he heard the sound of the trumpets and tabors, and the loud and earth-shaking reports of the mighty firing, he rose up from his camp with his heroes, who put on their arms[79]

That reference identifies the first reported context for actual drums in Ireland as being colonial and military, specifically at the end of the sixteenth century.[80] John Derricke's images from the period show the English with drums, the Irish with bagpipes. This also brings to mind the comments already made on the possible nature of the drum used by the earl of Desmond's soldiers in the same century, allowing for the likelihood of its being a captured English drum. The incidence and the associations of the English with drums is common, such as in the recitation 'The Wild Goose – The Irish Cavalier, 1690': 'When we shall see their colours wave and hear the Saxon drum'.[81] People in the country had everyday experience or knowledge of drums from the English military over the following centuries, as seen in a note from Dublin Castle in 1803 regarding the First Troop of the Muskerry Legion of Yeomanry Cavalry, County Cork which specifies 'one Trumpeter or Drummer for a company of sixty men'.[82] By contrast, the accounts of occasions of vernacular music from the seventeenth century are of widespread recreational dancing, and talk only of fiddles and pipes. As John Dunton describes recreation *c.* 1674:

> Sunday is the most leisure day they have in which they use all manner of sport; in every field a fiddle and the lasses footing it till they are all of a foam.[83]

He also describes a wedding where 'we had a bagpiper and a blind harper that dinned us constantly with their music, to which there was perpetual dancing'.[84] Yet even so, the fact that such reporters were one-off visitors, and were from outside the intimacy of local societies, does leave it possible that there may have been other music-making which could have included percussion, played on occasions separate from that which was observed by chroniclers, and independent of dancing. One reported recreational use of drums in 1602–3 does suggest this, in a 'humorous narrative of the holiday excursion of a knot of English officers in Ulster in the last days of Elizabeth's reign'.[85] The context appears to have been mumming in Lecale, County

▶ English military drummer, by John Derricke [*Courtesy The Blackstaff Press*]

3 THE IRISH TIMPAN: STRINGS OR DRUM?

Down, entertainment for Sir Josias Bodley, the man who in 1609 was to be appointed to carve up Ulster for distribution to loyal English, Scottish and Irish in the Ulster Plantation, and who considered

> Irish men-at-arms … a most vile race of men, if it be at all allowable to call them 'men' who live upon grass, and are foxes in their disposition and wolves in their actions

Describing hospitality at the house of Sir Richard Morrison, he recounts:

> once more to our Lecale, where, amongst other things that contributed to hilarity there came one night after supper certain maskers of the Irish gentry, four in number … they entered in this order: first a boy, with lighted torch; then two beating drums; then the maskers, two and two; then another torch … They were dressed in shirts with many ivy leaves sewn on here and there over them, and had over their faces masks of dog-skin with holes to see out of, and noses made of paper; their caps were high and peaked (in the Persian fashion) and were also of paper, and ornamented with the same leaves.[86]

The meaning of this is not quite clear, but it certainly suggests familiarity with some sort of mumming practice in which drums were used. Whether of Irish or planter origin is not clear, and the context might suggest military-style drums, for, apart from this incident, the only textual information on drums by this time is on those of the English military. Janet McCrickard indeed remarks on the conspicuous absence of the aesthetic or entertainment use of drums in early literature: 'one would surely expect that a drum with important magical uses or mythic connotations would appear somewhere; in the great Irish sagas, for example'.[87] Of course other references like the above Bodley reminiscence may well emerge in the future from scanning of as-yet-untapped collections

▲ 'Strings' reference for 'tiompán' in the Harp entry in O'Begly's 1732 dictionary

◀ Tambourine player on Beverly Minster in Yorkshire, one of seventy fifteenth-century wood and stone carvings that depict twenty or so instruments of all kinds, including bagpipes, fiddle, organ, tambourine, trumpet, flute, lute, psaltery, shawm and cymbals representing secular music. Similar instruments could have been known about in Ireland [EDI]

▶ O'Reilly's 'tiompán' dictionary entry, 1817

> Tiompán, *tiompan*, s. m. a timbrel, tabor, drum, cymbal
> Tiompán, *tiompan*, s. m. a jack for roasting
> Tiompánach, *tiompanach*, ⎱ s. m. a harper, a
> Tiompánuiḋe, *tiompanuidhe*, ⎰ drummer, a minstrel

of correspondence from earlier times, but the presently available information indicates that bodhrán, tambourine or any form of drum is not mentioned or portrayed in indigenous-Irish music-making contexts until the nineteenth century. But, still, it may simply have been invisible from outside, hidden by social stratification, the non-documented territory of what German ethnologist Leo Frobenius called 'counterplayers'. For then was a different scale of authority, society and communication. Poverty creates its own barriers, as does the special nature of music itself as a learned art with pride in its performance and territorial protectionism of the musician as regards ownership of music repertoire and equipment. Yet, fundamentally, the accounts of music-making that are found occasionally in literature typically involve fiddles, pipes and flutes, never a drum: Irish music is historically presented as a melody-based artform. Flute player, painter and sculptor Eamonn O'Doherty did however imply the possibility of a drum in his introduction to *The Northern Fiddler* in which he muses that the instruments in use in fifteenth-century Europe would be surprisingly familiar to an Irish folk musician today.[88] That thinking certainly applies to dance, for even though Eugene O'Curry could find no reference to it in the manuscripts from before the 1600s, the following century has ample evidence of it; so because dance was well established by then there must have been some precedent. All cultural expressions involve fashion, and they have to start somewhere, at some point in time, but can spread rapidly once popularised. At best it is a matter of speculation that there would also have been a drum among the poorer classes in Ireland, word of which did not reach the ears or eyes of the chroniclers.

'Cambrensis-ism' in dictionaries?
A coda to the timpan controversy is that lexicological thinking did not stay apace with the nineteenth-century re-evaluations, or Joyce's early-twentieth explanations. So the Irish-language dictionaries, the first port of call for most people studying the bodhrán, in the 1800s have significant omissions and contradictions regarding the term 'timpan'. Beginning with O'Reilly's 1817 Irish–English dictionary, 'tiompán' is given as meaning 'timbrel, tabor, drum, cymbal'. There is no mention of the actual Gaelic tiompán, yet a person who plays on the tiompán – *tiompánach, tiompánuidhe* – is given as meaning 'harper, drummer, minstrel,'[89] which implies that those were two instruments with the same name – or the unlikely meaning that the player of a drum can be called a harper. O'Brien's 1832 *Focalóir Gaoidhilge-Bhéarla* repeats the same confusing information,[90] so too Foley's 1855 dictionary where 'tabour' and 'tambourine' are given as *druim beag, tiompán*.[91] The same is continued in Patrick Dinneen's 1904 Irish–English dictionary,[92] with no indication that the Gaelic timpan/tiompán was a stringed instrument. His 1927 edition, however, remedies this by including 'cithernist',[93] which is stringed, but he does not clarify that the Gaelic meaning of 'tiompán' is 'strings', the European is 'drum'. In 1959 de Bhaldraithe's English-Irish

dictionary translated 'drum' as 'timpan',[94] still based on the old European meaning. But by 1977, Ó Dónaill's *Foclóir Gaeilge Béarla* dictionary does give a stringed-instrument reference for tiompán as 'metal stringed instrument of harp kind' (stringed, yes, but it is not a 'harp kind', it is a lyre – a guitar kind); he also gives tiompán as 'drum, tympanum, timbrel', and (amazingly) 'tambourine', each of those inapplicable to Gaelic Ireland.[95] An Gúm's 1986–2006 *Foclóir Scoile* backtracked even on that, and reverted to seeing tiompán as just a drum,[96] as did An Comhlacht Oideachais *Foclóir* in 2005.[97] Only by 2007 does the major Irish-English dictionary *eDIL* finally clearly come up with the dual meaning of strings and drum, although this is only in a digital assembly of information.[98] Dictionaries appear to either not have known what the manuscripts revealed (and what was in the main English-language dictionaries), or did not trust what O'Connor, O'Curry, Bunting, etc. spelt out. This may seem a pedantic point to labour, but faith is put in dictionaries, and research can easily get led astray, resulting in errors which – in this particular case – can still be seen even in some twenty-first century bodhrán literature.

None of this of course proves that there wasn't a frame drum in ancient Ireland, just that the timpan/tiompán' was not it. There may well have been a drum, not least because of other-nation parallels. And, as said, Cambrensis was giving an account of court music only, as indeed were the manuscripts quoted by O'Curry. But without evidence of drum objects, images or description, supposition cannot be documented as fact. Since the crux of the bodhrán story is the question 'Is today's bodhrán a timeless, ancient Irish percussion, or not?', it is not helpful that contemporary dictionaries do not consider the numerous well-documented rebuttals of the 'drum' interpretation of Cambrensis's Latin. Calling the Irish timpan a drum is an error which dictionary authority has facilitated being passed on uncritically like a Chinese whisper. Yet there are of course very numerous, better-read commentators who are well familiar with the timpan=strings issue.[99] So, there are two fundamental – and conflicting – opinions out and about. One is based on mistranslation and/or inadequate research, unchecked borrowings, or lack of confidence. The other is a rational deduction which draws on writing, images and manuscript data. And overlapping with both of these is a third attitude held by some emotionally-intuitive bodhrán players – a belief in a historical Irish drum, that is based on experience-led instinct – gut feeling rather than material, representational or handed-down evidence.

But there is yet more bumpy travel in the bodhrán – tambourine story, for the word 'bodhrán' itself is also spancilled by a double meaning, so a look at the documentation on that is now appropriate, starting with the oldest, the manuscript sources.

[1] O'Dwyer 2004, 28.

[2] Simon O'Dwyer writes on how (uniquely) he has worked on reconstruction of such instruments as horns (adharc) and trumpet (trumpa), and has devised techniques which permit playing them as accompaniment to melody, on modern instruments. Based on this potential, and consideration of legend, viz., 'The Romance of Fraoch', from the 70 BC 'Táin Bó Fraích', a 'wildly exaggerated' tale written down in the eighth century, rewritten in the twelfth, and translated from Scottish Gaelic in 1911, he speculates somewhat romantically on possible percussion music, social and orchestral-style playing scenarios for the adharc and trumpa, the former in a highly unlikely modern-session format with a bodhrán (O'Dwyer 2004, cover, and pp. 17–20).

[3] O'Donovan 1856, 217, c. AD 592, Dallan Forgaill composed this on the death of Colum Cille, 'Like the cure of a physician without light / Like the separation of marrow from the bone / Like a song to a harp without the ceis / Are we after being deprived of our noble'.

[4] O'Meara 1951, 11–12.

[5] Ibid., 13, from Dimock 1867, 351.

[6] O'Meara op. cit., 13; Brewer1861, 1 xl.

[7] Keating 1902, 153.

[8] Dimock 1867.

[9] O'Meara op. cit., 16.

[10] Ibid., 103–4; Wright 2000, 71–4.

[11] O'Meara op. cit., 104.

[12] Wright 2000, 71.

[13] O'Meara op. cit., 134.

[14] Sullivan 1873.

[15] Grattan Flood 1927, 26.

[16] Breathnach 1971, 6.

[17] Sullivan 1873, 543.

[18] Eugene O'Curry gleaned the of this poem from the conflation of data in two separate documents, 'The Book of Ballymote' in the Royal Irish Academy, Dublin, and from MS II.2.18 ('The Book of Leinster'), in Trinity College Dublin.

[19] O'Donovan 1860, 24–5.

[20] Radner 1978, 67–75. This translation is used on the Celt website, the major online repository of manuscripts at University College Cork. In *Irish Musical Studies* 1 Ann Buckley acknowledges it as an error. (Buckley 1995, 67).

[21] For instance, Benedict 2011.

[22] Such 1985, 10.

[23] O'Meara op. cit., 17.

[24] Benedict 2011, 124.

[25] O'Donovan 1856, xix.

[26] Ibid., xlii.

[27] Benedict op. cit., 126–7.

[28] Ibid., 117.

[29] O'Donovan 1856 Vol. III, 538–41.

[30] Ibid., 620–1.

[31] Ibid., 1180–1.

[32] O'Donovan 1856, Vol. VI, 2068–9.

[33] Ibid., 2127.

[34] Hennessy and MacCarthy 1887, 187.

[35] Williams 2007, 192–4, cited in Benedict 2011, 113.

[36] O'Sullivan Beare, 1625.

[37] Carolan 2001, 55 (translation of the *Zoilomastix* from the Latin).

[38] Ibid., 55–6. Writing in Latin, like Cambrensis O'Sullivan Beare also used 'tympano' as his translation of the Irish 'tiompan'.

[39] Ó Catháin 2009 (doi.org).

[40] Bunting in his 1840 volume, O'Curry in his 1869 lectures, and O'Curry's editor, W.K. Sullivan, in 1873.

[41] Walker Vol 1, 1786, 124.

[42] Walker Vol. 1, 1786, 88; 1818, 121.

[43] *Mr Pennant, speaking of the Welsh musicians, says, that the tabourers were reckoned among the ignoble performers. [*Tour in Wales*, v.1. p. 440].

[44] Walker Vol. 1, 1786, 122–3; 1818, 177–9.

[45] Walker op. cit., Appendix p. 21; 1818, 249–50; Also Ledwich 1804, 237.

[46] Bunting 1830, 30.

[47] Ibid., and Ó Súilleabháin 1974, 4.

[48] Bunting 1809, 4.

[49] Ibid.

[50] Ibid., 23.

[51] Bunting 1840, 56.

[52] Ibid.

[53] Reck1977, 80–1; Midgley 1978, 178, 183–4.

[54] Bunting 1840, 36.

[55] Ó Súilleabháin 1974, 4.

[56] McCarthy 2013, 987.

[57] Sullivan 1873, Vol. 3, 238 (O'Curry Lecture XXI).

[58] This remark refers to information from Dr Charles O'Conor (1710–91), whose papers are held at the Royal Irish Academy in Dublin.

[59] He does not presume O'Curry to be infallible either, saying in his preface that he had confidence in the writer's accuracy, even though he found that 'some of Professor O'Curry's translations are only free renderings of the original text, more or less paraphrased, but always sufficiently close and correct for the purposes for which they were used. However anxious I might be to make some emendations in those translations, such as he would have himself made if he had been spared to prepare his work for the press, I thought it due to O'Curry's memory to give his own words, except in one or two instances, where he gave rather an abstract than a translation' (Sullivan 1873 (Vol. 1), 9).

[60] Sullivan 1873, Vol. 3, 359–60.

[61] Ibid., 361–2.

[62] Ibid., 362–3.

[63] Ibid., 364.

[64] Ibid.

[65] Ibid., 265.

[66] Sullivan 1873 Vol. 1, dxxviii–dxxix

[67] Simpson and Weiner 1989, 783.

[68] Higden 1432–50, XXXV/70.

[69] Sullivan 1873 Vol. 3, 363; Simpson and Weiner 1989, 783.

[70] Online Latin dictionary.

[71] McCrickard 1987, 21–6.

[72] Guizzi 1988, 31.

[73] Morell, 1773.

[74] Merriam Webster, 2022. Webster's dictionary of 1828 carries similar meanings, and Webster's *New International Dictionary*, 1971 edition (p. 2475), has additional, more extensive information, noting numerous stretched-membrane similes.

[75] Webster's 1971 (Vol. 3), 2475.

[76] Joyce 1908, 85–6.

[77] Ralls 2000, 53–6.

[78] O'Donovan 1856, Vol. VI, 1957.

[79] Ibid., 2133.

[80] For instance, 'It was a fine pleasant day when unfurling their banners they marched without opposition over the smiling plain, to the sound of the trumpet, the music of pipes, and the beat of military drums, stimulating man and beast to combat' (Fynes Moryson, 1735, 297; LC1589.8 ['drum']; THI, 98, 112, 119, 129, 170 [late 16th c., 'drum']).

[81] Townshend 1904, 279.

[82] Day 1904, 1.

[83] Buckley, 1904, 99.

[84] From Edward McLysaght's quotation of Dunton in *Irish Life in the Seventeenth Century*, cited in Feldman and O'Doherty 1979, Preface.

[85] Reeves 1854, 326.

[86] Ibid., 343.

[87] McCrickard 1987, 21.

[88] Feldman & O'Doherty 1979, 3.

[89] O'Reilly 1817.

[90] O'Brien 1832.

[91] Foley 1855, 340.

[92] Dinneen 1904, 735.

[93] Dinneen 1927, 1211.

[94] De Bhaldraithe 1959, 208.

[95] Ó Dónaill 1977, 1238.

[96] An Gúm 1986, 384.

[97] Ó Luineacháin 2005, 253.

[98] eDIL 2019, 23 January 2022.

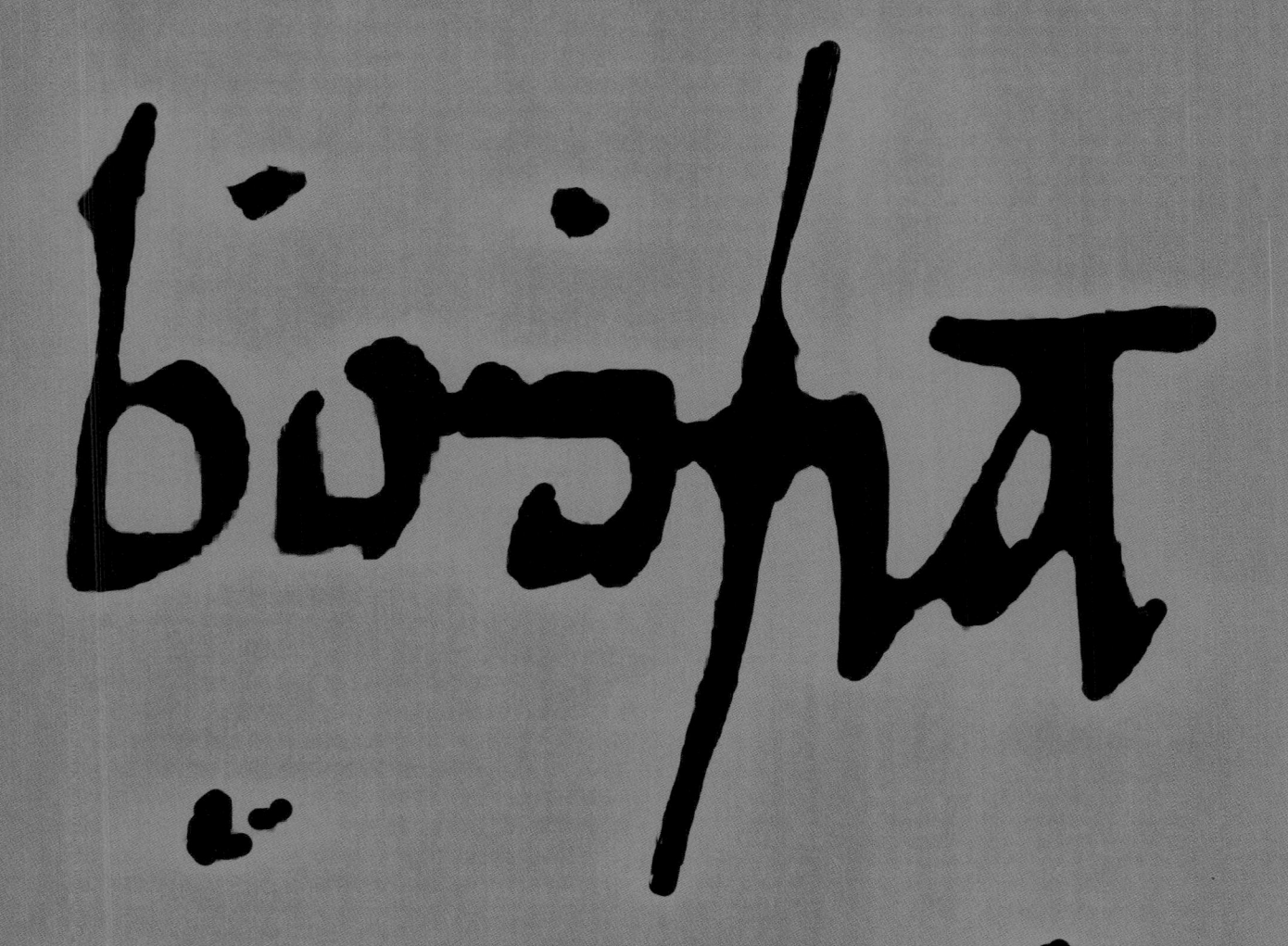

Detail in *Rosa Anglica* [*Courtesy The Board of Trinity College Dublin*]

CHAPTER 4
THE WORD 'BODHRÁN' IN DOCUMENTS

The previous chapter has said that melody was the dominant feature of music in Ireland, and that no indigenous drum form is spoken of. The next section looks at the written evidence around this – hand-scribed texts, and dictionaries as they emerged since the eighteenth century – and explores given and potential meanings of terminology. The oldest sources of such information are manuscripts which were hand-scribed on vellum, the historical record for Irish cultural and political affairs prior to the advent of printing. There are no references to any sense of a drum tradition in these documents which in their many mentions of music speak mostly of strings – harp (cruit) and lyre (timpan); a selection of them are given in Appendix 1. The printed word came after manuscripts, and it has a variety of mentions of 'bodhrán' and 'drums' – in dictionaries, books on music and newspaper reports. Dealing first with manuscripts, there are but two occurrences of words resembling 'bodhrán', the earliest from the ninth century, associated with deafness, the other much later, in the sixteenth, meaning a skin-on-frame device of some sort.

'The Paris manuscript', *c.* AD 900

The oldest manuscript to cite a word similar to 'bodhrán' is known as 'Paris Latin 10290', a tenth-century document which is referenced under 'bodhrán' in the Royal Irish Academy's dictionary of 1977:

> bodarán (bodar): bodaran gl. *surdaster* … *Études Celt,* xi 122. Cf. bodrán[1]

Dealing with the first part of the entry, the one word 'bodarán', this occurs only as a gloss (a correction or clarification) on a Latin transcription of a treatise by one Priscianus Caesariensis, known as Priscian, a Latin grammarian from *c.* AD 500 who was author of *Institutes of Grammar,* the standard Latin textbook for most of the Middle Ages and the Renaissance. In the manuscript Priscian quotes from Cicero's *Tusculan Disputations* where Cicero says: 'Erat surdaster M. Crassus' ['Crassus was somewhat deaf']. One gloss, in the margin, corrects the spelling of 'surdaster', because it had been written 'sordaster'. But the word 'bodaran' is also glossed above 'surdaster', indicating its Irish meaning (bodaran=a deaf person), the other meaning for the word, which appears later in the Irish dictionaries.[2] This has nothing to do with the bodhrán as either device or drum.

Yet, very interesting in that context, the word 'surdaster' (like 'bodhrán', a term for an almost-deaf person) historically does have a drum connotation – in Italy where it was applied to a loud, booming military drum type which was brought to the south of the country 'with the Ottoman troops during

▲ ◀ The Paris manuscript line 'bodaran', c. AD 900 [*Bibliotheque Nationale, Paris*]

the fifteenth and sixteenth centuries, starting from the capture of Otranto in 1480'.[3] Additionally, that large drum was associated with the smaller tambourine-like tamburello, and both were utilised in the treatment of scorpion and tarantula bites. Tarantism, a condition resulting from being bitten by a tarantula spider, was said to manifest itself as an uncontrollable compulsion to dance, and was prevalent in the south of Italy between the fifteenth and seventeenth centuries. The sound of the drum was supposed to neutralise the tarantula bite.[4] The tamburello was believed to be the remedy for tarantulas, while a war drum, of which the *surdastro* is a variant, was preferred for scorpion bites,[5] as to be effective the drum had to emit 'rather low and gloomy frequencies'.[6] This evidence of a drum culture in southern Italy is supported by much written and visual information, including this surreal 1784 description:

> for centuries, the drum, even in the Latin spelling *tympanum*, was included among the tools used to treat tarantulas in the sixteenth century ... while with some companions I walked through those squalid places of Puglia in the burning and the continuous heat of the sun ... many were playing, some with drums, and some with *zampogna* [bagpipe], and others with *piffari* [flutes] ... wanting to know the cause, we were told to take care in that place to avoid being bitten by the Tarantula.[7]

The tamburello is a tambourine of similar size to today's bodhrán (see p. 19). It was brought to London by Italian street musicians in the sixteenth – seventeenth centuries and, through this influence, is believed to be the drum model on which was based the eighteenth-century British military tambourines and subsequent orchestral ones.[8] Richard Graham holds that the playing style, which is still used in today's Marche region of Italy (see p. 323), was the basis of eighteenth-century tambourine style, aspects of which, from 1970s film footage shot in Doolin, County Clare, he sees in the style of older tambourine players there.

The second part of the reference to the Paris manuscript that is cited in the RIA dictionary entry – '*Études Celtique*' – says that the derivative word 'bodharán' is also the word used for a drum as played in Ireland: 'A conservé *bodhrán*: c'est le nom d'un tambourin dans les orchestres traditionnels'.[9] However that is a 1964 comment only, a side issue which was obviously informed by that (later) commentator's awareness of Irish music, which was well into revival at the time.

Overall, the meaning of the word in the manuscript concerns only deafnesss, and the reference serves to place the use of the word 'bodaran' for deafness at *c.* AD 900, as well as very indirectly associating that concept with a drum form. It can only be speculated whether or not the word at that time was additionally used in Ireland for the winnowing fan/utensil. However, the second manuscript, *Rosa Anglica*, clearly deals with the other definition of bodhrán, as a device.

Rosa Anglica, c. 1550

All that was required to make a bodhrán, wecht or dallán was a bent piece of supple wood, such as young ash, willow or sally, and a skin which could be secured by tucking it in on itself. Where the skin was not tucked in, strips of material – skin thong – would be used to bind it in position, simple technology. So it is likely that the making of these did not vary in any significant way for the *c.* 600 years before the second (and only other) Irish-manuscript reference to 'bodhrán' was made, in a document titled *Rosa Anglica*.[10] This source was also cited in the RIA dictionary in 1976, but its potential lay dormant, and untapped by music writers, until Liam Ó Bharáin's research for CCÉ's *Treoir* magazine in 2007–8. The RIA reference is succinct:

> Bodrán – tabor, drum, mar timpan, no mar tabur (bodhrán v.1), *Rosa Ang.* 268.15. Cf. bodarán).[11]

This introduces a bodhrán – a drum or drum-like object – and gives the source of that information as *Rosa Anglica*. The manuscript is a diagnostic medical document written in Latin in 1314 by John of Gaddesden, a reputed English physician and medical writer. There are four printed editions and a dozen manuscript copies of the original Latin-language work, none of them in English. It was, however, translated into Irish in 1400, reputedly by Nicholas O'Hickey,[12] with elements said to have been added from another Middle-Ages text; later translations were also made, two of which survive in Trinity College Dublin (one of them from 1460), and one in the Royal Irish Academy. Working with the Irish-language scripts, guided by a 1595 Latin copy held in Augsburg, Winifred Wulff edited an edition of *Rosa Anglica* in 1923, a study that was published by the Irish Texts Society in 1929 with the Irish and English on facing pages. She found that, because each of the

Irish translations of the manuscript was done by a different scribe, they differed in small measures. Only one word is relevant to the bodhrán, the item on 'tympanites', ('idropsis' / dropsy), a condition in which gas distends the stomach, which, when tapped, sounds hollow (the term 'tympanites' comes from the Greek for drum, 'tumpanon').[13] Expressed in the one of the translations into Irish, diagnosis of the condition could be made as follows:

> da fogruidhi an medhon re bualad mar timpan, no mar tabur …

From the MS copy this Wulff translates as:

> if the belly resound on being struck like a tympanum, or drum[14]

She adds a footnote which explains that in another, later, TCD *Rosa Anglica* manuscript the word 'tabur' is translated as 'bodhran':

> án meadhon re bhualadh mar thimpan nó mar bhodhran / if the belly resound on being struck like a timpan, or a bodhrán.[15]

In her glossary Wulff acknowledges this translation of 'tabur':

> Tabur, drum; 37a; R.A. tympanum; E1 bodhran

The date of that manuscript has been meticulously deduced by Liam Ó Bharáin to be mid sixteenth century, a landmark piece of information that locates the term 'bodhran' being used at that time. However, with regard to 'bodhrán', even though the intended acoustic meaning is clear, the nature of the device that the scribe intended to indicate is open to debate. He was certainly seeking to use a common object as a simile, one that he knew the readership would understand. Two things are therefore possible: either that there was an Irish drum called bodhrán, or that what was meant by the scribe was the household or winnowing bodhrán (see p. xiv). Tapping on either would give a hollow sound. However, there is no historical mention of an Irish drum in the sixteenth century, or before it, or for the following centuries – no named Irish drum which would be common enough for a medical person to consider using it as a then-familiar sound simile. But there can be no doubt that a utensil bodhrán was in wide use in that period and would have been in every house. So it does seem more likely that the scribe was referring to the device bodhrán in order to convey the sense of what the medical description intended. The word 'tabur' in the original English medical manuscript obviously meant a drum that was common in England at that time, the 'tabor', a small two-headed drum played in the sixteenth century, 'very different to the tambourine';[16] it was played by performers on the 'tabor pipe' (a one-handed flageolet) to accompany their own melody. The Irish translator of TCD MS 1435 is very likely to have considered that, since the tabor drum was not widely known or played in Ireland (it is absent from history and folklore), then a device which emits a similar sound should be used to illustrate the point. Hence the reference to the hollow-sounding bodhrán, because in a dry environment it would have had a drum-like resonance.[17] Supporting this likelihood is the fact that later, in the nineteenth century, there are many occurrences of words similar to bodhrán, all of which refer not to drums but to the simply-made utensils that were still in everyday use even three centuries after the *Rosa Anglica*

▶ Top: *Rosa Anglica* RIA MS 23, p.20, paragraph with 'tabur' cited [*Royal Irish Academy*]

▶ Middle: *Rosa Anglica* TCD MS 1435 p.155, paragraph with 'bodhran' cited [*Courtesy The Board of Trinity College Dublin*]

▶ Bottom: *Rosa Anglica* TCD MS 1435 p. 155, 'bodhran' line detail [*Courtesy The Board of Trinity College Dublin*]

4 THE WORD 'BODHRÁN' IN DOCUMENTS

translations were made. No actual drum-improvisation use of the device bodhrán is documented until *c.* 1820, and no similar drum is depicted anywhere until 1832, when a tambourine first appears, in a Daniel Maclise painting (see Chapter 8), so it is at least likely that the scribe was suggesting that tapping on the standard household implement known as 'bodhrán' (or a similar term) would give a hollow sound. That is, something like a drum, not an actual drum. And (if it was being done at that time) the scribe would also have been aware that casually, seasonally or ritually, the device bodhrán could double as an improvised drum.

The manuscript also says that tapping on a 'tiompán' would give the same kind of sound. The term 'tiompán' or 'timpan' in the Irish context has been established as meaning a stringed instrument (as detailed in Chapter 3), so the translator – again seeking to convey the idea of a resonant sound – suggests the simile of tapping on the hollow body of what was then a known stringed instrument – like tapping, for instance, on the back of a guitar, mandolin or bouzouki. Overall, Liam Ó Bharáin's investigation of *Rosa Anglica* highlights that the term 'bodhrán', or similar, was being used almost 500 years ago to describe a skin stretched on a hoop of wood. For the significance of that in dating the bodhrán, it actually matters little whether or not it was a drum, a utensil, or a utensil occasionally used as a drum.

It is indeed fortuitous that the researcher Winifred Wulff translated this document, that the RIA's lexicographer had sight of it and saw fit to include it r/e the word 'bodhrán' as a reference point in the 1977 dictionary, and that Ó Bharáin followed it up, for this is the only such old reference for the bodhrán as being some kind of device. And its existence in a medical manuscript suggests that the use of other non-music search parameters may well uncover further instances of the word. Considering the well-established domestic and agricultural use of the skin tray and sieve, such references would be more likely to be found in those contexts, rather than only in music. Even finding one such mention would help clarify the original derivation of, or meaning/s for, the word 'bodhrán'.

The two centuries after 1600 have many printed source materials that reference the paraphernalia of everyday living, but none of them have any reference to an indigenous drum as such. However, the dictionaries that come later provide a fresh array of possibilities.

Sifting out the words
Words for 'drum' begin to appear in print in Irish dictionaries during the eighteenth century, and those books have been the typical starting point for searching for a meaning for the word 'bodhrán'. They were complemented later by a major effort made towards the end of the 1800s via the Gaelic League's *Irisleabhar na Gaedhilge* journal which invited its readers to send in lists of words used in their localities. Those lexicons were published regularly, and some came to be gradually incorporated in the twentieth-century dictionaries, works which come in both basic-translation and word-meaning (etymological) formats. As regards the earlier publications, because English-to-Irish dictionaries provide meanings for words which were in use by English speakers, they may not necessarily reflect all of the vocabulary applying to the bulk of the rural-based, Gaelic-speaking Irish population. And the Irish-to-English versions too can be missing terminologies which were not in the experience of

▲ *Treoir* bodhrán researcher Liam Ó Bharáin

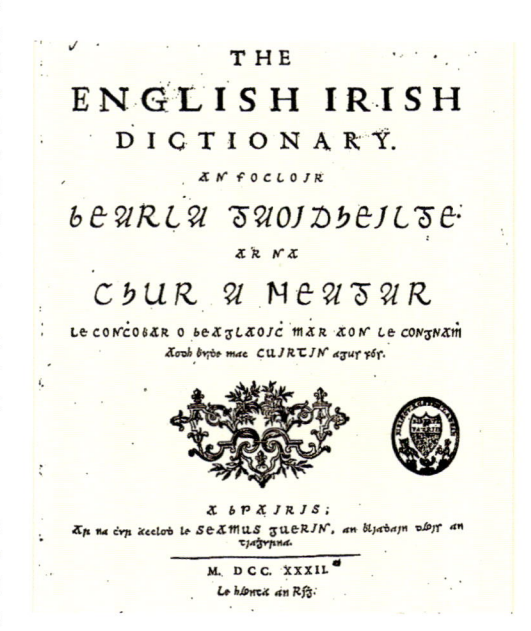

▲ O'Begly, 1732

▲ O'Begly's translation of 'drum', 1732

▲ 1768 O'Brien's dictionary

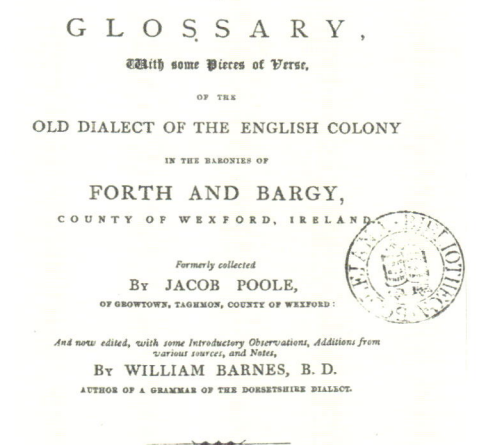

their compilers. No dictionary can be complete, despite its editor's intentions, as stated in the earliest of these books, *The English Irish Dictionary / An Foclóir Béarla Gaoidheilge*, by Conor O'Begly in 1732, in which there is a commitment to relevance, the editor saying that his work was 'as compleat as I could possibly make it, without swelling it with superfluous Phrases and antiquated Words, which would have been of very little use'.[18] Published in Paris with permission from King Louis XV, it was the first French book to use the Gaelic typeface, and was by its nature a strong political statement, being primarily for the education of Irish clerical students who were forbidden education at home under the Penal Laws, and who would be returning to minister and teach in Ireland. O'Begly's uncompromising, angry preface notes that for 500 years up until the time of publication, the same period in which 'most modern tongues of Europe have been polishing and refining', the sophistication of the Irish language had been declining at an equivalent inverse rate, a result of having been 'hitherto caryed down and ridiculed by the English in general'.[19] One should therefore expect topicality and accuracy appropriate to its era in its entries, even though a dictionary editor cannot have total familiarity with all dimensions of life and culture. The relevant words searched for in the dictionaries and local lexicons are 1/ those related to the word 'bodhrán' – 'bodhar', 'bodar', 'bodran' and 'bodaran' – as well as 2/ English words used for 'deaf', 'drum' and 'tambourine'; 3/ for a winnowing device or 'fan', and, related to this, 4/ where it occurs, the verb 'bother' and its equivalents.

The historic dictionaries
Taking the books in chronological order, in 1732 O'Begly gives 'drum' as, simply, *drumagh*, possibly in a similar phonetically-related manner as he gives 'bhilín' for violin/fiddle, and 'boghadh bhílín' for a fiddle bow. Since 'harp' is given as the terms 'cláirseach' and 'tiompán', both words familiar from old manuscripts, this suggests that drum as well as violin/fiddle were newer concepts. Consistent with later dictionaries, he also gives the alternative spelling 'boghar' for 'deaf', and 'boghradh' for 'to deafen'. Allowing for minor spelling variations, the same meanings are given in reverse three decades later in John O'Brien's 1768 Irish-English *Focalóir Gaoidhilge-Sax-Bhéarla*, also published in Paris: 'Bodhar, deaf, more usually written boghar', and also 'druma', a drum. Shaw's 1780 English-Gaelic dictionary has 'Deaf … bodhar' too, as well as 'Drum … druma' and 'Fiddle … fidhal', and his Gaelic-English translations are the reverse. He also has 'Dallan … A fan to winnow with'[20] (the 'dallan' is a device similar to the bodhrán, once used in Scotland and in the Isle of Man).

Relating roughly to *c.* 1800 is Poole's *Glossary* of terms from County Wexford, which has words used in the later 1700s. This was compiled by Jacob Poole, but had not been published by the time of his death in 1825. It was put in print in 1867, at which time it was edited for publication with additions from the later time (see below). The original 1825 glossary introduces '*Busk* … a small tambourine, or *booraan*, made of sheepskin stretched on a hoop'.[21] It is clear in this that a 'busk' is a drum, and it compares in construction with 'booraan', a device. An alternative spelling of the word is given as '*butheraan*'. This is the earliest mention of the word tambourine in an Irish gloss, glossary or dictionary, but it may have been intended to mean a tambourine-like object.

> Busk, pl. Buskès. A thick small cake of white meal, read in a song as "spiced bread," or a small tambourine, or booraan, made of sheepskin stretched on a hoop.

▲ Relating to *c.* 1800 is this entry in Jacob Poole's glossary.

From 1814, Thaddeus Connellan's English-Irish has: 'Deaf, *boghar*' and 'Drum, *drumagh*, *bobharan*', a landmark entry which shows that *bobharan* was then known as an alternative word for a drum. 'Drum', however, could also simply mean a generic cylindrical container (as in today's 'drum of paint') because in other, and later, contexts the bodhrán as a device is reported being used as a container for oats, potatoes, wool, etc.

Edward O'Reilly's 1817 *Sanas Gaoidhilge-Sagsbhearla / An Irish-English Dictionary* carries deafness associations, as well as *dallánach* for a winnowing fan, and *druma* and *droma* for drum.

1832, O'Brien's *Focalóir* has boghar = deaf, and droma/druma = drum, as in 1780.

In 1849 another Paris-printed *Focalóir Gaoidhilge-Sax-Bhéarla*, by Thomas De Vere Coneys, repeated the 'deaf' connection, but, like O'Reilly, did not acknowledge Connellan's 'drum' word.

Daniel Foley's 1855 English-Irish dictionary is similar to Connellan, with 'Drum … druim, bobharán' and 'Deaf … boghar'. Most interestingly, he has 'Bother … bodharaigh, bodhair',[24] and introduces the winnowing bodhrán as 'fan', types of which are translated as 'fuarán', 'gaothrán', 'buaireán'. The first two refer to a cooling fan, and the latter word – 'buaireán' – to the act of winnowing, or 'bothering'.[25]

In 1864 O'Reilly and O'Donovan's Irish-English dictionary only carries the '*bodhar* … deaf' and '*druma* … a drum'.

> [Booraan. A drum, tambourine. Irish, boġrán, a drum, also a sieve used in winnowing corn.]

▲ The Poole editor William Barnes' 1867 entry on 'booraan'

'The Poole Glossary'
This valuable source, already mentioned with regard to 1800, was published in 1867 in the book 'A Glossary With Some Pieces Of Verse of the Old Dialect of the English Colony in the Baronies of Forth and Bargy, County of Wexford, Ireland'. Referring to the late 1700s–*c.*1825, known as 'The Poole Glossary', it was edited by William Barnes, whose personal preface written in that year includes an extra note in order to clarify terminology that the originator, Jacob Poole, had used. Barnes himself gives us the additional information: 'Booraan. A drum, tambourine. Irish, *boghrán*, a drum, also a sieve used in winnowing corn'.[26] In this he links the drum form directly to the winnowing device by name, the first time that this is done in print. What this illustrates is that the word booraan/bodhrán, at the conclusion of the glossary's compilation, *c.* 1825, meant a tambourine-like object, but by

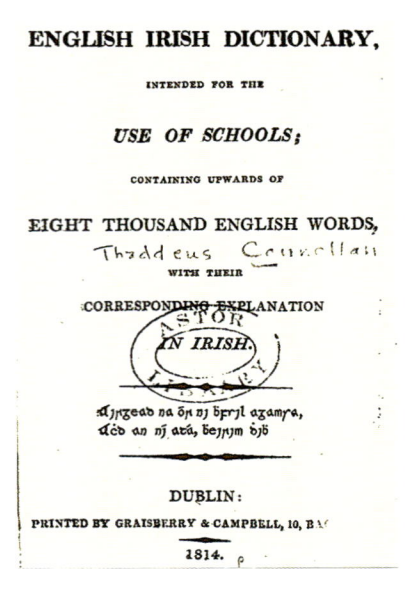

▲ Connellan's 1814 translation of drum as 'bobharán'

▲ Foley's, 1855

4 THE WORD 'BODHRÁN' IN DOCUMENTS

1867 when the glossary was published, the editor knew that 'booraan' at that time was also used to indicate a drum as well as a winnowing device. The interesting aspect of this is the Anglicised spelling 'booran', the same as that which writer Patrick Kennedy used for County Wexford a few decades later (see Chapter 6) and which could correspond to 'buaireán', a pronunciation and spelling which had been introduced by Foley in 1855.

Relating roughly to *c.*1900, Brian Ó Cuív's list of words used in Ballyvourney, County Cork has also the acoustic concept, linked to the idea of a drum: 'Bodhraí … "hollow" voice … sound of something empty (as a drum)'.[27] The device bodhrán would of course also have this quality.

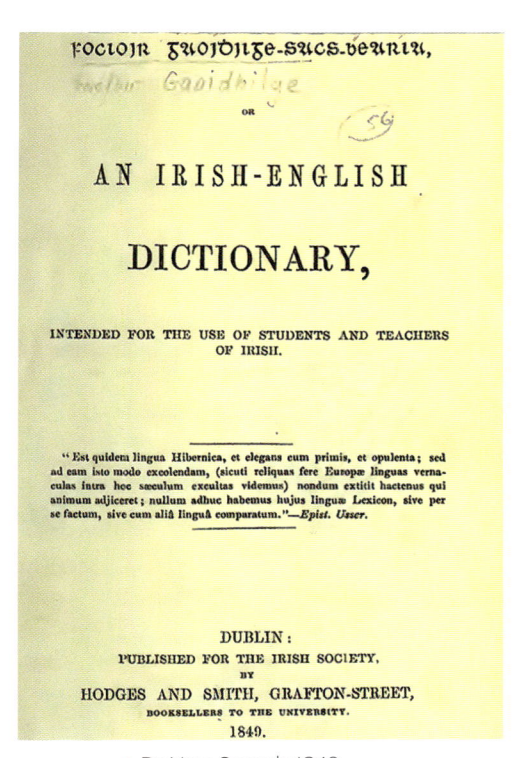

▲ De Vere Coney's 1849

▶ Foley's 'buaireán' word for a winnowing device, 1855

▲ *Irisleabhar* banner headline

Irisleabhar na Gaedhilge

The dictionary meanings in the previous paragraphs appear again from time to time in printed data that was published intermittently in the Irish newspapers but, in particular, in a systematic way, in *Irishleabhar na Gaedhilge/The Gaelic Journal*. That publication was initiated in October 1882 by The Gaelic Union for the Preservation and Cultivation of the Irish Language. Printed in Ireland on Irish-made paper, and dealing with Irish culture and language-related issues, in Irish and English it sought to expand the speaking of Irish through using topical journalism in Irish, inviting the engagement of readers in identifying and preserving Irish-language vocabulary that they were aware of in their local speech. Until it ceased in 1909 it published lexicons that readers contributed, among which were some entries regarding winnowing, including the meaning and application of the bodhrán:

- 1894: Sieve – made with wire or a sheepskin with holes burned in it.
- 1897: dallán – 'a blind riddle', i.e. with a leather bottom (this form of riddle is called a weight, wecht in some parts of the country, and buarán in Irish), is pronounced dullán in Meath.[28]
- 1900: dullán – a blind sieve made of sheepskin.[29]
- 1901: bodhrán – a circular tray, the bottom being formed with sheep skin. It is the size and form of a large sieve. As used in Wicklow, Wexford &c.[30]

▲ O'Reilly and O'Donovan, 1864

- 1901: bodhrán – a rim of ash, with a skin stretched on it, used for receiving corn as it comes from the winnowing machine.[31]
- 1901: bodharán – a tambourine; the frame of a sieve, with a piece of sack fastened on for a bottom, used for winnowing corn &c.[32]
- 1902: bárán – a riddle-shaped instrument with hide bottom, used for winnowing corn ['Irish words used in the spoken English of Farney in south Monaghan'].[33]
- 1902: bodhrán – a wooden frame covered with skin used for carrying oats &c. to horses, and in the County Wexford for kneading bread.[34]

These points certainly make it clear that in everyday speech a common name for the winnowing tool was 'bodhrán', or some phonetic relative of that, and so they challenge the idea of the origin of the bodhrán being as a drum. This, in turn, leads to the question of the literal meaning of the word 'bodhrán'. But because the dictionaries carried just the deaf-related meaning until *c.* 1800, and only began to indicate the word bodhrán as a winnowing tool *c.* 1867, this might well suggest that the original name 'bodhrán' did refer to a drum, or to a drum function, which by that time had almost been forgotten, and that at some point people began to colloquially refer to the similar-looking winnowing fans and wechts as 'bodhrán'. In the same way as, for instance, the device for sowing corn (a shoulder-mounted box with a scattering wheel operated by a push-and-pull, rod-and-twine hand lever) became known as a 'corn fiddle' on account of the similarity of holding it, and of the wrist and arm action, to fiddle playing. Against that, there is still the absence of a drum in written and folklore accounts of social music-making. That would suggest that, if such a music bodhrán did exist, it had limited, or seasonal, application and only among the poorer classes, and so was not part of what was formally regarded as 'music', and/or was beneath the line of sight of the lexicographers and so was not put on the record.

Dinneen's dictionary

In 1904 Patrick Dinneen in his *Irish-English Dictionary* continued with the deafness version, and with the functional device, but did not pick up on the music dimension:

> Bodhar ... deaf, bothered , Bodhrán ... a deaf person, person of indifferent hearing, one who speaks with an indistinct voice
>
> bodharán ... a sieve-like, shallow wooden vessel with sheep-skin bottom, a dildurn[35]

His inclusion of the latter definition reflects what had been appearing in the lexicons published each month in the Gaelic League's journal. His use of 'Druma ... a drum' was standard at this time, but he also introduced a third concept: 'Dallán ... a winnowing fan; sheep-hide; a wight'. Dinneen (1860–1934) was a lexicographer and historian, born near Rathmore, County Kerry. Ordained a Jesuit priest in 1894, he resigned in 1900 to devote his life to the study of the Irish language. He taught in his alma mater, Clongowes Wood College, and was a leading figure in the Irish Texts Society (founded in 1898) which was dedicated to restoring Irish language and literature. A minor novelist and playwright, he translated literature into Irish, but his best-known work is the Irish-English dictionary, *Foclóir Gaedhilge agus Béarla* (1904), the stock and plates of which were destroyed during the

Corn 'fiddle' from County Armagh showing bowing action: the 'bow' rod has a rubberised twine 'hair' which, lapped around a central axle, spins the grain-spreading wheel as the 'bow' is pushed from left to right in a fiddle-playing action [*EDI*]

Easter Rising of 1916; he expanded and republished the book in 1927.[36]

In 1910, Fournier's *An English-Irish Dictionary and Phrase-book* carries 'Drum … bobharán, druma'[37] as well as 'Tambour – tiompán'.[38]

Also in 1910, P.W. Joyce's *English as we Speak it in Ireland* has the first indication of the reality of the bodhrán, as well as a colloquial pronunciation. Monumentally, he says that the bodhrán can be used as an improvised tambourine, and that the tambourine can be called 'bowran', which was to be repeated by Ó Danachair in 1947:

> Bowraun, a sieve-shaped vessel for holding or measuring out corn, with the flat bottom made of dried sheepskin stretched tight; sometimes used as a rude tambourine, from which it gets the name *bowraun*; Irish *bodhur* [pron. bower here], deaf, from the *bothered* or indistinct sound. (south.)[39]

He also carries the term introduced by Dinneen in 1904: 'Dildron or dildern; a bowraun'.[40] The latter part of his statement presumably is intended to mean that the device bodhrán is named for the sound it can make when struck. His spelling 'bowran' is that which came to be used by the press for a decade or so from 1956 on.[41]

In 1917 Timothy O'Neill-Lane, in his *Foclóir Béarla-Gaedhlige*, follows Joyce in explaining the 'Dildurn' which Dinneen had mentioned. He also has 'deaf – bodhar' and 'drum – droma', but does not link them directly. He does however describes the dildurn:

> dildarn … a vessel like a sieve, but without holes, made of raw sheepskin stretched on a wooden hoop and allowed to dry (it is used in winnowing corn), bodhrán, or bodharán.[42]

In 1922 Lambert McKenna's English-Irish dictionary has 'Deaf … bodhar' and no entry for drum.

By 1926 bodhrán mór was being used as translation of 'big drum' in a marching band,[43] and this was recognised in 1927 by Dinneen's new Irish-English edition; this has 'Bodhar … deaf, bothered, confused … torann bodhar – a dead sound', and his two terms, which in 1904 had been separate, take heed of the variety of information by then in print, and are now conflated as

> Bodhrán *(bodharán)* … a deaf person … a shallow skin-bottomed vessel, a dildurn, a drum … *bodhrán mór*, a big drum[44]

He also has the range of acoustic associations that were to be used by Ó Danachair and Ó Riada in their interpretations of the drum: 'bodhraighe … deafness; hollowness as of sound … glór bodhraighe … the sound of a drum'.

1935. MacCionnaith's *Foclóir Béarla agus Goedilge / English-Irish Dictionary* has 'Drum – druma, dildurn, bodhrán, tiompán. Beating of – drumadóireacht';[45] 'tambourine – méisín ceoil'[46] [musical dish]; and 'dildurn – bódhrán'.[47]

1937. The word bodhrán, or versions of it, is recorded in **The Schools' Collection** (see Appendix 7) of folklore across fourteen counties – Carlow, Clare, Cork, Galway, Kilkenny, Kerry, Laois, Leitrim, Limerick, Mayo, Meath, Roscommon, Tipperary and Wexford. The greater number of these occurrences indicate the bodhrán as a utensil, either for winnowing (eleven occasions) or as a container (ten). It can also indicate deafness or a 'bothered' person, or a state of confusion (seven), and, significantly, only once does it

▲ Portrait of Patrick Dinneen by Jack B. Yeats

▲ Patrick Dinneen's 1927 dictionary

> **bóḋṙaḋ, -ḋaṙṫa,** *m.,* deafness, stunning, confusion; **b. leaṫ,** confusion attend you, bother you.
> **bóḋṙaim (bóḋṙuiġim), -aḋ,** *v. tr.,* I make deaf, I stun, I confuse; **ná bóḋaiṙ mé,** don't annoy me; **ná bí am' ḃóḋṙaḋ,** don't bother me.
> **bóḋṙán (bóḋaṙán), -áin,** *pl. id.,* *m.,* a deaf person; a person of indifferent hearing; one who speaks with an indistinct voice; *cf.,* **bóḋṙán ġan éiṙṫeaċṫ** (*Don. song*). See **bóḋaṙán.**

> **bóḋaṙ, -aiṙe,** *a.,* deaf, bothered; confused; annoyed; troubled.
> **bóḋaṙán, -áin,** *pl. id., m.,* a sieve-like shallow wooden vessel with sheep-skin bottom; a dildurn.

◀ Dinneen's 1904 entries showing that 'bodhrán' was understood to relate to deafness, and also to an agricultural device

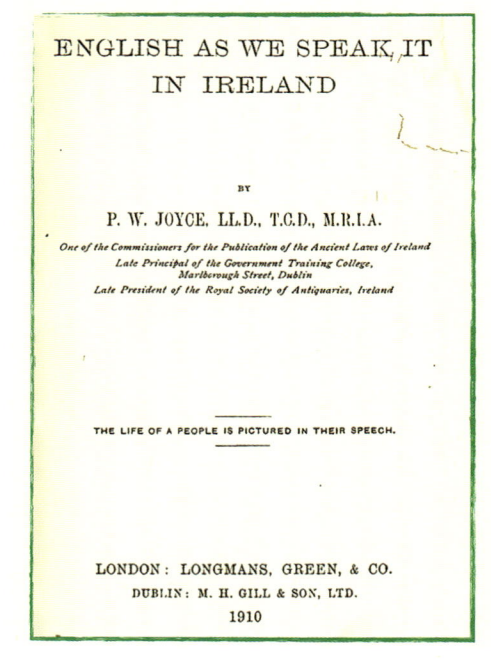

> **bóḋṙaḋ, -ḋaṙṫa,** *m.,* deafness, stunning, confusion; **b. leaṫ,** bother you.
> **bóḋṙaiġe,** *g. id., f.,* deafness; hollowness as of sound; (*al. a.,* bothered); **ġlóṙ b.,** a hollow voice indicative of ill-health, the sound of a drum, the sound of a stone being broken when it is at the breaking point.
> **bóḋṙaim (bóḋṙuiġim), -aḋ,** *v. tr.* and *intr.,* I make deaf, I stun, I confuse; I deaden (as an acute pain); **ná bóḋaiṙ mé,** don't annoy me; **ná bí am' ḃóḋṙaḋ,** don't bother me; *intr.,* I become confused, grow dull, bothered, deaf.
> **bóḋṙán (bóḋaṙán), -áin,** *pl. id., m.,* a deaf person; a person of indifferent hearing; an indistinct speaker; *al.* a shallow skin-bottomed vessel, a dildurn, a drum; **b. móṙ,** a big drum.

> ENGLISH AS WE SPEAK IT
> IN IRELAND
>
> BY
> P. W. JOYCE, LL.D., T.C.D., M.R.I.A.
> One of the Commissioners for the Publication of the Ancient Laws of Ireland
> Late Principal of the Government Training College,
> Marlborough Street, Dublin
> Late President of the Royal Society of Antiquaries, Ireland
>
> THE LIFE OF A PEOPLE IS PICTURED IN THEIR SPEECH.
>
> LONDON: LONGMANS, GREEN, & CO.
> DUBLIN: M. H. GILL & SON, LTD.
> 1910

▲ Joyce, 1910 [*NMI, Turlough, Castlebar*]

◀ Dinneen's 1927 entry

specifically refer to music, on the Wren. Where the word 'bodhrán' (or equivalent) is given as part of local vocabulary, any of the above meanings could apply.

By 1937 some newspapers were carrying lists of still-used, but local, Irish words, among which the deafness association was the only explanation of bodhrán. For instance:

> 'Boorawn' – Ir. 'Bodhrán', a deaf person. (Usually heard in 'As deaf as a boorawn'). [*Nenagh Guardian* 1937 0403 2]

In 1953, Michael Traynor's *The English Dialect of Donegal* has two interesting entries:

> Weight ... in forms waicht, weght (H), wecht, wight ... A hoop, with a skin stretched over it, used for winnowing corn ... used for filling winnowed corn ... A man stands out in the open with a few yards of sacking spread around, and in his hand a circular tray (a hoop with a shallow rim) about eighteen inches in diameter, and a tanned sheep-skin (the wool having been removed by lime) spread over it. He plies this in the wind, letting the grain fall on the sacking.[48]

> Bodhrán, bowraun. 1. A shallow drum-shaped vessel, made of sheepskin stretched over a frame, used for separating grain from chaff after flailing; a frame for carrying oats; After flailing, the grain is put into the bodhrán – a tall man was usually given the job: he tossed the grain away, into the wind. the chaff blew away, leaving the grain (KM, Kerry). 2. A kind of tambourine. [Dolan 1998]

In 1961 deafness appeared again, in Tipperary, but was extended to include the device:

> bodhar (bower) deaf. a 'bore'. Sé an bodhar é (nó í). Bodharán, a dildarn, or wide-meshed sieve. Bodhránaíl (bowránaí), one suffering from a head cold. [*Tipperary Star* 1961 1021 9]

The Scottish dictionaries

Scottish-Gaelic dictionaries seem more focused, dealing with fewer words and concepts. William Shaw's 1780 *Gaelic and English Dictionary* carries 'fan (for winnowing) *dallan*' and also the bodhar = deaf association. 'Dalan' comes from the Gaelic word *dall* meaning sightless, the suggestion being that this device was made the same way as a sieve, but with no perforations, i.e. 'a blind sieve'. The 1828 Highland Society of Scotland's *Dictionarium Scoto-Celticum*, without ambiguity carries the title of the device used for winnowing: 'Dallan – a fan to winnow corn with, and also Dallanach – a kind of winnowing fan'.[49] It also has 'Druma – a drum, tympanum', linking the drum and the European and English version of timpan.[50] In its English-Gaelic vol. 2, it back-translates 'Tambourine – druma láimhe',[51] and 'Winnowing fan – fasgain, dallan, dalanach'.[52] McAlpine's in 1866 gives Tiompán as 'timbril, cymbal, tabor or drum', acknowledging that this information is from the Bible, not from Gaelic sources; again, it includes the instrument-name 'tympanum', which is back-translated as 'drum'.[53] Alex MacEachen's 1936 Gaelic-English dictionary has bodhair etc. variously as 'deafen', and 'a hollow, low sound'.

The modern dictionaries

The dictionaries leave us with a choice of words, reflection on which is useful: *dallán, wight, wite, wecht, dildurn* all indicate a winnowing device. Bodhrán can also indicate the same, as already stated. But because by its construction – a skin stretched on a wood frame – the bodhrán resembles a tambourine, it is possible that the word 'tambourine' may be being used to indicate a similar generic construction. The later dictionaries re-use the translations from the early ones, but do not develop them. The word tambourine does not appear at all with regard to a music instrument in any lexicon until Tomás de Bhaldraithe's 1959 *English-Irish Dictionary* which has: 'Tambourine … *Tambóirín*', a phonetic approximation that is about sound, not about etymologically-derived nature or function. Coincidentally, this was in the same year that John B. Keane's play *Sive* introduced that instrument to the Dublin stage (see Chapter 10). But although the de Bhaldraithe dictionary separately explores 'drum' at some length, no reference is made in that context to either tambourine or bodhrán. In 1975 de Bhaldraithe's *Contributions to a Dictionary of the Irish Language*, and his 1981 follow-up work came closer with 'bodrán (bodhrán) tabor'. But the clear mentions of tambourine in relation to bodhrán have been Joyce in 1910, Michael Traynor in 1953, and, in 1977, Niall Ó Dónaill's Irish-English *Foclóir Gaeilge-Béarla*, which has 'bodhrán … Deaf person' and 'bodhrán … 1. Winnowing drum. 2. (Kind of) tambourine'.

The Royal Irish Academy dictionary

Also in 1977, the most comprehensive Irish-English work in the field in modern times was the *Dictionary of the Irish Language* (*DIL*), published by the Royal Irish Academy in Dublin. The dictionary was first projected at a meeting of the Irish Archaeological Society in November 1852, devised by the leading scholars John O'Donovan, William Elliott Hudson and Eugene O'Curry, who

> envisioned a dictionary that would be based on a thorough excerpting of old Irish manuscripts. The meanings of words were to be supported by citations. Etymology was not attempted apart from derivation within Irish itself and the giving of sources of loan words. These pioneering directions were adhered to throughout the compilation of the dictionary over more than a century.

The originators were dead by 1862, and the first instalment of the exacting work was not published until 1913. The remaining parts were completed by 1976, all twenty-four of them running to over 2,500 pages in a 'compact' edition. O'Donovan's contributions came from the 1817 O'Reilly's dictionary, and O'Curry's were from his own personal research. The *DIL* is based mainly on 'old- and middle-Irish materials, for all intents and purposes it is a "dictionary of early Irish"'.[54] Thus its entries relating to bodhrán should be notable, and indeed it has the two key manuscript links that have already been explored.[55]

The bodhrán 'in a bodhrán'

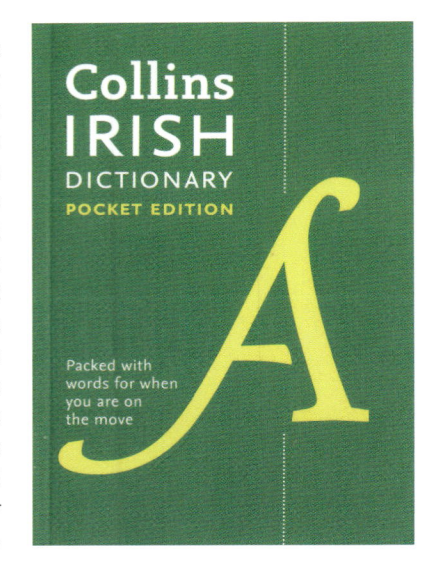

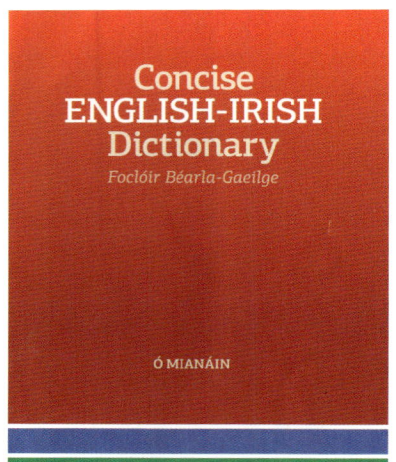

The most modern dictionary is Foras na Gaeilge's 2020 *The Concise English – Irish Dictionary / Foclóir Béarla – Gaeilge*, edited by Pádraig Ó Mianáin.[56] It does not cite 'bodhrán' in any context, an omission that invites the expression 'My head is in a bodhrán', which Kerry fiddle-player Julia Clifford used to express a sense of befuddlement,[57] for this immense, impressive work has no reference to the Irish drum even in its column of material on 'drum' that covers such terms as 'drummer' and 'drum machine'. 'Tambourine', however, is present, translated as the phonetic Gaelicisation 'tambóirín', the same as in Niall Ó Dónaill's 1977 book – implying, appropriately, that it should be understood to be an import. It is disappointing that a dictionary of 1,776 pages omits such a ubiquitous, thriving indigenous instrument as the bodhrán, even if the word and its translation are spelt the same. Absence of an entry by specific name may be totally understandable on account of the fact that certain objects, the terms for which originate in one language are the same in others.[58] But the Anglicised version of the word 'bodhrán' carries so many linguistic assumptions and loadings that it would seem to merit an entry, possibly as 'frame drum' (see pp. 66–7). That this dictionary omits mention of the bodhrán in the wider 'drum' context too is also a pity, though it is likely a consequence of both the modernity of this Irish form of percussion, and the traditional music field's own vagueness about the drum and its origins – is it 'bodhrán' in both Irish and English, or it is, as 1960s–70s music history could be interpreted as implying, 'tambourine' in English and 'bodhrán' in Irish? Whatever the reasoning, in the way that 'sleán', a turf-cutting spade, is also absent from the dictionary, reference to the bodhrán has been regarded as unnecessary, even though nine other specific types of drum, including 'snare-drum'[59] and 'bass-drum',[60] are covered. The dictionary is accessible online at focloir.ie.[61]

Another remarkable modern resource is the *teanglann.ie* website that hosts several digital, rapid-response major dictionaries, among them the Ó Dónaill Irish–English from 1977. As in its print edition, this offers 'bodhrán' with the same meaning as in the 1920s – '1. Winnowing drum. 2. (Kind of) tambourine' – and, otherwise, its listing of broader meanings for the actual word 'drum' includes everything except the music bodhrán. But *teanglann.ie* does also provide access to a more modern dictionary, from 1991, *An Foclóir Beag*, which explains terms as well as giving translations.[62] It sets a new level of information on the bodhrán: 'druma beag agus craiceann ar thaobh amháin de' [small drum with skin on one side]; for 'tambourine' it has 'cineál de bhodhrán' [kind of bodhrán]. So too with An Comhlacht Oideachais's *Foclóir* which has dispensed with 'winnowing', and pragmatically gives 'bodhrán' in its two present-day meanings of 'deaf person' and 'hand drum', as does the 2019 *Collins Irish Dictionary* which, additionally, has 'bodhránaí … bodhrán player'.

A distinct, purpose-defining original meaning for 'bodhrán'?

All of the dictionary words relating to the bodhrán are linked by similarities in their sound as well as by presumed meaning. But there is also such diversity among the spellings of the phonetic representations of 'bodhrán' in folklore, newspapers and literature that a variety of potential original spellings in Irish is at least possible. This must raise the chance of there being a meaning for the word 'bodhrán' other than the generally-assumed acoustic association of dull-sounding, or deafening noise. For instance, *'borrane'*, the English-language, phonetic spelling used by the Halls in 1842 (see p. 81) has an equivalent sound in Irish – *'borrán'*, variously translated as 'anger'[63] and also 'tumult'.[64]

P.W. Joyce addressed this in 1910, relating it to the word for bodhrán,[65] associating it with Ireland in particular, a point taken up also in The Oxford Dictionary:

> Bother … the earliest instances occur in the writings of Irishmen … and the word has long formed part of the vocabulary of the comic Irishman of fiction

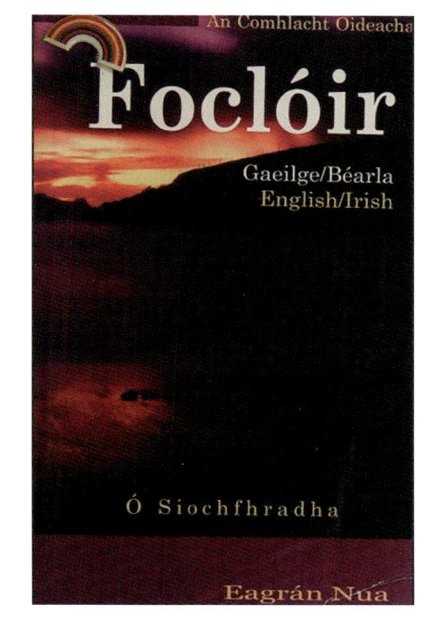

and the stage. This suggests an Anglo-Irish origin; but no suitable etymon has been found in Irish. The Irish bódhar deaf, and bódhairim I deafen (suggested by Crofton Croker), and buaidhirt trouble, affliction, buaidhrim I vex (proposed by Garnett) alike labour under the difficulty that the spoken words do not suggest bodder or bother ...

1. To bewilder with noise; to confuse, muddle; to put into a fluster or flutter.

2. To give trouble to; to pester, annoy, worry.[66]

The first of those is indeed one of the meanings of 'bodhrán', as it appeared in lexicons in the 1900s, and as quoted earlier from Julia Clifford. The second could suggest the physical action of winnowing grain. Related to this is the entry in Daniel Foley's 1855 *English-Irish Dictionary*, in which, as already stated, he introduces the winnowing bodhrán in relation to words for 'fan' – *'fuarán'* (for cooling), *'gaothrán'* (for blowing air, wind) – leading him to suggest *'buaireán'* for winnowing (pp. 58–9).[67] This is similar to the Wexford phonetic spelling given in the c. 1800 Poole Glossary, and by Patrick Kennedy in the 1860s (p. 79). It is the closest that the dictionary terms come to a word that visually describes an original functional feature of the utilitarian bodhrán.

Because that device's origin is to do with winnowing, with improvised drum use only largely a seasonal extra, could Foley's 1855 word be the original meaning of 'bodhrán'? Considering the variety among pronunciation-derived, Irish-language spellings given in print over the course of the years when the dictionaries were being solidified, there are several terms appropriate to consider as the origin of the name of our drum.

Spelling, pronunciation and meaning

As regards meaning, the various pronunciations of the word 'bodhrán' also offer clues. Today, each individual appears to use their own favoured pronunciation – typically 'bough-ran' or 'boh-ran', with equal emphasis on each syllable. Yet 'bough-*ran*' and 'bough-*rawn*' are quite commonly heard, and so too 'bo-*ran*' and 'bo-*rawn*' – in each case emphasising the second syllable. The first syllable is pronounced according to what Irish-language area the speaker comes from – roughly 'bough' in Munster Irish, and 'bodh' in Ulster Irish, and otherwise in line with regional Gaelic linguistic conventions. Since the second syllable has the á ('a-fada', the accented 'a'), that, technically, should be emphasised in speech, italics are used here to indicate that. Nevertheless, it is the first syllable of the written word – 'bodh' – that has become the more characteristic. Technically, in Ulster Irish it has the sound 'bo' (as in 'go' and 'sew'). But in Munster Irish it can rhyme with 'cow' and 'plough', as iterated in print as far back as 1910 by P.W. Joyce:

Bowraun ... Irish bodhur [pron. bower here][65]

Most people using the word, however, are not relating it to any language region, but would appear to be applying English-language colloquial-speech conventions, where the 'oh' sound can be pronounced 'ouw' – such as 'bold' / 'bould', 'hold' / 'hould', 'old' / 'ould' and so on (with many exceptions – for instance in names like 'Horan' and 'Moran'). So the term is very often spoken in English as 'bough-ran', with equal emphasis on both syllables – an

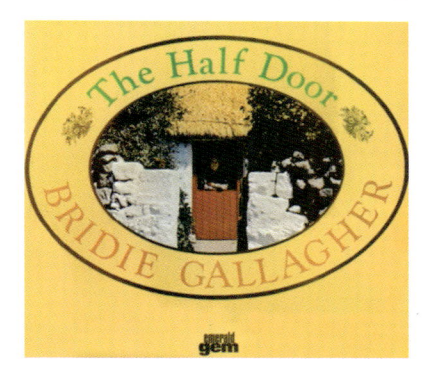

Anglicisation. In Irish, the earliest evidence in print is in the Munster Irish of Tomás Rua's poem cited on p. 144, which opens with:

> Is 'mdhó bean do bheadh ag clamhrán
> Nach tabharfadh uaithe bodhrán

This suggests the 'ow' sound for the first syllable. But the final verse is different:

> A Sighle mhaith Ní Mhódhráin
> Ó thugais uait an bodhrán

as the 'ó' implies the use of the 'oh' sound for the first syllable. An earlier, hand-written account by John Fleming of County Wexford concerning Aonach Bhearna na Gaoithe speaks of 'Tomás a' bhóghráin', using a spelling that also indicates a first-syllable pronunciation of 'oh' (see note 10, p. 155). This is the case too in the first two lines of a snatch of a rhyme collected in County Galway in the 1940s:

> Col ceathrair don chriathar an bodhrán
> Shiúil mé go mór agus chonaic mé mórán[68]

Seán Ó Riada, who ultimately based himself in County Cork used the pronunciation 'bough-*rawn*' in his 1962 radio essay (p. 267), yet many Irish speakers today refer to the drum as 'boh-*rán*', similar to the phonetic sound 'borrane' noted in County Cork by the Halls in the late 1830s (p. 81).

Audio evidence

The pendulum is also swung towards the 'oh' rather than the 'ow' by the earliest piece of audio evidence, a song recorded in 1926 titled 'Close the half-door' or 'The Half Door'. It was originally written and performed some time after 1916 by a Boston-Irish piper Shaun O'Nolan who had emigrated from Wicklow in 1898. It has the lines:

> She'd a bodhrán placed upon her knee
> It was full of potatoes I could see[69]

On O'Nolan's own 1926 Columbia recording he says 'boh-ran', and, subsequently, Peter McNulty on a disc in 1928 also pronounced it the same way, as did Donegal singer Bridie Gallagher who re-popularised the song on LP three decades later. Then, in line with revival times, The Grehan Sisters from Roscommon recorded in 1966 pronouncing the word as 'bough-ran'. Apropos meaning, it is interesting that when Connemara singer Seosamh Ó hÉanaí recorded it, he translated 'bodhrán', itself an interesting statement as to its meaning: 'She'd a basket placed upon her knee'. These audio testimonies are an unambiguous indication of how the word might once have been spoken, as well as offering a reasonable translation.

Wild card meanings

Occasionally the word 'boorawn' and even 'bodhrán' are found in press reports referring to the puffball, an edible fungus named from the Irish 'borrtha' meaning swollen, distended: 'I should prefer to smoke a piece of cane, dried turf or even a "bowran"'.[70] A satirical metaphor develops the fungal bowran idea:

> Lastly, there is the bowran question ... every new generation of farmer's

> children is less disposed than its predecessor to break bowrans ... apart from their responsibility as public men, they are nearly all reputed to be expert golfers, and breaking bowrans would be an ideal pastime for them and for the golfing fraternity generally. [*Southern Star* 1930, 0816 3]

As regards the actual bodhrán device, this 'bowran' bears no relation to either a bodhrán utensil or drum. The similarity of a dried cowpat to the puffball may have resulted in another colloquial usage of bodhrán *c.* 1900: '*bórán* – dry cow dung, often used as a fire material'.[71] This was also reported from County Cork in the *Schools' Collection*. Another wild card which muddied the picture was the substance called *baighreán*, described in folklore accounts, a thin gruel made by fermenting the post-milling husks of the grain, and then straining through a perforated sheepskin sieve. This was also called 'sowens' in northern counties, a drink, but by the 1950s the term was used to describe a similar preparation made from flax-seed husks for feeding animals. The same foodstuff in Wales was known as *bwdran*; today the substance is historic, but is known as flummery. Yet another tantalising morsel of diversion has been the *búran* in France. This was the name of the small houses used by transhumance farmers during the summers for making and storing the famous Cantal cheeses at high altitudes in the Massif Central. The cheeses were moulded and stored in wooden hoops over which was stretched a piece of animal skin, the same as is reported as done with cheese in England.[72] Such a visual similarity with regard to early Irish history would not unreasonably suggest a French, Norman connection, but other than the similarity in the devices and words used, it is not supported by any other information.

Linguistic speculation
Related to the container function of the original bodhrán is the Irish word to carry – *beir*. Adding the suffix -án as in a device for carrying, a carrier, would give 'beir-án', but there are no occurrences of such a pronunciation in published phonetics. Another speculative term might relate to the word for threshing – *bualadh* – which could give 'buailán', related to a primary purpose in winnowing, but applying to the flail, not to the container. A different 'bú' term is related to cattle in Dinneen, and to 'buarach', an owner of cattle. A witchcraft connection to the same word is 'buarach' as 'an unbroken hoop of skin cut with incantation from a corpse;'[73] 'búr' was a term for foreigner (boor). A final speculation is one proffered by County Kerry dramatist and writer John B. Keane in a 1970 television documentary:

> Bodhrán is a corruption of the word tambourine. It was always called the tambourine, then it was called the 'breen', then it was called a 'boreen' 'bóirín', eventually corrupted to 'bodhrán' which is the name given to the instrument everywhere now ... 'tamboran', 'tamboreen' ... 'bodhrán' is really a short way of saying 'tambourine'.[74]

Another Kerry writer, Bryan MacMahon, voiced a related opinion a few years later in 1978, saying that

> the use of the word 'bodhrán' for the drum derives from a process of accretion whereby the second two syllables of 'tambourine' become confused with the Gaelic word; thus '-bourine' becomes 'bodhrán'.[75]

NOTES TO CHAPTER 4

Both these opinions are based on accepting that the tambourine drum came in to Ireland, that we borrowed and copied it, and that the term 'bodhrán' used for it is a phonetic corruption of 'tambourine'. That being the case, as a word it would not exist in the older Gaelic lexicon, and therefore would have no meaning or history as a drum in Irish. And all objects titled 'bodhrán' in manuscript and other references would then irrefutably indicate only a device or an acoustic quality – not a drum. Overall, however, three distinct associations are identified by the manuscripts and dictionaries in their translations of bodhrán – 1/ deafness/noise, 2/ winnowing, and 3/ music-making.

And, among spellings and translations in early dictionaries, two interesting possible spellings stand out: 1/ Foley's 1855 'buaireán'; related to the act of 'bothering' in winnowing (p. 58), and 2/ Fleming's spelling 'bóghrán' which is related to the use of goatskin.

[1] RIA 1977, 133. The manuscript is held at the Bibliothèque Nationale in Paris, and can be read online. See Lambert 1982.
[2] Eamon O'Flaherty, PC 10 March 2022.
[3] Gioielli 2008, 15.
[4] Ibid., 11.
[5] Ibid., 13.
[6] Ibid., 19.
[7] Ibid., 15.
[8] Examples of both of these types can be seen in St Cecelia's Hall museum in Edinburgh.
[9] Bachellery 1964.
[10] Ó Bharáin 2007, 55 has established this MS to be between late fifteenth and very early seventeenth centuries and is essentially a sixteenth-century manuscript; the median figure is used here for convenience.
[11] RIA 1977, 133.
[12] Wulff 1929, xxxiv.
[13] It should not be confused with tympanitis, an infection of the eardrum, which affects reception of sound only.
[14] Wulff 1929, 268–9, from TCD MS 1432, p. 17.
[15] *Rosa Anglica*, TCD MS 1435, p. 155.
[16] Scholes 1970, 781.
[17] This is borne out by a test making of such a bodhrán, with a 'tucked-in' skin rather than a glued-on or nailed-on one (McNeela and Vallely, 2022).
[18] O'Begly 1732, Preface p. 3.
[19] Ibid., Preface.
[20] Shaw 1780, 124.
[21] Barnes 1867, 28.
[22] Ibid., 29.
[23] Ní Fhuarthán 2010, PC.
[24] Foley 1855, 47.
[25] Ibid., 132.
[26] Barnes op. cit., 27.
[27] Ó Cuív 1900, 32.
[28] Feis Laighean 's Midhe; ING Vol. 8, No. 88, 1897, 68.
[29] ING No. 3; Vol. 11, No. 132 1900, 154–5.
[30] ING Vol. 12, No. 138, 1902, 41.
[31] Feis Laighean 's Midhe, 1901; ING Vol. 12, No. 141, 1902, 96.
[32] ING Vol. 11, No. 175, 1901, 94.
[33] ING Vol. 12, No. 137, 1902, 26.
[34] ING Vol. 12, No. 139, 1902, 62.
[35] Dinneen 1904, 73.
[36] Hickey 1999, 178.
[37] Fournier 1910, 89.
[38] Ibid., 283.
[39] Joyce 1910, 222.
[40] Ibid., 217.
[41] *The Nationalist* 1956 0505 12, possibly the earliest use of 'bowran' in the press.
[42] O'Neill-Lane 1917, 454.
[43] An Lóchrann 1926, 82.
[44] Dinneen 1927, 105.
[45] MacCionnaith 1935, 365.
[46] Ibid., 1357.
[47] Ibid., 330.
[48] Traynor 1953, 324.
[49] HSS 1828, 326.
[50] Ibid., 374.
[51] Ibid., 800.
[52] Ibid., 502.
[53] McAlpine 1866, 262 and 526.
[54] RIA.ie.
[55] Ibid., 133.
[56] Foras na Gaeilge, founded in December 1999, is the Irish state's body responsible for the promotion of the Irish language throughout the island of Ireland.
[57] Hickey 1999, 57; see p. 203.
[58] One example of such is the German term 'shrapnell', which has a phonetic borrowing 'shrapnel' in English, and 'srapnal' in Irish.
[59] Ó Mianáin 2020, 1363.
[60] Ibid., 104.
[61] Focloir.ie, operated by teanglann.ie, developed by Foras na Gaeilge in parallel with the *New English-Irish Dictionary* project. The aim of the site is to provide users of the language with free, easy-to-use access to dictionaries and to grammatical and pronunciation information relating to words in the Irish language.
[62] *An Foclóir Beag*, 1991, leagan leictreonach inchuardaithe é seo de *An Foclóir Beag Gaeilge* – a foilsíodh i 1991.
[63] Dinneen, 1927, 111.
[64] Ó Dónaill 1977, 127.
[65] Joyce 1910, 221–2
[66] Simpson and Weiner 1989, 429.
[67] Foley 1855, 132.
[68] Williams 2021, 111 (286). Originally collected by T.S. Ó Máille, *Seanfhocla Chonnacht* (i) 1948-52.
[69] I am indebted for the audio reference here to a remarkable coincidence of academic conferencing, memory and scholarship involving Don Meade, Dan Neely and Alan Morrisroe. Meade and Neely were speaking about Mick Maloney at a Dublin symposium on Irish-American music, after which Meade told Neely of this bodhrán book, which reminded Neely (who is an authority on '78' records) of the song, and Morrisroe, who they were visiting, gave me a copy of the recording. Such a coincidence would not have happened had the event been an online, streamed one, and points to physical presence and resultant ongoing interaction as being vastly superior to remote options.
[70] *Tipperary Star* 1917, 0804 3
[71] Laighean 's Midhe, ING No. 3; Vol. 11, No. 132 1900, 154–5.
[72] McCrickard op. cit.
[73] Dinneen 1927, 136.
[74] Keane 1970.
[75] MacMahon 1978.

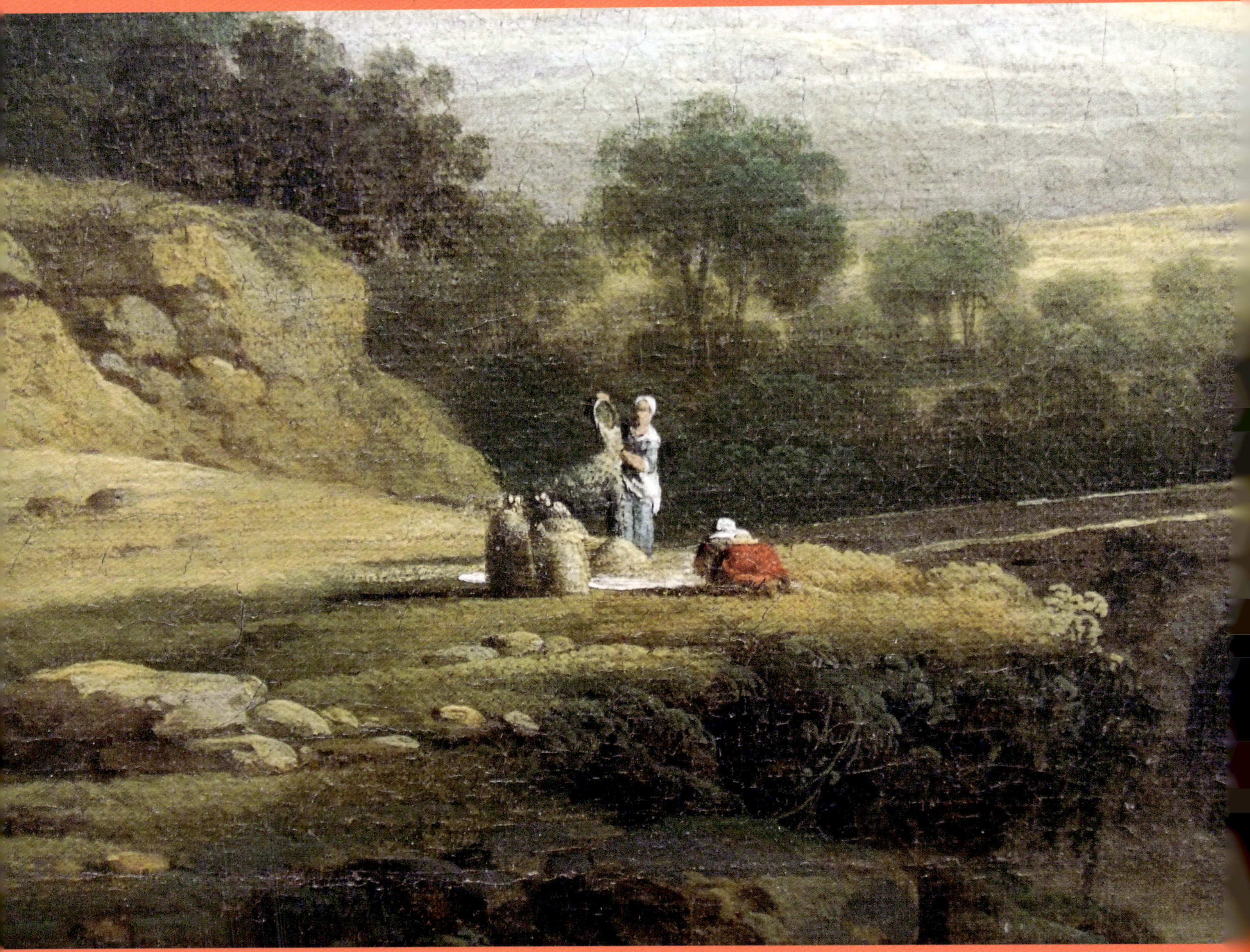

CHAPTER 5 | 'BODHRÁN': SOUND OR FUNCTION?

The earliest appearance of the word bodhrán in manuscripts dates to *c.* AD 900, at which time the given meaning was to describe a person who is without speech, and/or without hearing. This meaning persisted, repeated in later dictionaries and writing, but now is excluded in disablement-aware times from the most up-to-date English-Irish translations.[1] Related to deafness is the idea of 'sound' – dull, indistinct, booming and such – and this is the main meaning that is tracked in subsequent dictionaries. Since such sound is a quality of the device bodhrán when struck, this has come to be generally accepted as the reason for its having been so named. Because the deafness association appears in dictionaries from the start, in 1732, and runs parallel to the occurrence of the utensil meaning from 1800 on, it has become something of an obfuscation in thinking about the bodhrán as both a device and a drum.

Deafness, noise and dull sound

Prior to the twentieth century the word bodhrán appears in print mostly relating to deafness, in the 1732 O'Begly dictionary, and later appearing also in texts such as a 1768 sermon that cited the biblical line 'tá a radharc ag na dallaibh; atá a siubhal ag na bacachaibh; tá a n-éisteacht ag na bodhránaibh' [the blind have their sight, the lame can walk, the deaf can hear].[2] In Aodh Mac Domhnaill's poetry of 1850 the same concept is repeated: 'Na balbháin go labharfadh is na bodhráin go n-éistfeadh' [the dumb would speak, the deaf would hear].[3] This common usage is found not only in all the dictionaries, but also occasionally in twentieth-century newspapers' popular lexicons too:

> bodhrán, duine gan éisteach na gcluas aige [A person 'without the ability to hear with his ears']. [1931, *Sunday Independent* 0428 1 2]

> Seo é an fáth, ar seisean, mar cuireann an two-taw-tig a fhoghlamann sé sa sgoil bodhrán i mo chluasa … [the learning by rote that he learns in school deafens me]. [1931, *Irish Independent* 1001 8]

> Boorawn – Ir. Bodhrán, a deaf person. (Usually heard in As deaf as a boorawn). [1937, *Nenagh Guardian* 0403 2]

> an dall ag iarraidh radhairc shul / An bodhrán ag guidhe eisteachta / An balbhan ar lorg urlabhra / Gach duine aca go h-aindeis thruaghach [The blind one wanting to see / the deaf one wanting to hear / the dumb one wanting to talk] Writing by Seosamh Mac Grianna ('Máire'). [1939, *Meath Chronicle* 0617 8]

In the *Schools' Collection* of folklore – collected *c.* 1937 and relating to the turn of the twentieth century[4] – the word 'bodhrán' is given for deafness,

◀ *A River Landscape with Travellers on a Bridge and Women Winnowing*, by Thomas Roberts, late 1700s [*Private collection*]

▲ Detail of the winnowing process [*Patricia Vallely*]

a 'bothered' person, or a state of confusion, in seven counties. This is also linked to the already-considered range of dictionary translations in which the word 'bodhar' is associated too with 'dull', 'confusing', 'loud', 'hollow-sounding' and such, all acoustic terms which are related to the eardrum – auditory experiences. The suffix '-án' when added indicates a person or object with such sound-related condition, association or properties: thus for bodhar we have *bodhrán* meaning a deaf person. But the bodhrán was also an agricultural or domestic tool, so it would not be unreasonable to expect that its same-sounding word has another meaning which is related to its purpose – not to some feature of its nature. Allowing for spelling discrepancies, the earliest appearances of the full word similar to 'bodhrán' in print are *bobharán*, 1814, and *booranne*, 1825 (r/e *c.* 1800). In 1910 Joyce linked the device to the tambourine, based on the sound the device bodhrán made when struck, but it was not until Dinneen in 1904 that it was noted for the first time in a dictionary that 'bodhrán' is a deaf person as well as a winnowing tool.

By 1927 Dinneen also linked all three concepts – deafness/noise, the winnowing device, and a drum – thus setting a template which has been adhered to since.

While Dinneen was likely just including three actual meanings for the same word, his thinking could imply however that the drum use of 'bodhrán' predated its functional use, and that after the drum use passed (as said on p. 60), the device function took over. But it has been concluded that, based on spelling, in his trinity it is sound – or potential for dull, indistinct sound – which is the common denominator, not any practical aspect of the uses in winnowing, storage and music. At the time the term was first noted in a manuscript in the ninth century (see p. 51), there was but one meaning, and that was with regard to deafness. By the time of the second known manuscript citation of 'bodhrán' *c.* 600 years

▲ Winnowing at Cashel, *c.* 1780 [*'A south east View of the rock of Cashel'*, p. 149, in Edward Ledwich's 1804 The Antiquities of Ireland]

▼ Skin winnowing tray, Galway [Copyright National Museum of Ireland]

▶ Wood-mesh sieve and/or winnowing-bodhrán seller at Ballybricken Fair, Waterford City, *c.* 1900. The type of wide-mesh riddle that the seller is displaying would be for sifting straw out from flailed oats (see p. 78). The objects on the ground may also be sieves – possibly whited-out due to ambient light conditions? – or they may be flat-rim winnowing bodhráns, of the type used at Cashel, 1790s (opposite and above), or as mentioned later in a 1956 press report (see p. 82) [National Library of Ireland; courtesy Norah Byrne Kavanagh, Waterford]

later, this coexisted with the device meaning. Yet both meanings may well have applied all along, just have not been documented. The linking of the word bodhrán to a drum in some of the dictionaries may also have seemed apt, on account of structural similarity to the tambourine, and because the bodhrán as a device was in their time already on the way to extinction. Indeed, no-one could have even imagined that the frame drum would take off just three decades after Dinneen. The issue of the deafness connection will be left at this, as it is the device and drum meanings which are at the heart of this study.

The actual, original bodhráns

Bodhrán-style implements were everywhere in the past, on account of the fact that farming and domestic activities involved many different carrying and sifting practices. Central in these was grain processing and handling which used winnowing 'fans', riddles, sieves, shallow containers or measures, and trays. The earliest depiction of such usage is in a *c.* 1780 etching showing winnowing at Cashel, County Tipperary. Captioned 'A south east view of the rock of Cashel', this shows a tall woman spilling corn out of a bodhrán which she holds over her head, while another stoops to fill a bodhrán from a sack.[5] This use is noted among the many functional interpretations of 'bodhrán' which appeared in folklore records, such as in a blunt, 1862 comment from Loughrea, County Galway: 'The Bórán was used for winnowing oats an' bringing out oats to hens'.[6] These uses will be looked at separately.

◀ *Autumn* – woman winnowing with a bodhrán or sieve, 1845 [*Louisa Anne, marchioness of Waterford (1818–91)*]

▼ Winnowing oats with a skin wight, County Donegal, early to mid-1900s [*Photography by R.J. Welch, in Evans 1957, Plate 7, (pp. 81, 190)*]

▼ Thai woman winnowing rice with a fabric wecht [*Gender and Development Research Institute, Bangkok*]

Winnowing

Winnowing is the process by which the kernels of grains of oats, barley, wheat, rice, rye, etc. are separated from the surrounding inedible leafy material – known as chaff – which protects them while they grow. First, the grain and chaff are removed from the plant stalks, the straw, done by beating them on rocks or lashing with hand flails in older times, leaving a mix of grain, which is heavy, and light fluffy chaff. The chaff can be removed by letting air pass through the mix, achieved by emptying the grain from a height onto a sheet on the ground on a breezy day. The container used for this had various names, sometimes described as a 'winnowing fan', or large sieve which also had different names, including *bodhrán*, *wecht*, *dallan* and *dildurn*. These devices could also be used as containers, the ancestor of today's diverse plastic buckets, basins and trays. The folklore accounts gathered for *The Schools' Collection* in 1937 tell us that the original bodhrán served this purpose in eleven different parts of Ireland, so its story is taken to open at the point grain-growing began. This was *c.* 8500 BC in the Middle East, with wheat, barley, pea and lentil crops reaching Ireland in the neolithic period (late Stone Age) *c.* 4000 BC. The equipment associated

Boy Winnowing, 1840, by Daniel MacDonald, Cork [*Gorry Gallery*]

Les Vaneuses du Kerity, winnowers in Brittany, 1868 [*Felix Roy*]

Winnowing with a wight in the Mourne mountains, County Down, 1915 [*Green Collection*]

with such farming was initially rudimentary, and its use spread with people. Craft tools at the time were limited to those made of flint and porcellanite, so grain-processing equipment was without doubt simple. The grain was finally ground on a small hand-operated pair of millstones, a quern, and the flour was separated by passing through a perforated skin sieve. In northern counties, and across to Sligo, the winnowing device was known as a *wecht* or *wight*.[8] 'Bodhrán' (or some variant of that) was another of the names for the devices used in the process, as seen in an account from Inishbofin and Inishshark, County Galway, 1893: 'Querns are still in use, and in connection with them the boran, or sieve of skeepskin stretched over a wicker frame, used for screening the meal'.[9] The bodhrán is indicated for the east of the country too, in County Kildare in 1914: 'Bodhrán (buraun), a measure to hold corn, etc.; made from the rim of a sieve covered with a calfskin or sheepskin'.[10] It was in the centre of the country too, on the Westmeath–Longford boundary in 1948: 'bodhrán [bo:ra:n] shallow vessel, similar in shape to a riddle, with goat-skin bottom, used for lifting oats'.[11]

The devices they use in many of the pictures have a flat rim, suggesting that the membrane or mesh was by that time already being nailed or stitched to the rim, and if it was skin, there would also have been potential for use as a drum. Images similar to the Irish ones are common elsewhere in Europe, notably in Brittany where Karl Daubigny painted *Les Vaneuses de Kérity* in 1868, and Frederic Laguillermie *Jeune Bretonne Vannant du Blé Noir au Bord de la Mer* in 1874. Both of these show skin or mesh bodhrán-size frame devices, but there is no indication of what materials they are made from. Images with description, however, are more valuable, the earliest of which for Ireland is from *c.* 1840. The Irish painting on the title page of this chapter shows women winnowing in the Dublin mountains in the late 1700s, and another sketch by Daniel MacDonald shows a boy winnowing with a bodhrán too; the Wallace Collection has a photograph of a boy with a bodhrán or sieve in County Antrim or Down *c.* 1905. The advent of photography after the 1840s opened up a new potential for keeping records, as photographs retain actual images, and are less likely to be distorted or glamorised (as could be the case with paintings).

One such is of 'Winnowing at the Shillin Hill, County Down' [shilling = shelling].[12] All of these images are of the bodhrán, or similar device, as a utensil or container. The method of winnowing was the same in Ulster as elsewhere on the island, where the practice was still to be witnessed as late as 1940, historically the same as had been reported from 1812:

> In this district [Ulster] as well as in the greater part of Ireland, the corn is threshed on the highways, and is dressed by letting it fall from a kind of sieve, which during a pretty strong wind is held by a woman as high from the ground as her arms can reach.[13]

A 1954 press feature reminisced about the passing of the hand-winnowing process, illustrating the term used in Connacht:

> **THE DAYS OF THE REAPING HOOK, THE FLAIL AND THE BOURÁN**
> A man stood on each side of the layer of sheaves and swung the flail to beat the grain from the straw. Next came the winnowing. This was done by using a riddle or a 'bourán'. The 'bourán' was made by mounting a sheepskin on a hoop to make something like an African tom-tom. The grain was placed in this and it was held out and shaken in the wind to have the chaff blown away. The riddle was used in much the same way. [*Connacht Tribune* 1954 1204 3]

The folklore in the *Schools' Collection* has numerous descriptions of the use of device bodhráns in winnowing, its primary function in several areas:

Innishannon, County Cork: 'Before the machine for winnowing came into general use, the corn was winnowed with a "Bodhrán". On a windy day a person stood on a table or other elevated position, and let the corn fall from the Bodhrán to the winnowing sheet'.[14]

Timoleague, County Cork: 'Long ago before the winnowing machine was used the people used a kind of sieve called a "dildurn". It was shaped like a sieve and it was covered with a sheep skin. It was also called a Bodhrán'.[15]

Watergrasshill, County Cork: 'Then they used to winnow the oats with a bouran. This was made of sheep or goats skin fastened to a sally stick in the form of a circle … The person that used to hold the bouran of oats

◀ Boy with agricultural bodhrán, *c.* 1905, County Antrim, late 1800s [*Lawrence Photograph Collection, NLI*]

should stand upon a chair and leave the oats drop down and then the wind would blow away the chaff'.[16]

Kenmare, County Kerry: 'Tales of a Grandmother Born 1830 … Up to this year also wheat or barley or oats or rye was winnowed in a (Bodhrán) or dildarn, a sort of circular wooden vessel with a sheepskin bottom. It was held over the head on a windy day and shaken until the chaff had gone with the wind and the grain remained'.[17]

Brackloon, County Mayo: 'Names Adopted into English … Bodhrán (for winnowing corn)'.[18]

Multi-task bodhráns

> Bodhrán … shallow vessel, similar in shape to a riddle, with goat-skin bottom, used for lifting oats . É. Mhac an Fhailigh, 'A Westmeath (near Longford) word list (c. 1948) [*Éigse* V, 4, 257]

Bodhrán-like winnowing devices under various names – *bodhrán*, *wecht*, *dallan* – are seen often in paintings and in newspaper sketches. These are of most value when they are described in an accompanying text. Estyn Evans, in his 1957 *Irish Folk Ways*, does just this:

> the skin tray, the wecht or wight … The well-scraped skin of sheep, or sometimes of goat, is stitched on to a rim of ash, bog fir or … a ring of sugán. To secure the skin free of wrinkles is skilled work, and the finished product is not unlike a tambourine[19]

He suggests some of the uses mentioned by the Halls in the 1830s: 'There are also sieves, riddles and shallow baskets … for example the flat round potato *skib* – a communal self-service plate'.[20] The uses described for wights bring the word 'boran' into play also:

> The wight serves both to hold corn, in filling a sack for instance, and to convey peats from the stack to the fireside; perforated it becomes a meal-sieve (boran) for sifting the skins (seeds) from oatmeal, or a buttermilk sieve for taking out the last grains of butter from the churn. The winnowing tray or dallan is a larger version, and it, too, may be perforated to allow the wind to pass through as the corn is shaken out[21]

This concurs with the descriptions by Patrick Kennedy in early-1800s Wexford as described later in this chapter (p. 79), indicating not only slow change over a century and a quarter, but also the universality of both equipment and terminologies.

Further transcribed, spoken-word records at the Department of Irish Folklore at University College Dublin open up yet more possibilities, for the bulk of relevant information there is not about the bodhrán as a music instrument but as an agricultural implement associated with winnowing oats. They show that 'bodhrán' devices had been ubiquitous, and were known by different names, one being what Dinneen calls the 'winnowing fan', a form of the bodhrán not documented as having anything major to do with music. All of the department's spoken-word, folklore references to it are as a skin-covered tray, dish, winnower and container, a subsistence-era object which in its most basic form could be crudely home-crafted, requiring no financial outlay or sophisticated tools to make. Such devices were all over the island, in every rural home, farm and estate, beginning to disappear with the Great Famine, but lingering on until the early 1900s.

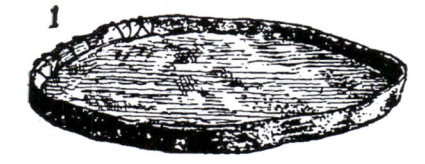

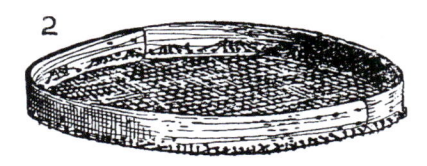

▲ Skin tray (top), and split-ash riddle sketched by Estyn Evans in *Irish Folk Ways*

▼ Perforated-skin bodhrán or dallan [*Copyright National Museum of Ireland*]

Sieves

A perforated bodhrán was used as a sieve, or riddle, to separate flour from seed husks after grinding corn; it was made from a skeepskin, with holes burnt through it using a red-hot nail. This account of making one is from County Donegal

> bhí rud acu a dtugadh siad rideall air ... an chomhdach a bhí ar an rideall seo craiceann na caoradh. Bhainthú an olann den chaora agus thriomochthaí an craiceann, agus nuair a bhí an craiceann sin triomaí acu thoiseachad agus chuirfead siad 'cowar' poill ann. B'fhéidir go mbeadh céad poll ná dhá chéad poll astoigh i gcionn acu seo agus nuair a bhéadh an coirce seo uilig go léir leathnáiste suas acu, chuirfead siad isteach ar an rideall seo é

> They had a thing called a riddle. The covering on this was sheepskin from which the wool had been removed and the skin then dried. When the skin was dry they would make holes in it. There would be perhaps a hundred or two hundred holes in the one skin, and when the corn was milled it was placed in this riddle[22]

Use by the more prosperous household and farm were described a century earlier in O'Curry's *Manners and Customs*:

> Different kinds of sieves were also used in cleaning the corn and separating the husks. The common sieve, the hoop of which was made of ash, was called a *criathur*, a fine kind of which was called a *criathur cumang* or narrow sieve. A hair sieve, *criathur cairceach*, was used to prepare flour to dust over buns, cakes, etc., to prevent them cracking or burning on the griddle[23]

Such essential devices had already been listed by the songwriter Tomás Ó Modhráin as being among the goods traded in the earlier-1800s song 'Aonach Bhearna na Gaoithe': 'Adhanta seínís, ruilleáin, créithre / China teapots, sieves and riddles'.[24] Sieves are a vast and vital technological field, with millions of applications worldwide still, notably at the molecular level. Nineteenth-century agricultural life depended on them just as much, part of a continuity as old as grain production itself. From the *Oxford English Dictionary* it can be seen too that indeed the terms 'sieve' and 'measure' could be interchanged, with the full of a sieve being a particular measure. A glimpse at an auction inventory for a self-sufficient, industrious, moderately-prosperous house with its own farm and numerous hired house and field workers in 1685 Lowland Scotland gives an idea of the variety among sieve and riddle devices as necessities. No fewer than fourteen different kinds were in everyday use, including skin trays. All are similar in basic principles, if not also construction, and though it is most likely (in this case) that they were made by specialist artisans, for poorer households they could also be improvised in a subsistence manner. Among the riddling devices listed are nine different types, at least five of them involving stretched skins:[25]

> Ane iron shuffell with ribs for riddling [building and gardening, for sand or soil]
>
> 2 seed boxes [for the outer husks of oats which are separated in grinding but were preserved for making sowens – a thin gruel, servants' foodstuff]
>
> A coall riddle [used in domestic heating]
>
> 2 corne riddles [for winnowing out chaff from grain after flailing]
>
> A wyde corne riddle [for removing straw from grain]
>
> A whit rainge [a wheat sieve, fine mesh, for bread flour]
>
> A beir [a kind of barley] riddle [used in animal feed, and in beer making]

▲ Wood-mesh meal sieve made for the National Museum [Copyright National Museum of Ireland]

▶ Sieve or winnower in a sketch in *Dublin Penny Journal*

▲ Wood-mesh riddle at Ulster Folk Museum [Courtesy of National Museums NI]

> 3 weights [*wecht*, a hoop with a skin stretched over it; for winnowing corn, and general carrying use]
> 2 way [*weeht*, a shallow hoop, 15 to 18 inches diameter over which a sheep or calf skin has been stretched] riddles [a perforated skin riddle][26]

With grain as a staple of food in Ireland, such equipment would have been everywhere:

> From prehistoric times to the close of the 17th century corn and milk were the mainstay of the national food … the land was ploughed for no other crop, except, perhaps, flax … The mill must have been one of the commonest features of the countryside[27]

An equivalent inventory from an Irish big house would show similar devices, going by the indications in literature in both Irish and English which widely document riddles, sieves and 'winnowing fans'.

The container bodhrán

In 1866, writer Patrick Kennedy from near Bunclody, County Wexford mentioned another utility use of the bodhrán – as a container, and the sieve as a measure. An astute observer of behaviour who wrote contemporary novels in English, for some time after 1822 he was a schoolteacher with the Kildare Place Society in Dublin, later running a bookshop in Anglesea Street in the city. On the household bodhrán he uses footnotes to explain:

> … the fire is getting low: take that *booran** out to the clamp, and bring in the full of it of turf …
> *A domestic article; shaped like an overgrown tambourine.[28]

> By Yarrow and Rue / And my Red cap too / Hie over to England.*
> *For the above formulary the words Borraun! Borraun! Borraun! are sometimes substituted. *Borran* is anger, *booraun* a domestic article mentioned already …[29]

Skin tray bodhrán used as a container for potatoes [*EDI*]

Modern-day household tray constructed in the perennial bodhrán format: a hoop of wood on which is fixed a flat membrane, in this case of wood [*EDI*]

Bodhrán like tray in use in a 1930s French, sugared-flowers confectionary factory [*Marcus Gibelin, Métiers et Savoir-faire de Toujours*]

This is further commented on in his glossary: '*Booran*, note, p. 167, should be *borrán*'.[30] A similar variant of the term is also used in the Poole Glossary. Kennedy's use of the term 'sieve' to describe the same kind of container is also interesting: '… there was one stable boy with a currycomb in his hand, and another with a bridle, and another with a sieve of oats, and another with an armful of hay'.[31] The earliest press references to the bodhrán are as the utensil or container, first being in an 1865 court report: 'when he came in for something to bring in the potatoes; she told him to take the bowrawn, as it was handier'.[32] *The Schools' Collection* has the word 'bodhrán' relating also to containers, or a sieve:

Carlow, Kildavin: 'Then they dug a pit and picked the potatoes on a bouran. The bouran was made out of a sheepskin. The sheepskin was first dried. Then they got a frame of a riddle and the sheepskin was tied or nailed on to the frame. The women picked the potatoes on the bouran, while the men dug them out. When they had the bouran-ful picked they put them in the pits'.[33]
Cork, Ballyvourney: '… fuair se Bodhrán agus chuir sé na leanbhaí go léir isteach sa Bodhrán …' [He got a bodhrán and put all the children into it].[34]
Galway, Kilmacduagh: 'Bouran. It's a basket used to bring in turf, e.g. Bring in a bouran of turf'.[35]
Galway, Cooloo: 'The man of the house would go to the mill and crush as much meal that would do the day. They would crush a Boarn (Bodhrán) full. A Boarn was a rim covered with a sheep-skin'.[36]
'About twenty years ago the people used things for filling oats which were called Bornes (Bodhrán)'.[37]
Laois, Loughteeog: 'Bodhrán – a vessel for carrying corn made by attaching sheep-skin to the rim of a sieve'.[38]
Wexford, Rosbercon: 'A bourawn (bodhrán) is used for carrying grain'.[39] Other references are found in literature, for instance in 1906:

> Nuair a chuir an capall a shrón sa bhodhrán, do chuir Muirtí an lámh chlé n-a mhaing [When the horse put its nose in the bodhrán, Muirtí put his left hand on its mane][40]

In **Connemara,** the artisan craft of making such bodhráns was considered

80

The Halls' 'borrane' household utensil, County Cork, 1842 [*Hall 1841, 83*]

important enough to be included in a Carna discussion on local industry:

> A class for horse hair rope and another for a bodhrán – a type of sieve made from sheepskin, were included [*Connacht Tribune* 1943, 042 7]

On the opposite side of the island too the same word was understood:

> Wicklow '98 Committee is to furnish Michael O'Dwyer's cottage at Derrynamuck in period style … the committee has to procure … old knives, forks and spoons, a crucifix, a wooden vat, a boorawn, a reaping hook, noggins and bowls [*Nationalist and Leinster Times* 1949, 0618 15]

The Halls' 'borrane', *c*. 1840

In the late 1830s Samuel Carter Hall and his wife Anna Maria researched an illustrated guide to Ireland, the first volume of which was published in 1842. Samuel was himself from Cork, and Anna Maria from Wexford, but they lived in London, moving in the same social circles as the painter Daniel Maclise.[41] The Halls' first book includes text, maps and illustrations, archaeological and cultural information, and details social experiences in various counties, including Cork. They provided images and descriptions of household items they observed there, among which was what they reported as a 'borrane', an Anglicisation presumably of bodh-rán. This, with image and text, is greatly informative:

> The borrane is formed of a scraped sheep-skin, drawn round a hoop; and is used instead of a sieve for winnowing corn, filling sacks with grain, holding wool when carded and ready for the spinning-wheel, or the feathers – plucked three times in the year from an unfortunate gander and his wives, and sometimes as a lordly dish – though of inexpensive workmanship – to hold the potatoes which constitute the family fare[42]

This is the earliest combined description and image of a standard bodhrán as we know it, but as a device, in daily use as a tray, or dish, and with an informed text which indicates that it was used for anything and everything, as ubiquitous indeed as today's plastic basin, bowl and bucket, or their tinware, enamel, wicker and earthenware ancestors. It is significant that no music function was mentioned for it. Other than this depiction, it is only occasionally that bodhráns, and large sieves, can be seen in sketches, generally hanging up high in a barn, to protect them from damage. All of these are typically the size of the larger bodhráns which were common in Munster by the 1950s.

Bodhrán as a music instrument?

Other than in dictionaries there is little historic literary indication of bodhrán as an instrument by name. But there was obviously use of the bodhrán as an improvised tambourine, seasonally at least, the earliest report being from *c*. 1800, in County Wexford where 'Jacob Poole (p. 57) referred to it as 'booran'. Other occurrences were in County Kilkenny *c*. 1820, and in County Kerry *c*. 1820 as 'bodhrán' on a hedge-school parade,[43] and with seasonal mumming in 1829.[44] It is mentioned only once in *The Schools' Collection* r/e *c*. 1900, from Ballyduff, County Kerry, in connection with the Wren: 'Irish Words and phrases still in use … We have a fine Bodhrán for the Wren's Day'.[45] The earliest newspaper reference for the word 'bodhrán' as a drum was for the Comeragh mountains in County Waterford, 1956, seen in a report on the jubilant occasion of an early fleadh at Carrick-on-Suir, County Waterford: 'Great interest was shown in the bodhrán, or

Curator Anne O'Dowd at the National Museum's bodhrán and sieve collection at Turlough, Castlebar, 2009 [EDI]

ancient Irish drum, which one musician brought in from the foot of the Comeraghs'.[46] The National Museum of Ireland has a small collection of such music bodhráns, most of which date to after the 1950s. The improvised use of the bodhrán as a tambourine is covered in Chapter 9.

Museum bodhráns

Curiously, despite the variety of device bodhrán uses, Eugene O'Curry does not mention it at all in his detailed inventory of artefacts – leather ones indeed – of Irish domestic life, even though he must surely have had experience of the term.[47] As mentioned, he does deal with sieves, but perhaps hand-winnowing tools had disappeared following the Famine, or perhaps he did not have occasion to see them, for, with prosperity, winnowing came to be done with a simple hand-cranked fanning machine which had already been around for a century by his time,[48] and the sieving process had moved on to use artisan-made sieves which had fine wood-strip or metal mesh membranes. However, some device bodhráns, sieves and riddles are preserved by Irish museums, these in a variety of forms and conditions, from which their fabrication methods can be readily deduced; all of the earlier ones were made of wood and animal skin. Museums in Britain and eco-museums in France have similar items, but in Ireland the major collection is at the National Museum at Turlough, Castlebar, County Mayo, with a smaller selection at the Ulster Folk Museum, Cultra, Holywood, County Down.

The National Museum bodhrán and sieve collection

Research for this book began with a visit to the National Museum at Turlough, Castlebar in early 2008 to view its collection of fifty-nine sieves, bodhráns and tambourines. None of these had been studied during the period of tenure there of their then curator, Anne O'Dowd. Twenty-four were found to be skinned, the remainder were wood-strip sieves and riddles. Of the skinned items, twelve were trays (for winnowing or carrying), four were perforated as sieves, and just eight were tambourines. All were measured, photographed and catalogued. Sight alone of them revealed the variety and similarities among them, the contrast in technologies used in their construction, and encouraged envisaging how the devices could be recycled or used as drums. There was not always a dating on the objects other than that of acquisition, but their counties of origin are revealing,

Spinning wool with an old Irish wool wheel (spinning wheel) with a flat rim [Fáilte Ireland, Dublin City Libraries]

Hand-cranked winnowing machine, invented in Scotland, 1737, by Andrew Rodger [EDI]

▸ Part of a catalogue made of the National Museum's tambourine collection [*EDI*]

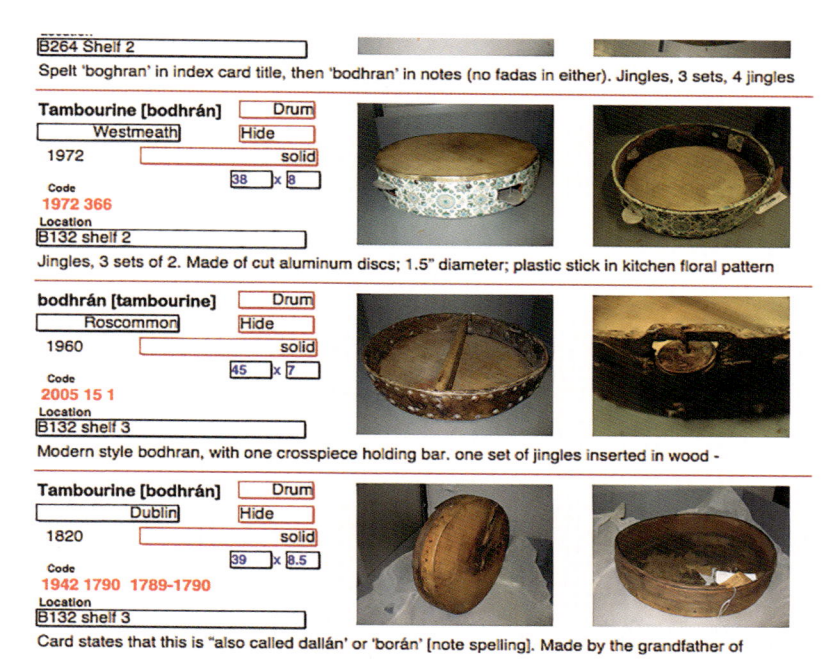

▲ Skin sieve at the National Museum [*Copyright National Museum of Ireland*]

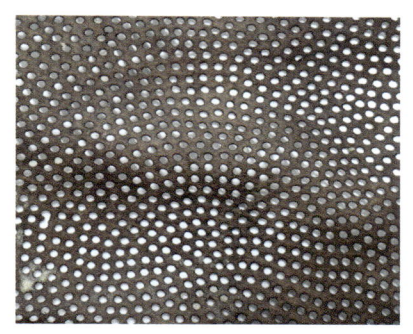

▲ Detail of piercings on a skin sieve at the Ulster Folk Museum [*Courtesy of National Museums NI*]

▼ Tucked-in style, 1933, bodhrán skin tray at the National Museum [*Copyright National Museum of Ireland*]

showing a wide spread over all of the island. The winnowing trays are a universal, as are the sieves, all relics of earlier grain-processing. The presence side by side of both skin and wood-weave sieves shows the lingering on of old technology in the presence of the new, something which is not unusual. Exact dating of most of the devices would seem impossible, because while a 1960s tambourine can look decrepit, a 1940s sieve could look new; indeed several of the sieves at the NMI had been specially commissioned in the mid-1900s from the last surviving sieve-maker. Measurements of diameters of the skin devices did not reveal much more than that their sizes were likely roughly determined by the size of the goatskin or sheepskin they were made from, allowing for the fact that tucked-in skins give a smaller diameter of device. But what stands out is that among the drums there are varying lengths of overlap in the jointing of the frames – a consequence of having to reduce the diameter of the improvised wood hoop in order to accommodate the skin. This, as well as the nature and condition of the rims of the drums in the collection, shows they are improvised. While the actual wood-weave sieves are purpose-designed and made, as were the skin trays and sieves, none of the drums/tambourines appear to have originally been purpose-made. All of those, judging from old holes and marks, and often excessive overlap of the ends of the bent wood, were crudely made from something else, typically a redundant sieve, and they had been repeatedly re-skinned. Also, as the keeper Albert Siggins valuably suggested, some have been made from the old Irish spinning wheel, a 'wool wheel', which has a thin, flat rim. It was apparent too, where decay permitted observation, that at least one skin tray had been made from the recycled rim of a more modern-style, wood-weave sieve.

What the overall examination yielded was awareness of the vital place of these bodhráns in agriculture, how they would have been a necessary and common presence in rural Ireland. Older, more simple forms are made with a tucked-in skin, but on more recent ones it is tacked on, giving a wider, tensioned skin which would be more efficient, and could be easily adapted where occasion demanded to serve as a tambourine, or drum. Additionally, as the Halls had said, their obvious utilitarian value reflected the fact that need for them was there throughout the island, as was the simple technology to make them, and which is why they were once ubiquitous. The older form of device – the skin tray or skin sieve – is intriguing for having its skin not nailed on but tucked in, perfectly adequate for containing or carrying, where that function was the main consideration. But for a drum, high tension in a skin is necessary. Yet the simplicity of the construction (only a knife is needed) and the availability of the only two materials needed to make them (a goat or sheep skin and a strip of wild wood), allied to the variety of essential uses to which it could be put, suggests that the bodhrán in this form was around for centuries, its only competitor in a subsistence society being a woven basket where reeds or sally wattles were available.

The Ulster Folk Museum collection
The non-public collection of frame devices held in this museum concerns only agricultural usage, and does not include any drum or tambourine. There are six objects – three coarse-mesh riddles, two skin-type sieves and one solid-skin bodhrán or wight. The riddles are artisan-made from woven strips of thin ash wood. One of the sieves is of perforated skin, with the number '1812', possibly a year, formed by the punched holes. The rim of this is in two semi-circular sections rather than in one piece, and the perforations are extremely regular in overlapping concentric circles. The skin is extremely thin, feeling almost like a plastic, and is secured by thongs which are laced through holes in the rim (see p. 87). The second sieve does not have a frame, but is shaped as if it had originally had one. Its material seems to be some kind of resin, rather than skin, and the hole patterning highlights the letters H+W. The holes are extremely regular in size and disposition, suggesting a more-modern, machine-made product, possibly made for the Harland & Wolff shipyard. The one actual bodhrán (wecht or dallan) is a superb example, with a naturally-patterned skin which is tucked in over an 8 cms deep, 42 cms diameter frame. The tucking is expert, and there is no skin distortion or rippling. It is labelled 'wight winnowing tray', and indicated as the kind of device used as late as 1920 for winnowing in the Mourne mountains, County Down. Its inscription reads:

> The seed to be winnowed was often held in a skin tray known as a wight, wecht or dallan. In south-west Ireland this type of tray was known as a bodhrán, and it was also used as a one-sided drum

It is identical in structure to some of the examples in the collection at Castlebar.

Sieve-making
There is an obvious similarity between all forms of the bodhrán, sieves and tambourines. Sieve-making in Middle Eastern cultures is a long-standing artisan profession, and is closely related to frame drum making, as both use a circular hoop of wood upon which is stretched a skin membrane or mesh. Structure and design thus relate drumming to the function of sieving, and in

▲ ▼ Yarn spinner deposits her spools in a bodhrán-like container, *c.* 1500, Holland [*Israhel van Merkenem*]

▲ Spinning wool with an old Irish wool wheel (spinning wheel) with a flat rim. The woman is placing her spun balls of wool in a bodhrán

▼ Bodhrán-type container used for keeping spun yarn, Brittany, 1905 [*Marcus Gibelin, Métiers et Savoir-faire de Toujours*]

Ireland the fact of redundant sieves being recycled as tambourines adds a further layer of association. That relationship can be seen in the National Museum's collection – a connection between the bodhrán as a device, sieves, crudely-made tambourines, and the bodhrán as an instrument. Early sieves had a tucked-in, perforated skin membrane; later commercial ones were made from meshed wood strips or metal wire mounted on a bodhrán-size frame. When such a commercial sieve wore out, its frame could be brought into service by fitting it with a skin to make either a household bodhrán or a tambourine. As to why it would occur to people at all to copy tambourines can be seen in the following chapter which documents the nature, presence and prevalence of imported tambourines during the 1700s and 1800s, the time when they came to prominence in Ireland. Their use may initially not have been among the poorer classes, but it was widespread enough to ensure that people at large knew what tambourines looked and sounded like, how they could be made, and what their attention-commanding potential was.

Bodhráns in photographs

Folklore and written accounts are unequivocal in that they account for the bodhrán as a device rather than a drum. Evidence in paintings and sketches, though slight, offers images of both winnowing devices and actual tambourine drums. Photography, which was developed after the Famine, has only a handful of early bodhrán images, as a container and winnower. The earliest of these, from 1895, shows a woman spinning, and depositing her balls of wool in a bodhrán – as indeed the Halls had reported a half-century earlier. The photo is similar to one from the same year in Brittany which shows exactly the same thing. In both cases the skin tray is being used as would a basket or plastic container today. And both reflect what had already been depicted 400 years previously in Holland as seen in a 1500s woodcut of a spinner depositing her spun bobbins in a bodhrán-like container (p. 84). An agricultural bodhrán or riddle features too in a photo from the Wallace collection at the National Library of Ireland (p. 76) and, more recently, Evans has a photograph of a man winnowing with a somewhat warped wecht or bodhrán in County Down (p. 75). One postcard photo shows a bodhrán-like device being used in sugared-flowers confectionery-making in France, and in Denmark Svend

Kjeldsen witnessed one being used for vibration-separation of lumps from finer particles in gunpowder-making. From the descriptions and images in these pages it becomes clear that the subject of 'bodhrán' covers three distinct items: 1/ the original bodhrán, a device which itself had three basic forms of winnower, container and dish/tray; 2/ the tambourine, a drum, which was copied and was being made rurally in Ireland during the 1800s; 3/ the post-1950s bodhrán drum, a tambourine without jingles. This book will now look at the tambourine, and its history in Ireland.

▲ Sieve in use at a windmill, near Mazamet, France [*EDI*]

◀ Bodhrán/wicht at the Ulster Folk Museum [*Courtesy of National Museums NI*]

◀ Wood mesh sieve at the Ulster Folk Museum [*Courtesy of National Museums NI*]

5 'BODHRÁN': SOUND OR FUNCTION?

▲ Laced-on perforated skin sieve at the Ulster Folk Museum, Holywood, County Down [*Courtesy of National Museums NI*]

◀ Sieve-maker John Hamilton from Naul, Co. Dublin, mid-1900s [*Copyright National Museum of Ireland*]

NOTES TO CHAPTER 5

[1] Foclóir.ie
[2] CCM 1907, 32.
[3] Beckett 1987, 105.
[4] See Appendix 6.
[5] Ledwich 1804, 148.
[6] CBÉ 1862, 199–200.
[7] Eight types of grain were grown in Ireland (Sullivan 1873 Vol. 1, ccclxii).
[8] McCrickard 1987, 2–10.
[9] Lucas 1953 08 03; Browne 1889–1901, 363.
[10] Mac Céachta 1914, 62.
[11] Mac an Fhailigh 1948, 257.
[12] Evans 1967, 185.
[13] Wakefield, 1812, 364–5.
[14] SC 0322, 117.
[15] SC 0318, 221–2.
[16] SC 0382, 091.
[17] SC 0461, 348.
[18] SC 0138, 353.
[19] Evans 1957, 211–12.
[20] Ibid., 212.
[21] Ibid., 213.
[22] Ó hEochaidh, MSS A1835, 48–9.
[23] Sullivan 1873, cclx. However, O'Curry did not give description of the tools used in the winnowing process which preceded the task he described here.
[24] Ó Gealbháin 2013, 112.
[25] Dalyell and Beveridge 1924, 344–70.
[26] For the house of General Thomas Dalyell, 21 August 1685.
[27] Lucas 1960, 1–3.
[28] Kennedy 1866, 160.
[29] Ibid., 167.
[30] Ibid., 351.
[31] Kennedy 1870, 110.
[32] *Waterford News and Star* 1865, 1027 4.
[33] SC 0911, 202.
[34] SC 0336, 004–7.
[35] SC 0047, 0203.
[36] SC 0081, 399.
[37] SC 0081, 459.
[38] SC 0837, 256.
[39] SC 0323, 0190.
[40] Ó Séaghdha 1906, 30.
[41] McCarthy 2008, 163.
[42] Hall 1841, 83-84.
[43] Fenton 1914, 106–7. See Chapter 9.
[44] Griffin 1829, 150.
[45] SC 0430, 123.
[46] The Nationalist 1956 0505 12.
[47] Sieves, as 'criathar', are listed, but not dallan or bodhrán (Sullivan 1873 Vol. 1, ccclviii).
[48] This machine was invented in Scotland c. 1737.

▲ Tambourine dance, 1854 [*Illustrated London News 1854 1104*]

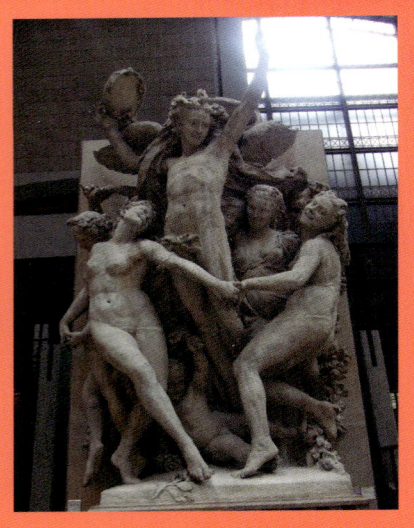

▲ Tambourine in ecstatic dance sculpture 'La Danse', by Jean-Baptiste Carpeaux (1827-1875) at Musée D'Orsay, Paris [*EDI*]

▲ Tambourine dance, 1854, detail [*Illustrated London News 1854 1104*]

▲ *The Cashel Dancers*, a 1990 sculpture by Rowan Gillespie at CCÉ's Brú Ború [*EDI*]

▲ Use of the Gillespie sculpture image on a display bodhrán in Brú Ború

CHAPTER 6
THE TAMBOURINE ON THE IRISH STAGE

Because the National Museum has both tambourines and bodhráns the question can be reasonably asked: how do we come to have tambourines? The answer lies in popular music in Ireland in the eighteenth and nineteenth centuries, a story that has been either largely unknown, or forgotten about.[1] Yet, as can be seen in newspaper advertising, the tambourine had two centuries of a head start on today's bodhrán. It had a prominent presence on popular-music stages all through the 1800s up until the 1920s. Dublin and other Irish cities and towns were part of the same music circuits as London, and got the same touring performers whose use of the tambourine made that drum visible through commercial entertainment, and, as will be shown, it became a common casual instrument with a popularity that lasted into the twentieth century. 'Tambourine' was romantically adopted in the 1700s as the title of a popular stage-dance form, the *tambourin* or *tambourine dance* which is reported as having been first performed in London as a solo dance by Marie Sallé at Lincoln's Inn Fields in 1730–1. Subsequently it was done as a solo, duet, or group dance up to the 1750s, and by the 1780s it had become a speciality performance that appeared in programmes on Irish city-theatre stages into the 1800s.[2] The first appearance of the word 'tambourine' in Irish newspapers was in 1741, the subject of a piece of romantic verse:

> When she strikes the Tambourine
>   Deckt with Roses
>   Gay with Posies
> Sure she seems some fairy Queen;
> Th' airy round her Dance composes
> All, all rejoyce but Barbarine,
> And the Paulanne, who die with spleen.

When she strikes the Tambourine / Deckt with Roses / Gay with Posies / Sure she seems some fairy Queen [*Dublin Journal* 1741, 0609 2]

The drum then comes up regularly in the early press, often, as said, in connection with 'the tambourine dance', in advertising for staged concerts in Irish cities, mostly Dublin:

> At the Theatre-Royal, on Monday the 7th of March, 1747 will be presented a Comedy called, The Double Gallant … new Entertainments of Dancing between every Act, by Monsieur & Madam. MECHEL. After the … Fourth Act, the Venetian Tambourine [*Dublin Journal* 1747 0227 2]

From then until 1830 the deployment of tambourines on stage ran from the accompaniment of stylish female singers to spectacular, acrobatic contortions and dramatic presentations. A Theatre Royal advertisement of 1783 announced: 'Harlequin will leap thro' a Fountain – a Tambourine six feet high'.[3] One such act was announced as:

> Tight Rope Dancing, By the Polish Olympian, Mr. Spillers … surprising Performances peculiar to himself with … Basket Boots, Fetters, Flags, Castanets, Tambourine [*Freeman's Journal* 1802, 0218 1]

This was still the case 110 years later in theatrical variety performances, often involving novelty:

> Miss Young will perform on the Slack Wire; on which she will play, in full swing, a variety of airs on the Violin and Tambourine [*Freeman's Journal* 1912, 0403 1]

Teaching and learning

There was a fad for tambourine learning and playing among young women of the upper classes around the turn of the nineteenth century (see pp. 24–5). Paintings from the period show them with the instrument, a fashionable depiction, and towards the 1800s it was clear that it was being 'treated as a serious instrument that could be in a girl's music education'. Composers scored for the tambourine, Muzio Clementi (1832–52) including it in his sets of waltzes, but the fashion was short-lived.[4] In 1803 Goulding's in Dublin was offering 'Ladies Tambourines' of different sizes,[5] and teaching of the instrument was being offered in the city in 1812:

> Violin, Piano Forte, Flute, Flageolet, Tambourine and Singing by Note, taught very reasonable; in private room, where Instruments are provided free, and Instruction given by the Lesson, from 6 in the morning till 12 at night [*Freeman's Journal* 1812, 0707]

Whatever about the neighbours, clearly there was demand at all hours. Learning to keep good time was obviously a useful social skill, for an advertisement by a Mr Cassidy for his dance-teaching services says:

▲ Muzio Clementi score for tambourine; London, 1802 [*researchgate.net*]

COWLAN,
(FROM LONDON,)
Military Musical Instrument-Maker,
No. 1, GREAT SHIP-STREET,
AFTER several years experience in the first Manufacturing Houses in London, has commenced Business as above, where he makes Military Instruments, Drums, Tambourines, Patent and Common Flutes and Flageolets, of Ivory, and Fancy Woods, Violins and excellent Roman and English Strings, and various Articles in the Music Line—Instruments of any timber, correctly, and neatly repaired or taken in exchange — Some choice Second-hand Instruments.

Freeman's Journal 1815 0202

They are fond of music and dancing; their instruments are a pipe of reeds, a sort of tambourine covered with goat-skin, which, when struck, makes a jarring sound; and a guitar, made of cocoa nut shells and thongs of goat-skin.

Article on Timbuktu, *Belfast News Letter*, 1816 1105

BEST MUSIC FOR BALLS,
COMPRISING Fiddles, Harps, Dulcimers, Basses, Tamborines, &c. by M. LEVINS, No. 126 Great Britain-street, five doors North of Great George's street.

Belfast News Letter 1818 0123

▲ Preston's tutor [Svend Kjeldsen]

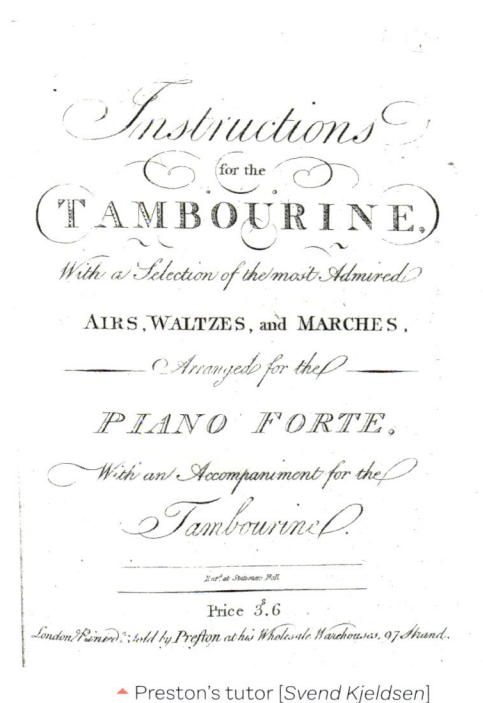

▲ Dale's tambourine tutor book, 1800 [Courtesy Svend Kjeldsen]

Mr. C. will teach the Tamborine and Spanish Castinets to such of his Pupils as are capable of learning the Dances appropriate to them; and those who play the Pianoforte will find a peculiar advantage in learning the Castinets as they give a perfect idea of time [*Freeman's Journal* 1813 1116 1].

Tutor books

Several tutor books for the tambourine were advertised in London – by Preston, 1798, Bolton, 1799 and Dale, 1800 – as were tambourines themselves. Literature of the period encouraged women to play, Bolton's tutor saying:

To Ladies, who wish to excel; and where the opportunity offers, experienced Masters, and Lady professors are particularly recommended [Bolton 1799, 50]

Indeed popular music fashions could be addictive, and affected all social classes, for the press advertising of tambourines, or reporting of performances where they featured, would have been heard about, and talked about. And such a knock-on visibility over a long period would build awareness and create interest. The availability of the tutor books for the tambourine from as far back as 1798 shows that there was a hunger for learning it at that time, which in turn means that people around the learner would have been aware of the instrument that the aspiring player worked on. Preston painted an attractive picture:

The Tambourine is an instrument at this time extremely fashionable; indeed none more so, and from its being sanctioned and performed on, by Persons of first distinction, there remains little doubt, but it will continue … no Instrument is better calculated to accompany a piece of music, with taste, and expression, than the Tambourine [Preston 1798, 2]

This booklet, and the others by Bolton and Dale, show that playing it demanded skill, but it was a method which is far from that used generally on today's bodhráns: performing on the tambourine was an extrovert act which used the hand, fingers, wrist and arms, rubbing, striking and shaking, with a great degree of physical engagement: 'Quasi-virtuoso techniques known as flamps, travales, gingle notes and bass notes in performance'.[6] Some folklore accounts describe older Irish-traditional players doing similar things in the past, and shades of those techniques can be seen in more expressive modern-day players, among them Tommy Hayes and Rónán Ó Snodaigh. The early books' instruction was graphic:

The Tambourine is held (and thrown round) with the left hand, the Performance is with the right; and it is customary. I may say necessary, to stand in an elegant attitude when performing … There is many other little elegances … such as beating it in various directions, producing different sounds, flourishing the hand, and the like, all of which depends on the ear and the taste of the Performer [Preston 1798, 2–5]

While this seems at odds with the politeness expected of ladies of the time, nevertheless it is clear that holding, and striking correctly with the hand, were critical to putting across the given style:

The Beat, No. 8: The Notes thus written … are considered to be beat with the first Joint & Nail of the first finger up & down alternately … But the necessary practice at first must be simply up and down, with the wrist out, & the Elbow even with the Hand, the Arm to be kept as still as possible, & the Tambourine turned a little from you [Dale 1800, 4]

The Gingle No. 14: Keep the fingers altogether & the Hand straight, then let the 2nd finger move from you round the edge of the Tambourine pressing so as to make it Gingle [Dale 1800, 5]

Dale's tutor book also advertised printed music which would not be unfamiliar to traditional players today, with tunes like 'Moll in the Wad', 'Merrily Danced the Quaker's Wife', 'The College Hornpipe' and Scottish reels – material which was scored for flute and for violin. Instruction was given for 'Common time, triple time (3/2) and 6/8 time', and the operation of the 'gingles' was expected to articulate this: 'Holding up, shaking … To turn one Gingle for each Note carrying the Hand over the Gingles so as to make them run round'.

Availability and role models

The instrument was already common enough in London at the end of the 1700s to be part of everyday experience, including provocative use among life on the streets, as this court report which appeared in a Dublin paper relates:

Barnett gave a tambourine, which he then had in his hand, to the other prisoner, and immediately came up to him, and gave him a violent blow in his mouth [*Finn's Leinster Journal* 1798, 0201]

Richard Graham believes that Italian street musicians brought the larger tamburello to the attention of music in London in the 1700s,[7] and that that instrument became the model on which contemporary military and orchestral instruments and styles were based. Its popularity among the plain people cannot be under-estimated, and Reg Hall's research shows that it entered into English folk music in the same period, and was still being played in duet with other instruments by such as Scan Tester in the 1950s.[8] Over the early years of the 1800s too, occasional incidents involving a 'tambourine' suggest familiarity among poorer urban people. In 1802 the Belfast press repeated a London story of a horse bolting with its carriage attached, plunging through a coffee-shop window, having been scared by a tambourine being played on the street.[9]

The earliest advertisement for tambourines for sale however did not appear in Ireland until 1803, in Dublin, from Goulding & Co. in Westmoreland Street, so clearly the drums were already popular by then. Goatskin was the preferred material for tambourine membranes in Ireland as well as elsewhere, as was reported in the *Belfast News Letter* for Timbuktu, west Africa: 'their instruments are a pipe of reeds, a sort of tambourine covered with goatskin, which, when struck, makes a jarring sound'.[10] Indeed, in Great Ship Street, Dublin, Cowlan's 1815 advertisement suggests a thriving instrument-making industry: 'Military Instruments, Drums, Tamborines, Patent and Common Flutes and Flageolets, of Ivory, and Fancy Woods'.[11] In Belfast too, off-the-shelf, ready-made tambourines were available. The cost of instruments varied, with MacLean's Cheap Commission Music Warehouse in Dublin being quite expensive, compared to the cost of keyed flutes: 'New Patent & Silver Key'd Flutes 3 guineas, Double flageolets, 2 Guineas, C Clarionets, 1 Guinea, elegant Tamborines 16s. 3d'.[12]

Evening Echo 1803 0120

▲ The earliest advertisement for tambourine in an Irish newspaper

Belfast News Letter 1818 0123 1

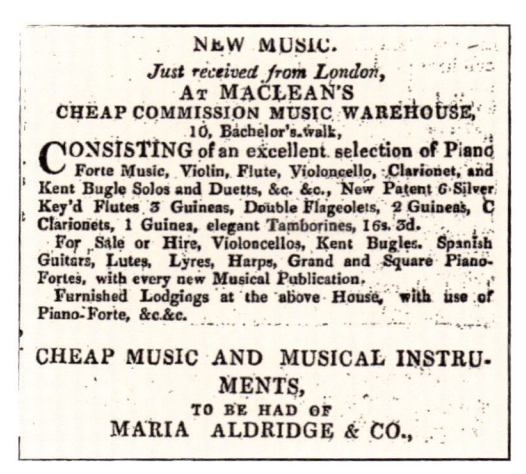

Freeman's Journal 1821 1224 2

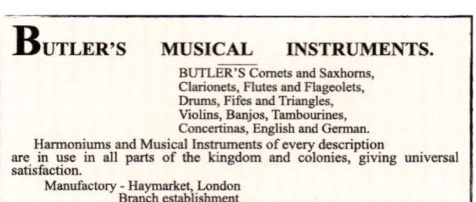

Irish Times 1859

6…THE TAMBOURINE ON THE IRISH STAGE

Londoner Joseph Dale who published the 1800 tutor and music was an enterprising manufacturer of tambourines, and prided himself in various models which were designed carefully, in differing sizes. Like today's makers, each had standards and patents:

> Dale feels himself extremely happy in having by his Invention of the Tambourine (for which he has obtained his Majesty's Royal Letters Patent) entirely removed the different Impediments so generally complained of, and brought it to such Perfection as to render it an Instrument of Science, and Competent to be Performed upon in Concert, or to Accompany any Piece of Music whether Vocal or Instrumental. The success he has experienced from the sanction of a Candid Public in the sale of them has induced many Artists to attempt and offer for sale mere Copies of such Improvement which tend not only to the Prejudice of the Patentee, but to deceive the Purchaser. The Public are therefore requested to apply at his Warehouses as above [Dale 1800, 1]

Dale's daughter Catherine, an able manipulator of the tambourine, married the often-vilified German composer Daniel Steibelt, and with him performed tambourine and piano works for salon recitals in Europe. They popularised the instrument in this way, and in Prague it was noted that interest in it led to demand for her teaching it, and consequently they 'sold a huge wagon full of tambourines'.[13] In the urban music trade in Ireland the relative cheapness of tambourines would have made them feasible to purchase by poorer people, especially for busking, and from press reports this could be deduced. In 1828 we read in the evidence given at a Tipperary murder trial how a party of people on one evening 'danced to the music of the tambourine, drum and fife'.[14] As stated in Chapter 2, the military bands of the later 1700s had already introduced the tambourine, bringing it into the experience of urban folk.

The 'minstrels', 1844 – c. 1905

National newspaper advertising does not alone prove country-wide experience of the tambourine, but it does mean that there was at least an increasing general awareness of the drum as the 1800s progressed. The

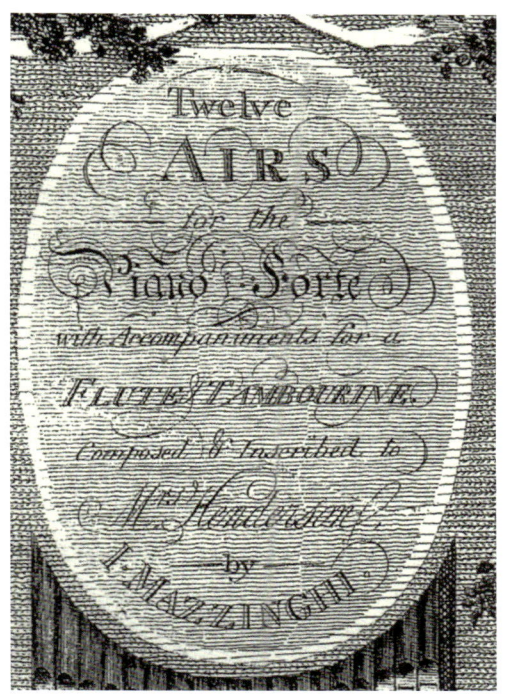

▲ Mazzinghi piano music scored with flute and tambourine accompaniment [*Courtesy Svend Kjeldsen*]

▼ 'Pandean Minstrels in Performance at Vauxhall, 1806'z, by engraver John Lee after Edward Francis Burney [*artandmusic.yale.edu*]

earliest swathe of tambourine fashion in European societies had been linked to military bands and the Classical Greek allusion. But the instrument really took off through a popular music genre which was devised in America and transformed in England – 'blackface' minstrelsy. This was white actors in black makeup 'delineating' blacks, performing dance and song with music and clowning. They used supposed African-American instruments – banjo, bones, tambourine and fiddle – and 'frequently combined popular British melody with words depicting white perceptions of African American life and dialect'.[15] Their virtuoso dances included hornpipe or jig and supposed imitations of African-American slave plantation performance culture. They also drew on Anglo-American folk forms. Thomas Dartmouth Rice shaped this practice as a solo act prior to the 1840s by taking on the character of 'Jim Crow'. He performed to great acclaim, and toured not only in east coast America but also in Ireland, Scotland and England.[16] By 1843 this was transformed into 'the minstrel show' by The Virginia Minstrels, a troupe led by the Irish-American Daniel Emmit, using a fixed group routine that became a standard format:

> they arranged their chairs in a semi-circle, with the tambourine and bones … players on the ends; to give the performance the aura of a real party and to provide continuity, they interspersed comic repartee between the otherwise unconnected songs and dances … they concentrated on songs and dance about Southern Negroes … the instruments they used – the fiddle, banjo, bones and tambourine – became the core of the minstrel band … it had such versatility and flexibility that it could immediately respond to its audiences' preferences[17]

All of the troupes included a tambourine, the origins of its inclusion said to lie in the tarantella dance via Italian migration to Britain.[18] The roots of the minstrel concert were in music-hall[19] variety concerts in late-eighteenth-century England, a form of popular entertainment that included groups of musicians regarded as 'minstrels'. A prototype of this ensemble was the Pandean Minstrels, c. 1810, who, while also playing Andean panpipes, each struck a percussion or concussion instrument, one of which was a tambourine. These kinds of shows had a high degree of novelty, even humour, but also included serious music abilities. The format was used in France too, known there as 'vaudeville' (from *voix de ville*/ urban voice, or *vaux-de-vire*/ satirical songs), a term adopted in England in the 1870s and America in the 1880s.[20]

The basis of the minstrel genre reflected the degraded condition of enslaved Africans and emancipated slaves as the lowest social class, an easy target for ridicule in stage sketches which presented them as stupid and frivolous, characterised them as comic fools,[21] not unlike the concept of the stage Irishman. Supposed African cultural practices and physical mannerisms were aped grotesquely and, beginning c. 1833 with T.D. Rice's 'Jim Crow' routine, were enacted by whites who painted their faces black using burnt cork and greasepaint. White audiences accepted being entertained by faux blacks, for though they were not able to deal with black people performing their own music, they could approve of whites mimicking it.[22] Minstrelsy is said to have contributed to the creation of the negative image of black people that continues to cloud human dignity in the United States in particular: it had an immense effect on the way mainstream society thought

▼ Daniel Emmit's music book: banjo dominates, with fiddle and tambourine

▲ The Ethiopian Serenaders, 1848

about blacks.[23] Yet as a music genre it is contradictory, tap dance authority Brian Seibert preferring to believe that 'most often, blacks were the vehicle, not the target'.[24] For the faux-African performers were not without artistic skill and ability (they were the elite of popular musicians and singers in their time) and, aided by developing print technology, publicity skills and transport networks, they became the first cross-nationality 'popular' music form in America, the foundation of Broadway; many of them were Irish.[25] The genre appropriated, dramatised, exaggerated and exoticised African-Americans' cultural style,[26] but it also included a wide variety of music genres which made it appealing to mixed-nationality audiences, and, not least, to Irish people in Ireland too, as he America-based, traditional-music authority Mick Moloney says:

> There were jigs, reels and songs old and new … sentimental ballads, Negro sermons, plantation sketches and steamboat sketches, and parodies and satires. There were thousands of Irish and Irish-American performers[27]

VIRGINIA MINSTRELS

Though the presentation concept can be historically abhorred, nevertheless in those ruthless, grasping, political-survival times this was the beginning of 'popular', one-audience music. The music quality and variety among the routines and skills of these performers earned admiration for the Virginia Minstrels from 1843 onwards. They toured the western world, including travelling to Ireland, England and Australia. Their first performance in Dublin was at the beginning of this period, 1844:

> First appearance of the celebrated Original Virginia Minstrels (from America), Messrs. F.M. Brower, R.W. Pelham, D.D. Emmit, in conjunction with Mr. J. W. Sweeny (leader), the Original Banjo Player ... Pelham, Tamborine; Emmit, Violin; Sweeny, Banjo; Brower, Bone Castanets [*Freeman's Journal* 1844 0424 1]

Their visits continued over the next three decades, and another troupe, The Christy Minstrels, which 'was more structured and refined' with an emphasis on musical content[28] became known island-wide too through repeated visits to Waterford, Cork, Dublin and Belfast. Their signature performance in 1860 centred on 'Banjo, Bones, Concertina, Tambourine, Violin &c'.[29] One of these American bands was led by women, announced for an 1850 performance in Tralee, County Kerry as 'THE FEMALE AMERICAN SERENADERS, with harmonised voices, bangoes, tambourines, castanets &c'.[30]

Authenticity or exoticism?
Following the American Civil War (1861–5) – which involved rejection of slavery – black entertainers were able to enter the minstrel space, performing now as themselves, though bound by stylistic conventions and political prejudice which disparaged them as a people. Despite the formidable contradictions involved (validation of the stereotype among the hostile whites), this was the only outlet for black performers, so opportunity and need over-ruled resentment of the implicit self-degradation. In the process, however, artistic skills and reputations had the space and economic support to develop in spite of being paralleled by continuing white-supremacist discrimination, hostility, assault and murder. Touring in Ireland and Britain was routine for them too, and black composers, such as the banjo-player and singer James Bland who wrote some 700 songs, thrived in the medium. This became the basis for the pushing out of the boundaries by African-Americans in popular music and their part in the world-sweeping forms of jazz and blues, leading to rock & roll and multiple genres through the twentieth century.

Consciousness about authenticity crept into the presentation of minstrel shows in America itself following the Civil War, eventually pushing the idea of whites masquerading as blacks out of favour. African-American artistic talent was real, and the desire to appreciate it led to demand that it had to be experienced for of a high calibre. This reforming, but exoticising, trend is seen in the appearance of such performers as Tambourine Voy in the Prince of Wales Theatre, Fishamble Street, Dublin in 1863.[31] Dundalk had already seen some of this kind of authenticity in Pell's Serenaders who performed with 'that wonderful youth of colour ... the Inimitable Juba', praise for whose extraordinary talent had been written about by Charles Dickens as 'new energy in the tambourine'.[32] Aside from political implications, this indicates that there was familiarity with and uptake of minstrel instruments,

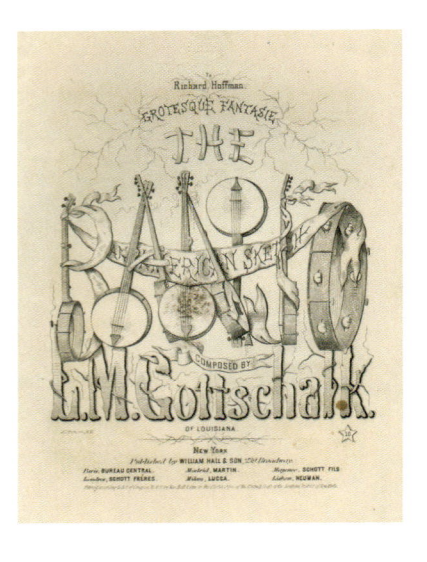

▲ Daniel Emmit's music book: banjo dominates, with fiddle and tambourine

▲ Blacked-up minstrel tambourine player [*Courtesy Mark Weems*]

THE FEMALE AMERICAN SERENADERS
These interesting vocalists has already appeared twice in Benner's large room before respectable audiences. *These ladies* gave several of their well-known Nigger songs with great spirit and correctness, particularly the choruses in which the several voices and appropriate in-struments, bangoes, tambourines, castanets, &c., harmo-nized most beautifully. Not being possessed of much musical knowledge, we are not able to criticise the several per-formances, as we feel they deserve. We can only say that they were highly amusing, and will well repay a visit

Kerry Evening Post 1850 0619 3

notably the tambourine which was also associated with sophisticated antics and routines. A charity concert in the 'Waterford lunatic asylum' in 1864, for instance, shows this, for among those playing were:

> one leading with a handsome silver-keyed concert flute, another a fife, – which caused a little discordance, as might reasonably be expected – others played a small drum, a tambourine and triangles [*Munster Express* 1864 0702]

A similar event in Cork also had 'tambourine, bones and concertina'.[33] The fashion for authenticity was reflected somewhat in advertising, such as for a concert at the Theatre Royal, Belfast which let its clientele know that:

> In the course of each evening a Troupe of Real Negros and Freed Slaves will introduce Songs, Glees, Hymns, Choruses, Banjo, Tambourine, and Bone Solos, representing Plantation Life in their Native Home [*Belfast News Letter* 1891 0901]

Portarlington, County Laois, heralded the newer version of minstrelsy too, featuring:

> Twenty-five Star Arttistes, including a number of Real Freed Slaves, who have just returned from a Tour round the World. And have appeared in all the principal Theatres of `America, Australia, New Zealand, India, China, Japan, Egypt, Holy Land, &c. Mr. Lewis begs the honour of your patronage during his visit, and desires to say that his Company is complete in every particular, comprising, as it does, beautiful Scenery, splendid Dresses, Bones, Tambourines, &c. [*Leinster Express* 1893 0603 4]

Such advertising marks the decline of whites pretending to be black, but nevertheless the concept remains alarming in its white-supremacist ideology, and the language and emphasis used in advertising shows that there was a long way to go to respect black artistes as human equals. One can only speculate as to how several generations in Ireland could have engaged so enthusiastically and apparently unselfconsciously with such a racist stereotype as the blacked-up white minstrels, for newspaper reports show that all over the country, just as in England and in America and Australia, these acts were not only well attended, and praised in the press, but were copied seriously in many counties. Since Ireland did not have a black population, all amateur participants blacked their skin with burnt cork, while the music trade cooperated by supplying the associated artefacts including African-hair wigs and key 'exotic' instruments – the banjo, the concertina, the bones

CHRISTY'S MINSTRELS
Were honoured by the Command of
THE QUEEN
To appear at BALMORAL CASTLE
On FRIDAY, 16th Instant.

From the Times of Monday, 13th Instant.
Court Circular.
"In the evening the Christy's Minstrels (Messrs Wilson and Montague proprietors) had the honour of performing before Her Majesty and the Prince and Princess Christian of Schleswig-Holstein, Princess Louise, Princess Beatrice, Prince Arthur, Prince Leopold, and the Prince and Princess of Teck, in the Ball-room of the Castle, where the Ladies and Gentlemen in Waiting and the entire household were assembled. Monsieur, Madame, and Miss Van de Weyer, and Sir Thomas and Lady Baddalph were also honoured with invitations"

FOURTEENTH ANNUAL VISIT

FOR TWELVE NIGHTS ONLY
Commencing on
MONDAY NEXT, NOVEMBER 2nd

Irish Times 1868 1029 1

and the tambourine. That the tambourine is listed in advertising for minstrel productions suggests it was an attractive feature of a music that was hugely popular. The fact that audiences for these shows were urban-based does not mean that rural people did not get to hear about them. On the contrary, this was 'popular' entertainment, and regional and local drama productions all went on to copy the format and the instrumentation.

Interest in minstrel music

Difference was the most compelling feature of minstrel music – its informality, newness and subversion of polite music norms. It

> mocked authority, formality and politics … a form of artistic expression that was in certain respects diametrically opposed to the prevailing aesthetic and direction of musical development of the period [34]

Yet the clowning and buffoonery were – on the surface – at the expense of the African American people who minstrelsy purported to imitate, and emphasised the fact that 'there were almost no blacks on antebellum [pre-Civil War] minstrel stages, almost no blacks on any antebellum stages at all'.[35] But it is argued that it mediated voices which were critical of the status quo in music; it pioneered improvisation, and its permitting of audience interaction gave it an engaging fluidity. The major troupes published their music arrangements, but on stage 'new material for the show … would often have emerged from intuitive group or individual responses to situations and problems arising out of live performance or rehearsal'.[36] Formally-scored arrangements were unlikely to have been used, playing from memory being the norm. The core melodies were carried by fiddle or by flautina (early accordion, later the concertina) with the banjo playing such thrilling variations that 'transformed even the simplest popular tune into something different – something "hotter" and more exciting'.[37] The voice too explored all potentials, breaking into the unusual, including falsetto and melisma, while the tambourine and bones acted as anchor and signal among the variety.[38] One such show by the British troupe Waterland and Readings band *c*. 1850 was described as

> a constant succession of songs and choruses accompanied by the banjo, the bones, the tambourine and flautina … ranging through all grades from the most deeply pathetic to the ultra-grotesque, filling the intervals with a running fire of conundrums, jokes and anecdotes[39]

The dance, which was a big part of the routine, and which eventually employed metal taps on shoes, was in tight measure with the melody and the tambourine, and powerfully expressive; from descriptions, it is reminiscent of today's *sean-nós* dance, as well as set-dance 'battering' dance practices:

> Minstrel dance interacted with the music to produce audible rhythmic patterns something like the percussion sounds produced by tambourine, bones, and minstrel hand-clapping[40]

Melody was vital as the line to hang all else on, and the fiddle could be used to produce 'extraordinary imitations of the bagpipes and other wind instruments', using open strings as drones, a novelty potential the possible fallout from which can be heard in Donegal fiddle player John Doherty's famous bagpipes rendering of 'The Enniskillen Dragoon'. The banjo's 'eccentricities' were so thrilling that that instrument was hugely popularised, developing a sophistication which in

TOWN HALL, MARYBOROUGH
ONE WEEK ONLY,
Commencing
MONDAY, JUNE 5, 1893
MR. R. B. LEWIS'S
WORLD-RENOWNED
American Dramatic Company.
Twenty-five Star Artistes, including a number of Real Freed Slaves, who have just returned from a Tour round the World. And have appeared in all the principal Theatres of America, Australia, New Zealand, India, China, Japan, Egypt, Holy Land, &c.

Leinster Express 1893 0604 4

▶ Poster for a London performance of the Ethiopian Serenaders with whom the celebrated Norwegian violinist Ole Bull junior played

▲ Ole Bull junior

America and Australia for instance led to the establishment of 'banjo academies, societies and banjo "orchestras" '.[41] In all of this, the tambourine and bones gave a dramatic accent with 'complex rhythmic and timbral embellishments'.[42] Indeed one 1845 programme's description of a tambourine's role shows all the hallmarks of today's 'bodhrán solo', as the minstrel player would:

> go through his imitative powers on the Tambourine, particularly where the locomotive runs off the track and bursts the Boiler, also the rattling of the Cannon in the distance … his Grist Mill grindings showing the power of steam … the rattling of a Cotton Mill and machinery. Language cannot convey any idea of his brilliant rapidity of execution on his Tambourine[43]

Minstrel music 'stirred popular imagination in the nineteenth century', its effect intensified on account of the distance of the audiences from its source, and the difference from listeners' normal everyday experience.[44] Being driven by vocals and thrilling dance routines, an ethos of roguery and a deceptive air of total improvisation, made the genre addictively attractive, and no doubt seemingly simple to reproduce, so it is small wonder that such music would be copied wherever minstrels toured.

Impersonating the impersonators
In the later 1800s, in communities island-wide in Ireland, the minstrels were mimicked, and their instruments and demonstrative style flowed inexorably into the Irish expressive palette. For instance, in a local music show in Killarney, County Kerry in 1866:

> the performers, who are all lads, protégés of the noble mistress of the ceremonies, were admirably got up as Ethiopian serenaders, and were armed with the musical instruments belonging to that particular line of the profession, as the banjo, tambourine, bones and so forth [*Cork Examiner* 1866 0822 2]

Music shops advertised frankly, in a manner which would not pass legal muster anywhere today.[45] In Belfast too, which was a centre of entertainment, awareness of and demand for the instruments of minstrelsy can be seen in music-shop advertising. All of such local music events were invariably reported as pleasant, the skills of local musicians in them praised highly. Dublin working-class familiarity with the tambourine can be seen in the fact that a locally-staffed 'Christy Minstrel' show at the Dublin Workingmen's Club in 1894 'was very largely attended; the hall of the club being crowded'.[46] Social mixing in rural areas had a similar effect on intra-class cultural appreciation and borrowing, such as seen in the Daniel Maclise painting 'Snap Apple Night' (see Chapter 8) of which has been said that 'Persons of superior position in society were to be found unaffectedly mingling with the poorest peasants of the parish'.[47] That the papers carry the names of tambourine players shows that the instrument was being taken up outside of professional music, and among these casual performers it can be seen that in Foxford, County Mayo, women were in the picture: 'Miss O'Donovan played the piano accompaniment, Miss May Seery the violin, and Miss Seery the tambourine'.[48] Such reports are numerous in the last years of the 1800s, most likely because of the expansion of newspapers and their coverage, so we hear of local minstrels in Sligo too, in 1894, where 'a novel and attractive feature of the concert was Miss H. Driver's tambourine solo'.[49] At a concert in Ardee, County Louth the same year the two 'new' instruments which were eventually to be espoused by Seán Ó Riada were present, in that 'The corner-men were Mr. M. Martin (bones), and Mr. McGowan (tambourine)'.[50] In Drogheda in 1897 too 'Messrs E. McAuliffe, T. Halpin and A. Murphy wielded the bones, and the tambourines were in the hands of Messrs M. McAuliffe, P. McKenna and W. Boyle'.[51]

Attitudes to slavery
The origins of the 'minstrel' concept in aspects of African slavery in America draws attention to the general abhorrence of the practice, understood most vividly in Ireland through political evocations on the subject nature of that country relative to England. But in the mid–1800s things were muddied by political expediencies. Daniel O'Connell, for instance, in the Irish-English domestic scene was unambiguously anti-slavery and vehemently outspoken in criticism of America regarding it. At one point he sent back 'with contumelious words' monies which had been sent from one of the southern US states in support of the Irish Repeal movement. He shared a platform with the black American abolitionist Frederick Douglass at an 1845 Limerick anti-slavery meeting to mighty acclaim, and Douglass himself addressed rallies in Dublin, Wexford, Waterford and Cork.[52] Despite such

The United Irish Parliamentary Minstrels.

▸ 1821 The Irish Parliamentary Party caricatured as minstrels [*Courtesy Terry Moylan*]

courageous stands against slavery, the seeming Irish public indifference to it[53] could possibly be influenced by the fact that the English manipulated slavery repeal in order to undermine Irish Repeal. This they did by supporting Irish landlords' clearances of the Irish 'surplus population', and proposing that they be replaced by freed slaves who could improve landlords' estates.[54] Still, anti-slavery principles were active in the political realm, seen in the 1795 songbook *Paddy's Resource* which carries two lyrics which indicate revulsion towards slavery: 'The Captive Negro' and 'The Dying Negro'. In another song the concept of slavery is compared to the political status of the Irish:

> Till you go to your graves
> You shall live and die – SLAVES

Familiarity

The minstrel genre was popular enough to be parodied in Lewis Carroll's 1874 *The Hunting of the Snark* in which his character, Banker, was depicted as a bones player in a minstrel's role: black of face and white of waistcoat.

> Down he sank in a chair, ran his hands through his hair
> And chanted in mimsiest tones
> Words whose utter inanity proved his insanity
> While he rattled a couple of bones[55]

Indications of familiarity with minstrels and their instruments can be seen too in a parody lyric of Stephen Foster's minstrel song 'The Old Folks at Home' which was published in *The Lepracaun*, 1908. This accompanied a cartoon by Thomas Fitzpatrick as a political satire which depicts Irish Parliamentary Party figures Tim Healy, John Dillon, John Redmond, T.P. O'Connor and William O'Brien in minstrel guise, blackness being an allegory for the condition of the Irish politicians.[56] Familiarity with the minstrel genre and

---

ENTERTAINMENT AT TENURE

The entertainment given at Tenure on Sunday evening, by the Christy Minstrel Troupe, Drogheda was, as we anticipated, from every point of view, a brilliant success. Seldom have the amateurs ap-peared to better advantage, or performed to a larger and more appreciative audience.

Drogheda Independent 1890 0524 2

Ballybay, County Monaghan young minstrels school band, 1905 [*Northern Standard*]

its instruments is seen as well in the work of the popular singer-songwriter Percy French, who got in on the minstrel fashion without apparent concern, as with a fellow apprentice Charles Manners he rehearsed duets to banjo and bones accompaniment.[57] In 1881:

> They decided to entertain the racegoers at Punchestown race course … they changed, blackened up their faces and as Christie.Minstrels boarded the train, where they endeavoured to entertain the passengers

French did not boast about the reaction to their partnership (possibly he was embarrassed?) but Manners reported that they were well received, and collected twenty-eight shillings.[58] This diversion led to French's writing two minstrel-style songs, 'The Hoodoo' and the carelessly racist 'Oklahoma Rose'. The minstrel genre persisted, developing its own tradition which was to last for another three or four decades, the political consciousness of the times still apparently uncaring, and certainly not obviously critical, of the implicit race-demeaning connotations.

The popularity of minstrelsy was made most clear by the widespread parodying of the parodists, done by local performers all over Ireland, and as late as 1905 *The Northern Standard* carried a report on a local national-school minstrel performance in Ballybay, County Monaghan, the participating lads looking at the camera no more self-consciously than might hurlers or footballers. Another such event was in County Longford in 1890 for a charity at Rathowen where the singing of a local version of 'The Kentucky Minstrels … was really heart-stirring (accompanied by banjo, triangle, tambourine and bones)'.[59] Local minstrels were out in County Louth too, and the 'Drogheda Christy Minstrel Troupe', who performed for a Catholic church event to great acclaim in 1890 at Tenure, listed among their players 'Tambourines – Messrs John Burke, James McConnon, Patrick McConnon'.[60] Among those who were experimenting with the newly-popular minstrel music, some had a particular aptitude for the tambourine. For instance, an 1893 Cork report says that 'Mr. Harris's tambourine solo was splendid, and fairly brought down the house'.[61] Belfast too was no stranger to local parodying of minstrel shows. At Mountpottinger Presbyterian Young Men's Association's final musical evening in 1895, the polite programme of song was concluded as 'Mr. Bradshaw brought a pleasant evening to a close with a tamborine solo'.[62] Such vigorous displays made performance on the tambourine attractive, even compelling, as seen in the case of a Dublin club with the appalling title Alabama Coons, dedicated to minstrel performance, which was instigated in the Ovoca Hall in 1896, an event marked by the troupe being presented with five tambourines.[63]

Mimicking of the minstrel genre, as already said, was inspired by the excitement, nose-thumbing to convention and authority, and novelty, its sheer difference to all other local music. It is likely also to have much to do with the gut appeal of tambourine and bones, something which is reflected in the post-1960s popular uptake of the bodhrán by otherwise-non-musicians. No doubt there were serious percussion novices among the tambourine players, but certainly there were enthusiastic audiences, so much so that Virginia Young Men's Club in County Cavan performed a Christy Minstrel Concert in 1897 at which two men played bones, and three tambourines. The venue 'was utilised to such accommodating capacities that scarce standing space could be found for the vast throng who had assembled'.[64] Cappoquin, County Waterford had its Magpie Minstrels show packed for two nights, including local clergy and nobility, the objective to raise money for a brass band. Dramatically-illuminated by acetylene gas, the twenty-three-strong troupe's

> exhibitions of vocal power and tambourine accompaniment were decidedly excellent. The manipulation of the indispensable bones by Mr. Donegan … gave a strong and broad support and sustaining power [*Waterford News and Star* 1897 0501 6]

Influence on music instruments in Ireland?
The actual American troupes had an influence from the earliest days of their touring. They got around the country, and in 1844 players were announced as giving 'Ethiopian Concerts' for a week at Belfast's Theatre Royal, part of the wonder being the unusual instruments they played – tambourine, banjo, concertina and bone castanets: 'each performer plays on an instrument such as the slaves use in the Southern parts of the United States'.[65] This was to continue, as an announcement almost fifty years later shows:

> THEATRE ROYAL: Mr. Charles Harrington and his great American Combination, Comprising the Largest TROUPE OF REAL NEGROES That has ever travelled in this country, who will introduce Songs, Glees, Dances, Hymns, Bango, Tambourine and Bone Solos [*Belfast News Letter* 1893 0508 1]

The influence of these shows must have encouraged the uptake and popularisation of the instruments they used. Their influence on the introduction and appreciation of, say, the concertina or banjo has not been assessed to date, but it has been remarked on by Mick Moloney as significant.[66] This would also have been the case for the bones, and for the tambourine, one can assume that since it is relatively easy to learn to play in a rudimentary fashion, it entered easily into the local instrumentarium. What is certain is that, as will be discussed in Chapter 9, the tambourine was known well enough in the early 1800s for it to be mimicked or improvised on the then ubiquitous household and agricultural bodhráns, dallans and wechts. By 1851, actual tambourines, popularised by the minstrels, were not only being imported and sold by the music trade, but were being made commercially in Ireland: 'Mr. Kirby, of 15, Lower Sackville-street [Dublin] … gives a vast deal of employment in the manufacture of … tambourines, racquets'.[67] Popularity inspired invention, and even mechanical tambourines were made too to fulfil the taste that was being cultivated for the thrilling percussive marking of beat in music, as had been done by military bands.[68]

Audiences for popular entertainments
Theatre entertainments were aimed at those with money, but Irish society was diverse and outside Dublin and Belfast, the regional centres had both urban and rural dimensions. The urban in the mid-1800s could be a

> mixture of elegant private gateways, trim lawns, and doorways with colonnades, shops with diamond-paned windows, mouldering hovels, cobbles, ruts, dungheaps and duckpuddles[69]

whereas rurally, the conditions of the 'peasantry' were grim, a life of subsistence with a huge dependence on the potato. Indigenous Irish music practice reflected all of this, with fiddles, pipes, song and dancing in the countryside, the harp, violin, piano and Thomas Moore being fashionable for the rising middle class in towns. In urban life on the streets 'music was not so refined. The frequent fair-days brought itinerant ballad-singer, fluters, pipers and chest-fiddlers whose songs were the news-sheets of the times',[70] a mixing bowl of styles, ambitions and influence. Post Famine, Dublin offered all classes of music diversion, for the wealthy and the poor alike. Connell's Monster Saloon, on the site of today's Olympia Theatre, was the first music-hall to open there, providing food and drink as well as variety entertainment, a hotbed of experience for the workers as well as for all classes of patrons. This was developed in 1879 as Dan Lowrey's Star of Erin Music Hall, on the opening night of which the clientele included a broad social mix of:

> the Architecht and members of the contracting firms, with artisans and labourers who had worked on the building ... Theatre managements, writers and journalists ... Trinity College students, soldiers of the Dublin garrison ... dockers, draymen, railwaymen, clerks, shopboys – Dubliners of all kinds ... all spruced up for the night and looking forward to a drink, a song and a bit of amusement under the same roof as the tophats and the solid-money members of society[71]

That was the reported amalgam of those engaging with popular music. Such premises were also therefore a window on to alternative and new music instruments from abroad. Among the performers for the eclectic mix, 'The rage for blacked-up acts was reflected in the Mad Minstrels Blanquin & Hearst, and in Craven & Cowley the Ethiopians'.[72] This, and other venues, notably the 'singing taverns' which 'blossomed all over town', thus gave experience of minstrels and their instruments to the poorer classes. Dublin in the late 1800s had a population of some quarter of a million, of whom 17,000 were the upper classes, and

> 150,000 of the humble sort – artisans, small shopkeepers, dockers, porters, workers in breweries and biscuit factories, railwaymen, tramway and canalmen, hawkers, casual labourers, inmates of the immense Workhouses and the beggarly hordes[73]

These were among those who sought diversion in Dan Lowrey's. Among the artistes in 1886 were the African-American Bohee Brothers, from Newfoundland, who had enjoyed huge favour in London where they were engaged to teach the royal infants the banjo; that fame gave them a full house at Dan Lowrey's.[74] Such

6...THE TAMBOURINE ON THE IRISH STAGE

was their effect that 'According to a son of Jack White, the Stage Carpenter ... all over Dublin boys were playing imaginary banjos with their fingernails';[75] the tambourine must also have made a similar impact. Thus the minstrel mimicking had no shortage of live role models, as Christy's Minstrels were such regular visitors in Ireland that even in 1868 *The Irish Times* could advertise them as fresh from a royal command performance for Queen Victoria at Balmoral Castle, on their 'Fourteenth annual visit, For Twelve Nights Only' in Dublin, including a Saturday morning show.[76] By 1887, Christy Minstrels were still among Dan Lowrey's artistes:

> 'Pure' music at Dan's ... had to be linked to the visible, the breath-taking, the comic ... such music was provided by American Christy Minstrels. A large Troupe of Twenty-five arrived in the Spring with a non-stop fund of song, dance and instrumentation. Quick pop-up gags, crass crosstalk, elastic legantics punctuated the incessant twanka-panka-panks of the banjo which the Bohees had made all the rage[77]

With the popularity of minstrelsy it is not surprising that the desire to play its instruments would spread, and the newspaper reports indicate local names in many places who had the ability to play variously on piccolo, concertina, bones and tambourine. The local parodists' repertoires included some Irish balladry as well as light 'parlour', classical lyrics, Irish-American vaudeville, and African-American and American popular songs,[78] all of which in this way added to Irish music taste. Additionally, some minstrel-type practices were used by the post-Christmas Wren tradition itself in addition to clowning, notably the process of 'blacking up':

▲ Dan Lowrey's Music Hall, the ancestor of today's Olympia theatre

> The Brosna Wren boys set flame to the turf sods dipped in paraffin and held them aloft on pikes. In the flare of these improvised torches it was possible to glimpse faces on which circles had been traced in burnt cork. Then to the tune of 'Rody McCorley' the Brosna Wren marched off to The Square [*Kerryman* 1961, 1007 3]

Where we know about the minstrels we are naturally embarrassed and may feel historically culpable as regards the insidiousness of the concept, even though we did not create it; it was a political phenomenon in fashion which though long-standing, nevertheless died away. Yet taste for it lingered for a considerable time, as seen in a photo of a community minstrel show in inner city Dublin in the mid-1900s (see photo overleaf). Surprisingly, the BBC revived the concept on television as *The Black and White Minstrel Show* in 1958, a programme which ran with blacked-up white performers for 178 shows for twenty-one years before political pressure stopped it.

▼ Minstrel show in inner-city Dublin, 1930s [*Courtesy Nicholas Carolan*]

For Ireland, the press record shows that the minstrel era is the longest period of Irish exposure to tambourines on stages, for about sixty years in all. So it needs to be considered, in an investigation of nineteenth-century music in Ireland, rather than it being over-flown to a cosy origin-myth for the Irish drum.

105

▲ Tambourine comfortably disposed in what could be a Gaelic League or Irish Musicians' Club orchestra with fiddles, flute, piano, harp, pipes and guitar, early 1900s. The piper is identified as Pat O'Neill, and the scene may be in America, as the picture came via piper Pádraig de Buitléar (Kilkenny and Cork) who was given it by a dealer in San Francisco from whom he bought O'Neill's Rowsome pipes. The amplifier is a 'Volutone', an American brand that dates to 1902 [*Photo courtesy ITMA; information thanks to Maeve Gebruers*]

▲ Late 1800 minstrels in the USA [*Courtesy Mark Weems*]

NOTES TO CHAPTER 6

[1] It is not included in *EMIR*, the main encyclopedia of music in Ireland, and, with the exception of Mick Moloney's study of Irish Americans in minstrel music, it does not appear to have been addressed significantly by any Irish research.

[2] Goff 2020.

[3] *Freeman's Journal* 1783, 0430.

[4] Girling 2018, Abstract.

[5] *Evening Echo* 1803, 0120.

[6] Ibid.

[7] Graham 2023, PC.

[8] Hall 2023, PC.

[9] *Belfast News Letter* 1802 0924 2.

[10] Ibid. 1816 1105.

[11] *Fermanagh Herald* 1815 0202 2.

[12] *Freeman's Journal* 1821 1224 2.

[13] Girling 2022, Abstract. The teaching and sales were reported in Stephen Thomson Moore's translation of memoirs of the Bohemian musician and writer Václav Jan Krtitel Tomásek (Wenzel Johann Tomaschek) (1774–1850), *Autobiography, Studies in Czech Music* No. 4. Hillsdale, Pendragon, 2017, p. 22.

[14] *Belfast News Letter* 1828 0408.

[15] Whiteoak 1999, 84; Nathan 1962, 160–88.

[16] Seibert 2015, 64–5.

[17] Whiteoak 1999, 85, from Toll 1974, 52.

[18] Graham 2023, PC.

[19] 'Music-hall', meaning an establishment which provided food, drink and entertainment, has its origins in seventeenth-century England, providing 'popular' acts and variety shows for all classes including the less well off.

[20] The variety of ethnicity-based acts included Irish music and dance, with many well-known Irish-traditional performers gracing the stages, including piper Patsy Touhey on uilleann pipes, his wife Mary Gillen dancing, accordionist John Kimmel and fiddle-player Michael Coleman.

[21] Mel Watkins, ex-*New York Times* critic, pbs.org.

[22] This same concept was revived in broadcasting in Ireland in the 1980s when it was forbidden for republicans to be interviewed on media, but it was acceptable if actors spoke their words as voice-over done to silent video of the real people on news bulletins.

[23] Mel Watkins, op. cit.

[24] Seibert op. cit., 73–5.

[25] Moloney 1999, 243; 2006, 383; 2011, 455.

[26] Deane Root, Center for American Music, University of Pittsburgh, pbs.org.

[27] Moloney 2006, 383.

[28] Whiteoak 1999, 87.

[29] *Waterford News and Star* 1860 0831 2.

[30] *Kerry Evening Post* 1850 0619.

[31] *Freeman's Journal* 1863 1216 1.

[32] *Dundalk Democrat* 1850 0202 3.

[33] *Cork Examiner* 1864 0406 2.

[34] Whiteoak 1999, 86.

[35] Seibert 2015, 77.

[36] Ibid., 89.

[37] Whiteoak op. cit., 107.

[38] Ibid., 92.

[39] Ibid., 105; Argus [Melbourne], 1850 0715 2.

[40] Ibid., 98.

[41] Ibid., 108.

[42] Ibid., 95.

[43] Ibid., 95; from Magriel 1948, 44–5.

[44] Nathan 1962, 183.

[45] Apology is offered for having to give sight to this data, but omission would be, as John Whiteoak believes, 'inaccurate and misleading'. It seems necessary that it be visible in these circumstances lest we lose sight not so much of how restricted our view of humanity once generally was, but how far political thinking has advanced in Ireland today.

[46] *Freeman's Journal* 1894 0206 7.

[47] Murray 2008, 98; quoted from anonymous article 'Memoir of Samuel Forde' in *Dublin University Magazine* XXV, March 1845, p. 355.

[48] *Western People* 1894 0922 5.

[49] *Sligo Champion* 1894 0206 7.

[50] *Dundalk Democrat* 1894 1124 4.

[51] *Drogheda Independent* 1897 0113 3.

[52] Kinealy, 2011.

[53] Mitchell 1861, 80–1.

[54] Ibid., 1861, 82.

[55] Gardner 1962, 91.

[56] Moylan 2020.

[57] O'Dowda 1981, 6.

[58] Ibid., 6.

[59] *Westmeath Examiner* 1890 0118 3.

[60] *Drogheda Independent* 1890 0524 2.

[61] *Munster Express* 1893 0121 8.

[62] *Belfast News Letter* 1895 0228 6.

[63] *Evening Herald* 1896 1114 3.

[64] *Anglo-Celt* 1897 0501 4.

[65] *Belfast News Letter* 1844 0514 3.

[66] Moloney 1998, PC.

[67] *Freeman's Journal* 1851 0515 4.

[68] Ibid. 1845 0920 1. Hand-cranked, card-programmed barrel organs often included a tambourine and triangle.

[69] Watters and Murtagh 1975, 9.

[70] Ibid., 10.

[71] Ibid., 22.

[72] Ibid., 23.

[73] Ibid., 43.

[74] Ibid., 83. James Joyce wrote in praise of them, but in quite inconsiderate racist language, 'Coloured coons … negroid hands … Flashing white eyes … smackful clacking nigger lips'.

[75] Ibid., 85.

[76] *Irish Times* 1868 1029 1.

[77] Watters and Murtagh 1975, 89.

[78] *Nationalist and Leinster Times* 1892 0604 12.

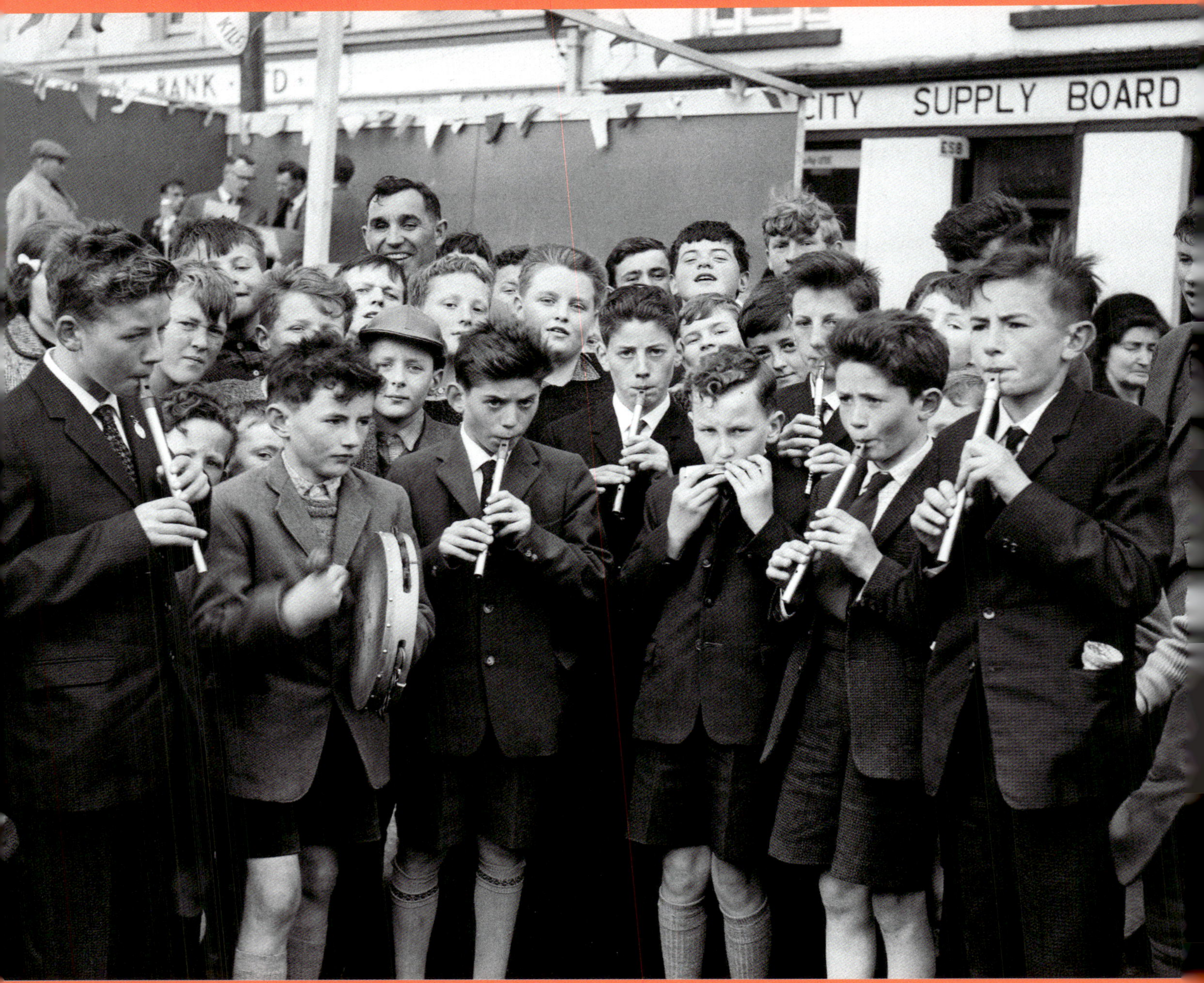
CITY SUPPLY BOARD
ESB

CHAPTER 7
TAMBOURINES AMONG THE PEOPLE

◀ Schoolboys with whistles, mouth organ and tambourine at Féile Castleisland, County Kerry, May 1965 [Kennelly Archive]

The previous pages show how the tambourine was known about in Ireland from the mid-1700s on, and how the later popularity of the minstrel show gave people in all parts experience or awareness of minstrel instruments and their alluring, exciting performance style. This had an influence too among poorer classes in society, complemented by the music trade selling the instruments that were popularised. And so the tambourine crops up with many other, and varied, associations which would have added further to its visibility and attraction for innovative music-makers. But there was already familiarity with the tambourine on the streets both at home and in exile before the minstrel troupes arrived, from military-band influence. For instance, a report from 1830 – a critique of a fair that had been washed out by rain – laments the absence of 'the merry and heart-stirring sounds of pipes and fiddle, tambourine and triangle, the very echo of which used make many a Paddy leap out of his brogues'.[1]

That indicates something which was already occasionally in everyday life on the streets before minstrels arrived. A few years later, in 1834, the accounting for the Dublin Sick and Indigent Room-keepers' annual ball included money from 'fiddler and wife, and tambourine player',[2] buskers perhaps, who had instruments which could have been originally purchased from such as the Harmonic Saloon in Westmoreland Street which by 1836 was selling 'Violins, Tenors, Guitars &c., Flutes, by the most approved makers; Tambourines and Accordions, in varieties'.[3] It is notable that the tambourine is here in the company of the accordion, which was primitive then, very much a prestige novelty, but by the twentieth century it had become a mainstay in traditional music.

This experience was not just gained in Ireland, but among Irish people as far away as Australia, where the professional performers were typically non-whites. A report from there in the year 1833 speaks of the township of Killarney, New South Wales which had 'the first race meeting of any importance outside the metropolis and so received much patronage from all classes … Black Simon playing the tambourine'.[4] In Ireland after the Famine, but in turbulent political times, and in the circumstances of the press advertising of minstrel performances, the development of local interest, uptake and expertise on the tambourine would be inevitable, as a report from County Waterford suggests concerning an 1862 party to celebrate the coming of age of a son of the Ussher family, the event had 2,000 guests, and 'dancing commenced and was kept up with animation to a late hour, to the music of violin, bagpipe, flute, pipes, drum, tambourine &c'.[5]

◀ Detail from George Heriot's, *Minuets of the Canadians,* 1807 [*Courtesy of Toronto Public Library*]

Reports from abroad

A few decades earlier, in 1829, reflecting a similar familiarity in England, the drum in popular parlance is seen in the name of a pub in London, *The Cow and Tambourine,* a place that Irish labourers were criticised for frequenting on a Sunday rather than 'attending mass and confessing their sins to the "praste"'.[6] Information about tambourines came via the press all through the nineteenth century, travel-style articles describing contemporary cultural practices elsewhere, such as this 1865 news report from France which was read about in Westmeath, one of the counties where the tambourine later became strong in Irish music:

> A New Military Cotillon [social dance] ... the dancers assemble in a close column and promenade the ball-room many times with military steps, whilst an obligato charivari is played on drums, tambourines and mirlitrons [*Westmeath Independent* 1865 0304 3]

This associates the tambourine with the formality of organised dance. And a similar familiarity with the instrument is also implied in a Tipperary newspaper's printing of a syndicated story in 1865 about Esquimaux (Inuit, north American) life: 'It is rare to find a village without its accompanying dance-house ... the walls are decorated with tambourines'.[7] A Roma burial in Berlin is shown to have had symbolic use of tambourines in this account in a Mayo newspaper of 1892: 'Close behind the coffin rode the six eldest members of the clan, beating tambourines, while they muttered prayers'.[8] And serenaders in Spain in 1895 are described as gathering round particular tables in restaurants 'making a disturbance with tambourines, castanets, fifes and guitars'.[9] In Ireland itself, scenes of emigration saw the deployment of tambourines:

> on Wednesday at the Listowel station a very pathetic sight was witnessed on the departure of some emigrants for America ... The delay was made interesting for a time by some juveniles from the country as they discoursed some nice music on the tambourine and other instruments which was greatly appreciated by those present [*Kerry Sentinel* 1892 0504 4]

Tambourine with 'dancing' bear, France c. 1920 [Marcus Gibelin, Métiers et Savoir-faire de Toujours]

The diversity of the application of tambourines included their use in travelling entertainments, as in 1899 when in a court case 'the constable stated that the quintette of foreigners were performing with three bears and two monkeys, and were putting them through various antics to the music of tambourines'.[10] In their time, the touring minstrels too were attractive on account of newness and difference. But they also created an opportunity to enter music-making at a rudimentary level, as can be deduced from comment on the opening of a hall for a working men's club in 1893, praise which noted that 'there is no parish in Ireland but would be proud of such a Club of young men, seeing the harmony that prevailed amongst them, harmony from the flageolet to the tambourine'.[11] This may have been somewhat arrogant in its implication that those instruments were seen as appropriate for a (mere?) workers' clubhouse, but it certainly makes clear that the tambourine was already commonly known and played.

Agitational tambourine

Use of the tambourine in public on the streets was, however, already visible by the early years of the nineteenth century. A County Clare parade for the Protestant O'Connell activist Tom Steele in 1828 reports one in celebratory circumstances:

> they had prepared a Chair, ornamented with green boughs, into which they put Mr. Steele outside the Chapel door, and with a flute, violin and tamborine, bore him in triumph over the bridge, near the cascade, through the street of Ennistymon [*Finn's Leinster Journal* 1828 0705 1]

From the opposite side of the political spectrum a prejudiced newspaper report in 1835 shows the tambourine deployed with O'Connell again, in Kilkenny:

> The public disturber, the arch-agitator, Daniel O'Connell, passed through Kilkenny on Saturday, on his way to the election for the city of Dublin. He was met a short distance from town by about fifty ragged, half-drunken ruffians, accompanied by a band of music (consisting of a bassoon, two fifes, a cracked clarionet, a broken-winded French horn, a big drum and a tambourine) who attempted to take the jaded horses from his carriage, and draw him into town [*Wexford Conservative* 1835 0121]

And it was on the edge of aggression too, as in Munster, at a rally:

> It was absolutely necessary for the safety of their lives to escort Mr. Stafford O'Brien, his Committee, and Agents through the streets, to their homes, with a troop of Dragoons to guard them from popular fury ... Another squadron has come in from Costlea and Hospital, mounted and dismounted, comprising 1,200 men, we suppose not 50 of them electors – bagpipes, Tamborine, and fiddle, in motion, and five Priests conducting the cavalcade [*Kerry Evening Post* 1838 0812 1]

Inevitably, the tambourine was in agitational politics, and evidence of its use in provocative or assertive music can be read between the lines of the newspaper court reports. More explicitly, an article from County Kilkenny in 1859 noted that the Phoenix Society used to 'meet in shebeen and other houses, on pretence of dancing, and the members are collected at night by the beat of drum or tambourine'.[12] The tambourine was occasionally being used much later in political parade or procession contexts, such as in north Kerry in 1910:

> Torch-lights were procured and all the available musical instruments – tambourines, concertinas, etc. requisitioned. A procession was then formed, with the torchbearer and the musicians leading. 'God Save Ireland' and other national airs were played, and on several occasions the music was completely drowned with the deafening cry from some hundreds of voices of 'Up Flavin!' [*Kerry Evening Star* 1910 0210 5]

▲ Tambourine used as a collection tray, Paris: *L'Escamoteur, Quart d'heure de Rabelais,* by Jean-Louis Ham, 1861

Religion and solemnity

As early as 1828 a report showed a colloquial religious affinity with the tambourine, such as when a Grand High Mass at the consecration of The New Chapel of Shanagolden in County Limerick was followed by a ceremony and assembly: 'They were dressed in flowers and ribands, with garlands and music. Flutes, violins, drums and tambourines met them on their approach'. So the tambourine was already known and being played by then, a couple of decades before the arrival of minstrels. A later travel tale in 1865 describes tambourines being brought to Rome by pilgrims celebrating the pope's birthday.[14] But tambourines were not just played by roaming Catholics and on parish stages, they were adopted with the biblical name 'timbrel' in the late 1800s too by the Salvation Army – proselytising, Protestant moral crusaders against whom the working and drinking classes took out their frustration occasionally in some dramatic incidents. Destroying the drums was the pinnacle of success in one such affair in Eastbourne, widely reported in the press in Ireland:

> The Salvationists were parading with a band ... they were attacked by a crowd of persons, who seized the bandsmen's uniforms, caps and tambourines ... The big drum and several musical instruments were smashed [*Belfast News Letter* 1891 0713 5]

Elsewhere, a Salvation Army band is described as using the drum, one ensemble described as having 'four tambourines, two fiddles, two drums and one penny whistle'.[15] There was familiarity with the instrument as part of the regalia of 'the Salvationers' too in later years in County Monaghan, 1901, where a discussion went on in the local authority about banning a Salvation Army band on account of their use of music, including the tambourine, in aggressive anti-Catholicism: 'You can hear them singing and playing their tambourines ... what religion can there be in that? (Laughter)'.[16] The tambourine associated with this group, however, in modern times has been the smaller one where the jingles are supreme.

▲ Salvation Army tambourine player

112

▲ Republican imagery on a bodhrán, 2022 [*EDI*]

▲ Painted-on Portuguese pandereta [*Sheena Vallely*]

▲ Tambourine frame used for embroidery, late 1800s

Tambourine as collection tray

Not unlike the actual old Irish bodhrán, the tambourine had a similar practical applicability as a container, particularly for collecting theatre entrance fees and for charity appeals, a practice noted in *Punch* magazine as early as 1846,[17] and done widely in the late 1800s. Tambourines were used for collection by buskers at Irish-community social events, such as one in New York in 1891:

> others hold tambourines in their hands, and all have some musical instrument – either a flute, fiddle, bagpipes, accordion, or concertina. They rush aboard and scramble for the choicest seats – that is seats in front of which were nice dancing spaces. There they kept up a continuous 'melody' until the boats returned at night, depending on the thousands of jiggers for their rewards [*Western People* 1891 0119 3]

Open display of money in tambourines in lean times could invite theft, as in Cork city in 1891:

> A man ... had just deposited a penny in the tambourine of one of the lady collectors when he was seen by a detective to pick up half a crown from the parchment in an adroit fashion [*Cork Examiner* 1891 1130 2]

A complementary symbolic, idiophonic sound is associated with the collection tambourine in Cork in 1892: 'The Red Cross badge was everywhere to be seen, the jingling of the tambourine was everywhere to be heard'.[18] As always, charm was a valuable skill in collection, and the use of a tambourine the following year made the handing over and reception of coins a less personal affair: 'A very handsome young lady took up the half-crowns in a tambourine, and a goodly sum was collected … it was impossible to resist her in that guise'.[19] In Munster for hospital fundraising 'the shaking of tambourines on behalf of our local hospitals is a feature in the 1890s of Cork city fundraising'[20] and 'at every street corner ladies with tambourines solicited subscriptions from the public'[21] 'at all corners and points of vantage young ladies with tambourines assembled in bunches of twos and threes'.[22] 'the Misses Royse had no difficulty in collecting £5 15s 3d in their tambourines'.[23] Reports of tambourines as collection devices in other cultures were printed in Irish newspapers, one an account of snake charming in Morocco:

> A trio of attendants beat a dismal refrain on a large tambourine and a couple of tamtams, which is repeated at intervals until the close ... at this point the boy passes around the tambourine, which receives a goodly number of sous [*Cork Examiner* 1895 0622 12]

Decoration and novelty

The painted bodhrán is nothing new either, for tambourines had decorative uses in the nineteenth century too, the art shops selling them specially for this purpose. A circular hoop on which was stretched fabric was the standard equipment for embroidery, but called a tambourine on account of its nature. The decorative tambourine was a popular wall hanging, perhaps doubling as a music instrument, as evident in this 1892 promotion for a craft fair:

> what lovers of music will be interested in – a pretty tambourine hand-painted with exquisite skill, and wanting only the magic touch of a master or mistress to awaken its latent harmony [*Drogheda Independent* 1892 1015 4]

A ball at Birr Castle in 1895 had lavish decorations, which included 'Spanish fans, tambourines, and festoons of the choicest flowers'.[24] And by the end of the century the fact that a tambourine was merely the twenty-first prize in a County Dublin raffle affirms the drum's common-ness at that stage rather than any prestige and novelty.[25]

Prejudices

Dismissal of non-classical music was part and parcel of upper-class society attitudes, despite the royals' one-time favour for the novelty of minstrelsy and its instruments. Occasional rants in the press indicate the scale of values, one commentator, in a lengthy tirade against street music (which may or may not have had racist connotations about perceived African-American music), saying:

> I am not aware whether a pair of bones, a Jew's harp, and a tambourine are musical instruments. Maybe they are; the cat is said to be a relation of the lordly tiger, and probably the above are some relation to instruments of music proper [*Southern Star* 1893 0603 3]

These attitudes prevailed right up until the 1960s, and undoubtedly still contribute to traditional-music players' occasional unease with the bodhrán today. The pervasiveness of the minstrel fashion was something seldom questioned critically as regards politics, but other comment on it appears to have been generally favourable, if patronising:

> All sorts and conditions of men, even those who regard stage plays as ungodly and music halls as dens of iniquity, cannot fail to perceive in the harmless eccentricities of the Christy Minstrel, and the untainted funniosities of the bones and tambourine an unfailing source of innocent merriment [*Irish Daily Independent* 1893 0214 7]

Minstrelsy being viewed in this way gives some idea of how the playing of tambourines, even on ritual occasions, would have been regarded somewhat patronisingly among the higher social classes; but it is clear that those who played them did so with enthusiasm and gratification.

Countrywide availability?

In Waterford city in 1863 F.T. Howard's Piano-Forte & Music Warehouse on the Quay had 'Concertinas, Accordeans, Guitars, Tambourines'[26] The latter are included in the inventory of goods for sale to schools stocked by a Belfast shop in 1895, among 'all apparatus for action songs, now so popular in our schools'.[27] The price of tambourines had increased by the late 1800s, as indeed had that of other instruments, but being sold well into the twentieth century suggests persisting popularity.[28] These were sold where there was a demand, and in places where there was not a specialist music shop, the local hardware business stepped in if there was profit to be made.[29] Tambourines for sale in Dublin were also advertised in the regional presses in the early 1900s, so awareness of their existence would have been high throughout the country.[30] Monaghan was among the towns which at the turn of the twentieth century offered tambourines for sale among other instruments that were to become central in traditional music revival sixty years later. Among his 'thousands of fresh goods for 1900' Robert Graham offered 'a splendid stock of melodeons and Concertinas, Violins, Flutes, Drums, Tambourines'.

LONGFORD SHOOTING CASE

Blowing of Horns and Beating of Tambourines

SCENE NEAR A FARM

Sergt. Foley stated that he was in charge of a protection post on a farm at Napogue, where the prisoners were working. On the 12th April, when the two Stratfords were returning to the farm with provisions, there were demonstrations at intervals along the road. When they came to Mr. Bourke's farm there were six people in a small garden, and as the Stratfords came along, three of the Burkes came up and lined themselves along the hedge.
One of them was armed with a tambourine,
ANOTHER WITH A HORN
and another with a tin can (laughter). The horse shied, and one of the Stratfords fired a shot. The other Stratford fired another shot, a third shot was also fired by the prisoners. After shots were fired stones were thrown. The prisoners have good character.

Evening Herald 1909 1208 1

[31] Local press advertising indicates indeed that trade in instruments was a viable business that catered for all tastes and pockets. The tambourine was also sold as a toy, supplied by the Varian Brush Company in Patrick Street, Dublin, 1853, which advertised that they had 'provided material for Fun during the Holidays … Pop-guns and Pistols, Swords, Drums, French Tambourines, Fifes, Small Violins'.[32] Yet tambourines were not particularly cheap in their time, and their place among popular instruments can be seen in an 1874 list, priced at three shillings, almost one third the price of a violin or English concertina, and little more than a German concertina. By 1905 an article in the County Cork *Skibbereen Eagle* titled 'The Industrial Cause in Skibbereen and Irish Tambourines' noted the local Gaelic League's desire to use only Irish-made tambourines for its language-week collection. They had the name of a Dublin manufacturer who told them 'his traveller has been in Skibbereen … and had succeeded in getting trial orders from every firm he called on'.[33] This shows use of, a demand for, and availability of, tambourines, certainly in west Cork.

Tambourine and the law

It is not surprising that the influence of the minstrel instruments spread into the communities that witnessed the shows, and so the tambourine, often with the flute, has been reported in the press in everything from religion to murder:

> Mary Shaughnessy … saw deceased on the day she was killed … Henry Meade … was at prisoner's house on the Sunday Biddy Fury was killed; it was before mass time; prisoner was there with his wife and five children … there was music – a tambourine and a flute [*Freeman's Journal* 1851 0305]

Tambourines were not only played, broken and sold, but were stolen too, as in County Laois, where

> Henry Delany summoned Thomas Donovan for stealing a tambourine of his, of the value of 3s 6d … dismissed because the complainant admitted … that he lent it to defendant [*Leinster Express* 1863 1003]

Tambourines are also involved in aggression: 'The prisoner said the complainant had assaulted his sister by striking her with a tambourine'.[34] The tambourine features in occasional trials, typically to do with assault and murder, showing that it was known among the poorer classes in society. It was obviously being used by buskers too at the turn of the twentieth century, going by a press report of the prosecution of one Mr. Smith for jumping from a moving train on the Dublin to Kingstown [now Dún Laoghaire] line:

> at Kingstown Station some itinerant musicians got into the carriage, and Smith had an objection to travel with them. To get rid of the musicians' company Smith attempted to leave the carriage. Mr. Swifte [prosecuting] said the conduct of the musicians could not be so bad that Smith could not suffer on from Kingstown to Sandycove. The Great Southern and Western Railway County have prosecuted some itinerant musicians for traveling in their carriages. Mr. Byrne [defence] pointed out that 'the Dublin and south Eastern Ccunty seemed to facilitate them. On Sundays one could not travel on the Kingstown line without having a tambourine thumping on one side of him and a bagpipes screeching on the other' (laughter) [*Evening Herald* 1907 0225]

AMUSING THE CROWD.
Tambourine Player and Mate Charged in Court.

Before Mr. Hannon, in the Dublin District Court to-day, Frank Jones and John Delaney, both of Chancery Lane, and described as of "no business," were charged by Guard Forde, 147B, with obstructing, on Saturday afternoon, the thoroughfare at Johnson's Place, near Mercer's Hospital, where Jones was engaged in playing a tambourine and Delaney in grinding a barrel organ. Their performances attracted a large crowd at the place.

The Guard stated that he found the carriage way blocked up. He accosted the defendants and asked them to move on, but they took no notice of what he said with regard to the obstruction of the traffic. They had with them
A DANCNG BOARD
which they utilised also for the amusement of the crowd. There had been complaints made with regard to the annoyance created close to the hospital.

The case against Jones was adjourned generally, and Delaney was discharged on his undertaking not to engage in such performances in future.

Evening Herald 1930 0609 1

The tambourine in folklore

The tambourine was put on the record in *Schools' Collection* accounts for the years around 1900 in twelve counties: Cavan, Clare, Kerry, Kilkenny, Leitrim, Limerick, Longford, Meath, Waterford, Westmeath, Wexford and Wicklow. The accounts are predominantly about making the tambourine for the Wren:

Cavan, *Freeduff:* … St Stephen's Day is a most delightful feast of the year. All the young folk and grown-ups both boys and girls in this district travel around on that day … most of them do have a lot of musical instruments, a mouth organ, a fiddle, a flute, a tambourine … [35]

Limerick, *Knockaderry:* … Long ago when the marriage ceremony was over … a batch of strawboys, sometimes girls, was sure to come … They were very much like the wren-boys. They wore cotton suits, tall hats decorated with feathers and also green and white sashes across their shoulders. They took with them violins, melodions, drums and tambourine and had great sport dancing … [36]

Longford, *Rathmore:* … the Wren Boys day. Men and boys go around in small bands about seven or eight in each. The usual musical instruments they used are fiddles, mouth-organs, melodeons, flutes or tin whistles. The leader also plays a tambourine.[37]

Westmeath, *Delvin:* It is mostly boys that go around with the wren … They usually have some musical instruments which are very often a mouth organ and a tambourine … One of the boys plays the music and the rest dance … [38]

Rattle or thump?

The tambourine has prevailed, but in different forms. The more robust, substantial one which was used by the British army bands and the American

▼ American minstrel tambourine

▲ American minstrel tabourine [*Courtesy Mark Weems*]

minstrel troupes is similar to that used on the Wren, but the small, leg-struck, rattle & shake version seems to had a currency too, suggested by a report on an 1893 concert in Cork in which 'the chorus "Seguidilla" – accompanied on the tambourine by Miss T. Taylor … was rendered in a careful manner'.[39] The same is likely the case for reports of school music too, for instance in Kerry at a 'Grand concert at the Presentation Convent, Killarney' where 'twenty youngsters who took part in it beat time on tambourines and triangles';[40] and in Monaghan, where a 1901 children's New Year festival concert for Ballyalbany Presbyterian Church had 'drum and tambourine accompaniment – by the little children'.[41] Such variety concerts were commonplace in the USA, Canada and Australia too from the early 1800s, where the tambourine was already played along with fiddles for dancing (see p. 110). By the mid-twentieth century schools were still using tambourines, seen in Drogheda in 1952 as part of 'a children's band … with many instruments including drums, tamborines, castinets, cymbals, triangles, etcetera',[42] so too at Ballina Feis, 1954 where were heard 'contrasting sounds of tamborines, cymbals and triangles'.[43] In Ireland it was still being reported as late as 1959, where, unconnected with the play *Sive*, familiarity with the the rattle-type tambourine is implied in such reports as one on a centenary concert celebration for the St Louis order of nuns held in Buncrana, County Donegal; this had a percussion band which included 'Tambourines: Lucy Barry, Teresa Byrne, Assumpta Doherty, Laurence McMorrow'.[44] In Kerry too that commercial tambourine was still being used in school bands in 1955, judging from photos of the Listowel Feis that year (p. 14) and of Féile Castleisland in 1965 (p. 108).

Tambourine sizes

One can only speculate as to the form of tambourine that was used in reported historic events, and on the manner of its being played, but jingles were certainly a key component. Going by sketches made in the early minstrel era, and from photographs later, it can be seen that the tambourine could be anything from *c.* 30 cm diameter up to the size of today's larger bodhráns. In earlier decades the instrument had been popular enough in English society to have music parts written for it, and, judging by pricing, it was made in different sizes. Typically it had a taut membrane which was struck, there was a thumb-hole for gripping, often a 'spinner' device for tricks, and the rim held numerous pairs of jingles which were activated by shaking, and by striking off the body. From art images it can be seen that tambourines were often of the larger size, more like the Italian tamburello, sometimes without, but generally with, jingles. But where 'tambourine' is mentioned in advertising and news reports, there is no indication of the size or the nature of the instrument. Looking at eighteenth and nineteenth-century images and paintings, the 'parlour' type of tambourine was larger, with a shallow rim. Military tambourines were bigger again, with a deeper rim, designed for making a carrying sound, a principle which, as said, is likely to have influenced Munster bodhráns.

American musician Mark Weems, who has researched this topic, says that minstrel tambourines were large in the early days, up to the 1870s, and made with skin, the objective being to get a strong, audible beat, with an emphasis on a solid, bass sound. Fifteen- and twenty-inch diameters (38 and 51 cm) were common in the early years, but since the high point of the fashion was before press use of photography there is little accurate visual record. No such tambourines are held by Irish museums, but those preserved in the USA and Europe are substantial instruments. Early-minstrel authority Robert Winans has written that 'the minstrel tambourine, being larger than the modern tambourine and having fewer rattles, was more a drum than a rattle'.[15] This type of instrument would have been a role model for some of the Irish tambourines, being similar to, if not derived from, the aforementioned Italianate one.

As regards playing style, there is no particular connection between west Africa and tambourines or bones, and there is no book describing a specific minstrel tambourine technique, so standard techniques as transmitted by the Italian street performers and as shown in the early tamborine tutors were most likely the stylistic starting point for minstrels. Some of these ways of playing are indeed referred to by older tambourine players in Ireland, with Peter Horan recalling that his mother used a 'thumb roll', a friction-controlled effect in which the thumb is used to 'bounce rapidly along the skin causing a series of continuous beats like a drum roll'.[16]

Copying the tambourine

The obvious use of the tambourine by the rural, poorer people, which is indicated in several of the newspaper reports, does leave it open as to whether or not there already had been a unique Irish frame drum, which would, naturally, be given the technically-proper name 'tambourine' in press coverage. But it is perfectly obvious too that, once having seen the commercial tambourine, and driven by the thrill of its effect, someone with appropriate skill and tools would make a tambourine copy. This would have been based on the examples seen, and on the local availability and sizes of goat-skins as used for the original device bodhráns, and would have used discarded rims of such as wool wheels and riddles. It would also have been simple to move from tucked-in, duller skins on the original device bodhráns to tensioned, tacked-on ones. One such craft genius from near Mallow, County Cork was Johnny Roche (c. 1800-80), a self-taught carpenter, blacksmith, miller and mason. He had been in America before the Great Famine, but returned home and set up a mill in 1870, completing an architecturally-quirky workshop near Doneraile which was nicknamed 'Castle Curious'. Among his diverse skills were dentistry, tailoring, baking, gardening, cobbling, tool-making, sculpting, wood-carving, and clock repair. His premises also hosted dancing, and he played fiddle and fife and sang. He made everything he used, including his bicycle, as well as 'violins, fifes, bagpipes, clarionettes, drums, tambourines ... and repaired all the musical instruments of the local musicians'.[17] Occasional press and other reports show that similar craft-oriented entrepreneurs in other areas would have also copied and made music instruments, including tambourines. But whether locally made or bought from the music trade, the newspaper reports show that tambourines were very common in Ireland right through the Gaelic Revival in the prelude to revolutionary change in the later nineteenth century.

▲ *The Broken Tambourine* [*Illustrated London News* 1873 0510 437]

The worn tambourine

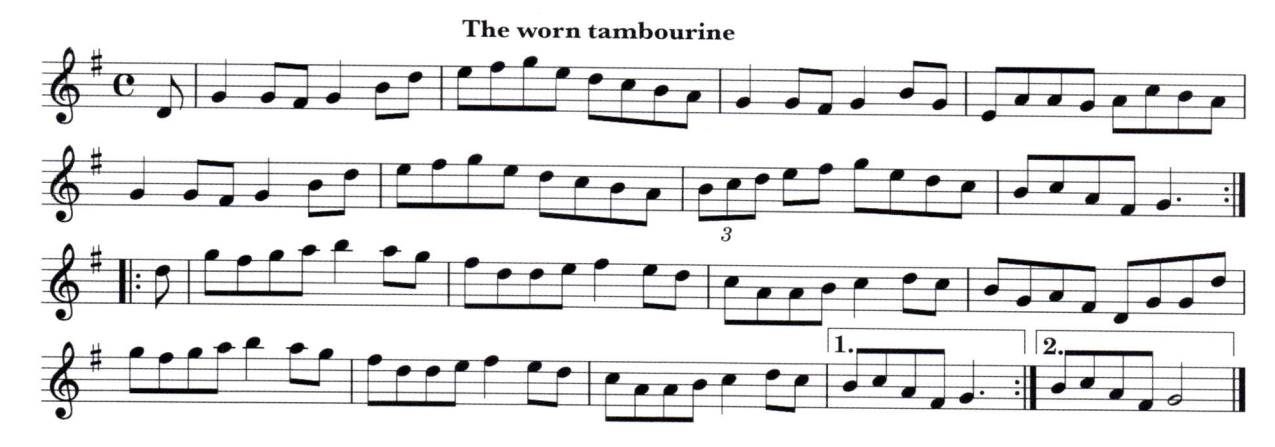

▲ 'The worn tambourine', a reel by Padraic Ganly, County Westmeath, published in his book of compositions in 1918 (see also p. 205)
[*Thanks to Fintan Farrell, and to Maeve Gebruers at the ITMA*]

Johnnie Lennon, a Longford man from Kilmahon townland, writing to an Irish priest in San Diego in 1949, speaks too of the skin being broken on his 'darling tambourine', this suggesting it was an instrument he often played, especially on the Wren. He was also a concert flute and trump player, and speaks of making music while in hospital with a Galway nurse would 'be whistling, lilting or singing'. Music is indicated as central to local life in his local Killoe parish, and the tambourine was not uncommon, as he says in a later letter: 'I have a bran new tambourine that was Tommy Dillon's that you beat on the evening you were here. It was busted the Wren Boy's night'.[48] Skins were scarce, but he managed to reskin it himself after recovering a dead goat that had been dumped a bog-hole.[49] Kilmahon is not far from the home area of John Reynolds (see p. 247), who played tambourine with Tom Morrison; this suggests a familiarity with tambourine playing in west Leinster/east Connacht from the late 1800s onwards.

NOTES TO CHAPTER 7

[1] *Carlow Morning Post* 1830 0830.
[2] *Freeman's Journal* 1834 0415.
[3] Ibid., 1836 0526 1.
[4] Ryan 1895, 114–15.
[5] *Waterford News and Star* 1862 0411 3.
[6] *Freeman's Journal* 1829 0905.
[7] *Nenagh Guardian* 1865 0617 4.
[8] *Ballinrobe Chronicle* 1892 0528 2.
[9] *Cork Examiner* 1895 0330 10.
[10] *Evening Herald* 1892 0726 2; *Freeman's Journal* 1899 1014 4.
[11] *Westmeath Examiner* 1893 1104 2.
[12] *Belfast News Letter* 1859 0125.
[13] *Freeman's Journal* 1828 0911.
[14] *Connaught Telegraph* 1865 0712 4.
[15] *Cork Examiner* 1891 0714 2.
[16] *Northern Standard* 1901 0112 3.

[17] *Punch*, 0101 146.
[18] *Cork Examiner* 1892 1107 5.
[19] *Evening Herald* 1893 0213.
[20] *Cork Examiner* 1894 1001 4.
[21] *Belfast News Letter* 1895 0930 5.
[22] *Evening Echo* 1896 0926 2.
[23] *Wicklow Newsletter* 1900 0224 4.
[24] *Evening Herald* 1895 0116 3.
[25] *Freeman's Journal* 1899 1014 4.
[26] *Munster Express* 1863 0530 8.
[27] *Belfast News Letter* 1895 0608 3.
[28] *Irish Press* 1948 1218 11.
[29] *Meath Chronicle* 1934 1215 7.
[30] *Westmeath Independent* 1916 1209.
[31] *Northern Standard* 1900 0120 4.
[32] *Cork Examiner* 1853 1221 2.
[33] *Skibbereen Eagle* 1905 0311 4.

[34] *Evening Herald* 1892 0409 4.
[35] Ibid., 0987, 114.
[36] Ibid., 0489, 199.
[37] Ibid., 0746, 596.
[38] Ibid., 0723, 278.
[39] *Cork Examiner* 1893 1223 8.
[40] *Killarney Echo and South Kerry Chronicle* 1901 0706 2.
[41] *Northern Standard* 1901 0112 4.
[42] *Drogheda Independent* 1952 1213 2.
[43] *Ballina Herald* 1954 0710 1.
[44] *Donegal Democrat* 1959 0501.
[45] Winans 1984, 73.
[46] Kjeldsen 2000, 74-5.
[47] J.W.B. 1904, 164.
[48] Devaney 1981, 126
[49] Ibid., 326

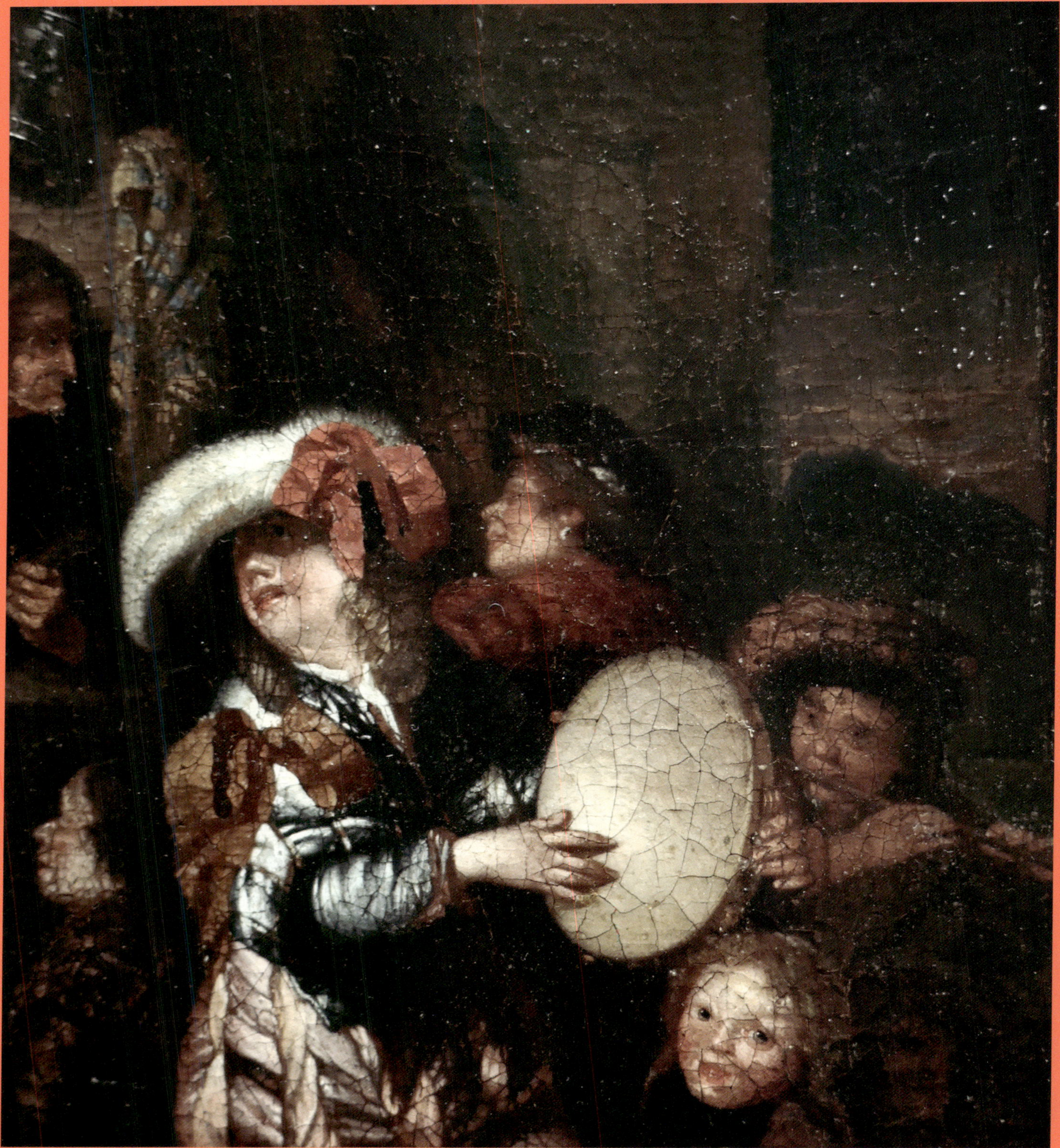

CHAPTER 8

SEEING IS BELIEVING: PRESENCE AND ABSENCE

Words alone cannot verify the existence of something in the past, but if they are backed by images a strong case is made.[1] The press did not carry photographs until the 1900s, so early reporting does not generally include images of what it describes, and when illustration began to be used, it was initially sketches and etchings. Those, and fine-art paintings, have been the standard visual record of aspects of music culture – 'more precise and richer than literature'.[2] This chapter observes the images, and notes too the absence of mention of, or images of, indigenous drums in Irish literature and in writing about Ireland.

The circumstances in which instruments are shown cannot, however, always be taken at face value, for as musician and writer Barra Boydell says:

> Musicians are portrayed in paintings as objects of interest, but often too as an exotic 'Other' for the well-to-do Irish or English art public … perhaps to be pitied … but observed at a safe distance from the comforts of the Victorian drawing room[3]

Many late-1800s images of music in Irish rural settings, he says, contain 'clichés of Irish peasant life',[4] and ignore the horror of the Famine period which had just preceded them. They tend to feature that which is more intricate, such as the Irish pipes, and it is of course possible that they may well have ignored – or not have observed at all – the use of any drum. Yet these are the only pictorial record of what was, and therefore are precious indications of the performers, as well as of the instruments that we had and how they were played, if not, generally, of the circumstances of performance. Boydell warns of the need for care in interpretation, that there is a need to establish 'the degree to which it [a particular image] can be accepted as a model rather than being dismissed as the product of inadequate observation or artistic licence'.[5] This is a general view of art which is quite separate from assessment of the actual quality or nature of the painter's talent. John Berger held that 'the way we see things is affected by what we know … or believe',[6] something which may have affected the images that we have. The winnowing bodhrán was depicted earliest – and more often – and displaying it was indeed a popular trope among nineteenth-century European painters, as seen in Chapter 5.

◂ Tambourine and flute players by Gerard Hoet (1658–1733), Holland. This may be the earliest European painting of a tambourine being played along with a flute

BEATING TIME. THE STORY OF THE IRISH BODHRÁN

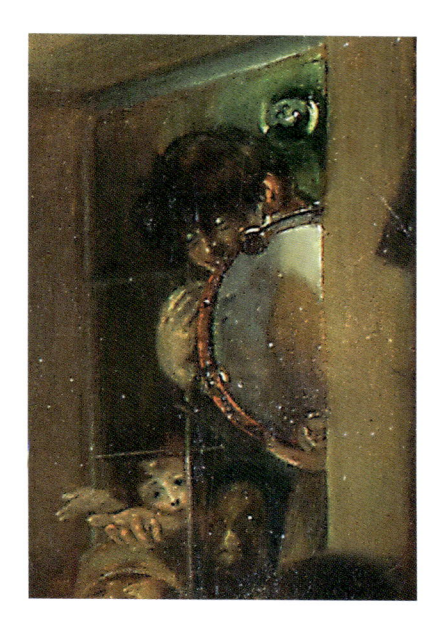

Snap Apple Night by Daniel Maclise, musicians and dancers, 1832 [*Photo James Carney*]

The first tambourine, 1832?
The earliest stand-alone image of a frame drum being played in an Irish recreational context is from 1833, in Cork artist Daniel Maclise's painting *Snap Apple Night*. His first substantial work, this was based on his attendance at an 1832 Hallowe'en party to which he had been invited by antiquarian Fr Matthew Horgan in Blarney, County Cork, an event at which he depicts musicians playing on pipes, flute, fiddle and a hand-struck tambourine. This is not only the earliest picture showing a seated group playing for dancers, but also of the use of a tambourine with music, and indeed of the tambourine in an Irish context at all. The image is clear, a boy playing a tambourine with the open fingers of his right hand, while gripping the drum on the bottom of the rim with his left, a perfect depiction indeed. Yet a painted image is not a photograph. Unusually, this event had been planned, and was well documented at the time, and the names and faces of several of the attendees are known.[7] But, necessarily, the components of the finished work were originally sketched by the artist separately, in groups, and afterwards reassembled in his studio to construct the final tableau.[8] Maclise was well familiar with rural mannerisms, and had already done drawings of scenes with people, one of which, a couple of years previously, was of a piper and dancers at a fair in Carrigaline, County Cork.[9] But, apropos what Febo Guzzi says with regard to representations of the Italian tamburello,[10] there is room for some doubt about the nature of the instruments that were actually being played in *Snap Apple Night*. This is suggested by the fact that the music is being led by a somewhat derelict-looking, sightless piper who is portrayed performing on a quite fabulous-looking set of silver-mounted union pipes rather than a more simple, plain wood or brass-adorned model as seen in paintings of men of his social class a decade later. The flute does not raise any question, as it is a short model, like a band-flute, perhaps pitched in B flat or C, which would have been common with the military at the time, and would work with pipes which at that time were pitched lower than today's D standard.

Interpretation of *Snap Apple Night*
The painting has been available from Chinese hand-painting copying houses for a number of years, and some of the poor-quality reproductions may not help interpretation. But, from a privileged examination of the original, it can be said without doubt that a quality tambourine is shown being played in it. However, as has been said about the piper, the wild demeanour of the fiddler and flute player raises the possibility that the tambourine boy might not have had such a well-presented item as a commercial tambourine. This proposition is supported also by the awareness that in Kilkenny and Kerry at that time there are reports of people improvising the tambourine on bodhrán skin trays, a practice which involves no cost, and which continued in Sligo up to the 1930s.[11] Also, considering that the actual tambourine is not likely to have been popularly known outside of Irish cities until a decade or so later than the painting, it is very possibly the case that on the night concerned the lad was indeed playing just on a locally-made, actual, bodhrán, the skin tray or wecht, a ubiquitous agricultural and household utensil. But, taking the licence of a professional painter, the artist gave him a perfect jingle-mounted tambourine, of which he would have had direct experience

on stages and streets where he lived and worked in London. It does seem unlikely that such a precise instrument with brass jingles as depicted would have been available in such otherwise poor surroundings. Considering that the painter, Daniel Maclise, was Cork-born, proud of his Irishness[12] and interested in antiquarianism, there is at least the question that, out of a sense of dignifying the gathering, if not with regard to showing the painting at the Royal Academy exhibition in London the following year,[13] he would feel it appropriate to glamorise the occasion. European art of the period has hundreds of fabulous paintings of tambourine players, all with substantial, fine instruments, so a degree of competition and precedent could easily have guided the artist into 'gilding the lily'. It is worth considering too that even if the lad in *Snap Apple Night* did have an actual local copy of a tambourine, it would probably have been smaller, would not have had brass jingles, and would have looked quite decrepit – like those used for the Wren. So, it is possible that in reality he may not have been holding a tambourine, but a bodhrán being played as a tambourine would be. Yet, of course, it still could have been the case that an actual tambourine was being used on that night, for the date makes that entirely possible, since the instrument had been known about on city theatre stages since the later 1700s, and one could have been borrowed from some local gentry who had travelled, loaned by them for what was a well-planned event. In the same painting, an actual sieve, riddle or bodhrán can be seen hanging high up in the rafters. But whether or not the lad is playing a tambourine or bodhrán is not as important as the fact that this is the earliest depiction of a frame drum played with music in Munster.

A Shebeen in Listowel, *c*. 1842
Art historian Claudia Kinmonth is of the opinion that professional artists could create or embellish at will. One of them, Erskine Nichol (who never depicted a tambourine player), had a studio full of props, including instruments, furniture and garments, which he used in setting up period scenes. Kinmonth also holds that, on the other hand, the amateur artist was much more likely to paint things as they actually were, and that may be the case for the next depiction of a frame drum in use in Ireland, an actual tambourine. It comes a decade after Maclise, in a painting by Bridget Maria Fitzgerald titled *A Local Squire Being Entertained in a Sheebeen in Listowel*. It shows two oddly-dressed males – possibly a father and son, or brothers – wearing military or fancy dress, one with a flute, the other playing, right-handed, a tambourine with jingles, the drum held up in the Italian or Arabic fashion; there is no glamorisation. No information is available on the scene, but it seems a reasonable portrayal of a big-house group taking their ease in a rural drinking emporium. A pig munches contentedly at a trough, some women by the fire look on politely, and hanging on the chimney breast is a domestic or agricultural sieve, wight or winnowing bodhrán. Art historian Claudia Kinmonth suggests that the dress and demeanour of the performers could indicate pantomime rather than indigenous music, as does the absence of anyone dancing. Nicholas Carolan, however, sees them as itinerant musicians, in which case the picture would indicate the practice of playing tambourine along with flute in sit-down, recital fashion, something which would mark the water-colour as a significant historical document. But regardless, here is

▲ Eccentric costume and hand-struck tambourine in *A Local Squire Being Entertained in a Sheebeen in Listowel*, by Bridget Maria Fitzgerald c. 1842 [*Courtesy J. Anthony Gaughan (from his book Listowel and Its Vicinity) and Loretto Dalton*]

an actual tambourine being played with a flute, for all the world in a similar fashion to many bodhrán and flute duets today. It does not seem likely that they would have been Wren-boys or mummers, not least on account of the absence of masks and of other lads and dancing. Terminology is everything too, and it is a matter of accuracy that the drum in this painting – as with that in the Maclise – should be described as it is depicted in its period, a tambourine, not as a bodhrán with jingles.[14] It is possible therefore that this painting is the earliest genuine sight of a tambourine in Irish art, and it is in Munster, in County Kerry, in the vicinity of Listowel. The image accords with Colm Murphy's reporting that one route for tambourines into Ireland has been speculated as being via big-house gentry, and this occasion (and possibly the Maclise event too) may well be a depiction of an instance of just that. Gentry would have had sight of tambourines on stage, and access to them through music shops in the cities, and via military experience, if not also on continental travels. The tambourine had been a fashionable and exotic instrument in music education of young, upper-class women in the decades before this, so it would not have been uncommon in their circles. And even though the painting may not be indicative of typical local practice – the players do not appear to be of the poorer classes and there is an attentive audience – such a happening would have had knock-on influence in its time in acquainting locals with the tambourine.

The Vinegar Hill tambourine, 1798 or 1854?
Historically, the next appearance of the frame drum-type is also an image of an actual tambourine, this one purporting to represent the year 1798. The drawing is by George Cruikshank, a highly-regarded illustrator, the best-known of his profession in the mid 1800s. Titled 'Camp on Vinegar Hill', this engraving was printed in Maxwell's 1854 *History of the Irish Rebellion in 1798*. It depicts a seated uilleann piper with a fiddler, accompanied by a woman playing on a tambourine replete with jingles, held high, using her fingers; this is supposed to be in an Irish camp in the course of the United Irish rebellion at Enniscorthy, County Wexford.[15] Maxwell, the author, was a military writer hostile to Ireland, and was only six at the time of the rebellion, so he was obviously working on second-hand information to begin with. And since he was dead before Cruikshank made the illustrations based on his text, he could not have been advising the artist. In any case, Maxwell's book does not make any reference to such music proper being played at Vinegar Hill in 1798, but it does say:

> Others were drinking, cursing, and swearing; many of them were playing on various musical instruments, which they had acquired by plunder in the adjacent Protestant houses, the whole producing a most disagreeable and barbarous dissonance[16]

Yet in the given image the players' demeanours are those of competent, if not professional, musicians, certainly not 'barbarous'. And since this does not tally with the idea of looters simply banging on pilfered instruments, it suggests that the artist, then at the height of his career, was merely inventively working from supposition, based on his considerable experience of observation of, and illustrative depiction of, people of all classes and occupations, including music-makers. He would have known of the likelihood that a tambourine would be among the luxury items in a wealthy big house,

▲ George Cruikshank's *Camp on Vinegar Hill*, published 1854 [*Maxwell 1854, 99*]

the property of a daughter for whom it was a fashionable music instrument at that time, and that this could have been looted by the insurgents. By 1850 the instrument was a common trope in European visual art as well as being a popular-music import in England, and would have been known through the military even in rural Ireland, so it would not be an unreasonable guess for Cruikshank. There is also the chance that the tambourine could have been taken from a British army bandsman (as described in Chapter 5). But in the absence of any supporting information, at best the illustration could mean that such a commercial tambourine was in the possession of either a British military bandsman or an Anglo-Irish family in Wexford in 1798 and had been pilfered by the United Irishmen. But, all things considered, the image is not a sighting of an indigenous Irish drum.

Tambourines in European art
The tambourine (or tamburello – which could be similar in size to today's bodhrán) was a common trope in nineteenth-century European artworks as a consequence of music fashion. In most of the images it is being held or played by women, their demeanour as depicted suggesting one or more of passivity, poverty or promiscuity, the portrayals highly conditioned by the male conventions of their era, the woman as object, the tambourine

a prop and a metaphor – the women who are painted invariably 'watch themselves being looked at'.[17] As already stated in Chapter 2, there has been an historical link between women, tambourines and sexuality in the early deployment of the instrument. Many of the art images also evidence this, as well as poverty and busking by children. And from the later 1600s onwards be-jingled frame drums feature in European paintings and illustrations, conveying a romantic view of music-making on the streets, but rendering visible the instruments of the times. Claude's 1664 'Figure Group with Dancing Girl' shows a tambourine with a bagpipe, while other images inform us about a huge variety of tambourine sizes, forms and contexts. The dating of the paintings shows clearly however that tambourines were both on the streets and in higher society during the eighteenth and early nineteenth centuries, the strongest indication that the drum had spread rapidly and socially-diversely before the advent of the minstrels. In Ireland, however, apart from Maclise there are no professional images, but the *Illustrated London News*, which had occasional fiddle, pipes and dancing graphics, carried one engraving in 1873 (see p. 118).

▲ Tambour D'après Justin Sanson – *Le Joueur de Tambourin*, 1865 [*Image courtesy invaluable.com*]

◄ Tambourine player – Mirjam Anselm Feuerbach, 1862 [*Image courtesy invaluable.com*]

▶ Eighteenth–nineteenth-century paintings [*Images from invaluable.com*]

8 SEEING IS BELIEVING: PRESENCE AND ABSENCE

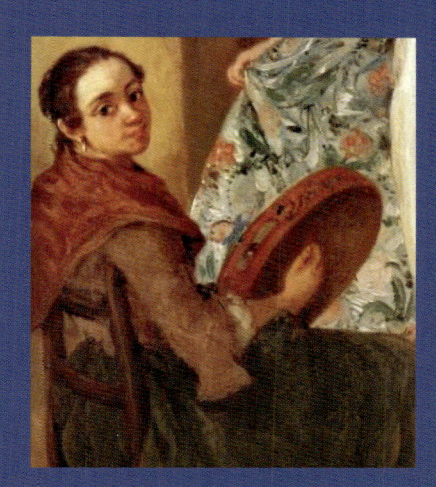

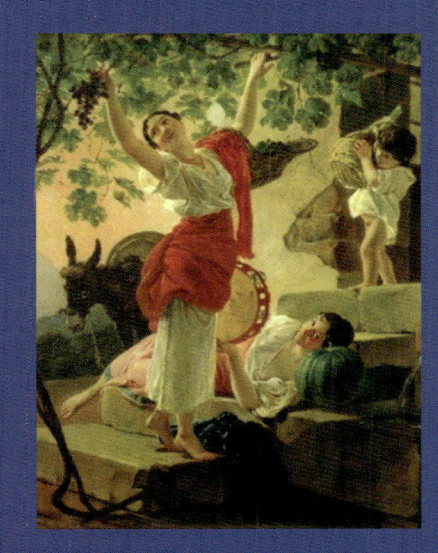

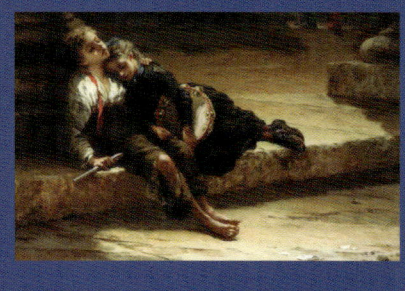

129

▲ Young Wrenboys at Athea, County Limerick, 1947 [*Caoimhín Ó Danachair, National Folklore Collection*]

Tambourines in Irish photographs
Mid-1900s photos show the tambourine being played in Europe as a rhythm for a dancing bear, a now-outlawed practice which was reported also in Ireland in 1899 (p. 111). There are no published photographs of bodhráns as such being played prior to the late 1940s. But there are early photos of the frame drum by Caoimhín Ó Danachair, from 1946, ´47 and ´55, showing the drums as used on the Wren by young boys. Though he calls the instrument 'bodhrán' in the later images, these are tambourine copies, and appear to have been called 'tambourine', most of them with jingles. In 1959, the photo of John B. Keane's *Sive* tambourine player (p. 156) shows a similar drum, but larger in diameter, and also with jingles. One remarkable sequence of photos taken by Padraig and Joan Kennelly in the late 1950s shows women dancing on a dance platform in Foley's Glen, near Tralee, County Kerry. A 'set-up' scene perhaps, possibly for visitors, but three bodhráns

▲ Tambourines with mouth organ being played for a platform dance at Foley's Glen, Tralee, 1957 [*Kennelly Archive*]

are present, along with a harmonica. This suggests that tambourines being played in dance-music contexts, though not common, was nevertheless being done, though not so widely until after the 1950s when it was seen more often – in County Clare in particular.

Absence – or out of sight?

There is a definite absence of commentary on a frame drum in rural Ireland in the centuries prior to the 1800s, no mention at all for social gatherings in rural Ireland. This can be interpreted as showing that there was no drum culture, but it could also be that it was just not noticed. Or else it was the case that rudimentary percussion had survived from pre-Christianity but by the 1800s was indulged in only by the lower social classes, and so was not approved by higher society or considered worthy of mention. Indeed, drums of any kind were not held in high esteem for aesthetically-oriented music-making in Ireland even by 1873, if W.K. Sullivan's introduction to Eugene O'Curry's lectures is anything to go by:

> The drum, which was not at all used by the ancient Irish, has unfortunately become the principal instrument of our popular bands. If the worthy Sebastian Virdung were to hear a temperance or trade band of our day, he

would be justified in his opinion that if beating and thumping make music, then coopers are musicians when they make barrels, and confirmed in his belief that the drum was invented and first made by the devil[18]

This makes it difficult to interpret the absence of drums in commentaries about life prior to the early 1800s. But that, including no mention in travellers' letters, may be no more than a matter of seasonality: if it was used exclusively on the Wren at mid-winter, well out of a tourist season, then it could have been missed by writers. But, to be considered as well is that the description of the Wren by the Halls in 1842 (p. 135) mentions no music at all, let alone any drum.[19] The absence of evidence of drums in accounts of major historical sites of socialisation and in commentary on culture and entertainment will now be looked at.

Music at ancient fairs
One would expect to find written mention of a drum if it had been part of the music-making which was common at fairs and patterns (patron saint's day revelry), especially those that came to be immortalised in song, but this is not the case. The oldest of such events which has been documented was the Fair of Carman held in County Kildare, a lengthy 1100s verse on which mentions music – the stringed timpan, along with harp, trumpet, horns and pipes, but no percussion[20] (see p. 31). Fairs on a European model, involving all sorts of commercial and recreational activities and 'letting go' over a period of eight days, might reasonably be hoped to provide some hard evidence of use of drums. Such events began in England after the Norman conquest in the 1200s, and others in colonial Ireland followed.

Donnybrook Fair 1200s–1855
Commissioned by the English monarch, and to be held in Dublin spread over fifteen days, this became the most important livestock and produce market in Ireland. It traded every kind of commodity including foodstuffs, fabrics and gold, becoming one of the great historical calendar events from c. 1215 until it was wound up because of social excesses in 1855.[21] It is celebrated in a lengthy verse which describes trades:

> There are carvers and gilders and all sorts of builders
> With soldiers from barracks and sailors from ships
> Entertainment is covered too:
> With pipers and fiddlers and dandies and diddlers
> All set in the humours of Donnybrook Fair

In this, the use of music implies dancing and the idea of the attractiveness of rhythm,[22] but there is no mention of drums in earlier times, though some curious lines have been suggested to imply improvised drumming by young women who would have been accustomed to winnowing:

> There's tinkers and nailers and beggars and tailors
> And singers of ballads and girls of the sieve[23]

However, 'sieve' most likely alludes to fortune-telling or the occult, and there is no report of women as music-makers elsewhere, let alone as drummers. But by 1828 the tambourine is mentioned at Donnybrook:

> Déanfad "tambuirín" (2) an cláirseac,
> An "French Horn" agus "clarionet,"
> An "Fife," an fliút, an "Flageolet,"
> An beirblín agus an bóg (3).

▲ Lines from Antaine Raiftearaí's poem 'Seághan Ó Branáin', in *Abhráin agus Dánta an Reachtabhraigh*, collected by Dubhglas de h-Íde, published by Foillseacháin Rialtais, Dublin, 1933

> mountain nymphs, with nimble feet merrily trippd it on the boarded platform, to some enlivening Irish jig, or mirth moving planxty, from the leathren lungs of the favourite bagpipe. Fiddles and flutes, tamborines and triangles, made the welkin ring with their jarrings and jinglings [*Freeman's Journal* 1828 0903 3]

This is the earliest reference to a 'tambourine' among the plain people in a social setting.

The sports of Easter Monday, Belfast, 1818

Another such event was an Easter Monday fair at Cave Hill near Belfast, thought to have begun in the 1760s, but likely to be pre-Christian. This too was immortalised in an epic, 1818 poem, by William Read, which details

> the fiddles flourish, and the bagpipe's grunting encouraged dancers to Hibernia's planxties [and] Caledonia's reels

> Some lightly springing, seem to leap on air / Some beat the earth with iron-studded heels

Writing about the event, Francis Joseph Bigger said:

> Dancing was the favourite pastime, reels, jigs, hornpipes, accompanied by fiddles, pipes and flutes[24]

Drums are not mentioned although, at that time, since Belfast's population was well familiar with military drums, mention of them may have seemed unnecessary.

Antaine Raiftearaí (1779–1835)

The tambourine was listed by this famous blind County Mayo poet and musician in a praise-poem which concerned the kinds of music instruments (as well as agricultural, domestic and industrial equipment) which a particular craftsman, Seán Ó Braonáin of Craughwell, County Galway supposedly could repair:

> Tamboureen is cláirseach / French horn agus clarinet
> an fife, an flute, and flageolet / An fhidil agus an bow

▼ Antaine Raiftearaí, from the preface to de h-Íde's book

Among the items he documents are the Irish pipes, all elements, including the 'regulators is na heochracha', as well as 'hautboy´s an spinet … dulcimer´s pianó'. Because nothing was a problem to the artisan, it becomes clear that the poet was being grandiose with his knowledge of contemporary music practices rather than describing common local instruments.[25] As press reports show, the tambourine was of course in Ireland at that time, and would have been known to those who had seen European instruments.

▲ Barndance illustration from William Carleton's 1844 *Traits and Stories of the Irish Peasantry* [1990 edition, Vol. 1. Buckinghamshire: Colin Smythe]

The Halls, *c.* 1840

These writers gave considerable detail on some social occasions of music, but they do not indicate any seasonal music, and no bodhráns or tambourines, not even in their description of the Biddy day, or the St Stephen's Day Wren; indeed their Wren engraving has no instrument of any kind. That does not of course mean that it was not used in those events, or for music, because the Halls, being of polite society, may well have missed – or avoided – aspects of the exuberant trampings of wild teenage boys and fun-loving adults:

> The national customs that prevail among the people of Cork are common to other parts of Ireland, with one exception … certainly to the southern districts of Ireland. For some weeks preceding Christmas, crowds of village boys may be seen peering into hedges, in search of the tiny wren … when one is discovered, the whole assemble and give eager chase to, until they have killed the little bird … the utmost excitement prevails; shouting, screeching, and rushing … From bush to bush, from hedge to hedge, is the wren pursued until bagged … On the anniversary of St Stephen (the 26th of December) the enigma is explained. Attached to a huge holly-bush, elevated on a pole, the bodies of several little wrens are borne about … by a troop of boys, among whom may be usually found 'children of a larger growth' shouting and roaring as they proceed along, and every now and then stopping before some popular house singing 'the wren boys' song … contributions are levied in many quarters, and the evening is, or rather was, occupied in drinking the sum total … This is, we believe, the only Christmas gambol remaining in Ireland of the many, that in the middle ages were so numerous[26]

William Carleton, 1843

Literature does not mention tambourines in widespread use among the plain people. For instance, one prolific writer, William Carleton, in his various books often has occasion to describe religious and secular social occasions where music is being played for dancing, but there is no mention of percussion or tambourines. Had drums been present, one would expect him to have mentioned that. For instance, in 1843: 'The dacentest of us went into the house for a while, taking the fiddler with us, and the rest, with the piper, staid on the green to dance[27]… Fiddlers, and pipers, and harpers, in short, all kinds of music and musicianers, played in shoals[28]… At such places [a saint's "pattern" day] it is quite usual to see young men and young women with all the marks of penitence and contrition strongly impressed upon their faces; whilst again, after an hour or two, the same individuals may be found in a tent dancing with ecstatic vehemence to the music of the bagpipe or fiddle'.[29] In this book too is an account of another saint's 'pattern' day, but, again, with only melody and dancing in focus: 'Every tent had a fiddler or a piper; many two or three …. the dancing, shouting, singing, courting, drinking, and fighting, formed one wild uproar of noise, that was perfectly astounding … fiddles were playing, pipes were squeaking … The ballad-singer had his own mob … '.[30] In the second volume, however, in the illustration for Phelim O'Toole's courtship, a device bodhrán or sieve can be seen hanging from the ceiling.

◀ Bodhrán, sieve or wecht hanging in a barn [*Illustration from William Carleton, 1844, 188*]

J.G. Kohl, 1843
Similarly, also published in 1843/4, the German travel writer, Johann Georg Kohl, though describing much social activity amid which was song and music, does not note any drum in his account of Kilkenny:

> On these and similar occasions of popular excitement in Ireland … In every corner of the great main street, which otherwise presented nothing very remarkable … bagpipes were snuffling, violins squeaking, melancholy flutes blowing, and ragged Paddies dancing; in a word, with the universal revelry was mingled a mass of misfortune, misery, and mourning, such as in any other country can very seldom be seen united[31]

'Aonach Bhearna na Gaoithe' / The Fair of Windgap, *c.* 1876
Another major such fair, that at Windgap, in County Kilkenny, also has a graphic song describing its happenings, but, again, no mention is made of a drum – only melody is indicated. The lyricist was Tomás Ó Modhrain, a singer who in later life accompanied himself on the original bodhrán (p. 144). The lyric's fifteen verses detail trades, foodstuffs and produce, eating and drinking, including music-making:

> Ceólta neuta, spórt, a's sgléip-suilt / *Delightful music, sport and revelry*
> An trumpa-béil ba bhinne leat é / *The Jews' harp, you'd think it sweet*
> Le Barra do mhéir a luigheadh air / *When touched by the tip of your finger*
> Bhí fliutín do'n leanbh ann … / *A flute for the child* …[32]

▲ Francis O'Neill sculpture at Tralibane, County Cork, by Jeanne Rynhart, 2000 [*EDI*]

The music alluded to is melody, with no sight of a drum, but there is also no mention of dancing, which must certainly have been going on. The tambourine was known in Ireland at that time, but since the songwriter himself played on it – indeed likely to accompany his own singing of this song – modesty may have prevailed, he himself must not have regarded it as significant enough to immortalise in the lyric. This suggests that he may have been a 'one-off' as regards his playing on the device bodhrán while singing.

Francis O'Neill, 1903–22

All that considered, perhaps it is no surprise either that the most effusive traditional-music voice at the turn of the twentieth century, Francis O'Neill, does not discuss any drum. But he does mention the tambourine, if only in a passing reference, in relation to the husband of fiddle-player Bridget Kenny:

> Mr. Kenny, however, does not confine himself exclusively to the Irish pipes, for he can take a turn with equal facility on the bass viol, fiddle, dulcimer and tambourine[33]

Considering the musicality of that household, this could well indicate that its practice was not uncommon, and not considered odd, though it was peripheral. O'Neill surely must have come across the tambourine himself on his visits to Ireland, since it was already being sold in music shops from before the time he was born in 1846.[34] It is unlikely too that he did not have experience of, or knowledge of, occasional drum improvisation on the device bodhrán. This suggests that he viewed the frame drum as being without any worthwhile music significance, as seasonal and impermanent, or as a mere import, or as a toy, not a serious instrument, and irrelevant.

He may also have held it in low esteem on account of its use in popular music, in 'blackface' minstrel troupes which he had experience of in the USA.[35] He would have been familiar with the instruments used by those (tambourine, bones, banjo and concertina), not only because the major performers among them were Irish,[36] but also on account of their being well documented. One biographer, Michael O'Malley, takes an extreme view on this: 'if we consider O'Neill's collecting … one has to ignore the influence of the minstrel shows'.[37] Indeed it is not unreasonable to assume that the title and structure of O'Neill's major opus, *Irish Minstrels and Musicians*, owed something to Irishman Edward Le Roy Rice's 1911 book on blackface minstrelsy, *Monarchs of Minstrelsy*, a copy of which is among O'Neill's personal literature held at the University of Notre Dame in Indiana, USA.[38]

O'Neill would have been aware that the tambourine, or the bodhrán improvised as a tambourine, was played seasonally in Ireland. But because his priority, and preference, was sophisticated melody and union pipes,[39] it is understandable that he would not have commented on it, not least indeed on account of the historical association of drumming, as such, with the English military. Socially too, his attitude to tambourines would have been related to his awareness of the lower social class or economic circumstances of such frame drum players as there were at the time: their marginalisation not only set them beyond his direct experience, but also outside his cultural interest. But it is more likely the case that his work was just very tightly focused, for he did not deal with or index any major instrument other than pipes and harp, and, marginally, the flute. For instance, his silence on free-reed instruments and banjos can in no way be taken to mean that he was not aware of them or that they were not around: he just chose not to discuss them, as O'Malley puts it: 'Francis O'Neill never listed banjo or accordion players in his accounts of Irish musicians … and banjos universally stood for the music of burned cork and greasepaint'.[40] So too for the tambourine, which, indeed, emphasising the frailty of inclusivity, and of the issue of perceived status or importance, is not mentioned either by O'Malley himself! Another factor is O'Neill's vision for Irish music as being decidedly of the soil and traditional in practice: as O'Malley says, he was not interested in any influence of modernity.[41]

O'Neill's attitude is reflected in the major studies of traditional music which followed his work, Breandán Breathnach's *Folk Music and Dances of Ireland* (1971), his *Ceol agus Rince na hÉireann* (1989), and Tomás Ó Canainn's *Traditional Music in Ireland* (1978). Both of them deal with Irish traditional music as an instrumental tradition but do not mention any accompaniment, and not the tambourine – or indeed the bodhrán, which had in their time become popular. Breathnach's erudition was clear from his statement that 'Irish music is essentially melodic',[42] and in response to a question about the bodhrán during a talk at CCÉ's headquarters in Monkstown, County Dublin, he was equally blunt: 'We didn't go in for that sort of thing'.[43]

But some people did, as the next chapter shows. From the early 1800s on there are documented glimpses of percussion musicians, so much part of life indeed that, as already seen, they made it into the dictionaries, though not into the chronicles of approved music-making.

▲ Flute and tambourine players in the 1842 *Síbín near Listowel* painting [*Bridget Maria Fitzgerald. Courtesy J. Anthony Gaughan and Loretto Dalton*]

NOTES TO CHAPTER 8

[1] Guizzi 1988, 28.
[2] Berger 1972, 10.
[3] Boydell 2007, 61.
[4] Ibid., 7 and 69.
[5] Ibid., 6.
[6] Berger op. cit., 8.
[7] Murray 2008, 96-98.
[8] Ibid.
[9] Ibid., 35.
[10] Guizzi op. cit.
[11] Such 1985, 11–12; Tansey 2022, PC.
[12] Levy 2008, 238.
[13] Ibid., 96.
[14] Ó Bharáin 2007, 55–6, uses the term 'bdhrán' for instance, as does Harte 2020, 11-13.
[15] Maxwell 1854, 100.
[16] Ibid., 99.
[17] Berger op. cit., 47.
[18] Sullivan 1873, dcxii.
[19] Halls 1841, 25.
[20] Sullivan 1873, 543.
[21] O'Dea 1958, 18.
[22] Hart 1990, 115, cites John Blacking's strong opinion on the importance of rhythm in all its forms to the very process of human evolution.
[23] O'Dea op. cit.
[24] Gray 2008, 197-203. Lyric lines from 'Hill of Caves', by William Read.
[25] De h-Íde 1933, 258; Uí Ógáin 1995, 85.
[26] Hall 1841, 23-24.
[27] Carleton 1843 Vol. 1, 77.
[28] Ibid., 42.
[29] Ibid., xxiv.
[30] Carleton 1843 Vol. 2, 193–5.
[31] Köhl 1844, 195–6.
[32] Ó Gealbháin 2013, 110–13.
[33] O'Neill 1913, 389.
[34] Advertisements for the sale of tambourines in Ireland are found all through the second half of the 1800s.
[35] O'Malley 2022, 57, 221, etc.
[36] Rice 1911; Moloney 2011, 455.
[37] O'Malley op. cit., 278.
[38] Dowling 2013, PC; this was suggested to me by Chicago-born musician Martin Dowling. The approach is the same in both books.
[39] The term for the Irish pipes at that time was 'union pipes', and its use in America lasted well into the twentieth century (Moylan 2022), but in Ireland it had changed to 'uilleann' by the early 1900s, in keeping with revival of the Irish language.
[40] O'Malley op. cit., 253.
[41] O'Malley 2022, PC.
[42] Breathnach 1971, 7; 1996, 94.
[43] Moylan 2022, PC.

▼ Peadar Mercier, bodhrán, Tony MacMahon accordion, Éamonn de Buitléar, Mel Mercier, bodhrán [*RTE Archive*]

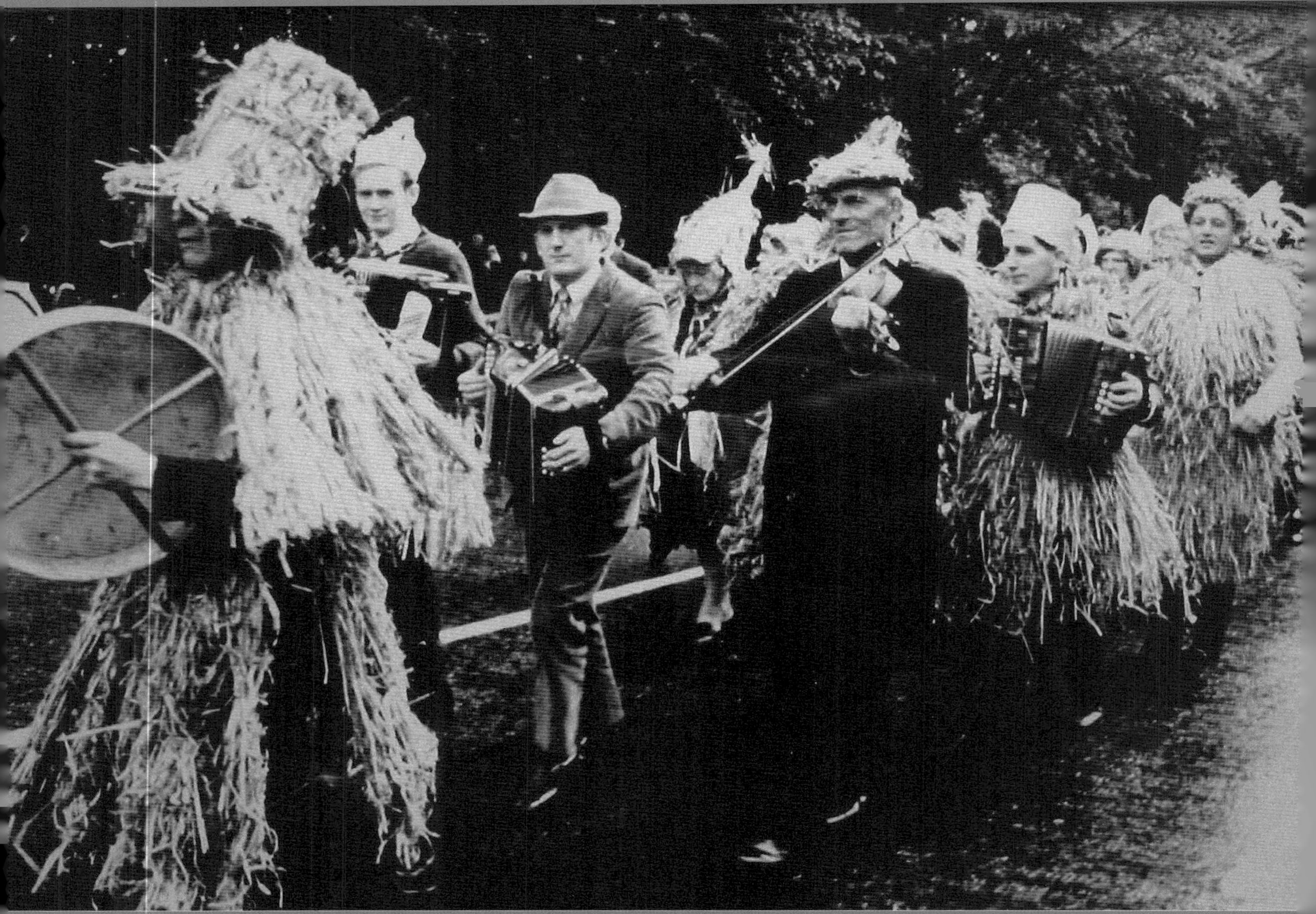

CHAPTER 9

IMPROVISING TAMBOURINE ON A BODHRÁN?

> Bowraun, a sieve-shaped vessel for holding or measuring out corn, with the flat bottom made of dried sheepskin stretched tight; sometimes used as a rude tambourine[1]

So wrote Patrick Weston Joyce in 1910. This chapter will look at the shaping and evidence of drumming with Irish music in earlier times and of how it is first reported as being done on improvised instruments. Everyone has witnessed people occasionally breaking into percussion on cardboard boxes and biscuit tins, drumming fingers on tables and dashboards. Beer-bottle tappers were common in the 1960s and ´70s. There is no reason to suppose that this was not a standard impulse in the past where there were no actual drums to hand.

The experience of the tambourine in the 1800s was initially among a social mix who paid to witness imported popular-music fashions; the mass of the rural poor were less likely to be involved. But as surely as the gun,

◂ Mummers with bodhrán, music and ccstumes, 1970s [*Anon, courtesy Renée Lawless*]

▾ The Armagh Rhymers at Omeath [*EDI*]

Wrenboys at Athea, County Limerick, 1947 [*Caoimhín Ó Danachair, National Folklore Collection*]

the bicycle, the car and television came to influence all classes, so too did the tambourine. And, as already said, for economic reasons its popular uptake rurally would have been more likely on copied instruments than on commercially-made ones. In early-1800s Kerry, music involving the tambourine is reported among rural people, indeed as a feature of the music of seasonal traditions other than the Wren, as Thomas Crofton Croker reported from the Glenflesk area in 1825:

> Mummers … appear at all seasons in Ireland, but May-day is their favourite and proper festival … They march in procession … the young men in the van … dressed in white or other gay-coloured jackets or vests … the young women are dressed also in light coloured garments, and two of them bear each a holly bush, in which are hung several new hurling-balls, the May-day present of the girls to the youths of the village … The procession is always preceded by music; sometimes of the bagpipe, but more commonly of a military fife, with the addition of a drum or tamboureen[2]

The inclusion of 'a military fife' in that parade suggests the likelihood of a link too between military practice and the tambourine. But while the fife would most likely be the real thing, young people also improvised the tambourine, the earliest account of which was being done on a device bodhrán, a dildurn. This is seen in a description a few years later by writer Gerald Griffin of an encounter with mummers in Kerry, 1829, a time when the tambourine was already known through the military and was visible on the streets and on theatre stages:

> One held a piccolo, another a fiddle, another a bagpipe. A fourth made a dildorn* serve for a tambourine ... *A vessel used in winnowing wheat, made of sheepskin stretched over a hoop[3]

Yet a treatise on Irish mummers given by songwriter P.J. McCall to the Irish Literary Society in May 1894 said that the instruments used in mumming were 'fiddles, flutes and perhaps a piccolo'. He made no mention of percussion of any kind.[4] He believed that mumming was 'not of native origin'; as he could find no references to it by Petrie, O'Donovan or O'Curry. He quoted Sir Walter Scott as saying that mummers' plays 'came from the east, probably carried back by the Crusaders on their return from Palestine;'[5] other local tradition has it that the practice was inherited from trade with Cornwall, or brought by shipwrecked Cornish sailors.[6] Any or all of those could have been the source or inspiration for the tambourine reported by Croker or Griffin. Indeed Daniel Maclise's 1838 painting of an English scene *Merry Christmas in the Baron's Hall* (see p. 229) shows mummers with a tambourine at an all-social-classes party. Absence of the word 'bodhrán' in the press does not, however, mean that it was not a term used for the drum, especially since *bobharan* was already in Connellan's dictionary as early as 1814. But literature has a sprinkle of links between tambourine and bodhrán in both the Irish and English languages.

These highlight it as both a device and an improvised instrument, a crossover from one function to the other which is not difficult to imagine, even where different construction methods applied. Crossover, or dual use, occurred seasonally, with mumming, or on the Wren. And, depending on how a bodhrán had been made, its effective sound would have varied: tucked-in skins being duller, 'fixed' nailed-on or stitched-on skins more ringing and resonant. From the earliest images of the winnowing bodhrán it is seen that they could either have tensioned skins (such as at Cashel, 1786, p. 73), or more flabby ones (as seen on some of the historic skin trays in the National Museum, as noted in Chapter 5). But both forms will provide a percussive sound, though with differing loudness, resonance and carrying power.

The Ballinskelligs battery
The winnowing bodhrán (*dildorn* or *wecht*) did not require any great tension in the skin but, because it was kept indoors for preservation, when the skin dried out on account of the warm atmosphere of the home, it could be resonant and loud when struck, a sort of drum.[7] Yet it is not on the record as having developed into an instrument of music *per se* in early times, certainly not as did lyres into harps, early timpans into fiddles, and triple pipes into bellows pipes, each of them becoming established in its own right as part of a melody-centred music, no doubt influenced by innovations and developments in music in neighbouring countries. But the bodhrán evidently kept a primary function as a tool or utensil until the early 1800s, by which time Irish people were well experienced with the drama of military drums, and were aware of the existence of the commercially-available, recreational frame drum, the tambourine. Such knowledge would have been a strong influence in leading an enterprising musician or singer to improvise drumming on a taut bodhrán, or to request of a maker that they tension the skin using tacks or thong lacing. The two early references to actual performance on this are in the Irish language, the first appearing

in print relating to some time between *c.* 1820 and the later 1840s. This links the domestic bodhrán to the actual tambourine, the former being used to mimic the latter, and confirms that there was some measure of casual percussion impulse and practice in Ireland, certainly in rural areas, if not indeed a common improvisation of the household bodhrán as a drum. The first source is a poem and associated commentary relating to the south-west Kerry poet Tomás Rua Ó Súilleabháin:

> Tomás and his 'apprentice' schoolmaster, 'An Camhlaobhach Caoin' … on the eve of the 'Pattern' of Gleanntan, near Ballinskelligs, the local scholars at the request of the master scoured the country side for bowráns: the bodhrán is an article resembling a small drum, and is used for holding carded wool. On this occasion they were to be used actually as drums by the pupils in promenading the village. A local woman, immortalised by the poet – Síghle Ní Mhodhráin – rushed to the school with her own bodhrán. Tomás tuned up the violin, handed the improvised drum to the Camhlaobhach Caoin and sang to an air similar to 'We'll have no prince but Charlie' the following pleasing strain:
>
> Is 'mdhó bean do bheadh ag clamhrán / Many's the woman would be complaining
> Nach tabharfadh uaithe bodhrán / Wouldn't bring over the bodhrán
> Is an Camhlaobhach Caoin / And Camhlaobhach Caoin
> De, Bhráthair Ghaoil / Your blood relation
> Ghá bhualadh le n-a mhéir mheádhoin! / Would strike with his fingers a sweet storm
>
> Cloisfear ins an nGleanntán / In the Glens will be heard
> Fothram an bhódhráin, / The resonance of the bodhrán
> Nach é an greann / Won't it be the fun
> Ag eirghe amach / Rising out
> Le cois an Bhaind ag máirseáil! / With the band marching
>
> A Síghle mhaith Ní Mhódhráin / O good Sheila Moran
> Ó Tugais uait an bodhrán / Who brought the bodhrán
> Is gearr gan mhoill / Quickly without delay
> Go bhfaghair do dhíoghal / So that you'd get your satisfaction
> Le ceól is rinnce is amhrán! / In music, dance and song![8]

Tomás a' Bhodhráin

Of similar vintage is the second story, possibly *c.* 1820, hand-written in a personal account by John Fleming of County Waterford in 1874, and printed by John O'Daly in 1876. This features Tomás Ó Móráin (no relation of Síghle), author of the already-mentioned descriptive ballad 'Aonach Bheárna na Gaoithe' / 'The Fair of Windgap' in County Kilkenny:

> Beárna na Gaoithe, Windgap, is a townland adjoining Four-mile-water … The fair was held I believe, towards the end of August, and was attended more for fun than for buying and selling. Among those who came to the fair, on a day, more than half a century ago was Tomás Ó Móráin, or Tomás a' Bhódhráin, this latter name he got from his skill in playing on the tambourine – a bodhrán is a dried sheepskin stretched on a hoop

Ó Móráin is elsewhere described as a ballad-maker

> He was a hedge schoolmaster for some time … his school in Cnoc a' Lisín … Having given up the teaching profession, during his lifetime afterwards he lived as a strolling minstrel, playing on the bódhrán, and singing to its accompaniment[9]

It is not clear from any of the versions of the story when he was born, or at what point he gave up teaching to take to the road of being a strolling minstrel, which would set a date for his use of the bodhrán as an instrument. Going by O'Daly's report, however, this may be the 1820s, as Ó Móráin died in the early 1830s:

> Tomas O'Modhrain; or Tomas an Bhoghrain, so called from his propensities as an expert player on the tambourine, and on that account was present at every social and merry-making meeting in the country, principally May Boys … We happen to know O'Modhrain well, he having spent a day at our house at Lickoran in 1820. In appearance he was low-sized, about five feet high, but very stoutly built, and always spoke and conversed in allegorical language[10]

His legendary status could be taken to imply that he was a one-off, rather than that singing to the bodhrán was a common practice, for the story was still being re-told as an item of folklore as late as 1952.[11]

John O'Daly's short biography of Ó Móráin is indeed the earliest description of a tambourine or bodhrán player, and, as the words suggest, of improvisation. That link between the agricultural or domestic tool and the tambourine crops up later, at the end of the nineteenth century in a vocabulary entry in *Irishleabhar na Gaedhilge*, which notes awareness of the dual use of the bodhrán: 'Bodhrán chun ceoil – tambourine'[12] [a bodhrán for making music – tambourine]. Such a use is confirmed by another account in that magazine in 1887:

> *wait, weit* – the name given to the dildurn or *bodharán* in the County Waterford. It is a circular wooden hoop covered over with calf or sheep skin, and can be played like a tambourine sometimes. The player, if nimble with fingers and elbow, can show off[13]

The improvised use was noted for *c.* 1900 in a Westmeath report in the *Schools' Collection*: 'A bodhrán is used to fill the oats into the winnowing machine. It is the rim of a riddle covered with a sheepskin. It is often used as a tambourine at the country dance'.[14] This was reported in the midlands as well: 'Bódrán' and 'Boorawn' – a kind of tambourine made with sheep skin.[15] A few years later in 1910, P.W. Joyce's alphabetic entry on 'Bowraun' in his book *English As We Speak It* verifies the use of the utensil as an improvised drum: 'Bowraun, a sieve-shaped vessel for holding or measuring out corn … sometimes used as a rude tambourine'.[16]

Drumming on the wecht

In modern time, Seamus Tansey, a keen observer of traditions, was the source of twentieth-century information on improvisation of a drum on the bodhrán/wecht/dallan, saying that:

> The *wite* was a skin drum just like a bodhrán but it had a rough surface … it was used for winnowing oats … They used to use it as a percussion instrument. It was played casually, but on only two days of the year, Midsummer's Day and Stephen's Day … religiously adhered to … but then it became a percussion instrument[17]

Indeed, in a region where the use of the tambourine was common in his own time, and has had a consistent practice since, Tansey did not use the term 'bodhrán', and only heard the word on one occasion, when it was

▲ Wrenboys with tambourines and band flute at Athea, Co. Limerick, December 1947
[*National Folklore Collection; photo by Caoimhín Ó Danachair*]

a reference to a hearing deficit. Tansey himself was too young to have witnessed a weit being played, as its agricultural use had ceased by his time, but he said that in his father's youth it would be done. Using her preferred term 'dallán' for the wight/wite, Janet McCrickard says of his account of improvised drumming which might follow a threshing:

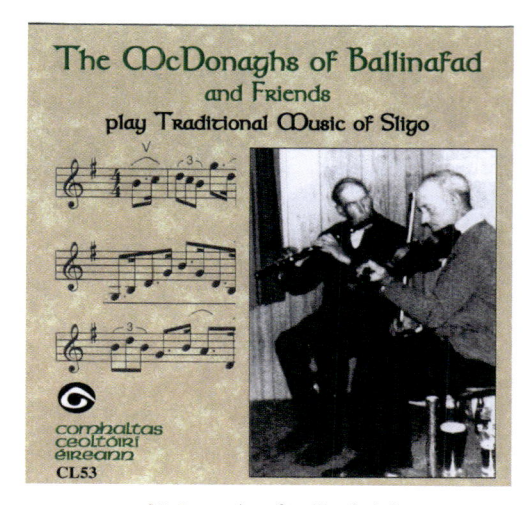

▲ McDonaghs of Ballinafad, foot percussionists

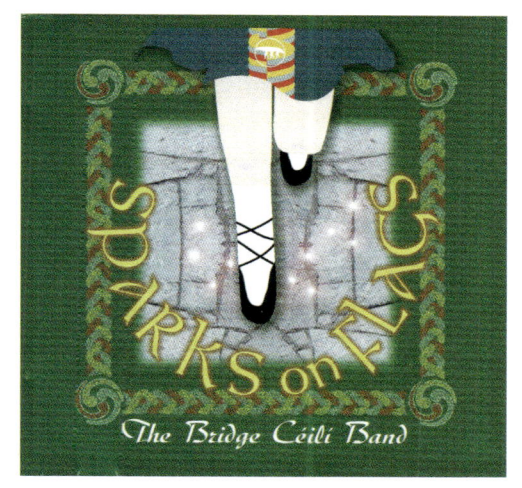

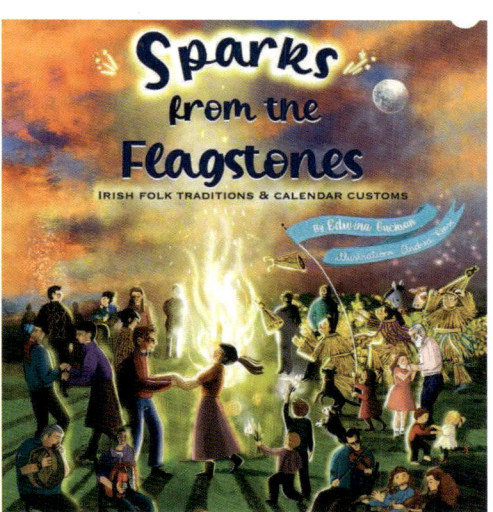

> The dallán, ready to hand with its natural resonance, was struck in imitation of the pleasing rhythms beaten out on the flags by the dancers' feet – and thus 'people learned to strike the wite'[18]

Such improvisation is not remarkable, and was not unique to Ireland of course, as reported about tourist sights such as Vesuvius in Italy where a Cork newspaper in 1895 wrote that 'children pelt each other with bits of hot lava, and the country people stroll around singing and beating tambourines or empty tins.'[19] Altogether indicating a human compulsion to make – and feel – patterned percussive sound.

Foot percussion
Janet McCrickard's words encourage thinking of the foot-noise of dancing on hard or hollow surfaces as not only impulsive percussion, but likely the most commonly-practised form of it. Writings from the thirteenth to the seventeenth centuries, and visual art in the 1800s, show that dancing was a vigorous recreation which inevitably produced percussive sound in tandem with its air-borne athleticism. Hard surfaces were sought out for dancing, such as on the compacted metal of public roads ('the crossroads') for dancing in summer, and hollow objects might be buried under parts of flagstone floors to add resonance to foot percussion in indoors quadrille social dance in the later 1800s.[20] Hollow, sprung wood floors were preferred for céilí dance from the 1920s to 1960s, and it is the end of that dance period that is indeed the beginning of the rise of the bodhrán as a popular element in the newly-reviving traditional music. All through these eras, actual choreographed step dancing in the formal, uniformed step-dance schools also took place, no doubt fulfilling the same impulse to engage bodily with music, as well as (as it eventually has become) an end in itself – the use of the feet to perform articulated, rhythmic detail, the application of the body in phrasing and framing of the melodies being danced to. But what is central to this observation is that in Irish traditional music, as in other northern-European musics, the impulse to rhythmically and percussively engage with music has been done mainly through dance – clogging in northern England for instance. This 'percussive impulse' has a vocabulary to describe it: the *slap* of feet on flagstones, the *whack* of hob-nailed boots on floors, the *scrape* of steel (shoe-sole studs) on stone, and, as used in a céilí band album title, dancers knocking '*Sparks from the Flagstones*'. So normal was this that County Galway accordionist Joe Burke could recall how a new maple-floor dance-hall in Loughrea banned hob-nail footwear.[21] Marching musics had a particular percussive dimension too before the invention of rubber: the regular, rhythmic beat of leather-soled, steel-clad boots on cobbled streets and drill-squares. The attractiveness of such a rudimentary percussion impulse was seen among musicians too, in such as the McDonagh brothers of Ballinafad, County Sligo, who, while seated playing, kick-danced rhythms on the flag floor under their chairs as an accompaniment to their own flute and fiddle; the Bridge Ceili Band used the concept for their album, and Edwina McGuckian used the same for her 2024 calendar. Cape Breton fiddle-player Tracy Dares, and others, do this also while playing the fiddle and piano. In gigs with Denis Cahill, Martin Hayes used to kick rhythmically on a piece of wood placed under his chair; he said that this was done by one of his

Tulla mentors, Joe Bane. Awareness of this dance feet-patterning is part of the multi-tonal, 'battering' stepping in set dancing. This was picked up on and brilliantly displayed in production by accordionist Tony MacMahon in his 1985 *I gCnoc na Graí* recording with concertina player Noel Hill and the Cooraclare set dancers, a classic demonstration – calculated, sophisticated foot percussion, like bodhrán playing. Such dancers as those are clearly conscious of this *felt* aspect of the 'battering' steps,[22] a synergy which indeed has already been mentioned (Chapter 6) as one of the highlights of minstrel performance. Dónal Lunny's *greadán* bodhrán playing on the opening track of the experimental band Cíorras's album *Silver Lining* has a patterning close to this set-dance battering.

Related to this is another form of body music, hand-clapping. This is mentioned in a religious context for the year AD 772 in the *Annals of Ulster*, where it was intended to simulate the sound of thunder on the feast of St Michael, at the 'Fair of the clapping of hands' *(oenach inna lam-comarthae)* … fire and thunder like the day of judgment'.[23] It is not seen anywhere subsequently except in modern-day song audiences. Many people have this impulse, but, unlike the practice in north African societies where it is an expert and enculturated part of music participation, European audiences do not always sustain a regular beat, so much so that singer Christy Moore has had to instruct his audiences not to clap while he performs. Yet other bands, such as Lúnasa, will encourage audience engagement via clapping to liven up the music.

From bodhrán to actual tambourine
With all of this mixed activity, at some point near the beginning of the 1800s, or earlier, and with the awareness of tambourines being supplied by the music trade and played on stage, it is obvious that those who were skilled at constructing sieves from woven wood strips, and making utilitarian bodhráns or wechts, would have experimented with tensioning skin. That small transition would create an Irish-made tambourine, the final act being copying too, as they did, the rim-mounted jingles using pieces of scrap metal. If such a transition was indeed made, why would the makers and the players call it anything other than 'tambourine', since that, as a device with the aura of some sophistication, was what was being copied? The evidence is that such drums were almost universally called a 'tambourine' at all times in all periods up to *c.* 1960, and the term 'bodhrán' was generally not applied to it. In Seamus Tansey's first book of recollections he consistently uses the term 'goatskin tambourine':

> we even played together on flutes at Gurteen cross-roads at a mid-summer eve bonfire in the early years of the 1960s … the boys and girls gathered and dance around the bonfire … Paddy Roddy struck a goatskin tambourine with his bare hand[24]

Yet, whereas the simplest, actual original bodhrán could be made with rudimentary tools, as it was just a hoop of tensioned, bent wood covered in a skin that used the natural pliability of young wood and the tough plasticity of skin, the inaugural rural tambourines would have required more robustness, notably a strong wood rim or shell to support a taut skin. From examples in the National Museum, and from makers' comments, this was achieved by making

"The bodhrán to me is so much part of our heritage and tradition here in west Limerick. And so too is the very unique style of playing with only one side of the stick which is associated with this area"
Michael Barrett, Carrigkerry Wren-boys

▼ Mike Barrett of Newcastle West [*EDI*]

▲ Bodhrán featured on cover of Munster Fleadh programme 2022

them out of something else – the pre-bent wood of an old meal sieve, a gravel riddle or the rim of an old Irish wool-wheel. It is only in the later twentieth century that the tambourines began to be purpose-made from scratch, taking on a more sophisticated look, and being created by tooled-up, specialist makers who experimented with materials, processes and melodic potential. Such drums today are for dedicated music purpose, but in the past, in their rougher form, they had been for the outdoors, theatrical, ritual letting-go that was associated with the Wren, May-boys and straw-boys, for whom volume and resonance were paramount, and finesse of finish was not a requirement. The Wren is predominantly an outdoor activity, a form of marching with an underlying military discipline and order, so it is not difficult to see how a drum type which has historically been associated with it might not be acceptable as part of dance-music performance. But there are exceptions and, by the 1920s, there are occasional reports of tambourines being played along with dance music in certain places, notably rural Munster, west Leinster and Connacht, possibly influenced by the Irish-American tambourine recordings. But by the late 1960s – in the form of the bodhrán – frame drums were being played across the island as an established music instrument, indoors as well as outdoors in fleadh music sessions (see p. 247 and also Appendix 10).

▲ Bodhrán players Jack Quaide and Mike Barrett with King of the Wren Joe Carrig and the Carrigkerry Wren at Newcastle West, 2022 [*Eddie Guiry*]

The Wren

The major writing on tambourines and, later, bodhráns is found in the press and in folklore and other accounts associated with 'the Wren'. This was recounted sentimentally by Seamus Tansey at Gurteen, County Sligo from his childhood days (*c*. 1950):

> Two young men with blackened faces put flutes in their mouths and another beat a goat skin tambourine with his head and face bent over the rim … It was the sound of those flutes over a goat-skin drum that sent a wave of elation and excitement but also a hitherto dammed up passion through my bloodstream as if some unseen force possessed my soul from then on … I ran after them bare-footed in the snow as if they were like the pied pipers of Hamelin piping my young heart away[25]

This post-Christmas, seasonal custom was once enacted all over Ireland, and still survives as a St Stephen's Day ritual in certain parts of the country, most notably in the south and west but now revived in many other localities. It is supposed to be a revenge act for the betrayal of St Stephen by a wren that sang on a bush under which he was hiding from Roman soldiers in early Christian times. The ritual and song involve a wren being hunted and killed, hung on a holly bush decked with ribbons, and paraded from house to house in front of a group of disguised young people who sing, dance and play music, requesting money 'to bury the wren'. The troupe of participants observe a kind of military order in their activity, and expect donations from houses visited, these to provide funds for refreshments and food for a 'Wren ball'.[26] All kinds of instruments have been played on it, but in west Limerick and North Kerry the tambourine featured strongly. Depending on the abilities of those taking part, the music can be good or indifferent, the dominant characteristic in the past being noise, for which tambourines, and even the household bodhrán, were prized. north Kerry and west Limerick have a strong history of 'the Wren', with some areas having several regular, seasonally-revived troupes, practised as a recurring tradition, age being no barrier. This came to be formalised as a spectacular festival in 1957, an event which has power, drama and spiritual association similar to a Swiss *Fasnacht* or a *Mardi Gras*. Since then, its popularity sustains a national competition annually, which draws Wren groups from all over the island.

The practice was not unique to Connacht and Munster, and among the occasional mentions of it in the late-1800s press is one reminiscence concerning the year 1905, about Wren-boys in County Kilkenny who

"Mention of the bodhrán sends my thoughts racing back to the early 1950s when as a youngster the beat of the tambourine on St Stephen's morning heralded the approach of the local Wrenboys. It also reminds me of a glorious day in 1977 when a lone piper and a troupe of fourteen bodhrán players led Uachtarán na hÉireann, Patrick Hillery, into our village of Templeglantine for the presentation of the Glór na nGael awards"
Tadhg Ó Maolcatha, cathaoirleach Chomhairle na Mumhan, CCÉ

▶ 'Hunting the Wren at Christmas – Procession of the Wren Bush and Wren Boys', 1850, by James Mahoney. Only fiddle and uilleann pipes are present [*The Print Collector / Alamy Stock Photo*]

◀ The Wren bush, Cork, c. 1840, as illustrated by Daniel Maclise. No music or drums are present [*Hall 1842, 42*]

9 IMPROVISING TAMBOURINE ON A BODHRÁN?

used to enliven the houses and villages of the Walsh Mountains with sheer entertainment ... the wren boys used to form in bands of eight or nine, each band would possess a kettle drummer, a vocalist, a comedian and dancer ... with their musical instruments of all descriptions they would drive the cobwebs of monotony and dull care away [*Munster Express* 1925 0103]

The Wren was being sporadically reported in all the provincial press by the mid-twentieth century, often flippantly – or impatiently – in the spirit of its being a wonderful old tradition, but which was presumed to be dying. Reports from places as diverse as Tipperary, Sligo, Carlow, Meath, Roscommon, Cork, Kerry and Wexford note the participation of masked youngsters, mostly males, in the custom, dressed in gaudy colours, women's clothes, hats and sashes, straw and leather masks, and outlandish disguise. Descriptions remark on a wide range of instruments, with piano accordion being mentioned by name generally, and mouth organs, bottomless buckets and tambourines noted in Carlow in 1942. By the 1940s, even though the tradition was being lamented as passing, and despite its preservation being desired, the Wrenboys were being occasionally upbraided for uncouthness, hammering insensitively on doors, being only interested in money and being associated with beggary and drinking – for quiet souls an intrusion on privacy. But commentary is generally positive, the custom being covered with a sense of pride. The press in Sligo and Roscommon note dancing being done by the Wrenboys, the presence of young women out on it is favourably commented on in one Limerick report, and the words of the Wren song, or its chorus, are often nostalgically quoted. All reports on the Wren appear in the first edition of the local press in January each year, and most are slight, often syndicated, repeating the same words from year to year – suggesting something either well-known and not really noteworthy, or, occasionally, annoying:

▲ Wrenboy parade at Athea, County Limerick, 1947 [*Caoimhín Ó Danachair, National Folklore Collection*]

On St Stephen's Day there was an organised din of tambourines and less provocative instruments, all day long, directing attention to the necessity for providing funeral expenses for the interment of a wren [*Limerick Leader* 1931 1230 3]

Ballymore, County Kerry: A number of young men marched through the town on New Year's Eve. they carried various musical instruments, including melodeons, mouth organs, tin whistles and tambourines [*Westmeath Examiner* 1931 0110 2]

The dulcid sounds of tamborines and the bold persistent knocking on closed doors ... 'Wren's Day' [*Kerry Champion* 1932 1231 6]

From noise to music

This emphasis on making an exuberant din and mildly aggressive spectacle on the Wren might be described as a *charivari*,[27] a feature of the tambourine's use on the Wren all through the twentieth century in Munster, Leinster and Connacht.

they played tin whistles, melodeons, fifes, fiddles and combs. No party was without a tambourine [*Drogheda Independent* 1932 0102 6] musical instruments of all types and brands were pressed into service, the tamborine predominating in almost all cases [*Kerry Champion* 1933 1230 5]

They were armed with all sorts of crude-looking holly bushes, new-fashioned drums, tambourines and a varied assortment of musical instruments from a mouth organ to a ukulele [*Munster Express* 1933 1229]

the wren boys thrilled the streets with the rattle of the tambourine, the bagpipes, and all the minor instruments, in and out of tune [*The Liberator* 1935 1228 2]

wet and dirty from headdress to pantaloons with the tambourines rattling and the melodeon and violin rasping out Irish jigs and reels and hornpipes … several batches of 'wren boys' visited Rathkeale. With their drums and tambourines and musical instruments [*Limerick Leader* 1936 0104 12]

They were masked and equipped, some with mouth-organs, often with tambourines and other musical instruments [*Kerryman* 1938 1231 7]

But the real highlight of the party were the tamborine players who pounded away on their home-made drum-like instruments … It is hard luck on the unfortunate goats, but the tamborines have to be provided somehow [*Kerryman* 1944 0101 7]

a cabriolet into which was crowded a band of musicians beating drums and tamborines to a piercing background of squeaky flute music [*Irish Independent* 1955 0720 3]

Santa Claus … was preceded by the famous Dirha wren boys' band … a selection of rousing tunes were played on tambourines, accordions and violins [*Kerryman* 1959 1226 11]

Change, decline and reorientation to new communications were part of the process, so, moving with the times, even by the 1930s Wrenboys were not always content to tramp many miles in the rain; this had an aesthetic fallout:

No more do we hear the sound of the tambourine floating on the morning air … instead the purring of motors, and the rattling of a full jazz band … The old simple system of mobilising at daybreak and tramping the country, with the tambourine man who was a highly efficient artist in his own line, at their head is gone [*Limerick Leader* 1932 1231 3]

The familiar broken melodies from their tin whistles or Santa Claus 'French Fiddles' [mouth organs] did not sound the same as in former years. 'Only a few faithful followers of the 'Tambourine Brigade' forced their noisy way past my terrier dog, and I felt that he, too, sensed their decline … Before I could express seasonal greetings, the leader of the party said: 'We'll sing … what would you like?… "Whatever will be will be" – or would you like one of Bill Haley's specials – "rock Around the Clock" [*Longford Leader* 1957 0112 2]

And the weather could interfere:

The young bloods hadn't the heart to come out … Neither tambourines nor whistles could shiver a note against the frosty nor western on the air [*Nationalist and Leinster Times* 1952 0105 5]

Preview commentary appears in print before Christmas, in both the daily press and in various editions of magazines like *Ireland's Own*, giving a fuller account of 'what' and 'why'. But, in common with most of the news reports, there is no particular information on instrumentation. In the gradual development of the Wren in 1943 the Sligo branch of the Gaelic League organised a 'Fleadh na Nodlag'.[28] In the same year the Wren-boys were using 'every available musical instrument' in Munster.[29] In Rosslare, County Wexford, in 1906 it was said that 'the custom has been continued annually without a break since the harbour opened'.[30] Caoimhín Ó Danachair's coverage, and film footage of the Wren on screen at the National Museum's Folklife department at Turlough, Castlebar, County Mayo, verifies the costumery, and the use also of accordion, along with flute and tambourines, whistles and an occasional bagpipe. The only other written document of the association of the frame drum with the ritual is in fiction, in Kerry writer Bryan MacMahon's 1952 *Children of the Rainbow* (see p. 159).

Wren catching
Thus the Wren had become the major outing for the tambourine in Irish cultural life, but, originally, this was only on one day of the year. The Wren was not seen as music *per se*, though it is of course an occasion for it. Its music's technical quality in the past, as reported, was lively but rough – more about making a good-natured beat for marching to or for dancing. The original traditional function which is described for the tambourine, however, was not about music at all, but to aid in catching a wren, by making an unpleasant din that would frighten the bird out of the bushes and facilitate its capture. But judging by the twentieth-century reports, the role of the tambourine in the custom has shifted to its becoming a symbolic part of a 'Wren orchestra'. In modern time these have become sophisticated, with a high standard of music, a concert recital of Irish music talent indeed. This can be heard not alone on the December Wren, but in the Wren-boy displays at Munster fleadhs where leading local musicians, singers, dancers and storytellers may take part. The drums used in the custom were called 'tambourine' until *c.* 1960 and, judging by the 1947 Ó Danachair footage and his still photos that are held in the National Museum at Turlough Park as well as by the 1977 film *Bodhrán* (see p. 177), these had taut, nailed-on skins mounted on somewhat-stressed, crude frames of mixed sizes.

This chapter has looked at tambourine improvisation on the device bodhrán, noting from early nineteenth-century writings that Tomás Ó Móráin is the earliest individual to be named doing that – possibly the first 'bodhrán' player as such in modern time? The use of the frame drum on the Wren enactment is also seen as the prelude to the use of both the tambourine and, subsequently, the modern bodhrán, in indoors, collective music performance. And, as the next chapter will show, the publicity trigger for that, perhaps ironically, was not music, but literature.

▸ Wrenboy with double-ended stick at Athea, County Limerick, 1947 [*Caoimhín Ó Danachair, National Folklore Collection*]

NOTES TO CHAPTER 9

[1] Joyce 1910, 222.

[2] Crofton-Croker 1825, 306. He was a friend of the painter Daniel Maclise, and Maclise indeed included him, complete with notepad, in the *Snap Apple Night* painting of 1832.

[3] Griffin 1829, 150. See Appendix 8 for the full quotation.

[4] Gaul 2011, 124.

[5] Ibid., 93.

[6] Leo Carthy, quoted in Gaul 2011, 122.

[7] Tansey 2022, PC.

[8] Fenton 1914, 106–7.

[9] *Irisleabhar na nGaedheilge*, Vol. 3, No. 25, 1887; Ó Gealbháin 92; Pléimeann 1887, 26–9, 43–6.

[10] Ó Gealbháin 91; O'Daly 1876, 53. Also, as part of a Royal Irish Academy request for people to write on the state of the Irish language and literature, one John Fleming of County Wexford contributed information on Ó Móráin as 'Tomás an Bhóghráin' [RIA MS 12 Q 13; thanks to Nicholas Carolan].

[11] Power 1952, 117.

[12] *Irisleabhar na nGaedheilge* Vol. 3, No. 26, 106.

[13] 'Peculiar Localisms', by Rev. D.B. Mulcahy, PP MRIA. 'Words in everyday use in Dalriada, North Antrim'; ING Vol. 3, No. 31, 1887.

[14] SC 0719, 369.

[15] *Westmeath Independent* 1907 0810 8.

[16] Joyce 1910, 222.

[17] Tansey 2022, PC.

[18] McCrickard 1987, 5.

[19] *Cork Examiner* 1895 0803 11.

[20] Ó Danachair 1955, 129.

[21] Burke 1997, PC.

[22] Vallely 2019, 150–1.

[23] Buckley 1995, 29.

[24] Tansey 1998, 113.

[25] Ibid., 53.

[26] Uí Ógáin 2011, 758.

[27] Pronounced 'shah-rivva-ree', a confusion of noise, sometimes written 'chivaree', it dates to at least the late seventeenth century. In France it was a coercive, insulting or goading mock parade with random, improvised noise-making. The term was used in Ireland in the *Westmeath Independent* newspaper in 1865 to describe a music movement played by a military band (see Chapter 8). In 1891 the term was used in an Irish-American song-sheet title, 'Patsey Doolin's Chivaree' (Vallely 2019, 161).

[28] *Roscommon Herald* 1943, 01 09.

[29] *Southern Star* 1943 0102.

[30] *The People* 1943 0102 4.

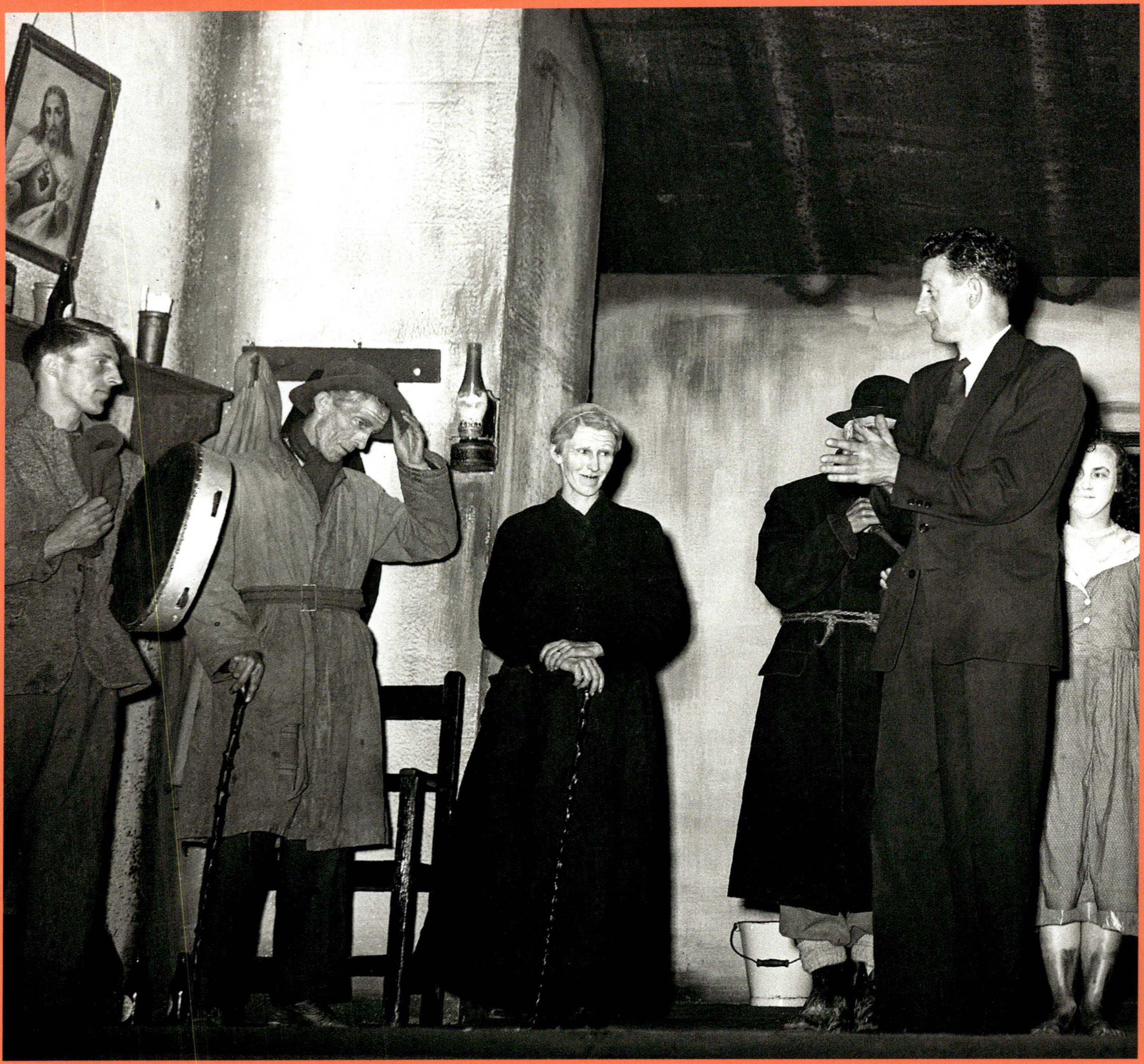

CHAPTER 10

THE LITERARY DRUM

As the twentieth century progressed, Ireland steadily challenged Anglo-Irish hegemony in attitudes to the arts. This process had been set in motion with the re-establishment of Gaelic culture over the course of the nineteenth century, culminating in movements in literature, drama, language and sport.[1] Things previously uncared for by the British establishment took on iconic and cultural value, and 'the plain people' began to have their voices heard and opinions regarded, particularly after 1921. Women, alas, were stuck in a second-class status, the gradual dismantling of which among other things nowadays manifests itself in the vastly greater participation of young women in music, something that has been facilitated by CCÉ. Huge changes have taken place in music practices and instrumentation, and one of the remarkable turn-ups has been not only the emergence in strength of what we call 'traditional' (indigenous) music, but also the coming into visibility of the next stage of the tamborine – the bodhrán.

None of the Irish museums display, or have, any of the tambourines as played by minstrel groups, nor have they any advertising material from these. This is likely a consequence of Irish attitudes to imported popular music, as well as to the impermanent nature of fashion. Numerous institutions in the USA, however, have collections and paraphernalia, among them the Library of Congress in Washington, D.C. The history of the tambourine is also represented in English, Scottish and European institutions. In the later 1800s the word 'tambourine' – perhaps as a respectable term, perhaps a reflection on borrowing – came to mean not the minstrel tambourine or the small, concussion tambourine, but a more robust one which is played today, re-configured *c.* 1960 as the bodhrán. This large-form tambourine 'just appeared', as if it had been waiting for its moment of resurgence. On the ground and in available records it had always been known as 'tambourine', and indeed this remained the case for many for quite a few years afterwards, as the following chapter will show. Evidence of the transition can be seen in folklore accounts, and is also quite clear in news reports, first in relation to the St Stephen's Day Wren tradition, then to do with CCÉ, the fleadh cheoil, competitions, and traditional music resurgence. But the impetus for the change could be said to have originally come not from musicians, but from fiction writers.

This intervention is relatively insignificant in the vast field of Irish writing, yet the morsel of literature which involves or celebrates the Irish frame drum does convey a great sense of the social use and function of the instrument in earlier times. Fiction of course is creative, imaginative invention, so one cannot expect to find life reflected accurately in it all of

◀ Sean Cahill plays the tambourine in the performance of *Sive* for the Abbey Theatre, 1959. Its midwife, John B. Keane, is on the right. This was the spark for renaissance of the tambourine, after which it was rapidly reconfigured as the bodhrán, and mushroomed into its status as a unique Irish percussion [*Irish Photo Archive*]

the time. But, outside of fantasy or science fiction, certain fundamentals of reality can be depended on – such as nature, mechanical devices, food and cuisine, agriculture, transport principles and systems, and the nature of music. Even so, names and terminologies do change with time. Shawls and capes were rendered redundant by coats, and coats by anoraks, kilts by trousers, leather shoes by 'runners'. In music, what are today universally called the 'uilleann pipes' were once called 'Irish pipes', and, originally, 'union pipes', and indeed the newer 'uilleann' term is, typically, often automatically back-applied in historic-literature references, because it remains the same instrument. The tin whistle in early competitions was titled 'flageolet', then became referred to as 'whistle'; the concert flute was always so called by older people, as a more polite term, but is generally abbreviated to the generic term 'flute', again, the same instrument. The fiddle (a generic term too, like 'car') is our most common instrument, in Irish *fidil*, yet older players have tended to call it by its proper title, 'violin', a word which came to be phonetically translated into Irish too, as *bhéidhlín*. In the case of the tambourine, the very first competition for it in 1962 was announced as for the 'tambourine', then the category label was changed after a couple of years to 'bodhrán', although the instruments and the players remained the same; these changes can be seen in competition and programme listings (see p. 181)

▼ Listowel Drama Group's Strawboys in Bryan MacMahon's play *The Golden Folk* (later *Song of the Anvil*) at Listowel, May 1960 [*Kennelly Archive*]

▲ Bryan MacMahon

▼ Bryan MacMahon's 1952 book which dealt at length with the tambourine and Wrenboys

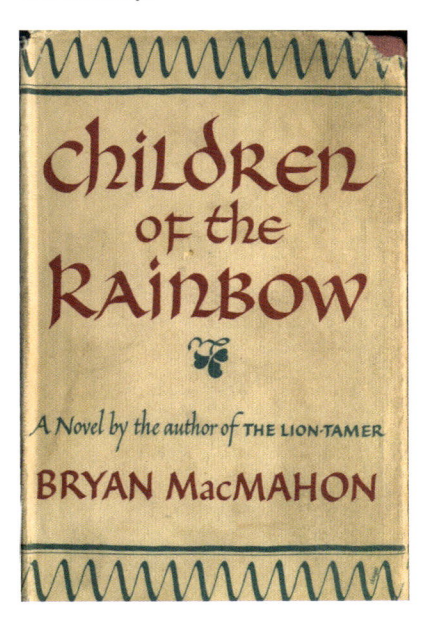

Twentieth-century tambourine

Indeed, today's bodhrán, without jingles, and generally played with a stick, is more or less the same as the pre-1960s tambourine, but, like all modern instruments, it has been hugely developed, and comes in all sizes, formats and pricings. Any of the instruments used in Irish traditional music are but vehicles on which to express it. The fact that, apart from harps and pipes, most are, originally, invented-abroad imports does not matter – accordions, concertinas, harmonicas, banjos, concert flutes, mandolins, Spanish guitars, Greek bouzoukis, tin whistles, violins, flutes, pianos and keyboards. As well as being adopted into Irish music use, some of these – such as button accordions and flutes – have come to be physically adapted to suit it too,[2] and most such are now also made in Ireland. It should not matter that the bodhrán we play is a twentieth-century, evolved cross-breed of native skin tray name and imported tambourine structure, for by now it is a distinctive instrument that is unique to Ireland. The fact that we retain for it the name of a similar-looking, onetime-household device and agricultural implement is quite a commemoration of something which was at the centre of survival for centuries. That name is much more noble indeed than our referring to free-reed instruments as 'box' (short for 'squeeze-box') or uilleann pipes as just the multiple-dimension generic type 'pipes'. Or indeed 'the car' for what could be anything from a rudimentary Fiesta to a driverless BMW. But the odd thing about the frame drum is the opposite, that until *c.* 1960 it was known universally by the 'proper' generic term, 'tambourine', yet we prefer to revert to the ancient word 'bodhrán' which has an indigenous ring to it. How some writers have dealt with the drum will now be looked at, showing that the transition from 'tambourine' to 'bodhrán' is no mystery, but is on the record in literature.

Rosa Mulholland

Possibly the earliest reference to the tambourine in Irish literature was by Belfast-born Rosa Mulholland in her 1883 novel, *The Wild Birds of Killeevy*:

> the bewitched mountaineers ... poured into the tents ... a gipsy with a banjo and another with a tambourine emphasised the time of the dances and drove the dancers wild with their quaint cries and snatches of foreign song[3]

Whether totally fictional or not, that writer drew on contemporary instruments which were being played popularly by minstrels in her lifetime.

Enter Bryan MacMahon

The next substantial reference after that, however, is, unchallengeably, local custom. This was *Children of the Rainbow*, a 1952 novel by Bryan MacMahon, a County Kerry schoolteacher who produced stories and drama that drew on rural life and customs, commenting on hardship among, and settled-community prejudice against, Travellers. The story was set in the mid-1920s,[1] its objective, the author states on the cover, being to celebrate simplicity, handed-on knowledge, and wonder in pre-machine, Irish rural life. In its quite surreal, vivid text the tambourine is described with the Wrenboys:

> Our musical instruments included four or five fiddles, three melodeons, one concertina, four kidskin tambourines and a mandolin. Neither the rib-bones, which

Jody Shea used as castanets, nor the mouth organ which Jack the Hibe played with palm-punching, were reckoned as instruments in the true sense of the word[5]

The tale does indicate music as being integral to social life – fiddles, concertina, mouth organ, set dancing and ballad singing.[6] But outside of the Wren, elsewhere in MacMahon's writing, in his mentions of music and recreation there is no percussion. By contrast, the use of music actually on the Wren is shown by him to be the opposite, for in this he indicates melody as being merely an adjunct to the drums, rather than drums being led by melody:[7] 'Our band was dominated by the skin and bell with the gadgets crushing down the slender hairline music of the fiddles[8]... Knuckles and wedges kept pounding heavily on the tambourines. The fiddler's elbows were working overtime ... the din of minor wrenbands floated to us from across the fields[9]... Dicky Hickey ... was carrying a tambourine which, in proportion to his size, seemed enormous[10]... Fiddlers, gadget-players, singers, mouth-organ players, dancers and tambourine strummers, we all followed'.[11] The rumbustious and aggressively-competitive nature of the rival Wren-boy groups is appreciated in the description of the way in which 'Dicky Hickey threw his tambourine at the cross an' touched it ... "We're claimin' that the village is ours!" '[12]

> The mannikin [little man, Hickey] was standing almost upright [in a pony trap] ... he continued to strike the pony's hindquarters with the flat of his tambourine. The cymbals of the tambourine agitated the pony more than did the lash of the whip ... he threw his tambourine at the cross [village monument]: it skidded off the limestone arm and went floating away into the crowd of onlookers ... Some-one threw him up his tambourine: he banged it in triumph against the cross ... One man was mourning for his broken fiddle, another was gaping at a great hole in his tambourine[13]

It is clear from this that the tambourine was the tambourine, and the term 'bodhrán', at the time of both the incident (mid-1920s) and the writing (1952), was not prominent, if it was used at all for the drum in that part of rural Munster. The same author's 1967 novel *The Honey Spike* covers a period some four decades later, *c.* 1965. It does not reference bodhrán or tambourine at all as a drum in Kerry, even though it deals with Puck Fair. That story is, again, somewhat surreal, a chromatically-vivid documentation of a tragic pony-and-trap journey from Antrim to Kerry by a young Traveller couple, the course of which is a kaleidoscope of excesses, emotion, chance, escapes, colourful characters, occasions and disputes. The only music *per se*, however, is a tremendously dynamic description of a pipes and drums band at Puck Fair in Killorglin: 'Then, its drums tapping time, the pipers' band passed ... The pipers were shrugging their green bags higher into their armpits. The drums were beating time'.[14] Yet the tambourine does not feature in the tale; it is introduced, but only via the thinking of the primal subject of the Killorglin fair, a goat which is confined atop a pole for the duration of the event. That reference indeed is a potted manual, a gem of instructional brevity and clarity:

> You are an old mountain billygoat ... You look out for the village lads, lest they push one of the nannies into a pool, stone her to death, skin her, bury the hide in dung, to be dug up later and stretched on the frame of a gravel sieve to make a tambourine[15]

At the time that was written in 1967 the Munster drum was still called 'tambourine', and its frame was still not always purpose-made, but could be improvised from something else. MacMahon's earlier book had come just five years before the first organisation of the Wren-boys' competition in 1957, an event in which he was honoured by being asked to adjudicate it. Joining him on that podium was John B. Keane, another County Kerry literary figure, who two years later himself introduced the tambourine to a much wider, national audience.

John B. Keane

The Irish tambourine's first formal appearance on a national theatre stage was in May 1959, in a play titled *Sive*, by John B. Keane, in which a singing actor accompanied himself on a tambourine. *Sive* (pronounced as the number 'five') was hugely popular at various festivals that year, culminating in its success at the All-Ireland Drama Festival in Athlone and a prestige

▲ Sean Cahill [*Irish Photo Archive*]

▶ John B. Keane [*Kennelly Archive*]

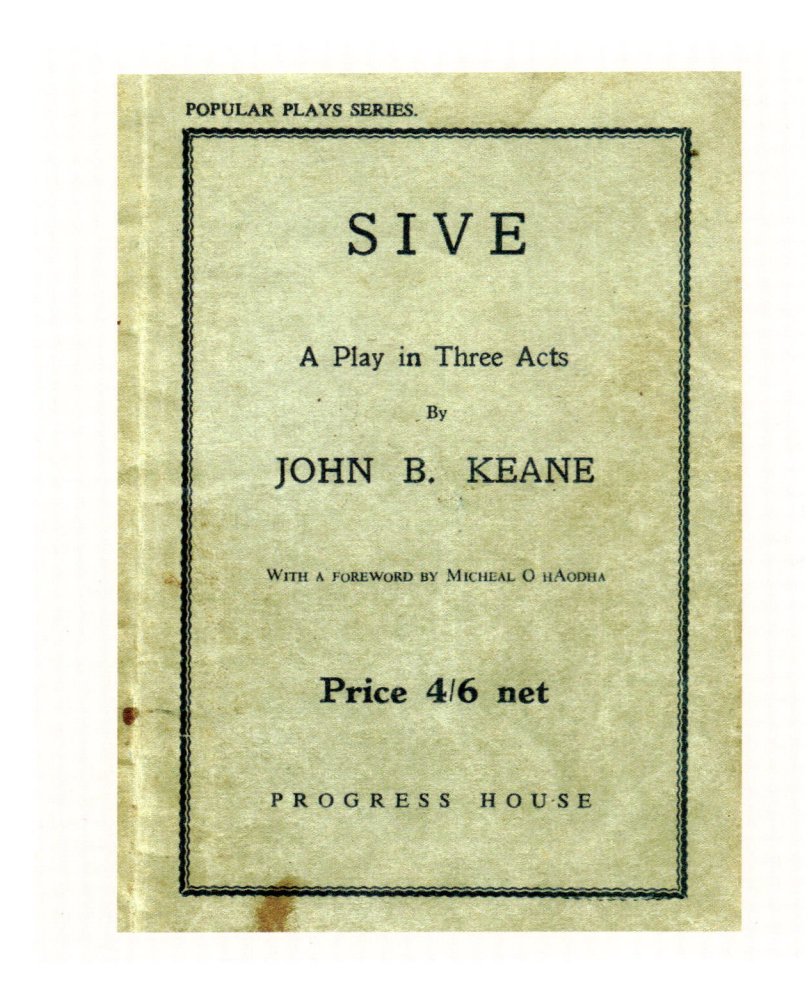

◀ Left: the original *Sive* cover from 1959
▼ Below: cover of the 1986 edition

performance for the Abbey Theatre, Ireland's national theatre. The play was recorded for radio, produced by Mícheál Ó hAodha, and broadcast nationally by Radio Éireann on 7 June the same year, in the week after the Abbey performance, spreading the information flow about the frame drum island-wide. Judging from press reports, it was the drum that became the focus of interest in the production:

> The Abbey is booked out for the week! Interest in a one-sided drum used in the production has caused enquiries to be made. It is a wren-boy's tambourine of a type which is seldom seen outside the south-west. Home-made, it is of goatskin drawn tightly over a hoop of wood. It is played by the knuckles of the hand. The tambourine … was made specially for the Killocrim Wrenboys and played on their annual St Stephen's Day outings. Sean Cahill … borrowed it from Jimmy Hennessy of Killocrim [*Cork Examiner* 1959 0528]

In its printed edition the play's stage instruction states, variously:

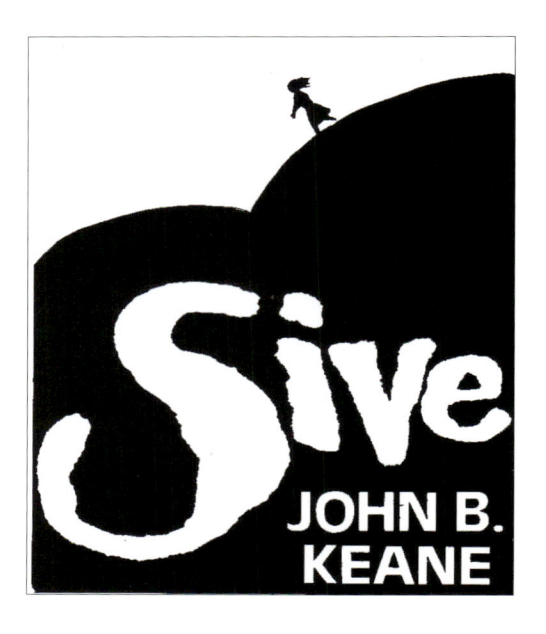

> In the distance but ever increasing is the sound of a tambourine and a voice singing …[16] Pats begins to tap again with his stick. Carthalawn begins to knuckle the tambourine.[17] Both assume dignity with the rhythm of the tambourine and blackthorn … The tapping of the stick is reduced, also the timbre of the tambourine …[18] Then unmistakably comes

> 'Sive' players' search for tambourine
>
> The Mallow Marian Players have struck a major snag in their preparations for their production of J. B. Keane's play "Sive".
>
> The two tinkers in the play use a wren-boys large tambourine for beating the tempo of their celebrated ballad "On the Road to Abbeyfeale. Such tambourines are unknown in the North Cork countryside. They are believed to be peculiar to North Kerry and the Mallow Players are now sending a "scout" to the Listowel area to get a suitable tambourine.

Evening Herald 1959 1027 4

> **PLAYERS ARE 'SAVED' BY DUBLIN MAN**
>
> MALLOW'S Marian Players are singing the praises of Mr. Paddy Latimer, No. 7 Wolfe tone Street, Dublin, and of the Evening Herald.
>
> Through the Herald they have found the large tambourine which will be one of the principal props in their forthcoming production of "Sive".

Evening Herald 1959 1031

> A Repeat by Public Demand
> LISTOWEL DRAMA GROUP presents
> **"SIVE"**
> By John B. Keane
> SUPER BALLROOM, LISTOWEL
> ON MONDAY, TUESDAY, WEDNESDAY,
> 11th, 12th, 13th MAY, 1959
> Admission 3/6 & 2/6. Doors open 7.45 p.m. Curtain 8.30 p.m.
> (Latecomers not admitted until end of Act)
> Booking: M. Kennelly, International Travel Agency, Market Street, Listowel. 'Phone 28.
> NOTE—Seats reserved for Associate Members on application.
> SEE — SIGH — SING — SOB . . . . "SIVE"
> ● THE STAGE SHALL NEVER DIE ●

Evening Herald 1959 1121 8

the sound of a tambourine in the distance, growing in volume ... The tapping of the stick is heard upon the door, in time with the tambourine ... the knuckles very gently tap the tambourine to slow time. Slow of voice and tenderly Carthalan sings'[19]

But in that early printed 1959 edition of *Sive*, in contradiction to the instruction in the actual script, a foreword by radio producer Mícheál Ó hAodha[20] (who was associated with traditional-music programming on Radio Éireann, and who had been instrumental in getting recognition for *Sive*) states: 'Pats Bocock and Carthalawn, with their bowrawns and cursing-songs, leave the audience breathless with excitement'.[21] This marks him as only the second person to link bodhrán and tambourine in print (the first was Ó Danachair, in 1947), as he, a Clareman

> **UNUSUAL DRUM**
>
> WHILE all the controversial talk about "Sive" at the Abbey Theatre continues in the theatrical circles, there is one important point which is overlooked. The Abbey is booked out for the week! Interest in a one-sided drum used in the production has caused enquiries to be made. It is a wren-boy's tambourine of a type which is seldom seen outside the South-West. Home-made, it is of goatskin drawn tightly over a hoop of wood. It is played by the knuckles of the hand. The tambourine

Cork Examiner 1959 0528 5

(and from Munster too), was aware of an overlap between tambourine and 'bowran'. That may or may not suggest that 'bodhrán' was a term that was better-known in Clare. A coda to the *Sive* saga was that in his 1969 memoir Keane refers to the drum as both tambourine and bodhrán in the one story-sequence: 'I found myself with a tambourine in my hand … The minute I lifted my hand to strike the bodhrán, the trousers came down'.[22] However, the play opened up both tambourine and bodhrán to national visibility in the year 1959.

Sive, the Munster finale ...

> An interesting feature of the broadcast will be the use made of 'boorawns', or homemade tambourines, to capture the wild intensity of the travelling men who, with their cursing sons, play an important part in the play [*Tuam Herald* 1959 0530 7]

> There can, I think, be no doubting that the intriguingly-titled play gripped the attention right from the moment one heard the distant boorawn thumping out its almost savage rhythm to the tragic close [*Evening Echo* 1959 0606 4]

Clearly some of the press had read the Ó hAodha foreword by calling the tambourine 'boorawn' (even if their attention to spelling was careless), but the 'bowran' word recalls P.W. Joyce's 1910 glossary (p. 61), and shows that that term was being used still in the 1950s; but 'tambourine' was the word initially favoured. Either way, the drum caught public imagination, and got terrific press when *Sive* was taken up by other drama groups. One 1959 headline ran: 'SIVE PLAYERS' SEARCH FOR TAMBOURINE'.[23] A follow-up of the saga was 'PLAYERS ARE "SAVED" BY DUBLIN MAN'.[24] And among the year's memorable drama moments in 1960 is cited 'the sound of the tamborine and the stick on the floor in *Sive*'.[25] In west Limerick and County Kerry, John B. Keane maintained a sustained promotion for the drum, trickling out the implication of a history, continuity and birthright, all of which he compounded later in his 1986 novel *The Bodhrán Makers*. That itself had the effect of helping to institutionalise the drum for Kerry county. Initially both his and Bryan MacMahon's fiction and folklore had spoken of the tambourine, but without missing a beat, so to speak, the drum was rechristened and reborn as bodhrán, which was the composer Seán Ó Riada's preferred term. In Keane's original 1959 script for *Sive* he has the instruction:

> (In the distance but ever increasing is the sound of a tambourine and a voice singing. The sound increases while the occupants of the kitchen await Pats Bocock and Carthalawn.

J. B. Keane tells all about the bowran

Evening Herald 1959 1121 8

In the 1986 edition, however, the instruction reads:

> (In the distance is the sound of a bodhran and a voice singing. The sound increases while the occupants of the kitchen await Pats Bocock and Carthalawn.

Seán Ó Riada, 1960 From: tambourine to bodhrán

J.B. Keane's *Sive* was performed in 1959 by The Listowel Drama Group for the Abbey at The Queen's Theatre venue in Pearse Street, Dublin.[26] This appearance in a sold-out, national-theatre play was the modern debut of the Irish frame drum on a Dublin stage – but as *tambourine*. Its effect was electrifying, expressed in the national press as a kind of wonder and pride, quite a fever of novelty interest that persisted for a couple of years. The *Sive* performance

▼ Seán Ó Riada playing stick-struck bodhrán with Ceoltóirí Chualann [*Gael Linn*]

> **MUSICIAN'S PLAY TO HAVE FIRST PRODUCTION**
>
> A play by a leading Irish musician will have its first production during the Dublin Theatre Festival. The author is Sean O Riada, 29-year-old director of music at the Abbey Theatre and composer of the "Mise Eire" film score.
>
> The play, "Spailpín a Rún", at Gael-Linn's Damer Theatre, deals with the unruly life of the 18th-century Kerry poet, Eoghan Ruadh O Suilleabhain, and the music, Sean O Riada says, is entirely traditional. There will be singers, fiddlers, pipers, and performers on the Kerry goatskin drum, the bodhran, which was introduced to Dublin audiences in "Sive". The author himself will play the harpsichord.
>
> Sean O Riada, who was born in Cork and is a graduate of U.C.C., makes a double contribution to the festival, for he also has written the incidental music for Bryan MacMahon's "Song of the Anvil", which will be presented at the Abbey. His score for the sequel to "Mise Eire", "Saoirse?", has been recorded by the Radio Eireann Symphony Orchestra.

Cork Examiner 1960 0902 13

> **Goatskin tambourine on two LPs**
>
> A GOATSKIN tambourine – beaten to suggest the roar of waves and scraped for the groaning of a ship's timbers – is used by Sean O Riada in two new LPs of traditional Irish music.
>
> The music in new arrangements by Sean O Riada is played by his folk orchestra, Ceoltoiri Cualann, and the records are issued by Gael-Linn.

Irish Press 1962 1219 15

on the tambourine was, however, independent of the music provided by the Abbey Theatre's orchestra, the director of music of which at that time was listed as John Reidy. In a 1988 interview, Keane said that at the time of the *Sive* production, Reidy

> was utterly intrigued when Johnny [Seán] Cahill came on the stage ... After the play he said to Johnny 'this is an instrument that has never been developed. I'll make good use of it'. And he did [27]

Reidy had worked in the theatre from July 1955 supplying interval music, including traditional music arrangements which included a set titled *Ceol Gaelach Reidy* [Reidy's Irish music] but always used Seán Ó Riada (his name in Irish) in the credits, and by which he was known as a composer. He began using his name in Irish-only for the Abbey programmes in July of 1960, the year following both *Sive* and his own major composition *Mise Éire* which had been commissioned by Gael Linn for George Morrison's film. In that year he was also preparing the score for *The Song of the Anvil*, a play by Bryan MacMahon, founder of the Listowel Drama Group, who had requested authentic traditional music for Wren-boy roles within the play (see photo on page 158). To perform this, Ó Riada (as he was known by then) formed a dedicated traditional-music ensemble, for which accordionist Éamonn de Buitléar had recommended the musicians.[28] These were Vincent Broderick on flute, Sonny Brogan on accordion, Sean Potts on whistle, John Kelly on fiddle and Paddy Moloney on pipes, with de Buitléar himself listed in the Abbey programme on bodhrán; Peadar Lamb also played bodhrán as a Wren-boy in this production.[29] Like *Sive*, this was also performed in the Queen's Theatre building.

An indication of Ó Riada's energetic engagement with traditional music can be seen in the fact that in the 1960 Dublin International Theatre Festival he arranged and performed music for both MacMahon's *Song of the Anvil* with the Abbey (12-24 Sept.), and his own drama, *Spailpín a Rúin*, at the Damer theatre (15-24 Sept.), with Peadar Mercier on bodhrán). For these overlapping performances he drew on a panel of musicians who were later to become his Ceoltóirí Chualann ensemble. His versatility was noted by the press:

> The first play of a leading Irish musician will have its first production during the Dublin Theatre Festival; the author is Sean O Riada, 29-year-old director of music at the Abbey Theatre and composer of the 'Mise Éire' score. The play, 'Spailpín a Rúin' at Gael-Linn's Damer Theatre, deals with the unruly life of 18th century Kerry poet, Eoghan Ruadh O Suilleabhain, and the music, says Sean O Riada, is entirely traditional. Onto the stage come singers, fiddlers, pipers and performers on the Kerry goatskin drum, the bodhrán, introduced to Dublin audiences in 'Sive' ... Ó Riada ... has a double contribution to the festival for he has also written the incidental music for Bryan MacMahon's 'Song of the Anvil' at the Abbey [*Kerryman* 1960 0910 3]

De Buitléar's playing bodhrán in the MacMahon play amounts to the national premiere of not only the drum in a formal ensemble, but also under its new name bodhrán.[30] Ó Riada developed the concept to become his experimental radio ensemble Ceoltóirí Chualann, which also did the music for another Gael Linn play at the Damer Hall in 1961, *Scéal ar Phadraigh*, by Seán Ó Tuama, the programme including 'Calypso, jazz and traditional Irish music on fiddle, flute and bodhrán'.[31] But the first formal concert debut of the bodhrán was by 'Ó Riada himself directing from the Bodhrán, or Kerry goatskin hand drum'.[32] This was with Ceoltóirí Chualann for the concert *Reachaireacht an Riadaigh* (Ó Riada's Recital), titled after his previous year's Radio Éireann radio programme. It was staged at the Shelbourne Hotel as the opening event for the Dublin Theatre Festival in September 1961. The bodhrán used by Ó Riada did not have jingles, and was used to achieve a kind of bass backdrop, a 'soft' yet articulate fill-in sound. The composer might not have been aware that in west Limerick and north Kerry it was called 'tambourine', but he went with the name which had a feeling of legacy about it, 'bodhrán', possibly from reading P.W. Joyce, or guided by Caoimhín Ó Danachair's opinion that older people occasionally used the terms tambourine and bodhrán interchangeably. Or perhaps he was told this by John B. Keane? The term 'bodhrán' was obviously more fitting for an ensemble of traditional musicians anyway, for it also symbolised an other-worldly, more primeval spiritual association or power; Ó Riada offered no reasoning other than this in a subsequent radio-lecture series.[33] And as he and Ó Danachair both believed (and what had been first said by Joyce in 1910), it was timbre – a dull, deep sound – that was the link between the name and the drum. The outcome was that what had been popularly known as the tambourine in *Sive* in 1959 was, now without jingles, *bodhrán* by 1960. So the composer Seán Ó Riada became midwife to the bodhrán as accompaniment in music, something not missed by the national press:

> Apart from the popularising effect which 'Sive' has had on the bodhrán, one of the greatest authorities on Irish folk music, Sean O Riada, has incorporated it into his unique traditional group known as Reacaireacht an Riadaigh. In all, it seems this fascinating instrument has quite a future [*Irish Independent* 1962 0517 7]

Ó Riada's efforts at authenticity did not go unnoticed, generating criticism from classical music aficionados, but also appreciation from at least one other far-seeing columnist:

> Ceoltóirí Chualann, so familiar to Radio Éireann listeners and originally formed for a Bryan MacMahon play, has been compiled with the main emphasis on authenticity and historical accuracy ... The re-appearance on the scene in this group of the 'bodhrán' – goatskin drum on iron frame as also featured in John B. Keane's 'Sive' – is a sign that Ireland's own 'trad' is looking back to its roots for its further development. A healthy sign for the future [*Evening Herald* 1963 0221 4]

Whatever about the 'iron frame' (presumably the journalist's assumption of the meaning of 'frame drum?'), Keane passionately promoted a sense of wonder about the drum, a mystique which he marshalled over subsequent years with comment and showmanship into a formidable pedigree. His own initial term 'tambourine' was replaced by 'bowran' in a short time, and the name was ferried further by Ó Riada through Ceoltóirí Chualann's captivating music arrangements. Visibility of these was made feasible and enhanced by public performances and a weekly show – *Fleadh Cheoil an Radió* – on national radio, a magical manifestation for the music devotees who had been variously revived, created and enabled by Comhaltas Ceoltóirí Éireann. Ó Riada's primary aim was to raise the status of traditional music to a nationally-deserved respect, and that meant dispensing with impediments such as the céilí band format and drum-kit, as well as the be-jingled tambourine.

HOME　MUSIC AT THE ABBEY　SOURCE MATERIALS

1960-09-02

Performance Date(s):
Thursday, September 22, 1960
Friday, September 23, 1960
Saturday, September 24, 1960
Known Number of Performances: 3
...
Programme Text
Thursday, Friday, Saturday, 22nd 23rd 24th September 1960
...
THE SONG OF THE ANVIL
A Play in Three Acts by Bryan MacMahon
...
MUSICIANS
SEAN POTTS Tin Whistle
VINCENT BRODERICK Flute
SEÁN O CEALLAIGH Fiddle
PÁDRAIG a MAOLDOMHNAIGH Chanter
PATRICK BROGAN Accordeon
EAMONN DE BUITLEAR Bodhrán
...
There will be Intervals of Ten Minutes between the Acts
...
Music by SEAN O RIADA

▲ Abbey Theatre programme details [*Courtesy Maria McHale and Abbeytheatremusic.ie*]

The Song of the Anvil 1960 (Abbey) by Bryan Mac Mahon

Opening Night:
Monday, 12 September 1960
Number of Performances: 9

Cast & Creative [Music]:
- Broderick, Vincent Musician [flute]
- De Buitléar, Eamonn Musician [bodhrán]
- O Ceallaigh, Sean Musician [John Kelly, fiddle]
- Ó Maoldomhnaigh, Padraig Musician [Paddy Moloney, uilleann pipes]
- Ó Riada, Seán (I) Music
- Potts, Sean Musician [whistle]

Venue
Queen's Theatre, Pearse Street, Dublin
Dates:
12-17, 22, 23, 24 September 1960

▲ Abbey Theatre programme details [*Courtesy Maria McHale and [abbeytheatre. ie/archives/production_detail/3756/]*]

▶ Local poet Michael Hartnett's welcoming words to the Irish president on his 1977 welcome to Newcastle West which was emblematically heralded by bodhrán players [*Courtesy Tadhg Ó Maolcatha*]

Michael Hartnett

The outcomes of the rise in visibility of the bodhrán are seen everywhere, not least in a reference by another literary figure, Newcastle West poet Michael Hartnett, in verses he made to welcome Irish president Paddy Hillery to Templeglantine, County Limerick to present Glór na nGael awards on 29 May 1977. His final stanza references the bodhrán as a significant local practice

> So, with the rumble of the bodhrán
> With music and feasting, with celebration and poetry
> Welcome to you President
> To Gaelic Templeglantine[34]

The Bodhrán Makers, 1986

Within a year of *Sive*'s first production, John B. Keane himself was using the term 'bodhrán' or 'bowran' all the time, and that was amplified by the press. As already mentioned, a subsequent print edition of the play in 1986 has all the 'tambourine' references changed to 'bodhrán':

In that same year the playwright developed his 'bodhrán' association further in fiction, the novel *The Bodhrán Makers*, which solidified the transfer of the word bodhrán to the tambourine. That book too is a powerful document about power, passion, poverty, social class, clerical oppression, bullying, factionalism and associated misogyny in rural Munster.

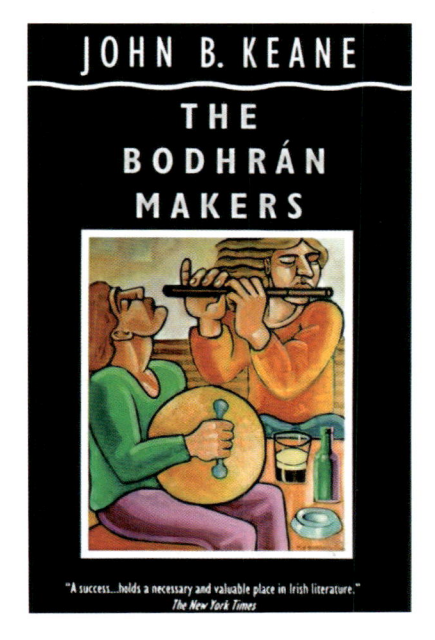

Essential to it is an image of day-to-day life involving bicycles and pony-and-trap which could be equally representative of any time from the 1890s to the 1930s, but modernistic tropes – such as the vehicles which are mentioned[35] – place it *c.* 1963, as do references to the magnet of economic opportunities presented by post-war rebuilding and development in England. The story is built around the power of the Catholic clergy as a socially-controlling iron fist, and identifies part of the emigration exodus as being the result of their moral and social anti-pleasure tyranny. The bodhrán drum is laced into this fabric of existence, suffering and survival in forty or so different references which link the Wren, traditional music and anti-clericalism, a synergy that ultimately consigns the main players to the emigration boat, and tips the punitive clergyman into dementia. Central to the plot is a local troupe of ageing Wren-'boys' who are determined to keep the Wren tradition alive. The symbol in all of that is not, however, tunes (melody), but the drum, termed 'bodhrán', presented in various contexts, including the priest's scathing denunciation of it: 'the spectacle of mobs of self-styled Wrenboys with their wretched drums, their so-called bodhráns'.[36] That remark could well imply that the cleric already knew the drums as tambourines, but the bodhráns in the story (like all drums) were also the expression of a kind of authority and a medium of communication: 'As the command was given the bodhráns sounded … ';[37] 'There's nothing like the sound of the bodhrán to rise the blood in a man';[38] 'He's the best bodhrán player in the country'.[39] A trophyism is alluded to: 'From a crook thereon hung a freshly-made bodhrán';[40] 'they awaited the thump on the bodhrán which would herald the music from fiddle, melodeon and concertina';[41] 'Father Dully was impressed by the Dirrabeg music, especially the bodhrán';[42] They sat in the lee of convenient turf ricks or hedgerows and spoke about 'football and bodhrán making'.[43] Mystification is catered to, as in any historico-cultural intervention. The mood described here is not unlike the kind of self-absorption that melody players are familiar with when a tune is going well, or, for manual workers, when a repetitive routine task becomes such a reflex action that the mind is permitted to stray elsewhere:

> Firstly he allowed his fingers to ripple the bodhrán's surface. Then he smote the drum with the clenched knuckle of his right hand. At once it vibrated into life … its varying tones now rippling, now plangent, now resounding were carried for miles across the still countryside … its clear tones racy, uninhibited and vigorous … felt a great satisfaction mingled with a physical ease he had never before experienced … a new mental tranquility … he felt like a superior being ….[44] Rubawrd Ring was shaving when the beat of the distant bodhrán assailed his ears ….[45] 'But what is a bodhrán doing up in the old fort in the middle of the day and such a bodhrán. It's like no drum I've ever heard'[46]

Male sexual fantasy, allegory and leprechauns enter the scene too in order to create a spice of unassailable other-worldliness for the drum:

> Around the wren dance fire Bluenose was reciting the saga of the bodhrán … 'You want this magic bodhrán? … didn't a door in the ground open and this tall woman climbed out. She wore no clothes … What did the creature do then but hand me the bodhrán and the cipín and instruct me to play'[47]

The player being in a trance completes the idea of transport out of reach of rational Christian control:

> There was silence now save for the beating of Dónal Hallapy's bodhrán … From where the curate stood the man with the bodhrán seemed to be possessed[48] … 'Throw that barbaric instrument away from you at once' [the curate] called out … 'it is the devil's drum' …[49] 'Canon Tett will go down as the man who purified Dirrabeg … By God you'll hear no bodhráns there for many a night to come'…[50] The drum he heard had been a bodhrán. He would recognise its distinctive and accursed throbbing anywhere…[51] In layman's language the Canon has bodhráns in the brain[52]

This is quite a variety and volume of commentary on attitudes to, and ethos of, the bodhrán. According to a note in the foreword of the book: 'The bodhrán is a shallow, single-headed drum of goatskin which resembles a tambourine, but is larger; it is played with a small stick called a cipín, or else with the hand'.[53] In its second edition in 2021 the author's son reflects on the 1959 play *Sive*'s role in the bodhrán's popularisation:

> the tinker duo Pats Bocock and his bodhrán-wielding son Carthalan ... *Sive* was the first time the vast majority of Irish people came into contact with the bodhrán. The now near-ubiquitous percussion was in its death-throes in 1959[54]

He concludes by paying tribute to his father's 'great friend, and often co-conspirator, Sonny Canavan ... the Antonio Stradivarius of bodhrán makers ... the last of the great bodhrán makers'. Yet he overlooks the fact that at the times of both *Sive*'s plot and its being written, the drum was known as 'tambourine', and that in his father's original version of *Sive* it was also referred to throughout as 'tambourine' despite its carrying Ó hAodha's foreword mention of the term 'bodhrán'. Worth thinking about too is the fact that *The Bodhrán Makers* charts Wren and music activity in north Kerry, something which is quite different to music further afield in the county and country-wide. Fiddle, concertina and melodeon played along with bodhrán[55] would have been unlikely to be the norm at that time (*c.* 1963?), for, certainly, the copious recorded and written documentation of north Munster music in that post-war period, and of dedicated music-revival players nationwide, shows that neither tambourine nor bodhrán play a significant part either at home or in English exile; this can be concluded too from Bryan MacMahon's references thirty-four years previously in 1952. There are of course exceptions and, even though *The Bodhrán Makers* is a work of fiction, its social critique has tremendous validity, opening eyes as it does to a crippling religious zealotry and economic stagnation.

Pointing out the tambourine-to-bodhrán transubstantiation is no mere pedantry; it is a call for accuracy. Keane was a major agent in that lexical genesis, something which was amazingly achieved in a short time by active promotion in press comment and interviews.

Gabriel Fitzmaurice, 2006

Something of a sequel to the previous story is offered in Gabriel Fitzmaurice's anecdotal *Beat the Goatskin Till the Goat Cries*, with its analysis of the use of music by Keane in the play *Sive*. Keane's original manuscript is taken as the source: 'Keane tells us in his stage directions, a "tambourine"'. But Fitzmaurice makes a clear distinction between bodhrán and tambourine: for him, the tambourine has jingles, the bodhrán has none:

> The tambourine was an ancient goatskin drum. The round, wooden rim was sometimes inset with the flattened metal tops of beer bottles which rattled in sympathy to the rhythm being played on the skin[56]

'Ancient' may not be appropriate for that particular use of beer-bottle caps, for they can only date to the appearance of the 'crown cork' for bottles, which, although invented in the USA, by an Irishman indeed, was not likely to be widespread in Ireland until at least the 1920s. But Fitzmaurice makes a further neat distinction, which is also at odds with Keane's lineage, and points to a different role for the tambourines outside music *per se*: 'Unlike the bodhrán, its more refined cousin of today, the tambourine was the instrument of the outdoors, of Wrenboys and Strawboys, the relic of a pagan Ireland'.[57] This separation of bodhrán and tambourine is valuable on two counts. First, it implies a belief in a historical continuity of ancient drum use, a speculative, imaginative narrative which suggests that ancient drumming had been abandoned by power structures, possibly due to Christianity, but was nevertheless retained, somewhat subversively, like vernacular traditional music, by the 'real' people – the poorer classes – and though that may well be the case, it is not provable from any folklore, history or manuscript documents. Second, and more importantly, in that distinction Fitzmaurice acknowledges that the bodhrán as we know it is of modern origin (though he does not indicate any awareness of the long-standing, island-wide existence of the bodhrán and similar devices as utensils and tools). Both sides of his view relate to music, one to a rough type for a tradition of noise-making – charivari – the other to a polished form which complements sophisticated melody. Mel Mercier has perhaps a more spiritual inference when he recalls his father, Peadar:

> When he taught himself to play the bodhrán in the mid-1950s, it was still primarily associated with the annual St Stephen's Day tradition of hunting the wren. It was considered to be a ritual instrument rather than a musical one[58]

▼ Ó Riada and large stick [*Gael Linn*]

A similar opinion was expressed to me too in 2022, much more bluntly, by a bodhrán player, Jack Quaide, at a CCÉ fund-raising session in Moore's of Carrigkerry, County Limerick, an area which is regarded as the home of the bodhrán: 'The "tambourine" is what we played for the Wren. The "bodhrán" came in when they started to play the Irish music on it. That fella Ó Riada was a classic'.[59]

In summary, it could be remarked that the tambourine was first brought to national attention by a Munster novelist, it was described as related to the bodhrán by a Munster folklorist, was given an iconic status in Munster by the establishing of the Wren competitions from 1957 on a trope prompted by a Munster playwright who gave it a national visibility, and then, under its new name, it was projected into universal use by a Munster composer. It is small wonder that it can be regarded as a Munster drum.

NOTES TO CHAPTER 10

[1] Matthews 2003, 5–34.
[2] *CITM* 2011, 5.
[3] Mulholland 1883, 56–7.
[4] The plot deliberately evades dating, but though motor vehicles are not mentioned, a small plane is, and that, and the execution in Belfast of a local lad for old-IRA border activity, indicates a date between 1921 and 1930.
[5] MacMahon 1952, 238.
[6] Ibid., 12 and 32.
[7] Ibid., 238–84.
[8] Ibid., 240.
[9] Ibid., 242.
[10] Ibid., 257.
[11] Ibid., 259.
[12] Ibid., 266.
[13] Ibid., 261.
[14] MacMahon 1967, 191 and 194.
[15] Ibid., 173.
[16] Keane 1959, 50.
[17] Ibid., 55. This usage of tambourine is properly acknowledged by some commentators (e.g. Ronan Nolan and Gabriel Rosenstock), but is generally not known by most.
[18] Ibid., 102.
[19] Ibid., 111.
[20] He was associated with the céilí-music programmes *Take the Floor with DinJoe, Balladmakers' Saturday Night* and *The Rambling House*.
[21] Keane, 1959, v.
[22] Keane 1969, 90–1.
[23] *Evening Herald* 1959 1027 4.
[24] Ibid., 1031 2.
[25] Ibid., 1960 0102 6.
[26] Keane 1959.
[27] Curran 1988, 13.
[28] De Buitléar 2014, PC; also Bradshaw 2022, PC.
[29] Ó Canainn 2003, 43.
[30] Abbey Theatre, 1960.
[31] *Evening Echo* 1961 0902 1.
[32] *Irish Times* 1961 0911 4.
[33] Ó Riada 1982, 76.
[34] See Appendix 4.
[35] The Morris Minor (pp. 129 and 263) was made from 1948 on; the Ford Consul (p. 362) from 1951 on; the Commer van (p. 90) from 1960 on.
[36] Keane J.B. 2017, 68.
[37] Ibid., 79.
[38] Ibid., 99.
[39] Ibid., 197.
[40] Ibid., 199.
[41] Ibid., 242.
[42] Ibid., 331.
[43] Ibid., 378.
[44] Ibid., 208–9.
[45] Ibid., 214.
[46] Ibid., 218.
[47] Ibid., 250–2.
[48] Ibid., 269.
[49] Ibid., 272–3.
[50] Ibid., 285.
[51] Ibid., 329.
[52] Ibid., 400.
[53] Ibid., ii.
[54] Keane C. 2017, 9.
[55] Keane J.B. 2017, 107.
[56] Fitzmaurice 2006, 128.
[57] Fitzmaurice, 2006.
[58] Mercier 2021.
[59] Quaide 2022, PC.

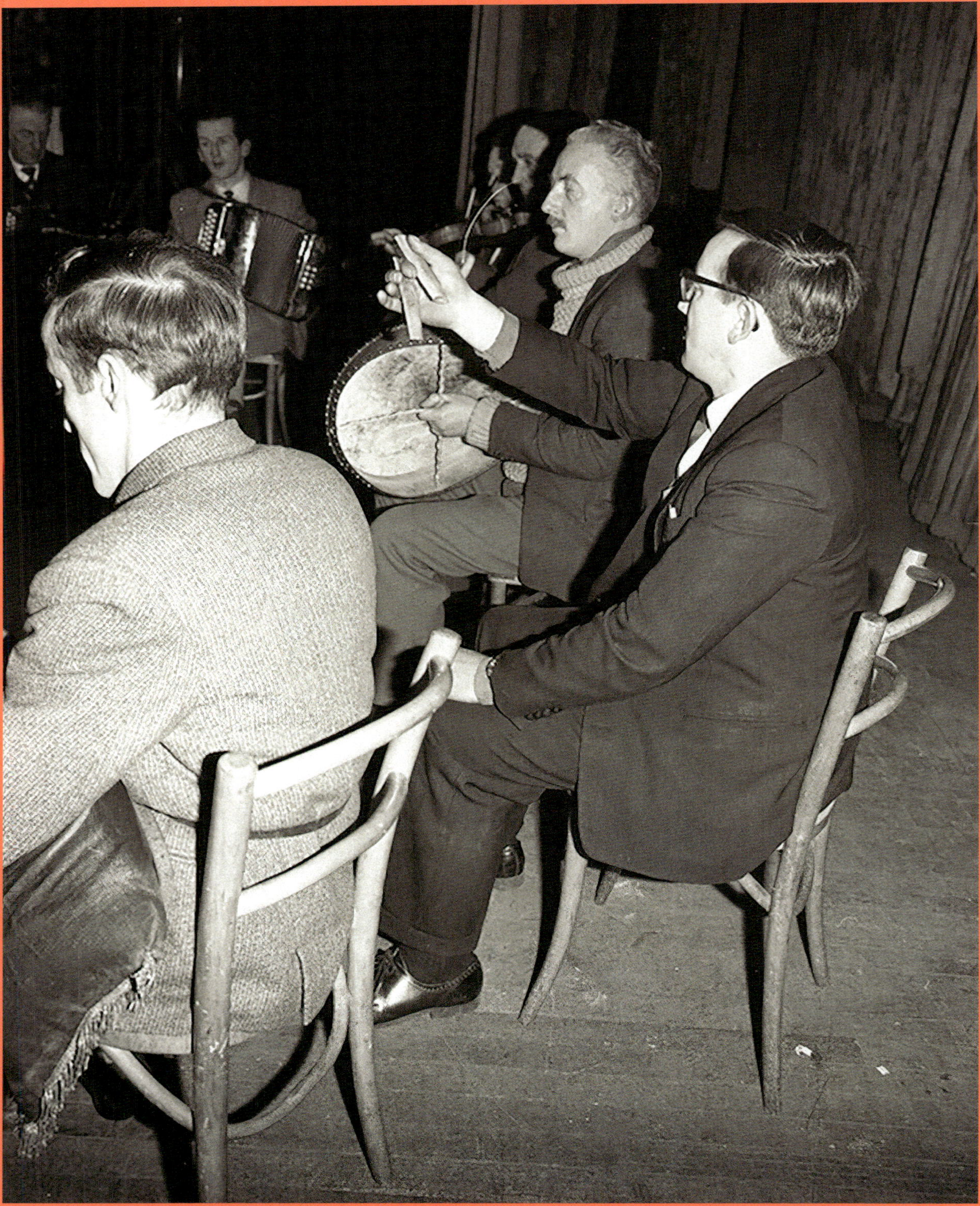

CHAPTER 11
FROM WALKING TO SITTING: TAMBOURINE TO BOWRAN

A 1958 radio interview with John B. Keane about the inaugural Wren-boy competition confirms then-standard use of the term 'tambourine'. Keane, who was one of those who came together to shape the Wren activity into a festival in 1957, told Radio Éireann's Ciarán Mac Mathúna that the participating Wren groups used 'three or four tambourines, five or six concertinas and melodeons and maybe three or four fiddles'. 'Tambourine' came to be dropped in favour of 'bodhrán' and the jingles were left behind over the course of the 1960s. 'Tambourine' had been most strongly associated with the Wren, with marching, its role like the side-drum in a marching band, while 'bodhrán' became part of sit-down music-display performance. This change in name and in roles is seen most clearly in the sequence of press reporting of the Wren itself and of music activities at major and minor fleadhs and in the cities. The quotations which follow have been selected from among many hundreds of such stories in a range of national and regional presses.[1] Prominent among them are highlights: the play *Sive*, Seán Ó Riada, the Wren, and tambourine/bodhrán competitions. In the excerpts, the gradual replacement of 'tambourine' to 'bodhrán' stands out, happening largely after 1959 and ´60, respectively the years of John B. Keane's play *Sive* and Seán Ó Riada's adoption of and name-change of the instrument. Some journalism is precise about terminology, but mostly it has inconsistencies, not surprisingly on account of the fact

◀ Left to right: Sonny Brogan and Éamon de Buitléar (accordions), Martin Fay and John Kelly (fiddles), Seán Ó Riada (bodhrán), Ronnie McShane (bones) and Paddy Moloney (uilleann pipes) at a recording of *Reachaireacht an Riadaigh* in 1971 [*Irish Photo Archive*]

▶ A variety of spellings are found in the press for 'bodhrán' as device and drum, and for 'tambourine'[1]

bodhrahn bobharan bodaran
boorawn bouraun badhran
tamborine bowran
bodran borrane tambareen
tambourine **bodhrán** bouran
bodhran boran bodharan tambarine
bowraw borra boorane
boarn tamboreen bourawn

173

The bodhrán used here as a noise-maker at a GAA hurling final [Sportsfile]

that in the 1960s even people in traditional music circles themselves were not familiar with the frame drum and its two descriptive terms, never mind Irish society as a whole.

But word did trickle down and, following the early traditional-music revival years, one consequence of the drum's widespread visibility is that it has come to be used as a visual marker of timeless authenticity in not only advertising and tourist promotions, but also in prestige events. It is used too as a definitively-Irish, team-support noise-maker in sports.

Tambourines on the sidelines

Today, bodhráns are seen being beaten enthusiastically by both GAA and soccer supporters, and one was reported too on the sidelines when Ireland won the ICC World Cricket League in 2010. The use of the bodhrán at sports matches need not, however, be considered either remarkable or new, for its ancestor the tambourine was used in this role before, reported for instance in 1930 at GAA Junior Cup matches in Croke Park:

> Drums, tamborines, bugles, bells, and whistles were brought into effective operation ... The singing of the various rallying songs ... with airs adapted from our most popular marching songs ... by over 1,200 youths [*Evening Herald* 1930 0307 2]

Parallel with this use in the twentieth century was the 'muscular' marching to the beat of the tambourine by rural Wren troupes. As well as this, better-

> **MELODEONS**, Accordions, Concertinas, Mandolines, Tambourines and Violins Selling Cheap. Also Buckets, Baths, Baskets, etc. A quantity Galvanized Iron and Slates, Sewerage Piping, etc. Still some Empty Barrels left.—McMenamin, Kells.

Meath Chronicle 1934 1215 7

> **Wren Boys Will Invade Listowel Next Friday**
>
> ST. STEPHEN'S Day may be three months away, but wren boys will invade Listowel on Friday next for the monster Wren Boys' band competition organised by the Carnival committee.

Kerryman 1958 0927 7

off society continued to entertain itself with versions of the tambourine too, but with more polite connotations: 'The dancing items included Irish jigs, reels and hornpipes and a tamborine dance in Gipsy costume'.[2]

Tambourines were still sold where there was a demand for them, so if there was no specialist music shop, a local hardware or bicycle shop stepped in as there was profit to be made, as in County Meath in 1934.[3] The instrument was still a popular item nationwide in the late 1940s, Cott's Stores, Kilcock, County Kildare, advertising:

> A big range of 1948 Battery-operated radios … Piano Accordians, Violins, Mandolines, Guitars, Flutes, Recorders, Xylophones, Flutinas, Jaw-Harps, Bagpipes, Flageolets, Tamborines, Trumpets, Trombones, Saxophones, also strings, etc. [*Irish Press* 1947 1011 2]

The price of tambourines had increased by the mid-twentieth century, as indeed had other instruments, confirming a continuing demand. Listed among toy or simple instruments were: 'Tambourines from 6/- … Tin whistles 1/6'.[4] Advertising too flew the tambourine flag, a sherry promotion announcing Spain as '... land of sunny splendour, or daring matadors, exciting women and rustling tambarines ..'.[5] And even as late as 1965, Christmas-presents inventories still continued to indicate popularity for the tambourine among children's interests in noise-making in this County Sligo list:

> The most popular presents, the ones that get the most use … are the functional ones that make as much noise as possible. Drums and trumpets, tamborines and castanets [*Sligo Champion* 1965 1217 12]

The new visibility given to the drum by John B. Keane and Seán Ó Riada steadily manifested itself in a heightened cultural awareness about, and excited 'new discovery' attitude to, the tambourine in the press, the instrument treated both curiously and patronisingly:

> suddenly we were attracted by music coming from the adjoining land … we found two young lads, one with an accordeon and the other with a tamborine, waltzing up and down the field putting the cattle to sleep [*Longford Leader* 1960 1001 8]

> Mr. Thomas Brewer, now known as 'the one man band', because of his remarkable ability to play three instruments at once, the mouth organ, the tamborine and foot drum [*Offaly Independent* 1960 1231 6]

> **10,000 Will Watch "Wren Boys" Contest**
>
> Ten thousand people are expected in Newcastle West, Co. Limerick, to-night for the annual Wren Boys Competition, which takes place at 7 o'clock. This is regarded as the All-Ireland Championship.

Cork Examiner 1963 0110 7

Transformation of the Wren

After the late 1950s the linking of the tambourine to traditional music took over from its Wren usage, its playing now on a year-round basis. But there was dramatic development of the Wren too, which, as one consequence of Bryan MacMahon's attention had evolved into a September competition, The Wren Boy's Bands Championship of Ireland, the first of which was held at Listowel in 1957. The custom, if not the event, obviously greatly impressed John B. Keane, perhaps influencing the creation of – but certainly powerfully enhancing reception of – his *Sive* production. Re-formation and rescheduling of the Wren to the autumn as a display and competition began with just three troupes in 1957, rising to eight in 1959, the event described in the press as featuring

> a group of adult 'Wren Boys', who will regale their audience with selections of Irish marches, etc., to the accompaniment of the ever-popular tambourine [*Kerryman* 1959 0103 8]

The practice gradually morphed into a carnival-style spectacle, with rehearsed routines from townland-specific, organised Wren-boy troupes. These, according to Keane,

> consisted of forty members and upwards … the greatest gathering of traditional musicians the Kingdom of Kerry has ever known … Out of Dirha west and Killocrim in north Kerry come the tambourine-tippers … From Bedford and the town of Listowel the concertina-players, the melodeon-players and the fiddlers make the stiff-backed streets rock to the strain of hornpipe and reel. Young blood and old respond [*Kerryman* 1960, 0924 6]

The tambourine was a key instrument in these, no longer a noise-maker to frighten the birds out of the bushes, but a percussion music. The very strangeness, sound, and feel of it implied a renaissance, a symbol of emergence from the dark, the opening of an atavistic route from the ancestors via a native music, a 'whup!!' of national sentiment, a football-final letting rip. It was certainly liberating for journalistic rhetoric which picked up on the energy and propelled it through the later years of the twentieth century. In the words of John B. Keane in his *Kerryman* column:

> The tambourines set the gay beat and away they go, one band after another, each fiercely proud and individual… This is the 'Wren boys' Bands Championship of Ireland' … It is the heart and soul of rural Ireland, crying out its thrilling and passionate music to the stars. It is the bond between us and those dead and gone before us [*Kerryman* 1960 0924 6]

▼ Warming bendirs at Tissardmine, Morocco, 13 October 2014 [*Detail from 'Morocco' by Missy Dunaway, pp. 96–7 from her 2021 book The Traveling Artist. New York: G Editions (©) – geditions.com*]

The press's coverage of the Wren reached a high with the competitions in the 1960s, still carried on today. The fervour and energy that Wren-boy festivals and competitions generate and engage with can be judged from press reports to be a phenomenal release, a sonic and visual drama and choreography:

> The wren boys assembled in the Presentation Convent grounds before parading through the town. In the darkness of the convent yard hundreds of strangely garbed figures were silhouetted against the glow of bonfires lit to heat the drums and tambourines to the p tch required to produce the requisite tone. Then as the drums, tambourines and bowrans gradually thawed, the deep, mysterious rhythm of the drums stole out through the darkness to the waiting thousands on the streets. The scene resembled a set for a motion picture fantasy with young men and boys huddling in groups about the leaping flames [Kerryman 1961 1007 3]

▼ Wren bodhráns at Newcastle West, 2022 L-R: Henry Keogh, Noel Mullins and Mike O'Connor [*Nutan*]

Beating out fervour

This energy is immortalised in the 1974 documentary *Bodhrán* by County Limerick film-maker Tom Hayes,[6] himself from the Newcastle West area. It was commissioned by the then minister for the Gaeltacht Tom O'Donnell (also from County Limerick), a formal state imprimatur for the bodhrán in recognition of the importance of the Wren tradition. In the film the drums are observed at Puck Fair, Killorglin, and also out on the Wren where four of them are seen being played along with accordion, fiddles, flute and banjo; rim shots are a feature of the exuberant playing to very fast music, with set dancing in houses on the Wrenboys' route. The drum is filmed being played too at the All-Ireland fleadh in Listowel, where there is a commanding female player, and at the Fleadh Nua in Dublin in the same year where multiple bodhráns are played, mostly by adult men, to which older men dance. It concludes with the wild, torch-lit, night-time spectacle of the Wrenboys' competition which by that time had been running for seventeen years. In all circumstances the bodhráns use a strong, solid stick-struck beat, there is crowd-thrilling showmanship by some players, notably by the legendary Jim Sheehy, and there are numerous shots of mass playing of the drum. Some of the the instruments have jingles, but most have not, showing that the new bodhrán had almost totally eclipsed the tambourine by then. But the various footages which are shown demonstrate that the making and the playing of tambourines in this way dates back to the end of the 1800s at least. It also makes clear that the drum came to traditional music via the Wren.[7]

Tambourine playing style in the Wren competitions in 1963 can be seen to be similar in articulation and detail to Lambeg drum performance – a flamboyant, double- and treble-beat which both matches and elaborates each note of the melody being played. Three or four bodhráns are heard in unison, played while walking, making a formidable backdrop to button accordions, flute and fiddle.[8] The associated passionate commentary rhetoric conjures up vigour in participants and viewers alike, and indeed is the very stuff of captivating television and film documentary. This sentiment was expressed in the opening of a Telefís Éireann programme on Puck Fair at Killorglin, County Kerry in 1969:

> Here and there throughout Ireland there are places, occasions and even festivals which echo the rhythms of an earlier way of life. They draw the imagination into areas where myth, history and religion meet and overlap, areas where scholars speculate and ordinary people do extraordinary things for reasons they no longer understand

The term 'tambourine' co-existed with 'bowran' and other bodhrán-derived words in 1960, though 'bodhrán' was initially much less often heard. But both words meant the same thing, and were used side by side, for it was the object, the frame drum, which was felt to be at the heart of local identity and pride, as dramatised by Keane:

> Our feet begin to tap when the step-dancers ascend the platform. Our hearts are lighter because we are country-people and this is our music and we are proud of it. Affectation and practised restraint fly skywards with the rattle of drum and barbaric beating of the bowran … a surge of national pride wells up inside of us … There is a music here that is our very own. You will shiver at the naked beauty of our past. From the flat fields of Finuge and Ennismore, from the dark lands of Dirha west and Shroneowen the clansmen are coming. There is pride here, pride in ourselves, pride in our townlands, in our parish, in our County and in our country. We can never deny what is our own – and why should we? This is the music of our country and it is coming into its own [*Kerryman* 1960 0924 6]

That same word 'barbaric' had previously had an opposite, derogatory, connotation. Hostile press commentary in Tipperary at the beginning of the 1900s, in the earliest press coverage, railed about the Wren that it had

> barbaric splendour of mixed garb and colours … barbarous songs or doggerels … It is about time that we had seen the last of the wren boys, anyway, for to many they are a real nuisance during the holidays [*The Nationalist* 1902 1231 3]

Such an old-establishment value was, however, well dissipated by the mid-century, the 'barbarism' by then clearly being appealing, invoking both a sense of liberation from convention and a historical continuity, a pride in local custom, central to which was the tambourine:

> The number of Wren Boys who visited the village on St Stephen's Day was well up on former years … after nightfall the tambourines were to be heard on all sides of the village [*Kerryman* 1960 0102 10]

> Christmas customs …. the *Farmers Journal* wants to hear about them from its readers. For example, Wexford has its mummers; Kerry has its wren boys

> "The tambourine is what we played for the Wren. The bodhrán came in when they started to play the Irish music on it"
> *Jack Quaide,* Carrigkerry Wren, County Limerick

complete with goatskin tambourines [*Irish Farmers Journal* 1961 1202 26]

Listowel: Santa Claus made a glorious and colourful arrival ... accompanied by the Killocrim Wrenboys and their band of accordions, tambourines and 'The bones' [*Kerryman* 1961 1216 9]

By 1963 another major competition at Newcastle West was 'a very keen and exciting contest between ten groups ... more than 200 Wren Boys'.[9] Bryan MacMahon said that this event – *Fleadh an Dreolín* [the Wren fleadh] – was attended by a record crowd of 8,000 people.[10] The Listowel Harvest Festival thrived on the Wren excitement too in 1964, with

> music ringing through the streets of the town and echoing from smoke-filled taverns ... modern and old, native and foreign, sweet and wild ... Perhaps the music that will appeal most to the visitors will be the wild notes sounded by the wren boys next Friday night [*Kerryman* 1964 1005 4]

> the Wren Boys Championship in Listowel is an event that is such a major attraction every year. People come from all parts of Kerry and west Limerick, which is the home of wren music in Ireland. The performance of men and boys from Brosna to Dingle sends the blood of excitement rushing through their veins and for a while they live in the pre-Christian times of their forefathers [*Kerryman* 1964 1005 4]

The deployment of the Wren-boys in the month of May indicates a rising cultural, artistic or entertainment profile rather than just ritual value, prompting John B. Keane, one of the organisers, to fan the spark he had already set:

> Everybody looks forward to the first mad belt of the bodhrán ... suddenly you want to go wild. The pagan stuff breaks out in you. The belting of the bodhráns and the notes from the old melodeons and the flutes and the bagpipes and fiddles are a mixture of pagan and Christian [*Kerryman* 1964 1005 4]

The tambourine was at the centre of the imagination, but the influence of Seán Ó Riada's use of the term 'bodhrán' can be seen to gradually alter the popular terminology in news reports, and often the two terms appear side by side as if they are different instruments. This may well indicate that jingled and non-jingled drums were in use, but is understandable too on account of either the newness of journalists to it, or their responsibility to the correct use of English. In 1965: 'wren boys and Biddy boys bands competing in the Festival of Kerry competition pared the town every night ... They carried the traditional bodhráns, tambourines and spoons'.[11]

Seán Ó Riada and the bodhrán in the press

The ascent of the Wren's popularity ran parallel to Ó Riada's new direction in music – coverage of this indicates his role in the relocation of the tambourine from on-the-streets, noisy use to sit-down, formal music in concerts and broadcasts with Ceoltóirí Chualann. All of this in turn drew its energy and audiences from the regeneration of traditional music by CCÉ, which had been going on since 1951 all over the island. Ó Riada's intervention has already been described, and the national press generally accepted the term 'bodhrán' that he had newly espoused, highlighting the drum's association with Kerry:

> "Everybody looks forward to the first mad belt of the bodhrán ... suddenly you want to go wild. The pagan stuff breaks out in you. The belting of the bodhráns and the notes from the old melodeons and the flutes and the bagpipes and fiddles are a mixture of pagan and Christian"
> **John B. Keane**
> [*Kerryman* 1964 1005 4]

> 'Spailpín a Rúin' at Gael-Linn's Damer Theatre … singers, fiddlers, pipers and performers on the Kerry goatskin drum, the bodhrán, introduced to Dublin audiences in 'Sive' [*Kerryman* 1960 0910 3]

But it was still being described literally – or generically – as 'tambourine':

> a Goatskin tambourine – beaten to suggest the roar of waves and scraped for the groaning of a ship's timbers. Ó Riada's folk orchestra, Ceoltóirí Chualann … known to listeners to the Radio Eireann feature 'Reacaireacht an Riadaigh' and have recently started a new programme, 'Fleadh Cheoil an Radio' [*Irish Press* 1962 1219 15]

By 1963, however the 'B' word was taking over, through Ó Riada's Fleadh Cheoil an Radio which created a certain amount of wonder on account of

> their ebullient conductor drummer-arranger Seán Ó Riada's most astonishing rhythmic effects on the boorawn (remember it in 'Sive'?) [*Evening Echo* 1963 0202 6]

His concerts with Ceoltóirí Chualann in the sixties attracted the attention of reviewers, not least on account of his prestige status as a composer. It was not always enthusiastic, but invariably it mentioned the 'bowran' as a key point of interest, though at times showing little empathy with traditional music:

> Anyone who doubted the popularity of the 'Cualann sound' had only to try to get a ticket for the concert given by Sean O Riada and his Ceoltoiri Cualann in the Gaiety Theatre … It would have been … a vain effort. It is in fact an attractive sound, if limited in colour interest, for a whole evening's listening. To the rather pastoral quality of uilleann pipes, flute and recorders [sic], strengthened with three fiddles, a discreet accordeon and the bowran [*Irish Independent* 1968 0331 15]

The tambourine competition, 1962

The increasing popularity and formalisation of the Wren inevitably demanded giving serious attention to the quality and presentation of the music as well as choreography. A logical spin-off was the tambourine finally getting formal recognition as an instrument by being admitted to competitions. The idea of competition may have been prompted by Seán Ó Riada's adoption of the instrument from 1960 onwards. But the Wren competitions, and the fact that the tambourine was being played occasionally with dance music in Connacht and Munster in the mid-1950s, would have been impetus enough. For instance, Ciarán Mac Mathúna had already recorded County Galway man Mícheál Ó Concannon (p. 206) playing tambourine with the hand in 1956, from which excerpt it was clear that the instrument was felt to add a tremendous lift to music – in that case the player's own lilting, as well as the fiddles of Máirtín Byrnes and Paddy Barrett. For the BBC Séamus Ennis had also been able to record stick-struck playing by Thady Casey along with Willie Clancy on pipes and Aggie Whyte on fiddle. Nevertheless, it is likely that Ó Riada's stated opinion about the bodhrán was quite an imprimatur for the tambourine and its offspring.

The first mention of a competition is, however, for 'tambourine' – for County Mayo, in connection with the Swinford All-Ireland of 1961. This appears to have been for the county or provincial fleadh which took place on the same weekend, and had been inaugurated the previous year at Westport. The only information available is the CCÉ PR statements that were issued to the press before the event; these announced entries from various instrumental performers, including 'tambourinists'. No result was

---

SWINFORD FLEADH CHEOIL

TWO thousand three hundred entries have been received for the Fleadh Ceoil which will be held in Swinford, Co. Mayo on Whit week-end (May 20th, 21st and 22nd).

The entries comprise traditional violinists, accordionists, flautists, pipers (war pipes and Uilleann), tambourinists, harpists, pianists, singers. They come from all over Ireland, Scotland, England and New York. Competitions for the first day (Saturday) are confined to Co. Mayo; it will in fact be the Mayo County Fleadh.

Connacht Tribune 1961 0422

Heartbreak end to a journey

MOST disappointed man in Swinford yesterday was Paddy Higgins, of Whiterock, Co. Longford. After cycling 70 miles to the Fleadh, he discovered that his entry for the tam-bourine class had arrived late. Paddy, who made his own tambourine, was still hoping last night that his entry would be accepted.

Irish Press 1961 0522 8

Ballyheigue Feis Tambourine Competition

Always with and eye on the unusual and the attractive, the committee have included in this year's programme of events, a Tambourine Competition.

To their minds Kerry is the home of the tambourine because of the famous wren boys and they feel that the new competition will be of great interest to both locals and visitors alike.

Kerryman 1962 0804 10

Fleadh Ceoil prizewinners

First prizewinners at Newcastle West Fleadh Ceoil were: All-Ireland Senior Tambourine Championship (Martinstown Branch Cup) — James Sheehy, Barnligue, Carrickerry, County Limerick.

Irish Press 1962 0605 4

published for any such competition, but because one upset tambourine player from Longford is reported as being disappointed after being deemed to have applied too late, it seems likely that the competition never actually took place – perhaps cancelled due to lack of advance entries.

County Limerick was next, in June, 1962, with CCÉ announcing a 'tambourine championship' which was to take place at the first County Limerick Fleadh Cheoil.[12] In August of that year another event responded to the rising profile of the frame drum: 'First tambourine competition announced for the annual Ballyheigue Feis':

> Always with an eye on the unusual and the attractive, the committee have included in this year's programme a Tambourine Competition. To their minds Kerry is the home of the tambourine because of the famous wren boys [*1962, Kerryman* 0804 10]

As competitive and engaging as a boxing match, 'the senior tambourine competition was expected to attract a record number of entries'.[13] Because the drum was known and talked about on the ground as 'tambourine', it is so listed in the programmes for the fleadhs which followed; the national press generally regarded it otherwise, apparently now regarding 'bodhrán' as the authentic term, and 'tambourine' as a colloquialism. This was despite the fact that the 1961–3 competitions were actually labelled and announced as 'tambourine':

> Who has ever heard of or seen a bodhrán competition up to this? No one at all, I should imagine. All praise then to the Limerick Comhaltas Ceoltóirí Éireann craobh for hitting on the novel idea of holding the bodhrán championship of Ireland during the Fleadh Cheoil Luimní at Newcastle West. [*Irish Independent* 1962 0517 7]

LIBRARY 3p.m.   TAMBOURINE   SENIOR
1. Michael Sheehy, Bullinabearna, Newcastlewest.
2. Patrick Mulvihill, Kiloughteen, Newcastlewest.
3. John Sanders, Kiloughteen, Newcastlewest.
4. Ml. Barrett, Newcastlewest
5. Tim Lane, Newcastlewest.
6. James Sheehy, Newcastlewest.

TAMBOURINE 14-18
1. John McKenna, Abbeyfeale.
2. Pat Cremin, Barnagh.
3. Bernard Lenihan, Barnagh.

TAMBOURINE under 14
Tambourine under 14
1. Padraig Ó Riardain, Ballybehy, Abbeyfeale.
2. Diarmud O Ceallachain, Tuar na Fola, Co. Luimni.
3. Eamon Roche, Tournafulla.
4. Michael Greene, Newcastle West.
5. Neil O'Reilly, Templeglantine West.
6. Kieran Aherne, Newcastlewest.

▲ Fleadh Cheoil Luimní, tambourine competitions, 1963 [*Courtesy Tadhg Ó Maolcatha*]

▲ Fleadh Cheoil Luimní, 1963, programme cover [*Courtesy Tadhg Ó Maolcatha*]

On account of this competition being the only such one in the country, the national press regarded it as an 'all-Ireland' championship. The adjudicators were Bryan MacMahon and Seán Ó Riada. Local presses hailed the event with glorious accounts of the instrument's ethnicity and elemental power, all related to its primary use up until then on the Wren on Stephen's Day, and in the Wren-boy competitions which had then been running for five years; the legendary Jim Sheeny was the winner in that inaugural year, and his brother Michael won it in 1963.

The silence of the tambourines
The transfer from tambourine to bodhrán did not happen overnight, as seen in the previous chapters which show that even into the 1970s, indeed beyond the eighties, the word 'tambourine' lingered on. But the change has by now become so thorough that, outside of north Munster and the sixty something age-group of musicians, nothing of 'tambourine' is known: all authorities speak only of the 'bodhrán'. That is of course absolutely fine, for the change was universally and enthusiastically accepted, not least because 'bodhrán' sounds more appropriate for an Irish-developed instrument. The feis, fleadh and other competitions were at the hub of this change.

Local presses, however, did generally continue to give all instruments their 'proper' dictionary, titles in the 1960s, as seen in the announcement that in 1963 'tambourine' competitions were planned for Lixnaw fleadh, as well as those for 'violin'.[14] Age, as always, and effort, were commended, attitudes likely underlain by a sense of respect for surviving cultural artefacts and personalities, if not wonder at the curiosity value of it all:

> Veteran amongst the players was 72-years-old Batt Daly of Kerrykyle, while there was one lone competitor – Mr. Pat Daly, Adare, who cycled 14 miles to attend the competition ... his solo contribution on a deerskin tamborine in which he accompanied himself on the mouth organ [*Limerick Leader* 1963 0119 19]

Still, 'bodhrán' crept in, its provenance analysed and praised:

> The bodhrán, a home-made, tambourine-like instrument made of hand-cured goat-skin mounted on a circular frame, provided the dominant note in the musical programme and the skill displayed by a number of the players was most favourably commented on [*Limerick Leader* 1963 0119 19]

The growing awareness of the change in terminology must surely have been mildly confusing, as the press reports show. Occasionally, tambourine and bodhrán were seen as being different, as in the citing of this quite prescriptive regulation:

> north Cork, east and north Kerry ... all parts of Limerick. These are now the main centres where wren parties are performed in the traditional fashion ... 'We will not accept any groups performing hot jazz or cool music. Songs must be the traditional ones' ... costumes must include the traditional straw and ivy. Their instruments will include the bodhrán, which is similar to a tambourine, and is played with a two-head stick. It is made from goat-skin, stretched over a frame [*Cork Examiner* 1963 0110 7]

Where such a difference was seen, it is probably in the nature of what makers Páiric McNeela, Malachy Kearns and others make clear – that the modern bodhrán does not have jingles. But other reports show that press commentators and music aficionados alike were not quite sure, as both

CALLING ALL TRADITIONAL MUSICIANS, Ballad Groups and Fleadh Ceoil followers, goat-skin bodhrain (tambourines), for sale and made to order. Prices quoted. Box 38208

Irish Independent 1964 1107 22

11 FROM WALKING TO SITTING: TAMBOURINE TO BOWRAN

GOATSKINS SOUGHT—FOR BODHRANS

Brosna (Co. Kerry) wrenboys, who have won numerous prizes at wrenboy gatherings, are at the present time looking for goatskins! The skins are required for the making of bodhrans, one of those drums quite familiar in the play "Sive".

Evening Echo 1963 0223 6

tambourine and bodhrán seem too to have been regarded as the same instrument, probably on account of how they were made and played. But the results of the earlier competitions demonstrate that 'tambourine' stuck as the dominant term by which the drum was known, and in 1964 it was still the one used in Kerry:

> A keen contest between two brothers for the All-Ireland tambourine championships proved one of the highlights of the Fleadh programme … James Sheehy, Glensharrold, last year's runner-up and winner two years ago, recaptured the title this year from his brother Mr. Michael Sheehy, Ballinabearna who was winner in 1963. The markings were extremely close [*Limerick Leader* 1964 0613 15]

Newcastle West's competition announcement highlights the name-transfer, indeed giving a historic pedigree: the air was clearing somewhat, as it must have become obvious that the winners under the titles 'tambourine' and, later, 'bodhrán' had not changed: the players were the same, the competition was the same, and the winners were the same. In 1964 it was announced that

> One of the highlights of Sunday's programme will be the contest for the Tambourine (Badhran) Championship of Ireland. This home-made, drum-like instrument, usually finished with goat-skin stretched on a circular frame, has been for generations the predominant instrument with wren boys groups in west Limerick and Kerry. The present holder is Mr. Mick Sheehy of Ballinabearna, Ardagh, who was awarded the championship last year after a very keen contest with his brother, Mr. Jim Sheehy, Barniegue … The reigning champion is very proud of his tambourine, in the making of which he departed from the old custom by substituting a deer-skin for the customary goat-hide. The brothers, it is of interest to note, inherited the talent from their grandfather, who was one of the most expert badhran players of his day [*Limerick Leader* 1964 0606 15]

BODHRAIN Under 14
1. P.J. Mulvihill, Newcastlewest.
2. Thos. Curtain, Newcastlewest.
3. A. Byrne, Arches Grove, Kilkenny.
4. C. Byrne, Arches Grove, Kilkenny.
5. Wm. Foley, Newcastlewest.
6. Ml. Greene, Newcastlewest.

BODHRAN Under 18.
1. Wm. Power, Newcastlewest.

BODHRAN SENIOR
1. Lorcan O Haimhirgin, Kilkenny.
2. Sean Flaherty, Croagh, Co. Limerick.
3. Patk. Murphy, Ardagh, Co. Limerick.
4. Maurice Foley, Co. Kerry.
5. Ml. Sheehy, Newcastlewest.
6. James Sheehy, Newcastlewest.
7. Patk Mulvihill, Newcastlewest.
8. Ml. Barrett, Newcastlewest.

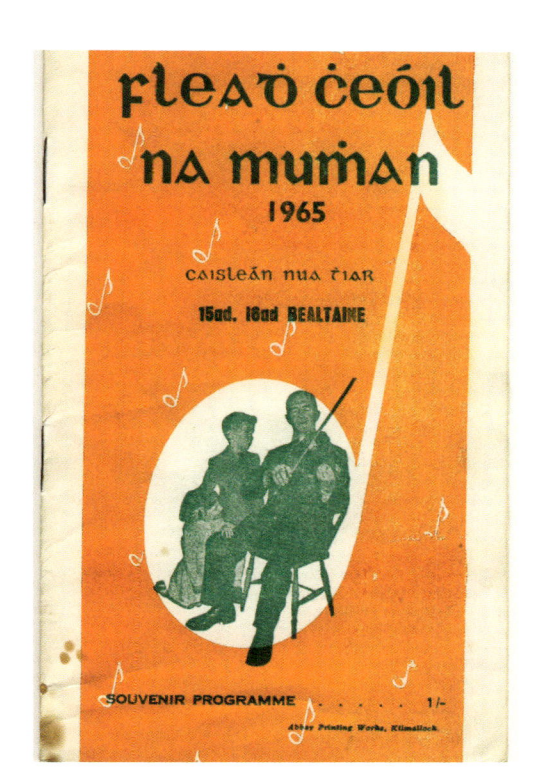

▲ ▶ 1965 Munster Fleadh programme
[*Courtesy Tadhg Ó Maolcatha*]

At the Newcastle West Munster Fleadh Cheoil of 1965 organisers persisted with the traditional terminology, a report announcing the winner of the 'All-Ireland Tamborine Championships – Patrick Murphy, Rooskagh'.[15] And following the same fleadh a dual title was indicated:

> Carmel Byrne (13) … Kilkenny, who won a medal and diploma by coming first in the final of the under 14 Bodhrán (Tabourine) competition in the Fleadh Ceoil at Newcastle West, Co., Limerick … her instructor was Mr. Lorcan Bergin, Kilkenny [*Kilkenny People* 1965 0521 5]

By 1965 the official name of the competition had changed: 'Competitions in the Munster Fleadh Cheoil at Newcastle West … include an all-Ireland bodhrán competition'.[16] Yet still, some in Limerick, and Kerry too, stuck to the old terminology twenty-five and more years after *Sive* and Ó Riada: 'Many Limerick winners at Fleadh Cheoil na Mumhan … Tambourine – M. Sheehy, Newcastle West'.[17] And in 1986: 'Following his recent victory on the tamborine at Fleadh Cheoil Chiarrai in Ballyheigue, Mr. Chohan [?] O'Grady will be competing in the Munster finals in Tipperary'.[18]

The *Sive* tambourine legacy
The legacy of the play *Sive* contributed to the increasing visibility of both tambourine and bodhrán. Subsequent comment changed the spelling to that introduced by Joyce in 1910, the phonetic 'bowran'. This became a standard Anglicisation that persisted for several years and, though it is now defunct in print, it is retained in pronunciation. The earliest *Sive* report in the national press to use the Joyce spelling of 'bodhrán' had actually been quite well informed:

> With the success of *Sive* we were effectively introduced to a species of tambourine, native to Kerry, the Bowran and what wonderful use of it was made in the play … First the Ivy Leaf, now the Bowran. I wonder how many other strange musical instruments are to be found here and there up and down the country [*Irish Independent* 1959 1225 6]

The 'ivy leaf' refers to the use of a leaf held between the sides of the thumbs and blown to make a reed-like music, a primitive improvisation which, like whistling or lilting, could be used for impromptu dance music where no regular instrument was available; the suggestion here was that the 'bowran' was a similar vernacular improvisation. Generally, after *Sive* the word tambourine began to disappear, pushed out by 'bodhrán' and 'bowran'. Yet press reportage often linked the two terms, and could be confusing

> local player Billy Vaughan got a lesson on the 'bowran' or wren-boy's tambourine from Listowel's Sean Cahill, who played Carthalawn … the Ballinasloe players had no tambourine worries, the 'bowran' was presented to the group by the author himself, John B. Keane [*Westmeath Independent* 1959 1107 9]

The presence of the tambourine in *Sive* was undoubtedly a factor in the play's huge popularity among other drama groups in Ireland. The drum, however, proved hard to find, generating requests in the national press in 1960: 'Sir – would some kind reader have in his, or her, possession a bowran or tambourine, as played by one for the tinkers in *Sive* that could be loaned?'[19] In the same year *The Irish Times* went for the name-change, saying of Ó Riada's first Ceoltóirí Chualann music: 'There will be singers fiddlers pipers, and performers on the Kerry goatskin drum, the bodhrán, which was introduced

---

Bodhran Competition

THE tinker couple in John B. Keane's "Sive" have raised the bodhran to a remarkable pitch of popularity and familiarity, but who has ever heard of or seen a bodhran competition up to this? No one at all, I should imagine.

All praise then, to the Limerick Comhaltas Ceoltóirí Eireann craobh for hitting on the novel idea of holding the bodhran championship of Ireland during the Fleadh Cheoil Luimni at Newcastle West on June 2 and 3.

Irish Independent 1962 0517 7

to Dublin audiences in *Sive*'.[20] A Connacht editorial in 1961 tried to explain the bodhrán and tambourine r/e *Sive:* 'there are many Connacht people who, [though] they have not heard hand-drumming on the bouraun, have heard of the tambourine by that name'.[21] The two terms overlapped, however, as in the same year mystery kept them alive: 'Then in the snug of this tavern there's a lot of talk about a drum-like tambourine called the Bowran. This curious instrument was in use in Keane's play *Sive*'.[22] The play continued to be enthusiastically performed, attended and reviewed, the drum still commanding attention: 'these nights the bowran can be heard as Páraic Burns goes through his paces',[23] and press reviews reflect the two names:

> Carthalawn, played by Padraic Burns, added much life and excitement to the play. It was interesting to learn that the Bowran, or tambourine used by Paraic Burns was made by Mr. Pat Connaughton of Eyrecourt a couple of years ago [*Connacht Tribune* 1968 0329 8]

Popularity continued into the 1980s, as did the term 'tambourine', use of it still in 1982 possibly related to its being in the original 1959 script from which local drama groups would have been working: 'Eamon Daly … gives a delightful portrayal as "Carthalawn". His singing and tamborine playing is a memorable feature of the show'.[24]

Travellers and the 'bowran'
Rural Ireland and traditional musicians generally took a certain gratification from the new high profile for the music and for the bodhrán through *Sive*, but Telefís Éireann's Proinsias Mac Aonghusa did not seem impressed, for he was

> neatly ticked-off by the great actress Siobhén MacKenna for suggesting that her defence of John B. Keane's play *Sive* was not sincere … He was afraid, he said, that if plays like *Sive* were seen by audiences outside Ireland it might give a completely erroneous picture of this country. Miss MacKenna … told her interviewer that he knew perfectly well such types existed in rural parts of Ireland … the tinkers in the play with their bowran and their incantations were quite true to life, she said, and should not be written-off as incredible simply because people like her interviewer had never met them [*Irish Press* 1964]

This mention of Travellers in relation to the bodhrán had been made also by Rosa Mulholland a century earlier (p. 159). It comes up again with maker Malachy Kearns, who says that the first time he heard a bodhrán was at the age of ten or eleven,[25] about 1963 in a pub in Mountcharles, County Donegal: 'What do you call that?' is what I asked the man beside me. "It's a tambourine yoke, a bodhrán. It's made out of the skin of a greyhound. The Travelling lads are great on them"'.[26] It was indeed being played by a Travelling man on that occasion, along with the fiddle-player John Doherty.[27] But other than Travellers picking up extant popular music and instruments to perform commercially, there is no record of a long-standing tradition of tambourine playing among them. The opposite impression was, however, given by Keane's casting of his tambourine player as a Traveller, and was focused on by the press, seen in such review comments as: 'The travelling tinkers with the bowran did not make the desired impact: they were not sufficiently forceful'.[28] This casting inference contrasts with MacMahon in his play *The Honey Spike* a year later which was clearly focused on settled people playing tambourines on the Wren.

Sive came to be performed all over the island, eventually all listing 'bowran' or 'bodhrán' rather than 'tambourine', but often highlighting the Traveller motif in relation to the drum, so creating two separate illusions – 1/ the Irish drum of the Wren was 'bodhrán' and 2/ it was a Traveller instrument.

Tambourine outside of Munster

The word 'tambourine', however, continued to be used outside of Kerry and Limerick as some event announcements in other parts of the country show, persisting until the 1980s both in connection with the Wren and otherwise. Apart from in Munster, the focus was more on the Wren than on the tambourine, which by that name still remained popular in, for instance, counties Westmeath and Meath. But it was becoming part of traditional-music entertainments and competitions:

> The sixth annual Rathconrath Aeriocht, under the auspices of Rathconrath Comhaltas branch ... included such well known artistes as: Frank Bavigan (accordionist), Agnes Gavigan (spoons), James Ballosty (accordion) and James Fox (tambourine) [*Westmeath Examiner 1962 0707 8*]

The tambourine was known well in north Mayo, south Sligo and Roscommon too and a report on a CCÉ concert in Ballymote notes that:

> an item which captured the imagination of the audience was the duet by 13 years old Seamus Leonard on the tin whistle, and 10 years old Tommie Underwood on the tamborine [*Sligo Champion 1962 0428 2*]

Still a novelty, the fact that the 'Tambourine of goatskin' was announced to be played at the fleadh in County Offaly by a child of seven merited coverage in regional press.[29] The main term used in both Connacht and Munster was 'tambourine', underlined by later reflection made by Connacht player Batty Sherlock: 'They used to call it a tambourine, but then in the later years, they changed that to the bodhrán'.[30] Underlining a certain resistance to the name-change, the term 'tambourine' persisted outside Munster too all through the 1960s, even when the new ballad groups began to absorb traditional instruments. One was the Dublin-based Ivy folk, in 1967, featuring 'double bass, banjo, guitar and tamborine',[31] while in Oldcastle, County Meath the same year the Show Hall 'Concert of the year' had 'Straight from Irish Club in London John Hiffins [Higgins] on The Gallanti with Tambourine accompaniment'.[32] In Sligo, 1967, 'tambourine' was what it continued to be, seen in the Leader label's *Masters Of Irish Music* series which listed Seamus Tansey and Eddie Corcoran as 'tin-whistle and tambourine'. In 1968 renowned flute-player, composer and singer Josie McDermott's band Flynn's Men was announced as playing in a CCÉ concert at the Town Hall, Omagh, County Tyrone, as 'FLYNN'S MEN (Co. Sligo) Ceili Band with tamborine'.[33] Interesting here was 'Guest Compere – Paul Lepari' [*sic*] of Magherafelt, who was father of Four Men and a Dog bodhrán-player-to-be Gino Lupari. Television broadcasting producer Tony MacMahon respected the local use of terminology for the drum: 'Radio Telefís Éireann's Bring Down the Lamp ... on which Kevin Daniels, Tullaree played the tambourine'.[34] Other commentators continued to take 'tambourine' for granted:

> Michael Hogan, Feighs, Banagher ... never failed, until this year, to 'beat the old year out and the New Year in' to Banagher at midnight on New Year's Eve. The music of his tambourine was sweet to the ears of his hearers the vast majority

---

Mini-Fleadh

Coming by invitation : Top traditional Fiddlers, Accordionists, Tin Whistle, Uilleann Pipes, Bagpipes, Bowran, Banjo, etc.

Free Car Park

ADMISSION (including Refreshments) 40p

Kilkenny People 1971 0723 18

of whom commented on its absence [*Westmeath Independent* 1969 0111 6]

To complete the foursome [the Carthy folk band] we have the only man in the group, drummer Sean, who is also an accomplished tamboreen player (or the bouran as some people call it) [*Leitrim Observer* 1970 1226 4]

At Rathmolyon Field Day, in County Meath, the parade was led by a group of talented musicians playing accordions, fiddles, tin whistles and tamborines [*Meath Chronicle* 1971 1002 12]

In Ballinamore, County Leitrim, too, in 1968. Wren Boys stuck to 'tambourine', the term regarded by Gabriel Fitzmaurice as applying to the outdoor version of the frame drum: 'The Band which numbers about 60, consists of Fiddles, Accordions, Tamborines, Whistlers, Lilters, Singers, Dancers'.[35] 'Tambourine' was still on the go at the end of the decade, at Knocknagoshel, County Kerry, 1969, where 'the rousing music of the accordions, violins, banjoes and tamborines could be heard all over the parish'.[36] And in Castlegregory the same year, on 'The Wren Day … groups toured the countryside with accordions, violins and tamborines'.[37] It is possible of course that newspaper reporters were

Ulster Herald 1968 0316 5

just using 'tambourine' as what they thought was a proper generic term for the frame drum, but they too gradually changed as the word bodhrán became more established and entered the major dictionaries.

In County Westmeath, 'Davey [Fallon] has a style of playing the tamboreen that would make anyone over forty feel twenty years younger;'[38] 'the Sheerin family Group … consists of father and mother, who play guitar and tamboreen and sing'.[39] As late as 1978 in County Louth the term 'tambourine' was still in circulation, retained possibly because of the older Wren association with it, one report listing:

> Juniors were: Derek Murtagh (accordion), brother C.J. (drums), Paul Gilroy (guitar), Frank Coleman (tamborine) … Seniors were: Jim Toole (accordion), David Murray and Paddy Tully (guitars and vocalists), Michael Rispin (mandolin), Kevin Toole (tamborine) [*Drogheda Independent* 1978 0113 7]

County Leitrim flute player Packie Duignan's band in 1979 was still resisting modern trends, as were many others up to the 1980s, including people in Tyrone, Longford, Leitrim, London and Offaly:

> Jack Campbell … born in Brooklyn … Josie his wife is a native of Newtownforbes, County Longford and she plays fiddle, tin whistle and Bodhrán … Six year old Kevin plays the tin whistle and tambourine. The youngest member of the family is Peter and he plays the tambourine [*Western Journal* 1979 0914 7]

> The surviving members of Fr. Conefrey's Band will take the stand with piano and tamborine accompanied to render selections of Irish music which they broadcast on 2RN Radio in 1934 [*Leitrim Observer* 1982 0605 11]

> The music still rings in my ears, though I know it's just a dream / But still I hear the fiddle, flute, and beat of tamborine. [Andy Foley, London] [*Munster Express* 1988 0115 10]

Good and convenient terms persist, and so 'bodhrán' is what we know today, regardless of how differently people recall the same event, even inside the one family. For instance Bryan MacMahon's son Owen said he had never heard his father calling it anything other than 'bodhrán', while his brother Jim, who is older, had never heard his father calling it anything other than 'tambourine'.[40]

The 'bowran' eclipse

The changing of its name to bodhrán does not appear to have caused any disputes. Perhaps 'bodhrán' was felt to be about newness, and was no more memorable a transformation than an electric kettle replacing one on the stove-top? Nevertheless, reports on bodhrán ran parallel with the reports on tambourine all through the 1960s and '70s, sometimes the two terms in the one sentence, suggesting that this was not controversial, supporting Caoimhín Ó Danachair's observation that the tambourine could also be called bodhrán. Verifying what he said too is the fact that, three years before *Sive*, at a 1956 fleadh in Carrick-on-Suir, County Waterford, the drum had already become an object of great curiosity, attracting a kind of antiquarian awe,[41] reported as 'bodhrán', possibly the earliest press use of the word, but by 1960 it had begun to be used in Kerry:[42]

> The 'Boys from Brosna' … took top honours … Close on forty sporting members from the locality … marched through the thronged town to the accompaniment of accordion, mouth-organ, fiddle, bodhrán and drum [*Kerryman* 1960 1006 7]

> **CONCERT OF THE YEAR !**
>
> THE SHOW HALL, OLDCASTLE
>
> ON SUNDAY, 12th MARCH, 1967
>
> Direct from Abbey Tavern Howth, The Amazing Pedalers Folk Group. Supreme Traditional Fiddler Tony Smith, Fleadh Cheoil Medalist.
>
> Winners of 1966 Tops of Drogheda. The newest on the showband scene—The Fabulous Sahara with star vocalist Paud O'Brien. Just released its first hit record. Well known McKenna Troup of Irish Dancing, All-Ireland Fleadh medalists. Straight from Irish Club in London John Higgins On The Gallanti with Tambourine accompaniment.

Meath Chronicle 1967 0311 14

Commentary on the dual identity of the Irish frame drum as both tambourine and bodhrán is found sometimes in reports, for instance in 1965: The Axills 'Cork's first beat group … use a bodhrán instead of a tamborine'.[43] Effort was made to be educational about the name-change, however, seen in this 1968 County Galway report: 'For the neophyte, a booraun is the native tambourine, made from the skin of a goat, preferably from Kerry'.[44]

The parallel bodhrán soundscape

The frame drum, now known as 'bodhrán', still commanded such curiosity value in 1964 that it could merit being singled out from all the instrumental paraphernalia of a fleadh cheoil for its ability to generate a seductive soundscape, as at the Clones, County Monaghan All-Ireland fleadh in 1964: 'All through the day, the throbbing of bodhráns, the clack of spoons or the beat of guitars drew crowds to where impromptu concerts were taking place;'[45] 'To the skirl of the pipes and the beat of the bodhrán the last of the 75,000 people who attended headed homewards'.[46] The drum began to feature widely in music ensembles, even in Dublin, 1964 where with 'St. John's Musicians, band Micheal Ó h-Allain runs the group which has bones, heard from Seán Ó Riada's Ceoltoiri Cualann. Gerry Byrne on bodhrán'.[47] Ó hAlmháin indeed went on to found the annual bodhrán festival Craiceann on Inis Oirr, off the Connemara coast. Connacht however retained the tambourine term generally, with Ballymote, County Sligo CCÉ concerts continuing to feature local tambourine players in their programmes. But there, with Fred Finn and Peter Horan, by 1964 they had updated the instrument's name in the announcement of 'a lilting bowran and tin-whistle trio'.[48] traditional-music visibility had increased as the 1960s progressed, and with it, so had knowledge of the bodhrán:

> splendid recitals of Irish traditional music, first by Pat and Mrs. Broderick, Cregg Castle on pipes and bowran [*Connacht Tribune* 1964 0415 19]

> Lorcan Bergin with his Bowran and merry spoons … gave the visitors a glimpse of the spirit of Ireland [*Nationalist and Leinster Times* 1965 1001 30]
>
> New Year's Eve was celebrated and the New Year ushered in by a 'scratch' band of melodeons, accordions, bowrans, fiddles and drums [*Kerryman* 1966 0108 4]

Role of the press

Journalists in 1966 seldom commented on the nature or quality of music played at fleadhs, since little was known about it outside of its small number of practitioners. Hence the attention which was given to the perceived and real distinction, and tension, between popular ballad singers and their clientele on the one hand, and the dance-music players and listeners on the other. The relative scarcity of the bodhrán can be seen in some fleadh reports:

> It was a long, loud night, a pitched battle between the casual balladeers and non-musical joy-seekers and the traditional musicians, who met in pub corners or in the middle of the street to merge fiddles, accordions, tin-whistles, pipes and an occasional bodhrán [*Irish Times* 1966 0531 1]
>
> In addition to the usual household musicians … Jimmy Martin, a new musician, played the bowran, its sound filling the Tower Room, tempting four people to dance a set. With a touch of slow, confident and exciting restoration, all that is best in our traditional life came back to us, listening to and watching this [*Limerick Leader* 1966 0716 6]

The creeping in of the word bodhrán in reporting of more formal music concerts did gradually become visible in the press, seen in the 1966 report that 'Martina Tighe, with songs, Joe Collopy, on the accordion, and Jimmy Martin, on the bowran, provided the musical interludes'.[49] Changing spelling and terminology is seen too in 1966, notable here on account of the fact that the same person had won two years before, in 1964, but on the 'tambourine':

> Members of the local branch of Comhaltas Ceoltóirí Éireann travelled to Lixnaw on Sunday last to compete in the Annual Féile Ceol and won several prizes. Pierce Godley, Ballyronan, won 1st prize in the Bodharan [*Kerryman* 1966 0917 5]

Bodhrán players' names began to appear on posters in large city music venues, and in press reports were given the same kind of status as melody players.

> The reputation Mark's Bar … Crowe St., Dundalk enjoys for its traditional music is known far and wide … released on an LP … recorded by Mr. Billy McBurney, proprietor of Outlet Recording Studio, Belfast … contributors were Liam Clarke (All-Ireland Champion Accordionist), Joe McKevitt (All-Ireland Champion Flute and Tin Whistle) … Ronnie Rosonin noted bodran performer and Jerry Quigley, a very fine accompanist on the spoons [*Monaghan Argus* 1967 1103 7]

The overlap of terminology was heard often, even up to 1981 when, after Jim Sheehy's death, Bryan MacMahon's son Gary mixed his terms when he said, either unconsciously or deliberately:

> the Sheehy brothers were the undisputed kings of the bodhrán, not alone in west Limerick, but in all Ireland. They were two highly talented exponents of the tambourine which they helped to promote to the high standing the bodhrán holds at present [*The Weekly Observer*, 2022 26]

> "Many 21st-century musicians proudly and confidently identify as bodhrán players, all of them standing on the shoulders of those who cemented this drum's place into the architecture of Irish traditional music"
> **Liz Doherty,** fiddle-player, music organiser, lecturer and teacher

▶ Jim (Rory) Sheehy with his own large and deep-frame bodhrán at Castleisland fleadh, May 1967 [*Kennelly Archive*]

Evening Herald 1967 0204 7

11 FROM WALKING TO SITTING: TAMBOURINE TO BOWRAN

> "There was a surge of bodhrán, spoons and bones in the early sixties that seemed to be welcomed by most musicians and listeners. For making the bodhrán in the countryside there were old sieves that had been used for cleaning soil off potatoes, bobbin winders and such, and access to goat skins. But in Dublin I had to buy a new gravel sieve, and once for a skin I used a page from old house deeds that were written on vellum"
> **Mary Jordan,** *ballad singer and bodhrán player*

◀ Mary Jordan on spoons with Paddy Moloney (pipes) and Barney McKenna (banjo) [*Courtesy Mary Jordan*]

▲ Joe Sweeney playing Mary Jordan's bodhran which was skinned with a vellum page from archaic house deeds [*Courtesy Mary Jordan*]

Bodhrán women

Women had been playing the tambourine and bodhrán over the same period, especially in south Sligo but also in Kerry, where in 1987 Jimmy Hennessy of Killocrim spoke of 'an old woman here and she was a terror for using her hand on the bodhrán … beautiful timing'.[50] Though they are prominent in early fleadh television footage, women only gradually became visible to the press. An early young pioneer was thirteen-year-old Carmel Byrne of Kilkenny who won the 'under 14 Bodhrán (Tambourine) competition in the fleadh ceoil at Newcastle West, Co. Limerick'.[51] Others emerged, by 1965 playing with leading musicians-to-be: 'Joe Heaney, the folk singer from Connemara, Tony MacMahon, accordion player; Patrick Keenan, piper; Mary Jordan, spoon and bowran player'.[52] MacMahon indeed had family involvement behind his respect for the role of the tambourine player, as seen from his programming on Telefís Éireann:

11 FROM WALKING TO SITTING: TAMBOURINE TO BOWRAN

▶ Paddy and Margaret Flavin demonstrate the bodhrán at the Living Crafts exhibition, Listowel Harvest Festival, 1970 [*Kennelly Archive*]

Mr. Tony MacMahon, the All-Ireland accordionist and concertina player and familiar to radio and TV viewers is an uncle to three members of the band [Tulla Junior Ceili Band], P.J. and Andrew McNamara and their sister Mary – whose twin, Anita, is joining the band on the bowran [*Nenagh Guardian* 1973 1027 9]

Women had already been known for playing the tambourine, however, Reg Hall recalling Mary Heffernan from County Limerick playing at London sessions in the 1960s. In Listowel 1970, Margaret Flavin played in a demonstration with her husband Paddy at the exhibition of living crafts during Listowel Harvest Festival. And, as already cited, there was a tradition of women playing in south Sligo, where Ted McGowan said that the custom was that 'women struck the tambourine at the end of sessions'.[53] Women are reported in the press as playing in other parts of the country too, as seen in regional press reports such as in 1975: 'Majella Gogarty and Catherine Givney (accordions) and Angela Callan (bowran) were a big hit'.[54] Like their male counterparts, women on the bodhrán not only could have 'name' status in advertising, but began to be noted as award winners; as can be seen from the All-Ireland fleadh results in subsequent years (Chapter 14) they gradually moved into the tambourine/bodhrán territory, achieving the highest awards, and in modern time many play or have played professionally.

Evening Herald 1967 0224 10

Evening Herald 1967 0217 10

Evening Herald 1967 0203 8

Mick and Jim Sheehy [*Weekly Observer*, County Limerick]

'The Bodhránry of west Limerick'

This expression was used to head a 2011 article by County Limerick journalist Tom Aherne, which detailed the achievements of two local tambourine players, the Sheehy brothers, Mick and Jim.[55] They stand out in 1960s press reports as the earliest names of repute in tambourine and bodhrán playing in post-1950s Ireland. From 'The Lane' area of Barnigue townland near Newcastle West, County Limerick they are celebrated in verse:

> From Barnigue's green woodland plain / The brothers focused their aim
> To perfect and to gain / Everlasting bodhrán acclaim and fame

Their sparring ground was the location for the inaugural County Limerick Fleach, at Newcastle West, in 1962 which had the first CCÉ tambourine competition. The area was noted as being highly regarded locally for the instrument:

> 'You can't beat a tradition after all', said Éamonn Ó Conaill, Headmaster of Newcastle West Vocational School … referring to the fact that almost all of the tambourine players – and there were many of them – were from the south-west part of County Limerick, a district where poetry and music have abounded for centuries [*Limerick Leader* 1962 0606 10]

The Sheehy brothers came from that area, born into an era in which the tambourine was known only for the Wren; they were at the heart of a local troupe known as 'The Laners'. Their village of Carrigkerry came to be

194

regarded as 'the home of the Wrenboys' due to the intensity of its local participation, and to those players' prominence in the All-Ireland Wrenboys competition. The area was noted for music too, and the Sheehy brothers' father Timothy (Tadhg) was a famous dancer, reputed to once have danced a hornpipe on a dinner plate on top of a kitchen table without damage to the plate.[56] Mick and Jim also had reputations, gained from winning County, Munster and All-Ireland tambourine and bodhrán titles. Born in 1910, Mick Sheehy was a labourer who also made tambourines. He experimented with different hides, and with a variety of woods for sticks. He once drummed with four sticks at a local Feis competition, a feature of his musicianship being the ability to hit every decorative melodic note, and to vary timbre from soft and gentle to sharp and loud. His brother Jim, who was born four years later, was a flamboyant entertainer who played whistle and sang as well. He too was a farm labourer, and worked on the beet harvest in England every year, playing at Irish-emigrant gatherings at *The Ship* bar in Birmingham. The brothers were fiercely competitive as well as musically brilliant, their challenges creating spectacle for the onlookers, not least on account of Jim's opinions, and sayings, such as 'I could drum anything from the seven deadly sins to the litanies from the Holy court of Rome – even up on an ass's back – into the city of Jerusalem'.

Despite the pride in the local west Limerick application of the tambourine, the story of the drum's beginnings there is open to the idea of the instrument being a borrowing. Local word had it that the first tambourine in Ireland was made there, by one Dan Hartigan who had been taught drum-making by a Clare man called Tierney who had deserted from the British army in Africa (likely the Boer War, 1899–1902); Hartigan ended up in west Limerick cutting turf during 'the emergency' (1939–45). While that might have been more a claim to regional exclusivity rather than the arrival of the first tambourine, nevertheless the story does suggest that skills of making and playing could have come from outside – the result of army band experience. Tierney is also said to have passed on his military drumming technique to Hartigan, whose own passing it on sparked a unique local style. Heirs to that tradition, the Sheehy brothers became synonymous with tambourine playing in the 1960s, and in the instrument's early revival stages they appeared at numerous CCÉ functions and on national television, guesting also with Ó Riada's Ceoltóirí Chualann, and featuring with the Carrigkerry Wrenboys in the state-sponsored 1974 documentary film *Bodhrán*.[57] Jim won the first, so-called 'All-Ireland Senior Tambourine Championship' at the Newcastle West fleadh cheoil in 1962,[58] and Mick won it the following year at the County Limerick fleadh which was also held in Newcastle West, with Jim second; one of the adjudicators was Bryan MacMahon. Two years later the same competition, at Newcastle West, was won by Jim, with Mick second; Seán Ó Riada was a judge.[59] The brothers continued to compete, still playing the same way, even though the competition title had changed to 'bodhrán'.

> "I have a vivid memory of the virtuoso bodhrán performance in the 1970s by the Sheehy brothers from County Limerick in a Fleadh Nua event at the National Stadium in Dublin. They captivated a capacity audience with fervour, fun and flamboyance, demonstrating what the bodhrán can do in the right hands. At times, it has the tribal resonance that one experiences with Wrenboys and Strawboys"
> **Labhrás Ó Murchú,** ardstiúrthóir náisiúnta, Comhaltas Ceoltóirí Éireann

The persistence of 'bowran'

The Leinster Wren Boys competition began to use both the old and new terms for the drum in 1968: 'the groups have lighted turf, tambourines (bodrans) and bones'.[60] In Kilkenny and elsewhere the drum was worthy of special mention: 'the well-known traditional fiddler Patsy Cooke, with Brendan Sheridan on the guitar and the bowran player, Peter Clarke'.[61] And the drum was already colouring the soundscape of the fleadh cheoil: 'the town will again hum with the lively music of the boorawns and the accordions ..'.[62] The 1970 Mummers' Fleadh at Woodford, on the borders of counties Galway and Clare, was a local CCÉ festival which highlighted the drum: 'streams of Mummers paraded up the hilly main street to the lilt of the accordeons and the heavy beat of the Bowrans'.[63] Meath and other counties feature in the stakes too:

> One of the finest performances of the evening was given by 92-year-old Mick Walsh from Ballivor with his playing of the bowran – a type of tambourine without tassels … The oldest performer in the contest, his contribution, not surprisingly, was greeted with thunderous applause [*Drogheda Independent* 1970 0313 15]

> Peter Clarke, Tubrid, Oldcastle, who has died, was a well-known figure at Irish-Ireland functions down the years. He was an expert at playing the bowran musical instrument and an expert at making them [*Meath Chronicle* 1970 1128 16]

> Ned Farrell 'doing his thing' impeccably as usual on the Bowran. With him were Michael Crehan, Frank Burke, and Charlie Lennon [*Nationalist and Leinster Times* 1971 0730 19]

By 1976, an obituary for the Meath player Michael Walsh found it no longer necessary to state the tambourine–bowran link in the announcement that 'Ballivor's oldest resident has died in the person of Michael Walsh … an accomplished player on the bowran'.[64] A 1976 concert at Mooncoin, County Kilkenny shows the popularity of and presumed knowledge about the drum in the announcement 'Sean Carroll (bowrawn) and Eamon O'Sullivan (bones)'.[65] The term 'bowran' had caught on, its spelling suiting all, regardless of whether it was pronounced in the Munster/Connacht or Donegal ways; the instrument was a universal. In 1977, 'One other person is heard on the new disc, Colm Murphy, who thumps a melodic bowran. Colm is a son of the late Seamus Murphy, sculptor and writer;'[66] 'Five brothers from Donegal, Na Casadaigh (two fiddles, guitar, pipes, bowran) rip exhilaratingly through Irish tunes'.[67] By 1979 Westmeath still had the 'ow' spelling: 'Music was provided by Mick Weir and Mick Bolan, on accordions, John Bolan on spoons, Peter Boland (bowran) and Mick Snee (concertina)'.[68] In Kerry, 1983 too, 'bowran' persisted: 'Ballyseedy May Sunday … music, song, dance, fiddle, accordeon, bowrán;'[69] 'music, song, dance, fiddle, accordion, bowran, etc. the organisers celebrated everything that was wholesome and traditional'.[70] And at Aughnacliffe, County Longford, a list for a 1986 community concert had 'McKenna family, Ballinamuck; Cornafean ceili group, Joe Doyle, John Murphy, Michael Kirwan on bowran'.[71] So too in the same town later that year 'Mr. Michael Curley, Moatfarrell, Champion Bowran player, paid a visit to Aughnacliffe on last Friday night',[72] the spelling still retained by 2008: 'Eric Trappe on the organ, Michael Farrell on the flute, Joe Feeney on the sax (yes sax), John Gilchrist bowran'.[73]

"A sapling and skin conundrum; originally hewn and moulded from the material affordances of the Irish countryside, this instrument/implement retains a domestic, primordial, and artisanal aesthetic and function, while simultaneously traversing and copper-fastening the global flow of Irishness rendered sonically and symbolically in mass-produced, rude forms"
Aileen Dillane, *musician, lecturer at IWAMD, Limerick*

"Johnny 'Ringo' McDonagh in a De Dannan concert was the first musician I ever saw perform an extended solo on the bodhrán. His dexterity and diversity left me slack-jawed in awe. I knew at once that virtuosity on the frame drum of Irish music was not only possible but actual. Even now, in memory, I still feel gobsmacked by what I saw and heard"
Earle Hitchner, *USA, former music writer for The Irish Voice, The Irish Echo, and The Wall Street Journal*

DOHERTY'S MOUNTAIN TAVERN

Sunday, June 24th — Traditional Musical night with
PACKIE DUIGNAN and HIS MEN
Flutes, Accordeons, Tamboreens

Leitrim Observer 1979 0623 7

So, through all performance media the bodhrán grew in popularity, and the phonetic 'bowran' spelling which had first been used by P.W. Joyce in 1910 persisted in parallel with the term 'tambourine' until at least 2008. And the instrument eventually arrived at the pinnacle of representational success, outdoing the pipes and harp, even the accordion, a trajectory noted by the press:

> Teach them the bowran and the tin whistle ... Anyone who can play the bowran or play a jig on the tin whistle is an Irish man and is accepted the world over [*Connaught Telegraph* 2008, 0319 1 1]

This chapter opened with accounts of the vitality of marching-format Wren performance on the tambourine. It moved through the gradual application of the term 'bowran' to the tambourine, and changed, as demonstrated – in both the press's use of the term 'bowran' for the tambourine in reportage, and in competition titling. It concludes on the new role for the modern-day bodhrán within dance music, now, like other traditional-music instruments, played by a seated performer.

NOTES TO CHAPTER 11

[1] All spellings of both terms – both accurate and inaccurate – are included as originally used in the presses in order to illustrate the process of change, but these can be considered as, basically, 'tambourine' and 'bodhrán'.
[2] *Meath Chronicle* 1941 0125 7.
[3] Ibid., 1934 1215 7.
[4] *Irish Press* 1948 1218 11.
[5] *Munster Express* 1950 0714 7.
[6] This can be accessed online at ifi.ie, the Irish Film Institute.
[7] Hayes 1974.
[8] RTÉ 1963.
[9] *Limerick Leader* 1963 0119 19.
[10] MacMahon 1963.
[11] *Kerryman* 1965 0904 10.
[12] *Irish Press* 1962 0605 4.
[13] *Kerryman* 1963 0921 8.
[14] Ibid., 0105 19.
[15] *Cork Examiner* 1965 0517 7.
[16] *Southern Star* 1966 0402.
[17] *Limerick Leader* 1984 0624 8.
[18] *Kerryman* 1986 0711 6.
[19] *Evening Herald* 1960 0330 13.
[20] *Irish Times* 1960 0902.
[21] *Connacht Tribune* 1961 0429 10.
[22] *Irish Press* 1961 1124 10.
[23] *Connacht Tribune* 1968 0315 6.
[24] *Leitrim Observer* 1982 0403 9.
[25] Kearns 2022, PC.
[26] Kearns 1996, 15.
[27] Ibid., 14.
[28] *Evening Herald* 1968 0116 5.
[29] *Nationalist and Leinster Times* 1962 0714 35.
[30] Kjeldsen 2000, 130.
[31] *Sligo Champion* 1967 0526 12.
[32] *Meath Chronicle* 1967 0311 14.
[33] *Ulster Herald* 1968 0316 5.
[34] *Kerryman* 1968 1207 5.
[35] *Leitrim Observer* 1968 0921 7.
[36] *Kerryman* 1969 0104 4.
[37] Ibid., 0104 6.
[38] *Westmeath Examiner* 1972 0610 9.
[39] *Offaly Independent* 1975 0725 1.
[40] McMahon 2022, PC.
[41] This contrasts with the earliest press mention of 'tambourine', 1741 (see Chapter 6).
[42] *The Nationalist* 1956 0505 12.
[43] *Evening Echo* 1965 0317 5.
[44] *Tuam Herald* 1968 0427 1.
[45] *Irish Times* 1964 0518 1.
[46] *Irish Press* 1964 0519 7.
[47] *Evening Herald* 1964 0218 7.
[48] *Sligo Champion* 1964 0404 9.
[49] *Limerick Leader* 1966 0723 8.
[50] Curran 1988, 30.
[51] *Kilkenny People* 1965 0521 5.
[52] *Evening Herald* 1965 0925 8.
[53] McGowan 1997, PC.
[54] *Meath Chronicle* 1975 1008 4.
[55] Aherne 2011.
[56] A similar feat has been reported in novelty music-hall minstrel performances.
[57] This was commissioned by the then minister for the Gaeltacht, Tom O'Donnell, from Oola-born director Tom Hayes as a celebration of the uniqueness of the bodhrán. In it, the Carrigkerry Wrenboys have an eight-minute feature.
[58] *Irish Press* 1962 0605 4.
[59] Aherne 2011.
[60] *Meath Chronicle* 1968 0329 6.
[61] Ibid., 1011 1.
[62] *Irish Independent* 1969 0917 11.
[63] *Irish Farmers Journal* 1970 0110 24.
[64] *Meath Chronicle* 1976 0410 6.
[65] *Munster Express* 1976 1224 16.
[66] *Evening Herald* 1977 0322 9.
[67] Ibid., 0804 8.
[68] *Westmeath Topic* 1979, 0524 11.
[69] *Kerryman* 1983, 0429 4.
[70] Ibid., 0527 6.
[71] *Longford Leader* 1986, 0207 8.
[72] Ibid., 0513 14.
[73] *Longford Leader* 2008, 0215 42 42.

"All the old lads I talked to around 1970-71 told me 'you take out the bodhrán any day of the year other than the 26th December and you're mad. It's like wearing shamrock on the 1st of June" *Prof. Mícheál Ó Súilleabháin*

CHAPTER 12
BELOW THE MELODICIST'S HORIZON?

The previous chapter demonstrated the tambourine's regional retention, and its persistence and popular appeal during the revival years. The pages which follow observe interest in percussion music, not only with regard to the wren, but in other applications of music in society.

> All the old lads I talked to around 1970, '71 told me 'you take out the bodhrán any day of the year other than the 26 December and you're mad. It's like wearing shamrock on the 1st of June'[1]

So said Mícheál Ó Súilleabháin in his summing up the difference between the bodhrán today and the tambourine in the past. This creates a picture that in Irish music history the Wren became a kind of training ground or waiting room where bodhrán-players-to-be bided their time all through the first half of the twentieth century, a shelter for the *sans-instrumentes*, those with the non-melodic music compulsion. Had there been no music revival their enclave may, like the minstrels, have come to be forgotten, but the post-Second World War valuing of national identities and folk cultures gave it oxygen.

And so it was the case that the Kerry writers then broke tambourines out of marginality into a space which had materialised aesthetically out of the revival movement which itself had been set in motion by the Dublin Pipers' Club and the founding of Comhaltas Ceoltóirí Éireann in 1951. It then became clear all through the 1960s that there was – and had been – an interest in percussion with Irish music, not only in the ranks of listeners but also among the melody players themselves. Most of those were adept at drumming the fingers on table tops anyway, and older, less self-conscious lads occasionally would tap out time with two coins on a beer bottle when among friends and neighbours – a practice that was appreciated enough for such concussionists to be included in major concerts such as that indicated on page 200. There were plenty of role models to drawn on in drumming, not least the céilí band drum-kit practice; in particular there were the side-drums used by the hundreds of marching bands which were everywhere weekly celebrating, intimidating, campaigning and commemorating for politics, feast-days and sport.

It could therefore be said that the formality of bands had been the main outlet for percussionists up until then – an association of ideology, marching and beat, a synergy that already had been proven – utilised efficaciously by military bands all over Europe. And just as the redundancy of musicians that followed the decline of traditional music for social dancing contributed to the rise of that music as sit-down, collective performance, so too the one-time band drummers and new percussion devotees found a fresh niche and themselves took to the chairs in sessions and groups with bodhráns.

◀ Prof. Mícheál Ó Súilleabháin, the first substantial commentator on the modern bodhrán [*Nutan*]

> COMHALTAS CEOLTOIRI EIREANN
> Liam Reynolds presents, by Special Request,
> **A GRAND VARIETY CONCERT**
> in St. Dominic's Hall, Kenagh, on Friday, Jan. 14
> Artistes include: Kieran Kelly, All Ireland Champion Accordeonist; Gerard Erwin and Sean McCormack, Pipes and Fiddle (Oireactas Prize-winners); Sean Ward, Songs with Pipe accompaniment; Michael O'Connor, Tenor; William Reynolds and John Healion, Pipes and Fiddle (Radio fame); Padraig Ledwith, Accordeon; Frank Slevin and Tony O'Brien, songs with Guitar; Peter Carberry, Pipes; Kevin Carberry, Banjo; Jim Donlon, Trad. Fiddle; Patrick Kilduff (Ballads); Chas. O'Brien, Trad. Fiddle (Radio Eireann); James Dolan (Uilleann Pipes); Master Bobby Kelly (Step Dancer); Michael McCarthy (Flute); W. Knight (Accordeon); Pat Duke Hickey (tunes on the Tamborine and pint tumbler); Simpson School of Irish Dancers, Athlone; Pat Brehony (Fiddle); Tom Derwin, Comedian; Sean Fitzpatrick, J. Daly (Fiddle, Recitations); J. J. Carr (Piano Accordeon); Tom Conlon (Trad. Fiddle); Walderstown Uilleann Pipe Trio. John Cawley (Flute). Programme Compere: Seamus McDonagh, N.T.
> Don't miss this great Feast of Music, Song and Dance.
> COMMENCING 8.15 p.m. ● ADMISSION: 3/- and 2/6
> (2-15-f)—431

Longford Leader 1955 0108 4

Once upon a time too the Wren was the territory of teenagers, but in the new formulation of an Irish state after 1921 it appears to have taken on the role of a manifestation of local pride, identity and tradition. And so it attracted cultural advocates who continued their involvement long after their teens, not a few of them into old age. Such is the pull of respect for tradition in this that many musicians today who are well beyond their fifth decade are still actively engaged in the Wren, no doubt gratified too by the sport-like adrenaline buzz of the competitions. Even back in 1966 things were similar, as was seen on one national news documentary about Kerry bodhrán maker Sonny Canavan. He made it clear that both he and his neighbour John (Jack) Duggan from near Listowel still took part in the Wren as well as making the drums. Duggan, born in 1887, said that he had played music for his first Wren *c.* 1899 at the age of twelve, on the concertina, and was still going out on it by the time of the broadcast, in 1966, when he was then in his seventy-ninth year. Apart from theme and costume, the common feature of the Wren wherever it is held on the island is the idea of the walk, the parade or the march done to music, with the drum being central: 'they'd never go without it, they're the cheapest instrument you could get'.[2] On the Wren itself there was a distinction made between performance in rural and built-up areas, for in Sligo Batty Sherlock also used a side drum:

> I used to have a kettledrum ... I used it mostly in the town ... march up the town ... and then when ... out to the country houses, you'd have the bodhrán, because the kettledrum would be too loud[3]

The act of group marching for a shared purpose is a universal, and engenders a 'heightening of fellow feeling', 'significant social bonding',[4] action made possible by the presence of music, and, in particular, of beat. The same was a basic factor in the pre-motor-transport era of movement of armies, where the speed of marching, which was critical to both planning and survival, was metered by beat. Like dancing, marching in unison is greatly enhanced by music.[5] The marching tunes and beats that are used on the Wren in Ireland add other significance, as they are often well-known patriotic and national airs. For instance, the tune which is marched to in the television coverage of a Wren competition in Newcastle West back in 1963 is 'Shane O'Neill's March', in a simple 4/4 time. But it is accompanied by four tambourines playing a fierce unison, semi-quaver battery to which the players step on cue, a more kinetic, dynamic experience for them, and a thrilling engagement for the observers. This having been the learning environment for a player, the transfer of that 'filled-in' style of performance to the complementary, less-assertive accompaniment required for the sit-down jigs and reels is quite a challenge to both skill and ego. Thus 'too loud', 'too fast' and 'taking over' arose early on as criticisms of bodhráns joining sessions in the 1960s. But more mature players who had had experience of both worlds could handle the different demands, and so were acceptable to melody players. Lads like these can be seen in many 1960s and earlier images, sitting on the edge of sessions utterly absorbed in their engagement, with fiddle, flute and accordion players all around, completely at ease. The beginning of this on a larger scale – ex-Wren tambourine players joining sit-down dance music at times other than the Wren season – dates certainly to the revival period from the 1950s on. But there already were other tambourine players too, and drummers who were not particularly involved in the Wren, including some who came out of fife and drum marching bands – from which, arguably, Wren practice had already picked up moves.

Fife and drum bands

> Hark! Who are these that I see in the distance
> Bearing green banners and beating a drum
> Cheering like men who are bent on resistance
> Steadily onward – O see how they come[6]

Fife and drum bands were popular through the 1800s. They were modelled on military bands, and used that format to generate order and sense of purpose, 'expanded emotional solidarity'[7] which could attract and hold participants and onlookers alike. They were a major promotion vehicle for the Temperance movement (anti-alcohol) which had started in New York in 1826, spreading to Dublin by 1829, and being particularly strong in Cork by 1838.[8] Bands sprang up all over Ireland, many of them fife and drum, and they were used also as a form of pubic entertainment, giving experience of the power and dramatic effect of drums along with melody to diverse communities. Formed and re-formed in various parts of the country, they serviced Daniel O'Connell's Catholic Emancipation rallies as well as Temperance parades, and got a fresh lease of life with the activities of the Land League towards the end of the century. Such is in the detail of a 2 January 1831 demonstration at Drumlease, Dromahair, County Leitrim, which is voiced in the verse above that was written about the event when 'Six marching bands led contingents from all the surrounding areas to the field of an evicted farmer Mr. O'Rourke'.[9] The fife and drum bands used side-drums and bass drum, but the tambourine is mentioned incidentally, though it was not quite a 'real' drum with them. In one recollection it was seen as more of a young person's instrument: 'I must have been nine years old at the time … I only had a tamborine … Soon afterwards I became a flute player, and in later years leader of the band, when we had real drums and flutes'.[10]

John Horkan of Carracastle, County Mayo recalls his band's activities while in the 'Blueshirts', the right-wing Army Comrades Association, which had junior and senior sections:

> The smaller ones had two tambourines and ten or twelve whistle players, and led off in front of the main band ... Austy Casey and myself were on the tambourines[11]

The seasonal custom of the Wren had the most visible use of the tambourine, certainly in the twentieth century, and that association is likely to have an overlap in repertoire and discipline with the music of political and other agitation. The power of drums among the poorer population cannot be underestimated in the age before broadcast or recorded sound, at a time when most entertainment was small-scale and local. Fife and drum bands have left their mark in local flute expertise and popularity in regions where the Land League was strongest, notably in Connacht.[12] After 1921 the bands remained popular in south Sligo and north Mayo with both pro- and anti-treaty loyalties. These shared marching tunes, different to what was played for dance music. The bands could occasionally be involved with the Wren:

> On New Year's nights we took out the fife and drum band together, welcoming the New Year in and the Old Year out in the company of Johnny Mullaney's drumming and other fifers[13]

The experience of witnessing or participating in drumming in the nineteenth century undoubtedly conditioned young minds to familiarity with it and created appreciation, and so the tambourine, as a drum, is mentioned in Connacht traditional-music contexts almost casually, naturally – not at all remarkable. How far back beyond 1900 that goes is difficult to establish.

Bodhrán territories

In 1988 John B. Keane was adamant that

> without question, the tradition here in north Kerry has always been the bodhrán ... This was the home of it, there's no doubt about it, 'twas the first thing when I was a child. And my father told me the same thing, that when he

▼ Mountainy Road Fife and Drum Band, Keady, County Armagh, 1930s was a child, the first thing he'd listen for on St Stephen's morning. He'd hear the beat of the drum and your heart would race[14]

Nevertheless, since Seamus Tansey expressed exactly the same sentiment for County Sligo, it appears that the practice was universal. Geographically, the two areas in which the use of the tambourine (and latterly the bodhrán) is reported as more extensive are north Connacht and north Munster, each of which is symbolic in traditional music. But in each place the use of tambourine has been visibly different in music. For instance, even though the Wren, with tambourines, has been strong in north Kerry, dance music appears to have not particularly involved the tambourine. Confirming this, Dónal Hickey's 1999 book on Sliabh Luachra cultural expressions describes its music as 'Soul – the heart and feeling that comes through the music … essentially dance music, with musicians and dancers synchronising and bringing out the best in each other'.[15] He speaks of a large number of fiddle-players, quoting accordionist Johnny O'Leary in a critique of the ubiquitousness of the TV set as saying that 'in his youth, there was an instrument in every home and people loved a few hours of music to pass away the time'.[16] Pipes, whistles, fiddles, accordions, singing, poetry and storytelling are described in the area, tambourine is not mentioned by Hickey, and the only reference to the word bodhrán was when Julia Clifford objected to the racket of young players in a rambling house at Maulykevane: 'Will ye shut up, my head is in a bodhrán',[17] meaning the noise had her head fuddled. While this indicates the supremacy, and distinctiveness, of melody, it still does not mean that tambourines were not there, but out of season they were not visible. However, the photo of a platform dance near Tralee in 1957 (p. 131) shows dancing to harmonica and hand-struck tambourines.

▼ Carracastle Fife and Drum Band *c.* 1912
[*Courtesy John Horkan*]

A Flute and Tambourine

'A Flute and Tambourine', composed by Padraic Ganly from Moate, County Westmeath, published by him in 1918 (see also page 119) [Courtesy ITMA]

Stevie McNamara playing the tambourine in O'Connor's pub, Doolin, County Clare, 1973. Note the thumb hole for grip – there is no question here of skin tensioning with the holding hand [RTÉ Archive]

Visibility of tambourines

Because tambourines were not that numerous, one is led to the view that historically, they played only a marginal role in the dance music – they were peripheral to the emphasis on melody which dominated cultural and recreational thinking after the 1500s. However, the trickle of mentions of tambourine being played along with dance music does show that this was likely not uncommon throughout the country. It is but a faded memory in many areas, but the tale of Tomás a' bhodhráin (p. 144) confirm that it was at least a peripheral practice in earlier times, and the recordings from the 1920s show that the interest in frame drum percussion with dance music was a valued sound. Emphasising this more firmly is the legacy of a Moate, County Westmeath fiddle-player Pádraic Ganly, born following the Famine,

> "Everyone hit the tambourine. Any house! ... The 'bodhrán' came in with Ó Riada ... The stick came in with the bodhrán"
> **Ted McGowan,** *The Róisín Dubh, Gurteen*

POBLACHT NA hEIREANN

110

ORIGINAL IRISH DANCE TUNES

---- AND ----

OTHER PIECES

---- FOR ----

VIOLIN, FLUTE, ETC.

COMPOSED BY

PADRAIC GANLY

▲ The Ganly collection, 1918
[*Courtesy ITMA*]

▼ Peter Horan (flute) and Ted McGowan
[*Nutan*]

who emigrated to Argentina in 1875. He was back in Ireland for a couple of years from 1900, but returned to Argentina, from where in 1918 he published a book of '110 original Irish dance tunes and other pieces for violin, flute, etc'. His titles are quite a social document of his home area, and among them is the significantly-titled reel 'A flute and tambourine' (p. 204); another is 'The worn tambourine' (p. 119). Both imply a common practice during his formative years in Westmeath, *c.* 1855–1875, either on the Wren or with dance music – or both. Prior to the 1950s there is little word of the tambourine anywhere outside of the Wren, such was its strict seasonality, as expressed in 1987 by Jimmy Hennessy in County Kerry:

> Twenty years ago, after St Stephen's Day being over, it was put away into a loft and 'twouldn't be seen again … and the man that used it at this St Stepher's Day, he might have gone to England or gone to America and he might never again see the bodhrán[18]

This was not least because, as he says, 'there were no sessions in the pub that time'. Michael Tubridy in County Clare said the same. Assumpta Curran's conclusion was that 'at least one bodhrán was thought necessary on St Stephen's Day, in parts of Kerry … where people even thought it improper to use the bodhrán in any other music'.[19] Yet, going by the press, tambourines had a commercial presence in Ireland from Antrim to Cork for all of the century prior to *c.* 1930. If music shops and dealers were offering them for sale, then there must have been an interest, and a demand. Poorer people in towns may have clubbed together to purchase such items, as they did for concertinas and accordions in the early 1900s, but considering the simplicity of structure of a tambourine, in rural areas the incentive would have been for people to make copies of the instrument themselves, as the reports of goat-stealing incidents in the next chapter show.

Either way, by the time of the Free State era after 1921 Ireland had had almost two centuries of experience, expertise and appreciation regarding the tambourine, so the stage was actually well set for the instrument's renaissance in the 1960s. Marching bands gradually disappeared as the relevance of their mobilisations lost steam or faded away, and so drummers lost their outlets. Some of them already played in céilí bands, and some moved to play dance music on tambourines, as did yet more of the 'homeless' céilí band drummers who had been made redundant by – yet were inspired by – Ó Riada's intervention.

An example of such skills transfer is seen in Sonny Davey of County Sligo who in the 1920s as a schoolboy played the tambourine at crossroads and country-house dances, 'often getting thrashed for not doing his lessons'. He also made and played the drum set for the local Rising Sun Ceili Band[20] as well as making tambourines. Occasional stories reveal the presence of tambourines playing along with dance music. One such is an anecdote from Finglas piper Pat Mitchell, writer and compiler of *The Dance Music of Séamus Ennis*, who recalls an occasion when as a younger man in the mid-1970s he accompanied the music collector Breandán Breathnach on a recording visit to Mícheál Ó Concannon, an older, revered singer at Annaghdown, County Galway, and was asked to play a tune on the pipes to break the ice. The singer found the playing so uplifting that he exclaimed to his daughter-in-law: 'Bring me out the tray!', upon receipt of which he enthusiastically joined in beating a terrific time. Hugely gratified, he said afterwards, that 'We used always hit tambourines with the music around here'.[21]

This not only affirms the use of tambourines with dance-music c. 1900, but the act of improvisation draws attention to how the old household bodhrán skin tray would easily have doubled as a spontaneous, rudimentary tambourine when the impulse or occasion demanded.

Like this occasion, despite what Ted McGowan, Micheal Tubridy and Mícheál Ó Súilleabháin said, tantalising snippets of information do surface which show that certain individuals did indulge themselves on the

▲ Cathy Jordan [*Nutan*]

◀ Malachy Towey [*James Fraher*]

"In 1999 I was at a ninety-ninth birthday party in Chicago for Malachy Towey from that bodhrán triangle there in east Mayo – Cloontia, Doocastle and Carracastle. He played a bodhrán with his hand. The same year I was at a 100th celebration for Tom Finn at Sliabh Mór and there were five hand-beaters. Tom said that he was delighted to hear the sound of the hand-beaten bodhrán and the flute: 'I remember it from when I was three years of age – ninety-seven years ago – that was the sound that rang around me when I was a young fellow'"
Joe O'Byrne, County Mayo, broadcaster, local historian

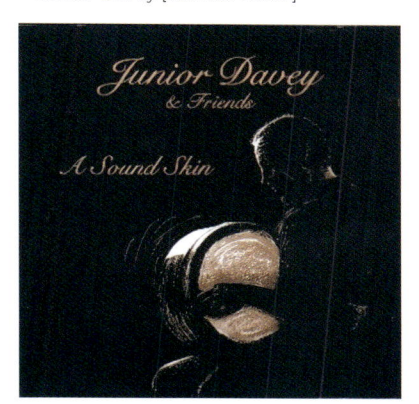

tambourine at times other than mid-winter. Among these were the County Kilkenny cousin of ancient horns pioneer Simon O'Dwyer (see p. 222), and Jack Cooley in east Galway as well as the various County Clare and County Meath players.[22] These were known and were accepted as part of local practice, and there can be no doubt that their music was generally appreciated as a complementary background or accent to melody. Their playing was most likely in the style heard on the American '78' tambourine recordings that were made of John Reynolds in 1927 and Patrick Carberry in 1938. If Michael Coleman, James Morrison and John McKenna inspired fiddle and flute players back in Ireland, the recordings of Reynolds and Carberry surely encouraged tambourine players.

Reg Hall in London implies this too in his recollection that he was captivated by his first hearing of Neal Smith's tambourine on the 1929 Packie Dolan's Melody Boys' recording.

▲ Junior Davey [James Fraher]

▶ Batty Sherlock [James Fraher]

▲ Breda, Sean and T.J. Smyth with Josie McDonagh at *Hanley's*, Strokestown, 1996 during RTÉ's filming of *The High Reel* [*Nutan*]

▼ Cathleen Taaffe and James Murray with the author, *The Róisín Dubh*, Gurteen, 1996 [*Gregory Daly*]

Connacht

In Connacht, the practice was different, certainly for local music-making in south County Sligo in the same period that Dónal Hickey deals with for Kerry. Svend Kjeldsen's County Sligo interviewees all indicated knowledge of and fondness for the use of tambourine along with the flute in particular, as described by bodhrán player Batty Sherlock:

> My other brother ... made the bodhrán ... every chance I get I'd take up the bodhrán ... maybe one tin whistle and maybe one flute at a time ... I was about eight or nine[23]

The Sligo bodhrán players do also speak a lot of the tambourine on the Wren, but as a somewhat different thing – they were clear about the two distinctive applications of it. They call it 'bodhrán' in those year 2000 interviews, in respect of the name-change, but all acknowledge that it was known to them as tambourine originally. Another player, Gerry Murray, underlines the seasonal use:

> St. Stephen's Day ... we had a country dance and the bodhrán was always very important ... but apart from that ... there wouldn't be many occasions where the bodhrán would be a necessity[24]

But the instrument had respect locally in music nevertheless, Ted McGowan testifying to people's familiarity with it: 'Everyone hit the bodhrán. Any house!',[25] similar to what Joe O'Sullivan said about west Limerick. But that it was not common in music-making gatherings was also suggested by McGowan from the experience of his decades of working in England: 'There'd be no bodhrán in London'.[26]

Galway

Pat Mitchell's anecdote about Mícheál Ó Concannon at Annaghdown suggests customary tambourine playing *c.* 1900 at least in west Galway, a deduction that is supported by the recording made by Ciarán Mac Mathúna of the same player in 1956 (see p. 206). Further hard evidence of this was brought to attention by Gaelic scholar Cathal Goan, a reference which also suggests that the tambourine was not uncommon by the turn of the twentieth century, and that there was demand, skill and style associated with it. This is in *Gan Baisteadh*, a 1972 book by Tomás Bairéad of Maigh Cuillinn near Loch Corrib, County Galway, who was writing on his younger life in the early 1900s. He recounts:

> Bhíodh fear an tambóirín ag dul thart i gcónaí le fear na feadóige agus é ag greadadh an tambóirín le cúl a mhéar agus ag tabhairt corrshonc den uillinn dó. Níor chuala mé aon ainm ariamh air ach 'tambóirín'

> The tambourine man was always going about with the whistle man, beating the tambourine with the back of his finger, and giving it a wallop of the elbow. I never heard the instrument called anything but 'tambourine'

The process of making it is neatly described, with the inclusion of jingles noteworthy:

> Craiceann gabhair nó pocaide, nó cúplphoc a bhíodh ann. Nuair a d'fheannfaí an t-ainmhí chuirtí aol ar an gcraiceann – agus chrochtaí amuigh sa scioból é. Níor dheacair an fionnadh a bhaint de ansin tar éis scaithimh. B'ócáid ar leith í an oíche a ndéantaí an tambóirín. Nuair a bhíodh na 'tincéirí' agus na píosaí stáin agus gach uile rud a dhéanfadh clingeadh agus gliogarnáíl air, bhí sé réidh le haghaidh an bhóthair

> The skin of a goat, he-goat or billy was on it. When the animal was skinned, lime was put on the skin – and hung up in the barn. It wasn't difficult to take the hair off the skin. It was a great occasion the night that the tambourine was made. When the 'tinklers' and bits of tin and anything that would make a clink and rattle were on it, it was ready to face the road

Likely on account of the new visibility of the bodhrán at the time of his writing the memoir, Bairéad goes on to make a clear distinction between the tambourine and the device bodhrán:

> Craiceann caorach a bhíodh sa bhodhrán tí agus scioból go hiondúil. Fearacht an chléibh choll agus an chléibhín ime agus na ciseoige (cliathóg) is fada imithe i móran gach uile áit é

> It was a sheepskin that was on the typical household and barn bodhrán. Similar to the related basket and the little butter-basket and the wicker-work creel that is long gone in most other places [Bairéad 1972, 50]

Clare

While the history of the tambourine in Kerry has been, in PR terms, somewhat 'noisy', its use in County Clare has been more understated. There are numerous photographs of older players in the late 1950s into the 1960s playing the larger be-jingled tambourines in fleadh sessions and with groups of musicians. Flute player and dance authority Michael Tubridy (b. 1935) from near Kilrush played with local Wrens during his younger years.

> The drum was known only as 'tambourine' in his time, and was made each year prior to the Wren. Following that it was forgotten about, and typically it decayed and had to be re-skinned the next year, resulting in something of an annual fever of activity about getting a suitable goatskin. The local knowledge of how to make it, he considers, was something that was passed on in the locality, as there was always someone who knew how it should be done. He also says, that while following the Wren parades, those who played on the tambourines would join with the other musicians in the Wren band in a house or indoor session afterwards, the 'wren ball', but the drum was not played with music at any other time of the year.[27] In this way, of course, playing skills – and traditions – would be gradually established. Photographs from the 1950s and '60s however show occasional older men playing with musicians, suggesting that there was acceptance and/or appreciation in the county of the tambourine being played as part of music outside of the Wren season. Among such players were Packie Russell, Thady Casey and Pat Kelly. This is similar to what has been said for counties Kerry and Limerick.

▼ Thady Casey at the 1957 Co. Clare fleadh in Miltown Malbay [*Courtesy ITMA. Photo by Jim Griffiths, thanks to Harry Hughes, Terry Wilson and Dal gCais*]

Tambourine among the 1950s London Irish

This is similar to the thinking of pianist Reg Hall, who immersed himself among the London Irish musicians from the 1950s on. He is of the opinion that tambourine players in the mid-twentieth century were not favoured – were just not 'fashionable' – considered not right for Irish music and 'didn't suit the image of it that the Gaelic League wanted to put across'.[28] The frame drummers came from what he classifies as the 'Rural Tradition, reaching back into the dim past', as opposed to 'Gaelic revivalism, concerned with the circulation of a constructed and idealised Irish culture'.[29] The effect of that selectivity would have implied inferiority, or non-authenticity, and would have discouraged players or would-be players from performing in public perhaps, so rendering the instrument somewhat invisible in the post-war years. But, obviously, this did not deter the sprinkle of tambourine playing which Hall went on to document in his work. His analysis of the instruments and players taking part in London Sunday-morning sessions at *The Favourite* bar in Holloway shows only three visiting tambourine players in 1967 out of a total of sixty names. He found that fiddle and flute players are 'most likely to have a place in popular memory', while 'less-esteemed players of the tin whistle, mouth organ, melodeon, concertina, tambourine, bones and spoons have been readily forgotten'.[30] Still, the cover of his online study features Ballingarry, County Limerick-born Gerry Wright playing a large bejingled tambourine, and another photo shows the same player as quite the centre of crack. That image is enhanced by a description of the typically-minstrelish supplementary performance features that Wright's mentor had passed on

▼ Gerry Wright on bodhrán with unknown spoons player, London, 1960s [Nutan]

to him, part of which was a pretend drunk act in which he would 'throw his tambourine up in the air and catch it, or miss it and let it fall.' Wright's cousin Mary Heffernan, herself a tambourine player, told Hall that there was a tambourine 'in nearly every house' in her part of County Limerick, and she played it each year marching with the Wren.[31] Yet others of Hall's informants, such as 'Danny McNiff who left Leitrim in 1952 never saw one in Ireland'.[32] But an interview with Paddy Malynn of County Longford let us know of the 'Carty family, who played the concertina, melodeon and tambourine',[33] and Lucy Farr tells of 'A mummers' dance … in Martin Kirwan's barn in Baunyknov, Ballinakill, County Galway … an informal band of up to fourteen fiddle and flute players and two tambourines.'[34]

Midlands

Affirming this wider popularity of the tambourine, Willie Reynolds, an uilleann piper and teacher with CCÉ in Mullingar, wrote in his 1990 *Memories of a Music Maker* about bodhrán players at sessions in Westmeath and adjoining counties, naming several others who used the drum in the 1960s, including The Chieftains' first player, Davy Fallon. This reflects what is reported for counties Meath, Westmeath and Laois in The School's Collection and press sources. Reynolds' information includes reference to the tambourine and the transition of its name to 'bodhrán':

> In my early days the performers on this accompanying instrument were few and far between … the Fleadhanna Cheoil brought it into popularity … Most of the players did not use the stick but the fingers … the 'tambourine' as it was called in the early days

He describes performance practices that suggest handed-down minstrel or professional tambourine technique:

> Paddy Kelly of Ballymore was the most stylish bodhrán player I knew. He could hit it off the top of his head and also off his elbow … Jim (Ghandi) Daly … was excellent …would not play without the few drinks and then he wanted to 'go to town on it'

Reynolds also mentions the con-cussion lobby:

> Peter Cassells could play the bodhrán and he could also do a nice turn with a penny and a porter bottle which sounds something like the spoons[35]

Dublin county

Interestingly it is Dublin county which uniquely has a folklore story that is linked to an actual, preserved tambourine that is held at the National Museum in Mayo. That story is narrated in a 1943 book of reminiscences by a Killinarden, Tallaght farmer Malachi Horan who was born in 1847. His memoir was documented from conversation interviews conducted by George Little, and the book was given the imprimatur of an introduction by Seán Ó Súilleabháin of the Irish Folklore Commission at UCD. In this, he expresses amazement at how such a richness of custom from earlier times could have persisted so close (just ten miles) from the capital city. Horan, whose education had been in a hedge school at 'Killinarden Four-roads', was ninety five when his words were taken down, and he died the following year. His comments about music that was used in social life concern 'the Bride Oge', a traditional festival celebrating St Brigid that ran 'from the 2nd February to Shrove'. In it:

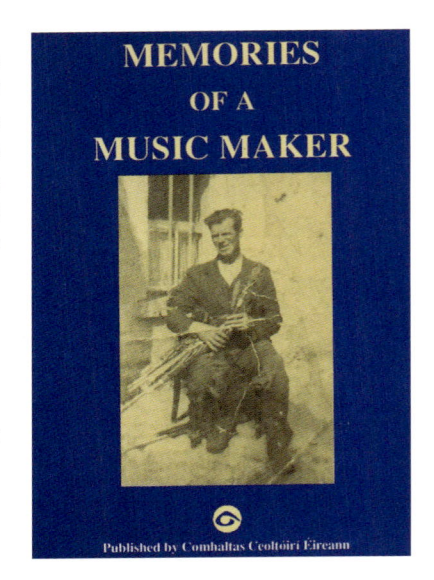

Cover of the 1976 Mercier Press reprint of the 1943 Malachi Horan story

'The Killinarden drum' which was played along with the fiddle for dancing and for 'the Brídóg' near Tallaght, County Dublin, and is reputed to have been made c. 1820 [Copyright National Museum of Ireland]

> The men dress up in long white shirts … When the feast starts, they do come to the neighbour's houses … they sing and dance to the music of the fiddle and the goatskin tambourine

'Tambourine' is explained in a footnote by the author, Little, as:

> composed of a round frame with ass-hide stretched over it. This utensil was used for carrying meal to chickens or oats to horses. Country boys when they wished to use it as a tambourine held it in front of the fire till the hide became taut. This was quite a usual practice in Meath. Irish = bodhrán or dolán[36]

It is quite remarkable both that the NMI has a tambourine said to be from the time of this story – donated to the NMI by George Little in 1942 – and that that writer shows familiarity with a primary use of this 'tamborine' as a device. His note shows that he was referring to how it was constructed, rather than what it was designed originally to be, and it certainly indicates awareness of improvisation on the device bodhrán, its having a seasonally-associated dual purpose. The date of Horan's recollection of the tambourine being played may be deduced as any time from *c.* 1857 up to the turn of the twentieth century. Remarkably, Little was able to source such a drum from Killinarden, though it is not known whether or not he got it from Horan himself. It is much larger than other bodhráns and tambourines in the NMI, and the depth of its frame, markings thereon, and the length of the overlap at the ends show that it was made from something else, most likely an old wool-wheel.

A further interesting aspect of the use of the tambourine in music in that second half of the 1800s is the fact of a woman playing it:

> Just past the door here, where the bohereen joins the mountain, was a great place for dancing of a summer Sunday long ago. Kitty Shea, the blind fiddler, would be there; and her daughter would be singing with her and keeping time on the tambourine … it was all jigs and hornpipes we danced[37]

Overall, this morsel of rural lore links familiarity with the tambourine of popular music to the bodhrán as a farm device in the years after the Famine. It also is in the same time-frame as the other accounts of improvising a tambourine on the device bodhrán

Social class and style

Despite the working-class connotations in the London emigré scene, back in Ireland the tambourine had a middle-class presence in Irish music too. This is seen in a photograph from around the turn of the 1900s which has a quite formally-attired group of musicians in an orchestral, stage setting playing with a full-size, Italian or military style bejingled tambourine. Since this was likely a Gaelic League function, the instrument obviously did have a currency. Other images in Ireland from several decades later show poorer, rural players with more crude, warped tambourines – generally with jingles – so the instrument would seem to have had a cross-class and all-regions appeal and practice. The manner of performing is an interesting issue, according to some descriptions of older players in the past which indicate an extrovert technique, like the documented eighteenth-century fashion and that of the nineteenth-century minstrels. This prompts consideration of a question that myself and Tim Lyons were once asked while on a tour in Scotland: 'Is Irish traditional music culture or entertainment?' The paradox is that dedicated players who are sometimes regarded as 'musicians' musicians' have a clear view of what they want to hear and emulate – a handed-down, cultural ideal in sophistication and technique, their condition typically – tritely – dismissed as 'purism'. On the other hand there are 'the plain people', for whom music is desired to be response-provoking, uplifting and satisfying. So, as well as being familiar and culturally acceptable, for them it must also be an invitation and opportunity to emotionally participate, trigger an impulse to let go, give relief from daily tedium. Travelling musicians, including pipers, on account of survival, economic savvy and necessity managed this variety by having tunes for every occasion. Tambourine players had their physical antics too, in addition to the skill and power of beating time on the frame drum. So it can be appreciated that in the pre-broadcasting age there would have been an audience for Tomás Rua back in the mid-1800s singing to his bodhrán or improvised tambourine, as much as there was for Paddy Conneely on the pipes in the same period. In the USA, Patsy Touhey performed on the pipes with his wife dancing, both of them dressed in symbolic 'Irish' attire; they could not have survived had their vaudeville theatre performances not been a mix of humour and pastiche as well as serious talent.

And so, part of tambourine players' routine was being extrovert and attention-seeking when younger. As they got older, those players became the classic 'ould boys' who are seen sitting at the edge of dance-music making in the mid-1900s: the odd tambourine player, beer-bottle tapper and spoons beater in the course of the early fleadh and session years. As long as there have been tambourines, there have been tambourine players in Ireland, in small numbers, yes, but a definite presence nevertheless. And looking at the occasional pieces of video footage from the 1960s shows that the melody players were at ease with them one way or another. Yet until the post-*Sive* years, this was observable only by those who travelled to fleadhs, and indeed such players were maybe even missed by the pundits on account of the low profile of the instrument relative to the superior status of and wonder for the melody instruments.

◀ Marcus Walsh with thumb-hole tambourine, Denis Murphy on fiddle, and whistle player Joe Coneen, at the Leon bar, Kilrush fleadh1960s [*Courtesy ITMA; thanks to Harry Hughes and Eamonn McGivney*]

▶ Three legendary figures in the bodhrán story: Colm Murphy, Mel Mercier and Mícheál Ó Súilleabháin [*From The Dolphin's Way album, courtesy Helen Phelan*]

NOTES TO CHAPTER 12

[1] Ó Súilleabháin 1996, par. 43.
[2] Batty Sherlock, in Kjeldsen 2000, 195.
[3] Ibid., 137.
[4] McNeill 1995, 8.
[5] Ibid., 9, 'Everyone has seen people dancing all night. But take a man and make him dance for a quarter of an hour without music and see if he can bear it' (pp. 30–1 in Maurice de Saxe's *Reveries on the Art of War*, trans. Thomas R. Phillips. Harrisberg, PA, 1944).
[6] Ibid.
[7] Ibid., 23.
[8] Kearney 1981, 3.
[9] Donohoe 1985, 16.
[10] *The Nationalist* 1926 0327 7.
[11] Byrne 1998, 48.
[12] Vallely 2004, Chapter 10, etc.
[13] Tansey 1997, 113.
[14] Curran 1988, 12.
[15] Hickey 1999, 32.
[16] Ibid., 115.
[17] Ibid., 57.
[18] Curran op. cit., 38–9.
[19] Ibid., 38.
[20] *Irish Press* 1977, 0627 4.
[21] Mitchell 2022, PC.
[22] O'Dwyer 2022, PC.
[23] Kjeldsen 2000, 131.
[24] Ibid., 182.
[25] Ibid., 193.
[26] Ibid., 194.
[27] Tubridy 2022, PC.
[28] Hall 2023, PC.
[29] Hall 2016, 1.
[30] Ibid., 828.
[31] Ibid., 429.
[32] Ibid., 392.
[33] Ibid., 372.
[34] Ibid., 373.
[35] Reynolds 1990, 38.
[36] Little 1943, 34.
[37] Ibid., 35.

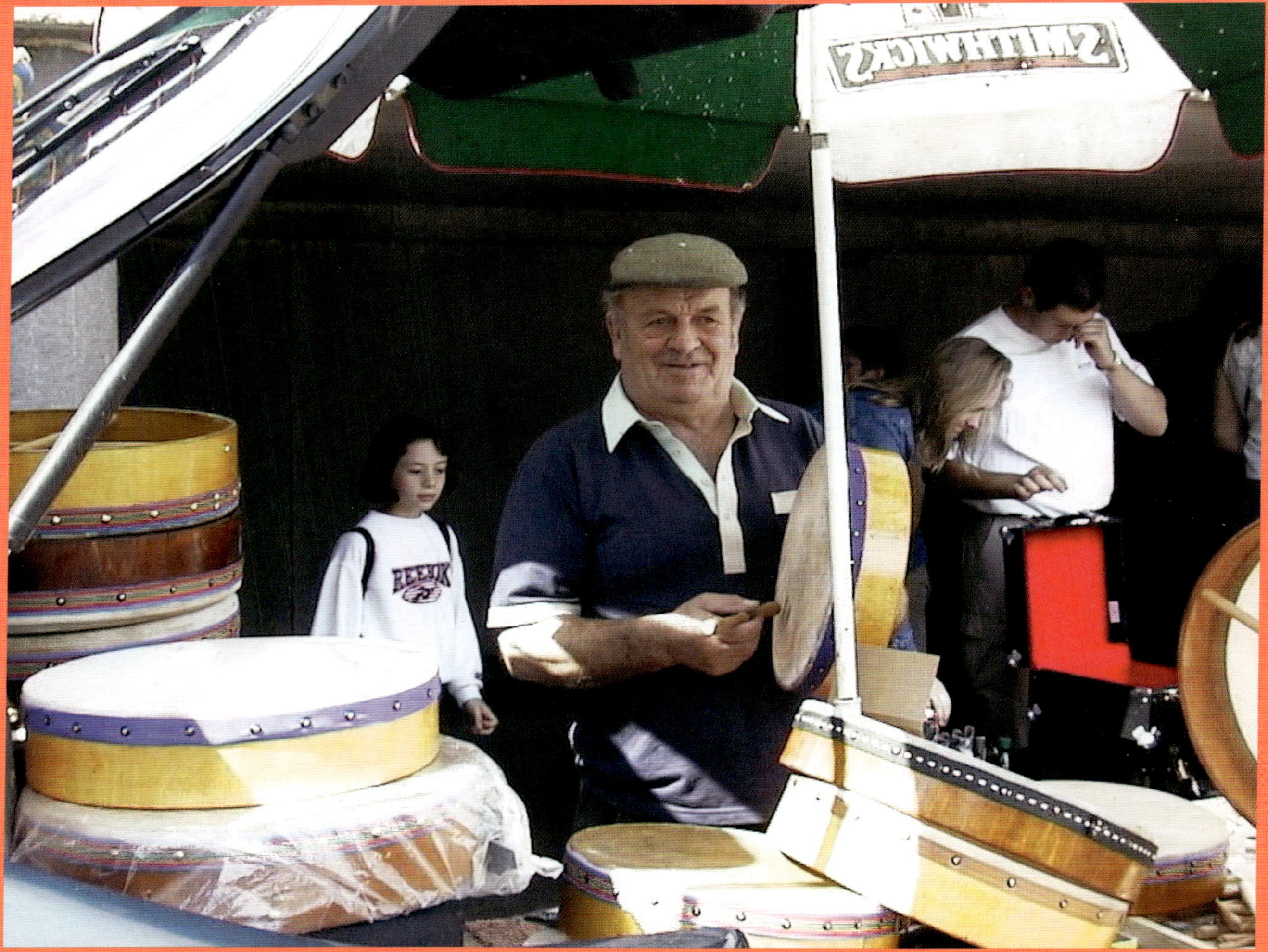

CHAPTER 13

THE *ACTUAL* BODHRÁN MAKERS

Interest in the tambourine and the bodhrán has been shown to be quite intense not only in various specific localities, but also, notably, island-wide among traditional musicians. This creates the need for drums, and in order to service that, there has for at least a century been a sprinkle of part-time, artisan makers. Rising popularity however led to increased demand, and to specialisation in order to fulfil that. The numerous modern-day makers learnt their basic skills from the older generation, but, driven by performance sophistication, have gone on to develop frame drum making with a high level of innovation. Oral documentary evidence charts this from more than a century ago.

From the *Schools' Collection* of folklore we learn that the tambourine was noted in twelve counties *c.* 1900. Some of these give rudimentary information on how they were made within a poor, subsistence-based rural society:

> Goats were to be found in abundance in this district. They were killed and the flesh was used for food the hide was very often used in the construction of the instrument we call the tambourine (Illaunbaun, County Clare)[1]

> This is how to make a tambourine. Get a goat and skin him. Take the hair off the skin and draw it. Then put the skin up in the chimney and leave it get hard. Then take it down and tack it on to the ring (Co. Kerry)[2]

Making bodhráns and tambourines draws on leather- and wood-working expertises, both of them common in earlier society. Knowledge of curing skin and of making simple frames was very much in the folk experience at all times in Irish history, with certain individuals becoming specialists. Elsewhere in the world where there were drum cultures, knowledge about drum-making would have been passed down through the centuries from ancient times when making drums for shamanistic practices is said to have been specialised and sacred.[3] That may or may not apply to Ireland but, according to the thinking of Ann Buckley, we cannot rule out something just because we have no record of it.[4] We do have to consider that what is known to have been the case in neighbouring countries may also be applicable for us – yet there is neither folklore nor manuscript evidence of it. Rather, because Irish music has been melody based, with drums playing no part in it, until the twentieth century the making of percussion instruments has not been a major specialist craft. The Lambeg drum – a sophisticated development out of a military instrument – is the only other Irish drum form, but it dates to just *c.* 1871.[5] Device bodhráns had been made for centuries, but the making of tambourine copies most likely did not begin until the early 1800s,[6] and that could be accomplished by those who

◂ 'The Limerick Bodhrán Maker', Paddy Clancy of Ballingarry [*EDI*]

already had the experience of making the older skin trays, containers and winnowers. Folklore records have many descriptions of the making of the latter devices, and some describe making tambourines. Firstly, a look at conditions for the rural Famine and post-Famine communities during the tambourine era in Ireland will illustrate why people had to, or would have been spurred to, make their own drums.

Poverty and making do

From the folklore accounts it is clear that there were degrees of specialisation in casual manufacture of both the utilitarian bodhrán and, later, the tambourine. One description is from County Meath, a January 1949 interview with Michael McMahon, a farmer aged eighty-four from Carnakelly, Kilmainhamwood who had a wealth of integrated information on all aspects of local culture and topography.[7] His childhood began in the mid-1860s when the memory of the Penal times was still marked by the reverence for a mass rock on the edge of their farm, and by 'mass pads', local tracks originally established to access this. He could recall the lean times when he was a teenager in 1879:

> 'Parnell's meal' ... before the coming of the Champion potato ... A Famine was starting, people dreaded another Famine like the one in '46 and '47 when the Scotch potatoes failed. The potatoes failed again [in 1879] and Parnell went to America and ... brought home thousands of pounds. That money was used to buy Indian meal ... There was a committee formed in every parish. The meal was given out on a ticket ... we had a shop at the time and people came with their tickets and got so much meal according to the size of their families – I saw that, my father and my mother and my sisters weigh it out for them ... the committee would meet every week in Moynalty.

This sets a climate of absolute scarcity in which improvisation would be standard, as also would be the inclination of young people to entertain themselves with subsistence music-making, self-entertainment, perhaps a central thing in their week. In that area the winnowing tray was called a *woit*, which by 1949 McMahon had not seen in a long time, likely meaning since the 1890s:

◀ Donncha Gough (bodhrán and pipes) with Charlie Byrne [*Nutan*]

It was used for winnowing oats where they had no winnowing machine ... The woit was round and about three feet in diameter. It had a light wooden rim and the rest of it was a goat-skin or a calf-skin that was tanned and tacked on to the rim ... There was no skin as good for the purpose as a goatskin [8]

Since in other places it is sheep-skin that is described as being used for bodhráns and wechts, perhaps the goatskin is significant evidence of the crossover to music, as McMahon continues: 'It was great for making a tambourine. There's a tambourine in Red Paddy Lynch's of Newcastle, and it makes a sound like a drum'.

▶ Bodhrán by Charlie Byrne [*James Fraher*]

Making tambourine copies

The role model for this improvisation was the fact that commercial tambourines were for sale in city music shops, no doubt alluring to the rhythmically-inclined. It might seem likely that cash would be gathered up to purchase a music-shop tambourine, as was done for melodeons, concertinas and, later, mouth organs, which were bought from enterprising grocers or travelling salesmen; there are many such accounts of saving up or pooling cash for melody instruments. But there are no such reminiscences about tambourines. It seems more likely therefore that, in addition to the household bodhrán or wecht being improvised on, it was also the case that people made their own tambourine copies with a tight, tacked-on skin. Going by examples in the National Museum, such devices might not look so good, especially when they had been re-skinned multiple times over the years, and playing on them was largely seasonal. Performance on tambourines likely was considered marginal, the territory of wild youth, or 'far-gone' ould boys, subject to a degree of disapproval that may be an aspect of the anti-bodhrán attitudes which prevailed in the 1970s. The urge to mimic marching bands with household bodhráns has been commented on in Ballinskelligs (Chapter 9), as has the fact that the device bodhrán was being improvised on as a tambourine at other times in the first couple of decades of the 1800s. The earliest method of the making of the original will now be looked at as a stage in the story of the bodhrán as a drum. A 1974 account by Thomas Pierce, a farmer from Kylemore, County Galway, indicates the more primitive tucking in of the skin to secure it:

"My first ever music session was at a County Galway fleadh in 1970. There I was so impressed by an old man playing a loud bodhrán that when a lad came into the pub selling them later I bought one for ten shillings. He turned out to be Charlie Byrne, the best maker I have ever come across! I played it first along with rock-'n-roll records, then with the Tulla Ceili Band's first LP"
Johnny 'Ringo' MacDonagh

> 'Twas made with a sheepskin. Lay down the sheepskin on the floor, an' leave the rim down on the skin, the wool side underneath. There was no trouble in gettin' a sheepskin because plenty o' sheep were dyin', an' they'd skin them an' keep the skins; if the wool was long they'd shear it off. You'd be putting the skin inside on the rim all the way about, and tight too, and put it inside the skin again. If you hadn't it tight lumps would come outside on the rim[9]

◀ Rough, experimental bent-willow frame for the original type of bodhrán [EDI]

Pat Mitchell was told of such a lime and horse manure method when he was planning to make a bodhrán in 1961. Deer-skin had been suggested to him and, when he went in search of one in a national park in County Galway, Ned O'Brien, the ranger there, welcomed him with the words 'Come in, lads, it's deer skin you need – that's what is always used'. Mitchell had been advised by Michael Duignan, professor of Celtic archaeology at UCG, that

> In ancient times the bodhrán was assembled by making a frame of flexible willow branches bent round a 'form' and woven together to make a circular frame on which the skin was stretched, brought up the sides, then down the inside and tucked under the top skin, this being possible because the wetted skin is very flexible and can be stretched easily. When this assembly dried out the skin shrank, thereby holding the whole assembly together[10]

This method concurs with folklore skin-tray bodhrán instructions given in the *Schools' Collection* r/e *c.* 1900. The same method was described by Gerry Hallinan in 1988 for 1930s County Roscommon,[11] and it can be seen in the skin trays and winnowers held at the National Museum of Ireland and the Ulster Folk Museum. Caoimhín Ó Danachair too was familiar with it in his 1955 description of how both the device bodhrán and the music one were made:

> The rim of the bodhrán is made of split ash ... about one and a half inches [4 cm] thick ... Usually the head is of goatskin ... well softened by soaking in water, stretched over the rim ... secured in position by a row of brass-headed upholstery nails. Formerly a different method of securing the skin was used: the soft wet skin was stretched tightly over the rim, carried down on the inside of the rim and pushed under the rim and inside the outer covering of skin. Thus the rim was entirely covered by the skin which gripped tightly upon itself in shrinking[12]

▲ The tuck-in method of securing the skin on skin trays, as reported in *The Schools' Collection*

The *Schools' Collection* of folklore has several sets of instructions for making tambourines and bodhráns using rudimentary materials. These have been described for the original bodhrán, but for a taut-skinned tambourine the method is not so different, as can be seen in this case from Listowel, County Kerry:

> My brother William Cahill of Craughatoosane, Listowel made a tambourine out of a goat's skin. This is the way he made it. He got the skin of a goat and put it down the glaise for about six weeks and he put a grain of lime on it the way there would not be a smell and he put a grain of salt in it the way it would not rot. Then he got the rim of a screen and put the skin on and pulled it well and then got 2d worth of brass tacks and put them on it and then got the covers off of polish boxes and flattened them out and then made holes in the rim. Then he got the tongs and reddened it and put it into the holes and made them nice and long. Then he rubbed a small piece of resin to it and it made it very hard. Then he put it up and let it dry. Then he put wires along the back of it[13]

At Cloughaneely, County Donegal, the percussion compulsion led enterprising young people to make crude bass drums *c.* 1835:

> Chuireadh siad craiceann na caorach – ba ghnách le baraillí a bheith acu a bhí a coinneail plúr fadó shin agus ní raibh siad ró-mhór ... chuirthí dhá craiceann caorach air agus ba gnách leo craiceann na gcaorach seo poill bheag a dhéanamh ionntu ins a dóigh nuair a bhuailfeá tuaim air go dtiocfadh an tuaim amach ar gach fuile thaobh ... Agus fídeogaí stáin le cuid acu, cuid eile acu a raibh plátaí leo – cláraí, cannaí – in a mbuaileadh go dtí go siúladh siad fríd an áit uilig[14]

> They would put a sheepskin on both ends of a flour barrel, which wasn't too big ... and make holes in the timber to let the sound out; some played on tin whistles, some banged on cans or plates while marching through the whole place

Drums were improvised from barrels in County Mayo too in the early 1900s, with John Horkan recalling that 'Michael Casey's father made the drum out of an old "bacon" barrel ... and he put a goatskin on each end'.[15] This was also done in Kerry where Jimmy Hennessy said in 1987: 'There are barrels going now – plywood barrels – and there's good rims cut out of them'.[16]

Home-making of instruments

Fiddles and flutes were occasionally home-made in the past; fiddles could be made from tea-chest plywood, and rudimentary flutes are reported on occasion as being fashioned from cart spokes, chair legs and bicycle pumps:

> In those days there were lots of bicycles about and there was a black celluloid pump with them. It looked similar in size to a concert flute, so I ... drilled six holes in it with a hot iron and also made a mouth hole and to my great surprise the flute could be played[17]

▲ Home-made fiddle played by a Traveller musician at Puck Fair, Killorglin, County Kerry, 1955 [*Kennelly Archive*]

▼ Top: flute made from flexible plastic tubing [*EDI*]
▼ Bottom: flutes made from Japanese Knotweed [*EDI*]

In County Kerry, *sean-nós* singer Jimmy O'Brien remembered seeing his uncle

> making a flute from the branch of an alder tree. The centre of the branch was scooped out and Paddy then reddened six-inch nails to make holes for fingers … A neighbour … made a fiddle with wood from a tea chest and used ordinary timber for the neck of the instrument[18]
>
> Many useful instruments were also made. Patrick Dunne of Newtown, near Galboystown, made a fiddle out of bog ash, and Bob Lalor made a tambourine from the hide of a goat[19] [Galboystown, County Meath]

Dessie Wilkinson reports in *CITM* that Roscommon flute-player Josie McDermott and John Blessing in Fermanagh could recall improvised flutes made out of 'boor-tree' (elder) and 'fuarawn' (from the Irish *fuarán* – hogweed – similar in its noded stem structure to bamboo).

◀ Stick-struck tambourine made in the mid-1930s by Eddie Phelan of Lavistown, Co. Kilkenny, a paternal cousin of ancient horns pioneer Simon O'Dwyer. The rim is from a sand riddle, and the skin, given by a local traveller woman, is donkey; the jingles are pennies, and the gripping wire was used to tension the skin. The drum was played by Eddie's brother Joe in a small band up to 1940, and the fact that he was known for a particular 'march triplet' that he had learnt from a man who was in his 70s indicates a local tambourine tradition [*EDI; information courtesy Simon O'Dwyer and Maria Cullen O'Dwyer, Ancient Music Ireland*]

Tambourines were home-crafted too by people of modest ability, and the fact that those skills existed at all, and persisted, suggests an ongoing, historic practice which certainly dated at least to the nineteenth century. The most challenging part of the process was getting a suitable rim, and most popular for this was a moribund sieve, riddle or 'sand-screen'. This was confirmed on radio by Listowel maker Jack Duggan, who told Ciarán Mac Mathúna that 'You kill either a dog, or a goat, and skin it … put that skin down with a shake of lime on the hairy side down in stable manure, to tan it … you will have to have a rim – such as a sieve, about a foot and a half in diameter'. He also said that this preparation for the Wren was the same as he had known in all his fifty-five years of taking part in it.

Recycling the riddle
From the various accounts it is clear that, long before the entry of Seán Ó Riada, tambourines were being made for the Wren in a rudimentary craft way. Mel Mercier recounts this for his father Peadar, who played with The Chieftains: 'He made his first drum using the old methods, soaking a goatskin in the bath at home for a week before stretching it over the rim of

13 THE ACTUAL BODHRÁN MAKERS

a garden sieve'.[20] Such drums might be made by Wren-boys themselves, but the process also involved specialists who either handed on lore or who generally made tambourines part-time; various improvisations, especially for the rim, were the norm. Patricia Lynch relates what she was told when enquiring about the making of the 'bowran' as used in *Sive*:

> Get a goatskin first ... There's nothing like a goatskin for a tambourine ... sprinkle it with lime. Bury it for a fortnight in an old manure heap rolled up tightly ... Take it out and you will find the hairs will rub off ... Clean it well ... stretch it, pull it gently. Get a wooden frame, the round of a garden sieve is just the thing. Wire it on and yer tambourine is made. 'Tis ready to play then [*Kerryman* 1961, 1111 17]

Use of a discarded implement for the frame is most common, and comes into the instructions for making tambourines in Leinster too, where the drum was played both on the Wren and in dance music, as the list of 'Museum Acquisitions for a proposed County Museum at Stradbally, County Laois' shows:

> No. 1 is a tambourine, which was home-made and used by Mr. Patrick Kelly, a noted Timahoe boxer, about sixty years ago [c. 1903]. The wooden portion was fashioned from a coal riddle, and covered in goatskin [*Leinster Express* 1963, 0309 7]

Bryan MacMahon, himself an authority on the Wren and on the making of the tambourine in Kerry and Limerick, gave the same recipe:

> You get the skin of a goat or some similar animal and it's stretched over a frame. The usual frame they use is the rim of a sieve ... and behind it's made taut by two iron bars or wires, then it's nailed around the rim[21]

Jimmy Hennessy in Kerry also spoke of using riddles, but indicates the move to specialised rim- or frame-making:

▲ 1948 Wren tambourine from County Clare [*Copyright National Museum of Ireland*]

▶ Specialist maker Eamonn Maguire, Belfast [*Matt Kavanagh, Irish Times*]

that's the rim for the bodhrán yes, for sieving sand, the timber work that's in the sieve and the sieve part would be taken off the rim you see, and the rim part would be cleaned and polished and you'd have a proper rim for your bodhrán ... years ago they used to buy the sieve, take off the wire and meshing you know, and make a bodhrán with the rim of the sieve. And other times they used to get plywood and they used to do it with hot water until they got it into the shape [22]

Interviewed by Svend Kjeldsen, Sonny Davey in County Sligo was frank about improvisation in construction materials: 'The Dowds had an old bodhrán of mine for thirty two years. It had thumbholes in the rim, there was no stick and it was played with hand, with two fingers. That one I made from a sand riddle'.[23] Players confirm how common this practice was. Among these was Batty Sherlock at Doocastle, County Mayo, who recalled his brother making a tambourine but, unable to find a discarded sand-screen (gravel riddle), they improvised: 'The sieves were a very valuable piece of machinery ... them times ... we couldn't find one, so we decided we'd make a square rim, about four inches deep'.[24] Joe McDonagh of Gurteen, County Sligo had been making bodhráns since schooldays too: 'With Tansey [Seamus] and other school friends. Caught a goat and killed it. 1956 or '7. Made a bodhrán for the Wren boys'.[25] Bending the wood was the major problem, so they too utilised a discarded circular frame: 'We couldn't make the rim of it ourselves ... but Kelly got the rim of a sand-screen ... Took off the wire ... We made a very good bodhrán from that'.[26] Another of Kjeldsen's forthright interviewees had a similar story: 'The rims got very scarce ... we couldn't find them, and there wasn't money to go buying them ... Worn-out sand-screen ... sometimes we cut it down to make it smaller'.[27]

Specialisation

> Sonny Canavan ... is a maker of tambourines or bowrawns and he has a herd of fifty goats. He sells the bowrawns at eight pounds a time and finds it hard to keep up with the demand [*Limerick Leader* 1969, 1004 14]

As the tambourine expanded out of seasonal Wren use into year-round music accompaniment after 1960, demand increased, and makers had to develop woodwork skills and have more raw materials to hand. The stepped-up scale of making required sourcing suitable timber, and using craft methods of bending it, skills which were already in the community, used by professional sieve and wool-wheel makers in the past, and also by contemporary artisan woodworkers. Before the advent of plywood, instructions for the making of the tambourine frames in Kerry involved what appears to have been a flat piece of wood made by slicing a length of young ash timber:

> A rim of green ash is then prepared, in shape resembling the rim of a hand gravel-sieve. Four circular pieces of tin are threaded on a thin wire and the wire inserted, each end to the longer sides of the rectangular slits. The skin is drawn taut and tacked about the rim ... The tambourine, or bowrawn, is then held near the fire, not too near [*Kerryman* 1960, 0924 6]

Sonny Davey in County Sligo could chart his move away from riddles too, as reported by Mary Gaffney in 1977:

> James Davey of Killavil, County Sligo has been one of the more visible of the older generation of smalltime makers. He gave up farming at the age of 64 to specialise in the drums, having made his first one at the age of twelve under

---

UNIQUE NEWCASTLE WEST CASE.

Alleged Stealing of Goat to Use Skin for a Drum.

Sergeant Hickey, Tournafulla, said the larceny of a goat was reported to him. In the course of his subsequent inquiries he interrogated the defendant at the residence of his employers in Kilmeedy. At first Doherty denied all knowledge of the affair but later said he might as well tell the truth.

He then made a statement in the course of which he described in detail how himself and three other men had taken the goat to get the skin for the purpose of making a tambourine for St. Stephen's Day.

The Liberator 1934 1016 4

SKIN OF GOAT FOR TAMBOURINE

The killing of a goat, and the utilisation of the skin for the purpose of making a Tambourine, were mentioned during the hearing of an amusing larceny case at Ferbane District Court on Thursday ...
Justice: "Did you say you were going to use the skin of the goat for a tambourine?"
Defendant: "I did, sir. (Laughter)".

Witness: "There was to have been a dance at a house named Horan's about that time, but he did not attend it"
Justice: 'If he had the tambourine ready he would have been invited ...' (Laughter)
'There is some romance about this case' remarked the Justice".
The witness, in further cross-examination, said he did not know what it would cost to make a tambourine. He never made one.
Justice: 'Do you mean to tell me that you killed the unfortunate goat in order to make a tambourine?'
Witness: 'Not exactly that ...'
Justice: 'I order that the skin be returned to Reddin so that he can proceed with the making of the tambourine. I presume that is really the most valuable part of the goat'

Offaly Independent 1927 1119 5

> TAMBORINES and DRUMS have just arrived, also Recorders, Flagolets, Mouthorgans, Castanets, Jaws Harps, Tin Whistles stocked. DENNISTON, Longford.

Longford Leader 1969 1112 6

instruction from flute-player Tom McDonagh. The first bodhrán, made with an old sand screen, was rough and unpolished compared to his present work … His drums are from 15 to 17 inches in diameter, and were pitched carefully prior to sale. He only used goatskin, considering sheepskin malodorous in the proximity of a fire. At his peak, he made two each week, as well as making souvenir-type ones. He began making in 1925, his drums travelling to England, USA, Europe and Sweden [*Irish Press* 1977, 0627 4]

Professional manufacture led to commercial retail potential, and to advertising by the music trade. The description too moved with the times, from 'tambourine' to 'bodhrán', with O'Reilly's of Dublin by the 1980s selling all instruments, including 'Bowran'.[28] This marks a shift of the bodhrán from home- or craft-made object to a commercial product, a coming of age of the Irish drum.

Desperate measures

The famous Kerry maker Sonny Canavan lived in an isolated farmhouse without electricity, and made tambourines and bodhráns from the skins of goats he raised himself on the surrounding moorland.[29] But for those with no land or financial resources in earlier days, getting a goatskin could be a problem. The urge to drum on the Wren created a seasonal peak in the demand, and could lead to unorthodox methods of acquisition which often landed people in court:

> himself and three other men had taken the goat to get the skin for the purpose of making a tambourine for St Stephen's Day [*The Liberator* 1934, 1016]

> they took Cotter's goat and killed it in order to get the skin for a tambourine for the 'Wren Boys' [*Limerick Leader* 1934, 0611 4]

> WANTED GOAT'S SKIN FOR THE WREN. Seven youths were charged … Supt. Burns, who prosecuted, said these boys were making preparations for the 'wren'. They had a few instruments and wanted the skin of a goat to make a tambourine. The defendants took the goat and decided that the best way to kill it was to drown it [*Kerryman* 1959, 1212 21]

Sons Steal Father's Goat To Make A Tambourine!

WITH the intention of using the skin to make a drum or tambourine for their role as "wren boys," two youths stole their father's goat, which they slaughtered. The story was told at Shanagolden Court, when the boys were charged with stealing the animal.

JUSTICE C.S. KENNY, at Shanagolden Court on Wednesday, was told the unusual story of how two youths, with the help of companions, stole their father's goat and killed the animal for the purpose of making a tamborine from the animal's skin. Before the Court as a result of the occurrence were Patrick and Michael Hanley, two brothers, of Moig, Shanagolden, and they were charged with the larceny of a goat, the property of their father, Richard Hanley, of the same address, on 11th December last. Arising out of the charge, Patrick Hanley, the first named defendant, was also prosecuted for alleged cruelty to the goat, and with leaving the carcass unburied.

Supt. M. McKenna, Newcastle West, prosecuted, and defendants, who were not professionally represented, admitted taking the goat.

FATHER COMPENSATED.

Richard Hanley, Moig, gave evidence of having missed the goat early in December. He estimated the value of the animal at £2 and said that no one had authority to take the goat. Witness added that since the occurrence defendants, out of their savings, had compensated him for the loss of the goat.

Patrick Hanley, in evidence, admitted taking the goat and, with some other youths, killing the animal with a knife which he got from another boy. One of the youths, Patrick Duggan, witness said, had since gone to England.

CRUELTY ASPECT.

Supt. McKenna said that the alleged cruelty was the most serious aspect of the case. In their attempts to kill the goat the defendants first tried to smother the animal and they eventually killed it by stabbing it in the neck with a knife. Their motive was to get the goat's skin for the purpose of making a tamborine or drum for Wren's Day.

CHARGES DISMISSED.

In view of the fact that the father had been compensated for the loss of the goat and that the carcass had been subsequently buried, the Justice dismissed all the charges against the defendants.

Kerryman 1957 0105 8

'Wren boys' kill Kerry goats to make music

Evening Herald 1959 1209 5

> The goat-stealing season has opened around Listowel for the demand for bowrans will be great and nothing is better than the skin of an old buck. Men are staying up these nights around Listowel to see that nothing happens to their puck. An authentic bowran costs about £30 and even at that it is not a profitable business [*Evening Herald* 1976, 1123 7]

In 1959, *Sive* drew attention to the frame drum which had not in recent time been heard of by the greater number of people on the island. The prevalence of comment on how it was made from goatskin created a fascination, a kind of mystique which generated its own mythology. This, in turn, resulted in making it attractive, generating a compulsion to get one at all costs among young lads, a sudden demand which could not be met by the tiny number of part-time makers, and resulted in spates of thefts of goats. Early on, John B. Keane stated that 'more goats are being stolen this year than in any other year I can remember – and they are being killed for the making of bodhráns'.[30] The national press reported:

> Many of the farmers are laying the blame for the increased goat stealing on the popularity of the two bodhrán-strumming tinkers in *Sive*. There are about ten recognised bodhrán-makers in north Kerry, but these … often rear their own goats. One of them told me: 'There is always some goat-stealing around Christmas time. But from what I have heard, this year is a record' [*Evening Herald* 1959, 1209 5]

▲ Sophisticated jingles, including bells, on a tambourine played in Tenerife [*Nutan*]

The jingles

The primary difference between the tambourine and the bodhrán is that the the tambourine typically had jingles. These were on the bulk of Irish tambourines until the early 1960s, usually improvised from available pieces of already-circular metal like shoe-polish tin lids, brass door-knob trims, pot-menders, beer-bottle caps, and even low-currency coins – pennies or ha'pennies. Scrap tinplate and discs of easily-cut metals such as discarded aluminium household utensils were also used, anything to rattle or buzz. It can be seen from mid-1900s tambourines in the National Museum that the slots for these were often roughly cut. And in Caoimhín Ó Danachair's 1950s, west Limerick Wrenboy photographs the jingles could be just crudely tacked on to the outside of the rim – perhaps tokenistically, for tradition's sake; in some cases there are no jingles at all. The National Museum's earliest frame drum, from Killinarden, Dublin (p. 228), said to have been used with dancing in the early 1800s, has no jingles either, making it too an interesting landmark in the bodhrán to tambourine transition. Similarly, by 1974 in the film *Bodhrán* some tambourines have jingles, some have not. The photo of Jim Sheehy at Castleisland (p. 191) shows that by 1970 his drum prototype was very large and deep-rimmed and had no jingles. The objective perhaps was volume, and a richer tone – a scale and perfection no doubt driven by his highly-competitive extrovert showmanship. Ó Danachair – from the same area as Sheehy, and a contemporary of his – noted in 1947 that the north Munster bodhrán could be 'from eighteen to twenty-four inches' (46–61 cm). That drum may suggest that he – and/or his brother – were pioneering the jingle-free tambourine, the bodhrán. Jingles can be heard on John Reynolds' 1927 tambourine recording, but are faint, prompting the suggestion that they may have been suppressed by taping. If so, that would mark Reynolds as the medium between the tambourine with jingles and the

▼ Improvised coin jingles–a 1960 halfpenny–on a tambourine at the NMI [*Copyright National Museum of Ireland*]

13 THE ACTUAL BODHRÁN MAKERS

▲ Jingles on a stick-struck tambouine, Athea, County Limerick, 1946 [*Photo Caoimhín Ó Danachair, courtesy National Folklore Collection*]

▶ Improvised aluminium jingles on a 1960s tambourine at the NMI [*Copyright National Museum of Ireland*]

◀ Brass door knob trim jingles on a Westmeath tambourine [*Copyright National Museum of Ireland*]

▲ Polish-box lids used as jingles on a County Clare bodhrán at the NMI [*Copyright National Museum of Ireland*]

▶ Jingles on a tambourine at a fleadh in Roscrea, 1964 [*CCÉ*]

227

one without them – the bodhrán. That taping-up theory is raised again by journalist Ronan Nolan for the revival period, noting that, when forming The Chieftains c. 1960, Paddy Moloney got their Westmeath tambourine player Davy Fallon to 'tape up the jingles so only the drum could be heard'.[31] That demonstrates that Moloney was aware of the nature of the transfer from be-jingled tambourine to jingle-free bodhrán – a move from solely being for entertainment excitement to having additional complementary aesthetic rigour in serious music-making – which was already in vogue in north Munster a decade earlier. But perhaps it was prompted by his mentor Seán Ó Riada's decision to use a tambourine without jingles in Ceoltóirí Chualann? For although John B. Keane said that Ó Riada's first sight of an Irish frame drum was the be-jingled tambourine used in *Sive*, the composer's questing nature is likely to have made him aware of Caoimhín Ó Danachair's 1955 comment that the use of jingles on pre-1960s drums appeared to be 'in imitation of the jingles of the tambourine'.[32] In that view, the bodhrán drum was seen to be an evolution from the device bodhrán, and the use of both the jingles and the term 'tambourine' was simply a temporary, innovative stage of that evolution. In this thinking it is easy to understand the acceptance of the co-existence of the terms 'tambourine' and 'bodhrán'. Looking at Sheehy's drums it is clear that he as both maker and player was innovatory in abandoning the jingles. This was happening in Connacht as well, for Ted McGowan in County Sligo made his tambourine at the end of the 1940s, and it had no jingles. Where it started is difficult to pinpoint, since it appears that there were not any in-depth interviews done with older makers and players. It is all a moot point of course, relevant only to pedantic history, but the jingle-free tambourine was the starting point for the remarkable scale of innovation and invention which marks today's makers – the outcome of maker, player and maker-player interactive innovations since the 1960s.

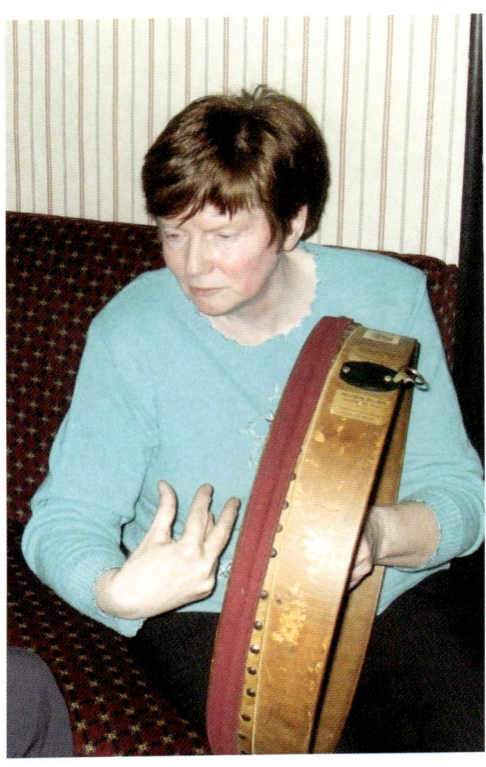

▲ Kathleen Gray, hand-striker
[Gregory Daly]

The 'stick', *cipín* or 'tipper'

Historically, as described in Chapter 2, the tambourines used in the Janissary-inspired military music in England were reported as being large, bodhrán size, and images show them being played with the hand.[33] In Daniel Maclise's 1838 painting *Merry Christmas in the Baron's Hall*, a boy with mummers in England plays on a tambourine too, but with a stick, which likely mimics military side-drum or tabor drum practice. If that was being done in England it need not be surprising that people in Ireland would have tended to do it as well, and indeed a stick could be used with medieval tambourines in Europe too. But the majority of playing on frame drums world wide in the past and today is done directly with the hand. In the developing culture of public sessions in the 1960s Dónal Lunny recalls that Ned Farrell in *Pat Dowling's* bar in Prosperous, County Kildare 'as often as not struck the skin with a knuckle rather than a bodhrán-stick, or tipper'.[34] The earliest popular press descriptions of Irish tambourine playing say the same, that 'it is played by the knuckles of the hand',[35] and the earliest film images show just that – as well as indicating the presence of jingles. Sonny Canavan in Kerry had strong opinions on the subject: 'Borans is, like, very nice music, if you have got the right tipper'. He himself played with the hand, being of the opinion that 'The real tipper is with the hand, from the wrist downwards '.[36] But today most bodhráns are played with a beater of some sort, which has

▲ Frank McGann (Roscommon) and Ted McGowan (Sligo). Stick-striking and hand-striking [*James Fraher*]

▶ Mummers with stick-struck tambourine in Daniel Maclise's 1838 *Merry Christmas in the Baron's Hall* [*National Gallery of Ireland*]

▼ Tony MacMahon with Seán Ó Riada hand-striking [*Gael Linn*]

transformed playing potential. This is variously called a *'cipín'* [twig, little stick] or 'tipper', typically referred to as a 'stick'. The use of it came to define regional style and attitudes in the past, expressed by Seamus Tansey from Sligo as 'The hand was what the tambourine was played with in Connacht; the stick was used in Munster'. He himself, like his neighbour Josie McDonagh and other local players Kathleen Gray and Geraldine Towey, did not use a stick – they played in the manner of casual improvisation on the wicht in the past. The use of the stick, like the term 'bodhrán', Tansey associated with Seán Ó Riada.[37] This opinion was also held by Ted McGowan in Gurteen, who also regarded himself as playing the tambourine, and he was blunt in pin-pointing the name-change: 'The bodhrán came in with Ó Riada', and 'the stick came in with the bodhrán'.[38] The use of the hand thus is another casual marker of difference between tambourine and bodhrán, significant enough for Svend Kjeldsen to title his 2000 thesis and subsequent lectures *The Coleman Hand-strikers*. This was the old way universally.

But a yet further distinction is made in the stick-playing regions, with west Limerick being regarded as the home of a single-ended stick, as described by Mícheál Ó Súilleabháin in 1974, and as seen with the Sheehy brothers earlier, as described in Chapter 11. But in neighbouring north Kerry a double-ended stick was said to be typical. The use of a stick was highlighted by Caoimhín Ó Danachair's image and description of a two-ended stick in 1946 and '47, and thereafter it has often been mentioned: such an implement is useful on a vertically-held, one-sided drum. As a possible origin for the two-ended stick, an interesting sequel indeed could well be what was mentioned by one maker: 'But ye must use a bone with a knob at each end or if ye've the right kind of knuckles on yer fist, use them, till they bleed! there's no music like it'.[39] This mention of a knobbed bone is an interesting variant of the two-ended stick, and indeed may

▲ Páidí Ó Dubháin, County Down [*EDI*]

"When I first saw and heard a bodhrán I was fascinated by the sound and the way it was played – love at first sight. I have been making it full time since after the 1990s, putting a lot of time into development. The deeper I get into it, the more I understand how complex and versatile it is, with limitless possibility. My love and passion for it have grown over the years and keep me coming up with new ideas"
Christian Hedwitschak,
bodhrán maker

◀ German bodhran-maker Christian Hedwitschak at Craiceann, 2012 [*EDI*]

13 THE ACTUAL BODHRÁN MAKERS

be its precursor (if it was not just a personal, pragmatic solution). This provokes thinking of the colloquial term for a two-knobbed fowl leg-bone in cuisine – the 'drumstick'. From 1897, an Irish newspaper report of culture in 'Qumevadjik' spoke similarly concerning the Ichuktobis people who were said to have one musical instrument: 'a tambourine made of fish skin, beaten with a seal bone'.[40] The already-cited 1949 interview with Michael McMahon from County Meath also includes a comment that a stick was used there, so pushing the date of an implement other than the hand being used on the tambourine back to the nineteenth century; that is a half-century earlier than Caoimhín Ó Danachair's 1947 Kerry report, and also means that a stick-struck tambourine was known and was being made a couple of hundred miles north of Kerry:

> You hold a little bit of a stick in the middle – you hold it between your two fingers, and you 'time' a tune by striking the tambourine with each end of the stick. Some fellows were great at it[41]

▲ Stick-struck large tambourine with jingles, County Limerick, 1946 [*Caoimhín Ó Danachair, National Folklore Collection*]

First mention of 'stick' in the press

Press reportage of the tambourine occasionally mentions playing with a two-head stick in the revival period, as a kind of curiosity which was presumably seen as odd, being different to the typical one-headed drumstick.[42] The effect of this was noted in the decade before Bryan MacMahon's first writing, showing that the tambourine was already well established at that time:

> When played by an expert with a double-sided drumstick the instrument is capable of producing an alarming volume of sound that its not too unlike distant thunder or heavy gunfire [*Kerryman* 1944, 0101 7]

The *cipín* these days comes in huge variety, each form designed to produce particular effect or timbre. Dublin bodhrán maker Páiric McNeela makes them from weighted sections of discarded fiddle-bows. Stick styles – single- and double-ended, and made from myriad materials – indeed merit a study on their own.

▲ Profiled, carved beater stick [*EDI*]

▶ Bodhrán beaters [*EDI*]

231

Bodhrán makers and the media

Makers in the past have typically been small farmers who made tambourines on a specialised but part-time basis. The most valuable sources of information on them are television and film archives, among which RTÉ has two short documentaries involving Kerry maker Sonny Canavan. The first of them was broadcast in 1966, when Canavan and another maker John (Jack) Duggan from near Listowel were interviewed about the Wren and making bodhráns. On making the drum, Duggan confirmed that it had been a minor craft when he said, 'First of all you look out for a worn sieve, for sievin' oats or gravel … a good firm rim'.[13] As for the drum's name, although he was being asked by the interviewer about 'the bodhrán', he did not himself use that term – for in winding up, he said that in the final part of the process 'You can heat the tambourine on the fire then'. Sonny Canavan, of Dirha west, Listowel was also interviewed on another documentary eleven years later in 1977. In this he was identified as the maker of the bejingled tambourine for John B. Keane's *Sive*, but by that time he was using purpose-made bodhrán shells made from bent plywood, and no jingles. He chats over the half door with John B. Keane who sings a verse from the *Sive* song and accompanies himself on the drum.[14] This emphasises the new popularisation of the bodhrán and a consequent rise in demand that had generated full-process, specialist making rather than using redundant sieves or riddles. The other major visual celebration of the bodhrán was rather more spectacular, the already-mentioned 1974 film *Bodhrán*, by Tom Hayes. In it, the bodhrán is seen being made from scratch by Joe O'Sullivan of Carrigkerry, County Limerick, the third generation of his family with the expertise. He too was using purpose-made rims by that time.

▲ Sonny Canavan [*Courtesy RTÉ Archive*]

▲ 'Bodhrán Billy', a 2020s fantasy, goat-to bodhrán postcard by Mike Lancaster [*mikelancasterportraits.co.uk*]

◀ Sonny Davey with the writer, 1997 [*Courtesy Davey Family*]

▲ Sonny Davey [EDI]

▼ Seamus O'Kane playing a tambourine he made which is modelled on the 1832 Maclise image [EDI]

Part-time specialists

The original, seasonal use of the tambourine did not require full-time manufacture. But its new popularity is emphasised in printed interviews with makers, notably with Sonny Davey from County Sligo in 1995: 'I had the bodhrán all to myself for years – there was no-one playing, or even making it. Now they're making them all over the place, even abroad'.[15] He was a part-time maker who eventually became full-time as demand for bodhráns increased in the 1960s. The new popularity put a spotlight on rural part-timers, one of whom was pictured as part of an *Irish Times* crafts feature in 1970 (p. 216), Ned O'Connor of Tournafulla, west Limerick;[16] David Shaw-Smith featured Malachy Kearns in his 1984 book *Ireland's traditional Crafts*; and Méabh Ó'Hare's TG4 *Ceird an Cheoil* documentary dealt with Dungiven, County Derry maker Seamus O'Kane. From folklore and other accounts the making of tambourines and bodhráns can be seen to have once been a rudimentary craft, but it was guided by handed-on lore and skills. Early makers appear to have been doing it as a seasonal or other adjunct to running a small farm, some on a year-round (but not industrial) scale. Certain makers had their own purpose-reared goats, others got sufficient skins from adjacent farmers whose goat had died naturally. John Duggan said that the skin of a young greyhound was very suitable; these were available as a consequence of a dog having to be put down due to track injuries. The many modern makers today not only have a vastly increased market, but have the advantage of access to high-class machine tools, and to skins imported from Pakistan and elsewhere, and, consequently, have

TUCK-IN SEQUENCE

Maker Padraig MacNeela working through the tuck in bodhrán making sequence

▼ Tuck in bodhrán at the NMI Castlebar

13 THE ACTUAL BODHRÁN MAKERS

developed factory-style fabrication routines and prestige reputations. Waltons have their bodhráns made in a specialist factory in China where the workers are skilled in making this one product. In Ireland, however, all makers took advice from older makers, notably from those in counties Tipperary, Kerry and Limerick, but most have gone their own way in the years since. The drum is now universally called bodhrán, and is no longer made with jingles. Tuneable versions, with patent screw-adjustment tensioners – an early form of which had been used already in the eighteenth century – have become both sophisticated and common, and certain makers are revered, their drums sought after. Each of them has come to making from radically different places, and each has an independent philosophy.

Testing the theories

As part of the research which this book prompted, three drums were made. One was a copy of the tucked-in-skin style of household, skin tray bodhráns which are held at the National Museum of Ireland – Country Life in County Mayo, and at the Ulster Folk Museum in County Down, the purpose in making of which was to test the feasibility of both the 1988 instruction given by Gerry Hallinan, the description r/e c. 1900 in the *Schools' Collection* of folklore, and the writings of Caoimhín Ó Danachair – to see if the task was feasible; Páiric McNeela contributed to the thinking in this.

Two types were tried, the first, the skin tray type following Hallinan's directions of how they did it as boys in Roscommon in the 1930s: year-old willow rods were bent into hoops to use for a frame, using three layers to get depth (p. 220). MacNeela stretched a skin on this rim (pp. 234–5), a native one provided by Malachy Kearns. It was secured by tucking it in and, when dried, the bodhrán gave a dullish tone, but when heated was resonant.

The second one was made by attempting to use a flat wood rim for a tuck-in skin, but this proved very difficult, though folding over the skin on the flat rim and lightly tacking it on without tucking in permitted higher tension and produced a loud ringing tone like any standard bodhrán, a much brighter sound when struck than when a bent willow frame was used. This would suggest that, when tambourine copies were being made in the past, it is flat wood that would be needed, and any previously-bent material such as a riddle would be eagerly sought after, as described earlier in this chapter.

The third was a copy of the Maclise tambourine, as a purpose-made tambourine with hammered-out brass jingles and tacked-on, tensioned skin, crafted by Seamus O'Kane; this can be seen being played by him on page 233.

The testing and proving of these three forms of bodhrán – skin tray, flat-rim bodhrán and tambourine – has contributed considerably to the major conclusion of this study – that early percussion players, such as buskers and those on the Wren, could reasonably improvise a tambourine on the historic device-bodhrán, even where these were not made with a tensioned skin. This habit would have paved the way to transitioning to copying the tambourine – making tensioned-skin drums – and, eventually, the suitability, logic and acceptability of applying the old term 'bodhrán' to the new drum form. The many makers in modern times are mostly new-school, so to speak, among them those who have investigated technical qualities of not only skins and skin treatment, fixing and tensioning, but also frames and frame materials, and sticks and stick materials. A few only will be mentioned here, on account of their visibility and contrasting philosophies.

▼ Original tuck-in, flat-rim skin tray bodhrán at the NMI Castlebar [*Copyright National Museum of Ireland*]

FLAT-RIM FOLD-OVER BODHRÁN MAKING SEQUENCE

▸ Páiric McNeela fixing the skin in a fold-over manner on a flat frame [EDI]

▸ Sequence of tasks in the completion of making the bodhrán [EDI]

Charlie Byrne

One of the best-known, old-style, bodhrán makers was Charlie Byrne of Tipperary. He made his first drum for his daughter Carmel, who won one of the earliest bodhrán competitions in 1965, and he continued making in response to the new demand created in that decade. Like all such makers he had to devise his own system, and so developed a practical assembly of equipment which included an open-fire-heated metal trough for steaming wood for bending the rims, and various jigs and forms for assembling and skinning the drums. He was generous with his knowledge, and shared it with other aspiring makers over the years, including Seamus O'Kane and Páiric McNeela. Leading bodhrán players place great faith in his drum-making skills, among them Johnny 'Ringo' MacDonagh and Colm Murphy. The process of this charismatic maker's industrial-style method can be seen in James Fraher's exclusive 1980s photographs on these pages, the result of a fortuitous visit to the maker to pick up a bodhrán in 1982.

13 THE ACTUAL BODHRÁN MAKERS

Charlie Byrne pictured in his workshop [*James Fraher*]

Seamus O'Kane

Regarded as one of the entrepreneurs in bodhrán construction, this highly-regarded maker had from childhood been obsessed with percussion of all kinds. When he first heard a bodhrán in 1968 or so 'on an early Dubliners LP', he became hooked. Being an engineering and technology teacher in Dungiven, County Derry, he had a wide range of skills which he was able to bring to experimenting with all aspects of making the drum from 1969 onwards, a decade before the other new-generation makers. Early on he constructed a steam tank in which he bent light birch planks to make rims, then used standard pigskin drumheads that he bought through the music trade. Parallel with this he was learning to play himself, initially self-taught, 'using entirely the wrong method', eventually settling to a comfortable style using a *c.* 8-inch stick. Demand was not great in those early years, nor was competition, for only the old, established makers were working at bodhráns, like himself producing small numbers of them. O'Kane's testing and evaluation system was to loan out the prototype instruments at a time when there was no shortage of demand, and each subsequent new drum he produced benefited from player feedback on the previous one. So, as the drum's popularity expanded

▲ ▶ Seamus O'Kane [*Nutan*]

▲ O'Kane's tambourine copy which he modelled on the image of that which is being played in the Maclise painting of 1832 [*EDI*]

"When a song is being sung the singer concentrates on the words, melody players focus on the music, and drummers on the beat. From a very young age I was always mad about drumming and making drums and sticks. It has been compulsive"
Seamus O'Kane, bodhrán maker, Dungiven, County Derry

in traditional music he was able not only to sell all he made, but to evolve his designs, so building a reputation, and found himself making to pre-orders. He was constantly on the lookout for new direction, observing and discussing methods used by others as well as noting innovations described by an old jazz drummer he knew, and by bodhrán players. He talked to older makers as well as the younger ones, and applied response-enhancing modifications such as taping the edge of the skin, eventually settling for a system devised originally by Johnny 'Ringo' McDonagh. In response to interest, his part-time making gathered momentum following his retirement from teaching. He had moved to making tuneable drums already by 1975, prompted by observation of the tensioning of banjo heads, but using an internally-placed mechanism. This he refined over the years in response to feedback given to him by leading players, and today he uses hand-turned adjustors to tension the skin. Being in County Derry which has a history of harping and harp-making, including a harp school in his hometown, perhaps not surprisingly he diversified into making harps eventually, producing three superb copies of the County Derry 'Downhill' harp used by Denis Hempson in the 1700s, and seven others.[17]

Malachy Kearns in his workshop [EDI]

Malachy Kearns

This Sligo-born, ex-Dublin, Connemara-based bodhrán maker has been most visible in Ireland and the world through a business-oriented promotion that demonstrates his emotional engagement with the ethos of the drum. For him, the bodhrán's music is 'a sound-experience that goes straight past our head and heart and right into our gut (the life centre) … part of us for those magical moments … at our soul level we experience the bodhrán sound'.[48] The first time he heard a bodhrán was 'at the age of ten or eleven'[49] about 1963 in County Donegal, but it was another fifteen years before he began making the drum, influenced not least by the fact that The Chieftains' first bodhrán player Peadar Mercier had once been his next-door neighbour. He sees Mercier as a pioneer in performance technique, as, in his opinion, it was Mercier who developed 'the controlled rolling rhythm style of playing … a hand tucked behind the skin … moving, varying the tone – both hands interacting'. Prior to this he says that 'in the 1960s the bodhrán was just tapped or thumped on stage', as – he considers – 'it was in the play *Sive*'. The bodhrán's identification with traditional Irish music he concedes is modern.

"The bodhrán touches your gut, where the life-centre is, rather than slowly going through your head and heart. It's a very quickly-felt experience. That makes it special"
Malachy Kearns, *bodhrán maker, Co. Galway*

▲ Páiric McNeela making bodhráns on the street at Scoil Samhraidh Willie Clancy in 1999 [EDI]

"Seán Ó Riada elevated the status of not just this lowly Irish drum, but of traditional Irish music itself to a genre worthy of theatres and concert halls. The humble bodhrán drum shared in this prestige"
Páiric McNeela, bodhrán maker, County Dublin

Páiric McNeela

A Dublin-based bodhrán maker, he has been developing his skills since he was shown the ropes by Charlie Byrne whom he had first encountered at Scoil Samhraidh Willie Clancy c. 1979, and later met at fleadhs. He spent considerable time experimenting with equipment, tools, templates and materials, consulting too with existing makers. Out of this he established an efficient working method based on modern equipment, and set up in business making bodhráns initially from home, but also on the street at fleadhs and festivals. Within a decade his enterprise had grown into a family business which now sees him not only making and selling bodhráns, but other instruments, including Irish-made flutes and other music tutor-books and equipment. He makes all the components of the drums, producing a range of forms from decorative through to high-spec for professional players, some of the latter with double skins and many with tuning mechanisms. These he sells all over the world as well as at major music events in Ireland. He sees the bodhrán *as part* of Irish music: 'Percussion is the pulse behind the music … gives music its flavour, its kick and ties it all together'. This says that there is a natural place for it in Irish music, that it adds to it. He relates the Irish drum to a world culture of frame drums, and notes that 'regardless of its origin, the bodhrán was not commonly played in traditional Irish music until the 1960s. The modern bodhrán-playing style that exists today is a very recent development'. The Wren he sees as important in the history of the drum, which is 'often described as the "heartbeat of Irish music"'. He attributes its popularity to Seán Ó Riada.[50]

O'Kane, McNeela and Kearns are each new to bodhrán making and playing, something which is typical of all of today's major makers. Their attitudes reflect much of what bodhrán players themselves say – mainly that they know the bodhrán to now be intrinsically, but newly, part of traditional music. They acknowledge its modernity in various ways, while also relating to its personal emotional pull and expressivity for players and listeners, and they see Ó Riada as the starting point for its contemporary popularity. As much as the stylists in the top tier of players have been pioneers and innovators, so too have been the makers, who have had an equal role in the expansion of the field. This is also the case with flute, uilleann pipes, fiddle and concertina makers, and, as with them also, the resultant variety in instrument appearance, quality, music potential, aesthetic style, availability and cost all render the manufacturers productively highly competitive, a subject of ongoing animated brainstorming, critique and debate, and of tremendous importance in Irish traditional music. The skills have moved outside Ireland too, with top makers now based also in Europe, all of whom bring other experience to the drum, particularly with regard to tuning, an aspect which prompted Dónal Lunny to have tuneable bodhráns made – by Brendan White in Tipperary, and Davey Stewart in Christchurch, New Zealand.

Still moving on with new ideas, at the Craiceann bodhrán festival on Inis Oirr in 2014, Lunny's meeting with Christian Hedwitschak, a German maker of high-precision bodhráns, resulted in a prototype bass bodhrán with a cutaway rim to allow easier application of pressure to the skin. This Lunny terms 'Dordrán', so named from 'dord', the Irish word for bass, hum or drone.[51] To date, there is an immense variety of bodhrán models available, each using different permutations of rim-structure, skin thickness and lamination, and tuning mechanism, and each owing something to a synergy of the ingenuity of makers and the virtuosity-driven demands of leading players.

▲ Siobhán O'Donnell, Craiceann festival, 2023 [*EDI*]

"I was immersed in Traditional music and singing when growing up, but I was drawn to the bodhran's bassy tone, and learnt to play it listening to guitar and piano accompaniments, picking out similar rhythmic patterns. As the tuning of bodhrans developed, that influenced my style, and now I vary pitches so that the bodhran can at times sound like a double bass. I tune to a low base note – ideally the exact key of the music – hitting this on the beat or every second beat to add depth"
Siobhán O'Donnell

"The bodhrán was often a despised and unwelcome intrusion in sessions in the past because of ignorance and insensitivity among those who played it. The Craiceann festival has contributed much to improving things by raising not only the standard of playing but also awareness of the sensitivities and demands of playing with other musicians"
Mícheál Ó hAlmháin, Director of Craiceann, the annual Inis Oírr bodhrán festival

NOTES TO CHAPTER 13

▲ Mícheál Ó hAlmhain leads a final rally with whistle at the conclusion of the Craiceann bodhrán summer-school on Inis Oírr, 2023

[1] SC, 0622, C07.
[2] Ibid., 1126, 420.
[3] Hart 1990, 161–92.
[4] Buckley 2005, 745–73; see Chapter 2.
[5] Schiller 2001, 89 and Scullion 1981, 36.
[6] See Chapter 9: Fenton 1914, 106–7; Ó Gealbháin 2013, 91; O'Daly 1876, 53.
[7] CBÉ 1160, 539–40; he was interviewed by P.J. Gaynor from Bailieboro', County Cavan.
[8] CBÉ 1160, 543.
[9] CBÉ 1862, 199. Collected by Ciarán Bairéad.
[10] Mitchell 2023, PC.
[11] Hallinan 1988, PC.
[12] Ó Danachair 1955, 130.
[13] SC 1126, 414–15.
[14] CBÉ 1835, 246, 'Craiceann na gcaorach mar ghléas ceoil', bailitheoir S. Ó hEochaidh, l. 167–8.
[15] Byrne 1998, 49.
[16] Curran 1988, 42.
[17] Byrne 1998, 33; also 24 (interview with Michael Cronnolly, flute maker, east Mayo).
[18] Hickey 1999, 36.
[19] SC 0725, 0166.
[20] Mercier 2021 1129 (rte.ie).
[21] MacMahon 1963.
[22] Curran 1988, 42.
[23] Vallely 2004, 340.
[24] Kjeldsen 2000, 129–30. Interview with Batty Sherlock, 25 March 2000.
[25] Ibid., 156; interview with Joe McDonagh.
[26] Ibid., 162. Ibid.
[27] Ibid., 177; interview with Gerry Murray.
[28] Irish Independent 1986, 0425 23.
[29] O'Shannon 1970.
[30] Evening Herald, 1959, 1209 5.
[31] Nolan, 2.
[32] Ó Danachair 1955, 130.
[33] Farmer 1912, frontispiece.
[34] Lunny 2023, PC.
[35] Cork Examiner 1959 0528.
[36] Canavan 1970.
[37] Tansey 2022, PC.
[38] McGowan 1997, PC.
[39] Kerryman 1961, 1111 17.
[40] Evening Echo 1897 0416 4.
[41] CBÉ 1160, 539–40.
[42] Cork Examiner 1963 0110 7.
[43] Canavan 1966.
[44] Ibid., 1977.
[45] John Finn, 1995, 'County Sligo, the Deep South', cited on p. 341 of Vallely, 2004.
[46] Irish Times 1970 0825 9.
[47] O'Kane 2022, PC.
[48] Kearns PR.
[49] Kearns 2022, PC.
[50] MacNeela, 2022.
[51] Lunny 2023, PC.

"I heard a bodhrán first on Raidió Éireann, with the song from John B. Keane's play Sive, and then heard it played by Seán Ó Riada with Ceoltóirí Cualann at his GPO radio recordings. In the mid-sixties at Newcastle West I heard the Sheehy brothers play against each other in the only bodhrán competition held at any fleadh – they played very big bodhráns with two and three sticks. I bought my first bodhrán there for £3"
Kevin Conneff, *Dublin*

"My first experience of the bodhrán was seeing young girls being taught by Róisín Nolan, the rhythms reverberating around the school yard, an image that both looked and sounded powerful. It resonated deeply with me, much like those who describe it as the 'heartbeat of the music' and 'soul of the ensemble'. Its grounding nature strengthens one's ability to connect, allowing for a greater sense of purpose within our musical experience"
Aimée Farrell Courtney, *bodhrán player and teacher*

"I first encountered the Bodhrán at 1960s sessions in Dowling's of Prosperous, County Kildare, where it was played by Ned Farrell. In those days the player most often struck the skin with a knuckle rather than a stick, and rhythms were simple and constant, a steady support to the tune. I discovered however that I could enhance the music by tuning to a specific note – tensioning the skin with the heel of my hand to go with tunes in different keys. My high point in this was on a Bothy Band track 'Music in the Glen' where I played a complete octave descending from E2 to E1"
Dónal Lunny, *Offaly and Dublin*

▲ Bodhrán trio with Kevin Coneff, Aimée Farrell Courtney and Dónal Lunny [*Nutan*]

CHAPTER 14

TWENTIETH-CENTURY BODHRÁN

The first national radio broadcast of the tambourine was in J.B. Keane's *Sive* on 7 June 1959 following the show's stage debut. The first public Dublin performances on the bodhrán, by that name, were, as said on page 165, with Seán Ó Riada's music for two plays, *The Honey Spike* for the Abbey Theatre, and *Spailpín a Rúin* at the Damer Theatre in 1960. Ó Riada's radio programme *Reachaireacht an Riadaigh* was also recorded as an LP – the first broadcast and the first recording with the bodhrán by name. Paddy Moloney's group The Chieftains, whose members overlapped with Ceoltóirí Chualann, were next to record, with Davy Fallon playing, on their inaugural LP in 1964. There had already been a few recordings featuring the tambourine, back in the 1920s, of John Reynolds, originally from near Drumsna in County Leitrim, and Patrick Carberry, both of whom recorded in New York. Reynolds accompanied flute-player Tom Morrison on six '78' sides, the first in 1927. In an interview with broadcaster Harry Bradshaw, Morrison's son Jim recalled that, as a child in the 1930s, he saw a tambourine player among the fiddle, flute and pipes players who took part in sessions in their house in the Irish-settled, Navy Yard district of Brooklyn. Since those musicians included flute player Tom Morrison, it is likely that that tambourine player was John Reynolds.[1] Described as 'Flute and Tambourine', their discs were made in 1927 and 1928, with re-issues two decades later; Morrison recalled that player striking the tambourine with the thumb of his fist.

◀ ▼ '78' Records by Tom Morrison and John Reynold with flute and tambourine. Recorded in 1927.

247

The next such recording was by Patrick Carberry, playing with Michael J. Grogan as a duet, recorded in 1946, described as 'Accordion and Irish Tambourine'. In Reynolds' playing the jingles can be heard occasionally, faintly, but the nature of their sound, and their low volume relative to the strength of the hand-striking, might explain their quietness, especially with regard to recording pick-up quality at that time. On Carberry's playing there is no hint of jingles but, again, the emphasis in the recordings was on the strength and solidity of the tambourine rhythm. Both Reynolds' and Carberry's tracks are freely available for listening on the internet. The Irish-American band Packie Dolan and his Melody Boys also used tambourine, played by Neal Smith,[2] who accompanied on spoons too on some tracks.[3]

From the hard, solid, steady sound of both Reynolds and Carberry their tambourine appears to be hand-struck on these recordings, and the fact that these were made in the USA at a time when there is no word of tambourine accompaniment in Ireland, might well suggest that the inaugural use of tambourine in an accompaniment role was an innovative American thing [see Appendix 10]. Whether or not a stick was used on the first tambourine recording in 1927 may be debatable. But another intriguing recording, of the Flanagan Brothers in 1926, has a short burst of a multiple-beat, stick drumming done to a marching tune played on accordion and banjo. The rapidity of the strokes resembles a modern-day, two-headed stick bodhrán style, though close listening most strongly suggests that the drum used is a muted snare-drum (and, indeed, on a Flanagans' recording of a similar piece the following year the drum they use is unmistakably a standard snare). The 1926 performance is, however, the earliest recording of a stick-struck, multiple-beat percussion style matched to traditional tunes – setting the stage perhaps for typical modern bodhrán style?[4]

▲ 1927 '78' record with flute and tambourine

▼ Painter Brian Bourke celebrates his exhibition opening with son Malachy and with Frankie Gavin [EDI]

14 TWENTIETH-CENTURY BODHRÁN

Colm Murphy [Nutan]

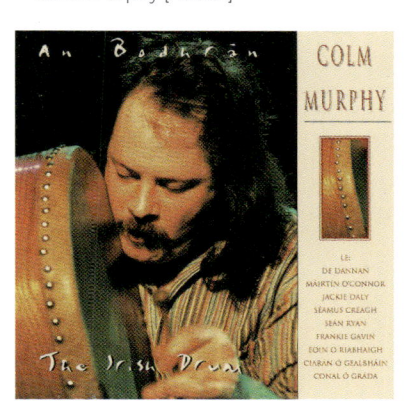

Bodhrán soloists

Tambourine is scarce on field-recordings made for early Irish radio, possibly the only one being that made by Ciarán Mac Mathúna of Mícheál Ó Ceannabháin in 1956. The bodhrán is scarce too, explained by another story from Harry Bradshaw who tells how a bodhrán player who attended a lecture he once gave on the recording work of Ciarán Mac Mathúna asked him why he had not included any bodhrán tracks. Bradshaw's answer was that Mac Mathúna had not recorded it. This was partly a consequence of its absence or scarcity in traditional music in the key era of Mac Mathúna's recording from 1954 through to the 1970s.[5] But also because getting 'the real thing' – melody – was the objective in field recording, broadcasters had to choose carefully what they considered important; they were not anthropologists or folklorists, and their time was limited. So, considering that the most visible role of the tambourine in those early years was in Wren activity, and took place only in the aftermath of Christmas, tambourine recordings could be expected to be scarce. But in the period after Ó Riada's and The Chieftains' leads from the early 1960s on, the bodhrán features on many recordings. Some are dedicated to it, such as Tommy Hayes' *An Rás* in 1991, and Colm Murphy's

▶ John Joe Kelly with Flook

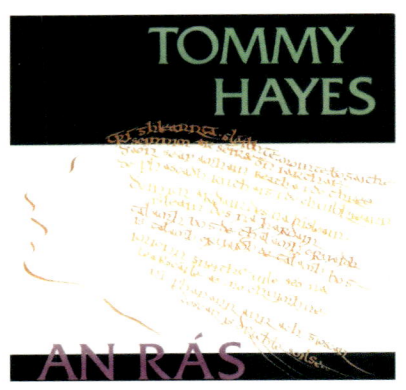

▲ Tommy Hayes CD *An Rás*

▶ Robbie Harris's compilation CD carries a selection of old and new playing styles from 18 players which can be listened to on bandcamp.com

14 TWENTIETH-CENTURY BODHRÁN

▲ John Joe Kelly.[Nutan] ▼ Gino Lupari [*Nutan*]

1996 *An Bodhrán: The Irish drum*, wherein he demonstrates his technique with a variety of instrumentalists. Murphy accompanied Jackie Daly and Seamus Creagh on their celebrated 1976 duet album, and also Máirtín O'Connor and whistle-player Sean Ryan. An album which is dedicated to a historic vista of the bodhrán is Robbie Harris' 2000 compilation *Pure Bodhrán*, which samples the playing of Tommy Hayes, Ronan Ó Snodaigh, Jimmy Higgins, Damien Quinn, Donnacha Goff, Dave Donohue, Cathy Jordan, Brian Fleming, John Joe Kelly, Christy Moore, Kevin Conneff, Johnny 'Ringo' McDonagh, Gino Lupari, Glen Velez, James McNally, Dónal Lunny, Colm Murphy and Harris himself, as well as, by way of both comparison and an indication of style evolution, a clip of John Reynolds on tambourine from 1927. This was followed by Andrew Junior Davey's *A Sound Skin* in 2005, and Colm Phelan's *Full Circle* in 2012.

▼ Dónal Lunny with the author, Rathmines 2022 [*Nutan*]

Stylistic change

In all of these recordings an ongoing stylistic change can be heard. Dónal Lunny recalls that the rhythms played in the 1960s were 'generally quite simple and constant, giving a steady support to the tune being accompanied'. But this has given way to 'a more varied and decorative approach, which, while being more exciting, can often be more distracting than supportive'. Lunny, who has pioneered the bodhrán's potential more than most players, observed early on that when bodhrán skins are evenly tensioned and played

▲ Dónal Lunny's *dordrán* [dord, meaning bass] drums made by Christian Hedwitschak [*Dónal Lunny*]

▲ Julie McNamara, 1991 [*Maria Pedro*]

'open', a very pure fundamental note is generally produced. But he realised that it was possible to tune the skin to a specific note – to further enhance rather than just support the music being accompanied. The most useful note he found was a low D, the same as the drones on uilleann pipes. He took it further by applying tension to the skin with the heel of his hand, changing the note to go with tunes in different keys – such as E, when accompanying a tune in E-minor. He found too that that was easier if the bodhrán had a crossbar to brace the hand which was applying pressure to the skin, and he was able to achieve a natural progression to change the note up to G by applying further pressure. Applying yet more pressure he could generate higher pitches, eventually achieving 'a kind of breakthrough when I added bodhrán to the track "Music in the Glen", on the Bothy Band's second album, *Old Hag You Have Killed Me*, and played a complete octave descending from E2 to E1'.[6] This 'pitching' is now a feature of much modern-day playing, but it co-exists with the basic style that mushroomed in the 1960s.

Media and myth

The widely-differing schools of thinking about, of making, and of playing the bodhrán all engage in some way with versions of the drum's history and the psychology of its being played. So too for entertainment media when they come to feature it. Television programmes have been powerful in showing the making and playing of the drum, but film and drama are more inclined to feature it as a striking background to social activities. In those, unchecked assumptions about the drum's vintage can yield rather unlikely scenarios, notably the inappropriate placing of modern-day, balanced traditional-music bands in earlier social settings. The film *Titanic*, for instance, features a bodhrán being played with pipes, fiddle, mandolin and accordion among poorer passengers, for dancing. Whatever about a home-made tambourine being present, a post 1960s bodhrán is as out of place in 1912 as a mobile phone. Advertising often uses traditional music as a badge of authenticity, applying such terms as 'precious heritage', 'cream of tradition', 'rich tapestry' and 'noble pedigree'. The modern bodhrán features strongly in many of these cameos, especially for seasonal, tourist-oriented performance and presentations, and it is also part of 21st-century mass consumption in big-show promotions, soundtrack on films and, especially, for selling items as diverse as dairy products, motor cars, soccer and electronics.[7] The bodhrán has been popular too for adding percussive riffs in radio advertising and programme signature music. It has appeared as well on postage stamps, but its most significant symbolism today is at quite an ambassadorial level where it is presented along with harp, fiddle, flute, whistles and dancing shoes, in the company of two minstrel instruments – banjo and accordion – as a background image of culture in the Irish passport. This is quite a promotion, especially considering that the uilleann pipes, which was granted UNESCO 'important and unique cultural heritage' symbolism in 2017, is not represented on this premium Irish ID document.[8]

▲ 1953 An Tóstal with harp

▲ 1990s stamp with bodhrán, pipes and dance

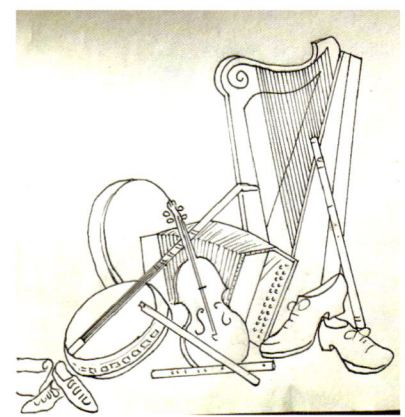

◀ Bodhran depicted on the Irish passport [*Courtesy Department of Foreign Affairs; detail sketch Patricia Vallely*]

▶ The bodhrán was one of the instruments depicted on the 2001 Irish postage stamp to commemorate the fiftieth anniversary of the founding of CCÉ.

▶ ▶ Bodhrán on a 1997 postage stamp

▼ Bodhrán chosen as emblematic of Ireland on this 2014 Europa postage stamp

▲ Stamp featuring The Chieftains in 2006

▲ Polish and Algerian stamps

▲ Doira on a 1990 CCCP stamp

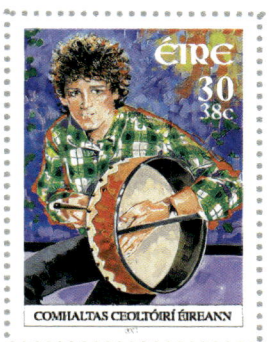

State representation of bodhrán popularity and status

Irish postage stamps developed as a vehicle for national reflection and celebration after the mid-1900s. Earlier imagery used on them had included the harp, incidentally, as an aspect of Irish identity, but advances in printing opened up the possibility of marking a broader spectrum of cultural matters. This followed the lead of central-European countries, which tended to celebrate their national, classical and traditional musics on postage stamps. The earliest strong statement of Irish culture symbolised on stamps by music was the use of the harp on those marking the national *An Tóstal* festival of 1953. But it was not until forty years later that an uilleann piper made it on to a 1993 stamp, for the centenary of Conradh na Gaeilge, a deviation from the supremacy of the harp. This was followed soon however by an image of the bodhrán, along with pipes, whistle and dance, giving significant status to the drum. And in 1997, to mark the seventy-fifth anniversary of the setting up of the state, it was again featured, played by maker Malachy Kearns – quite a statement on representation.

The series of stamps to celebrate CCÉ's fiftieth anniversary also included bodhrán and in 2006 a stamp honouring The Chieftains shows Kevin Conneff playing that drum too. The supreme tribute, however, was paid in 2014 when the bodhrán was featured independently on a *Europa*-issue. sixty-cent stamp in a series of only two titled 'Gléasanna Ceoil Náisiúnta / National Musical Instruments'; its partner was a harp (albeit on the more expensive ninety-cent stamp!). Uilleann pipes – an instrument at the core of the music's revival – were not shown in this way as being nationally symbolic, but did come to be honoured in 2018 for the fiftieth anniversary of the founding of the pipers' organisation, Na Píobairí Uilleann. The series of instruments featured on Irish stamps over those three decades is a visual meter of the rise in popularity of, and consequent respect for, Irish traditional music itself and, within that, the harp is seen to have receded, the bodhrán advanced. Elsewhere, accordions are the most popular among representations of music on postage stamps world-wide, but some frame drums have featured, notably the Soviet Union with the *doira*, Poland with the *bębenek* tambourine, and Algeria the *târ*, which is central to its music. With the marginalisation of the use of the postal service that is a consequence of email and telephone texting today, however, postage stamps feature little in the consciousness of most Irish people, and so their visual message is of a much lesser significance than it was before the year 2000.

Competitions

Bodhrán competitions were not part of the All-Ireland honours system in traditional music until 1972, but before that, regionally, in the early years of fleadhanna ceoil, when there wasn't a rigid routine in such contests, Kerry and Limerick ran tambourine competitions from 1962 on, then bodhrán; there seems to have been a certain autonomy accorded to local, County and provincial fleadhnna as to what competitions they offered, and how those were titled. In announcements for these, the greater tendency has been to use the Irish-language translation of instrument names, but in many places the English was used, depending on the local expertise in Irish, or in deference to local opinion perhaps. As regards instruments, the category Miscellaneous / Rogha Gléas [choice of instrument] could cover anything, and indeed in the early 1950s fleadhanna the concertina appeared only in this spot; at the County Limerick fleadh of 1963, the instruments in this category were banjo, bagpipes and spoons. Bodhrán, as far as can be ascertained, was either not prevalent enough to merit inclusion, or it was considered to be purely an accompanying, rhythmic instrument rather than one on which at that point it was not considered appropriate, or possible, to articulate pitch or melody. Competitions for the Wren-boy troupes started in pre-John B. Keane time, in 1957, but the first which were exclusively for the frame drum as an instrument only emerged following Keane's drama *Sive* and the subsequent promotion of the tambourine as a Kerry and north Munster music symbol. As dealt with in pages 180–81, the first competitions for the bodhrán were for the tambourine (so to speak), in Munster, from 1962 on:

> Always with an eye on the unusual and the attractive, the committee have included in this year's programme a Tambourine Competition. To their minds Kerry is the home of the tambourine because of the famous wren boys
> [*Kerryman* 1962 0804 10]

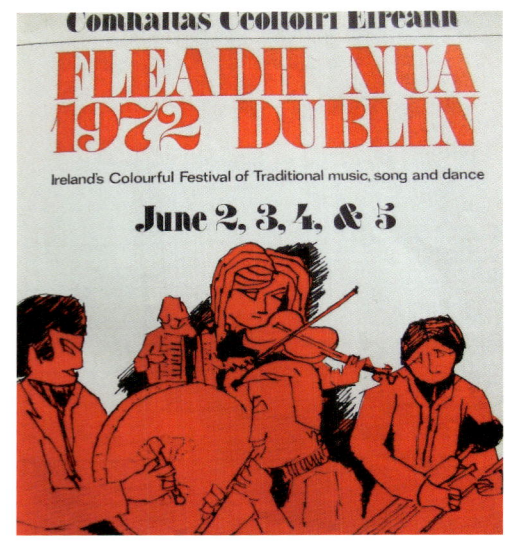

▲ 1972 Bodhrán on cover of CCÉ *Treoir* magazine

The tambourine/bodhrán event remained local only, in Munster, for more than a decade, however, after which the category was included in the All-Ireland fleadh in 1972. Fleadh results in the 1970s show the entry of later stylists, such as Colm Murphy who won at Minor level in 1975, and even players who went on to achieve prominence on other instruments, such as fiddle player Breda Smyth of Mayo at Minor level in 1981, and the Coventry-born accordion player and singer Verena Commins winning at Minor level in 1985 and at Junior the following year. Fleadh results speak for themselves however as the figures in the following pages demonstrate.[9]

The bodhrán in the All-Ireland Fleadh

So-called, the bodhrán was first admitted as a competition category in the All-Ireland Fleadh in 1972 when it was, appropriately enough, won by Michael ('Rory') Sheehy, he who had been the victor (though on tambourine) at the first regional fleadh competition. The following year it was won by John Dwyer, the first England-based player to do so. Thereafter the Limerick flag held sway only briefly, championed in 1975 and '76 by Tommy Hayes of County Limerick, the second Munster player to win.

The Munster supremacy did not kick in again at Senior level until 1981 when Corkman Michel Dwyer took the honours, followed by Maurice Griffin from County Tipperary in 1985, then Fabian Ó Murchú from Cork

▲ Frank Torpey of the band Nomos at *Chief O'Neill's*, Dublin, 1999 [*EDI*]

in 1986, '87 and '89. Sligo came into the reckoning with Andrew Junior Davey in 1990, '93, '96, '97 and 1999. The first female to get the title, in 2004, thirty-two years after the bodhrán was first recognised, was Serena Curley from County Galway, followed in 2005 by Sligowoman Siobhán O'Donnell.

The first Munster woman to become All-Ireland Senior Champion was Niamh Fennell of Waterford in 2018. Considering where the bodhrán competitions first started, it is not surprising that there have been five Limerick victories at Senior level, even if they were but a memory for four decades after 1976 until Séamus Ó Conchubhair's win in 2017.

▼ Tommy Hayes, Senior bodhrán champion 1975 and '76

◂ Niamh Fennell, County Waterford, tutor at Craiceann 2023, playing with Cormac Ó hAlmháin [*EDI*]

Geographic expansion

But with regard to the drum's first exposition and exuberant promotion by a Kerryman, it may seem surprising that Kerry has only featured once in the forty-seven years of the Senior All-Irelands (Eamonn O'Sullivan, second in 1974) and once only as a winner at Junior level (Thomas Buckley in 1977). Limerick, in contrast, had wins at Junior as well as Senior level, Michael Donegan in 1973, and Ronan Ó Maoldomhaigh in 1992 and '93. What the trend in the competitions shows clearly is that the bodhrán drum, though it came from nowhere in academic terms, and from west Limerick, north Kerry and north Connacht geographically, has moved out, and been developed and practised widely to the highest levels of stylistic proficiency in all parts of the island and its music diaspora. The competition statistics which use three categories: Senior (over age 18), Junior (roughly from age 14 to 18), and Minor (roughly from about 11 to 14, within which are classifications that fluctuate over the years). Provincially, Leinster leads with forty-five all-categories first places, Ulster almost ties with forty-four, Connacht has forty, while Munster has had thirty-three. In the statistics here the island of Ireland is regarded in total geographically as the four historic provinces. This is because music, like accents, travels without regard to political boundaries. So too are Scotland, England, America and Europe considered, effectively, 'provinces' of Ireland and its cultural diaspora.

> "The bodhrán has evolved through the years both in relation to players' styles and technical abilities, and to the production of bodhráns. I see it as an instrument that provides a wonderful complementary element to a session, and I am constantly being inspired by players who are absolute masters of their craft, among them the many prominent and renowned female players in the Irish traditional music scene"
> *Niamh Fennell, County Waterford*

Ulster

Ulster has had 44 All-Ireland first-place wins across all grades since 1975: Antrim (fourteen), Down (thirteen) and Donegal (six) dominating, and Armagh (three), Cavan (four), Derry and Fermanagh (one each) and Monaghan (two). Six of these were at Senior level, twelve at Junior, and twenty-eight in Minor categories. Overall, five winners were female, and thirty-nine were male.

The earliest Senior win was in 1994 by Michael McElwee from Tyrone, the only winner in any group for his County over all years; all of the Senior placings were males.

The first Junior win was Bernadette McMahon from Antrim in 1985 who was also the first Ulster female to win such; and the second female winner was Sheila Rooney from Down in 2004.

In Minor age groups there were twenty-eight first-place wins over all decades from 1975 to 2018, three of them by females, twenty-eight by males.

At second-place level, Ulster has fifty-six, among whom were four females and fifty-

▲ Brian Morrissey [*Nutan*]

"My first bodhrán at the age of twelve was the catalyst for an explorative journey in and through rhythm, influenced by set-dancing, percussive dance and the playing of bodhrán masters. My fascination with pitched bodhrán was awakened by Dónal Lunny, and led me to dovetail with harmonic accompanists. It is inspiring to see bodhrán players now collaborate with other drum and dance traditions, and I am excited about the next stages of our drum's development"
Brian Morrissey

two males, including nineteen Senior, thirteen Junior, and twenty-four Minor.

At the third place level the province has thirty-four, among them five females, and including eight Senior, twelve Junior and fourteen Minor.

Munster

Munster has had thirty-three All-Ireland first-place wins across all grades over the period since 1972: Limerick and Cork (ten each), Waterford (six) and Tipperary (four) dominate, with two from Clare and just one from Kerry (Thomas Buckley at Junior level in 1977).

Thirteen were at Senior level, one of whom was female; ten were at Junior level, two of whom were females, and ten at lower age levels, including one female. Overall, four were female, twenty-nine male.

The first Senior win was in the competition's inaugural year of 1972, by the legendary Michael Sheehy of County Limerick. The first Munster woman to win was Niamh Fennell from Waterford in 2018, forty-six years after the competition's inception.

The first Junior level win was by John O'Brien of Tipperary, in year one, 1972. Two of the Junior winners have been female, earliest being Aoife Drohan of Waterford in 1996. Colm Murphy of Cork was the earliest at minor level in 1975, and Sharon McCarthy of Waterford the earliest female in that category, in 1994.

Munster seconds total thirty-four, including seven females, and with eight Senior, ten Junior and sixteen Minor.

Munster thirds are thirty-eight, including eight females, and with seven Senior, seven Junior and twenty-four Minor.

Leinster

Leinster has had forty-five All-Ireland first-place wins across all grades since 1975, Dublin dominating with sixteen, Wexford with eight, Laois seven, Offaly four, Westmeath three, Meath, Longford and Carlow two each, and Kilkenny one. Overall, ten were at Senior level, seventeen at Junior, and eighteen in Minor age-groups; five were female, forty male.

The first Senior win was in 1980, Michael Gaynor of Meath. No female has as yet won at this level. The first Junior winner was Fergal Ó Brollachain of Dublin in 1976, and at that level Maura Egan from Offaly was the earliest female winner, in 1984. The earliest Minor winner was Noel Carberry of County Longford in 1975, and the first female in that category was Derville Dolan in 1983, joined almost three decades later by three others – in 2012, '16 and '17.

Leinster Seconds are forty-one, including five females, and with nine Senior, ten Junior and twenty-two Minor.

Leinster Thirds number fifty-seven, including thirteen females, and with fifteen Senior, fifteen Junior and twenty-seven Minor.

Connacht

Connacht has had forty All-Ireland first-place wins across all categories since 1974, almost evenly divided between Galway (fourteen), Mayo (thirteen) and Sligo (thirteen); Leitrim does not feature among firsts. Eleven wins were at Senior level, three at Junior level, and twenty-six at Minor levels. Thirteen of the winners were females, three of them at Senior level – a record among all provinces, not least for the fact that among them is Serena Curley of Galway who was the first ever female Senior All-Ireland bodhrán champion, in 2004. One female first was at Junior level, and nine were Minor.

The earliest Senior winner was Johnny Ringo McDonagh of Galway in 1974, with five wins later by Andrew Junior Davey of Sligo in the 1990s.

There were three wins at Junior level, the first of these by Louise Ní Neillinigh of Sligo in 1987.

◀ Maria Ní Cholmáin (right), U-15 All-Ireland bodhrán winner 2012, with accompanist Niamh Casey [*CCE*]

"The bodhrán has taught me how to value my heritage – where I've come from, and my own traditions. I believe that one should have a deep respect for the music, take only what serves us, but don't be afraid to put our own stamp on things. This little drum has helped me turn the best bits of myself into useful tools for the future while leaving behind what I no longer need"
Cara Wildman

At Minor levels, twenty-six wins are spread between 1976 and 2013, these including nine females, earliest being Fionnuala Collis of Sligo in 1976 (she was also the earliest Minor-level female bodhrán champion).

Connacht Seconds are twenty-eight, including seven females, and with six Seniors, seven Junior and fifteen Minor.

Connacht Thirds are thirty-five, including eleven females, and with seven Senior, five Junior and twenty-three Minor.

Out-of-State wins

England leads these for the bodhrán – twenty-three firsts, of which five were Senior, five Junior and thirteen Minor; two were Junior females and one was a Minor female.

Seconds were sixteen, including one female; three were Senior, four Junior and nine Minor.

Thirds were twenty-two, including two Junior and Minor females, with – overall – three Senior, six Junior and thirteen Minor.

Scotland has had thirteen overall prizes including three Senior and one Minor firsts, two Senior and two Junior seconds, four Senior and one Junior thirds.

America has had nine victories including three Senior third places, one of these a female player, Cara Wildman in 2019; one each of Junior first, second and third places; one each Minor second and third.

Europe credits began with the French Josselin Fouinel who was a Senior second in 2004.

▲ Cara Wildman, USA [*Rebecca Eggar, Cast Iron Photography*]

All-Ireland all age-group 1st, 2nd & 3rd places, both genders

Province/ region	Firsts	Seconds	Thirds	Aggregate	Percent
Ulster	44	56	34	134	23.6%
Munster	33	42	30	105	18.5%
Leinster	45	41	57	143	25.1%
Connacht	40	28	35	103	18.1%
America	1	3	5	9	1.6%
England	23	16	22	61	10.7%
Europe	0	1	0	1	0.2%
Scotland	4	4	5	13	2.3%

▲ All bodhrán winners at 1st, 2nd and 3rd level, all years [Fintan Farrell, Rebecca Draisey-Collishaw]

Considering that the differences between firsts, seconds and thirds can be minor, it seems appropriate to combine them to come up with a visual in the form of an aggregate figure for the four provinces. This shows Leinster and Ulster counties at the top overall, Munster and Connacht similar, but all provinces close enough in the share of first places:

All-Ireland all age-group 1st, 2nd & 3rd places, females

Province / Region	Firsts		Seconds		Thirds		1,2,3 Aggregate	Female Percent
Ulster	5	17.2%	4	17.4%	5	11.6%	14	14.7%
Munster	4	13.8%	7	30.4%	9	20.9%	20	21.1%
Leinster	4	13.8%	5	21.7%	13	30.2%	22	23.2%
Connacht	13	44.8%	6	26.1%	11	25.6%	30	31.6%
America	0	0.0%	0	0.0%	1	2.3%	1	1.1%
England	3	10.3%	1	4.3%	4	9.3%	8	8.4%
Europe	0	0.0%	0	0.0%	0	0.0%	0	0.0%
Scotland	0	0.0%	0	0.0%	0	0.0%	0	0.0%

▲ All female bodhrán winners at 1st, 2nd and 3rd level, all years [Courtesy Fintan Farrell and Rebecca Draisey-Collishaw]

As regards the changing image of instruments, and the uptake of all of these across the genders, the figures for female competitors show Connacht leading, dramatically so in first places, with Munster and Leinster on a par, Ulster well down, but on a par in firsts with the other two provinces.

All-Ireland all age-group 1st, 2nd & 3rd places, MALES

Province / Region	Firsts		Seconds		Thirds		1,2,3 Aggregate	Male Percent
Ulster	39	24.2%	52	31.0%	29	20.0%	120	25.3%
Munster	29	18.0%	35	20.8%	21	14.5%	85	17.9%
Leinster	41	25.5%	36	21.4%	44	30.3%	121	25.5%
Connacht	27	16.8%	22	13.1%	24	16.6%	73	15.4%
America	1	0.6%	3	1.8%	4	2.8%	8	1.7%
England	20	12.4%	15	8.9%	18	12.4%	53	11.2%
Europe	0	0.0%	1	0.6%	0	0.0%	1	0.2%
Scotland	4	2.5%	4	2.4%	5	3.4%	13	2.7%

▲ All male bodhrán winners at 1st, 2nd and 3rd level, all years [Fintan Farrell, Rebecca Draisey-Collishaw]

The corresponding figures for male competitors shows Leinster and Ulster leading on a par, with Munster and Connacht similar, and England well represented; Ulster and Leinster lead in first places.

All-Ireland Senior 1st, 2nd & 3rd places, both genders

Province/region	Firsts	Seconds	Thirds	Aggregate	Percent
Ulster	6	19	8	33	23.1%
Munster	13	8	7	28	19.6%
Leinster	10	9	15	34	23.8%
Connacht	11	6	7	24	16.8%
America	0	0	3	3	2.1%
England	5	3	3	11	7.7%
Europe	0	1	0	1	0.7%
Scotland	3	2	4	9	6.3%

▲ All-Ireland senior level 1st, 2nd and 3rd winners, all years [Fintan Farrell, Rebecca Draisey-Collishaw]

As regards stylistic finesse at No. 1 Senior level Munster emerges on top in this prestige category, but Ulster is a formidable voice in second places. Much can be read into such figures, as is done with sports results, but, as in other competitions, what they demonstrate is a high level of application and commitment by learners, teachers and organisers alike, a synergy of interests which propels the popularity and fortunes of the bodhrán forward.

From the figures it is clear that the drum is by a large margin male territory in Ulster counties, but in Connacht there is a more cross-gender spread. Overall, there is an increase in female participation from the mid 1970s until the late '80s, it drops off in the '90s and 2000s, then picks up somewhat after 2014.

14 TWENTIETH-CENTURY BODHRÁN

▼ Cathy Kirk, County Monaghan, bodhrán player with CCÉ National Folk Orchestra of Ireland

▲ Japanese Irish-traditional musicians busking in Galway, early 2000s [*EDI*]

[1] Bradshaw 2022, PC.

[2] Information from Don Meade, New York, sourced in a discography of ethnic music in America compiled by Dick Spottswood and Philippe Varlet.

[3] Kjeldsen 2013, 108, says that bones were played on these recordings also. A kit of such instruments was referred to in the music trade as 'traps', the abbreviation for 'contraption' (Hart 1990, 61).

[4] Neely, 2025, PC.

[5] Bradshaw 2022, PC.

[6] Lunny 2023, PC.

[7] For instance, Kilmeaden cheese used the beating of a bodhrán as its badge of authenticity over several years. This ran with the voice-over 'We do things the way they were done before "modern" things were invented'.

[8] Éire – Ireland Pas; Passport, p. 19 [Moylan

NOTES TO CHAPTER 14

2022]. The harp has cultural heritage status as well, granted by the United Nations Educational, Scientific and Cultural Organization (UNESCO) in 2019.

[9] The figures have been culled from privileged access to musician Fintan Farrelly's immense database of fleadh results which was assembled from CCÉ's *Treoir* magazine reports and from gleaning newspaper articles in the years prior to the initiation of those.

Cartoon by Cormac (Brian Moore). [*Courtesy Brian Moore estate*]

CHAPTER 15

BODHRÁN THEORIES AND OPINIONS

The preceding chapter shows that the bodhrán has a popular practice all over Ireland today. This is despite the fact that there is no long-established lore of drum-playing in traditional music that is comparative to – say – fiddle, uilleann pipes and harp practices. Such information as exists is peripheral, found in rural folklore studies rather than in music *per se*. And so, aside from the occasional accounts of improvisation of the tambourine on the bodhrán in the 1800s, which are noted in Chapter 9, the earliest serious commentary on the frame drum in traditional music did not begin until the mid-1900s, and since then it has been appearing in the form of academic music-magazine features, folklore discourses and introductions to tutor books. The chronology of this information shows a general progress in thinking – as well as misinterpretations, wrong information and uncritically repeated errors.

The earliest account of the bodhrán or tambourine – as such – was given in 1947 by Caoimhín Ó Danachair (also known in his writing by the English form of his name, Kevin Danaher) late of Irish Folklore at University College Dublin. Filed in that department under the term 'Ceoltóireacht', he offered the to-be-significant comment:

> Musical (?) Instrument, Athea, County Limerick. A percussion instrument still widely used in this district is the Bodhrán or Tambourine. (Both names are used, the latter is more usual now.) This is a large tambourine, diameter about 18 to 24 inches, of goat-skin stretched on a circular frame. It is played with a double-headed stick about eight inches long. Nowadays it is used chiefly by wren-boys on St Stephen's day[1]

The use of 'still' indicates that he considers that this was a long-standing practice; the use of 'more usual now' suggests that 'bodhrán' had been a more widely-used term for the drum in the past; 'nowadays it is used chiefly by' suggests there was a more widespread use in the past in actual music. But he may also be simply recognising that in the past the device bodhrán had a dual use as an improvised drum.

In 1955 Ó Danachair explored this further in an article which dealt exclusively with the bodhrán as a single-headed drum, drawing on Dinneen's 1927 given meanings:

> The name bodhrán appears to be derived from the word bodhar, which means both 'deaf' and 'dull sounding'; it would seem, then, that the name comes from the noise made by the instrument[2]

He was thus the first to attempt reason out meaning and effect for both the word and the object bodhrán, but, as in his 1947 opinion, he does leave room for reconsideration by using the term 'appears to', and the expression 'it would seem that'. But he explores the device meaning as well, stating:

▲ Caoimhín Ó Danachair / Kevin Danaher at Dún Chaoin, 1946 [*Dúchas, the National Folklore Collection*]

> The fact that the word bodhrán means a skin tray (of identical or similar make to the percussion instrument) in many areas where its use as a drum is not now known seems to indicate a much wider use in former times[3]

By 'not now known' Ó Danachair again could mean 'not known any more', implying that there was once an earlier drum which had been abandoned and forgotten about, the name passing on to the winnowing device and container. But his remark could mean 'not known at this point in time', i.e. that there had been an earlier primary, utilitarian, function for the device that we know as 'bodhrán', one which has come to be superceded by its music use. Ó Danachair's only allusion to the tambourine is that the use of jingles on 1950s drums 'appears to be a recent innovation in imitation of the jingles of the tambourine'. This too implies that he saw the bodhrán as already existing, not as a copy or derivative of the tambourine. But again he leaves room for re-thinking by saying 'appears'. And he does not specify what he means by 'recent'. Is it recent historically, as perhaps in the previous hundred years, or is it recent as in during, or just before, the end of the 1940s? Being from west Limerick, he was obviously well aware of both the bodhrán and the tambourine, as his deep interest was in valuing all aspects of the past and the present, regardless of how mundane objects might be. Yet, still, even though he was a prolific commentator, in his other writings his references to 'bodhrán' and 'tambourine' seem fleeting and circumstantial, relating only to the Wren and to a few Munster counties.

This suggests that either it was not readily visible out of season, or else that he did not consider, or (unlikely) was not aware, that this percussion was a meaningful part of traditional music practices. So, as with other writers, such as Francis O'Neill, any conclusions about the frame drum in music outside of the Wren can only be deduced from his illustrative information – it was either present but un-commented-on, or else absent. For instance, almost thirty years later in his 1984 book *That's How It Was*, dealing with years *c*. 1923, he reported that 'there was not a townland without three or four musicians, and hardly a house without a fiddle, a flute, a melodeon or a concertina, or at the very least a tin-whistle'.[4] If bodhráns, or even tambourines, were used, were significant or present, or in memory in music at that time, why would he not have mentioned them? This suggests that they were not part of what was customary for music for dance, although they were part of the Wren annually, and may have occasionally joined in with music. Comment in Ireland on frame drum percussion along with dance music only becomes visible in later years, when it appears in County Kerry fiction literature, initially as the tambourine, then, amended later, as the bodhrán (see Chapters 10 and 11).

This points to the bodhrán's modern role as the percussion associated with Irish music to be the result of a transfer from obscurity to visibility, from an independent, seasonal *charivari* function which was not experienced, or perceived, as music *per se*, to actual music accompaniment as we know it today. That idea was implied by Ó Danachair's next article, 1955, in which he explained the bodhrán's context as well as how it was made and played:

> In many parts of Munster, and especially in south-west Clare, west Limerick and north Kerry … the loud vigorous drumming of the bodhrán, a percussion

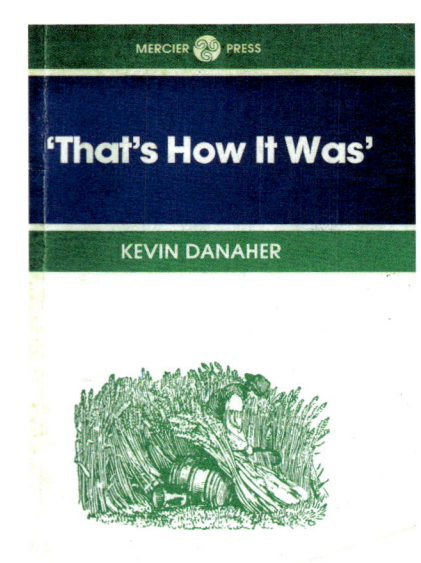

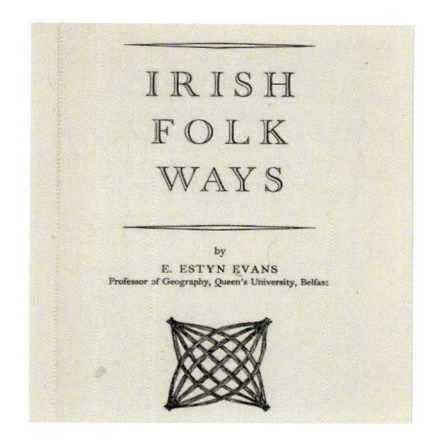

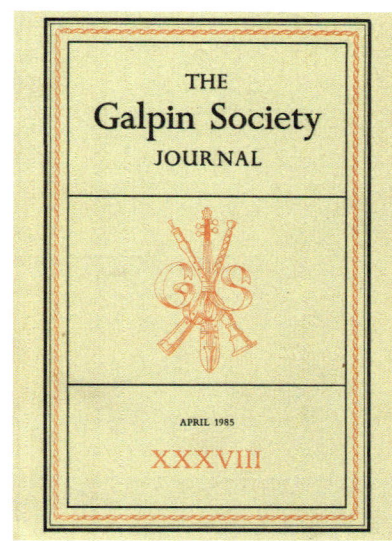

instrument upon which was beaten an accompaniment to the flutes, fiddles and melodeons which made up the wren boys' orchestra[5]

It was found, he says, associated with the Wren tradition on St Stephen's Day, but seldom heard otherwise. This analysis seems most likely to have influenced Seán Ó Riada in his adoption of the term bodhrán.

Shortly after this, Estyn Evans in his 1957 book *Irish folk Ways* described and provided drawings of both wecht and tambourine as artefacts of rural, grain-related agriculture and seasonal ritual, relating these to 'boran': 'the skin tray, the wecht or wight … closely resembles the Eskimo caribou drum. Irish Wrenboys carried a skin tambourine which they beat when hunting the wren', and this he illustrated, describing it as having a deep rim, nailed-on skin, and jingles.[6]

Seán Ó Riada was first to spell out a role for the bodhrán in Irish traditional music. This was in his radio essay series *Our Musical Heritage* that was broadcast on Radio Éireann in 1962 (see Appendix 11). In this, Ó Riada summed up all the relevant issues – winnowing, seasonal celebration, and music. Some aspects of his zealous dogmatism in that essay – about piano in particular – have subsequently been repudiated. But at the time his words were a radical, idealistic spoken polemic that was hugely influential in the revival of traditional music. His statement on group instrumentation – which was demonstrated in his band Ceoltóirí Chualann – effectively invented the bodhrán: 'our native drum – the bodhrán or tambourine, whose history goes back well into pre-Christian times … it probably goes back at least to the Bronze age, and possibly earlier'. He gave no reference to support this dating, but added that 'Until fairly recently it was used in some of the more primitive parts of the country for its primary purpose, which was separating wheat from chaff. I imagine that this was always its main purpose, and that because of this it became associated with harvest festivals'. Regardless of the ambiguity, Ó Riada on a national media platform acknowledged the bodhrán's original, primary function as a winnowing tool, implying the opportunity for it to be improvised on as a drum, which he also called 'tambourine'. And judging by his statement that the bodhrán is 'a most suitable instrument for accompanying Irish music', he preferred to believe it to have an ancient history as a drum, so planting an idea that was to be raised often among subsequent commentators.[7]

Almost a decade later in 1974 Mícheál Ó Súilleabháin became the first to attempt a methodological investigation of the bodhrán. Writing in CCÉ's magazine *Treoir* he gave a comprehensive and concise analysis of the bodhrán, observing its lineage as possibly involving the *wecht*, but also citing three other parallels, an Eskimo, Indian and north American shamanistic routes, prior to the AD 470s Roman tambourine period, and to the Arabian frame drum connections. He left open whether or not the bodhrán developed from the *wecht*, but raised the issue that it might also be an imitation of the tambourine. He saw the way in which Edward Bunting interpreted Cambrensis' Latin word *tympano* as 'drum' as 'a mystery', and, like Ó Riada, he did not acknowledge that the Wren drum was known primarily as 'tambourine', rather than 'bodhrán'. His main source for contexts and for information on construction of the bodhrán was Caoimhín Ó Danachair's 1955 article. He noted the role of literary attention in the promotion of the drum, but also took the radical stance that he saw the bodhrán by 1974 to be already 'as characteristic an instrument as the Uilleann pipes are in Irish music today or as the harp was in the music of several hundred years ago'.[8] He describes bodhrán making and playing in north Kerry, south Tipperary, and west Limerick, the playing method and the use of the stick, noting in particular the west Limerick style of single-end stick playing. He did not speculate as to which came first, the skin tray and sieves on the one hand or the drum on the other, but used Evans' 1957 drawings to illustrate the similarity; he did not himself have sight of the National Museum's collection.[9] Following Ó Súilleabháin came a slew of bodhrán-related booklets and articles, all drawing in some way on his range of references.

The commentators included Nancy Lyon in 1979, with a concise article in *Sing Out!* magazine in which she acknowledged the utilitarian origin in agriculture, but laces in speculation about possible Viking and Laplander importation in the ninth century and also the Romans theory: 'tribes of Celts were playing it long before it reached Irish shores' She believed that few people who pick up a bodhrán take it seriously as an instrument, but also that even though such bad bodhrán players are rightly criticised, this does not happen to poor players of other instruments.[10]

A decade later, in 1982 Seán Ó Riada's radio essay *Our Musical Heritage* appeared in print, edited by poet Thomas Kinsella and piper Tomás Ó Canainn. A significant obfuscating textual change was the editor's removal of 'tambourine' from his lead statement (see Appendix 12), but the ambiguity of whether or not the bodhrán's ancient pedigree was in agriculture or music remained.[11]

In 1983 Mícheál Ó Súilleabháin took his research further, and published a bullet-point summary of 'Contemporary Developments in Bodhrán Performance Technique' contrasting Old and New aspects of the 'how', 'where' and 'on what'. These he itemised as 1/ Social factors, 2/ Morphology (drum structure) and 3/ Performance (technical detail of playing);'[12] this is reproduced in Appendix 4. He summarised his research to date the following year, 1984, in a player-oriented tutor book for Waltons' *The Bodhrán: a practical introduction*, in which he acknowledges getting information from both old and new players and musicians, and ethnomusicological inspiration from John Baily and John Blacking. He moves thinking forward and dispels the mystery by saying that what he terms an 'Irish frame drum' he sees as having 'spread from a rural to an urban setting, from amateur to professional status, from being exclusively male to including female performers, from an outdoor to an indoor performance situation, from having the combined function of skin tray (or sieve) and percussion instrument, to being exclusively the latter, and from being tied to such folk rituals as "hunting the wren" on St Stephen's Day … to being a freely-used instrument'.[13] Also in 1984 David Shaw Smith covered Malachy Kearns' drum-making in his book on artisan crafts, believing that 'the origin of the bodhrán is obscure … thought to date from pagan times'.[14]

In 1985 David Such, writing in the *Galpin Society Journal*, gives a full, scholarly treatment of the instrument, wherein he took the bodhrán as it was, specifically its relatively recent introduction, remarking that 'no other instrument of Irish folk music has shown a comparable rate of development', its players having 'mastered complex rhythmic phrasing and ornamentation with the stick while incorporating … varying the pitch of the tone'.

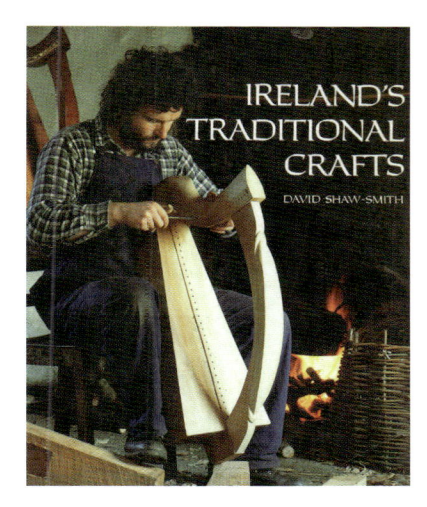

He speaks of dual use, primarily as a utensil, but also as a drum. His article also dwells heavily on expressions of hostility to the bodhrán with regard to poor rhythm and excessive volume, which were a feature of the early years, and which set a fashion for criticism that still persists, and leaves the role of the bodhrán player always subject to question. However, he found that it is necessary to make a distinction between amateur and skilled bodhrán players, but that even where a bodhrán player is good, and accepted, they may well still feel their role as questionable and uncertain.[15]

Ciaran Carson, the County Antrim poet, flute player, writer and one-time music administrator who was guided by a strong aesthetic sensibility, wrote in 1986 with a whiff of understated wit on the bodhrán in his *Pocket Guide to Irish Traditional Music*. His commentary relates to the fact that the music is melody-centred, and it becomes difficult to play if the intricacy of the melodic line is clouded. Advocating common sense and manners, Carson details a challenging courtesy and preparation process for a bodhrán player joining sessions. This amounts to first, learning to lilt a variety of tune-types or to play on another instrument, then learning how to strike the bodhrán. After this, when in public, the bodhrán player must wait for an invitation from other musicians – but only if the protocol of 'one bodhrán at a time' in sessions can be met. In the unlikely event of this stringent regulation being implementable at all, he then, generously, exhorts the bodhrán player to hold their head up: 'The obverse of the ignorant and insensitive is the paranoiac and guilt-ridden player who cannot enjoy himself for fear of spoiling others' enjoyment. If you must play the bodhrán, then play it'.[16]

This was followed in 1987 by Janet McCrickard who gives the most complete and wide-ranging account of all aspects of the bodhrán and its frame drum and tambourine cousins, starting with its antecedents the skin trays and winnowing utensils. Her study is exemplary for its breadth of references and thoroughness, notably its exploration of mystic, spiritual and shamanistic uses of frame drums, a direction which guided her personal appreciation. She cites Bryan MacMahon as the first writer to deal with the drum, John B. Keane the second, in his play *Sive*, though not acknowledging that both writers actually called it 'tambourine'. She explores the frame drum exhaustively back through the centuries and countries, emphasising that it was once played only by women with spiritual significance, and wittily and knowledgeably critiques the various 'madhouse' romantic, wishful thinking and daft-origins theories, hoaxes and 'tall tales', while categorically regarding the bodhrán as a modern tradition of international significance.[17]

Nicholas Driver, in his *Bodhrán & Bones Book* in 1988, speaks of the obscure history of the frame drum, seeing it as native to the south-west, linked to pre-Christianity and the Wren, but believing that any attempt to reconstruct the origins and past of the bodhrán must rest on nothing more than reasoned speculation and circumstantial evidence.[18]

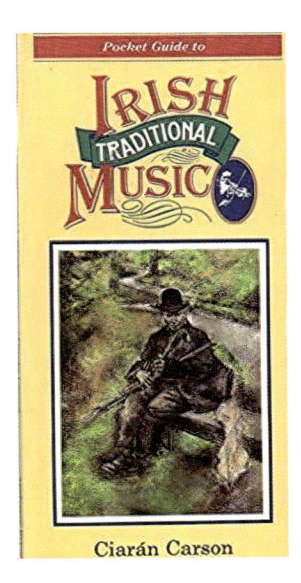

Assumpta Curran's unpublished fieldwork-based survey in 1988 which looked at the use of the bodhrán on the Wren in County Kerry carries an interview with John B. Keane that is significant firstly for his cited importance of the bodhrán to the Wren: 'a band without a bodhrán was considered no band'.[19] This opinion is the opposite to what she herself deduced – that for the Wren music, any kind of drum would suffice, she observing that in Steve MacDonogh's 1983 book on the Dingle Wren there is no mention of tambourine or bodhrán at all,[20] and that, from a Mícheál Ó Súilleabháin interview, it was clear that that drum was 'peripheral to the main activity'. She also reports Keane telling her that his play *Sive* was Ó Riada's first sight of the tambourine, and also that for the Wren competitions people had to be enticed by adjudicators' marking strategies into playing the bodhrán at all rather than more glamorous instruments.[21]

The same year, 1988, tambourine and bodhrán player Sean Halpenny in his *Secrets of the Bodhrán* booklet also sees origins as 'lost in the mists of time', but permits the theory that it 'metamorphosed from a work implement'. As a drum he believes it is ancient, though he sees its use in traditional music as such as recent. He acknowledges the use of the term 'tambourine' prior to 1960, but sees this as a different instrument, being replaced by the bodhrán rather than it being a copy of the tambourine or, as appears to be more the case, a modification.[22]

Stefan Hannigan in *The Bodhrán Book* in 1991 reasons that the bodhrán may have come from outside the country 'like many of the instruments used in Irish traditional music'.[23]

Tommy Walsh and Jim Kelly in the 1994 *Walton Bodhrán Tutor* state that the bodhrán's 'origins are lost in the mists of antiquity', but cite two opposing stories: 'an ancient utensil converted to a musical instrument', versus an actual drum with native, pre-Christian associations, 'coming to us courtesy of the Romans', or 'brought from Lapland by the Danes'.[24]

Erick Falc'jer-Poyroux and Alain Monnier in 1995 wrote 'Il semble qu'il ait été tour d'abord utilisé soit comme tamis, soit pour séparer les grains de blé de livraie'/ originated as a winnowing sieve, and they see it as 'il n'est pas un instrument propre à l'irlande' / it is not an instrument unique to Ireland.[25]

Professional, large-scale maker Malachy Kearns, in his 1996 personal account *Wallup*, sees the bodhrán as 'one of Ireland's oldest products', but, like Halpenny, considers that the actual tambourine was replaced by the bodhrán, and is 'now more or less defunct'.[26]

Returning to the picture in 1996 at the *Crosbhealach an Cheoil* conference, Mícheál Ó Súilleabháin broke new, concise ground, dwelling on the modern bodhrán's newness, and that in its playing 'two musical languages' had arisen, one the standard 'open hand playing, open skin, "hunting the wren" – the sort of Wren-boy sound … this was an open air, pastoral sound', and the other involving 'the hand moving in at the back, dampening the skin, pressing against the skin'. He believed that modern bodhrán styles, which included stick development and skin-tensioning, were 'a new flowering … a different thing, for it breaks loose from the Wren ritual in the nineteen fifties', the marking of a transition to engaging in music sessions, which was demonstrated by 'the bodhrán's emergence onto the streets for sessions in the fleadh cheoils of the fifties and sixties'.[27]

In 1997 Layne Redmond published *When the Drummers Were Women: A spiritual history of rhythm*, a unique, detailed history of the frame drum and its ancient religious associations. It does not relate specifically to the Irish bodhrán, but sets the tambourine's ancestors in pre-Christian society where the god-heads were female, and where the frame drum was both symbol and instrument of their spiritual leadership in society. Based on research and travel in the Middle East and in southern Europe, Redmond's work gives a pictorial chronology of representations of the single-headed, shallow-frame, hand-struck drum. The earliest of these dates to Çatal Hüyük in present-day Turkey, *c.* 5600 BC, a proliferation of statuettes, carvings and imagery that continues well into the Christian period, *c.* 400 AD. A drummer herself, the author details the history and meaning of female drumming in ancient spiritual traditions in Mesopotamia (present-day Turkey, Syria and Iraq), in the Nile Valley, Egypt, and in Greece, Rome and India. She identifies the silencing of both women and drumming by patriarchy, and examines the reappearance of drumming in the modern age and its potential as a medium for transformation. The book's spiritual axis offers a reference point for modern-day belief in a pre-historic use of the frame drum in religion in Ireland: it brings together mythology, history and prehistory, personal experience and scientific information to posit a theory on the historical healthful and transformative effects of drumming. Remarkably, it locates the first named frame drummer in history – a Mesopotamian priestess, Lipushiau, who lived in Ur (in Iraq) *c.* 4,400 years before our time.[28]

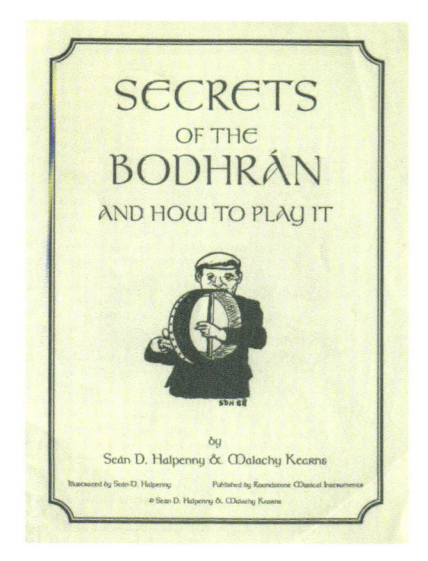

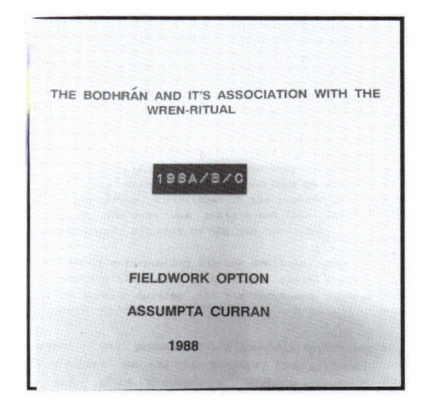

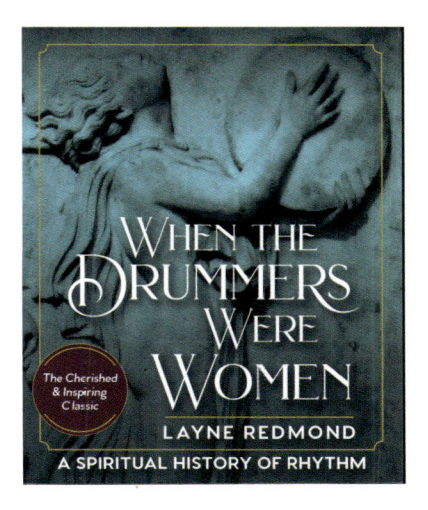

Redmond's collaboration with the drum authority Glen Velez established that from 3000 BC to 500 AD the tambourine-style drum was the main form of percussion, and most of its players were female – goddesses or priestesses – who struck with the hand, whereas northern-hemisphere shamans used a stick or bone beater. The frame drum spread to Egypt 'somewhere between 2000 and 1500 BC', its performers women. Some of the drums were rectangular, such as one held in the Cairo Museum, *c.* 1400 BC that was found in a female burial chamber. Redmond believes that rites involving frame drumming 'can be used to rouse and shape group emotion and behaviour, developing a continuous shared consciousness' and that 'Music vibrationally transmits states of mind directly from consciousness to consciousness', resonating simultaneously on emotional, spiritual, intellectual and physical levels, with the power to 'affect vast social and economic cycles'.[29] All of this chimes with some modern-day opinions – particularly with what is implied by those proposing the 'pagan' thesis and other spiritual dimensions of bodhrán lore in Ireland. But it relates to far-away places, for in the ancient past the religious cults that used the frame drum were centred on such figures as Aphrodite in Cyprus, where the frame drum was prominent from at least 1000 BC.

A greatly-illuminating study, this book is remarkable for its compilation and detailing of so much actual material evidence. But its Ireland references involve much supposition: 'A skin tray or sieve used in rites associated with the Celtic grain goddess Brigid is identical to the bodhrán, an Irish frame drum. The bodhrán is thought to have been used originally in religious processions'[30] and 'The bodhrán, the large frame drum still used by traditional Irish musicians, was closely associated with folk ritual and played in religious and festival processions'.[31] Neither statement is supported by evidence (though of course what they say could have been theoretically possible in ancient Ireland).

In 1999 the first edition of the encyclopedia *Companion to Irish Traditional Music* (*CITM*) set the bodhrán in a range of similar drums internationally, saw it being originally with the Wren, not having a role in Irish music historically, and noted modern-day romantic misunderstandings about it. The bodhrán's move to being commercially made is charted, as are developments in tuning systems and playing styles, and the rhythmic similarity to step-dancers' footwork is suggested as a stylistic influence.[32]

By far the most exacting researcher has been Danish bodhrán player Svend Kjeldsen, who in his 2000 (unpublished) University of Limerick MA dissertation 'The Coleman Hand-strikers: old style bodhrán playing in south Sligo' gives a rigorous, intelligently-structured and thought-through study based on substantial interviews with key contemporary players. His planned, systematic questions come from inside the field, and cover origins-ideas, past and present playing styles, ritual use and the Wren, and extant publications and recordings. He sees that 'Ó Riada brought the instrument from a completely rural setting to the concert hall … radio broadcasts enabled many Irish people to hear the bodhrán played possibly for the first time',[33] and concludes that 'until the end of the 1950s the bodhrán was played only on the west coast of rural Ireland'.[34] This is a detailed scientific account of the bodhrán's development, of its playing techniques today, its Connacht stylists, and of information gathered from musicians.

Also in 2000 the *Ceolas* website has an interesting turn of phrase by Josh Mittleman: 'The bodhrán is an old drum but a young musical instrument', and '… the drum languished for centuries outside the realm of musical performance'.

The following year Rina Schiller with *The Lambeg and the Bodhrán* in 2001 did a comparative study of the bodhrán and the Lambeg drum, the only other Irish form of percussion. While a history is not the purpose of her work, nevertheless she gives a detailed account of contexts and construction for the bodhrán, though she does not acknowledge the presence of the tambourine (as such) in Irish society; rather, drawing on Caoimhín Ó Danachair's words, she cites the Wren as the bodhrán's link to pre-history, and articulates symbolic differences between the two drum forms. The Lambeg is observed as being most visibly and historically associated with political declaration of loyal-British, separatist identity as well as having a wider, specialised, aesthetic appeal which is expressed via competitions involving serious performers. On the other hand, the bodhrán is an artistically and recreationally devised instrument the players of which regard themselves primarily as artistically-performing musicians; their primary role is musical, not political, even though the instrument has accrued a marginal, but significant political symbolism. Context and use have thus come to visibly differentiate and define the drums, as each is associated and identifies with, respectively, political and cultural expression in their own present-day host societies.[35] She uses only the new generic term 'bodhrán' throughout, emphasising that she views the frame drum primarily as a contemporary instrument. Her reporting that CCÉ only belatedly accepted the drum as a bona fide instrument supports this attitude, something which may also help one appreciate the tendency of melody musicians to impulsively dismiss, or to be prejudiced against, percussion in traditional music circles. But that opinion, as the author valuably asserts, merely mirrors the same general tendency to deride drums that exists within western art music.[36] Awareness of such attitudes has, she says, resulted in a sensitivity among bodhrán players about their role, especially as regards multiple drums participating simultaneously in sessions. It has also promoted a currency of tongue-in-cheek bodhránist satire in jokes and songs.[37] Schiller's reporting too of opinions that the

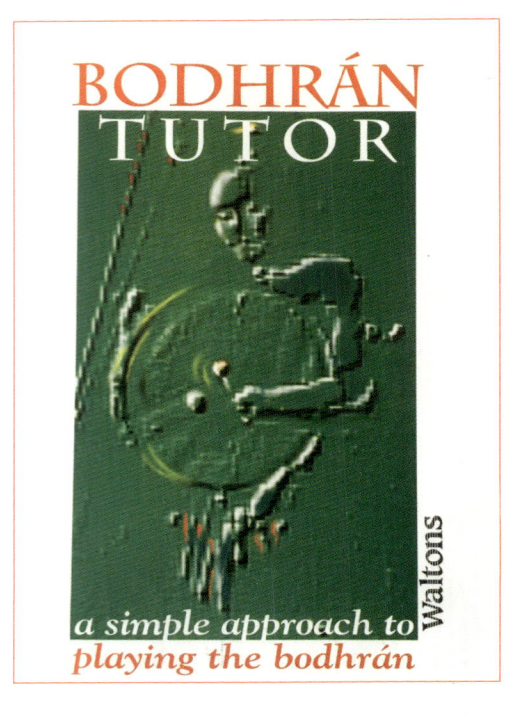

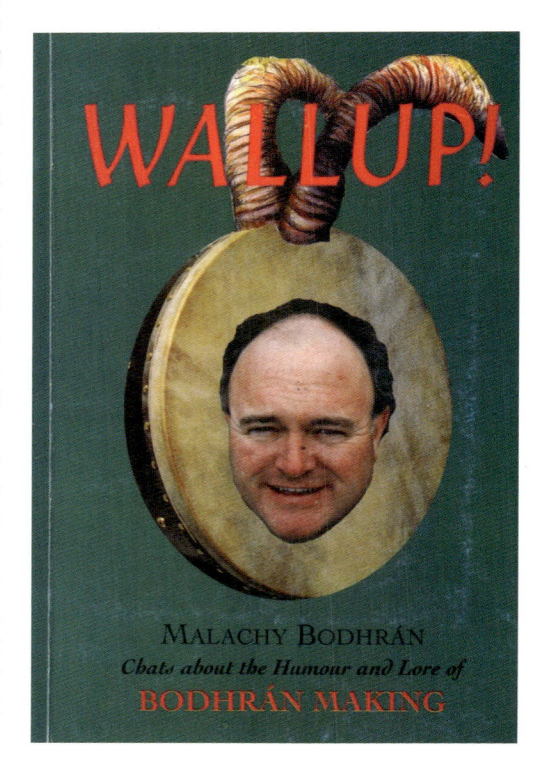

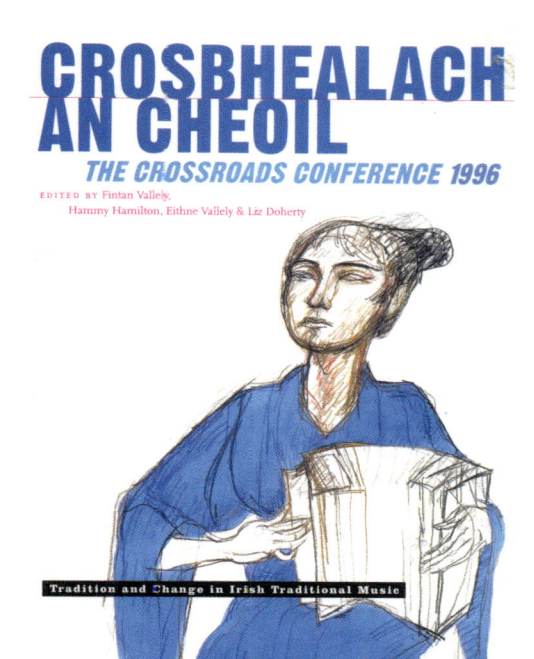

European mind associates drumming with the military, particularly through the fife and drum band, does tie in with the history of the actual tambourine in Europe, and implies a subliminal authority aspect of the bodhrán even in its recreational or artistic performance contexts.[38] She sees seasonal practice as a possible route back to a medieval precedent for the bodhrán, and that the skin tray may well have been improvised as a drum on a seasonal basis,[39] which accords with Janet McCrickard's research, particularly on wechts and on historical spiritual usage.[40]

Geoff Wallis and Sue Wilson, in *The Rough Guide to Irish Music*, 2001, see the bodhrán as having 'rarely featured in traditional music … primarily associated with the arcane ritual of the Wren Boys', and remark on the fact that 'Older versions of the bodhrán often had jingles inserted in the frame, like a tambourine, but these have virtually disappeared'.[41]

Similarly, Dorothea Hast and Stanley Scott, in their 2004 *Music in Ireland*, cite Schiller and Ó Súilleabháin, seeing the bodhrán as originally 'a skin tray for separating chaff, baking, serving food, and storing food … use as a musical instrument in rural Ireland was restricted to ritual occasions … but it did not appear on the concert stage or recordings until the 1960s'.[42]

Berliner Moritz Wulf Lange, in his 2004 *Handbuch für Bodhránspieler*, sees a dual purpose as device and seasonal instrument, with the drum developing from the tray, but after the 1930s it has increasingly been used solely as an instrument.

Simon O'Dwyer went furthest in speculation in his book *Prehistoric Music Ireland*, also in 2004, saying that he regards the bodhrán as belonging to pre-historic music, though as a dual-use winnower,[43] which in its music role 'may be a major influence' on today's traditional music. Though unsupported by any sources, the value of such an opinion from a researcher who is deeply acquainted with sophisticated ancient instruments is that one can indeed only imagine much of what there was in the past, and how much we have aesthetically lost from it.

A tutor by Peter Houlihan in 2007 gives a modern, detailed process of construction and of playing, but historically he speaks of 'a total lack of references in both modern and ancient literature', arguing that 'any historical dissertation can only be based on guesswork and speculation … the origins of the bodhrán are shrouded in the mists of time'.[44]

Liam Ó Bharáin, in three editions of CCÉ's *Treoir* magazine of 2007–8, gives an extensive exploration of all aspects of the bodhrán's history and international relatives. His article has four key arguments. First is his study of the *Rosa Anglica* manuscript, from which he shows that the term 'bodhrán' as some kind of device was already known *c*. 1550, and is interpreted by him to mean a drum. Second is his bringing of fresh attention to the County Wexford *Poole Glossary* which he believes locates the bodhrán's presence as a drum at the end of the 1700s. His third point concerns the derivation of 'bodhrán' from words relating to deafness and noise, and his final detail involves interpretation of visual images from the nineteenth century. Overall, his information constitutes a thesis which for him identifies and places the bodhrán as originally an Irish drum in the sixteenth, eighteenth and nineteenth centuries. His work is notable for its exceptional unveiling of *Rosa Anglica* and the *Poole Glossary*, the landmark verification of the earliest dating of the 'skin on a frame' object called bodhrán.[45]

Bill Woods, in *Bodhrán: the basics*, 2009, warns against frame drums with decorations: 'painting a Celtic design on it doesn't make a bodhrán any better, no more than painting large numerals on the family sedan makes it a race car'. He sees it that its regular use as an instrument in Irish traditional music only took off in the 1960s, and 'its incredible dynamic and melodic range didn't start until the 1970s'.[46]

Ronan Nolan's website irishmusicweb.ie, also from 2009, took a sanguine, catch-all view, acknowledging Ó Riada to 'stick his neck out, brazenly describing the bodhrán as "our native drum ... its history goes back to pre-christian times"'. His overall view is refreshing for his thinking on the absence of jingles on the bodhrán, for his researched information on J.B. Keane's original use of the term 'tambourine' in *Sive*, and for the instrument's progressive visibility and popularisation via Fallon, Peadar Mercier, Kevin Conneff in Prosperous, Christy Moore (Planxty), Robin Morton (Boys of the Lough), Tommy Hayes (Stockton's Wing), Johnny Ringo McDonagh (De Dannan), Colm Murphy, Donnchadh Gough (Danú) and so on up to John Joe Kelly (Flook). He also notes that rural tambourines, as used on the Wren in Kerry, were obviously made from riddles or sieves.[47]

Sean Williams, in her 2010 book *Focus: Irish Traditional Music*, calls the bodhrán 'an old style of drum', but which 'is neither historically popular nor particularly traditional', seeing it as having a history with the Wren, yet having had an 'extraordinary revival in the later half of the twentieth century'.[48] The following year, 2011, the second edition of *CITM* identifies the original bodhrán as a device, noting the different terms for this and for its varied applications, including evidence of improvised drum use, images of tambourines in nineteenth-century art, the use of the term 'tambourine' for the bodhrán up until the Ó Riada period, and introducing the idea of influence from touring minstrels.[49]

In the following year Svend Kjeldsen visually explored the bodhrán from a transcultural perspective, observing Norse, Middle East and Breton frame drums as well as the influence of sixteenth-century Turkish military, the tamburello in nineteenth-century London, orientalist portrayals of female tambourine players, and tambourines as used by the British military. Kjeldsen views the similarity of the device bodhrán and the European tambourine as leading to the Irish tambourine, initially the crude Wren versions, and eventually to today's sophisticated contemporary bodhrán, which is described as 'a music instrument'.[50]

In 2013, in a 'Statutory Public Lecture' for the Dublin Institute for Advanced Studies Fergus Kelly voiced a *belief* in a historic Irish frame drum, but valuably speculating that 'bodhrán' was 'a word for a low prestige instrument ... which may have been in general currency during the earlier period, but simply did not make it into the texts'. Reflecting what Ann Buckley has said, this is food for thought regarding manuscript interpretation and the invisibility to history of the poorer classes and their cultural practices.[51]

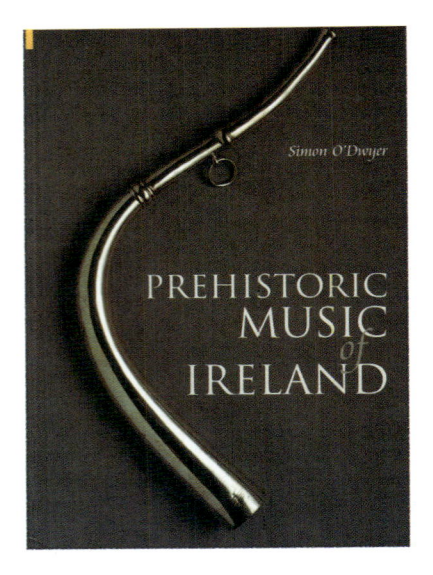

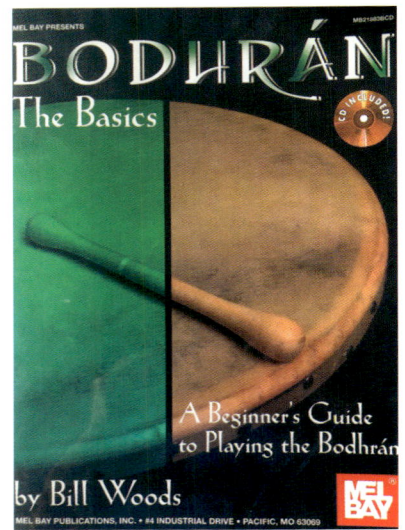

Svend Kjeldsen again addressed the history in 2013 as an *Encyclopaedia of Music in Ireland* entry, concluding that 'there is no scientific evidence' to support the idea that the bodhrán is directly related to (or derived from) other frame drums or 'that it came to Ireland from abroad'. This nativistic confidence did however acknowledge that '... folklore studies and linguistic research have revealed an overlap between the instrument as a drum and as a rural utensil'.[52] Colin Harte's 2020 *The Bodhrán* was the first full-length book devoted to the Irish drum, carrying observations and interviews on playing style, organological developments, innovation, professionalism and cosmopolitanism; the skin-tray/device is acknowledged, but interpretation of the drum's history is disappointing, as is the use of the term 'bodhrán' to describe tambourines in three early paintings and on '78' discs.[53]

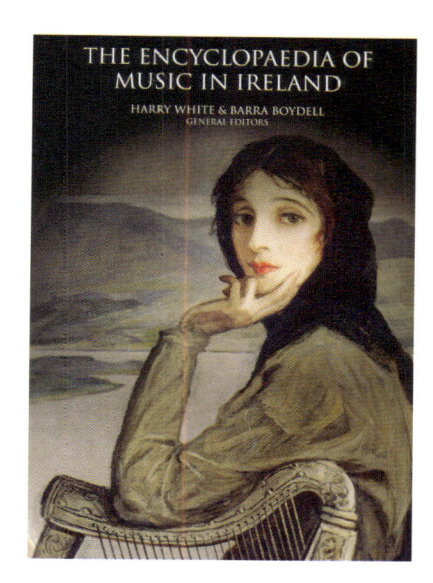

Rolf Wagel's website (bodhran-info.de) gives a tight summary history which carries useful leads, and audio links to two recorded tambourine players – John Reynolds, and Neal Smith with Packie Dolan – and cites Willie Reynolds' valuable memories of the 1940s. He chooses, however, to overlook the description 'tambourine' on the recordings, and indeed throughout his article he back-applies the term 'bodhrán' to pre-1960 tambourines.

Ruairi Glasheen rounds off the analytical commentary superbly however, in a 2023/4 series of four films posted on YouTube, an hour and a half of detailed exploration through interviews of history, popularisation, developments and makers, and players and style. The original device bodhrán, skin trays, sieves and tambourines at the National Museum are studied, speculating on dual or improvised use as a tambourine. The mid-1900s are dealt with visually in eloquent recollections by John B. Keane's son Billy and others, drawing intelligently on Telefís Éireann's and Caoimhín Ó Danachair's film footage and still photos. The back-application of 'bodhrán' for the Irish frame drum by some of the interviewees can be misleading, but these compelling documentaries carry all the facts about the modern bodhrán vividly and creatively.

In addition to these texts there are numerous documents available on the internet, many of them excellent, if brief, but some are shallow, some misleading, and the odd one plain daft. Omission of mention of them here does not by any means imply criticism or rejection: the internet is simply much too big a field to tackle in the present already-bursting-at-the-seams book. The next chapter will consider the sum of these commentaries and proffer additional conclusions based on their information and on the body of data which has been sourced as described in the chapters to date.

▶ Film-maker and bodhrán player Ruairi Glasheen with Netherlands-based bodhrán maker Brendan White [*Courtesy Ruairi Glasheen*]

276

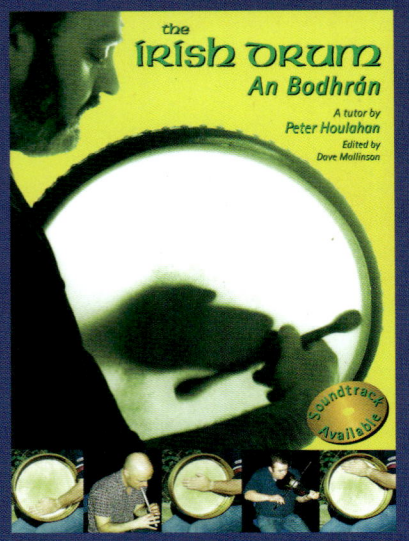

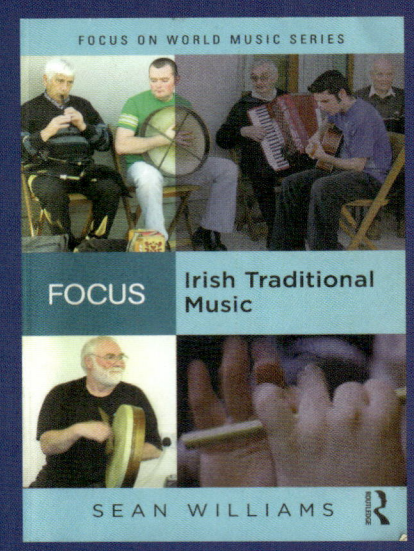

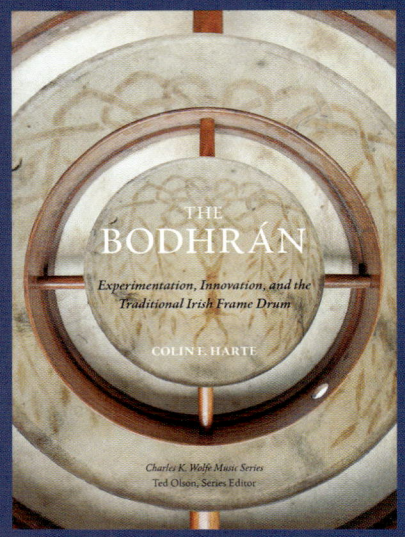

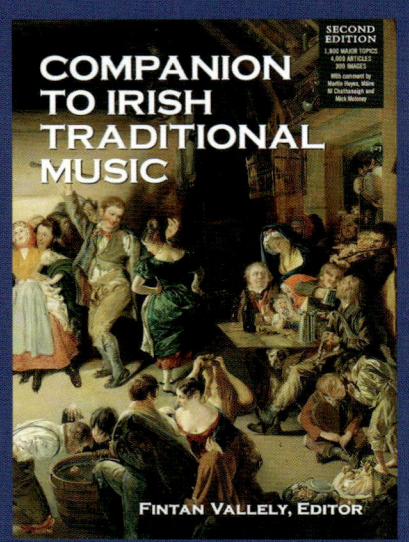

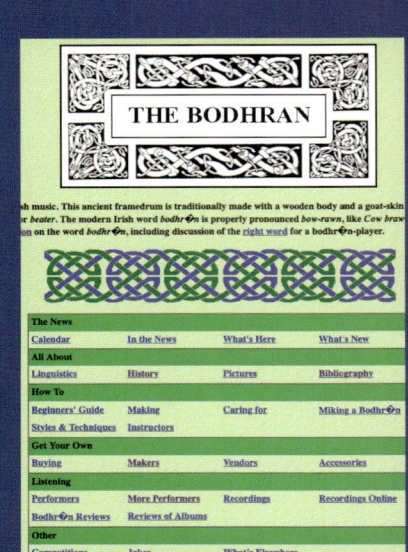

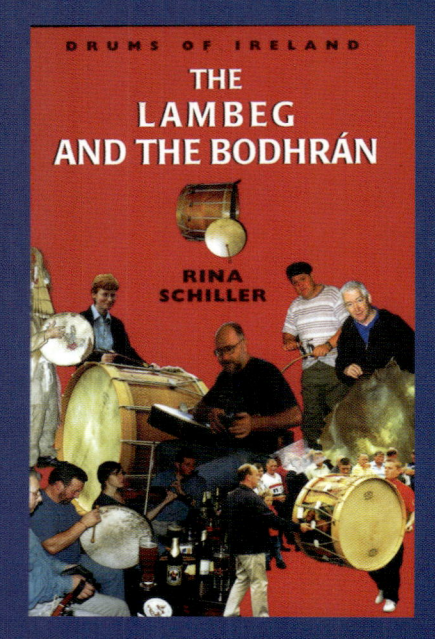

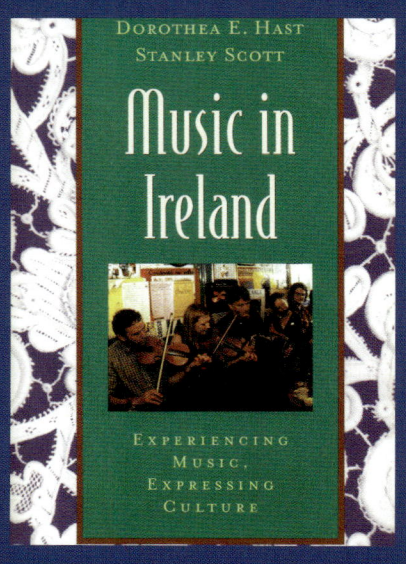

15　BODHRÁN THEORIES AND OPINIONS

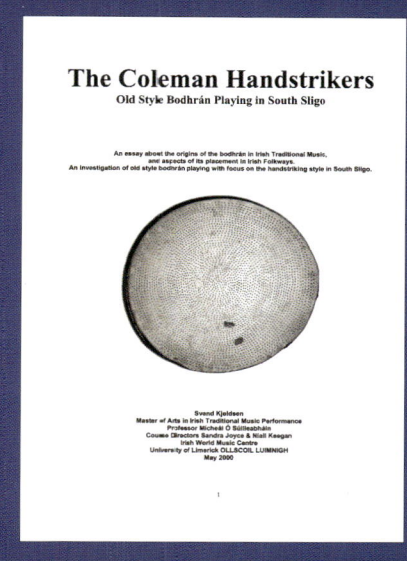

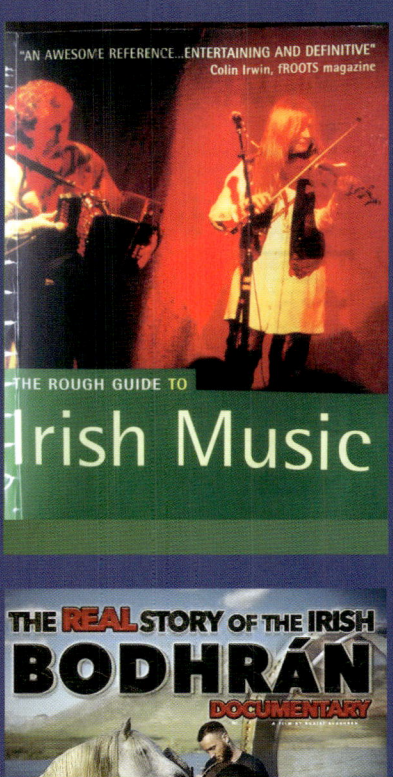

▲ The band Porterhead, Galway [*Colm Keating*]

NOTES TO CHAPTER 15

[1] CBÉ, 'Ceoltóireacht'; 1947 0103.
[2] Ó Danachair 1955, 130.
[3] Ibid.
[4] Ó Danachair 1984, 56.
[5] Ibid. 1955, 129–30.
[6] Evans 1957, 211–12.
[7] Ó Riada, 1962.
[8] Ó Súilleabháin 1974, 5.
[9] Ó Súilleabháin 2014, PC. This collection was not accessible until the 2000s. He may, however, have been using the term 'bodhrán' in its modern, generic, sense.
[10] Lyon 1979, 3.
[11] Kinsella 1982, 74–7.
[12] Webber 1983, 43.
[13] Ó Súilleabháin 1984.
[14] Shaw Smith 1984, 110.
[15] Such 1985, 16–17.
[16] Carson 1986, 39.
[17] McCrickard 1987, 55.
[18] Driver 1988, 21.
[19] Curran 1988, 11.
[20] Ibid., 5.
[21] Ibid., 12.
[22] Halpenny 1990, 1.
[23] Hannigan 1991, 69.
[24] Walsh and Kelly 1994, 6.
[25] Falc'jer-Poyroux and Monnier, 1995.
[26] Kearns, 1996.
[27] Ó Súilleabháin 1996.
[28] Redmond 1997, 48.
[29] *DRUM!* magazine, Vol. 9, No. 8, Dec. 2000.
[30] Redmond op. cit., 47.
[31] Ibid., 133.
[32] Vallely 1999, pp. 28–30.
[33] Kjeldsen 2000, 10–11.
[34] Ibid., 30.
[35] Schiller 2001, 106.
[36] Ibid., 103.
[37] Ibid., 116–19.
[38] Ibid., 83.
[39] Ibid., 95.
[40] Ibid., 96.
[41] Wallis and Wilson 2001, 533.
[42] Hast and Scott 2004, 81–2.
[43] O'Dwyer 2004, 17.
[44] Houlihan 2007, 4.
[45] Ó Bharáin, 2007–8.
[46] Woods 2009, 3.
[47] Nolan, 2023.
[48] Williams 2010, 144.
[49] Vallely 2021, 68–72.
[50] Kjeldsen 2012.
[51] Kelly 2013.
[52] Kjeldsen 2013, 103.
[53] Harte 2020.

▲ Aimée Farrell Courtney, Kevin Conneff and Dónal Lunny [*Nutan*]

CHAPTER 16

RE-THINKING THE BODHRÁN?

Because much of the information in these pages has not been widely known, the term 'bodhrán' has passed without question into general parlance and so has prevailed for the drum among its post-1960s audiences. There is nothing wrong with that in itself, but there has been a gap in thinking which has come to be filled with a potpourri of the good and the bad – fact, intelligent speculation, imagination and wishful thinking. Much of that damages no-one, but it does seem better that things be more clearly understood, hence this book. The first actual analysis of the Irish frame drum by Mícheál Ó Súilleabháin in 1974 gives the bodhrán a musicological legitimation as a drum by placing it in an international pedigree-tree of frame drums. Janet McCrickard went further, introducing the element of mysticism, spirituality and ritual. Subsequent obsession with this dimension by others has had two outcomes: a tendency to cloud reality, as well as to spark a new imaginative but logical rationalisation which takes its information from parallel cultures in other places. The strength in the published opinions and arguments is a passion for the bodhrán which affirms it as a highly-developed Irish percussion. But the weakness to date has possibly been the apparent need to find an ancient, indigenous drum for Ireland other than the Lambeg – which is the other drum form evolved on the island, but which carries anti-Irish political connotations. Awkward things and chunks of time have consequently been skimmed over.

▼ Street players at SSWC, 2019 [*Colm Keating*]

The gap – no outside influence?

Almost all of the opinions published to date note that the bodhrán, the single-sided Irish drum, is generally played with a stick, and sometimes the open hand. Some see the bodhrán as a tambourine without jingles, others see the tambourine as a bodhrán with jingles. Some say the bodhrán drum evolved from the device bodhrán, while others speculate that the drum came first. But most know that in the Irish context 'tambourine' and 'bodhrán' mean more or less the same thing. Some of the commentators have simply cited each other, and some have misinterpreted the limited visual evidence, likely on account of having had poor access to it. But it is surprising that most appear not to have considered the nineteenth century, which is otherwise a century of immense significance not only in Irish culture and politics, but for instruments played in Irish music. This could mean that society has blocked it out or has tactfully forgotten about it – because in the nineteenth century we did enthusiastically consume popular minstrel music. And as with all popular musics it is impossible that this did not have some kind of influence on music here – as did, for instance, the guitar in the twentieth century. But it can also be explained by the fact that popular-music fashions are ephemeral, and, by definition, those that have gone before are rapidly replaced by those which follow.

No 'minstrel boys' on the drum?

Many of the studies and summaries do, however, acknowledge the possibility of an original Roman, shamanistic or military original source for a tambourine-type drum here, and the relevance of the ancient bodhrán

▼ Tommy Sherlock, Ennistymon, applies a practical solution to tensioning skin in Cruises' during a fleadh in Ennis, 2016 [*Colm Keating*]

winnower or container is frequently cited. But if the original was the device bodhrán that would have been likely to be improvised as a drum, then what particular relevance would any early-Christian period import have? And, too, if the bodhrán, by that name, as a device, is of Ireland, but did not originate as a drum, and only evolved from a device to become a drum, then the possibility of a function-related meaning for the term 'bodhrán' is raised, i.e. what does the word 'bodhrán' actually mean? The tambourine is a separate issue, and is mentioned by some of the commentators, but where it is cited, it is to say that it is a different thing (i.e. it differs by having jingles).

In leaping over the nineteenth century, however, a period is skipped that does seem to be every bit as challenging in the world of recreation as it was in politics, firstly for the very presence of the commercial tambourines, and secondly for the post-minstrels use of the tambourine – by that name – on the Wren. It seems remiss too to not consider the possibility of outside influence from somewhere close to modern time, not least on account of the fact that such awareness is standard in analysis of other aspects of music. For instance in song, where the movement of ballads among Ireland, England, Scotland, USA and Canada is hugely important. So too with harp and pipes, where global sharing and applicability of the instruments are key factors. And if we are analysing, say, the accordion, or the banjo, we don't even have to pause to think about looking beyond Ireland itself, and to the nineteenth century in particular. Jumping the nineteenth-century gap has consequences in what passes for fact, and so it is not at all surprising that some choose to say the bodhrán's history is 'lost in the mists of time'. But misinformation breeds misinformation, seen, for instance, in 2022 in data posted by a peripatetic music-teaching service which deals with more

▼ Liam Weldon at the launch of a Gypsy and Travellers' Centre in Greenwich, London, 1989 [*Colm Keating*]

than a hundred schools in Ireland. In a brief to announce the institution of a bodhrán class it erroneously states: 'The bodhrán is one of Ireland's oldest traditional musical instruments ... one of a small select family of Celtic instruments that is stated to pre-date Christianity'.[1]

The 'pagan' bodhrán thesis

For a few of the commentators, pre-Christian 'paganism', so called, does indeed arise occasionally. This is cited as a likely origins-theory, implicitly with spiritual connotations. But underlying that would have to be a belief that the bodhrán was originally primarily a drum, not a device that was fundamental to survival in a grain-dependent society.. 'Pagan', a term dating to the fourth century AD, has many meanings, but it is assumed that in the drum context it is intended to relate to primeval, pre-Christian worship involving nature, cosmology, seasons and the earth.[2] With regard to this thinking, as has already been shown in press quotes, 'pagan' and 'pre-Christian', as well as 'barbaric', were used early on during the post-*Sive* excitement by John B. Keane and others when speaking about a Wren event in Listowel: 'The pagan stuff breaks out in you'[3] (see p. 179). Such tremendous words are matched indeed by the 1974 film *Bodhrán*, in which players' intense vitality can be easily appreciated in dramatic scenes of the torchlit Wrenboys' competition parade. But that is an organised, choreographed event, akin in its objective and energy to *Mardi Gras* or a thrilling football final. And it began only in 1957. Over the years that followed, numerous commentators who were moved by the bodhrán=pagan romance continued to pass it on, notably Seamus Tansey in his didactic concerts, setting his brilliant playing in an ever-expanding, extrovert mythic matrix. As expressed by his accompanying bodhrán player Josie McDonagh: 'Tansey would think of it

▲ Trevor Bury, Cavan [*Martin Gaffney*]

▼ Conor Lyons teaching teaching at Bodhrán Buzz, October 2014 [*Colm Keating*]

▼ Session players in Miltown Malbay, Niall McQuaid on bodhrán, 1990s [*Nutan*]

▲ Teaching circle at Robbie Harris' Bodhrán Buzz workshop at Áras Chrónán, Clondalkin, County Dublin, 2014 [*Colm Keating*]

as a pagan instrument … It'll go back to pagan time … two thousand years'.[4] Writer Gabriel Fitzmaurice picked up Keane's elemental pagan ball too in 2006: 'The tambourine was the instrument of the outdoors, of Wrenboys and Strawboys, the relic of a pagan Ireland'.[5]

Romantic rhetoric?
The commercial world has capitalised on the Pagan thesis too, as seen in the PR used for the bodhrán-based drums constructed by Malachy Kearns for the massively-successful *Riverdance* show. Made at the request of composer Bill Whelan, and hugely powerful in a militaristic manner in the production, these drums served to swell the myth of a 'drum past' with their PR citation: 'From the battlefield to the concert hall, drums have played an important part in our history … evoke feelings going back to Tribal and Pagan rituals of days gone by'. In modern time, yes, but deployed by colonisers from the seventeenth century on only – and not in spirituality, for it is not the case that drums are an ancient marker in Irish identity. War aside, 'tribal and pagan rituals' is not beyond questioning, for (aside from blood sacrifice) the suggested spirituality is a long way from 'battlefield', and, anyway, there is no folklore or manuscript evidence of either indigenous-Irish military, or ritual spiritual frame drum use. But the intimation of an original militaristic function for drumming elsewhere isn't itself far off the mark, and indeed it is the ancestor of the worldwide use of drums by football supporters. The loudness and authority of drumming are no doubt what invoke the 'primitive' in people's minds – 'what really stirs my blood' as one Lambeg drum fan put it[6] – for drums of all kinds have been associated with politics as well as music theatre and music spectacle, and are profoundly influential as regards transporting the listener 'out of themselves'.[7] The wild side of drumming is by now somewhat tamed, re-deployed and corralled as cultural expression (as theatrical as is war by sport), but it is central to most music genres. Drums were originally introduced into war to inspire, encourage, intimidate, frighten, dominate and subjugate, but there is no evidence that we had any such drum culture in ancient Ireland: we inherited a melodic one which has been appreciated as introspective, uplifting, inspirational, enabling, symbolic, emotionally fulfilling, communicative, collaborative and motivational. Music, as such, and primal instinct do seem like two different things, but on occasion they do overlap on all instruments in a powerful synergy. Veneration of antiquity is vital to our understanding and appreciating who we are and where we came from, but it is not useful to apply it exclusively or uncritically.

Another aspect of the 'Pagan' thesis is that *all* serious forms of music, music-making or music-instrument practice speak to the same deep emotional or spiritual aesthetic. All earlier-society music forms, including drumming, can be felt – and are often desired to be felt – as more fundamentally expressive than modern ones. But music appreciation is also a matter of taste. Achievement of an 'other' elemental spiritual state is not unique to communing with the past: it is the very essence of contemporary practice in all artforms, in all musics, and on all instruments, whether old or new. *Any* serious music can bring us to 'another place', as can any specialised instrument – for some it is strings, for some pipes, free reeds or flutes; occasion, genre and politics count too. If this was not the case, then

▲ Sandra Joyce [*Nutan*]

"Playing the bodhrán is an act of personal entrainment for me, especially in the context of the session. I find a deep, embodied connection between the tunes being played and my rhythmic and tonal response to them through the resonance of the bodhrán. I experience music in a very different way when I am in this state of flow"
Sandra Joyce, IWAMD, Limerick

▲ County Cavan multi-instrumentalist Ted Sweeney [*Martin Gaffney*]

"Drumming is about making people dance" *John Joe Kelly*

instruments other than drums would be irrelevant. And they are not. Even so, most of the perceived origin-tales for the bodhrán have elements of truth, and many of them see it as productive that the modern-day bodhrán's transformation was facilitated and encouraged after the late 1950s by Keane, marginally, and by Ó Riada, profoundly. The opinions documented in all publications agree that the bodhrán took off to its present state of popularity *c.* 1960, though they differ in details and accuracy of historical interpretation. The skin tray or winnower is acknowledged as the bodhrán's precursor, following the lead of Dinneen, Ó Danachair and Ó Súilleabháin, but this is not investigated any further. Some take the view that the bodhrán has been dual purpose by design, rather than, as this book has suggested, being a tool which in addition to its vital practical functions came to be, or had originally been, merely *improvised* as a drum. Some are aware of the name-change from tambourine to bodhrán, but most are not, or else do not attribute it any significance. And not all commentators connect the present drum with the imported commercial tambourine, although some do note the possibility of a military connection. The meaning of the bodhrán's name is not considered beyond the status quo 'noise' either, though there are alternative possibilities. And, for instance, was it for aesthetic reasons that in the mid-1900s we tacked the by-then-obsolete skin tray's name on to the similar-looking tambourine which we had already borrowed and had been copying for more than a century? Or was the term just applied in jest, innocently and derogatorily, to players of the tambourine: 'Would you ever get away out of here with that ould *bodhrán!!*', or, 'Him and his ould bodhrán!'.

Awareness of the minstrel phenomenon is not indicated by most Irish commentator, nor is the sale of tambourines throughout the nineteenth century by the music trade. Both 'tambourine' and 'minstrels' are generally absent from Irish nineteenth- and twentieth-century music references,[8] so if academic musicology has overlooked them, it is not surprising that bodhrán aficionados do so too, and it is understandable that the term 'bodhrán' can come to be used without qualification when talking historically. Sometimes this is through unawareness of the pre-1960s term 'tambourine', but it may also be on account of a pragmatic decision to ignore the burden of history and so to use the modern term 'bodhrán' in a generic sense.

Closing the file

This study was sparked by the degree of speculation and mystery in the bodhrán story as we have known it. It has looked mostly at the written, visual and artefact evidence, with some interviews and other personal communication. There are of course other quite different books to be done on spiritual, aesthetic and music-related aspects of the drum, on players, on the development of playing techniques, and on drum-making history and advances, none of which this book has done any more than allude to. The search in these pages began with the question whether or not there was an indigenous Irish drum which had somehow been lost, or had gone deep underground, but came to be revived in the 1960s. The wide variety of information sources consulted does not support this idea, or of an historic Irish drum-music culture: Ireland's music has been melody-centred for many centuries, with the percussive impulse only implied – in articulate, detailed dance steps. All the information sources show that the original bodhrán was a skin tray, container and winnowing device which initially had only a taut, low-tension skin, but in the 1800s evolved to have a higher tension and a drum potential. Following the paper trail has involved journalism, academic and historical reading and process, digital archives and traditional-music experience. Trawling through large volumes of data has yielded many surprises which dictated ongoing re-evaluation of thesis, regularly upending what had earlier been considered certainty. This applies not only to printed sources, but also to people's opinions, for every avenue of exploration has had unanticipated, productive side-roads, depressing cul de sacs and diversionary red herrings. Inevitably, the information that has been collected has, variously, confirmed, questioned and contradicted the numerous strands of received wisdom which by 2022 had come to be taken for granted.

The making of Irish tambourine copies with tensioned skins was visible by the late 1800s, the size of the drums being dictated by military and minstrel prototypes and the dimensions of the available skins, but affected too by the desire to create louder, more carrying sound. The original device bodhrán disappeared from all but subsistence farming during the decades after the Great Famine, replaced by more modern equipment, though it did linger on in some places for another century. On account of similarity – and awareness and feasability of dual use – the name 'bodhrán' had come to be occasionally applied to locally-made tambourine copies in north Kerry by 1910 or earlier. In modern time, the tambourine became nationally visible again following its being facilitated by CCÉ and the fleadh, and its introduction to national theatre audiences by playwright John B. Keane in 1959. Subsequently it was adopted by composer Seán Ó Riada who played an instrument without its characteristic jingles, and did not call it tambourine, but 'bodhrán'. The re-naming was promoted by Keane as well, and caught the imagination within the traditional music revival scene, press reports showing that inside just a handful of years the Irish tambourine had become the bodhrán.

Waving the flag

Elements of the information in these pages have been known by many of those who have written about the bodhrán, more so with some, less so with others. The disparities among commentators have produced – variously – incomplete, confused or conflicting pedigrees for the drum, the result of both absence of information, and a driven need to believe in an historic Gaelic, pre-Gaelic or pre-Christian percussion. The latter idea is articulated by Mel Mercier when he says that Seán Ó Riada was perhaps more interested in this drum's 'distinctive Irishness'.[9] But wherever or however the bodhrán originated, and whichever term is used for it today, do not matter. The device is a frame drum, the form is a tambourine, the Irish type is a bodhrán. That it was once known as tambourine and is now known as bodhrán is indeed appropriate, not least on account of the fact that the word 'tambourine' has so many other independent meanings and international cultural connotations. The Irish bodhrán is a distinct instrument which may be generically a type of tambourine, but it is different to all other frame drums in how it is held, how it is played, what its role in music is, how it has been developed, and how it has come to be symbolically regarded.

"I went to University College Cork in 1987 to study music with a shiny new trumpet from my dad under my arm. I came home to Galway a fortnight later with a bodhrán in a bin bag, and my father nearly fainted. I had fortunately picked up the bodhrán bug in Cork and the instrument has gripped me ever since – a primal experience that can boom and excite, pacify and soothe"
Jim Higgins

▲ Colm Murphy, Cork 2022 [*Nutan*]

From marching Wren to sit-down music

It is not possible to say for sure if there was or was not an ancient, indigenous drum in Ireland, though evidence from other countries implies that it would be unlikely if there was not such an instrument type. And it is clear from numerous references in these pages that there was a largely-unacknowledged tambourine and improvised-tambourine drumming practice all through the 1800s and early 1900s.[10] Such as that has been, it was certainly of peripheral music significance. But in modern time, the information in these pages makes it clear that there have been two applications of an Irish frame drum: 1/ rurally, as the tambourine, with marching on the Wren, and, 2/ since the 1950s, as the bodhrán in largely-urban, classicised sit-down music. Once exclusively male in uptake, it is now also played by females, its players are of all ages, and it has a substantial professional life. The nature of the drum and its potential roles, styles and techniques have all progressed so immensely that in its new life it has moved too from just being an accompanying instrument to now also having solo-performance, 'break' potential.

Today's bodhrán has evolved inside Irish music in Ireland, and has developed unique performance skills since the 1960s in response to music fashions, player innovation, available technologies, and instrument development. These mark it as one of the newest instruments used in Irish music, a role in which it has been both controversial and thrilling, and it has enhanced, and at times propelled, the music's national and international appreciation and uptake. It has mediated percussive satisfaction and expression for both its players and for those passionate about its music. In artistic terms, the skills of its advanced performers now match the attention to finesse and subtlety which has been the hallmark of expert performance of melodic Irish music for some 900 years. And, not least, as well as being emblematic of music-making traditions in west Limerick and north Kerry, the bodhrán now remarkably shares with the harp and uilleann pipes symbolism of not only Irish music, but of Ireland itself.

NOTES TO CHAPTER 16

[1] The Mobile Music School, 2022.

[2] This, rather than to its (other) typically assumed meaning of 'irresponsible pursuit of uninhibited seeking after sensual pleasures and material goods', irreligious hedonism (Webster's 1971, 1620).

[3] *Kerryman* 1964, 1005 4.

[4] Kjeldsen 2000, 164.

[5] Fitzmaurice 2006, 128.

[6] McNamee 1992, 16 (opinion of David Bushe, Ulster Society r/e Orange music and drum traditions).

[7] This is the experience in other drumming forms, including in rock music, described, for instance, as 'becoming entranced' by Mickey Hart (Hart 1990, 62).

[8] Bones, however, are covered within it, and minstrels are mentioned in connection with them (Kjeldsen 2013, 107–8), as well as in the entry on banjo (Smith 2013, 56).

[9] *The Real Story of the Bodhrán*, film no. 2 on Ruairi Gleeson's Youtube channel, interview with Mel Mercier, @ 11'50".

[10] This element of likelihood is referenced where appropriate over the course of this book; see, for instance, pages v, x, 12, 121, 131, 135, 137, 141, 144, 148 and 206.

▲ Cathy Jordan with two of her band Dervish's members Michael Holmes (bouzouki) and Tom Morrow (fiddle) [Colin Gillen]

CHAPTER 17

A BODHRÁN PORTRAIT GALLERY

▲ Jacques Piraprez Nutan

▲ James Fraher

▲ Martin Gaffney

These concluding pages offer a selection of portraits of contemporary players as well as photographs from the archives. There are contributions from two photographers in particular – our commissioned camera-man Jacques Piraprez Nutan and James Fraher.

Jacques Piraprez Nutan

Jacques Piraprez Nutan was born in Belgium and studied art from a young age, influenced by major Belgian and French Dadaist and surrealist painters including his childhood neighbour René Magritte. Moving to Ireland in 1969, he went on to lecture at the National College of Art and Design, Dublin, and in Sligo, Waterford and Galway art schools. As a photo journalist he has published in the leading presses including *Time*, *Stern*, *National Geographic*, *New York Times* and *Geo*. He has made the west of Ireland his home, and Irish topography, people and music his life's work. A member of the Paris agency RAPHO, he has photographed the antiquities of Ireland for government agencies, and has published some twenty-one books of his work. Passionate about traditional music, he has had his photos grace album covers for leading artists including Sharon Shannon, Martin Hayes, Altan, Frankie Gavin, Peter Horan and Ben Lennon. He has exhibited in Ireland, Europe and the USA, and his work has earned him the major Benson and Hedges Gold and Pentax Gold international awards.

James Fraher

James Fraher's passion for creating portraits of musicians stems from playing and listening to music and a desire to meet its creators and performers. His work includes *The Blues is a Feeling, Voices and visions of African-American blues musicians* (1998), and he collaborated with Houston writer Roger Wood on *Down in Houston: Bayou City blues* (2003), and *Texas Zydeco* (2006). In Irish music he worked with Gregory Daly to produce *In Nearly Every House: Irish traditional musicians of north Connacht* (2020). His photographs have appeared on album covers and in publications and media including *Irish Arts Review*, *Irish America*, *Living blues*, *Rolling Stone*, *Chicago Tribune*, and in Martin Scorsese's *The Blues* series. He has co-produced recordings including Kevin Henry's *One's Own Place*, Johnny Henry's *One Out of the Fort*, and Colm O'Donnell's *Farewell to Evening Dances*. His photographs have been exhibited in museums and galleries in the USA, Ireland, Scotland, Italy and France, and his work will eventually be archived at The Irish Traditional Music Archive, Dublin.

Martin Gaffney FIDI

Multi-instrumentalist Martin Gaffney is a award-winning specialist in visual communications design who studied photography with Nutan in Sligo at the turn of the 1980s. He went on to found the Dublin studio Designworks in 1983, and was president of the Institute of Designers in Ireland (IDI) in 2004. From Killeshandra, County Cavan, he was grounded in traditional Irish music from childhood, and has been pivotal in the design of scores of traditional-music album sleeves and books, most recently Robert Harvey's unique *Feadail, The Whistling Tradition in Ireland*. A passionate performer, and a music teacher with CCÉ's Craobh Naithí in Dublin, he was CCE's national PRO from 2003 to 2008, and with them organised brand and PR workshops, as well as the design concept for the Cavan All-Ireland fleadhs in the mid 2000s. As an artist and designer, he is deeply interested in the synergy of design, photography and traditional Irish music culture.

▲ Niamh Fennell [EDI]

▲ Siobhán O'Donnell [*Nutan*]

▲ Charlie Byrne [*James Fraher*]

▲ Mel Mercier [*Nutan*]

Colm Murphy [*Nutan*]

17 A BODHRÁN PORTRAIT GALLERY

▲ Aimée Farrell Courtney [*Nutan*]

▲ Kevin Conneff with one of the experimental bodhrán forms skinned by Páiric McNeela [*Nutan*]

▲ Brian Fleming [Nutan]

"My bodhrán has an inscription on the inside: 'Bodhraíonn an ghléas seo faiscistí'. It's a nod to 'this machine kills fascists' on Woody Guthrie's guitar, only more nuanced, for it could be a jibe at those in the music who don't appreciate the virtues of this most traditional and versatile of Irish instruments. For me the bodhrán has been a kind of passport. Without it I'd be a refugee among traditional percussionists, but with it, I have an identity and something to share" **Brian Fleming**

17 A BODHRÁN PORTRAIT GALLERY

"Getting the bodhrán changed my life, and I am still finding new playing ideas. It is such a part of my body that if I ever had to stop playing it would be like losing an arm" *Johnny 'Ringo' MacDonagh*

▲ Johnny 'Ringo' McDonagh [*Nutan*]

▲ Tommy Hayes [*Nutan*]

"Like most instruments the bodhrán is very easy to play badly and has gained a disagreeable reputation for that reason, but it should be considered that there are melody players out there who have poor rhythmic sense too: without rhythm it's just a bunch of notes. The bodhrán in the hands of a skilled player who knows how to keep a groove going, and has a knowledge of the melodic patterns of traditional Irish music, has the power to elevate the mundane to a thrilling level." **Tommy Hayes**

"When I got my first bodhrán in 1991 from Seamus O'Kane, little did I think the remarkable journey it would take me on. The access it would give me to the most incredible musical experiences. The sheer joy I would feel losing myself in the beat of the bodhrán. It was to become my heartbeat outside my body"
Cathy Jordan

▲ Cathy Jordan [*Nutan*]

▲ Gino Lupari [*Nutan*]

▲ John Joe Kelly [*Nutan*]

▲ Svend Kjeldsen [*Nutan*]

▲ Sandra Joyce [*Nutan*]

▲ Dónal Lunny [*Nutan*]

▲ Jack Cooley [Nutan]

▲ Donnchadh Gough, Danú [*Frankie Lloyd*]

▲ Black Isle, Scotland bodhrán maker Iain Campbell, 2002 [*EDI*]

▲ Cormac Byrne at the Royal Albert Hall, London, April 2023 [*Natalie Shaw*]

"The first player I heard was the late Ned Farrell of Prosperous, Co Kildare back in 1966. He was at the heart of the Comhaltas Sessions in Pat Dowling's pub – thats where Dónal Lunny and I first encountered Liam Óg Ó Flynn. Dónal got me started on the drum when Planxty kicked off in 1972. For a while I used a beater, but for the past thirty years I've used the forefinger of my right hand – skin on skin. Singing a capella to the beat of the drum has become part of my work"
Christy Moore

▲ Christy Moore playing with the hand
[*Adam Sherwood*]

▲ Cara Wildman, USA [*Andrew Simmons*]

▲ Colm Phelan, Portlaoise, member of the band Goitse. The inaugural 'World Bodhran' champion in 2006, he was a Junior winner at the All-Ireland fleadh in that year and in 2005 [*Courtesy of AMG; photo by Eddie Kavanagh*]

▲ Robbie Harris [Christian Staunton]

"As a young fella I spent hours tapping rhythms on any surface and played knitting needles on biscuit tins. I had drumsticks at six, and at thirteen was drumming with a pipe band. Then I got a bodhrán and was drawn to its simplicity and complexity, a hypnotic beat that draws people in, but whether accompanying a fiddle or driving a song has endless expression and creativity if you have a strong passion for the music and its culture" **Robbie Harris**

▲ Polish bodhrán player Patrycja Betley [*EDI*]

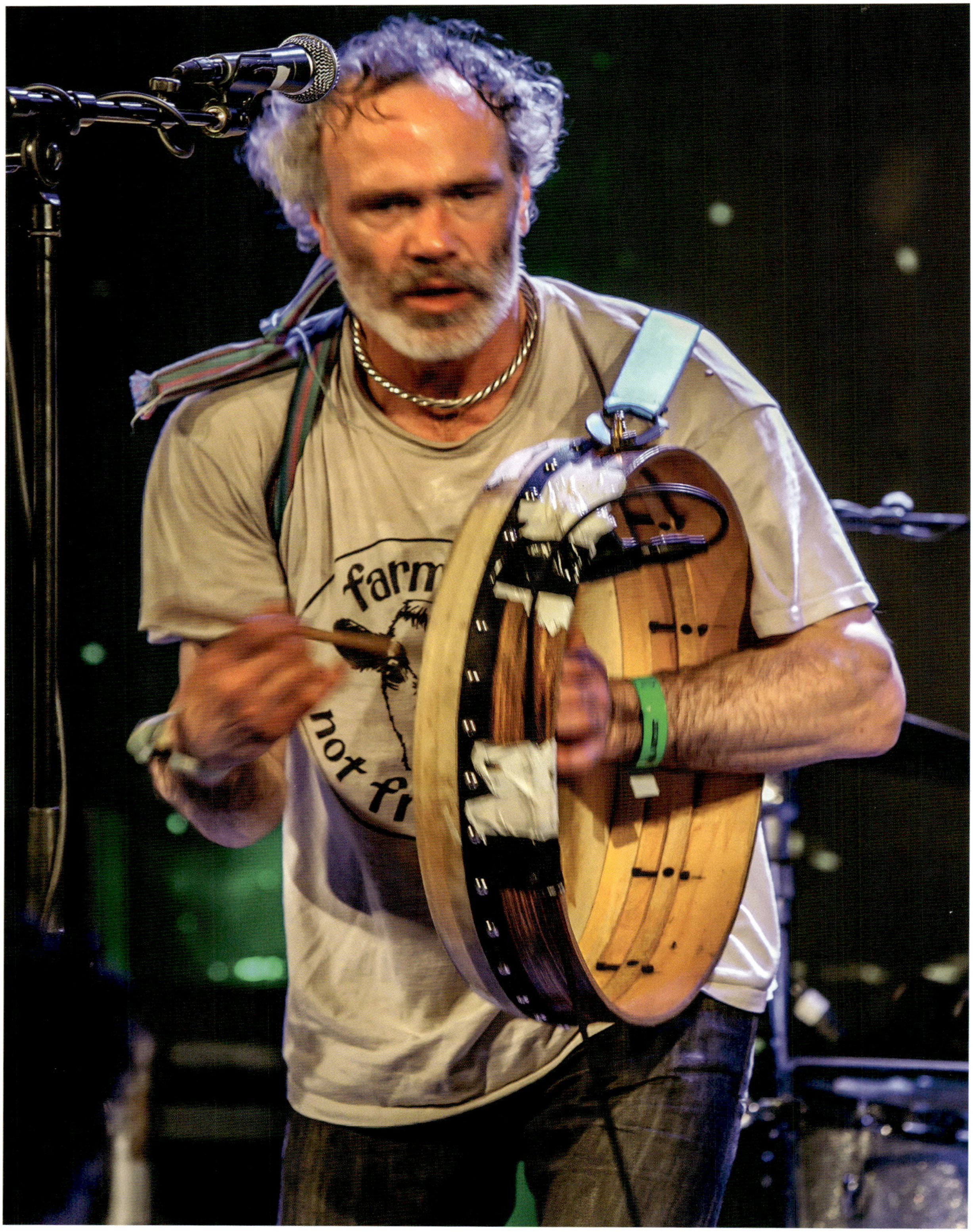

17 A BODHRÁN PORTRAIT GALLERY

▲ Sculpture at Lisdoonvarna, County Clare by Cliodhna Cussen [*Courtesy of Clare County Council (EDI)*]

◀ Ronan Ó Snodaigh of Kila at Mountshannon Traditional Festival, 2015 [*Debra Reschoff Ahearn, Dreamtime.com © Debra Reschoff Ahearn | 246275392 Dreamtime.com*]

APPENDIX 1.
The Eugene O'Curry lectures: notes on the timpan

Lecture XXXI (31)

1/ From Imtheacht na Trom Dhaimhe, or the Adventures of the Great Bardic Company:

Marbhan requested a music performance from Seanchan and his company, vocal music *(Cronan)* and instrumental. One of the musical company was Casamel the Cruitire, who was asked which of them was the first invented, the *Cruit* or the *Timpan?* Out of this it emerges that a woman Canoclach Mhor had once been lulled to sleep by the music of the wind sounding the exposed fine sinews of a decayed whale on a beach, which led to her husband Cuil constructing a *Cruit* from wood and stringing it with whale sinews, the first harp.[1]

2/ Marbhan then recounts a tale of a son of Noah who brought a *Timpan* into the ark, which was greatly appreciated. After the deluge Noah was reluctant to part with it until a bounty had been paid in the form of the instrument being henceforth named after him: Noah, Timpan of the saints.[2]

Lecture XXXII (32)

3/ From the tale *Iubhar Mic Aingis*, a tale of great antiquity, from *The book of Leinster*, c. AD 234: Eoghan, the son of Oillioll and Lughaidh Mac Con, his stepbrother, set out to pay a visit to Art, the son of Con [monarch of Erinn], their mother's brother … as they were passing over the river Maigh [at Caherass in the County of Limerick], they heard music in a yew tree over the cataract, [and saw a little man playing there]. After that they returned back to Oillioll with him … he was a little man, with three strings in his *Timpan* … he played for them the crying tune *(Goltraighe)*, and he put them to crying and lamenting and tear-shedding, and he was requested to desist from it. And then he played the laughing tune *(Geantraighe)*, till they laughed with mouths so wide open that all but their lungs were visible. He then played the sleeping tune *(Suantraighe)* for them, until they were cast into a sleep from that hour till the same hour next day.[3]

4/ A modern reference, c. 1680 shows how late the timpan persisted, a figurative reference mentioned in a poem by Eoghan O'Donnghaile:

> I perceive in the middle of thy Timpan
> Small their power; bitter their sound;

Even so late as the close of the seventeenth century, the *Timpan*, or *Tympanum*, was known in this country as a stringed instrument and not by any means as a drum instrument of any kind.[4]

5/ In the Brehon Laws *Timpan* is mentioned in conjunction with *Cruit*, as the only species of music; that is, it is the only profession of music which is entitled to be ennobled … Here again we have the *Cruit*, or harp proper, and the Timpan as a species of harp, placed in such a relative position as to render it difficult to distinguish between them, although there is certainly a marked distinction.[5]

Lecture XXXVI (36)

The biggest volume of information on the timpan is given in Chapter 36, fifteen pages in all (351–66), the data presented in tales, descriptions and extracts from the Brehon Laws.

6/ The next place in which I meet the word *Timpan* is in the free translation of the *Book of Exodus* in the *Great Book of Dun Doighre*, where we are told … the assembly of the women around … Mirian the daughter of Amram and sister of Moses, and she playing a *Timpan*. The following reference clearly indicates not the Irish stringed timpan, but the timbrel, a hand drum mentioned often in the Bible:

> So Mary the prophetess, the sister of Aaron, took a timbrel in her hand, and all the women went forth after her with timbrels and with dances

… at the present day [that] would mean a tambourine or some such instrument, though it is certain that such was not the instrument which the Irish translator had in view.

7/ The word Timpan next occurs in the ancient historic tale of the *Battle of Magh Lena* (p. 50) where Eoghan Mór, king of Munster in the second century, on his return from Spain to the Island of Cregraidhe in Berehaven, is received by the lady Eadan, whom he addresses with the following words '… dost thou still survive in this island, where we were once before?' Eadan answers: 'Yes; the splendid chess-board still is here, on which we played on the noble couch, the pleasant sunny chamber also remains, Where the sweet-stringed *Timpan* was heard'.

8/ In the tale of the *Loinges Mac Duil Dermaid*, or the *Exile of the Sons of Duil Dermaid*, Cuchulain landed upon the island and came to a house with pillars of *Findruine*, or white bronze, in which he saw three times fifty couches, with a chessboard (Fidchell). A draught-board (Brandub) and a *Timpan* hung up over each of them but the particular nature of the *Timpan* is not described.

9/ Another reference is in *Agallamh na Seanorach*, or *Dialogue of the Ancient Men*… In which Cailte is asked by the King of Munster near Cashel why an ancient earthen fort was called *Lis an Bhanntrachta*, or the *Mansion of the Ladies*. The women there had a source of pleasure and delight beyond any other known company of ladies, namely a *Timpan*, which was played by the three daughters of the king of Ui Ceinselaigh (a district in the present county of Wexford) … And this … was the description of the *Timpan*. It had its *Lethrind* (other treble strings) of silver, and its pins (or keys) of gold, and its (bass) strings of *Findruine* (or white bronze).[6]

10/ Another short but curious description of *Timpan* is found in the ancient tale of the *Forbais*, or *Siege of Dromdamhghaire*, now Cnoc Luinge or Knocklong in the south east corner of the County of Limerick.[7] In it, Cormac was accustomed to shut himself up in a sacred chamber for the purpose of studying the laws and the wisest mode of administering them … He described an aisling-style, spiritual meeting in verse form, including the verse

> He held a silver Timpan in his hand
> Of red gold were the strings of that Timpan
> Sweeter than all music under heaven
> Were the strings of that Timpan.

We may consider that we have arrived at a clear determination of the hitherto undecided difference between the Cruit, or harp, and the Timpan, as well as of the latter being a stringed instrument, and not a drum, such as the name would imply. And this description will go far also to sustain our former view of the misnomers of the Welsh Telyn and Cruth, as there can now be little doubt that our Cruit is their Telyn, and our Timpan their Cruth.

One short reference more to the character of the Timpan; and the difference between that instrument and the *Cruit* or harp, and I have done with the subject. In a vellum MS in TCD, on the Brehon Laws there is a 'curious note', standing by itself, and unconnected with any other subject.

11/ There are three qualities that give distinction to a *Cruit* (or Harp), namely, the Crying Mode, the Laughing Mode, and the Sleeping Mode. The Timpanist has a wand, and hair, and doubling (or repetition). The harper has exclusive harping at this day against these. The Timpanist has exclusive timpaning (or *Timpan* playing) at this day against these.

First it [this] shows distinctly that the Cruit was of a very different and of a higher order than the Timpan … And secondly, it proves beyond all controversy that the *Timpan*, like that described by king Cormac, was played with a wand and hair, or, in other words, with a bow. It is also seen from the passage that both the harp and the *timpan* were common to the same performer.[8] Further deductions as regards dating are made from the above-quoted note:

12/ The MS in which this note was found was transcribed on the brink of *Loch Senain*, or St Senan's lake, in the year 1509 by Edmund O'Deórain. The lake had its name from the circumstances of St Senan, the founder of the churches and round tower of Scattery island *(Inis Cathargh)*, near Kilrush, in the lower Shannon, having been born there about the year 540. This lake is well known to me. It lies about five miles to the east of the town of Kilrush in the County of Clare; and the ruins of an ancient church and oratory still mark the spot on which St Senan was born; they are situated on the north side of the lake, near the east end. This book, then, having been compiled in the year 1509, the note on the harp and *Timpan* must have been copied from an older book, or written by the scribe himself for the first time, that year. In either case it is plain that at this time, or possibly long before, the playing on the harp and on the *Timpan* had become distinct professions, notwithstanding that, as a matter of course, any person might play both instruments, though [be] the professor of but one. From many sources we have authority to believe that the *Timpan* came down concurrently with the harp to the close of the seventeenth century; but what became of it then, or whether it merged into our present fiddle, I am quite at a loss to know. We find the harp, *Timpan*, and fiddle, mentioned in the ancient poem on the fair of Carman … and we have them again mentioned in Eugene O'Donnelly's poems about the year 1680; but from that time down, I am not certain of having met with any reference whatsoever to the *Timpan*. A passage from the Brehon Laws which provides for wounds and compensation also mentions timpan:[9]

13/ If the top of his finger, from the root of the nail, or above the black, has been cut off a person, he is entitled to compensation for his [injured body] and a fine [for his outraged] honour, in proportion to the severity of the wound. If the blood has been drawn while cutting his nail off, he is entitled to the fine for blood-shedding for it. If it be from the black [circle] out that his nail has been taken off him, he is entitled to the same fine as for a white [or bloodless] blow; and if he be a Timpanist then there is a quill [or feather] nail for him besides, by way of restitution.[10] This last reference to the *Timpan* so plainly implies its character, that nothing more need be said upon the subject. A question, however, for the first time arises out of the above extract from the Brehon Laws, and it is this: was the quill really used as a substitute for the bow, or, as we have it in this law, was it used as a substitute for the nail of the finger, or for the thumb perhaps? It is not easy to determine this question with certainty but it may easily be conceived as affording an explanation of how the two extra strings of the instrument now called *Cruit* by the Welsh were played. We may imagine the *Timpan* in fact to have been a kind of fiddle, played with a bow, but with two additional deeper strings, struck with the thumb or thumb-nail, so that if that nail were injured, it would be necessary to supply it with an artificial one.

14/ It is remarkable too … how constantly we find the *Cruit* and the *Timpan* accompanying each other, and that this is no modern confusion of the one with the other may be seen from a passage of the *Tochmarc Emire*, or courtship of the lady Emir … r/e the splendour of the palace of the Royal Branch of the kings of Ulster at Emania, in the time of king *Conchobhar Mac Nessa*… 'Great and numerous were the assemblies of that royal house; and of admirable performers, in gymnastics; and in singing; and in playing; for gymnasts contended; and poets sang; and Harpers and Timpanists played there.'[11]

15/ Of the relative power and compass of the *Timpan* and *Cruit* we have a curious instance in the Book of Lismore, in … the *Agallamh na Seanorach*, or Dialogue of the Old Men. The outcome of this makes it clear that on November Eve … The Tuatha Dé Danann came to see the hurling; and there was brought to them a chess *(Fitceall)* for every six of them; and draughts *(Bronnaib)* for every five; and a *Timpan* for every ten; and a Cruit for every hundred; and a vigorous, accomplished tube-player *(Cuisleannach)* for every nine.[12] According to the scale of value or power suggested in this account, it will be seen that the *Cruit* was considered to have that of the *Timpan*, or, in other words, that one *Cruit* was deemed equal to ten Timpans … the very superior place which the *Cruit* held above the *Timpan*...[13]

16/ A–Z list of the professional performers on the Gaelic instruments as given by O'Curry, including those on the timpan:

Buinnire, who performed on the *Buinne*, some sort of tube, possibly flute or fife or clarionet kind.

Cnaimh-fhear, bone man, mentioned in the Fair of Carman, unknown type of instrument.

Cornair, great horn blower. The *Cornaire* has a place with the *Buinnire Cruitire* or harper, in a special place in the Banqueting Hall of Tara, accompanied by the *Timpanach*, or *Timpan* player.[14]

Cuisleannach, playing the *Cuisleanna Ciúil*, musical tubes; these were grouped with the *Cruitire* and the *Timpanach* in playing Congal Claen, the prince of Ulster, to sleep on the eve of the battle of Magh Rath.

Fedánach, performer on the *Fedan*, a shrill pipe or whistle. *Fead* is still the common word for a whistle with the mouth; and *Feadan* is still the name for any thin tube or pipe … among the lower class of musicians mentioned in the Brehon Laws, as attending great fairs and assemblies.

Fer-cengail, man of ties, bonds or bindings, only mentioned in the Fair of Carman, maybe not a musician;

Graice (literally croakers), who are otherwise called *Coirne*, or horn players, and who … were not entitled to any legal recognition of their profession in the Brehon Laws.

Pipaire, piper, in the Brehon Laws among the lower class of artists, ranking with the mechanics. The piper and fiddler are referred to in the fair of Carman. *Ergolan* and *Scalfartach* are names of a piper preserved in some of our latter-day glossaries; but, as both words imply loud noise, they must apply to that species of pipes which we know at present as the Highland Pipes of Scotland.

Stocaire, performer on the *Stoc*, or short curved horn or speaking trumpet, the ancient *Buccina*.

Sturganaidhe, performer on the *Sturgan*, or Lituus of the ancients

Timpanach or Timpan-player.[14]

Appendix 2. Music-professionalism references in manuscripts

[AU – Annals of Ulster; AFM – Annals of the Four Masters; AC – Annals of Connacht] Mention in manuscripts of musicians, professors of music, and deaths of musicians indicate a status for melodic music in ancient Ireland:

AD 630: The two sons of Aedh Slaine were slain by Conall, son of Suibhne, at Loch Trethin, at Freamhain, namely, Congal, chief of Breagh, ancestor of the Ui Conaing, and Ailill Cruitire, i.e. the Harper, ancestor of the Sil Dluthaigh (AFM L1).

AD 634: The killing of two sons of Aed Sláine by Conall son of Suibne at Loch Treitni opposite Fremainn, i.e. Congal king of Brega, and Ailill the Harper, ancestor of Síl Dlúthaig (AU U634.1).

AD 1110: Bran ua Bruic, elder of Iarmumu, Gilla Pátraic ua Duibrátha, lector of Cell dá Lua, and sage of Mumu, Ferdomnach the blind, lector of Cell Dara, i.e. a master of harping, died (AU U1110.11).

AD 1168: Amhlaeibh Mac Innaighneorach, chief ollamh of Ireland in harp-playing, died (AFM L2).

AD 1369: John Mac Egan, and Gilbert O'Bardan, two accomplished young harpers of Conmaicne, died.

AD 1357: Donslevy Mac Caroll, a noble master of music and melody, the best of his time, died.
AD 1360: Gilla-na-naev O'Conmhaigh, chief professor of music in Thomond, died.
AD 1361: Magrath O'Finnaghty, chief musician and tympanist to the Sil-Murray, died. (AFM L3).
AD 1379: William, the son of Gilla-Caech Mac Carroll, the most eminent of the Irish in music, died.
AD 1396: Matthew O'Luinin, Erenagh of Arda, a man of various professions, and skilled in history, poetry, music, and general literature, died.
AD 1399: Boethius Mac Egan, a man extensively skilled in the Fenechus law, and in music, and who had kept a celebrated house of hospitality … died.
AD 1404: Gilla-Duivin Mac Curtin, ollav of Thomond in music, died.
AD 1429: Matthew, the son of Thomas O'Cuirnin, ollav of Breifny, and universally learned in history and music, died in his own house (AFM 4).
AD 1469: Ruaidri son of Donnchad son of Eogan Oc O Dalaig, the most musical-handed harpist in all Ireland, died. (AC 7).
AD 1490: John Oge, the son of John More of Ilay, was treacherously slain by Dermot Mac Carbry, an Ultonian harper, who was one of his own servants … Mac Carbry was quartered for this crime.
AD 1490: Finn O'Haughluinn, Chief Tympanist of Ireland, died . (AFM 4).
AD 1512: Niall, the son of Con … Lord of Trian-Congail … a successful and triumphant man, who had not paid tribute to the Clann-Neill or Clann-Daly, or to the deputy of the king of England, a man of very long prosperity and life, and a man well skilled in the sciences, both of history, poetry, and music, died on 11th of April (AFM 5).

Appendix 3.
Verses written by Newcastle West poet Michael Hartnett to welcome Irish president Paddy Hillery to Templeglantine to present Glór na nGael awards on 29 May 1977.
[*Courtesy Tadhg Ó Maolcatha*]

Leis an ndán álainn seo chuir an file cáiliúil Mícheál Ó h-Airtnéide, fáilte roimh Uachtarán na h-Éireann, Pádraig Ó h-Irghile go Teampall a' Ghleanntáin chun duaiseanna Ghlór na nGael a bronnadh ar an 29ú lá Bealtaine 1977.

Appendix 4.
Ó Súilleabháin, Mícheál: 'Contemporary developments in bodhrán performance technique', in Webber, N. (Ed.) Studies in traditional music and Dance V & II, p. 58. London: 1983.

Contemporary Developments in Bodhrán Performance Technique

OLD v NEW

SOCIAL FACTORS:

1. Ritual usage — Session/Concert hall/competition/media
2. Exclusively rural — Rural and urban
3. Regional styles — Breakdown of regional styles
4. Exclusively male — Mostly male, occasionally female
5. Outdoor — Indoor
6. Exclusively amateur — Occasionally professional
7. Skin tray/sieve as well as drum — Drum only
8. Flamboyant personality — Flamboyance absent

MORPHOLOGY:

9. Jingles present occasionally — Jingles rarely present
10. 'Cross bar' of various types — Cross bar' sometimes omitted
11. Variety of construction methods — Construction methods modernised in some cases
12. Single skin tacked on — Some experimentation
13. Hand carved stick — Stick sometimes 'turned'

PERFORMANCE

14. Variety of styles using hand or stick — Stick used only
15. Played while standing or walking — Played while sitting
16. Skin and rim sometimes alternated as playing surfaces — Playing directly on rim avoided
17. Left hand not used in sound production — Left hand used to dampen and to alter skin tension
18. Constant 'non-pitch' sound — 'Approximate pitch' introduced including melodic contour
19. 'Follow the tune' approach — Increased tendency towards independent rhythmic patterns
20. Seen as an accompanying instrument — Emergence of bodhrán solo
21. 'Thumb roll' used in some styles — 'Thumb roll' not used
22. Level dynamic — Dynamic variation
23. Non-rehearsed improvisation — Some pre-arranged synchronisation
24. 'Acoustic' sound — PA system common

Ó Súilleabháin, Mícheál. 1983. 'Contemporary Developments in Bodhrán Performance Technique', p.58 in Webber, N. (ed.) Studies in Traditional Music and Dance *V & II*, London 1983

[Permission courtesy of Helen Phelan]

Appendix 5.
Caoimhín Ó Danachair / Kevin Danaher, biography
Caoimhín Ó Danachair (1913–2002) was a pioneer of Irish ethnological studies. Born at Athea, County Limerick, he was educated there and in Limerick city, and studied archaeology at UCD. At twenty-one he collected oral folklore of his home area for the Irish Folklore Institute. From 1948 to 1952 in his field work he recorded singers, musicians and storytellers – in particular uilleann piper Johnny Doran in 1947 – as well as documenting the Wren in photographs. A lecturer at the Department of Irish Folklore at UCD from its inception in 1971, his prolific writing includes key journal articles regarding the bodhrán, and, contextually for music, numerous books on rural folklife.

Appendix 6.
Video, film and online links
rte.ie/archives/2016/1214/838897-wrenboys-and-bodhrán-making/
Sonny Canavan and John (Jack) Duggan interviewed by Ted Nealon talk on the Wren and making bodhráns on RTÉ's *Cross Country*, broadcast on 20 December 1966. Available on the RTÉ archives. John Duggan, born 1887, played music first on the Wren *c.* 1899 at the age of twelve, on the concertina, and was still going out on it in 1966 at the age of seventy-nine. A bodhrán maker himself, on making the bodhrán he said, 'You look out for a wooden sieve for sievin' oats or gravel … you'd have a good firm rim'.
rte.ie/archives/2017/0130/848715-bodhrán-maker-sonny-canavan/

Eleven years later Sonny Canavan, Dirha west, Listowel, County Kerry (1977) interviewed by Brendan O'Brien on RTÉ's *Newsround*, broadcast on 13 January 1977. In this, Canavan is seen with a purpose-made bodhrán shell, made from bent plywood, and talks to John B. Keane for whose play *Sive* he made the tambourine; Keane sings a verse from the play's song and accompanies himself on the drum.
Bodhrán, the film by Tom Hayes, accessed on vimeo.com/727710094. It is the second of two films on this link, Le Reve Celtique AB392 / AB535 Bodhrán MV6113. In it the bodhrán is observed at Puck Fair, Killorglin, and drums being made from scratch by Joe O'Sullivan of Carrigkerry who uses a purpose-made rim, and at that time was the third generation making the drums. The bodhrán is observed out on the Wren where four of them are played along with accordion, fiddles, flute and banjo; rim shots are a feature of the exuberant playing to very fast music, with set dancing. The drum is filmed being played too at the All-Ireland fleadh, where there is one female player, and at the Fleadh Nua in Dublin in the same year. The playing is mostly by adult men, and involves a strong, solid stick-struck beat, with crowd-thrilling showmanship by Jim Sheehy, and there are numerous shots of mass playing of the drum in the Wren-boys competition. Occasional bodhráns have jingles, but most have not.

Video of a full set of tunes with a group of older male musicians in *O'Connor's* pub, Doolin, 1970s: oconnorspubdoolin/videos/2049910852006190

14th Annual World Creole Music Festival in Dominica, 2 December 2010: discoverdominica.com.

Italian tamburello
Gran Bal Trad Vialfrè 2017 Corso tamburello marchigiano. Tamburello demonstration from the Marche region of Italy – Ancona, Macerata and Fermo provinces – youtube.com/watch?v=GPi11-0XSnU&t=84s
Tamburello and tambourine website: http://www.nscottrobinson.com/gallery/tamburello.php; also http://www.rhythmweb.com/andrea/

Bubny, Ukrainian frame drum, 2020. First video instruction on playing a traditional instrument: youtube.com/watch?v=B7jigm5-feA
The village of Gogolevo, Velykobagachansky district.
Leiko Victor Nikolaevich, born in 1949 (tambourine); Ladyvir Vladimir Alekseevich, born in 1963 (accordion).

ITMA video references and DVDs (access is in-house only).
The REAL Story of the Bodhrán, a four-part film series by Ruairi Glasheen. Among the numerous bodhrán videos on YouTube, a remarkably comprehensive independent production. (v=YjMEOzfDDBY).

ITMA video (in-house access)
• 4.2.5LX 2508 News: Fleadh an Dreolín, Newcastle West, County Limerick, 1963. Brian MacMahon on bodhrán and Wrenboys competition.
• 4.2.697D00049 The west Clare Wren, rec. Dec. 1979: Wrenboys (Kilbaha, Couty Clare).
• 5.12.302D01100 Newsbeat, tx 30, Apr. 1970: Sonny Canavan (Kerry). Speech and demonstration: making bodhráns. Reporter Cathal O'Shannon.
• 5.12.402D01107 Newsround, tx 13, Feb. 1977; Sonny Canavan, J.B. Keane, etc. (Kerry). Speech, demonstration, music, making bodhráns etc. Reporter Brendan O'Brien.

Appendix 7. Folklore: *The Schools' Collection*

Bailiúchán na Scol – The Schools' Collection was a scheme run between 1937 and 1939 by the Irish Folklore Commission, under the direction of Séamus Ó Duilearga and Seán Ó Súilleabháin, in collaboration with the Department of Education and the Irish National Teachers' Organisation. A quite astonishing project in the new 26-county state, it was driven by the political need and compulsion to identify, categorise and assemble elements of lived and recalled Irish cultural heritage in the wake of extraction from the previous provincial colonial hegemony.

More than 50,000 schoolchildren were involved, in 5,000 schools of the then Irish Free State. These were asked to collect folklore from their parents, grandparents and neighbours in their home districts, including oral history, topographical information, folktales and legends, riddles and proverbs, games and pastimes, trades and crafts.[15] Their 288,000 original pages of data were written up in standard school jotters in the contributors' first languages, both Irish and English as appropriate, and overall the scheme produced more than half a million manuscript pages, all of which are now indexed and bound in a total of 1,128 volumes. In these, each school has a title page with the name of the school, the parish, the barony, the county and the teacher. Some 40,000 of the original copybooks are stored at the National Folklore Collection, and by 2022 the bulk of the materials had been digitised and made available for consultation on-line, in both original hand-written formats and as an unrestricted, rapid-response digital text catalogue. This resource is a privileged window onto the nineteenth century, as it involves the earlier memories of the parents and others who were interviewed, these dating to, roughly, the late 1890s. In this way it is a hidden voice of rural people, containing as it does the material which does not appear in printed histories. It is complementary to newspaper and other writing of the last couple of hundred years, and equivalent in an inverted-timescale manner to the ancient lore which was drawn upon by Eugene O'Curry and others from the far side of the rise of the printed word, the manuscript era. For this study it was accessed in February 2022, and digital searches made for major key terms 'bodhrán', 'tambourine' and 'winnow'.

The Schools' Collection information is clear about distinguishing between the bodhrán as a device, and the tambourine as a drum. It provides information on the device bodhrán for the earlier decades of the twentieth century, and on the casual, ubiquitous making and application of the tambourine. This information corroborates speculation about the tambourine being played as a kind of undercurrent to life in rural Ireland in the later 1800s into the 1900s, something which undoubtedly was the foundation for the rise in popularity of the frame drum after the 1950s. While deeper research is required on the time-line of music on the Wren, nevertheless it is clear that this ritual has had at least a century of association with the tambourine, and that the drum gradually accrued its more melodic identity as the twentieth century progressed.

Appendix 8. Gerald Griffin: extract from *The Collegians*, 1829

The earliest account of the tambourine in mumming, such as the Wren, indicates that not much has changed in almost two centuries, as Gerald Griffin's 1829 *The Collegians* indicates. Remarkable and exceptional in this quotation is the detail of how one lad improvises the tambourine on an actual bodhrán, called here a 'dildorn', something considered important enough for the writer himself to explain in a footnote:

On a sudden, as they approached an angle in the road, the attention of our loiterers was caught by sounds of boisterous mirth and rustic harmony. In a few seconds, on reaching the turn, they beheld the persons from whom the noise (for we dare not call it music) proceeded. A number of young peasants, dressed out in mumming masquerade with their coats off, their waistcoats turned the wrong side outward, their hats, shoulders, and knees, decorated with gay ribbands (borrowed for the occasion from their fair friends), their faces streaked with paint of various colours, and their waists encircled with shawls and sashes, procured most probably from the same tender quarter. Many of them held in their hands long poles with handkerchieves fluttering at the top, and forming a double file on either side of half a dozen persons, who composed the band, and whose attire was no less gaudy than that of their companions. One held a piccolo, another a fiddle, another a bagpipe. A fourth made a dildorn* serve for a tambourine, and a fifth was beating with a pair of spindles on the bottom of an inverted tin can, while imitated with much drollery, the important strut and swagger of the military Kettle-drum. Behind, and on each side, were a number of boys and girls, who, by their shrill clamour, made the discord, that prevailed among the musicians, somewhat less intolerable. Every face was bright with health and gayety, and not a few were handsome …The musicians struck up a jig, and one of the young men, dragging out of the crowd, with both hands, a bashful and and unwilling country girl, began to time the music with a rapid movement of heel and toe, which have rough grace of its own, and harmonised well with the vigorous and rough-hewn exterior of the peasant … *A vessel used in winnowing wheat, made of sheepskin stretched over a hoop.[16]

[New York: J.J. Harper, 1829]

Appendix 9. *The Kerryman*, 1944 Report on the Wren and tambourine in west Limerick

The Kerryman
All the news of interest
TRALEE, SATURDAY, JANUARY 1, 1944.

By "The Rambler"

SEASONAL COMMENTARY ON THE WREN, 1944 by Sean Coughlin a.k.a. 'The Rambler'

And then, of course we had St. Stephen's Day, when men and boys rallied forth to pay tribute to the "King of Birds", and solicit subscriptions from all and sundry in honour of the occasion.

In many parts of the country they call it "Ran's" Day, and the more enterprising of the "ran-boys" still capture and display on the time-honoured holly-bush corpses of the harmless little bird. Custom has even handed down an old song in honour of the bird.

I'm sure they seldom trouble to capture the "wren" nowadays, but the song still persists and the pennies are still collected until they mount up to shillings and pounds and wind up in an all-night "Wren" party with a half-barrel or two of porter and the free-for-all dance on the mud floor of a big kitchen.

HECTIC PARTIES
Of course these festive occasions are not merely as numerous as they used to be in the countryside. In these enlightened days the young folk, even in the remoter rural parts, prefer the modern ballroom, in which there is no place for the "half-set" or the "jig" or the more robust strains of the old-fashioned melodeon. But coming bac to my original idea, I was pleased to observe the "wran boys" were as numerous as ever this year.

They turned out at all ages, from advanced old-age pensioners to little mites who evidently had just acquired the useful art of walking. They were attired in every conceivable make or colour of dress from cast-off fashionable ladies' frocks to discarded undergarments.

They utilised all makes and shapes of musical instruments and availed, in fact, of anything and everything that emitted noise. Some of the musicians were skilled artists and others just succeeded in making sounds that were anything but pleasing to the ear. But we tolerated them all and smiled charitably, even when they all but threatened to break in our front door in their efforts to put up the collection of something or anything for the "wran". It's an old Irish custom and who amongst us would want to end it?

MERRY PARTY
I was myself fortunate on Sunday to come into direct contact with a big bunch of "Wran boys" who, I was told hailed all the way from little known and remote Knockanare, somewhere round the Limerick-Kerry border.

The scene was a wayside inn at a picturesque spot called the "Old Mill", a few miles from Newcastlewest, on the road to Athea. There were at least eleven of the "boys", some of whom were not quite so young. The Party included a smallish old violinist, who gave us quite a good rendering of many old-time Irish airs, while one of the younger lads treated us to some popular native ballads and a lively exhibition of step-dancing. Two old-timers, with the stamp of the years marked indelibly on their weather-beaten countenances, looked on with evident enjoyment on the scene that may well have recalled to their fading minds memories of days that were filled with the glory of enthusiasm of youth.

"TOM TOMS"
But the real highlight of the party were the tamborine players who pounded away on their home-made drum-like instruments that sounded something like the terrorising "tom-toms" used by the natives of Africa on occasion of festivity or war.

The tamborine, by the way, is one of the most essential parts of the make-up of the true "wran" party. It reminds one of a sort of kettle-drum with only one side made of well-seasoned boat skin. The skins are generally "acquired": off adult goats, begged, borrowed or stolen from neighbours a month of two before Christmas. This custom, no doubt, accounts for the mysterious disappearance of a number of these useful animals around November.

It is hard luck on the unfortunate goats, but the tamborines have to be provided somehow. When played by an expert with a double-sided drumstick the instrument is capable of producing an alarming volume of sound that its not too unlike distant thunder or heavy gunfire.

But the rhythm is nearly always perfect, and a good tamborine player is the pride of any "wran" party. The boys from Knockanare had no less than three good "tamborinists", and as they departed into the darkness of the road that leads to Carrig we could still hear the rumble of their nerve-shattering "tom-toms."

Kerryman, 1944 0101 7
By The Rambler

Appendix 10. The '78' recording discs

John Reynolds, with Tom Morrison and Piano Accompaniment Ed. Gegan [Geoghegan]. Flute and Tambourine:

1927: A: 'The Dunmore Lasses' (reel). B: 'The Sweet Flowers of Milltown' (barndance), 'The Boys From Knock'.

1928: A: 'Indian on the Rock', 'The Jolly Plowboy', 'The Fox Chase'. B: 'The Tenpenny Bit' (jigs).

1928: A: 'The Connaught Reel', 'The Shepherd's Daughter'. B: 'Maggie in the Woods' (polkas).

1929 & 1946: A: 'The Boys from Galway'. B: 'The Holy Land', 'The Star of Kilkenny' (reels).

1929 & 1946: A: 'The Roscommon Reel'. B: 'The London Clog' (Irish hornpipe).

Packie Dolan's Melody Boys, with violin, flute, piano and tambourine:

1928: A: 'The Steampacket', 'The Flogging' (reels). B: 'First of May'.

1928: A: 'Royal Charley' (old-time set tune)' B: 'The Windy Gap' (reel).

1928: A: 'The Lady of the House' (reel). B: 'One, Two, Three'.

Patrick Carberry with Michael Grogan – Accordion and Irish Tambourine:

1946: 'Joy of My Life'/'Banks of Lough Gowna' (jigs) and 'Green Groves of Erin'/ 'Sligo Maid' (reels).

Appendix 11. Transcription extract from Seán Ó Riada's *Our Musical Heritage* radio essay series broadcast on Radio Éireann from 7 July to 13 October 1962

Now, I think that our native drum, the bodhrán or tambourine, whose history goes back well into pre-Christian times, would be very suitable. And to provide variety with the bodhrán, since variety is the keynote, the bones, which are played traditionally as castanets. The bodhrán is a drum measuring from – well, some of them are fifteen inches in diameter, up to, say, two and a half feet in diameter, resembling the tambourine. It consists of a shallow wooden cylinder, usually not more than three or four inches deep – usually, in fact, the frame of a sieve – and across one side of which is stretched the drum head. The drum head is generally of cured goat-skin, or dog skin, although sheepskin has been occasionally used.

It probably goes back at least to the Bronze Age, and possibly earlier, and it's still quite common in various parts of the country, mostly along the western sea-board, although it used to be played in county Wicklow up to a few years ago. Until fairly recently it was used in some of the more primitive parts of the country for its primary purpose, which was separating wheat from chaff. I imagine that this was always its main purpose, and that because of this it became associated with harvest festivals, the old pagan harvest festivals. It is certainly true that in parts of Limerick, Kerry and Clare, it is still associated with, and played on the occasion of, Hallowe'en, which is of course the old pagan Samhain harvest festival. It's also associated with that other pre-Christian festival of the winter equinox, which is now made to coincide with St Stephen's Day, when the Wren-boys, wearing straw costumes, parade playing flutes and bodhráns. It is thus an instrument of tremendous antiquity. with a wealth of tradition behind it. Apart from all that the instrument itself is particularly suited to accompanying Irish music. The random frequencies of the skin are richer than those of even the orchestral bass drum, and thus tend to fill out and even provide the illusion of a harmonic bass for a band. Further, these frequencies can be readily changed: that is, the pitch of the bodhrán can be raised or lowered very simply, by pressing the fingers of the left hand (in which it is usually held) against the inside of the skin, thus tightening it a little. It is sometimes beaten by the hand alone , but more usually a stick is used, and this is also used to beat the rim of the drum producing still another kind of sound. All in all, the versatility of this instrument, the variety in timbre produced by playing on the rim or on the skin, by playing with a stick or with the hand, and the variety of pitch available, make it challengeable, particularly in a band, and particularly when it is supplemented by the bones. [*Courtesy RTE Archive*]

Appendix 12. '…Our native drum, the bodhrán…'.

Amended opening words in print version of O'Riada's lecture (pp. 74-5 of *Our Musical Heritage*, [Kinsella, 1982]).

▲ Val Byrne's 'Ignatius with his bodhrán' [*Courtesy Val Byrne*]

Appendix 13. Comparison of various players' striking styles as noted by Svend Kjeldsen

Hand-struck Connacht players comparison:
1/ Ted McGowan with Peter Horan (flute)

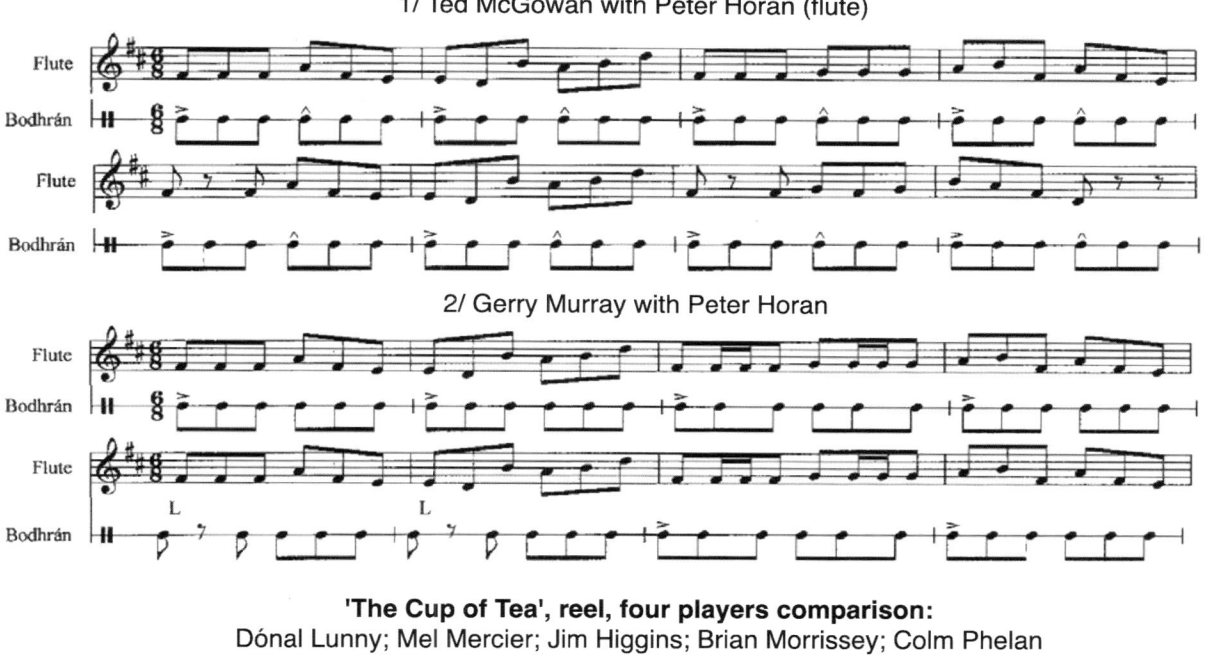

2/ Gerry Murray with Peter Horan

'The Cup of Tea', reel, four players comparison:
Dónal Lunny; Mel Mercier; Jim Higgins; Brian Morrissey; Colm Phelan

Dónal Lunny (with bass bodhran)

Mel Mercier

Jim Higgins

Brian Morrissey

Colm Phelan

▲ Comparison of various players' striking styles [*Svend Kjeldsen*]

Appendix 14. Singing about and slagging off the bodhrán

Reflecting the widespread suspicion about or aversion to percussion in traditional music is the fact that the bodhrán is the only instrument to have had detailed songs devoted to it. These eloquently lay out the prejudice and assumption vocabulary of melodicist superiority. The first one came about in 1988 on a Schitheredee tour in the magical landscape overhanging the Summer Isles beyond the port of Ullapool in north-west Scotland. Following a whisky and prawns gig in Andy Wilson's *Fúarán Bar* at Achiltiebuie, Brian O'Rourke succumbed to a state of back-seat unconsciousness brought on by an excess of bodhrán-maker Ian Campbell's seductive malt. Tim Lyons was driving us, and under the cover of the silence while heading for Skye he expostulated on an idea for a song about the bodhrán – from the point of view of the goat. He thought nothing more about the brainwave until after that night's gig in the *King Haakon* Bar, Kyleakin, when Brian presented us with this superb song, the idea for which had come to him in a dream.

▲ Songwriter Briain O'Rourke [*Courtesy Carlow Nationalist*]

WHEN I GROW UP
(**air: 'In Belfast There Is No Hope'**)
Oh I am a year-old kid, I'm worth scarcely twenty quid
I'm the kind of beast that you might well look down on
But my value will increase, at the time of my decease
For when I grow up I want to be a bodhrán

If you kill me for my meat, you won't find me very sweet
Your palate I'm afraid I'll soon turn sour on
Ah, but if you do me in, for the sake of my thick skin
Then you'll find I'll make a tasty little bodhrán

Now my parents Bill and Nan, they do not approve my plan
To become a yoke for every yob to pound on
But sure I would sooner scamper, with a bang than with a whimper
And achieve re-incarnation as a bodhrán

I look forward to the day, when I can leave off eating hay
And become a drum to entertain a crowd on
And I'll make my presence felt with each well delivered belt
As a fully manufactured concert bodhrán

For when I'm killed then I'll be cured, and my career will be assured
I'll be a skin you'll see no scum or scour on
But with studs around my rim, I'll be sounding out the tim – bre
And I'll make a dandy, handy little bodhrán

Oh! My heart with joy expands when I dream of far off lands
And consider all the streets that I will sound on
And I pity my poor ma, who was never at a Fleadh
Or indulged in foreign travel as a bodhrán

Now all sorts of cats have nine lives, and they may well be fine
And dogs I think have not too much to growl on
But it's when you are a goat that you can strike a merry note
Provided you have first become a bodhrán

For a hornpipe or a reel, a dead donkey has no feel
Or a horse or cow or sheep that has its shroud on
And you can't join in a jig, as a former Grade A pig
But you can wallop out the lot if you're a bodhrán

So if ever you feel low, to a session you should go
And bring me there to exercise an hour on
And you can strike a mighty thump
On my belly, back or rump
But I'd thank you if you'd wait till I'm a bodhrán

And when I dedicate my hide, I'll enhance my family's pride
Tradition is a thing I won't fall down on
For I'll sire a few young kids, who'll be glad of the few quid
That they'll get for their ould lad to make a bodhrán

328

Now I think you've had enough, of this rubbishy ould guff
So I'll put a sudden end to this wee amhrán
And quite soon my bleddy bleat
Will become a steady beat
When I start my new existence as a bodhrán
© Briain O'Rourke, 1989

THE BODHRÁN SONG

In response to the tourist music scenario all round him the whole summer long in Galway, Tim Lyons, himself a bodhrán player, retaliated with an original yarn about the bodhrán in song in which he lets the goat get away. Sensibly enough he robbed the tune of the three-part hornpipe 'The Cuckoo's Nest' to lay his tonic eggs in – to eliminate the possibility of any non-singer ever learning it.

Oh, me name is Heinrich Schnitzel
And from Germany I do come
Of all the music in the world
I much do like the drum

These last days I've been to Irelant
Where musicianers play till dawn
It was there I meet and fell in love
With a drum they call 'BOH-RAWN'

One day I'm going to Doolin famed
In music, song and dance
And as I did hug my Fürstenberg
My mind was in a trance
For there behind two whistles
In between a box and flute
A thunderous bang, and a goaty whang
The air it did pollute

This hairy drum my mind did numb
In love with it I fell
And I strongly did desire one
Despite the awful smell
Enquiries then I soon did make
Me mind being sorely bent
As to how and when and where and how
I'd procure such instrument

▲ Tim Lyons at *An Góilín* singers' club, Werburgh St, Dublin, 1989 [*Derek Speirs*]

I approached this bodhrán driver now
Being drunken with the sound
'To purchase one of these yokes
Will cost you fifty pounds'
My mind did race, at a gross pace
About my wallet thick
He then did roar 'SIXTEEN POUNDS MORE -
FOR CANVAS BAG AND STICK!'

Oh mein gotten! I'm exclaiming now
This is most expensive loot
At home ve are not paying this
For a silvery concert flute
'It isn't likely known', says he
'And I don't give a hoot, but
Why don't you lend a gun from off some-one
And your own goat you can shoot?'

Now this seemed to me a bright idea
And became my sole intent
For we German ones, are good with guns
And brainy to invent
That very day without delay
A shotgun I did borrow
Says I 'I'll haff my goatskin now
This evening or tomorrow'

So, upon the Burren mountain top
I stealthily did creep
O'er its craggy hill tops
Into its valleys deep
When there suddenly appeared to me
A herd of shaggy goats
With horns high, and yellow eye
Great manes and shaggy coats

As they thundered by I then let fly
Me Ely's Number 5
When the smoke had cleared
It soon appeared
These goats were still alive
I pursued them with alacrity
Till me legs were nearly lame
But in vain I stood, it was no good
Back to Doolin then I came

And as I walked up by Fisher Street
My spirits dragging low
I heard a thick and a heavy voice
Cry out 'HALLO, HALLO!
I observe a deadly weapon –
Pray, tell me, is it your own?
Where is the licence for this gun –
To me it must be shown'.

'Oh the truth to you I'll plainly tell
Nix licence have I got
For I just borrowed it from Gerry Smith
To have a sporting shot'
'GER SMITH! HOW DO! I'm arresting you
A subversive you must be
From some revolting movement
In far off Germany'

So now I lie in Ennis jail
Lamenting my condition

◀ Goats on Inis Mór, Aran Islands, 2021 [EDI]

The jury found me guilty
Ten pounds fine and extradition
The sergeant swore me life away
The judge he called me barmy
Said 'You're a Bader Meinhof refugee
And a member of Red Army'

So farewell to Ireland's fields of green
Far famed in song and poem
Farewell to Burren's rocky slopes
Where wild bodhráns do roam
If ever I return again
I'll shoot no goat or kid
And when I want to bate me drum
I'll pay up me fifty quid
© *Tim Lyons, 1989*

CONFESSIONS OF A BODHRÁN PLAYER

This song started out life as an introduction to Tim Lyons', addressing the spiritual appeal of the bodhrán for many, and the mispronunciations of its name.
(Air: 'Ould Rigadoo' / 'Jolly Beggarman')

I'm a new-age, vegetarian, Greenpeace, PC chap
I save whales, and as a male,
I don't talk sexist crap
I eat brown rice, and bread – instead of bacon, meat and chops
I dress in 'threads', sleep in Futon beds
And I don't talk – I rap
Now this lifestyle's most appealing, and by all the outward signs
I've left the structured feelings, of consumer life behind
But I'll confess that I've a failing, that I can't control, I find
I need percussion music's beat to regulate my mind

CHORUS:
Rup, rup, ruppety buppety bup
Ruppetty buppety ruppety buppety
Ruppety bup bup bup

So you might want to know why don't I have a go at flutes
Rebabs, or Balalaikas, Saz, Gadulkas, Lyres or Lutes –
But the ruthless, brutal truth is –
I couldn't give a hoot,
That I can't pluck, pick bow
Strum, squeeze, sing, yo-dell, Tinkle, rasp or Toot
For I have another problem, with an ideological root -

Factory instruments, on principle I must refute
So the bodd–ran hued from bended wood
A goatskin, nails and glue, is the closest thing to nature
That in style (and price) will do
CHORUS:

And yes, I know it's con-tra-dict-ry – I'm exploiting a goat's hide -
For leisure, when all other leather yokes I won't abide
So I just close my ears to pressure from those slashers who would thrash me
For bashing it with pleasure even after it has died
Yes, I'm happy just to wallop time with others of like mind
While intolerant, melodicists are pompously unkind
With their smart-ass, smug pre-ten-tious-ness
Guffaws, and glib pis-eógs
About 'Semtex', 'onions', 'Radox foot-spas'
'Sand', 'rats', 'pen-knives' and 'brogues'
CHORUS:

▲ Tim Lyons [*Music Network*]

▲ Bodhrán already established as an icon in Irish cultural assertiveness in mid-1970s, 'troubles'-era Belfast: Ceoltóirí Goill, the Ó Maoleoin family from Downings, Donegal / Belfast, their band named for the Rosguill peninsula, County Donegal [*photo by Bill Doyle, 'the Irish Cartier-Bresson'; courtesy Slógadh/Gael Linn*]

So, truthfully I'd rather have us gathered in some room
With treble-glazing cladding, to preserve our sonic boom
Where we'd lather up the batteries, like a mighty Samba school
And raise a Harvey Smith to all self-righteous ethnic rules
So youse Ugandans, Turks, Nigerians –
Afghanis, Sikhs, Ghanese
Hindustanis, Pakistanis, Jap-pa-pan-ies, Indo-nese -
You can shove your talkin' drums
Your oul' tablas, kotos and tarambukas -
We can do it better on our instrumental pookas

CHORUS:

So, farewell, Mustapha Tettey Addy, and ye Drummers of Burundi
Ye Lambeg-totin' Paddies, Sabri brothers and Dónal Lunny
Mel, Ringo, Colm, Cathy, Joh-Joe, Tommy Hayes and Kevin Coneff
Any bum can thump for fun, and be an instant drummer
And come all ye music dreamers, who're originally eccentric
Buy a bodd ran – and it seems
That you're indigenously authentic
But, if Ó Riada could phone home
He might say he 'hadn't really meant it' – yet

'If the Bowrán hadn't been around some fecker would invent it'
CHORUS:
© *Fintan Vallely, 1990*

THE GOAT'S REPLY
On a visit to Peadar Ó Doirnín mystic country for the magnificent October Forkhill Singers' weekend some years later, Liverpudlian Fred McCormick took a dislike to Briain O'Rourke's misrepresentation of the thoughts of an intelligent kid. After all, wouldn't only an eegit want to be a bodhrán? (Air: 'In Belfast There is No Hope')

I'm a poor downtrodden kid, from whom justice has been hid
Whose head threats constantly rain down on
For my loftiest ambitions, face parental opposition
And I'm told I'm only fit to be a bodhrán
My parents, Nan and Bill, have tried to subjugate my will
To force my hand they've turned the verbal power on
But I would rather go with the divil that I know
Than wind up in Düsseldorf a lonely bodhrán

My noble kith and kin, bequeathed me a gentle skin
It's the kind you'd pour the Chanel Number Five on
And I would surely love, to be a handbag or kid glove
There's lesser bastes well fit to be a bodhrán

There are elephants galore, tigers, gnus, giraffes and boars
Dogs, llamas, wildebeests, gazelles and lions
If the fishes in the sea were utilised instead of me
You could even play a scale upon a bodhrán

A subscription I will pay now to the ISPCA
To keep me from the paws of any moron
Who, the moment I have died, will stretch and tan my hide
And wallop my backside as a new bodhrán

Now I'd have no objection if I'd choice in resurrection
I'd return as fiddle, flute or an accordion
For with my luck some tuneless shit, or mindless thumpin German git
Will possess me if I end up as a bodhrán

If the glories of the Celt depend on belt and bang and welt
On a baste that's long deceased, then I'd call down on
The entire Irish race, humiliation and disgrace
With special doses for the ones who're making bodhráns

But there's bards and kings and chiefs, there's elaborate motifs
There's a language that's served many's a fine amhrán
There's Beckett, Yeats and Joyce, you can easy take your choice
Any one of those well bates the bodhrán

I've often heard it said that a drum should have two heads
And I'll bet there's some with three or four on
But how many goats have died, for a drum with just one side?
You're not just dead meat, but incomplete, when you're a bodhrán
So I hope I've said enough, in this elaborate rebuff
And I've given drummers guilty thoughts to drown on
Goats won't have peace of mind, till there's no value on their rind
When humanity abolishes the bodhrán.
© *Fred McCormick, 1995*

Briain O'Rourke's song can be heard on his album *Chantal de Champignon;* Tim's and Fintan's songs are on the CD *Big Guns and Hairy Drums;* Fred's song is on his album *The Song I'm Composing.*

NOTES TO APPENDICES

[1] Sullivan 1873 Vol. 3, 235–6.
[2] Ibid., 237. Quoted from Connellan's translation in *Transactions of the Ossianic Society*, Vol. 5, p. 96.
[3] Ibid., 259–60.
[4] Ibid., 265.
[5] Ibid., 266.
[6] Ibid., 359–60.
[7] Ibid., 361–2.
[8] Ibid., 363.
[9] Ibid., 364.
[10] Ibid.
[11] Ibid., 365.
[12] [Book of Lismore, fol. 237. b.a.]
[13] Ibid., 366.
[14] Ibid., 367–8.
[15] Dúchas 2022.
[16] Griffin 1829, 150.

Bibliography

Monographs, Articles, Websites and Other Published Works

Abbey Theatre. 1960. www.abbeytheatremusic.ie

Aherne, Tom. 2011. 'United We Stand', *The Weekly Observer*. 2020 0821 26. Newcastle West: *The Weekly Observer*.

An Lóchrann (ed.). 1926. 'Glóire Bhaile an Choiligh', *Páipéar Gaedhilge in Aghaidh Gacha Mí*. Sraith 3, Uimh. 11. Cork: An Lóchrann.

Anon. 1945. 'Memoir of Samuel Forde', *Dublin University Magazine* 25 (Mar.), 355.

Bachellery, Édouard. 1964. 'Les gloses irlandaises du manuscrit Paris Latin 10290', *Etudes Celtiques* 11, no. 1, 100–30.

Baily, John. 1988. *Music of Afghanistan*. Cambridge: Cambridge University Press.

Bairéad, Tomás, *Gan Baisteadh*. Dublin: Sairséal & Dill, 1972.

Begg, E. 1985. *The Cult of the Black Virgin*. London: Arkana.

Beckett, Colm (ed.). 1987. *Aodh Mac Domhnaill: Dánta*. Dublin: An Clóchomhar.

Benedict, Jeffrey W., 2011. 'References to Pre-Modern Music and Performing Arts Culture in the Irish Annals: A Survey of Common Themes', *Eolas 5, Journal of the American Society of Irish Medieval Studies* 5, 2011, 90–118.

Bhagavad Gita. 2022. Bhagavad Gita, Chapter 1, Verse 13 (www.holy-bhagavad-gita.org).

Boesch, Christopher. 1991. 'Symbolic Communication in Wild Chimpanzees', *Human Evolution*, 6, no.1 (1991), 81.

Boydell, Barra. 2007. 'Constructs of Nationality: The literary and visual politics of Irish music in the nineteenth century', in Michael Murphy and Jan Smaczny (eds), *Irish Musical Studies* 9. Dublin: Four Courts Press, 52–73.

Broderick, George. 1979. 'The Dollan: A Traditional Manx Hand-Drum', *Béaloideas* 45/47 (1977–9), 27–9.

Browne, Charles E. 1893–6. 'The Ethnography of Inishbofin and Inishshark, County Galway', in *Proceedings of the Royal Irish Academy* (1889–1901), vol. 3, 317–70. Dublin: Royal Irish Academy.

Buckley, Ann. 1990. 'Musical Instruments in Ireland from the Ninth to the Fourteenth Centuries', in Gerard Gillen and Harry White (eds), *Irish Musical Studies 1 – Musicology in Ireland*. Dublin: Irish Academic Press, 13–57.

———. 1995. 'Music as Symbolic Sound in Medieval Irish Society', in Gerard Gillen and Harry White (eds), *Irish Musical Studies 3 – Music and Irish Cultural History*. Dublin: Irish Academic Press, 13–76.

———. 1997. 'Music and Manners: Readings of Medieval Irish Literature', *Bullán. An Irish Studies Journal* 3, no. 1, 33–43.

———. 2005. 'Music in Ireland to *c.* 1500', in *A New History of Ireland, I: Prehistoric and Early Ireland*, Dáibhí Ó Cróinín (ed.) Oxford: Oxford University Press, 744–813.

Buckley, James. 1904. 'A Tour in Ireland in 1672–4', *Journal of the Cork Historical & Archaeological Society*, 10, no. 62, 85–100.

Bunting, Edward. 1809. *A General Collection of the Ancient Music of Ireland*. London: Clementi.

———. 1969. *The Ancient Music of Ireland*. Vols. 1–3. Dublin: Waltons.

Byrne, Joe (ed.). 1998. *Fíf agus Fideog: Fluters and whistlers of east Mayo*. Achadh Mór, Mayo: Joe Byrne.

Canavan, Sonny. 1970. Interviewed by Cathal O'Shannon on Telefís Éireann's *Newsbeat*, 30 April 1970. Broadcast on *Come West Along the Road*, Series 5, Programme 12 (TTMA CID 22640).

Carleton, William. 1843. *Traits of the Irish Peasantry*, Vol. 1. Dublin: W. Curry.

———. 1844. *Traits of the Irish Peasantry*, Vol. 2. Dublin: W. Curry.

Carolan, Nicholas. 2001. 'Philip O'Sullivan Beare on Irish Music', *Éigse Cheol Tíre. Irish Folk Music Studies* 5–6 (1986–2001), 47–57.

Carson, Ciaran. 1986. *Pocket Guide to Irish Traditional Music*. Belfast: Appletree Press.

CCM (Connradh Chuilm Naomhtha). 1907. *Seanmóirí Muighe Nuadhad* II. Dublin: M.H. Gill.

Crellin, A.M. 1923. 'On Some Things Manx, Now Obsolete', *Yn Lioar Manninagh 2, Proceedings IoM Natural History and Antiquarian Society* (Sept.), 265–70. Web: isle-of-man.com.

Crofton Croker, Thomas. 1825. *Fairy Legends and Traditions of the South of Ireland*. London: John Murray.

Curran, Assumpta, 1988. 'The Bodhrán and Its Association with the Wren Ritual' (fieldwork dissertation). Music Dept., University College Cork.

Dalyell, James and James Beveridge. 1924. 'Inventory of the Plenishing of the House of The Binns *Proceedings of the Society of Antiquaries of Scotland* 58, 344–70. [Web: soas.is.ed.ac.uk p. 7609].

Danaher, Kevin, see Ó Danachair, Caoimhín.

Day, Robert. 1904. '1st Muskerry Cavalry', *Journal of the Cork Historical & Archaeological Society*. 10, no. 62, 1–11.

Dean, Matt. 2011. *The Drum: A History*. Lanham, MD: The Scarecrow Press.

de h-Íde, Dubhglas. 1933. Abhráin agus Dánta an Reachtabhraigh. Dublin: Foillseacháin Rialtais.

Doherty, Richard. 2022. https://royal-irish.com/stories/tyrone-militia, accessed 2 October 2022.

Dolan, T. P. and Diarmaid Ó Muirithe (eds). 1979. 'Poole's Glossary with Some Pieces of Verse of the Old Dialect of the English Colony in the Baronies of Forth and Bargy County Wexford', *The Past: Organ of the Uí Cinsealaigh Historical Society* 13, 5–69.

Doubleday, Veronica. 1999. 'The Frame Drum in the Middle East: Women, Musical Instruments and Power', *Ethnomusicology* 43, no. 1, 101–35.

Dunton, J. (1699) 'Conversation in Ireland' [unpublished letters, 1698] in R. Head, 'The Western Wonder' part reprinted, ed. James Buckley, as 'A Tour in Ireland in 1672–4', pp. 85–100, *Journal of the Cork Historical & Archaeological Society*. 1904, Vol. 10, No. 62.

Evans, Emyr Estyn. 1957. *Irish Folkways*. London: Routledge & Kegan Paul.

———. 1967. *Mourne Country: Landscape and Life in South Down*. Dundalk: Dundalgan Press.

Evans, Emyr Estyn and Brian S. Turner, (eds). 1977. *Ireland's Eye: The Photographs of Robert John Welch*. Belfast: Blackstaff Press for the Ulster Museum and the Arts Council of Northern Ireland.

Falc'jer-Poyroux, Erick and Alain Monnier, 1995, 'Le Bodhrán', pp. 46–7 In *La musique irlandaise*. Kerangwenn Coop Breizh.

Feldman, Allen and Eamonn O'Doherty, 1979. *The Northern Fiddler*. Belfast: The Blackstaff Press.

Farmer, Henry G. 1904. *Memoir of the Royal Artillery Band*. London: Boosey & Co.

———. 1912. *Military Music and Its Story: The Rise and Development of Military Music*. London: W.M. Reeves.

Fitzmaurice, Gabriel. 2008. *Beat the Goatskin till the Goat Cries: Notes from a Kerry Village*. Cork: Mercier Press.

Foster, Stephen. ND. 'Blackface Minstrelsy', American Experience. USA: Public Broadcasting Corporation, accessed 10 June 2022.

Galpin, F.W. 1956. *A Textbook of European Musical Instruments: Their Origin, History and Character*. London: Ernest Benn.

Gardner, Martin. 1962. *The Annotated Snark*. London: Simon & Schuster.

Gaul, Liam. 2011. *Glory O! Glory O! The Life of P.J. McCall*. Dublin: The History Press.

Gillen, Gerard and Harry White (eds). 1990. *Irish Musical Studies 1 – Musicology in Ireland*. Dublin: Irish Academic Press.

Gioielli, Mauro. 2008. 'Sulle tracce del surdastro, uno strumento musicale del tarantism' [On the trail of the surdastro, a musical instrument of tarantism], *Utriculus* 46 (Apr.), 11–20.

Girling, Sam. 2018. 'Clementi and the Tambourine – The Waltzes Opp. 38–9 in the Context of Domestic Music-making in Early Nineteenth-century Britain', in Luca Sala and Rohan Stewart-MacDonald (eds) *Muzio Clementi and British Musical Culture: Sources, Performance Practice and Style* (ch. 9). Oxford: Routledge.

———. 2022. 'The Tambourine, Joseph Dale's Grand Sonata and Its Role in the Appearance of Women Musicians in the Salon', in Bennett Zon (ed.) *Nineteenth-Century Music Review*. Cambridge: Cambridge University Press, (online) 2022 0207.

Goff, Moira. 2020. 'The Most Popular Entr'acte Dances on the London Stage, 1700–1760', www.danceinhistory.com, accessed 7 April 2022.

Grattan Flood, W.H. 1927. *History of Irish Music*. Dublin: Browne & Nolan.

Gray, John. 2008. 'The Sports of Easter Monday', *Irish Pages* 5, no. 1, Language and Languages, 197–211.

Griffin, Gerald. 1829. *The Collegians*, in two volumes. New York: J. & J. Harper.

Groce, Nancy. 1996. *The Musician's Joke Book: Knowing the Score*. New York: Schirmer.

Guizzi, Febo. 1988. 'The Continuity of the Pictorial Representation of a Folk Instrument's Playing Technique: The Iconography of the Tamburello in Italy', *The World of Music* 30, no. 3, Musical Iconography, 28–58.

Hall, Reg. 2016. *A Few Tunes of Good Music: A History of Irish Music and Dance in London 1800–1980 and Beyond*. Croydon: Reg Hall and Topic Recording.

Hall, Samuel Carter and Anna Maria. 1841. *Ireland: Scenery, Character, &c*. Vol. 1. London: How & Parsons.

Hamelman, Stephen. 2011. 'The Beatles and the Art of the Tambourine', *Studies in Popular Culture* 33, no. 2 (Spring): 95–116.

Hardiman, James. 1831. *Irish Minstrelsy, or Bardic Remains of Ireland, with English Poetical Translations*. London: Joseph Robins.

Hart, Mickey and Jay Stevens. 1990. *Drumming at the Edge of Magic: A Journey into the Spirit of Percussion*. San Francisco: Harper.

Harte, Colin. 2020. *The Bodhrán: Experimentation, Innovation and the Traditional Irish Frame Drum*. Knoxville: The University of Tennessee Press.

Hast, Dorothea and Stanley Scott. 2004. 'The Bodhrán', pp. 81–2 in *Music in Ireland: Experiencing Music, Expressing Culture*. New York and Oxford: Oxford University Press.

Hennessy W.M. and B. MacCarthy (eds). 1887. *Annals of Ulster, otherwise Annala Senait, Annals of Senat: A Chronicle of Irish Affairs from AD 431 to AD 1540*. Dublin, 1887–1901.

Hickey, Dónal, 1999. *Stone Mad for Music: The Sliabh Luachra Story*. Dublin: Marino.

Higden, Ranulphus. 1422–92. 'Liber Primus', in *Policronicon* [translated by John of Trevisa, 1380s]. Westminster: Wynkyn de Worde.

Houlihan, Peter. 2007. *The Irish Drum / An Bodhrán*. Edited by Dave Mallinson. Cleckheaton UK: Mally Productions.

Inniskillings. 2018. 'The Tyrone Militia, 1793–1919', www.inniskillingsmuseum.com, accessed 3 October 2020.

Irish Central. 2022. www.irishcentral.com/roots/history/newgrange-winter-solstice, accessed 21 December 2024.

Joyce, P.W. 1908. *The Story of Ancient Irish Civilisation*. Dublin: M.H. Gill.

——. 1910. *English as We Speak it in Ireland*.

Dublin: Wolfhound Press.

J.W.B. (1904), 'County Cork Celebrities: Johnny Roche', pp. 160–7 in *Journal of the Cork Historical & Archaeological Society*, Vol. 10, No. 62.

Kartomi, Margaret J. 1990. *On Concepts and Classifications of Musical Instruments*. Chicago: University of Chicago Press.

Keane, Conor. 2017. 'Foreword', *The Bodhrán Makers* by John B. Keane, 2nd edition. Dublin: Brandon, pp. 9–11.

Keane, John B. 1959. *Sive: A Play in Three Acts*. Dublin: Progress House.

——. 1977. Interview with Brendan O'Brien on RTÉ's *Newsround*, 13 Feb. On ITMA CID 22640 – Come West along the Road. Series 5, Programme 12.

——. 1986. *The Bodhrán Makers*. Dublin: Brandon. Reprinted by O'Brien Press, 2021.

——. 1986. *Sive: A Play in Two Acts*. Dublin: Progress House.

Kearney, Aiveen, 1981. 'Temperance Bands and Their Significance in Nineteenth-century Ireland' [MA diss.] Cork: University College Cork.

Kearns, Malachy. 1996. *Wallup!* Roundstone: Roundstone Music.

Kelly, Fergus. 2013. 'Early Irish Music: An Overview of the Linguistic and Documentary Evidence', Statutory Public Lecture for the School of Celtic Studies at Trinity College Dublin. Dublin Institute for Advanced Studies –DIAS, https://www.dias.ie/2014/11/24/dias-recordedlectures/ (accessed 3 February 2017) [this has since been removed].

Kennedy, Patrick. 1866. *Legendary Fictions of the Irish Celts, Collected and Narrated by Patrick Kennedy*. London: Macmillan & Co.

——. 1869. *Evenings in the Duffrey*. Dublin: McGlasker & Gill.

——. 1870. 'The Greek Princess and the Young Gardener', in *The Fireside Stories of Ireland, Irish Fireside Folktales*, 51. Dublin: McGlashan & Gill. Reprinted by Mercier Press (Cork), 1969.

Kinealy, Christine. 2011. *Daniel O'Connell and the Anti-slavery Movement*. London: Pickering & Chatto.

Kinsella, Thomas, with Tomás Ó Canainn (eds). 1982. *Our Musical Heritage* [by Seán Ó Riada, 1962]. Mountrath: The Dolmen Press.

Kjeldsen, Svend. 2000. 'The Coleman Handstrikers: Old Style Bodhrán Playing in South Sligo', MA dissertation (unpublished), University of Limerick.

——. 2013. 'Bodhrán', in *The Encyclopaedia of Music in Ireland*, Harry White and Barra Boydell (eds) 103–4. Dublin: UCD Press.

——. 2013. 'Bones', in *The Encyclopaedia of Music in Ireland*, Harry White and Barra Boydell (eds) 107–8. Dublin: UCD Press.

Köhl, Johann Georg. 1843. *Reisen in Irland*. Dresden und Leipzig: Arnoldische Buchhandlung.

——. 1844. *England, Wales and Scotland*. London: Chapman & Hall.

Ledwich, Edward. 1804. *The Antiquities of Ireland*. Dublin: John Jones.

Levy, Nancy. 2008. 'Daniel Maclise Paints for the Government: Analysing Meaning in the Westminster Murals', in Peter Murray (ed.) *Daniel Maclise, 1806–1870: Romancing the Past*, pp. 232–43. Cork: Crawford Art Gallery & Gandon Editions.

Little, George A. 1943. *Malachi Horan Remembers Rathfarnham and Tallaght in the 19th Century*. Dublin: M.H. Gill; Cork and Dublin: Mercier Press, 1976 reprint.

Lover, Samuel (ed.). 1833. 'Tales and Sketches Characteristic and Descriptive of the Manners, Customs, Superstitions of Our Peasantry, Hallow Eve No. 11', *The Irish Penny Magazine* 1, no. 48 (30 Nov.).

Lucas, A.T. 1960. 'Irish Food Before the Potato', *Gwerin: A Half-Yearly Journal of Folk Life* 3, no. 2, 8–43.

Lyon, Nancy. 1979. 'The Mighty Goatskin Drum: The Irish Bodhrán', *Sing Out! The Folk Song Magazine*, 27, 3–7.

Mac Céachta (do bhailigh). 1914. 'Béarla Chille Dara. Focla Gaedhilge atá in Usáidh ag Béarlóiribh Chille Dara', in *Scéalta, Gaeilge i mBéarla Chill Dara*, pp. 62–97. Dublin: Na Caipísinigh.

MacCurtain, Margaret and Mary O'Dowd (eds). 1991. *Women in Early Modern Ireland*. Dublin: Wolfhound.

MacDonogh, Steve. 1983. *Green and Gold: The Wrenboys of Dingle*. Dingle: Brandon Books.

Mac Grianna, Seosamh. 1969. *An Druma Mór*. Dublin: An Gúm.

MacLysaght, Edward. 1939. *Irish Life in the Seventeenth Century After Cromwell*. Dublin: Talbot Press; London: Longmans. Reprinted by Irish Academic Press (Dublin), 1979.

MacMahon, Bryan. 1952. *Children of the Rainbow*. New York: E.P. Dutton.

——. 1963. Interview on RTÉ TV news, broadcast on Come West Along the Road, Series 4, Programme 2. (ITMA CID 22623).

——. 1967. *The Honey Spike*. Oxford: The Bodley Head. Reprinted by Poolbeg Press (Dublin), 1993.

——. 1978. 'Mourn the Ivy Leaf and Sound the Saw', *Treoir*, 10, no. 6.

Matthews, P.J. 2003. *Revival: The Abbey Theatre, Sinn Féin, The Gaelic League and the Co-operative Movement*. Cork: Cork University Press and Field Day.

McNeill, William. 1995. *Keeping Together in Time: Dance and Drill in Human History*. Cambridge (MA): Harvard.

Magriel, Paul (ed.). 1948. *Chronicles of the American Dance from the Shakers to Martha Graham*. New York: Da Capo Press, 44–5.

Maxwell, W.H. 1845. *History of the Irish Rebellion in 1798 with Memoirs of the Union and Emmett's Insurrection in 1803*. London: Baily Brothers.

——. 1854. *History of the Irish Rebellion in 1798*. London: H.G. Bohn.

McCarthy, Darina. 2013. 'Timpán / Tiompán', in Harry White and Barra Boydell (eds) *The Encyclopaedia of Music in Ireland*, Dublin: UCD Press, 987.

McCarthy, Tom. 2008. 'Bad Company for D. Maclise', in Peter Murray (ed.), *Daniel Maclise, 1806–1870: Romancing the Past*. Cork: Crawford Art Gallery and Gandon Editions, 160–7.

McCrickard, Janet E. 1987. *The Bodhrán: The Background to the Traditional Irish Drum*. Devon, UK: Fieldfare Arts and Design. Reprinted by K. O'Connell (Devon, UK), 1996.

McGann, Cliff. 1996. 'An Bodhrán', *Celtic Heritage* https://www.ceolas.org/instruments/bodhran/mcgann.shtml, accessed 21 December 2024.

McHale, Maria. 2007. 'Singing and Sobriety: Music and the Temperance Movement in Ireland, 1838–43', in Michael Murphy and Jan Smaczny (eds), *Irish Musical Studies* 9. Dublin: Four Courts Press, 166–86.

McHale, Maria and Catherine Ferris (eds). 2011. *Music at the Abbey Theatre*, www.abbeytheatremusic.ie, accessed 6 June 2022.

McNamee, Peter (ed.) 1992. *Traditional Music: Whose Music?* Belfast: Institute of Irish Studies.

MacNeela. 2022. www.mcneelamusic.com, accessed 21 December 2024.

Meyer, Kuno. 1906. *Contributions to Irish Lexicography*. London: David Nutt.

Midgley, Ruth, and Susan Sturrock (eds). 1976. *Musical Instruments of the World*. London: Paddington Press.

Mitchel, John. 1861. *The Last Conquest of Ireland (Perhaps)*. Glasgow: R&T Washbourne.

Mittleman, Josh. 2007. 'History of the Bodhrán', Ceolas Celtic Music Archive, https://www.ceolas.org/instruments/bodhrán, accessed 6 June 2022,

Mobile Music School. 2022. www.mobilemusicschool.ie, accessed 17 September 2022.

Moloney, Mick (2006). 'Irish American Popular Music', in J.J. Lee and Marion Casey (eds) *Making the Irish American: History and Heritage of the Irish in the United States*. New York: New York University Press.

Montagu, Jeremy. 2002. *Timpani and Percussion*. New Haven, CT: Yale University Press.

——. 2010. 'The Tabor: Its Origin and Use', *The Galpin Society Journal* 63, 209–16.

Mulholland, Rosa (Lady Gilbert). 1883. *The Wild Birds of Killeevy*. London: Burns, Oates & Washbourne.

Muller, Sylvie. 1996. 'The Irish Wren Tales and Ritual. To Pay or Not to Pay the Debt of Nature', *Béaloideas* 64, no. 5, 131–69, Web: doi.org/10.2307/20522463, accessed 21 December 2024.

Murray, Peter (ed.) 2008. *Daniel Maclise, 1806–1870: Romancing the Past*. Cork: Crawford Art Gallery and Gandon Editions.

——. 2008. 'Snap-Apple Night', in *Daniel Maclise, 1806–1870: Romancing the Past*, 96–9. Cork: Crawford Art Gallery and Gandon Editions.

Musgrave, Richard. 1801. *Memoirs of the Different Rebellions in Ireland from the Arrival of the English*. London: Milliken & Stockdale.

Nathan, Hans. 1962. *Dan Emmett and the Rise of Negro Minstrelsy*. Oklahoma: Oklahoma University Press.

Norris, John. 2012. *Marching to the Drums: A History of Military Drums and Drummers*. Cheltenham: The History Press.

Nolan, Ronan. 2009. www.irishmusicweb.ie.

Ó Bharáin, Liam. 2007. 'Bodhrán: Its Origin, Meaning and History – Part I: Etymology', *Treoir* 39, no. 4 (Nov.), 50–6.

——. 2008. 'Bodhrán: Its Recent History – Part 2: Making and Playing the Bodhrán', *Treoir* 40, no. 1, 47–52.

——. 2008. 'Bodhrán: The Origin, Meaning of the Word – Part 3', *Treoir* 40, no. 2, 49–55.

Ó Canainn, Tomás. 2003. *Seán Ó Riada: His Life and Work*. Cork: Collins Press.

Ó Catháin, Diarmuid. 2009. *Dictionary of Irish Biography*, s.v. 'O'Conor, Charles', doi.org/10.3318/dib.006652.v1, accessed 21 December 2024.

Ó Crohan, Tomás. 1978. *The Islandman*. Translated by Robin Flower. Oxford: Oxford University Press.

Ó Cuív, Brian (ed.). 1947. *Cnósach Focal ó Bhaile Bhúirne i gCunndae Chorcaí: Mícheál Ó Briain (1866–1942) a Bhailig*. Dublin: Institiúid Árd-Léighinn Bhaile Átha Cliath.

O'Curry, Eugene. 1873. 'Of Music and Musical Instruments in Ancient Erinn', in *On the Manners and Customs of the Ancient Irish: A Series of Lectures Delivered by the Late Eugene O'Curry*, Vol. 3, edited with an introduction by W.K. Sullivan. London: Williams & Norgate, 212–409.

O'Daly, John (ed.). 1876. *The Irish Language Miscellany, Being a Selection of Poems by the Munster Bards of the Last Century*. Dublin: John O'Daly.

Ó Danachair, Caoimhín. 1955. 'The Bodhrán: A Percussion Instrument', *Journal of the Cork Historical and Archaeological Society* 60, no. 192 (Jul./Dec.), 129–30.

——. 1958. 'Happy Christmas', *Biatas: The Beet Grower* 12, no. 9 (Dec.), 556–60.

——. 1959. 'Hunting the Wren', *Biatas: The Beet Grower* 13, no. 9 (Dec.), 667–72.

——. 1962. *In Ireland Long Ago*. Ireland: Dufour Editions.

——. 1966. 'King of All Birds', *Ireland of the Welcomes* 15, no. 4 (Nov.–Dec.), 27–30.

O'Dea, Laurence. 1958. 'The Fair of Donnybrook', *Dublin Historical Record* 15, no. 1 (Oct.), 11–20, jstor.org/stable/30103825, accessed 21 December 2024.

O'Donnell, Edward T. 2011. '156 Years Ago: Frederick Douglass in Ireland', *The Irish Echo*, 2011 0216, www.group.irishecho.com/2011/02/156, accessed 12 September 2022.

O'Donovan, John (1860). *Three Fragments Copied from Ancient Sources by Dubhaltach. Mac Firbisigh, and Edited with a Translation and Notes from a Manuscript Preserved in the Burgundian Library at Brussels*. Dublin: The University Press, for The Irish Archaeological and Celtic Society.

O'Donovan, John (trans. & ed.) (1851). *The Four Masters – Annals of the Kingdom of Ireland, from the Earliest Times to the Year 1616, Edited from MSS in the Library of the Royal Irish Academy and of Trinity College Dublin, with a Translation, and Copious Notes*. Vols 1–7. Dublin: Hodges, Smith, 1851; Dublin: De Búrca Rare Books, 1990.

O'Dowda, Brendan. 1981. *The World of Percy French*. Belfast: The Blackstaff Press.

O'Dowd, Anne and Mairead Reynolds. 1986. 'The Wren Hunt', in *The Second Irish Christmas Book*, ed. John Killen. Belfast: Blackstaff Press, 131–5.

Ó Gealbháin, Ciarán. 2013, 'Diversion Aerach: An tAmhrán "Aonach Bhearna na Gaoithe" agus an Saol in Éirinn sa Naoú Haois Déag'. *Béaloideas* 81. Dublin: An Cumann Le Béaloideas Éireann, 88–113.

O'Meara, John (trans., ed.). 1951. *Gerald of Wales: The History and Topography of Ireland*. Dundalk: Dundalgan Press, 1951; Dublin: Dolmen, 1982; London: Penguin, 1982.

O'Neill, Francis. 1910. *Irish Folk Music: A Fascinating Hobby*. Darby. Reprint Pennsylvania: Norwood, 1973.

——. 1913. *Irish Minstrels and Musicians: With Numerous Dissertations on Related Subjects*. Chicago; reprint Cork: Mercier Press, 1987.

O'Neill, Timothy P. 1977. *Life and Tradition in Rural Ireland*. London: Dent & Sons.

Ó Riada, Peadar, 2024, *Ceoltóirí Chualann*. Cork: Mercier

Ó Riada, Seán. 1962. *Our Musical Heritage*. See Kinsella, 1982.

Ó Séaghdha, Pádraig. 1906. *Annéla na Tuatha, Cuid a Dó*. Dublin, Conradh na Gaeilge.

O'Shannon, Cathal. 1970. Telefís Éireann's *Newsbeat*, 30 April, documentary clip on Sonny Canavan. Broadcast on *Come West along the Road*, Series 5, Programme 12 (ITMA CID 22640).

O Súilleabháin, Mícheál. 1974. 'The Bodhrán'. *Treoir* 6, no. 2: 4–7.

——. 1974. 'The Bodhrán 2'. *Treoir* 6, no. 5: 6–10.

——. 1996. 'Crossroads or Twin Track: Tradition and Innovation', audio, paper given at Crosbhealach an Cheoil – The Crossroads Conference: Tradition and Innovation. Dublin.

——. 1983. 'Contemporary Developments in Bodhrán Performance Technique', in N. Webber (ed.) *Studies in Traditional Music and Dance* V & II, London, 58.

Pléimeann, S. 1887. 'Aonach Bhearna na

Gaoithe'. *Irishleabhar na Gaedhilge* 3, no. 26: 26–9.

———. 1887. 'Aonach Bhearna na Gaoithe'. *Irishleabhar na Gaedhilge* 3, no. 27: 43–6.

Poole, Jacob. 1867. *A Glossary with Some Pieces of Verse of the Old Dialect of the English Colony in the Baronies of Forth and Bargy, County of Wexford, Ireland*. Edited by William Barnes. London: J. Russell Smith.

Porter, James. 1795. *Paddy's Resource, Being a Select Collection of Original and Modern Patriotic Songs, Toasts and Sentiments Compiled for the Use of the People of Ireland*. Dublin.

Power, Patrick. 1952. *The Place-names of Decies*. Cork: Cork University Press.

Pyle, Hilary. 1997. *The Sligo Leitrim World of Kate Cullen 1832–1913: A 19th Century Memoir Revealed*. Dublin: Woodfield Press.

Quirey, Belinda. 1976. *May I Have the Pleasure? The story of Popular Dancing*. London: Dance Books, 1976.

Radner, Joan. 1978 (ed.). 'Fragmentary Annals of Ireland'. Dublin; online copy, https://celt.ucc.ie/published/T100017.html, accessed 21 December 2024.

Reck, David Benedict. 1977. *Music of the Whole Earth*. New York: Scribner.

Redmond, Layne (ed.). 2018. *When the Drummers Were Women: A Spiritual History of Rhythm*. Brattleboro, VT: Echo Point Books & Media.

Rees, Stephen. 2011. 'Welsh Harp (telyn)', in Fintan Vallely (ed.) *Companion to Irish Traditional Music*, 2nd edition. Cork: Cork University Press, 732.

Reeves, Bishop (trans.). 1854. 'Bodley's Visit to Lecale, County of Down, AD 1602–3', *Ulster Journal of Archaeology* 2, 73–95, jstor.org/stable/20608711, accessed 21 December 2024.

Reynolds, Willie. 1990. *Memories of a Music Maker*. Dublin: CCÉ.

Rice, Edward Le Roy. 1911. *Monarchs of Minstrelsy, from 'Daddy' Rice to Date*. New York: Kenny Publishing Company.

Royal Irish Academy. 2022. 'Historical Irish Corpus, 1600–1926', corpas.ria.ie, accessed 10 June 2022.

RTÉ. 1963. Footage of Fleadh an Dreolín, Newcastle West, County Limerick, December. Broadcast on *Come West along the Road*, Series 4, Programme 2. (ITMA CID 22623).

Ryan, James Tobias. 1895. *Reminiscences of Australia: Containing 70 Years of His Own Knowledge, and 35 Years of His Ancestors*. Sydney: George Robertson & Company.

Salvador-Daniel, Francesco. 1915. *The Music and Musical Instruments of the Arab*. New York: Scribner.

Schiller, Rena. 2001. *Drums of Ireland: The Lambeg and the Bodhrán*. Belfast: The Institute of Irish Studies, Queen's University Belfast.

Scholes, Percy and John Owen Wards (eds). 1987. *The Oxford Companion to Music*. Oxford: Oxford University Press.

Scullion, Fionnuala. 1982. 'The Lambeg Drum in Ulster', MA thesis, Queen's University Belfast.

Scully, Louis. 2015. http://www.worcestershireregiment.com/black_drummers.php, accessed 21 December 2024.

Seibert, Brian. 2015. *What the Eye Hears: A History of Tap Dancing*. New York: Farrar, Straus & Giroux.

Shaw-Smith, David. 2003. *Traditional Crafts of Ireland*. London: Thames & Hudson.

Skinner, Anthea. 2003. *The Tambourine: A Fertility Symbol for the Goddess*. Melbourne: Monash University.

Skinner Sawyers, June. 2000. *The Complete Guide to Celtic Music, from the Highland Bagpipe and Riverdance to U2 and Enya*. London: Aurum.

Smith, Chris. 2013. 'Banjo', in Harry White and Barra Boydell (eds), *The Encyclopaedia of Music in Ireland*. Dublin: UCD Press, 56–7.

Such, David G. 1985. 'The Bodhrán: The Black Sheep in the Family of Traditional Irish Musical Instruments', *The Galpin Society Journal* 38 (Apr.): 9–19.

Sullivan, William Kirby. 1873. *On the Manners and Customs of the Ancient Irish: A Series of Lectures Delivered by the Late Eugene O'Curry*, Vol. 1. London: Williams & Norgate.

Tansey, Seamus. 1998. *The Bardic Apostles of Innisfree*. Craigavon: Tanbar Publications.

Townshend, H. 1904. 'The Wild Goose: The Irish Cavalier, 1690', *Journal of the Cork Historical & Archaeological Society*. 10, no. 62, 278–9.

Uí Ógáin, Ríonach. 2002. 'A Tune off the River: The Lore of Musical Instruments in the Irish Tradition', *Béaloideas* 70, 127–52.

———. 1995. 'Traditional Music and Irish Cultural History', pp. 77–100 in H. White and G. Gillen (eds.) Music in Irish Cultural History. Dublin: Irish Academic Press.

Vallely, Fintan, 2004. 'Flute Routes to 21st Century Ireland: The History, Aesthetics and Social Dynamics of Three Centuries of Recreational and Political Music', unpublished PhD thesis, Dublin: National University of Ireland, University College Dublin.

———. 2011. 'Bodhrán', in Fintan Vallely (ed.) *The Companion to Irish Traditional Music*, 2nd edition, substantially revised and expanded. Cork: Cork University Press, 68–72.

———. 2019. 'Clattering Feet and Thumping the Bodhrán: The Percussive Impulse in Irish Music', in Brian Vallely (ed.) *The William Kennedy Lectures – Lectures from 25 years of the William Kennedy Piping Festival*. Armagh: Armagh Pipers' Club, 146–58.

———. 2020. 'Di-rum-ditherum-dan-dee: Trauma and Prejudice, Conflict and Change as Reflections of Societal Transformation in the Modern-Day Consolidation of Irish Traditional Music', in Terrezas Gallego (ed.) *Trauma and Identity in Contemporary Irish Culture*. Oxford: Peter Lang, 185–210.

———. 2011. 'Bodhrán', in Fintan Vallely (ed.), *The Companion to Irish Traditional Music*, 3rd edition, substantially revised and expanded. Cork: Cork University Press, pp. 89–96.

Wakefield, Edward, 1812. *An Account of Ireland Statistical and Political*, Vol. 1. London: Longman & Co.

Walker, Joseph Cooper. 1786. *Historical Memoirs of the Irish Bards. Interspersed with Anecdotes of, and Occasional Observations on, the Music of Ireland. Also, an Historical and Descriptive Account of the Musical Instruments of the Ancient Irish, and an Appendix Containing Several Biographical and Other Papers, with Select Irish Melodies*. Dublin: Joseph C. Walker (printed by Luke White).

Watters, Eugene and Matthew Murtagh. 1975. *Infinite Variety: Dan Lowrey's Music Hall 1879–97*. Dublin: Gill & Macmillan.

White, Harry and Barra Boydell (eds). 2013. *The Encyclopaedia of Music in Ireland*. Dublin: UCD Press.

Whiteoak, John. 1999. *Playing Ad Lib: Improvisatory Music in Australia, 1836–1970*. Sydney: Currency Press.

Williams, Bernadette. 2007. *The Annals of Ireland by Friar John Clyn*. Dublin: Four Courts Press.

Williams, N.J.A. 1988. Cniogaide Cnagaide – Rainn traidisiúnta do pháistí. Dublin: An Clóchomhar.

Wilson, Anthony M. (ed.). 1995. 'A Visit to Lecale by Josias Bodley in 1602', *Lecale Miscellany* 13, 18–27.

Winans, Robert. 1984. 'Early Minstrel Show Music 1843–1852', in Glenn Loney (ed.) *Musical Theater in America: Papers and Proceedings of the Conference on the Musical Theater in America*. Westport, CT: Greenwood Press.

Worcester. 2022. www.worcestershireregiment.com, accessed 21 December 2024.

Wright, Thomas (ed.). 2000. *Giraldus Cambrensis: The Topography of Ireland*. Translated by Thomas Forester. Cambridge, Canada: In Parentheses Publications.

Wulff, Winifred (ed.). 1929. *Rosa Anglica: An Early Modern Irish Translation of a Section of the Medieval Medical Text-book of John of Gaddesden*. Irish Texts Society 25. London: Simpkin, Marshall.

YouTube. 2022. www.youtube.com/watch?v=ujDxn0mtmks, accessed 21 December 2024.

Dictionaries

An Gúm. 2006 (1st edition 1986). *Foclóir Scoile – English-Irish / Irish-English Dictionary*. Baile Átha Cliath: An Gúm.

Connellan, Thaddeus. 1814. *An English Irish Dictionary Intended for the Use of Schools*. Dublin: Graisberry & Campbell.

de Bhaldraithe, Tomás. 1981. *Innéacs nua-Ghaeilge don Dictionary of the Irish Language*. Dublin: Acadamh Ríoga na hÉireann.

———. 2022. 'English-Irish Dictionary (de Bhaldraithe, 1959)'. Dictionary and Language Library. Dublin: Foras na Gaeilge, teanglann.

ie/en/eid, accessed 21 December 2024.

de Vere Coneys, Thomas. 1849. *Foclóir Gaoidhilge-sacs-Béarla, or an Irish-English Dictionary, Intended for the Use of Students and Teachers of Irish*. Ireland: Irish Society.

Dinneen, Patrick. 1904. *Foclóir Gaedhilge agus Béarla* (new edition, revised and greatly enlarged). Dublin: M.H. Gill for The Irish Texts Society and The Gaelic League.

———. 1927, 1934. *Foclóir Gaedhilge agus Béarla*. Dublin: The Educational Company of Ireland, for The Irish Texts Society.

Dolan, T.P. 1998. *A Dictionary of Hiberno-English*. Dublin: Gill & Macmillan.

Donohoe, K. 1985. *The Land League in Leitrim* (pamphlet). Leitrim: Donohoe.

eDIL. 2019. *Electronic Dictionary of the Irish Language, Based on the Contributions to a Dictionary of the Irish Language*. Dublin: Royal Irish Academy, dil.ie, accessed 8 June 2022.

Foclóir. www.focloir.ie/ga/dictionary/ei/deaf+mute, accessed 21 December 2024.

Foley, Daniel. 1855. *An English-Irish Dictionary Intended for the Use of Students of the Irish Language, and for those who wish to translate their English thoughts, or the works of others, into language intelligible to the present Irish-speaking inhabitants of Ireland*. Dublin: William Curry.

Fournier, E. 1910. *An English-Irish Dictionary and Phrase-book*. Dublin: MH Gill.

Gove, Philip Babcock (ed.), 1971. *Webster's Third New International Dictionary of the English Language, Unabridged*. USA: G. & C. Merriam Company.

Highland Society of Scotland. 1828. *Dictionarium Scoto-Celticum: A Dictionary of the Celtic Language*. Vols. 1 and 2. Edinburgh: William Blackwood.

Lhuyd, Edward. 1707. 'A Comparative Vocabulary', in *Archaeologia Britannica*, Vol. 1 Glossography. Oxford: Edward Lhuyd, 41–179.

———. 1707. 'Foclóir Gaoidheilge-Shagsonach … An Irish-English Dictionary', in *Archaeologia Britannica*, Vol. 1 Glossography. Oxford: Edward Lhuyd, 310–440.

Mac an Fhailigh, Éamonn (Edward Vincent Nally). 1945. 'A Westmeath Word-list', *Éigse* 5, 256–66.

MacCionnaith, L. 1935. *Foclóir Béarla agus Gaedhilge: English-Irish Dictionary*. Dublin: Oifig Díolta Foillseacháin.

Maceachen, Alex. 1922. *Faclair Gaidhlic is Beurla le Eobhan Mac-Eachainn: Maceachen's Gaelic-English Dictionary*, 4th edn. Inverness: Northern Counties Newspaper and Printing and Publishing Company, 1936.

McAlpine, Neil. 1866. *A Pronouncing Gaelic Dictionary*. Edinburgh: MacLachlan & Stewart.

McKenna, Lambert Andrew Joseph. 1922. *English-Irish Phrase Dictionary*. Dublin: M.H. Gill & Son.

Merriam-Webster. 2022, merriam-webster.com, dictionary. S.v. tympanum, accessed 8 June, 2022.

Morell, Thomas (ed.) 1773. *Robert Ainsworth's Dictionary, English and Latin*. London: Charles Rivington & William Woodfall.

Mulcahy, D.B. 1887. 'Peculiar Localisms: Words in Everyday Use in Dalriada, North Antrim', *Irishleabhar* 3, no. 31.

Ó Beaglaoic, Concobhar (Conor O'Begley), with Aodh Bhuide mac Cuirtín (Hugh McCurtin) (eds). 1732. *The English-Irish Dictionary. An Foclóir Béarla-Gaoidheilge*. Paris: Seamus Guerin.

O'Brien, John. 1768. *Focalóir Gaoidhilge-Sax-Bhéarla or an Irish-English Dictionary*. Paris: Nicolas-Francis Valleyre.

———. 1832. *Focalóir Gaoidhilge-Bhéarla, or an Irish-English Dictionary*, 2nd edn. Dublin: Hodges & Smith.

Ó Dómhnaill, Niall. 1977. *Foclóir Gaeilge-Béarla*. Dublin: Oifig an tSoláthar.

Ó Dónaill, Niall and Padraig Ua Maoileoin (eds). 2013–22. 'An Foclóir Beag Gaeilge (Ó Dónaill agus Ua Maoileoin, 1991)', Dictionary and Language Library, Dublin: Foras na Gaeilge, www.teanglann.ie/en/fb, accessed 21 December 2024.

Ó Mianáin, Pádraig (ed.). 2020. *The Concise English-Irish Dictionary / Foclóir Béarla-Gaeilge*. Dublin: Foras na Gaeilge.

O'Neill Lane, Timothy. 1917. *Larger English-Irish Dictionary [Foclóir Béarla-Gaedhilge]*. New edn. London: Funk & Wagnalls.

Online Latin Dictionary, www.online-latin-dictionary.com, accessed 21 December 2024.

O'Reilly, Edward. 1817. *Sanas Gaoidhilge-Sagsbhearla. An Irish-English Dictionary, Containing Upwards of Twenty Thousand Words that Have Never Appeared in any Former Irish Lexicon. With Copious Quotations from the Most Esteemed Ancient and Modern Writers, to Elucidate the Meaning of Obscure Words; and Numerous Comparisons of the Irish Words with those of Similar Orthography, Sense, or Sound in the Welsh and Hebrew Languages*. Dublin: John Barlow.

———. 1864. *An Irish-English Dictionary … Edited with a Supplement by John O'Donovan*. Dublin: James Duffy.

———. 1877. *An Irish-English Dictionary. A New Edition, with a Supplement*. Dublin: James Duffy.

Ó Luineacháin, Dáithí. 2005 (1st edition Ó Siochfhradha, Mícheál, 1959). *Foclóir Gaeilge / Béarla – Béarla-Gaeilge / Easy Reference Irish-English – English/Irish Dictionary*. Baile Átha Cliath: An Comhlacht Oideachais.

Quin, E.G. (ed.). 1984. *Dictionary of the Irish Language: Based Mainly on Old and Middle Irish Materials*. Dublin: Royal Irish Academy.

Simpson, J.A. and E.S.C. Weiner. 1989. *The Oxford English Dictionary*, 2nd edn. Vol. XVIII. Oxford: Clarendon Press.

Shaw, William. 1780. *A Galic and English Dictionary. Containing All the Words in the Scotch and Irish Dialects of the Celtic that Could Be Collected from the Voice, and Old Books and MSS*. Vols 1 and 2. London: William Shaw.

Toller, Thomas Northcote (ed.). 1898. *An Anglo-Saxon Dictionary: Based on the Manuscript Collections of the Late Joseph Bosworth*. Oxford: Oxford University Press.

Traynor, Michael. 1953. *The English Dialect of Donegal: A Glossary Incorporating the Collections of H.C. Hart*. Dublin: Royal Irish Academy.

Tutors

Bolton. Thomas. 1799. *Instructions for the Tambourine*. London: Bolton.

Caswell, Chris. 2005. *How to Play the Bodhrán*. DVD059. Fort Bragg Lark in the Morning Inc. Video recording, DVD.

Dale. 1800. *Dale's Instructions for the Tambourine, with an Explanation of the Different Characters*. London: Dale's Music & Musical Instrument Warehouses.

Driver, Nicholas. 1994. *Bodhrán & Bones Tutor*. Horsham: Gremlin.

Gracy, Mance. 1992. *Playing the Irish Drum: Getting Started*. Video recording, DVD. www.mance.com, accessed 21 December 2024.

Halpenny, Sean. 1988. *Secrets of the Bodhrán and How to Play It*. Roundstone: Roundstone Musical Instruments.

Hannigan, Steáphán. 1991. *The Bodhrán Book*. With demo cassette. Cork: Ossian Publications.

———. 1991. *The Bodhrán Video*. Cork: Ossian Publications OMB-OSV1. VHS Video Cassette.

Hayes, Tommy. 1993. *Bodhrán, Bones, and Spoons*. Ireland: CW Productions. DVD. 105 minutes.

Lange, Moritz Wulf, 2004, *Bodhrán: Handbuch für Bodhránspieler*. Berlin: Schell Music.

Mercier, Mel, with Seamus Egan. 1994. *Bodhrán and Bones*. Alfred Music 00-VH1071. Video recording.

Ó Súilleabháin, Micheál. 1984. *The Bodhrán: An Easy to Learn Method for the Complete Beginner Showing the Different Regional Styles and Techniques*. Dublin: Waltons.

Preston, T. 1798. *Instructions for the Tambourine*. London: Preston.

Ralls, Karen. 2000. *Music and the Celtic Otherworld*. New York: St Martin's Press.

Smith, Robin M. 1993. *Power Bodhrán Techniques: A New Approach to the Celtic Drum*. West Melbourne, FL: Mid-East Mfg., Inc.

Sullivan, Tony. 2006. *Bodhrán Tutor: Instructions for Playing Irish Jigs and Reels, etc.* United Kingdom: Halshaw Music HM306. Compact disc and A5 booklet.

Wallis, Geoff and Sue Wilson, 2001. 'Percussionists', in *The Rough Guide to Irish Music*. London: Rough Guides.

Walsh, Tommy and Jim Kelly. 1994. *The Walton Bodhrán Tutor*. Dublin: Waltons. Book with cassette tape.

Woods, Bill, 2009. *Bodhrán: The Basics*. Pacific, MO: Mel Bay.

Manuscripts

Lambert, Pierre-Yves. 1982. 'Les gloses du manuscrit BN Lat. 10290', *Études Celtiques* 19, 173–213, https://codecs.vanhamel.nl/Lambert_(Pierre-Yves)_1982_19php, accessed 21 December 2024.

Lucas, A.T. 1953. record cards, National Museum of Ireland, 1953 08 03.

Moryson, Fynes. 2010. 'The Commonwealth of Ireland (1735)'. Corpus of Electronic Texts Edition T100072. Translated by Charles Hughes. compiled by Beatrix Färber, celt.ucc.ie/published/T100072, accessed 21 December 2024.

O'Donovan, John 1860 (ed.). *Annals of Ireland: Three Fragments Copied from Ancient Sources by Dubhaltach Mac Firbisigh; and edited with a translation and notes, from a manuscript preserved in the Burgundian Library at Brussels [extracted from a Vellum of Manuscript belonging to Nehemias Mac Egan, Senior, a Man most Learned in Irish Law, in Ormond, by Mac Firbisigh, for the Use of the Rev. Doctor John Lynch. From approximately AD 571 to about the Year 910.* (RIA MS 23 P 24: Cat. No. 138).

Ó hEochaidh, Seán. Interview with Joe MacEachmhaonaigh, Doire Chonaire, Gaoth Dobhair, Co. Donegal. MSS A1835, 48–9. Department of Irish Folklore, University College Dublin.

O'Sullivan Beare, Philip [1621]. 'Chapters Towards a History of Ireland in the Reign of Elizabeth'. MS 988. National Library of Ireland, Dublin.

——. *c.* 1625/6. 'Vindiciae Hibernicae contra Giraldum Cambrensem et alios vel Zoilomastigis Liber Primus, 2, 3, 4 et 5 et contra Stanihurstum'. Autograph manuscript, H. 248. Universitetsbibliotek, Uppsala, Sweden.

Anon. 2002. 'Annals of the Four Masters'. Corpus of Electronic Texts Edition T100005A Translated by John O'Donovan, compiled by Emma Ryan, celt.ucc.ie/published/T100005A/index.html, accessed 21 December 2024.

Anon. 2008. 'Fragmentary Annals of Ireland'. Corpus of Electronic Texts Edition T100017. Translated by Joan Newlon, compiled by Beatrix Färber, Maxim Fomin, Emer Purcell, celt.ucc.ie/published/T100017.html, accessed 21 December 2024.

Anon. 2008. 'Annals of Loch Cé'. Corpus of Electronic Texts Edition. Translated by William M. Hennessy, celt.ucc.ie/published/T100010A/index.html, accessed 21 December 2024.

Personal communication, conference paper, radio

Boydell, Barra. 2005. Information given in the course of a paper to ICTM in Dublin.

Bradshaw, Harry. 2022. Information given in the course of a phone call to check home-place of John Reynolds.

Browne, Peter. Information given 2010, 2018, 2023.

Burke, Joe. Discussion on percussive foot sounds, at Kilnadeema, April 1997.

Carolan, Nicholas. 2010, 2014, 2023, 2024. Numerous discussions on the occurrence of bodhrán references in print and in imagery.

De Buitléar 2014, discussion on Ceoltóirí Chualann.

Dowling, Martin. 2009. Comment in discussion about O'Neill and minstrels, County Clare.

——. 2011. Suggestion from the floor during a lecture on the bodhrán at Queen's University Belfast.

Graham, Richard. 2022. Discussions on the military and Italian associations of the tambourine.

Hall, Reg. 2023. Discussion by phone on tambourines in the London-Irish scene and in English social history.

Hallinan, Gerry. 1988. Information given in conversation during a speaking tour by the author for Irish American Cultural Institute at Rochester, NY.

Hamilton, Colin. 2022. Discussion on improvised flutes and other instruments.

Kearns, Malachy. Conversation at his workshop, Connemara, May 2022.

Kelton, Jane. 2012. Discussion r/e Norman influence, at Catskills Irish music summer school, New York.

Kinmonth, Claudia. Information in the course of a discussion on the painting 'Síbín in Listowel', June 2018.

Kjeldsen, Svend. 2010. Information given in discussion about the nature of the bodhrán.

——. 2012. 'The Bodhrán Was Not a Drum – The Tambourine Was Not a Bodhrán', presentation at Musical Instruments in Cultural Encounter: Transculturation, Hybridisation and Organology, seminar at University of Limerick, 28 November.

Lunny, Dónal. 2023. Information exchange.

McMahon, Jim and Owen. 2022. Discussion at the launch of Kerry Writers' Museum exhibition, 7 May.

Meade, Don. 2023. Discussion on Shaun O'Nolan's recording of 'The Half-Door Song'

Mercier, Mel. 2021. *Documentary On One: Bodhrán Legend Peadar Mercier Remembered*, https://www.rte.ie/culture/2021/1126/1262941-documentary-on-one-bodhran-legend-peadar-mercier-remembered, accessed 21 December 2024.

McGowan, Ted. 1997. Comment made in discussion on the tambourine in Sligo.

Moloney, Mick. 1998 and 2022. Discussion on articles for *Companion to Irish Traditional Music*.

Mitchell, Pat. January 2023. Discussion on early bodhráns.

Morrisroe, Alan. 2023. Discussion on early recordings of tambouine in the USA; access to Shaun O'Nolan song.

Moylan, Terry. 2022. Discussion, and contribution of references and checks r/e 1798, Lewis Carroll, John Mitchel and Percy French.

Neely, Dan. 2023, 04. Information on Shaun O'Nolan's 'The Half Door Song'.

——. 2025, 01. Information on The Flanagan Brothers' use of modern bodhrán style, muted snare drum on '78' rpm recordings.

Ní Fhuarthán, Méabh (musician, lecturer and writer, NUIG). 2010. Comment made following lecture on the bodhrán at the Irish Studies Seminar, University College Galway, February. 2022. Information given in discussion about her interim work on drums in céilí bands, 25 July.

O'Flaherty, Eamon. 2022 (Scholar). Translation of MSS and information given, 10 March.

O'Malley, James. 2022. Stated in a paper delivered on Francis O'Neill, NPU Notes and Narratives, Dublin, 19 July.

Ó Súilleabháin, Mícheál. 2009. Information given in conversation at University of Limerick.

Quaide, Jack. 2022. Discussion in Moore's of Carrigkerry, 7 May.

Tansey, Seamus. Information given in the course of a phone call to check how his quoted words had been interpreted, May 2022.

Tubridy, Michael. 2022. Information given at Ritchie Piggott's book launch, Teachers' Club, Dublin, 27 October.

Turrisi, Francesco (contemporary composer, musician, bendir player). 2022. Discussion on the route of entry of tambourines to the minstrels. Greystones, 14 December.

Vallely, Fintan. 2010. 'Hunting for Borr-án: Shaking a Stick at Theories on the Famous Irish Drum', Irish Studies Seminar, University College Galway, 11 February.

Weems, Mark. 2022. Telephone discussion on minstrel tambourines, 8 April.

▲ Waltons bodhrán band promotion at Milwaukee Irish Fest, 2000 [*EDI*]

Acknowledgements

Sincere thanks are due to so many people without whose knowledge, tolerance, generosity, thinking time, life experience, musicianship, humanity, wisdom, funding decisions, sense of priority and indeed commercial enterprise this book could never have reached fruition. The process began with my mother back *c*. 1965 whose craft intuition was able to advise me in making a bodhrán for my cousin Niall from an old sand riddle (but who also had the wisdom to facilitate my learning to play the flute). The many bodhrán players whom I encountered over the years since then have all contributed morsels of information, legend, lore and wild assumptions which added to the picture. The slagging, denunciation and self-perceived patience of the melodicists of my world also filled in many gaps regarding taste, intolerance, pragmatism and human compulsion, in particular songwriter Tim Lyons' socially-caring lyrical wit. For the work proper I owe thanks to the one-time research body An Foras Feasa and my then boss Eilís Farrell and Dundalk Institute of Technology for both research time and support; to the Ireland Fund of Monaco for the amazing opportunity of a month's residency at the Princess Grace Irish Library, and to librarian Judith Gantley there, a most unlikely location in which to have become obsessed with so mundane an object, the polar opposite of the oligarchical, be-schoonered and engineering splendour in which that facility is located. I must thank Cristóir Mac Carthaigh at the Department of Irish Folklore at University College Dublin for direction, Fiona Burke, Curator of History at the Ulster Folk Museum, Clodagh Doyle and Anne O'Dowd at the National Museum at Turlough, Castlebar, and also Albert Siggins on the floor there.

For photographic images I am mainly indebted for superb portraits to Jacques Piraprez Nutan, with whom I worked on *Blooming Meadows*, *Ben Lennon: The Tailor's Twist*, the *Compánach* audiovisual concert and the *Turas* DVD. Deep thanks also to James Fraher, who kindly consented to the use of images from his superb 2020 book with Gregory Daly *In Nearly Every House*, and – fortuitously – his unique, splendid visual narrative of Charlie Byrne. So too Colm Keating for images from his vast archive of Dublin photos, Siobhán Ní Chonaráin at CCÉ, and Eddie Guiry in Newcastle West, as well as several private collections. Numerous others are credited in these pages for generous permission to use archive photos, notably The Kennelly archive, Comhairle Bhéaloideas Éireann at University College Dublin, and Dúchas.

John Whiteoak in Melbourne gave valuable prompts, reading and information, and Mark Weems in North Carolina provided key minstrel pointers and images; Nick Roth opened a valuable stream of eager exploration and discussion on the tambourine by Francesco Turrisi, and fresh research by Richard Graham who himself gave detailed and patient insights to me.

Martin Gaffney must be thanked for his magnificent, patient design and print set-up which give the third dimension to the overall book, and fundamental to this of course has been what made it possible, and brought it all forward by several years, An Comhairle Ealaíon's Deis award which financed photography, book design, copyright and commercial-archive access payments as well as coaxing the project to conclusion.

The use of the amazing facility and generosity of Andrew Martin at the Irish Newspapers Archive has been invaluable in opening the curtains on the hidden years of the nineteenth-century heyday of the tambourine in Ireland, as have the Corpus of Electronic Texts (CELT) at University College Cork and

▲ Tommy Hayes plays Seamus O'Kane's 1832 *Snap Apple Night* tambourine copy [*Nutan*]

Corpas at the Royal Irish Academy, each a tremendous asset for manuscript references from the centuries before journalism. In the latter regard too, the conscientious attention of the staffs at Trinity College Manuscripts Department and the Royal Irish Academy was vital to verifying the manuscript links, as was advice from Bernadette Cunningham and Pádraig Ó Machain, and assistance in literature from Maeve Gebruers and Róisín Conlon at the Irish Traditional Music Archive, and Mary Mitchell Ingoldsby at UCC's traditional Music Archive. Discussions with Steve Chambers and with Tom Sherlock, and with Micí Walsh at Newry and Mourne District Council sparked early speculation. Niamh Parsons did interview transcription, Don Meade gave American information, Dan Neely and Alan Morrisroe opened up vital channels and images, Eamon McGivney and Harry Hughes filled important gaps; my brother Jamesy was immense help through his Craobh Rua book agency's locating old texts and first editions needed for the timeline, and Michael Kelly of Barna was a valuable contact, facilitated by Joe Byrne in Achadh Mór, County Mayo. But the most considerable direction has come from the numerous writers on the subject, notably the pioneering Mícheál Ó Súilleabháin, Janet McCrickard and David Such, the rigour and interviewing of Rina Schiller and Assumpta Curran, and, in particular, Svend Kjeldsen who has been a tremendous psychological ally for his hard-nosed wisdom and his generosity in sharing access to his meticulous, savvy-question research in which the comments of his interviewees like Batty Sherlock are greatly valued; Reg Hall too gave freely and generously of voluminous research. I am particularly indebted to Barra Ó Seaghdha for early copy-editing and guidance, to Barbara O'Connor, and Svend too, for critical reading and structural advice, and to Terry Moylan for invaluable comment, extra references and direction as well as undertaking note-checking and proof reading.

To Liam Ó Bharáin we all owe considerable gratitude for his perceptive unveiling of the *Rosa Anglica* and the *Poole Glossary*, each of them a vital milestone on the journey; indeed, had I known of his 2007/8 articles (and, too, of Svend's 2000 thesis and Janet McCrickard's 1987 work) I would not ever have felt the need to embark on such a study as this; but ignorance, in this regard, though eating up social life, has added something to posterity

Among the many individuals I have to graciously acknowledge are Gerry Hallinan of Roscommon for information given to me in Albany, New York in 1988, and Ted McGowan and Sonny (James) Davey for interviews in Gurteen in 1999, Gregory Daly, while as researcher at the Michael Coleman Centre in Gurteen and while editing with James Fraher. Michael Tubridy gave me Clare information, Harry Bradshaw gave me data on Longford and John Reynolds, Jim and Owen McMahon from Kerry gave me insights on their father Bryan, Colin Hamilton introduced to me the earliest painted images, Eamonn O'Flaherty translated 'the Paris manuscript', Ian Ó Caoimh brought contacts, Michael Cronin of DCU and TCD gave names and advice, Michael McDonnell of Kilkenny brought interesting leads, Ríonach Uí Ógáin gave key clarifications. Tommy Hayes' opinions a directional shake-up, my sister Patricia painted terrific historic-image copies, and Helen Phelan generously permitted the inclusion of the Ó Súilleabháin summary.

On-the-ground most important direction for west Limerick was received from chance meeting flute-player Joe O'Sullivan at the TG4 Gradam preview, and through him Mike Barrett of Newcastle West and journalist Tom Aherne of Carrigkerry. Jim McNamara's hospitality at Knockaderry was invaluable, so too the diligence of Tadhg Ó Maolcatha of Tournafulla, Munster chair of CCÉ who was most helpful with sight of key documents. Peter Browne passed me terrific morsels which supported my intuition of improvisation on original bodhráns, as did Nicholas Carolan, Cathal Goan, John McIntyre and Pat Mitchell who threw in provocative and revealing data and anecdotes, each a link in the thinking. I must also thank Rebecca Draisey Collishaw for making sense of the bibliography, and David Gardiner at *New Hibernia Review* for his editorial diligence which was the catalyst for the momentum that tipped what was once a mere article into the chasm of being a book.

The numerous bodies which permitted me to air my ongoing findings in talks and lectures have been a tremendous help in clarifying the picture for me through feedback, among them Armagh Pipers' Club (which also published a lengthy paper), Na Píobairí Uilleann, NAFCo in Derry City 2012, Comhaltas Ceoltóirí Éireann at the Cavan All-Ireland, Scoil Samhraidh Willie Clancy, the Catskills Irish Arts Week, Mícheál Ó hAlmhain and the Craiceann Festival on Inis Oírr, Adrian Scahill at NUI Maynooth, Méabh Ní Fhuartháin at University College Galway, and Martin Dowling at Queen's University Belfast. I have to thank Páiric McNeela in particular for his wisdom and skills in trying out the ancient bodhrán recipes, Malachy Kearns for experimental skins, Seamus O'Kane for the Maclise tambourine copy, and Caoimhín Mac Aoidh and Hammy for improvised instrument comment. But without the incredible patience and tolerance of my bean céile Evelyn Conlon the whole operation could never have got beyond the first beat; may she never again have to hear the B word.

▲ 'The Bodhrán Player' by George Campbell (1917–79) [*Courtesy George Campbell estate*]

◀ John Say, London playing the first bodhrán made by Ian Campbell (p. 309) [*Sheena Vallely*]

ACKNOWLEDGEMENTS

"The first time I heard the sound of a bodhrán was when De Dannan, with Johnny Ringo McDonagh, played their premiere Danish concert at the Skagen Festival in 1981. It became a life-changing experience. A defining moment of an Irish music performance is when the bodhrán traces a deep groove within it and adds a pulsating flow of lift and energy to the entire rendition"
Svend Kjeldsen, *bodhrán player and researcher*

▲ Svend Kjeldsen and Fintan Vallely [*Nutan*]

Index

African-American 94–9, 104–6
Aherne, Tom 194
Albania 19
All-Ireland fleadh 1, 9, 31, 177, 189, 193
All-Ireland tambourine competition 184
American Civil War 96
American Revolutionary War 22
An Bodhrán: The Irish Drum CD 249
An Rás CD 249
Ancient Britons 22
Ancient Music of Ireland 37
Anglo-Irish 127, 157
Annaghdown 206, 209
Annals of Ulster 35, 148, 320
Aphrodite 18
Armagh Rhymers 141
audio evidence 67
authority of drumming 284
Axills folk group 189

Babylonia 15
Báiréad, Tomás 209, 210
Ballinskelligs 143
Ballybay 102
Ballybricken fair 73
Ballyheigue feis 181, 184
Ballymote 49, 186, 189
Bane, Joe 148
Bantry Bay 23
barbaric 168, 178, 282
Barnes, William 58
Barnigue 194
bass drum 13, 21, 201, 221, 326
battering 98, 148
Bavigan, Frank 186
bear 111
Bergin, Lorcan 184, 190
Betley, Patrycja 315
Beverly Minster 20, 46
Biddy (Bride Oge, Brideog) 135, 179, 213
big drum 24, 61, 111, 112
big house 26, 79, 124, 126
Bigger, Francis Joseph 133
Birmingham 195
Black and White Minstrel Show 105
blackface 25, 94, 138
Blessing, John 222
Blueshirts 201
bobharán 58, 61, 72
Bodhrán (film) 177, 232
bodhrán competition 181, 184, 238, 246, 256
bodhrán women 192
Bohee Brothers 104
Boland, Peter 196
bone tipper 230–1

bones 1, 94–105, 114, 118, 159, 172, 179, 189, 196, 326
Book of Leinster 31, 49
Boston 22, 67
bother 57–61, 66, 69
Bothy Band, The 13, 246, 253
Bourke, Brian 6, 248, 330
bow 17, 41, 42, 44, 57, 319, 320
Bradshaw, Harry 247, 249, 342
Breathnach, Breandán 138, 206
Breatnach, Cormac 13
Bring Down the Lamp 186
British army 116, 127, 195
Brittany 75, 85
Broderick, Pat 189
Broderick, Vincent 165–6
bronze age 29, 267, 326
Brooklyn 188, 247
Brosna 105, 179, 188
buaireán 58, 59, 66, 69
Buckley, Ann 17, 49, 217, 274
Buckley, Thomas 258, 259
Burke, Fiona 340
busk 57
buskers 22, 109, 113, 115, 236
Byrne, Carmel 184, 190, 192
Byrne, Charlie 218, 219, 238–9, 259
Byrne, Cormac 310
Byrne, Gerry 189

Cahill, Sean 157, 161, 162, 184
Cahill, William 221
Callan, Angela 193
Cambrensis, Giraldus 28–32, 35–39, 41, 47–8, 267
Campbell, Iain 309, 328
Campbell, Josie & Peter 188
Canavan, Sonny 169, 200, 224, 225, 228, 232, 323
Cape Breton 147
Carberry, Noel 260
Carberry, Patrick 207, 247, 248, 326
Carleton, William 135, 136
Carolan, Nicholas 7, 21, 121, 124, 197, 342
Carracastle 201, 203, 206
Carrigkerry 148, 171, 178, 194–5, 197, 232, 323
Carroll, Lewis 101
Carroll, Sean 196
Carson, Ciaran 269
Casey, Austy, 202
Casey, Thady 11, 180, 210
Cashel 72–3, 88, 318
Cassells, Peter 212
Castlebar 62, 72, 77, 82–4, 154, 236, 340
Castleisland 108, 190, 226
Çatal Hüyük 15, 271

Catholic Church 35, 102
Catholic schools 35
Catholic University of Ireland 39
céilí 8-12, 166, 199, 206
CELT 32, 49
Celtic design 274
Celtic studies 39
Ceolas 272
Ceoltóirí Chualann 164, 166, 179, 180, 184, 195, 228, 247, 267
chaff 63, 74, 76, 77, 78, 267, 273, 326
charivari 110, 152, 170, 266
Chieftains, The 13, 17, 212, 222, 228, 242, 247, 249, 255
Christianity 19, 33, 131, 170, 269, 282
Christy Minstrels 96, 100-5, 114
cipín 168–9, 228, 230, 231
Clancy, Willie 11, 180, 243
Clarke, Peter 196
classical music 114, 166
Clementi, Muzio 90
Clifford, Julia 64, 66, 203
climate 15, 17
Coleman hand-strikers, The 230, 272
Coleman, Frank 188
Coleman, Michael 207, 341
collection tray 112, 113
Collis, Fionnuala 260
Comeraghs 81–2
Comhaltas Ceoltóirí Éireann (CCÉ) 9, 12, 166, 171, 180, 181, 186, 189, 190, 194, 195, 196, 199, 212
Commins, Verena 11, 256
competitions 9, 150, 157–8, 161, 171, 173–5, 180–196, 256–263
concussion 21, 94, 157, 199
Connaughton, Pat 185
Conneely, Paddy 214
Conneff, Kevin 246, 255, 274, 297
Connellan, Thaddeus (dictionary) 58
Connemara 67, 80, 189, 192, 242
container 15, 58, 61, 68, 73–7, 79–86, 113, 266, 281, 286
copying the tambourine 118, 148, 219, 236, 285
Corcoran, Eddie 186
corn fiddle 60
corruption 68–9
Coughlin, Seán 325
court music 32, 48
Craiceann 189, 244, 245, 258
Croker, Thomas Crofton 142
Crosbhealach an Cheoil 270
cross-breed 159
Cruikshank, George 22, 126
Cruit 17, 31, 38, 40, 318, 319, 320
Crusades 8, 20

crwth 41
Curley, Michael 196
Curley, Serena 257, 260
Curran, Assumpta 205, 269
Cussen, Cliodhna 317
Cybele 16, 18, 19, 20, 42
Cyprus 18, 271

Dale, Joseph 23, 93
dallan 57, 63, 74, 77, 84, 87, 145
Daly, Batt & Pat 182
Daly, Gregory 208, 228, 289, 340
Daly, Jackie 12, 252
Damer, An 165, 180, 247
Dan Lowrey's Music Hall 104–5
Daniels, Kevin 186
Dares, Tracy 147
Davey, Andrew 'Junior' 223, 252, 257, 260
Davey, James 'Sonny' 206, 224, 232, 233
De Bhaldraithe, Tomás 47, 64
De Buitléar, Éamonn 139, 165, 173
De Dannan 13, 189, 196, 274, 343
De Vere Coneys, Thomas 58
deafness 51–3, 58, 60–3, 69, 71–3, 274
decorative tambourine 2, 3, 113, 244
deerskin 182, 220
Derricke John, 21, 34, 44
Dickens, Charles 96
dildorn 143, 324
dildurn 60–3, 74, 76, 142, 145
Dillane, Aileen 196
Dingle 179, 269
Dinneen, Patrick 47, 60–2, 67–9, 72–3, 77, 265, 285
Dionysian 18
Doherty, John 98, 185
Doherty, Liz 190
Dolan, Derville 260
Dolan, Packie 207, 248, 326
Donabate 17
Donegan, Michael 258
Donnybrook Fair 132
Dordrán 244, 253
Douglass, Frederick 100
Dowling, Pat 228, 246, 311
Doyle, Clodagh 332
Doyle, Kevin 310
Driver, Nicholas 269
Drohan, Aoife 259
drum-kit 8, 9, 12, 166, 199
drumstick 231, 314, 325
Duggan, John (Jack) 200, 222, 232, 323
Duignan, Michael 220
Duignan, Packie 12, 188
Dunton, John 44
Dwyer / O'Dwyer, Michael 31
Dwyer, John 256

EDIL – Dictionary of the Irish Language 48
Egan, Maura 260
Egypt 16, 18, 38, 97, 271
emigrants 5, 110, 195
EMIR – Encyclopaedia of Music in Ireland 107
Emmit, Daniel 94, 96
English military 35, 44, 46, 138
Ennis, Séamus 13, 180
Estonia 19
Ethiopian Serenaders 95, 99, 100, 103–4
European art 124, 127–9
Evans, E. Estyn 77, 267
Exeter 16, 20

Fair of Carman 31, 32, 40, 132, 319, 320
Fair of Windgap 136, 144
fairs 31, 132, 320
Falc'jer-Poyroux, Erick 270
Fallon, Davy 228, 247
Farr, Lucy 212
Farrell-Courtney, Aimée 246, 278, 296
Farrell, Ned 196, 228, 246, 311
faux 94, 95
Favourite, The 211
Féile 109, 117, 190
Feis 15, 117, 181, 182, 195
Female American Serenaders 96
Fennell, Niamh 257, 258, 259, 290,
fife 21, 93, 97, 110, 111, 115, 118, 133, 142, 152, 201, 202, 219, 273, 320
fife and drum 201–3, 273
fine-art paintings 121
Finn, Fred 189
Fitzmaurice, Gabriel 169, 187, 284
Flavin, Elizabeth 18, 97
Flavin, Margaret 192, 193
Fleadh an Dreolín 179, 329
fleadh ceoil 166, 180, 181, 184, 189, 195, 196
Fleadh Cheoil an Radio 166, 180
Fleadh Nua 177, 195, 323
Fleming, Brian 215, 298
Fleming, John 67, 144, 155
Flynn's Men 186
Foclóir Béarla agus Gaoidheilge 61
Foclóir Gaedhilge agus Béarla 60
Foley, Andy 188
Foley, Daniel 58, 66
foot percussion 147–8
Forde, William 26
Fouinel, Josselin 260
Four Masters' *Annals of Ireland* 33, 320
Four Men and a Dog 7, 186
Fragmentary Annals of Ireland 32
Fraher, James 238–9, 289
France, 82, 85, 86, 94, 110
Free State 4, 206, 324

free-reed 5, 159, 284
French, Percy 102

Gael-Linn 165, 180
Gaelic culture 39, 157
Gaelic League 60, 65, 115, 154, 211, 213
Gaelic Revival 118, 211
Gaelic song 7
Gaffney, Martin 289, 340
Gaffney, Mary 224
Gallagher, Bridie 67
Galpin Society 268
Ganly, Padraic 119, 204
Gavigan, Agnes 186
Gaynor, Michael 260
gender 74, 262
gentry 25, 46, 124, 126
Gilchrist, John 196
Gillespie, Rowan 88
Gipsy 19, 159, 191, 281
Girling, Sam 25
Glasheen, Ruairí 275, 323
Glenflesk 142
Goan, Cathal 209, 342
goat killing 224, 225
goat stealing 205, 226
Goddess 16–8, 271
Gorman 26
Gough, Donnchadh 218, 274, 308
Graham, Richard 25, 27, 53, 92, 340
grain growing 74
gramophone 7
Grattan Flood W.H. 31
gravel/sand riddle – see 'riddle'
Gray, Kathleen 228, 230
greadán 148
Great Famine 77, 118, 219, 286
Grehan sisters 67
Griffin, Gerald 142, 324
Guadeloupe 22
guitar-like instruments 38
gunpowder 19, 86
Gurteen 148–9, 189, 204, 208, 224, 230, 341

Hall, Reg 13, 26, 92, 192, 207, 211
Hall, Samuel C. & Anna Maria 81
Hallinan, Gerry 220, 236, 341
Halpenny, Sean 270
hand-clapping 98, 148
Hannigan, Stefan 270
harmonica 10, 131, 159, 203
harpers 32, 36, 135, 320
Harte, Colin 275
Hartigan, Dan 195
Hartnett Michael 167, 321
Hast, Dorothea 273
Hayes, Martin 147, 289
Hayes, Tom 177, 197, 232, 322

Hayes, Tommy 91, 249, 250, 256, 257, 300, 340
Hedwitschak, Christian 187, 244, 253
Heffernan, Mary 192, 212
Hennessy, Jimmy 162, 192, 205, 221, 223
Hickey Donal, 203, 209
Higgins, Jim 286
Hill, Noel 148
Hillery, Paddy 150, 167, 321
Hitchner, Earle 196
Hogan, Michael 187
Holloway 211
home making of instruments 221
Horan, Malachi 212–3
Horan, Peter 118, 189, 205, 289, 327
Horkan, John 201, 203, 221
Houlihan, Peter 273

Iceland 17
Illustrated London News 23, 26, 88, 118
impersonating 100
improvising 15, 56, 61, 66, 78, 80–3, 98–9, 103, 137, 141–7, 184, 206, 213–4, 219–230, 281, 285, 324
India 20, 271
Iraq 15, 271
Irish Folk Ways 77, 267
Irish language 4, 35, 47, 53, 59, 60, 64, 69, 139, 143
Irish Parliamentary Party 101
Irish stage 89
Irish Traditional Music Archive 7
Irisleabhar na Gaedhilge 56, 59
Isis 18
Italian street musicians 53, 92, 114

Janissary music 21–5, 228
Japan 16, 38, 97, 263
jazz 8. 9, 96, 153, 165, 182, 241
Jews 19, 43, 136
Jim Crow 94
Jingles 226–8
Jordan, Cathy 13, 172, 206, 252, 288, 301
Jordan, Mary 192
Joyce, Patrick Weston 42, 61–2, 66, 72, 141, 145, 163, 166, 184, 197
Joyce, Sandra 284, 305

Kavanagh, Nóra Byrne 9
Keane, John B. 64–8, 130, 157–71, 173, 175, 184–85, 202, 226, 228, 232, 269, 275
Kearns, Malachy 182, 185, 233, 236, 242, 255, 270, 284
Keating, Geoffrey 30
Kelly, Fergus 274
Kelly, Jim 279
Kelly, John Joe 176, 250–1, 274, 285, 303
Kelly, Pat 210

Kennedy, Patrick 59, 77, 79, 80
Kentucky Minstrels 102
King, Johnny 259
Kinmonth, Claudia 124
Kirk, Cathy 263
Kirwan, Martin 212
Kirwan, Michael 196
Kjeldsen, Svend 7, 23, 86, 91, 93, 188, 209, 224, 230, 272–5, 327, 333
Kohl, JG 136

ladies tambourines 90–1, 113, 318, 325
Lamb, Peadar 165
Lambeg 21, 178, 217, 272, 279, 284
Lambeg and the Bodhrán, The 272
Land League 201, 202
Lapland 268, 270
Lawlor, Helen 10
Le Roy Rice, Edward 138
Leahy, Frank 10
Ledwich, Edward 31, 37, 72
Lennon, Johnnie 119
Library of Congress, USA 157
Limerick Fleadh Cheoil 181, 195, 256
Listowel Drama Group 158, 164, 165
Listowel Harvest Festival 179, 192
Little, George 212–3
London 23, 26, 92, 107, 118, 124, 186, 188, 192, 207, 211, 213
Louvre 15
Loyal-British 46, 272
Lunny, Donal 13, 148, 177, 228, 244, 246, 252, 253, 255, 259, 306, 311
Lupari, Gino 251, 302
lute 26, 35, 38, 46
Lyon, Nancy 268
Lyons, Tim 1, 214, 328, 328–31

Mac Aonghusa, Proinsias 185
Mac Mathúna, Ciarán 173, 180, 209, 222, 249
MacDonald, Daniel 75
MacDonogh, Steve 269
MacKenna, Siobhán 185
Maclise tambourine copy 236, 341
Maclise, Daniel 56, 81, 100, 123–6, 128, 136, 143, 155, 228, 229, 233
MacMahon, Bryan 68, 154, 158, 159–60, 165, 166, 175, 179, 188, 195, 223. 269
MacMahon, Gary 190
MacMahon, Tony 139, 148, 186, 192, 229
MacNamara, Anita 192
MacNamara, Stevie 204
Madden, Joanie 12
Maguire, Eamonn 223
Mainzer, Joseph 26
Malynn, Paddy 212

Marche region of Italy 19, 26, 53
marching 9, 20–5, 61, 144, 147, 149, 154, 173, 199–206, 212, 219, 221, 248
Mardi Gras 150, 282
Martin, Jimmy 190
May, Imelda 3
McCall, P.J. 143
McCarthy, Sharon 259
McCormick, Fred 333
McCrickard, Janet 17, 18, 46, 146–7, 269, 279
McDermott, Josie 186
McDonagh brothers 147
McDonagh, Joe 224, 245
McDonagh, Johnny 'Ringo' 196, 219, 241, 252, 260, 274, 299, 343
McDonagh, Josie 208, 230, 282
McDonagh, Tom 225
McElwee, Michael 258
McGann, Frank 229
McGowan, Ted 189, 192, 204, 205, 206, 209, 228, 229, 230, 327
McMahon, Bernadette 259
McMahon, Michael 218, 231
McNamara, Julie 253
McNeela, Páiric 4, 182, 231, 234–7, 243–44, 342
McNulty, Peter 67
McShane, Ronnie 172
Meade, Don 69, 263, 341
meal sieve 79, 149
measure 73, 75, 78, 79
media 253, 267
melody instruments 3, 16, 214, 219
Mercier, Mel 13, 138, 170, 215, 222, 286, 291–2
Mercier, Peadar 13, 138, 165, 242,
Mesopotamia 15, 16
Middle Ages 17, 19, 51
military bands 8, 22, 94, 104, 127, 199, 201
military drum 20, 24, 35, 44. 51, 133, 143, 195
mimicking 94, 103, 105
minstrel routines 96–9, 176
Mitchell, Mary 342
Mitchell, Pat 12, 206, 209, 220, 342
Mittleman, Josh 272
modern dictionaries 63–5
Moloney, Mick 95, 103, 107
Moloney, Paddy 165, 172, 228, 247
Moore, Brian (Cormac) 264
Moore, Christy 13, 148, 311, 252
Morisroe, Alan 69, 341
Morocco frame drummers 113, 176
Morrison, James 119, 207
Morrison, Tom 247, 326
Morrissey, Brian 177, 259, 327

Moylan, Terry 8, 101
Mulholland, Rosa 159, 185
Mullaney, Johnny 202
mummers 140–3, 196, 212, 228
mumming 44–6, 81, 143, 324
Murphy, Colm 7, 13, 19, 126, 196, 214, 238, 249, 256, 259, 274, 287, 295
Murray, Gerry 209, 327
musichall 104–5, 114
myth 33, 46, 105, 178, 226, 253, 271, 282, 284

Na Píobairí Uilleann (NPU) 7, 255, 342
National Museum 1, 82–9, 148, 154, 219–20, 226, 236, 268, 275
National Museum, Folklife department 82–3, 227, 236
Neely, Dan 69, 85, 341
Newgrange 16
Ní Mhóráin, Sighle 66, 144
Ní Neillinigh, Louise 260
Nolan, Ronan 171, 228, 274
Nutan, Jacques Piraprez 289

Ó Beacháin, Niall 12
Ó Bharáin, Liam 53–6, 69, 139, 273, 341
Ó Brollachain, Fergal 260
Ó Canainn, Tomás 138, 268
Ó Conaill, Éamonn 194
Ó Concannon, Mícheál 180, 206, 209
Ó Danachair, Caoimhín (Kevin Danaher) 65, 154, 166, 188, 220, 226, 228, 230–1, 236, 265, 323
Ó Dónaill, Niall 48, 64, 65
Ó Donnghaile (O'Donnelly), Eugene 40, 319
Ó hAlmháin, Mícheál 189, 244; see also *Craiceann*
Ó hAodha, Mícheál 162, 163
Ó hÉanaí, Seosamh 67
Ó Maoldomhaigh, Ronan 258
Ó Mianáin, Pádraig 64
Ó Modhráin/Ó Móráin, Tomás 144, 145, 154, 155
Ó Murchú, Fabian 256
Ó Murchú, Labhrás 195
Ó Riada, Sean 23, 65, 100, 164–6, 170–80, 182, 184, 195, 204, 228, 243, 244, 326
Ó Snodaigh, Ronan 91, 252, 317
Ó Súilleabháin, Eoghan Ruadh 165
Ó Súilleabháin, Mícheál 38, 198, 199–206, 215, 230, 267, 268, 270, 279, 322
Ó Súilleabháin, Tomás Rua 144
Ó Tuama, Seán 165
O'Begly, Conor 46, 56, 57, 71
O'Brien, Jimmy (Kerry) 222
O'Brien, John (bodhrán) 259
O'Brien, John (dictionary) 47, 57, 58

O'Brien, Ned 220
O'Byrne, Joe 206
O'Carrol, the Harper 36
O'Connell, Daniel 100, 111, 201,
O'Connor, Máirtín 252
O'Connor, Ned 217, 233
O'Conor, Charles 31, 35–6, 38, 49
O'Curry, Eugene 38–43, 47, 49, 64, 82, 121, 318
O'Daly, John 145
O'Doherty, Eamonn 47
O'Donnell, Fionn 4
O'Donnell, Siobhán 244, 257, 291, 331
O'Donnell, Tom 177, 197
O'Donnelly, Eugene – see Ó Donnghaile
O'Donovan, John 32–39, 64, 74, 143
O'Dowd, Anne 82, 340
O'Dwyer, Michael 81
O'Dwyer, Simon 49, 207, 222, 273
Ó'Hare, Méabh 233
O'Kane, Seamus 172, 233, 237, 240, 244, 342
O'Leary, Johnny 203
O'Meara, John 30, 31
O'Neachtain, Shane 38
O'Neill-Lane, Timothy 61
O'Neill, Francis 137, 266
O'Nolan, Shaun 67
O'Reilly, Edward 47, 58, 64, 67
O'Rourke, Brian 328
O'Sullivan Beare, Philip 35, 49
O'Sullivan, Eamonn 196, 258
O'Sullivan, Joe 209, 232, 323
Old Testament 15
Olympia Theatre 104
otherworld 16
Ottoman 20, 21, 52
Our Musical Heritage 267, 326
oversize tambourines 23
Oxford English Dictionary 41, 42, 66, 78

pagan 169, 179, 268, 271, 282, 284, 326
Pakistan 236
Palestine 15, 20, 143
Pandean Minstrels 93, 94
panderetta 113
Paris Latin manuscript 51
part-time specialists 223, 226, 232–3, 241
passport image 254
performance style 98–9, 206, 213
Petrie, George 34, 143
Phelan, Colm 252, 313
Phoenix Society 112
photography 75, 85
Pierce, Thomas 219
pitch/pitching 3, 10, 177, 225, 244, 253, 256, 259, 268, 326

Planxty 274, 311
plastic 74, 81, 84, 85, 148
plywood 221, 224, 232, 323
politics 19, 98, 111–2, 114, 199, 280, 281, 284
Poole Glossary 57, 58, 80, 81, 273
postage stamps 254, 255
poverty 47, 127, 128, 167, 218
Presbyterian 102, 117
price 114, 115, 175
priestesses 271
professional musicians in ancient Ireland 320
pronunciation and meaning 59, 61, 66, 67, 196
Prosperous 228, 246, 274, 311
Puck Fair 160, 177, 178, 221, 323
puffball 67, 68
Pure Bodhrán 250, 252

Quaide, Jack 149, 170, 178
quern 75

Racism 97, 102, 107, 114
Radio Éireann/Radio 1 (RTÉ) 162, 166, 173, 232, 246, 267, 272, 323, 326
Raiftearaí, Antaine 133
Rambler, The 325
Reachaireacht an Riadaigh 165, 173, 180, 247
Redmond, Layne 7, 18, 270
Reidy, John 165
religion 18, 19, 112, 115, 178, 271
revival 3–9, 53, 114, 169, 174, 195, 199, 201, 228, 231, 255, 286
Reynolds, John 119, 207, 226, 247, 248, 252, 275, 326
Reynolds, Willie 212, 275
RIA – see Royal Irish Academy
Rice, Thomas Dartmouth 94
riddle 1, 80, 145, 149, 160, 222, 224, 232, 236, 274
Rising Sun Ceili Band 206
Riverdance 284
Roberts, Thomas 71
Roche, Johnny 118
rock & roll 96
role models 23, 25, 92, 105, 199, 219
Roma 19, 110
Rooney, Sheila 259
Rosa Anglica 53–6, 273
Rosonin, Ronnie 190
Rotunda 23
Royal Irish Academy 39, 49, 51, 53, 55, 64, 355
Rural Tradition 211
Russell, Packie 210

Sallé, Marie 89
Salvation Army 19, 112
sand-screen – see 'riddle'
Santucci, Gian Franco 26
Say, John 342
Schiller, Rina 7, 272
Schools' Collection, The 68, 74, 220, 236, 324.
Scoil Samhraidh Willie Clancy/SSWC 11, 243, 342,
scorpion 52
Scott, Stanley 273
Scottish dictionaries 63
sean-nós 35, 98, 114, 222
sexuality 18, 19, 128
shamanism 1, 7, 8, 16, 17, 217, 267, 269, 271, 280
shamrock 198
Shaw Smith, David 268
Sheehy brothers 24, 177, 183–4, 190–5, 230, 246
Sheehy, Jim 177, 183, 190, 194, 226
Sheehy, Michael 183, 259
Sheerin family 188
Sherlock, Batty 186, 200, 209, 224
Sherlock, Tommy 280
Shebeen in Listowel 124
sheepskin 57, 59, 61, 68, 63, 75–8, 80–3, 141–5, 210, 220, 221, 225, 324
Sicily 19
side-drums 173, 199, 200, 201, 228
sieve making 84
sieves 56–87
sit-down music 5, 124, 173, 179, 199, 201, 287
Sive (the play) 161–164, 184–5
skib 77
skin tray 56, 77, 80–7, 123, 143, 206, 218, 220, 236, 237, 266, 267, 268, 272, 273, 275, 285, 286
slavery 96, 97, 100, 101
Sliabh Luachra 203
Smith, Neal 207, 248, 275
Smyth, Breda 208, 256
Snap Apple Night 26, 100, 123–4, 236, 340
snare 8, 13, 20, 65, 248
social class 22, 26, 91, 94, 114, 123, 131, 138, 167, 213
social dancing 9, 19, 199
solo tradition 10
soloists 249
Spailpín a Rúin 165, 180, 247
Spain 20, 39, 110, 175, 318
specialisation in making 217, 218, 224
spectacle 22, 39, 152, 168, 176, 177, 195, 284
spinning wheel, see 'wool wheel'
spoons 12, 179, 186, 189, 180, 192, 196, 211, 212, 214, 248, 256
Sports 2, 133, 174, 262
St Cecelia's Hall 24
Stanihurst, Richard 35
Stewart, Davey 244
Stowe MSS 36, 38
strawboys 116, 159, 169
striking styles 327
stylistic change 252
Such, David 7, 268, 341
Sullivan, W.K., 39–41, 49, 87, 131
Swinford All-Ireland fleadh tambourine competition 180
symbolism 166, 254–5, 272, 287

tabor drum 20, 30–8, 44–7, 53–4, 63, 228
tambourine competition 181
Tambourine dance, The 88–9
Tambourine Frazier 22, 23
tambourine sizes 16, 83, 90, 93, 117, 118, 128, 154
tambourines for sale 92, 114, 219
tamburello 19, 22, 26, 42, 52–3, 92, 117, 127, 323
Tansey, Seamus 145–9, 186, 203, 224, 230, 282
taping-up 226, 228, 241
tarantella 19, 94
tarantula 52
teaching and learning tambourine 90, 91
temperance 26, 131, 201
Templeglantine 150, 167, 321
testing theories 234–7
The Bodhrán Makers 164, 167, 169
The half-door song 67
The Honey Spike 160, 185, 247
The Northern Fiddler 47
Theatre Royal 89, 90
thumb roll 118
timpan 29–48
Titanic 254
Tomás a' Bhodhráin 144
Toole, Kevin 188
Topographia Hibernica 29, 30
Torpey, Frank 256
Tournafulla 217, 233, 342
Towey, Geraldine 230
Towey, Malachy 206
Travellers 159, 185
Traynor, Michael 63
Treoir 53, 256, 263, 267, 273
tribal 195, 284
Tubridy, Michael 205–6, 210
tucked-in skins 84, 234–6
Tulla Céilí Band 8, 219
tuning 244, 246, 271
Turkey 15, 271
Turkish music 16, 22, 274

tutor books for bodhrán 267–74
tutor books for tambourine 91, 92
Tyrone Militia 23

Ukraine 19
Ulster Folk Museum 82–7, 220
Ulster Plantation 46
Underwood, Tommie 186
United Irishmen 23, 127
University College Dublin 39, 77

vaudeville 25, 94, 105, 214
Velez, Glen 7, 252, 271
Victoria 105
Vikings 7, 268
Vinegar Hill , 23, 27, 126, 127
Virginia Minstrels 94, 96
Virginia Young Men's Club 103
Voice of the People 26

Walker, Joseph Cooper 31, 33, 36
Wallace Collection 75, 85
Wallis, Geoff 273
Wallup 270
Walsh, Mick (Michael) 196
Walsh, Tommy 270
Walton Bodhrán Tutor 270, 330
War of Independence 23
Ward, Cornelius 23
weather 153, 325
Weems, Mark 118
Weldon, Liam 281
When the Drummers Were Women 18, 270
White, Brendan 275
Whiteoak, John 107, 340
wicker 75, 81, 210
wight/wecht 60, 63, 74, 75, 77, 84, 124, 146, 267
Wildman, Cara 260, 312
Wilkinson, Dessie 222
Williams, Sean 274
willow 53, 220, 236, 237
Wilson, Sue 273
Windgap 136, 144
winnowing 53, 58–69, 72–87, 121, 124, 132, 143–5, 219
winnowing machine 82
wite 63, 145–7
women 157, 192, 258–63
Woods, Bill 274
wool ('spinning') wheel 81–5
wool-wheel 83, 85, 148, 224
Wren ball 150, 210
Wren competitions 171–8
Wren-boys 142, 149, 150, 152, 154
Wright, Gerry 211
Wulff, Winifred 53–6,

Zoilomastix, The 35

◀ Brian Bourke from a painting by Jay Murphy [*Courtesy Jay Murphy and Brian Bourke*]